# The Trails of Virginia

THIRD EDITION

# The Trails of Virginia
## Hiking the Old Dominion

## Allen de Hart

The University of North Carolina Press
Chapel Hill and London

Unless otherwise credited, all photographs are by Allen de Hart.

The paper in this book meets the guidelines for permanence and durability of the Committee on Production Guidelines for Book Longevity of the Council on Library Resources.

Library of Congress Cataloging-in-Publication Data

De Hart, Allen.
The trails of Virginia: hiking the Old Dominion / Allen de Hart.—
3rd ed.
    p. cm.
Includes bibliographical references and index.
ISBN 0-8078-5471-9 (pbk.: alk. paper)
1. Hiking—Virginia—Guidebooks.    2. Trails—Virginia—Guidebooks.
3. National parks and reserves—Virginia—Guidebooks.
4. Virginia—Guidebooks.    I. Title.
GV199.42.V8 D4    2003
917.55'0444—dc21                                        2003012090

07   06   05   04   03      5   4   3   2   1

# Contents

# Illustrations

# Acknowledgments

It was a full day's adventure in a forest of autumn colors. My mission in that late September coolness was a search for an old, lost trail. To locate it I had to first find and hike a narrow, unnamed and unsigned forest road. I hiked the road to its gated end where Clay Lick Trail should begin. There was not a trail sign, but a former forest road continued beyond the gate to end on the east side of Snake Hollow Mountain. I soon found a deer path up an embankment that became an unsigned, unblazed, and unmaintained foot trail. I ascended it to the south side of Cabin Ridge, where among scattered hardwoods the view south was magnificent. I could see multiple ridges—Stony Point and Clover Lick—and rugged peaks surrounding Clay Lick Hollow, a deep chasm where the trail would mysteriously end. I began a descent on a faint trail among large patches of mint, mullein, and white snakeroot.

I would not have found this trail without directional assistance. In this adventure my help came from Robert Tennyson of Dry River Ranger District in the George Washington and Jefferson National Forests, and from a National Geographic Trails Instructional Map. These pages of acknowledgment honor Robert and hundreds of others who have given me counsel, hiked many miles with me (sometimes in hazardous conditions), or provided hospitality.

Other national forest district rangers and trail staff who provided assistance are Steve Parsons and Tom Holland of Dry River; Cindy Holland and Michael Gallegly of Deerfield; Anne Downing, Sharon Mohney, Yvonne McAlister, and Chazy Nicely of James River; James Smalls, Donaly Sawyer, and Dean Kelly of Lee; Pat Sheridan, Ralph Egan, and Dawn Coulson of Warm Springs; Terry Bussey, William Compton, David Collins, and Diane Artale of New River Valley; Sten Olsen, Lynda Hubbard, and John Stallard of Clinch; Pat Egan, Dave Benavitch, Kathy Hall, and David Wagner of Glenwood/Pedlar; Frank Beum and Jerry Jacobsen of New Castle; and Doug Byerly, Tim Eling, and Ginny Williams of Mount Rogers NRA. Additionally, there was counsel from William Damon, supervisor of districts, and among his staff Al McPherson, Ted Coffman, David Olson, Toni Preston, and Bob Young. Because of new and altered trails, and a major change in authorized usage in the Lee Ranger District, I re-hiked all its trails with the exception of the ATV routes. Providing me with outstanding trail direction and assistance for this district was volunteer Wil Kohlbrenner of the Potomac Appalachian Trail Club.

Shenandoah National Park rangers Shawn Green, Steve Bair, Rolf Gubler, and park volunteer editor Joanne Amberson assisted me with information on changes and conditions of the park's trails and other service systems. Blue Ridge Parkway staff who edited my descriptions were Tammy Keller, Bruce Bytnar, and Larry Hultquist. Updated material on the Appalachian Trail was provided by the Appalachian Trail Conference headquarters staff. Direction changes in the Cumberland Gap National Historical park were provided by Ries Collier.

In this third edition more than 300 new trail descriptions have been added. Among the complete new trails or revised trails are some in the Virginia State Parks. The superintendent and staff who assisted me are Scott Schanklin of Belle Isle, Danette McAdoo of Chippokes Plantation, Mark Shuppin of James River, Douglas Graham of Lake Anna, Tony Widmer and Caroline Gander of Shenandoah River, Mark Hufeisen and Eric Houghland of Shot Tower and New River Trail, and Timothy Vest of Staunton River Battlefield. For the state's Natural Area Preserves, Curtis Hutto was a source of information. Lee Walker provided information for the Virginia Wildlife Management Areas.

New parks with trails or older parks with revised trails are also among counties, cities, and towns. For the counties, I received help from the following people: Patrick Mullaney of Albemarle, Terri Kolodziej-Simmons of Clarke, Lynn Tadlock of Fairfax, Larry Miller of Fauquier, Christina Roberson of Fluvana, Chris Smith of Gloucester, Brad Ashley of Hanover, Wes Malcomb of Henrico, Debra Weir of Isle of Wight; Paul Tubach Jr. of James City, Suzanne Grobbel of Loudoun, Clyde Crissman of Patrick, Jeff Balon of Roanoke, Marcus Ordonez of Shenandoah, and Ray Koltz and Dan Hutton of Wythe.

In the cities, help came from Fran Hart in Bedford; Dean Crane and Darren Coffey in Blacksburg; Pat Plocek in Charlottesville; Cyndy Perkins and Lennie Luke in Chesapeake; Karen Cross, Norma Howard, and Joe Ceizkowski in Danville; Linday Baily and William Ross in Fredericksburg/Stafford; Chris Hickman and Lourine Press in Hampton; Pat O'Brian in Luray; Andrew Reeder in Lynchburg; Michael Poplawski in Newport News; and Liz Belcher and Charlie Hammersley in Roanoke. Assistance for the Northern Regional Park Authority was provided by Carol Ann Cohen.

Assisting in the identification of the state's flora and fauna were Shirl Dressler of the Wildlife Diversity Division of the Department of Game and Inland Fisheries; Steve Croy, professor of biology at Virginia Polytechnic Institute and State University; Alexander Krings, professor of botany, and Charles Mitchell, agricultural extension agent, from North Carolina State University.

A prominent source of allied information about the state's recreation and environmental systems is the 452-page *Virginia Outdoors Plan*, published by the Virginia Department of Conservation and Recreation in 2002. Advising me on the document's coverage of natural resources, recreation (greenways, blueways, and trails), heritage, and services of local, regional, state, and federal parks and forests was Scott Bedwell, environmental program planner.

My appreciation goes to the staff of UNC Press for making this third edition possible, and particularly to David Perry, editor-in-chief; Pamela Upton, assistant managing editor; and Laura Cotterman, copyeditor. Some of the families and individuals who provided personal hospitality for my comfort and safety, or shuttle service, or places to camp or park for sleeping in my van, are Robert Dillon, Lawrence Pitt, the Emmett Snead III family, the Atlas Parker family, the Steve Belcher family, Ron Barnett, Pat Morgan, Don Ethington, Chris Sturgill, the Jeff Jansen family, and John Kiefer.

Throughout many years of hiking, backpacking, and camping on the trails of Virginia, before and during the three editions of this guidebook, I have had many faithful companions. Among them are Todd Adcock, Chris Addison, Jeff Ayscue, Scott Bailey, Robert Ballance, Joyce Barbare, Steve Bass, Mike Batts, Dean Belcher, Steve and Kim Belcher, Kim Bendheim, Lilian Benton, Tom Bond, John and Jimbo Borum, Dale Bowman, Chris Bracknell, Jeff Brewer, Jason Burgess, Richard Byrd, Lori Clark, Travis Combest, Gray Conner, Noel Copeland, Steven Cosby, Laura Davis, Flora de Hart, Rob Dillon, Robert Dillon, Lindy Eagle, Ronnie Echols, Craig Eller, Greg Frederick, Nancy Freeman, Paul Girard, Steve Guyton, Bernd and Jorn Haneke, Rudy Hauser, David Hicks, Rocky Holloway, Barry Jackson, Heather Jakeway, Becky Johnson, Mike Johnson, Billy Jones, Johnny King, Steve King, Terrel Knutson, Michael Lambert, Sarah Lancaster, John LeMay Jr., Jack Lewis, Mike Lewis, Ed Liberatore, John Lohmeyer, Gus Lucast, Chad McLane, Jason Mason, John Matthews, Walter May, Matt Morgan, Win Neagle, Robert Old, Debe Pacher, Kevin Parker, Dennis Parrish, Todd Phillips, Lawrence Pitt, Julia Pope, John Rohme, Bill Ross, Virginia Rynk, Chuck Satterwhite, Sandy Satterwhite, Todd Shearon, Brad Shuler, Emmett Snead, Eric Springer, David Stinchfield, David and Tim Straw, Kenneth Tippette, Jon Toppen, Ed and Seth Washburn, Ryan Watts, Dan Watson, Buster White, Charlotte Wicks, Rob Wilfong, Meredith Wilkins, Mary Willete, Darrell Williams, Chuck Wilson, Tony Woodard, and Autumn Wright.

In addition to this team of hikers, some of whom have hiked with me regularly for fifty years, I am grateful for the support of my parents, brothers, and sister. My oldest brother, Moir (who died in 1979), was a personal inspiration. Twelve years my senior, he took me on my first hiking and camping trip near Smith River Falls in Patrick County when I was five, and he taught me in my childhood to appreciate and care for the natural environment. My middle brother, Willie Lee (who died in 1953), and my youngest brother, Richard (who died in 1999), followed me into the forests to build and hike trails, canoe the rivers, hunt and fish, and explore. We all must have had a great influence on the youngest in the family, Virginia. She has taught her children and grandchildren to appreciate the beauty of nature, something our beloved parents and Moir taught us.

# Abbreviations

In an effort to save space in this book, some abbreviations may be used frequently.

| | |
|---|---|
| **AT** | **Appalachian National Scenic Trail** |
| ATC | Appalachian Trail Conference |
| ATV | all-terrain vehicle |
| BRP | Blue Ridge Parkway |
| BSA | Boy Scouts of America |
| CCC | Civilian Conservation Corps |
| CO | county road in West Virginia (e.g., CO 636) |
| elev. | elevation |
| FR | U.S. Forest Service road (e.g., FR 186) |
| GPS | global positioning system |
| GW&JNF | George Washington and Jefferson National Forests |
| GWNF | George Washington National Forest |
| I | interstate highway (e.g., I-81) |
| jct. | intersection/junction |
| JNF | Jefferson National Forest |
| KY | major Kentucky primary road (e.g., KY 80) |
| mi. | mile/miles |
| mp | milepost (on the BRP) |
| Mt. | Mount (used in proper names) |
| NC | North Carolina primary road (e.g., NC 8) |
| NE | northeast |
| NF | National Forest |
| NP | National Park |
| NPS | National Park Service |
| NRA | National Recreation Area |

| | |
|---|---|
| NVRPA | Northern Virginia Regional Park Authority |
| NW | northwest |
| NWR | National Wildlife Refuge |
| ORV | off-road vehicle |
| PATC | Potomac Appalachian Trail Club |
| Rd. | Road (used in proper names) |
| RR | railroad |
| RS | ranger station |
| RV | recreational vehicle |
| SE | southeast |
| SR | state secondary or county road (e.g., SR 635) |
| SW | southwest |
| TIS | Transportation Inventory Survey |
| TN | major Tennessee primary road (e.g., TN 91) |
| US | federal highway (e.g., US 11) |
| USFS | United States Forest Service |
| USGS | United States Geological Survey |
| VA | Virginia primary road (e.g., VA 41) |
| WMA | Wildlife Management Area |
| WV | West Virginia primary road (e.g., WV 17) |
| YACC | Young Adult Conservation Corps |
| YCC | Youth Conservation Crops |
| 4WD | four-wheel drive vehicle |

# The Trails of Virginia

*And this our life, exempt from public haunt,*
*Finds tongues in trees, books in the running brooks. . . .*
WILLIAM SHAKESPEARE

# Introduction

The purpose of this book is to inform the public that hiking a trail can be a wholesome educational and recreational experience. There is history to learn; there are trees, flowers, and animals you may have never seen. There are mountains to climb, and paths of springtime fragrance never experienced. And as Shakespeare said in the remainder of the quote above, there are "sermons in stones, and good in everything." The Bard was repeating, in meaning, what Saint Bernard had said 500 years before him. With the same attitude, the late professional hiker and author Edward B. Garvy of Virginia stated, "I like every trail I see, and I clean it up if it needs to be."

The information in this book is organized to give you a catalog of hundreds of trails in Virginia. Something is good in all of them. This introduction provides some information on how to prepare for your journeys on Virginia's trails. Although Saint Bernard stated "you will find something more in woods than in books," I hope you will take this book into the woods with you to prove his statement.

Hiking trails usually have official names, names that help define their location or identify the reason for their existence. A trail develops as a passage of interest, and is sometimes called a path, pathway, footway, walk, walkway, beaten path, towpath, lane, course, shortcut, tract, or greenway. The latter is likely to have a surface of asphalt (it is the effort to provide green grass, trees, and shrubs on the trail sides that matters). You may notice in this third edition that some familiar trail names are missing. That may be because of the astonishing increase in bulldozing for more housing developments and vehicular expressways. There are also many new names in this edition. Some are simply name changes. An example is at Kerr Reservoir where **Eagle Point Trail** is now **Robert Munford Trail**, in Mr. Munford's honor. Among new trails are the **Greensprings Trail** in James City County and the **Lick Run Greenway** in the city of Roanoke. An example of an extended trail is **Pickem Mountain Trail** from High Knob Tower to Flag Rock Recreation Area in the Clinch Ranger District of the George Washington and Jefferson National Forests. Another extension is the **James River Heritage Trail** in Lynchburg where it follows an island in the James River. Plans are to re-cross the river toward Appomattox.

This book is comprehensive, often giving space to unknown places or to short trails with special attributes. In Appendix C, I have suggested some "best" trails for the most adventurous outings, some for family trips with children, and trails for the physically disabled. I have found something new on each trail I re-hiked to complete this edition, and I believe you will experience some of the same. The diversity of trails in Virginia provides enormous options.

In a 2002 public report from the Virginia's Department of Conservation and Recreation, there were 2,964 state, local, and regional recreational facilities (excluding schools) comprising 689,815 land and water acres. If schools are included, the numbers are 4,136 and 710,172. Additionally, there are 238 federal facilities (such as national forests and parks, preserves, reservoirs, and military establishments) comprising 2,516,818 land and water acres. And there is more. Private facilities number 2,235, and they comprise 493,582 land and water acres. The opportunity represented by applying the learning philosophy of Saint Bernard and Shakespeare to a total of 3,720,572 acres is matchless. And we left out a factor unknown to them and our forefathers: facilities. Current day hikers and bicyclists have difficulty imagining travel with the frugal rations and services available to John Lederer and other early explorers of what is now Virginia. Today our facilities provide everything from drinking water and electricity to luxurious food and lodging, drug stores, food chains, and specialty shops.

Within the space and facility options, what are our *trail* options? Again, using the state's Department of Conservation and Development as our authority, we can choose between 5,363 miles of foot (pedestrian) trails, 2,708 miles of equestrian trails, and 3,136 miles of canoe trails. The department did not report a mileage list for bicyclists, because bicycles in Virginia are considered vehicles. A report from the Department of Transportation indicated the agency was not tracking bicycle trails by name or distance at this time. The Virginia Bicycle Association did not have a report.

There is a report, however, from the U.S. Forest Service that shows bicycle (particularly mountain bike) usage available on 1,411.2 miles of multi-use trails on USFS property. In the New River Ranger District, there is a 22.2-mile system created and named specifically for mountain bicycling. According to a report based on the state's Department of Conservation and Recreation's 2000 Virginia Outdoor Survey, bicycle routes on state and local properties and the interstate bicycle trails total at 4,380 miles. The survey also showed that 67 percent of the population hiked for pleasure; 39.7 percent of the population biked for pleasure; and 6.2 percent do horseback riding. In my descriptions here, I indicate where bicycle and horse traffic are included with hiking trails.

One of your questions when planning a hike may be, "Will the trail provide a 'warm harmonious glow of mind and body'?" a feature claimed to be significant for the pleasure of walking by Christopher Morley in his essay "The Art of Walking." According to Morley, "you never know when an adventure is going to happen" because you are by nature an adventurer, a discoverer. Walter Teller, in "Country Walks," a section of his book *Area Code 215*, says, "To be a discoverer you must go looking for something." That something may be in Shakespeare's trees, brooks, and stones.

Before thinking about your preparations for discovering the trails, I recommend that you read the next section on the history and development of trails in Virginia for a comparison of past trail usage and trails of today.

## Virginia's First Trails

Native Americans may have been in the area of what is now Virginia and North Carolina as early as 5000 B.C. during the Archaic Period. But archaeological study is more specific for the Woodland Periods, the first around A.D. 1600, and particularly the Late Woodland Period after A.D. 900. During this period Indian settlements were more stable, with agriculture, ceramic ware, domestic crafts, and ceremonies. By the time the English settled at Jamestown in 1607, the entire Chesapeake Bay area was the Powhatan chiefdom. This vast territory for about 13,000 indigenous inhabitants extended from the Potomac River south to the Nansemond River. The westward boundary was along the fall line, the James River Falls at Richmond being an example. The eastern territory included the southern half of the Eastern Shore.

Powhatan's (Wahunsonacock in the native language) area probably included thirty-one territorial units, each with a chief (*weroance*). All the chiefs were at least partially subject to Powhatan, and most of the units were Algonquian speaking. Some of the groups were captured by Powhatan; others, such as the Werowocomocos and the Chiskiacks on the York River, were likely inherited. West of the fall line were hostile Monacans and Mannahoacs, whose language was Siouan. Iroquoian-speaking groups such as the Nottoways and the Meherrins were on the southern side of Powhatan's claim, and farther south into present-day North Carolina were Algonquian-speaking groups such as the Chowanocs and the Roanokes. Communication between the diverse groups was by canoeing (some dugouts were large enough for forty people) and travel on land trails. The width and usage of the forest trails depended on the degree of trade and social exchanges between the chiefdoms.

In 1612 William Strachey wrote about the network of trails among the Powhatans in *The Historie of Travell into Virginia Britania*. John Smith also wrote about the trails not only along the riverside but across the necks between rivers (James, York, Chickahominy, and Rappahannock). Pocahontas (Matoaca in the native language, but Rebecca after her marriage to John Rolfe) at the age of twelve or thirteen was familiar with the trails between Jamestown and the Powhatan village because she escorted John Smith, after his release from Powhatan, through Paspahegh Indian territory to Jamestown.

Trail design was "dry, level, and direct" and sometimes wide enough for sociable groups. The English called them "plain roads." The Indians regularly removed brush and stones from the trails but left the large logs. It was traditional courtesy among the Indians to welcome travelers and give them food and drink. The hosts would also pick out briars and thorns from the travelers if the journey had been on a rough trail. Salves were used for bruises and sores. Whether a family encampment or a settlement, the rules were for the hosts to be hospitable. If the traveler was on a business trip or representing a diplomatic mission, the settlement chief would meet the guests. This could mean pipe smoking, banquets, and dancing. A few Indian units, such as the Nottoways, had thatched guest houses. Siouan-speaking Indians provided female companionship ("trading girls") for the male travelers. Forerunners of the modern lean-to were bark shelters, observed and described by a number of the European writers. But not all Indian travelers used shelters. One writer, Benjamin Hawkins, described seeing healthy, athletic Indians sleeping through a storm with rain falling on their faces.

Travelers carried their own bedding and knives. Warriors and hunters packed leather for moccasin repair and weapons for food foraging. Among foods frequently carried were chinaroot bread and parched cornmeal. They also ate sap and cambium from trees such as maple, birch, beech, poplar, and willow. Other foods in season were berries, wild potatoes (*wapatos*; *Saggittaria* spp.) and roasted ground nuts (*Apios americana*). Trail markings indicated trail conditions, food sources, threat of enemies, and assurances of the right path.

Long-distance trails, particularly for traders, were never well maintained; they were narrow but usually as straight as possible. It was customary for Europeans to have local or experienced guides for risky explorations into the backcountry to settlements of other groups or tribes. Traveling traders transported mica, cooper, flint, hides, dried fish, pearls, medical roots, salt, shells for gorgets, and steatite (soft stone for carving bowls). Also on the market was a poisonous root (*Cicuta maculata*, probably harvested on the Eastern Shore), which could be used to kill an enemy. Color pigments came from plants such as the red puccoon (*Lithospermum caroliniense*), likely from the Nottoway Indians in present-day Sussex County. White pigments from the hoary puccoon (*Lithospermum canescens*) came from the Blue Ridge Mountains, or farther away.

The Powhatan chiefdom first met Europeans when Spaniards attempted to build a settlement in the Chesapeake Bay area in 1566. In 1570 Spanish Jesuit priests sailed up the James River to what is now Chippokes and crossed the peninsula to the York River to settle. They were killed, except for a boy who escaped, in 1571. When Pedro Menendez arrived with a supply ship in 1572, he retrieved the boy and vengefully executed a number of Powhatans (see *Powhatan Foreign Relations, 1500–1722*, by Helen C. Rountree).

Friend and foe to the English, the Powhatans could have killed all the English settlers the first year, but instead they shared enough food to keep some of the disease-ridden colonists alive. After Powhatan's death in 1618, a year after a peace treaty had been signed, his younger brother, Opechancanough, took command. Less friendly to the English, he conspired the Massacre of 1622, which killed 347 men, women, and children. For the next ten years the trails of tidewater Virginia were stained with blood as the English and Powhatans fought, and the Indian groups fought and raided one another. Again in 1644 Opechancanough plotted another slaughter of more than 500 English settlers. Opechancanough was captured and brought to Jamestown by a group of soldiers led by Governor William Berkeley. While under confinement Opechancanough was shot by a soldier assigned to guard the chief's quarters. The Powhatans appealed for peace. In a treaty settlement the Indians were granted the "hunting grounds north of the York River," and no Indian "was to come south of it, except as a messenger." Trails from Jamestown upriver to the falls (Richmond), downriver to the Chesapeake Bay, and across the peninsula to the York and Pamunkey Rivers would be safer for English settlers. Five years later a colonist wrote in an essay titled "A Perfect Description of Virginia," which was published in London: "Virginia is the earthly Paradise. It is full of trees and the hum of bees . . . and a bird we call the *mockbird*. . . . In this happy Virginia there is nothing wanting to produce plenty, health and wealth."

By 1648 there were 15,000 English settlers in the quiet and prosperous colony, and they lacked great concern about the civil war that had begun in England in 1642. Although Charles I was condemned for treason and beheaded in 1649, not until 1652 did parliamentary commissioners come from England to demand the colony's surrender to Oliver Cromwell. Governor Berkeley bitterly signed the decree, left the state house in Jamestown, and retired to his manor in Greenspring to sulk in his silk and lace. Not completely silent during the Cromwellian years, he supported the Cavalierian cause (of church and king) by inviting Cavalier immigrants to Virginia. When Charles II was returned to the English throne in 1660, the Virginia House of Burgesses reinstated Berkeley as Virginia's governor. During the 1660s the population continued to increase, farms and plantations expanded, and old trails became better roads for horses and carriages on the Virginia Peninsula. Occasionally there were attacks by Doeg and Ricahecrian Indians on the frontier.

The trail routes beyond tidewater Virginia had long been of interest to the English. They were intrigued by a "China boxe" lined with taffeta, which chief Patawomeck said came from a trader south of the mountains (Blue Ridge Mountains). There was speculation that the item came from Spanish ocean traffic in Mobile Bay, a southern trailhead with trade routes to the **Lower Cherokee Trad-**

ing Path, the **Saponi Trail**, and the **Occoneechi Path**. By 1650 not only were the routes of interest to the English, but there were plans to explore the frontier with packhorses and Indian guides where trails did not exist. Some of these early explorers were Edward Bland and Abraham Wood in the 1650s; John Lederer, a former German physician, in the late 1660s and early 1670s; and Captain Thomas Batts and Robert Fallam, and James Needham and Gabriel Arthur in the early 1670s. But credit for opening the frontier goes to Abraham Wood, who under the governorship of Sir William Berkeley spent much of his life as commander of a large trading post at Fort Henry (Petersburg) and who discovered and named the New River in 1654. He also financed and sent Batts and Fallam in 1671 to explore north and west of what is now Radford. Their expedition went as far west as Tug Fork (Kentucky state line), a tributary to Big Sandy and the Ohio River.

Lederer, who made three excursions to the Blue Ridge Mountains (climbing to the top for views of the Shenandoah Valley in 1669), was the first to travel mainly alone for a two-month loop to include part of North Carolina. Sent and financed by Governor Berkeley in the summer of 1670, Lederer probably went west to the base of the Blue Ridge Mountains between Charlottesville and Lynchburg, then south to Sapon at the Staunton/Roanoke River (near Brookneal). His travels continued south to Occoneechee (Clarksville) and into North Carolina near Oxford and to Sara (Durham). A place called Wesacky is likely to be near the confluence of the Haw and Cape Fear Rivers. His course turned east to Katearas (Rocky Mount) and north to current Weldon for a return to Fort Henry. Lederer's survival convinced Abraham Wood that it was time to send trading representatives to Indians never before contacted.

In 1673 Wood sent Needham and Arthur to discover the "south or west sea," which Wood believed was not far beyond the Blue Ridge Mountains. With Appomattox Indian guides, they left Fort Henry, followed the **Occoneechi Path** and other trails to the Catawba River and Hickory Nut Gap (east of Asheville) in North Carolina, and southwest to the village of the Tomahitan Indians (near Rome, Georgia). Later Needham returned with a report to Fort Henry, but on his return to Arthur he was slain by Indian John, an Occoneechee guide, near the Yadkin River. Indian John also laid plans to murder Arthur. Arthur was safe as long as he stayed with the king of the Tomahitans, a friend to the English. For nearly a year Arthur roamed the Southeast with the Tomahitans, learned their language fluently, and faced death on at least three adventurous occasions. In May 1674 the king of the Tomahitans began a journey to Fort Henry with a trading team, Arthur, and a boy of Spanish/Indian heritage. Near Sara, Indian John was waiting to murder Arthur and other associates. But Arthur and the boy escaped. They continued to the village on Occoneechee Island in the Staunton/Roanoke River and in the cover of darkness crossed safely. In their flight on the **Occoneechi Path** for a week they had only huckleberries for food. They arrived at Wood's home in mid-June 1674. Nearly a month later the king of the Tomahitans, who also had escaped and taken the **Saponi Trail**, arrived to visit Wood. The young Arthur, who did not read or write, had walked 2,500 miles (and canoed 1,000) from Virginia to Mobile Bay, to Port Royal on the Atlantic, to the Ohio River, and back to General Wood, to whom he was indentured. Historians would record him as Virginia's most adventurous English hiker of the seventeenth century.

Virginia's population increased to 40,000 by 1670; of this number 6,000 were white servants and 2,000 were black slaves. Commerce increased, and tobacco remained the colony's chief export. In May 1676 a party of Doeg Indians attacked and killed some of the settlers on an estate owned by Nathaniel Bacon near the falls at Richmond. Bacon requested a commission from Governor Berkeley to head a team for a retaliation attack. The governor refused, but Bacon defied him by leading a party of settlers to rouse the Doegs in a bloody fight near what became known as Bacon Quarter Branch in eastern Richmond. This was the first act of what became Bacon's Rebellion for five dramatic months. Bacon was a member of the Governor's Council; therefore his rebellious behavior came to the attention of the House of Burgesses. The twenty-eight-year-old Bacon was a graduate of Cambridge University and a tempestuous orator. His opposition to the governor's restricted franchise and high taxes on farmers was shared by the majority of the population. He persuaded the burgesses to appoint him general and commander in chief against the Indians. Governor Berkeley was helpless and furious. The governor soon fled to Accomack on the Eastern Shore.

During the summer, Bacon's forces crossed the James River at Curles (near Hatcher Island) and followed the Indian trails to kill or disperse the Appomattox Indians (near Petersburg). They also followed the **Occoneechi Path** and other trails to kill and disperse the Nottoway Indians and the Occoneechee Indians at the Roanoke River (near Clarksville). Governor Berkeley returned on a flimsy fleet to recapture Jamestown in September but was defeated by Bacon's troops, who in the fight burned the colony's government headquarters. In late October, Bacon died of a fever at Gloucester and was secretly buried by his friends. Governor Berkeley returned and tyrannically killed enough Virginians to cause Charles II to say, "That old fool has hanged more men in that naked country than I have for the murder of my father." Recalled to England by Charles II, Governor Berkeley died of natural causes in 1677.

The early trails of Virginia west of the James River were becoming roads for expanding settlements, and new trails were developing beyond the fall line toward the Blue Ridge Mountains. In 1716 Governor Alexander Spotswood led an expedition of sixty-three men and seventy-four horses to the Shenandoah Valley. Later known as the Knights of the Golden Horseshoe, they left from the Mattaponi River and traveled northwest to the Rapidan River. From there they followed rough paths to and wilderness routes over the Blue Ridge Mountains (probably at Milam Gap) to the Shenandoah River (near the current community of Alma). Their one-month expedition exposed them at worst to rattlesnakes and hornets (plus an attack of measles). They claimed the area for King George's health and camped, fished, hunted (and had bear steaks), and drank at least ten varieties of liquor, plus punch and cider.

Not until the eighteenth century did Virginians explore the colony's longest trail, the **Great Indian Warpath** through the length of the Shenandoah Valley. In the southwest it connected with the **Warrior's Path** (later known as the **Wilderness Trail** through the Cumberland Gap into Kentucky). It also extended to trails in the Northeast (Pennsylvania, for example). The 1928 trail map by W. E. Myer shows a similarity in this and other Virginia trails to current highway routes. Examples are I-81 (and US 11) for the **Great Indian Warpath**; I-85 for the **Occoneechi Path** from Charlotte, North Carolina, to Petersburg; and part of the **Saponi Trail** from Greensboro, North Carolina, to Charlottesville on US 29.

## How To Use This Book

This book is divided into sixteen chapters. They cover national forests and parks, battlefield and historical parks, the significant points on the **Appalachian National Scenic Trail,** national wildlife refuges, state parks and wildlife management areas, state historic sites, county and municipal recreation areas, regional park systems, military and U.S. Army Corps of Engineers installations, and private holdings. Each chapter has an introduction to acquaint you with the area's natural and cultural environment, major features and topographical location, and support facilities such as campgrounds. There are addresses and telephone numbers listed at the conclusion of each description of a forest, park, refuge, recreation area, or privately owned site. You will find references to other guidebooks throughout this book, and a bibliography is provided. Addresses and telephone numbers of public and citizens' organizations are also listed in Appendix A. There is a trail numbering system to assist you in determining the general location on the maps.

FORMAT FOR TRAIL DESCRIPTIONS: In the chapters on national forests (Chapters 1 and 2), the districts are arranged in geographical order. They begin with Lee Ranger District, whose boundary is the farthest north near Winchester in the George Washington National Forest (now administratively joined with Jefferson National Forest). The order follows southwest along the mountain slopes and valleys to Clinch Ranger District in the Jefferson National Forest to the Kentucky state line at Pennington Gap. An effort has also been made to describe the trails in the same geographical direction with only a few necessary exceptions. The trail, or group of trails, is set in pockets or areas likely to be near campgrounds of that particular district. The description will also refer to the proximity or boundary to other districts. For the Blue Ridge Parkway and the Shenandoah National Park (Chapters 4 and 5) the format is the opposite. The trails are numbered with descriptions from north to south because the mileposts in both parks are in that order. The **Appalachian Trail** description format is either north or south. The **Allegheny Trail** is described from south to north, though the West Virginia Scenic Trail Association has organized the descriptive routing in the opposite order. There is not a format pattern for state parks, with the exception of the **New River State Park Trail**. Its description is from south to north, though the former railroad markers may be opposite. (Consistent with this description, the **Virginia Creeper Trail** in Chapter 1 is also described south to north.) In all the other chapters the parks and refuges are listed alphabetically. Trails are not listed alphabetically in the description; instead they are described according to trailhead and connections in order of trail routing. On all trails throughout the book, the descriptions usually begin at the most accessible trailhead. Parentheses are used to indicate side trails or connecting trails from a main trail.

TITLE AND NUMBER: The trail name is from the most current source, but references may indicate that it was formerly known by another name. Some trails will carry a double name because two trails run together for a distance. An example is where the **Appalachian Trail** may follow the **Virginia Creeper Trail**. The USFS trail numbers listed at the close of a trail or trails description are from the Transportation Inventory Survey (TIS), on the USGS topographical maps modified for USFS boundaries, and the USFS district maps. On these maps the **Appalachian Trail** is always number 1. The other numbers in each district are not consistent (and may follow the age of the trail rather than a pattern of proximity). In this book the USFS trail numbers are listed in order of their appearance in the description. For example, in the Little Wilson Creek Wilderness Area, the first two trails listed are in Grayson Highlands State Park, thus without forest numbers. The **Scales Trail** number is 4523, the **First Peak Trail** is 4524, the **Kabel Trail** is 4606, and the **Big Wilson Creek Trail** is 4607. You may not need to use these numbers, but if you do, they will be there as a reference point for your study of the USFS maps. There is another number I have assigned to each trail solely for the purpose of having a numerical order in the book and for cross-referencing with the book's maps. The first trail is the **Massanutten Mountain East Trail** (no. 1), and the last trail is the **Hollow Tree Trail** (no. 1403). These numbers appear in bold type in the outside margins of the page. They are also listed in the index to serve as an easy and general location reference on the maps.

LENGTH: The trail length is always within the nearest 0.1 mile (with the exception of short trails that may be described in feet or yards). All numbers followed by *miles* or *mi.* indicate the distance from one trailhead to the other of each trail. If the mileage is followed by *round-trip*, the distance is doubled as either backtracking or forming a loop. If the word *combined* is used, the main trail and other trails are combined as a group. Some trail networks offer a hiker a diversity of distances and even backtracking to choose a shorter or longer trail in the group, but altogether you will have an idea of the total distance. If neither *round-trip* nor *combined* is used, the trail distance is linear with trailheads accessible by vehicle at both ends. I have used a 400 Rolatape measuring wheel (which registers each foot) on all the trails.

DIFFICULTY: Trails are described as *easy* (has a gentle grade, may be short, and does not require rest stops); *moderate* (has a greater change in elevation or rough treadway that requires some exertion and likely rest stops); and *strenuous* (has high or steep elevation change and requires exertion and perhaps frequent rest stops; requires some skill over rough treadway). Elevation changes on some of the strenuous trails are listed.

CONNECTING TRAILS: Where a single trail is listed with a number of connecting trails, some of the trails may be covered in more detail under another heading. If so, they will be enclosed in parentheses. Although reading about a connecting trail may create a temporary break in your chain of thought, a return to the main description usually will start with the words *to continue* or *continuing ahead*. The objective is to give you an option on how far you wish to hike before backtracking, making a loop, or staying on the main trail. If continuing, you can ignore the paragraphs in parentheses, but the information is there if you change your mind.

FEATURES: Some of the trails have features that are more distinctive, rare, or outstanding than trails in general. I found something attractive or scenic about all the trails, but I have made an effort to avoid repetitive superlatives. Appendix C contains a brief list of suggested trails for special populations such as adventurous backpackers, families with young children on short trips, and people with disabilities. (Disabled hunters should contact the district rangers in the USFS for information on special hunting roads.)

TRAILHEADS: Where possible, access to a trailhead is described from the Virginia official highway map. But in a number of places a county map or city map will almost be essential for you to find your way if there are multiple trailheads. Also, I recommend the *Virginia Atlas and Gazetteer* by DeLorme Mapping Company, P.O. Box 298, Yarmouth, ME 04096 (phone: 207-846-7000). This map is usually available at bookstores and convenience stores. (See other maps listed under Maps, below.) An identifiable place on the regular maps is listed, an intersection is named (usually with road junction numbers), and the distance from that point to the trailhead is given. Access may also be described from the opposite direction. If the trailhead has more than one access point, the easiest and nearest to an identifiable place is described first.

ROADS: Virginians call every road, even an interstate, a *route* (not to be confused with a rural mail route, or RFD, that has not been changed to a name or number or both). A single word for all roads can be confusing to outsiders and to some Virginians who depend on many types of road systems when driving to trailheads. Road conditions affect your decision on what type of vehicle to drive. In this book, roads are described according to the systems used by the Department of Highways and Transportation as follows: *I* denotes an interstate highway, with red, white, and blue shield. (A green shield is an alternate or business route.) *US* indicates a federal/state arterial system, with black and white shield. *VA* is used for the major state primary system, with black and white, rounded, three-corner shield, numbered from 1 to 599. (Numbers generally do not duplicate a US route number.) *SR* indicates a state secondary or county road (the bulk of the state's road system), paved or gravel, with black and white round signs (but rectangles are used on the official highway map), numbered from 600 up, with numbers often repeated in other counties. *T* is for town and county combinations in towns with populations of 3,500 or less; these are rectangular, may be blue, and are numbered 1000 and above. In addition the USFS has its own numbering system on forest roads open to the public (but sometimes gated, depending on hunting season). The road sign is usually rectangular in brown and yellow and is listed in this book as *FR*. The USFS roads are not shown on the state's official highway map. County roads in West Virginia are listed with a *CO*.

Once you have located the trailhead, the next decision is where to park. Parking areas are described in the book, but a relocation may have occurred between my visit and yours. Some trailheads do not have parking areas; only roadside parking is available at these locations. Unfortunately, there are parking areas with a high rate of vandalism and theft. Always lock your vehicle doors, and lock your valuables in the trunk or leave them at home.

INTRODUCTION: A long trail or a group of trails may need an introduction to provide more information than is usual for the description. This may include history, an expanded description of the features, or physiography.

DESCRIPTION: This is the heart of the trail focus. It begins at the trailhead and guides you across the ridges, over the streams, and into the wonderland and mystery of the forests, fields, and plateaus. It offers milepoints, sometimes frequently to reaffirm that you are on track. References may be made to the plant and animal life along the way. Spur trails to overlooks and grand views are listed at milepoints. Sometimes campsites are suggested, and I have made an effort to make you feel part of an adventure. You will have individual experiences with plant and animal life, weather, and a sense of comfort in the woods, but the description (though you are not likely to have a measuring wheel) is supposed to chart your passage from every significant point to the next.

Descriptions include the value of trail connections, frequency of usage, and the change in elevation. Most of the trails are described as *main* or *primary* (blazed, marked, or maintained); some are *primitive* (the opposite of primary). Others are as follows: A *side* or *spur* offers a shorter route or a path to a point of interest. A *multiple* trail is used by equestrians, bicyclists, or hikers. *Jeep* indicates mainly old forest or hunting roads used by 4WDs. A *manway* or *wilderness* trail is exceptionally primitive, overgrown, or obscure. *Special* indicates a trail used for special populations, such as the physically impaired. A *gated trail* may be a foot trail only for pedestrians during a protected season for wildlife, but may be open to both hikers and vehicles at other times. A *seeded trail* is usually a former logging road planted with grass for soil stabilization. There are numerous paths used by hunters and fishermen that may be called *fisherman's trails* or *hunter's trails* on both public and private lands. Some mountain trails are used as *ski trails* in winter. Other trails may be described as *recreational* (for jogging, exercise, and fitness); *historic* (emphasizing heritage or historical districts or sites); and *nature* (including interpretive, botanical displays). Any or all of these trails may be described as ascents or descents to creeks and ridge saddles and as easy access to highways in the event of an emergency. At the end of the descriptions are listings of the USGS maps that have detailed topo lines for the trails and the USFS trail number.

ADDRESS AND INFORMATION: This is found at the end of all districts, parks, or administrative organizations responsible for a single trail or group of trails. The "available are" listing enables you to have an idea of what to ask for when you write or call. Telephone numbers are the most recently known at press time. (With the increase in population, you may notice early changes.)

SUPPORT FACILITIES: Campgrounds and their facilities are usually described in the introductory section of the district, park, or recreation area. At other times a store or shopping center is listed. Restaurants, telephones, and service stations may also be mentioned.

SIGNS, BLAZES, AND MARKERS: Virginia's Native Americans left hatchet marks on the trees to guide themselves home. Today trailblazers leave ax marks, painted logos, and plastic, diamond-shaped cards. But not all of Virginia's trails are currently blazed or signed. Examples are in the national forests.

The flagship of all Virginia trails, the **Appalachian Trail** is overall the most blazed, marked, signed, and manicured (see Chapter 3). The **AT** mark is always a white 2×6-inch vertical blaze, with side/spur trails (usually for water) painted blue. An exception is where it joins other primary trails, such as the yellow-blazed **Allegheny Trail**. It is maintained primarily by volunteer clubs of the Appalachian Trail Conference with help from the forest and park staffs. Neither of the national forests has a policy or guidelines for consistency in trail blazes, colors, or signage in the districts. The most likely colors are yellow, blue, and orange. Occasionally there will be other colors or a white/gray on such trails as the **Wild Oak Trail** in the Deerfield District. (The usfs boundary marks are red and should not be confused with trail blazes. Also, some trees slated for timbering may have a variety of color markings, even color banding.)

Do not expect to see blazes in the wilderness, but you may see trailhead signage. Vandalism of signs in the national forests is a problem especially in isolated areas. Signs and trailhead outdoor board maps are frequent and clearly designed in the Shenandoah National Park. The Blue Ridge Parkway also has good signage and trail directions. State parks have well-marked trails, and some are color coded. In areas where blazes are faint, I have made an effort to emphasize natural markers—rock formations, flora, streams, viewpoints, bridges, roads, and power lines. If the blazes disappear, I recommend that you backtrack to the last blaze seen to determine if a sharp turn or other change in the trail went unnoticed.

MAPS: An official Virginia highway map is essential. It is available at service stations, convenience stores, drug stores, and newsstands. It can also be ordered (free) from the Virginia Department of Highways and Transportation (phone: 800-367-7623, ext. 00, in Virginia; see Appendix A for address), or the Virginia Division of Tourism (phone: 800-847-4882 [for ordering free travel guide only] or 804-786-2051 [for state highway map]; see Appendix A for address). The tourism office will send you an annual travel guide that covers the state's attractions, activities, and accommodations, plus brochures on horse trails, hiking trails, and bicycle trails. The *Virginia Atlas and Gazetteer* (cited under Trailheads, above) is exceptionally valuable, with many details. Detailed county maps are available from county courthouses, local chambers of commerce, and statewide from the Department of Highways and Transportation at a nominal cost. City maps are available from city newsstands, bookstores, and chambers of commerce for a small charge. Other significant maps are *ADC's Street Maps* of the cities and metropolitan suburbs. Such a map of northern Virginia, for example, is necessary to hike or bike on a labyrinth of trails in a megalopolis unless you live there. Colorful and detailed, it shows all streets, parks, town/city boundaries, streams, lakes, streets/roads/interstates, airports, shopping centers, schools, hospitals, churches, zip code numbers, and much more. Contact the ADC Map People, 6440 General Green Way, Alexandria, VA 22312 (phone: 703-750-0510; fax:

703-750-3092; web: ⟨www.adcmap.com⟩). The map/magazine is available at convenience stores and newsstands.

If you plan to hike in a wilderness area, a topographical map and compass are recommended to prevent disorientation. The USGS maps most commonly used and referred to in this guidebook are on the scale of 1:24,000 (1 in. = 2,000 ft.); they are of considerable assistance in locating roads, residences, lakes, forests, and streams and, with the contour line, in determining elevation. The USGS maps used by the national forests have a modified printing that shows all forest boundaries. For each trail or group of trails described in this guidebook there is a USGS map noted at the end of the description. If your local blueprint store or outdoor sports store does not have the map you desire, you can order from Branch of Distribution, USGS, Box 25286 Federal Center, Denver, CO 80225. Because you must pay in advance, write for a free Virginia map index and order form. Expect two to four weeks for delivery. You may also contact the national forest headquarters.

There are two other sources of maps for your hikes. On the **Appalachian Trail**, the best map to use is the one numbered for a particular district and supported by the **Appalachian Trail** guidebooks of that area (see Chapter 3). These may be ordered from the Appalachian Trail Conference in Harpers Ferry, West Virginia. For other areas, you can obtain a contour map from each of the forest ranger districts. Some of the maps are outdated and have titles such as "Map" or "Sportsman's Guide." They are supposed to show all the trails by name and number, forest roads and number, and all secondary and primary roads and number. They cut off trails at their boundaries and rarely show their continuation or connection in the adjoining district. They can be purchased (for a small fee) at the district office or at forest headquarters. Call or write for a list of these and other maps (some free) of the districts. The maps also list and describe all the recreation areas, including campgrounds. In 2001 the National Geographic Society prepared *Trails Illustrated*, topographic maps for all the national forests in Virginia and the Shenandoah National Park. The multicolor maps are identified by district names and map numbers. These are the most informative maps on the market. (The few mistakes can be removed by the next printing.) Contact your local bookstore or USFS office, or NGM, P.O. Box 357, Evergreen, CO 80437; phone: 800-962-1643 or 303-670-3457; web: ⟨www.trailsillustrated.com⟩.

For hikers and birders there are eighteen color-keyed maps in *Discover Our Wild Side: Virginia Birding and Wildlife Trail (Coastal Area)* for circuit highway routes to private and public parks, forests, preserves, natural areas, memorial sanctuaries, colleges, and historic sites. The maps are in a 100-page book of illustrations and descriptions of wildlife, and many of the locations enhance what is described in this guidebook. The map/book is free. Plans are to publish similar books on the state's central and mountain areas. For more information or copies, contact the Wildlife Diversity Division, Virginia Department of Game and Inland Fisheries, 4010 West Broad Street, Richmond, VA 23230; phone: 804-367-1000, or 804-367-0940; fax:

804-367-0488; web: ⟨www.dgif.state.va.us⟩. For extra copies of trail highway loop and site maps contact the Virginia Tourism Corporation at 866-VABIRDS.

WILDERNESS: The George Washington and Jefferson National Forests have seventeen wilderness areas, described in the introductions and narratives of Chapters 1 and 2. Not all have trail networks, but trail life in these areas is different from all the other areas. Wilderness management is guided by the Wilderness Act of 1964, whose purpose is to preserve and protect natural ecosystems and values. A basic factor in wilderness guidelines is the provision of a unique experience for the visitors without evidence that anyone has visited. Therefore, when planning trips into the backcountry, remember that a trip to a wilderness area is considerably demanding.

In wilderness areas no timber is harvested, and no roads, dams, or reservoirs are constructed; there are no power projects with transmission lines and no developed recreational facilities. Recreational usage is not promoted, and facilities, if any, are not designed for comfort. Maintenance occurs only when users are adversely affecting the soil or vegetation on the treadway. Shelters may be absent or in the process of being phased out. Signage and blazes are kept to the minimum; only ax blazes may give some direction, or signage may be of metal or unpainted routed wood. Where there are roads, they usually serve the USFS for safety reasons, fire suppression, and the treatment of diseased trees.

A few set policies are prescribed for hikers and campers. Basics include no-trace planning, no-trace travel, and no-trace camping. The regular backpacking rule of "pack it in, pack it out" applies. The maximum group size is ten. Camp stoves are strongly encouraged, and campfires must be from only dead and down wood. Topographical maps, compass, first-aid kit, and water purifier are essential. Use of horses is not encouraged because of limited trail maintenance. Hunting, fishing, and trapping may occur but are subject to appropriate state and federal laws. Law enforcement personnel check for litter, vehicle usage, and adherence to fire regulations. For information, consult the district ranger and request the "Leave No Trace Land Ethics" brochure. You may also wish to purchase *Field Guide to Wilderness Survival* by Tom Brown and the *Wilderness Guide* by Peter Simer and John Sullivan for the National Outdoor Leadership School. The contents cover the impact of camping on the environment, how to dress and what equipment is necessary for the backcountry, cooking, maps, first aid, weather, and more.

## Plants, Animals, and Minerals

This book does not attempt to describe in detail any of the plants, animals, or minerals seen on the trails. References are made in general terms, but more specific details are given for places where I encountered unusual or impressive scenery. Hikers may see the same thing, or something entirely different during a different season. Therefore, I have used common names for a single or multiple species. For example, *oak* may be used to name any of the twenty-six species of oaks. If there are exclusive groves such as chestnut oak (*Quercus prinus*), I may be more specific and give the botanical name. The same is true for the eleven species of rhododendron, except for outstanding displays of rosebay, great laurel (*Rhododendron maximum*), purple (*Rhododendron catawbiense*), flame (*Rhododendron calendulaceum*), or the rose (fragrant) (*Rhododendron roseum*). The latter is unforgettable on the **Appalachian Trail** in Nelson County during May. Residents of the Appalachian Mountains usually call rhododendron "laurel," and mountain laurel (*Kalmia latifolia*) "ivy." To save space, I frequently refer to "wildflowers" rather than describe all the various flowers in a given location. Sometimes one wildflower will be more profuse, and I include it specifically. An example is the beds of lily-of-the-valley (*Convallaria majalis*) on North Mountain near New Castle. Once the botanical names are given, only the common names are used thereafter.

Virginia has more than 85 species of ferns and more than 3,400 species and varieties of other vascular plants. Some occur statewide, while others occur in only one or a few areas. Among the books for serious examination are *Atlas of Virginia Flora*, volumes 1 and 2, by Harvill, Stevens, Ware, and Bradley (contains maps showing county-by-county occurrences of the known species); and two scholarly sources, *Flora of West Virginia*, volumes 1–4, by Strausbaugh and Core, and the *Manual of the Vascular Flora of the Carolinas* by Radford, Ahles, and Bell. These books have most of the plants found in Virginia. Otherwise, for basic information, use Lawrence Newcomb's *Wildflower Guide*, the *Peterson Field Guide*, or the *Audubon Society Field Guide for North American Wildflowers*. All are concise, colorful, and easy to carry. The nonvascular plants in Virginia consist of more than 25,000 species and include algae, lichens, fungi, liverworts, and mosses. Again, consult with the field guide books for basic use. If you are interested in the wild plants for food, read the *Field Guide to Edible Wild Plants* by Bradford Angier. For medical usage, try Mannfried Pahlow's *Living Medicine*. (For a book on the poisonous plants, see Health and Safety, below.)

From among the seventy-five species of terrestrial mammals known in Virginia, you will be lucky to see a dozen in one day or hear the nocturnal ones at night. Your chances of seeing birds is better because of their daily activity. There are approximately 400 species, with some overwintering in Virginia during the migratory periods. On trails where I have seen an unusual number of bird species, I have indicated the information in the description. Two excellent books for birding are *Virginia's Birdlife*, published by the Virginia Society of Ornithology, and *Birds of the Blue Ridge Mountains* by Marcus B. Simpson Jr. The state's herpetofauna consists of 144 species and subspecies almost equally divided: 75 amphibians and 69 reptiles. Some occur statewide, but most have a rather limited distribution.

The remaining vertebrate animals in the state, the fish, are known to occur in more than 200 freshwater species and in an almost equal number of marine and estuarine species. Additionally, invertebrates represent at least 90 percent of the animals in the state. They include insects and mollusks. A few of many recommended books for the hiker interested in wildlife are *Amphibians and Reptiles of the Carolinas and Virginia* by Martof, Palmer, Bailey, Harrison, and Dermid; *Mammals of Virginia* by John W. Bailey; *Snakes of Virginia* by D. W. Linzey; *Mammals of the Carolinas, Virginia, and Maryland* by Webster, Parnell, and Biggs; and the popular Audubon field guides on butterflies, mammals, fish, insects and spiders, and others. Virginia has a number of rare plants and animals, some of which I have referred to in the trail descriptions. Most are rare because of habitat destruction, not natural occurrence. A good overview of this subject is found in *Endangered and Threatened Plants and Animals of Virginia*, edited by D. W. Linzey. Another book, by Christopher White, is *Endangered and Threatened Wildlife of the Chesapeake Bay Region* (of Delaware, Maryland, and Virginia). A list of Virginia's endangered or threatened species is in Appendix B of this book.

White-tailed deer (*Odocoileus virginianus*) and wild turkey (*Meleagris gallopavo silvestris*) are perhaps the most likely to be seen game animal and nonmigratory game bird in the forests and parks. Other game species frequently sighted are squirrel, fox, rabbit, and raccoon. Black bear (*Ursus americanus*) and bobcat are elusive and rarely seen by hikers. (Hikers have reported seeing bears on the AT and on trails in Shenandoah National Park.) The state's deer population in 2002 was about 1 million, with 200,000 harvested by hunters. The highest density was in Bedford, Botetourt, Southampton, and Loudoun Counties. The black bear population is about 3,500, with about 890 killed each year. (The Virginia Department of Game and Inland Fisheries restricts hunting of the bear to one per person per year.) The turkey flock is about 100,000, with 26,000 harvested annually.

If you hike in the mountains of southwestern Virginia, you will become aware of the seven counties with bituminous coal on the Appalachian plateau, and layers of sandstone and limestone. Many of the valleys are underlain with shales and carbonates. Faulted rock formations are prominent. The state's highest concentrations of oil and gas are also in this area. Farther northeast the geological makeup of the Blue Ridge Mountains includes more metamorphic and igneous rock. Limestone is noticeable throughout the Shenandoah Valley, and shale is sometimes found in mountainside slides in both the Allegheny and the Blue Ridge Mountains. Slate is prominent in central counties of the state, particularly Buckingham. Other rock formations in the state are of feldspar, granite, quartz, greenstone (both in the Blue Ridge Mountains and near the fall line in Prince William County), gneiss, schist, and soapstone. Virginia is the only state in the nation that produces aplite, an acidic granite of quartz and feldspar. In a number of areas along the Blue Ridge Mountains you will see the remains of old iron mines and furnaces, which were prominent before the late 1880s. The state has three physical geographical divisions: mountains (from the Blue Ridge Mountains west to other Appalachian Mountain chains at the borders of Kentucky and West Virginia); piedmont (between the fall line and west to the Blue Ridge Mountains, about 40 mi. in the northeast to 185 mi. along the southern border); and tidewater (coastal and level plain of alluvial soil). The fall line runs from Alexandria slightly southwest to Fredericksburg, Richmond, Petersburg, and Clarksville/South Hill (a navigation factor that influenced the location of Native American and European settlements). Unique to the fall line is a distinctive break in the piedmont's crystalline rock formation. For a source on minerals, consult *Mineral Resources of Virginia* by Thomas Watson.

## Health and Safety

Trails may appear to be a safe retreat from the dangers of an industrial world, except for the fact that you can encounter precipitous rocks, streams to be forded, falling tree limbs, poisonous plants and animals, and stormy weather. Hikers must go prepared. Even a minor injury or bacterial disorder can ruin an otherwise pleasant trip. Although veteran hikers know how to prepare for a journey and how to face emergencies, there are some commonsense suggestions for the novice: Do not take chances at dangerous places. Observe official regulations and guidelines. Use care in the use of fires, knives, tin or glass cans, and fishhooks. Do not go swimming in unfamiliar waters. Avoid unfiltered or unapproved drinking water. Make certain you have enough warm clothes and that your boots fit properly. Take a first-class first-aid kit. Do not hike at night. Do not become over-exhausted. Avoid getting cold and wet. Do not carry firearms unless you are hunting wild game. Be prepared for stormy weather. Take precautions against getting lost. For overnight or long hikes always have an emergency plan. You may wish to take your first backpacking trip with trained or seasoned hikers who can give you additional suggestions.

FIRST-AID KIT: The following items are recommended for your first-aid kit: adhesive bandages (a variety of shapes and sizes for small or large wounds, fingertip cuts, and scraped knuckles); sterile gauze pads and tapes; cleaning pads (water may not be available); antibiotic cream; cortisone cream; phenol for insect bite or blister relief; lotion or cream for chapped skin and cold sores; sunscreen; tweezers; elastic bandage for twisted ankle or knee; acetaminophen or aspirin (ask your doctor about stronger pain killers); repellents against ticks, mosquitoes, and other biting insects; antihistamines for allergic rhinitis/hay fever; tablets for stomach upsets or acidity; moleskin; and your personal medical prescription. One rule is to not take something you do not know how to use. Although you may think this list is long, properly packaged it should not take up much space. You may wish to have a professional first-aid kit instead of making a kit for yourself. If so, contact Chinook Medical Gear, Inc., 120 Rock Point Dr., Unit C, Durango, CO 81301 (phone: 800-766-1365; fax: 970-375-6343; web: ⟨www.chinookmed.com⟩), or Adventure Medical Kits, P.O. Box 43309, Oakland, CA 94624 (phone: 800-324-3517; fax: 510-261-7419; web: ⟨www.adventuremedicalkits.com⟩). You may also wish to check with your local outdoor sports store for a kit to suit your needs. (See Planning Your Trip, below.)

SAFETY EQUIPMENT: In addition to the first-aid kit, there are other important safety items. Take a Swiss army knife (which should have scissors if you have not included a pair in the first-aid kit); waterproof matches (this is also a good storage place for first-aid needles); maps, pencil and note paper, compass, and flashlight (preferably one with krypton bulbs); batteries; multifrequency whistle (for SOS calls); 75 to 100 feet of nylon rope; biodegradable soap; safety pins; and water filter. The day has passed when you could dip your Sierra cup in any bubbling mountain stream without fear of acquiring *Giardia* (bacteria causing severe diarrhea). Water purification is necessary unless you are at campgrounds or recreational areas where water is officially tested safe. Boiling water is still one method (a full boil for three to five minutes), and iodine crystals may help against some pollutants, but not against *Giardia*. Inexpensive filters are available from your outdoor sports shops. The snakebite kit, recommended in the past as being essential, is no longer preferred for treatment of poisonous snakebites. Immediate transportation to a hospital emergency clinic is considered the best response. If you are hiking in a poisonous snake environment, have a hiking companion and wear protective legwear.

POISONOUS PLANTS AND ANIMALS: Virginia has three types of poisonous snakes: rattlesnakes (habitat mainly in the mountains), copperheads (general locations), and cottonmouth moccasins (chiefly in the state's southeastern swamps and backwater). The rattlesnake is thought by some to be the most deadly, and its bite requires immediate treatment.

The female black widow spider (*Latrodectus mactans*) is usually under benches, picnic tables, and around old stumps and logs. Her bite may go unnoticed until the victim experiences severe abdominal pain (much like appendicitis) and profuse sweating. Treatment should be at an emergency clinic. Black widows can be identified by their red underbelly.

Bites from yellow jackets, wasps, bees, and hornets can cause pain and swelling. To some hikers with allergies a single sting can be serious, and multiple stings life-threatening. A pharmacist can recommend an effective product for quick insect bite relief, or take an emergency insect-sting allergy kit obtained with a doctor's prescription.

Most common among poisonous plants are poison ivy, oak, and sumac, with ivy

(*Toxicodendron radicans*) being the most profuse. Its oil, urushiol, is colorless and may not show its effect until hours or days after contact. Treat with cortisone or calamine lotion or medication prescribed by a doctor. Remember, "leaves of three, leave it be." To avoid this nuisance, be able to identify the leaves and berries.

The berries of the Virginia creeper and the American holly are poisonous when ingested. Also toxic are buckeye, wild cherry, jimsonweed, white snakeroot, ground cherry (except the ripe fruit), lupine, nightshade, and lily-of-the-valley.

Among the toxic mushrooms are the destroying angel and the greengill. Avoid eating mushrooms unless you know them with certainty. A recommended book is *Plants That Poison* by Ervin M. Schmutz and Lucretia B. Hamilton.

Lyme disease, for many years difficult to diagnose, is contracted only through the bite of an infected deer tick (the deer being the carrier). Currently, the disease is more serious in a few states outside Virginia, but caution should be taken. At first a large circular red rash may appear followed by stages of lesion expansion. After a few months or years, aches and pains and paralysis develop. It is treatable with doxycycline or amoxicillin, but prevention is simple: use a repellent with deet or permethrin, and check yourself daily.

Coping with other bugs such as mosquitoes, black flies, deerflies, no-see-ums, and red-bugs (chiggers) requires knowing their habitats, wearing long and light-colored clothes, and using repellents.

HYPOTHERMIA: Fatalities are rare on Virginia's more than 5,000 miles of trails, but when they occur, the causes are mainly drowning, falling, or hypothermia. The latter occurs when the body core temperature falls below normal. It can develop unexpectedly in weather temperatures up to 40–50°F when the hiker has wet, cold clothes and may be physically exhausted. Usually the first sign is uncontrolled shivering, which consumes an already low energy reserve. The result is a lack of reasoning, and the victim seems to be unaware of a loss of control. Without immediate treatment the hiker can collapse, unable to speak, and may become unconscious. Companions should be aware of symptoms other than shivering, such as slurred speech, memory loss, and stumbling. Avoid the causes by staying dry and out of wind and rain or snow, and wear adequate clothes and rain or snow gear. Treatment must be immediate with a change into warm, dry clothes and sleeping bag, a warm drink (no alcohol), warmth to face and head, gentle handling, and evacuation to an emergency hospital.

WEATHER: The Old Dominion has moderate weather conditions with average temperatures for Norfolk in winter 42°F, in spring 58°F, in summer 77°F, and in fall 62°F. Farther west in Roanoke the temperature in winter averages 37°F, in spring 56°F, in summer 74°F, and in fall 57°F. Temperatures are always lower in the state's higher elevations, such as at Mount Rogers (the state's highest).

Snow is most likely from January through March in the western half of the state but infrequent in the Chesapeake Bay area. Without warning there can be rapid changes in the weather and in temperatures on Mount Rogers and in the Allegheny Mountains and Shenandoah Mountains bordering West Virginia. Hikers should be prepared with proper clothing and equipment and calls to the local ranger districts or local weather stations.

Lightning is the most serious threat in the summer months. (It strikes about 1,800 people, of whom 300 are killed, each year in the United States.) Lightning may strike directly, when you are the primary target, or indirectly, when it bounces from a tree or other object. Safety suggestions are to stay away from conductive materials such as water, metal boats, carbon fishing rods, and even metal framed backpacks. Do not stand under a single tree or in open areas or rock crevices. If in a group, do not cluster. If possible choose a shrubby area, squat low, balanced on the balls of your feet with feet together. Some guides suggest you choose this position on your sleeping bag or foam mattress to prevent being a conductor. Even though a victim of a lightning strike may appear unconscious, a persistent effort using CPR or mouth-to-mouth breathing may resuscitate the person.

SEARCH AND RESCUE: One way to avoid being lost in the forest is to not venture off the trail unless you have adequate maps or are familiar with the territory. However, if you get lost, the following is recommended: Do not panic; rest and examine your maps with a compass. If you are lost on a trail, try to remember directions to where you saw the last blaze or sign; otherwise, stay in place. Make a fire and keep warm. Use an sos of three sounds. Conserve your food and water. If you are able to walk and if after a reasonable number of hours or days you are not rescued, follow a stream to a road and perhaps a house or store with a telephone. Leave a message at the site you left and indicate your intended plans or route. (You could carry a walkie-talkie or cellular phone with you, but most hikers feel this compromises the wilderness experience. Furthermore, rescue teams are complaining that they are receiving trivial calls from the inexperienced.)

If you are in a group when another hiker is seriously injured, a litter may be the best method of transport. A pole litter can be made with two seven-foot poles and two thirty-inch poles for a rectangular frame. Use rope interloops. Remember, do not create additional victims by careless or risky evacuation. Helpful in search and rescue plans are Bernard Shanks's *Wilderness Survival* and Paul Gill's *Pocket Guide to Wilderness Medicine*.

## Planning Your Trip

Getting started is as simple as having the interest in going, but the distance and length of time on the trails will determine, and delay, your preparation. If you plan to hike all of the **Appalachian Trail** in Virginia (550 mi.), you may need five to six weeks (plus time for diversions). If you are in a group (more than two), expect to take longer because groups usually slow the pace, and the housekeeping of camping becomes cumbersome. You may plan for other activities besides hiking, such as bicycling, horseback riding, fishing and hunting, long-term camping, water sports, or mountain climbing. Or you may wish to take only a daypack from your vehicle and, like John Muir, just pack some bread and tea in a sack, or a modern prepacked luncheon. Whatever your plans as an outdoors aficionado, there are some basic guidelines. Below are some examples of what to take, mainly recommended by the writers and guides of the trail community.

Decide on who and how many are going; what are their limitations and special considerations? Are you taking grandparents, children, or a physically impaired relative or friend? If you are on a challenging backpacking trip into the wilderness, will you go alone or take a companion or companions? If you are going into the wilderness with others, choose only pleasant and agreeable companions, those you can trust to finish the journey and support you in a crisis or emergency. In your planning, contact forest or park officials for information on maps, permits, restrictions, accessibility, weather conditions, rank of trail traffic, campgrounds, shelters, water, and trail hazards. Determine your objective and who is the leader in the trek. Make a checklist, which you will probably change a number of times: the essentials (must-have items); partially needed items (may decide on after you weigh your backpack); and optionals (frills, extra comforts, or perhaps a heavy zoom lens). Do not take firearms.

Basic items to take are sleeping bag; tent; hiking boots (with insoles and socks); backpack or daypack; food (if freeze-dried, take some onions and bell peppers or sauce mix for improved flavor); canteen; cookware; stove; mattress; water purifier; first-aid kit with other items listed under *Health and Safety* (above); clothing (prepare for stable to radical weather); pen/pencil and note paper; and personal hygiene kit. Do not forget to service your vehicle, one that will certainly get you to and from the trailheads but, if stolen, will not cost four years of mortgage payments to replace. Dress realistically; dealing with stinging bugs and bees and poisonous snakes and spiders requires more the Daniel Boone type than a tennis player in *lederhosen* (though you may see **Appalachian Trail** through-hikers in only boots, shorts, and a pack). If your trip is to include canoeing and bicycling and you plan to take the equipment on top of your car, take extra time for long-range planning. Of help will be *The Camper's Companion* by Rick Greenspan and Hal L. Kahn. Experienced hikers know of *The Complete Walker IV* by Colin Fletcher. If you are a beginner, his book is worthwhile for what *Field and Stream* has called "The Hiker's Bible." His thorough checklist covers every subject on which you are likely to have a question.

TRAIL COURTESY: As the trail user population increases (42 million in the United States in 2002), so does the need for good trail relationships between all users.

*Lewis Fork Trail, Mount Rogers NRA (Courtesy U.S. Forest Service)*

Within the past decade there has been a major change from single usage of trails to multiple usage. Many of the trails were created for pedestrian usage only and are not wide enough for an influx of other users. To accommodate multiple users some of the trails were simply widened to provide usage for hikers, mountain bikers, equestrians, joggers, roller skaters, and skateboarders. On some of the USFS trails, all-terrain vehicle (ATV) drivers also became a user. The polite expression of dissatisfaction to another person whose radio is keeping you awake at a campsite can suddenly shift from courtesy to justified anger when you are disturbed or injured by an ATV, or those who violate personal and public property regulations.

In June 2002 the Appalachian Trail Conference staff appealed to conference members for financial assistance to combat the usage of ATVs on the environmentally sensitive *Appalachian Trail*. The message indicated that usage of ATVs exists from Maine to Georgia, and that the environmental damage and the safety of hikers were urgent issues. Damage could be permanent to the "nation's most treasured footpath." It is not just the **Appalachian Trail** that has this problem; aggressive violation of trail regulations is occurring on other trails in the national forests and parks. If you encounter a problem with an ATV user, or a poacher, make an effort to remember as much as possible about identity and location in reporting your complaint. Sometimes courtesy is best demonstrated by not saying or doing anything. There are other times, for example when you see trail users building fires in no-fire zones, that a verbal complaint without courtesy is justified.

Although it is not a safety issue, the quality of courteous feelings are tested at a tranquil campsite when another trail user arrives with a loud two-way radio, or TV, or solar-powered satellite telephone, or portable computer. For some trail users these modern services undermine and disrupt the traditional trail experience. An all-night barking dog or unleashed dogs disturbing you or wildlife is also a courtesy tester, particularly if you are in a zone where any type of pets are forbidden. For a cooperative experience on any trail, other people's differences have to be accepted or reasonably tolerated. If the level of toleration becomes unacceptable, then you have to risk your judgment on a solution. Some trail users are more outspoken; they simply demand you cease what is offending them.

On trails where camping or shelter space may be a significant issue, consider always having a tent with you. Courtesy or not, one should not be timid about requesting another user to respect cleanliness of the water supply, or violating the "carry in–carry out" waste principle. Hikers appreciate bikers using a warning bell or other sound to not startle them from behind, and equestrians appreciate both bikers and hikers who refrain from surprising the horses. Because the trails are there for the benefit of all users, it seems only civil that we find solutions for minor personal grievances, yet also remain aggressive in reporting violations of forest and park rules and regulations.

## Trails for the Future

If you have recently been on some of the most popular trails in Virginia, you will notice how crowded some of them are becoming. The Virginia Division of Parks and Recreation, the Appalachian Trail Conference, the USFS, the NPS, and county and municipal departments of parks and recreation report an increase in usage of facilities and trails. Many visitors to the parks where trails exist take short walks either for a leg stretcher or seeing the scenery. Others hike them daily and completely. Within the past few years the National Park Service has been reporting that more than 275 million Americans annually visit national parks. One of those parks, the Blue Ridge Parkway, has about 20 million visitors annually. The reports indicate that many in the national number make from three to ten visits at the same or a variety of parks during the year. Imagine the significance of usage when we add up the numbers for all national forests, state parks, preserves, and neighborhood parks. There will always be a need for more trails for all user groups. On November 5, 2002, the Virginia legislature passed a $118 million bond referendum for the purchase and development of new state parks and for developing new and upgraded services. If you are interested in Virginia's plans, including trail plans for the future, request a copy of the 2002 "Virginia Outdoors Plan" by the Department of Conservation and Economic Development (804-786-2556). (The plan is revised every four years.) Also, consider becoming more than an active trail user; join a neighborhood or state recreation organization that assists in the construction and maintenance of current trails and trails of the future (see a list of state organizations in Appendix A). Welcome to the trails of Virginia.

*Much of our 2,000-mile network of trails is maintained by volunteers in partnership with U.S. Forest Service. The American people benefit enormously from the help of these dedicated people.*

BILL DAMON, FOREST SUPERVISOR, 2003

# PART I. National Forest Trails

In 1995 the George Washington National Forest (GWNF) and the Jefferson National Forest (JNF) were administratively combined to form the George Washington and Jefferson National Forests (GW&JNF). The total area of the combined unit is 1,764,237 acres, of which 1,658,769 are in Virginia, 104,507 are in West Virginia, and 961 are in Kentucky. These national forests are among the nation's 156, and among 35 in the Southern Region's (Region 8) 14 states from Texas to Virginia. The Virginia headquarters for both forests is in Roanoke. Virginia's national forests border each other at the James River, and both have boundaries that spill over into West Virginia. The JNF also extends into Kentucky and borders the Cherokee National Forest at the Tennessee state line. The GWNF also shares a state line boundary with the Monongahela National Forest in West Virginia.

National forests and national grasslands are under the management of the USFS, a federal agency, in the Department of Agriculture. Additionally, the Department of Agriculture administers programs such as the Agricultural Stabilization and Conservation Service, the Animal and Plant Health Inspection Service, the Economic Research Service, the Science and Education Service (for watershed, soil, and air research), and the Natural Resources Conservation Service.

The purpose and management of the USFS have been controversial from the beginning in 1905 when President Theodore Roosevelt appointed conservationist Gifford Pinchot as the agency's first chief of staff. Considered to be the founder of professional forestry, Pinchot said that to make the national forests "accomplish the most good the people themselves must make clear how they want them run." (His observations led eventually to the National Forest Management Act of 1976, which requires forest supervisory staff to hold public forums and respond to thousands of letters before a long written plan among alternatives is approved.) Another conservationist, John Muir, attempted to convince President Roosevelt that all national forests (as with national parks, begun in 1872) should be preserved. How the silviculturists interpreted the federal policies has remained a major part of the public controversy.

Since 1905 more than twenty-five congressional acts have been passed that affect the national forests. Among them is the Weeks Law (1911). It authorized the purchase of lands for timber production. In 1960 the Multiple Use–Sustained

Yield Act reemphasized the basic purposes of forests for outdoor recreation, watershed, range, mineral resources, wildlife and fish, and timber production. The Wilderness Act of 1964 established a system for preserving special areas from timber harvesting, mining, or other development. The National Trails System Act (1968) established a protective system for national recreational and scenic trails. (An example is the *Appalachian National Scenic Trail*, which passes through both the JNF and the GWNF in Virginia. The act is administered by the National Park Service of the Department of the Interior.) The National Environmental Policy Act (1970) requires all federal agencies to prepare formal environmental impact statements on the environmental effects of all planned programs and actions. In 1974 the Forest and Rangeland Renewable Resources Planning Act required the USFS to prepare long-range programs concerning forest administration, roads and trails, research, and cooperative ventures. It was amended by the National Forest Management Act of 1976, which requires full public participation in the development and revision of land management plans and periodic proposal of a Land and Resource Management Plan (hereafter referred to as the Forest Plan). The environmental impact statements and the Forest Plan are the most revealing documents for hikers who wish to know about the stewardship of the USFS.

In January 1993 the GWNF released an Environmental Impact Statement for the Revised Land and Resource Management Plan. In March 2001 the GW&JNF released a volume entitled *Detailed Monitoring and Evaluation Report of Land and Resource Management Plan*. Some of the public issues remain the same as in earlier management plans of 1985 and 1986. Examples are ATVs, access needs, development of mines and energy resources, below-cost timber sales and timber roads, clear-cutting, multiple-use trails, and wilderness areas with mineral rights.

Geographically the George Washington National Forest extends southwest from near Winchester to between Lexington and Roanoke, and the Jefferson National Forest continues southwest to the Kentucky border. The forest trails are described in this book contiguously southwest rather than alphabetically. You will notice the order of contents matches this order of descriptions for Lee Ranger District to be first and Clinch Ranger District to be last.

There are 2,000 miles of trails listed on Virginia's national forests Transportation Inventory Survey (TIS). The USFS does not have the staff or the money to keep them all maintained, blazed, and signed. To understand the needs of the USFS, its position in the crossfire of public demands, its adaptation to the new management policies, and its future plans, I recommend the following to all trail users: Become knowledgeable by examining the long list of topics found on the USFS southern region's website under headings such as About the Forests, Recreation, General Information, Forest Management, Forest Plan Revisions, and Other Information of Interest ⟨http:/www.southernregion.fs.fed.us/gwj/⟩. Additionally, study the Forest Plan and environmental impact statements, become active in a hiking/

maintenance organization, and visit usfs district ranger offices for personal contact information, maps, and brochures.

HEADQUARTERS ADDRESS: George Washington and Jefferson National Forests, 5162 Valleypointe Parkway, Roanoke, VA 24019; phone: 540-265-5100 or 888-265-0019 (toll free); fax: 540-265-5145.

*Trees and stones will teach you that*
*which you can never learn from Masters.*
ST. BERNARD (1091–1153)

# 1. George Washington National Forest

The 1,061,080-acre George Washington National Forest (GWNF) celebrated its 85th birthday in 2002. Its history began six years after the Congressional Weeks Law authorized the purchase of land to form national forests. Shenandoah and Natural Bridge were two of the first forests, but President Herbert Hoover decreed in 1932 that the Shenandoah National Forest would henceforth be the George Washington National Forest. In 1933 the Natural Bridge National Forest was added to the GWNF, but part of it went to the JNF, which was formed in 1936.

The GWNF spreads from the James River and south of Covington in the south to near Winchester in the north. On its eastern boundary are Shenandoah National Park and the Blue Ridge Parkway (BRP, which sometimes is in the forest). Its western boundary shares two districts—Warm Springs and part of James River—with the Monongahela National Forest in West Virginia. In the center of this vast and resplendent domain is the idyllic Shenandoah Valley, where pioneers began to settle and farm in 1728, and where battles were fought in the Revolutionary and Civil wars. The national forest covers parts of 17 counties, including 4 in West Virginia. It has 1,287 miles of streams (called creeks, runs, forks, or branches) and rivers, and 3,190 acres of lakes, ponds, and tarns, the largest of which is Lake Moomaw. There are high, windswept peaks, knobs, and balds over 4,000 feet (Reddish Knob), cascading waterfalls (Crabtree), damp and dark drafts (Ramseys), natural springs (Wiggins), and native trout rivers (Jackson). The GWNF has eight wilderness areas totaling more than 42,500 acres: Ramseys Draft, St. Mary's, Rich Hole, Rough Mountain, The Priest, Three Ridges, Barbours Creek, and Shawvers Run. There are six ranger districts.

At least 46 areas and about 51,000 acres of unique botanical and zoological habitats have been identified by the U.S. Fish and Wildlife Service and Virginia Natural Heritage Program. As a result, the forest service has set a primary goal of protecting the endangered, threatened, and sensitive species of flora and fauna. Examples of threatened vascular plants are swamp pink (*Helonias bullata*), usually found in mossy cold seeps, and Virginia sneezeweed (*Helenium virginicum*), located near borders of dry ponds in only two counties. Smooth rockcress (*Arabis serotina*), on shaley slopes, and northeastern bulrush (*Scirpus ancistrochaetus*) are federally listed as endangered. Paper birch, which grows only in the Dry River

Ranger District, is listed by the state as sensitive. American ginseng (*Panax quin-quefolium*) is considered threatened in the state, but harvesting is allowed with a license. It grows usually in rich, mesic coves. Two federally endangered mammals are the northern Virginia flying squirrel (*Glaucomys sabrinus fuscus*) and the Indiana bat (*Myotis sodalis*). Both are in the Warm Springs Ranger District. A complete status list of all flora and fauna is in Appendix F of the 1993 *Final Environmental Impact Statement* of the forest. There are about 1,400 species of plants in the GWNF, 70 species of trees, and 71 terrestrial mammal species. In the past few years large segments of hardwoods have been defoliated by the gypsy moth, the hemlock by woolly adelgid, and the dogwood by anthracnose, a fungal disease. The cost of treatment for the gypsy moth is exorbitant, and the only known enemy is the spores of a moth-killing fungus, *Entomophaga maimaiga*. Entire stands of Virginia pine and table mountain pine have been destroyed by the southern pine beetle. However, plant pathologists in the USFS have stated that recovery will occur through adaptation.

Because the GWNF is within a day's driving distance of more than 57 million people, the administrative policy of its managers is to provide a varied catalog of services to meet the diverse interests of the public. An example is the partnership between the national forest and the Wildlife Center of Virginia for a 400-acre facility in the Glenwood/Pedlar Ranger District, south of Waynesboro. The environmental education center provides classrooms, activity labs, universal interpretive trails, and learning stations. Another environmental awareness program is Eyes on Wildlife (also called Watchable Wildlife) in cooperation with Defenders of Wildlife. One of its purposes is to monitor healthy ecosystems for all plants. The GWNF is also active in providing accommodations for people with disabilities. Anglers, for example, have piers at Bealer's Ferry Pond (9 mi. north of Luray, off SR 684) in the Lee Ranger District, Elkhorn Lake (near Stokesville) in the Dry River Ranger District, and Bolar Flats Picnic Area (at the marina at Lake Moomaw). In the Warm Springs Ranger District, at Hidden Valley Recreation Area, is an ATV and motorcycle route for hunters with disabilities. Another special region is the Shady Mountain Disabled Hunter Area in the Glenwood/Pedlar Ranger District. (The USFS provides a list of all disabled hunter's road.) The GWNF has cooperative programs with Ducks Unlimited, Trout Unlimited, and the Virginia Department of Game and Inland Fisheries. An example of these programs is Kids Fishing Day, usually held in late April. Some of the participating areas are Elkhorn Lake in the Dry River Ranger District, Sherando Lake in the Glenwood/Pedlar Ranger District, and Dunlop Creek in the James River Ranger District. In addition there is the outdoor classroom for young people at Augusta Springs in the Deerfield Ranger District. To help local rural areas with long-term economic development, the GWNF began a program in the early 1990s to obtain grants through the Rural Revitalization Forest projects.

There are ninety-eight recreation areas containing twenty developed campgrounds in the GWNF. From these areas are many trails that offer a variety of recreation. Of the more than 900 miles of trails, there are foot trails for back-packers and hikers, equestrian trails, bicycle trails, trails for motor vehicles, trails for the disabled, and multiple-use trails. Three long-distance trails pass through the forest: 57 miles of the **AT**, 40 miles of the **Tuscarora Trail**, and 10 miles (with at least 18 more mi. planned) of the **Allegheny Trail**. Examples of long internal trails are the **Massanutten Mountain Trail** (East, South, and West), 91.4 miles in the Lee Ranger District; the **Shenandoah Mountain Trail** (South and North), 28 miles in the Deerfield Ranger District; and the **Wild Oak Trail** (circuit), 26 miles in the Dry River Ranger District. One of the long trails for motor vehicles is 12-mile **Rocky Run Trail** for ATVs and 4WDs in the Dry River Ranger District.

During the 1980s a large percentage of the trails lacked maintenance, signage, and blazing, and improvements began in the 1990s. The Lee and Pedlar Ranger Districts, closest to metropolitan areas and volunteer groups, have a better record of trail upkeep. Maintenance is more difficult, and more commensurate with usage, in some of the rugged areas of other districts, termed "remote highlands," of which there are about 143,000 acres. But trails in these areas often appeal to the more experienced hikers who desire less manicuring of trails for a more wilderness atmosphere. Trail management policy is described on pages 3-141–142 of the 1993 *Final Revised Land and Resource Management Plan* (usually called *The Plan*).

ADDRESS AND INFORMATION: George Washington and Jefferson National Forests, 5162 Valleypointe Parkway, Roanoke, VA 24019; phone: 540-265-5100. Available for free are GWNF news information, brochures, and Forest Visitor Guide. Materials available for a fee are National Geographic maps #788, 789, 791, 792; GWNF map of Virginia and West Virginia; all district recreation maps; topographical maps; and wilderness maps of Ramseys Draft, St. Mary's, and Lake Moomaw.

## Lee Ranger District

Lee Ranger District has 189,082 acres in (Rockingham, Shenandoah, Page, Frederick, and Warren Counties) Virginia and (Hampshire and Hardy Counties) in West Virginia. Unlike the other districts in the GW&JNF, its acreage is about evenly divided in two elongated sections. One is on both sides of Great North Mountain where half (51,950 acres) is in West Virginia. The other section is east of the wide Shenandoah Valley on the Massanutten Mountain range and other mountain ridges to its west and south. In the north-central part of this section is Fort Valley, a scenic 17-mile strip of private farmland. Parallel to the east side of Massanutten Mountain is the Shenandoah River and Shenandoah National Park. On the southwestern corner the district adjoins Dry River Ranger District. Cities closest to the Lee Ranger District are Harrisonburg in the south and Winchester in the north.

*Big Schloss Mountain Trail, George Washington NF, on Virginia/West Virginia border*

Some of the highest peaks in the district are along the Virginia/West Virginia border. One is Big Schloss (2,964 ft.) and another is Devil's Hole Mountain (2,833 ft.). The latter does not have a trail to its peak, but the mountain is noted for its long and narrow ridge on which travel 1.8 miles of SR 691. In the Massanutten Mountain area is Signal Knob (2,106 ft.), southeast of Strasburg, and Kennedy Peak (2,560 ft.) on Massanutten Mountain. Predominate rock formations are shale, limestone, and resilient sandstone. The district's forests are mainly hardwood with scattered white pine and hemlock groves. Frequent understory shrubs are rosebay rhododendron and mountain laurel. Damage is extensive to pines from the southern pine beetle, and infestations by the gypsy moth on oaks and a fungal disease on dogwoods have also caused defoliation. Bear, deer, grouse, turkey, and raccoon are among the most prominent game animals. There are approximately 175 species of birds.

Human history in the district is illustrated at Elizabeth Furnace Recreation Area, where there are remnants of the iron ore industry that flourished 150 years ago. Signal Knob had breastworks during the Civil War, and Sherman Gap Road, a Revolutionary War redeployment route for General Washington's army, is east of Fort Valley. There is archaeological evidence of a Native American village that existed between 3000 and 1150 B.C. at "The Point" of the South Fork of the Shenandoah River.

Also on historic soil are two developed fee campgrounds, Elizabeth Furnace and Camp Roosevelt, which have the usual facilities. Other recreational areas are Trout Pond Recreation Area with campground facilities including electric hook-ups, and Hawk Campground in West Virginia. In Virginia are High Cliff Canoe Camp near Bixler's Ferry Bridge by the South Fork of the Shenandoah River, Little Fort near Detrick, Tomahawk Pond west of Broadway, and Wolf Gap on SR 675. A list of directions, fees, and open seasons are available from the district office. Massanutten Visitor Center is on US 211 (exit 264 off I-81), 3.8 miles east of New Market. On the staff are knowledgeable volunteers to assist with printed material including books and maps. Nearby are interpretive trails and a picnic area. Visitor Center hours of operation are 8 A.M. to 4:30 P.M. daily from April 15 through October 31, and weekends only during the first two weekends in November.

The district estimates that it has about 2.5 million annual visitors who see or utilize the services of its total acreage. Among the most frequent activities are hunting, fishing, camping, hiking, bicycling, horseback riding, bird-watching, nature study, and sight-seeing.

Many visitors choose the district for its first-class trail network. The district's 2002 trail inventory shows 109 color-coded, paint-blazed, user-designated trails of which 14 include motorized vehicles (ATV/ORV, motorcycles). Of the other 95 trails, 27 (88.4 mi.) are in West Virginia and 68 (223.1 mi.) are in Virginia. Accounting for the popularity and quality of the trail system are the district's leadership in trail development, the volunteer assistance in planning and preservation of trails by the Potomac Appalachian Trail Club and other volunteers, and the accessibility and proximity of the district to metropolitan areas.

The district differs from most in its policy of designating almost all its trails as multiple use. Only 11 of its 109 trails on inventory are listed as suitable for hiker use exclusively, a total of 10.2 miles. These trails are mainly interpretive, or for the handicapped. Others, such as **Meneka Peak Trail**, is described as being a "block field," which means that stepping from rock to rock and maintaining your balance are required. The district has three other "suitability" ratings: nonmotorized trails (coded with blue dots on maps) suitable for mountain bike and hiker use; non-motorized trails (coded with brown dots) suitable for equestrian, mountain bike, and hiker use; and motorized trails (coded with brown diamonds) suitable for motorized vehicles (when indicated), equestrian, mountain bike, and hiker use. This policy is interpreted by the PATC as a method of "keeping horses off trails where they are likely to be injured and to keep bicyclists from having to carry their bikes over long distances. But all trails are good hiking trails." All but a few road trails, mainly for hunting, are included in the descriptions ahead. Some of my trail measurements may differ from those of the USFS.

The district's longest trail is the **Massanutten Mountain Trail**. It has three connected sections (east, south, and west) with a total of 91.4 miles. In the summers of 2000 and 2001, PATC workers extended **Massanutten Mountain West Trail** on Kerns Mountain for a connection between Moreland Gap Road and Jawbone Gap, and accomplished a partial relocation of **Waterfall Mountain Trail** to **Duncan Hollow Trail**. With these changes there is now a ring of 71.1 miles for the west and east sections. (These changes were made after the publication of the National Geographic Society's *Trails Illustrated* map for Lee Ranger District #792, in 2001.)

Another long trail, which connects with the **Appalachian Trail**, is the **Tuscarora Trail** (formerly the **Big Blue Trail**), with 55 miles in Virginia, of which 36 miles are in this district. It is blazed with a blue vertical bar shaped like the **Appalachian Trail** white blaze. You may see sections of the **Tuscarora Trail** on preexisting treadway with names such as **Tuscarora/Doll Ridge Trail**.

The district has six interpretive trails. The jewel is **Lions Tale Trail** on FR 274, 1 mile south from Camp Roosevelt. In a mature forest beside Passage Creek, this 0.3-mile loop, partially on a boardwalk, is an education for all ages. It is constructed for the physically handicapped and has information signage in Braille. **Discovery Way** (0.2 mi.) and **Wildflower Trail** (0.5 mi.) are linear paths with emphasis on history and biology. Both are at Massanutten Visitor Center on US 211. From the Visitor Center traveling 1.5 miles north on FR 274 is **Massanutten Story Book Trail** (0.6 mi. round-trip). It begins on a serpentine bridge and provides a study of geology. At the end is a rock outcrop with views of the Luray area and Shenandoah National Park beyond. The **Pig Iron Trail** (0.3 mi.) and **Charcoal Trail** (0.6 mi.) loops at Elizabeth Furnace are described in the **Massanutten Mountain East Trail**.

The Lee Ranger District trails in Virginia and five trails on the West Virginia boundary of Great North Mountain are covered in this guidebook, but I have covered all the other trails of West Virginia in *West Virginia Hiking Trails*, published by Appalachian Mountain Club Books. (For information and to order, telephone 800-262-4455, or contact a local bookstore.) A comprehensive statewide guidebook such as *The Trails of Virginia* cannot provide as much detailed mapping as the National Geographic map #792 or maps by the Potomac Appalachian Trail

Club. For information and to order the PATC guidebooks and maps, contact PATC at 703-242-0693; general information is available at 703-242-0315, hikes and activities at 703-242-0965, or use their website <www.patc.net>.

ADDRESS AND INFORMATION: Lee Ranger District, 109 Molineu Rd., Edinburg, VA 22824; phone: 540-984-4101; website: <www.southernregion.fs.fed.us/gwj/lee>. At junction of I-81, exit 279 onto SR 675, go east and take first left onto Windsor Knit Road. The next left is Molineu Road. Hours are 8 A.M. to 4:30 P.M. Monday–Friday.

## MASSANUTTEN MOUNTAIN EAST AREA
*Shenandoah, Warren, and Page Counties*

### Massanutten Mountain East Trail (MMET)                                    1–17
LENGTH AND DIFFICULTY: 35.86 miles (57.4 km); moderate to strenuous
CONNECTING TRAILS: **Shawl Gap Trail** (4.5 mi.), **Pig Iron Trail** (0.3 mi.), **Charcoal Trail** (0.6 mi.), **Tuscarora Trail** (9.1 mi.), **Sherman Gap Trail** (5.9 mi.), **Veach Gap Trail** (3.2 mi.), **Milford Gap Trail** (3.1 mi.), **Tolliver Trail** (1.8 mi.), **Indian Grave Ridge Trail** (2.5 mi.), **Habron Gap Trail** (1.5 mi.), **Stephens Trail** (4.7 mi.), **Kennedy Peak Trail** (0.3 mi.), **Duncan Hollow Trail** (9.3 mi.), **Gap Creek Trail** (2.4 mi.), **Scothorn Gap Trail** (3 mi.), **Waterfall Mountain Trail** (1.2 mi.)
FEATURES: historic sites, old iron furnace, iron mine, wildlife, wildflowers, scenic overlooks, solitude
TRAILHEADS: Access to the northern trailhead is officially from a parking area on SR 619 south of the Virginia Fish Cultural Station. It is also accessible on the **Shawl Gap/Tuscarora Trail** from Elizabeth Furnace Recreation Area on SR 18 678. For either approach turn south off I-81 at exit 296 on VA 55 or exit 298 on US 11 into Strasburg where the two highways join, but after 0.2 mile follow VA 55 east. After 5.1 miles to Waterlick, turn right on SR 678 (7.2 mi. west of Front Royal). Follow SR 678 (Fort Valley Rd.) for 1 mile and turn left on SR 619. After 1.2 miles there is a small parking area, right, with sign for **Massanutten Trail**. To approach Elizabeth Furnace Recreation Area from the junction of SR 678 and SR 619, continue south on SR 678 for 2.5 miles to large Signal Knob parking lot, right, and another 0.5 mile to the trail access at picnic parking space, left. The campground is ahead, 0.5 mile, left, on SR 678. (To reach Camp Roosevelt camping area [at milepoint 25.8 of the trail] drive south on SR 678 for 14.1 mi. to juncture with SR 675 and Kings Crossing. Turn left on SR 675 and after 4.2 mi. the campground is on the left.) For the southern access on US 211, 2 miles east of the Massanutten Visitor Center at New Market Gap, the shortest road distance from Camp Roosevelt is to take FR 274 (Crisman Hollow Road) 9.2 miles to the visitor center. **Massanutten Mountain West Trail** connects at **MMET** milepoint 34.0 and **Massanutten Mountain South Trail** connects at 35.8.

INTRODUCTION: The Elizabeth Furnace Campground is an excellent base camp for hiking trails in the north area on both the Massanutten Mountain and adjoining ranges. The camping and picnic areas are open from April to October and have trailer and tent sites, flush toilets, warm showers, and waste disposal. At the picnic area are the **Pig Iron Trail**, a 0.3-mile interpretive loop trail explaining how pig iron was made at the furnace, and the **Charcoal Trail**, a 0.6-mile interpretive loop trail explaining charcoal processing. In the nineteenth century the iron ore was mined, purified, and hauled by wagon over the Massanutten Mountain for boarding on the Shenandoah River to Harpers Ferry. This old wagon road is part of the **Shawl Gap Trail** described ahead. The **Tuscarora Trail** (143 mi.) passes through the picnic area on its western route from the **Appalachian Trail** (**AT**) at Mathews Arm in the Shenandoah National Park to West Virginia for 55 miles, and north through Maryland and Pennsylvania to connect with the **AT**. This section of trail has only one shelter—at Veach Gap about one-third of the way—and there is a USFS campground more than two-thirds of the way. Water sources on the ridgeline are absent for the first 25 miles except at Veach Gap. In your planning pack sufficient water. Between Camp Roosevelt and US 211, water sources are frequent.

DESCRIPTION: If using the yellow-blazed **Shawl Gap Trail** (also the route of the blue-blazed **Tuscarora Trail**) to approach the **MMET**, begin at the northeast end of the bridge over Passage Creek to the Elizabeth Furnace Picnic Area. The trail passes the iron furnace and connections with **Pig Iron Trail** and **Charcoal Trail** to parallel downstream by Passage Creek. The forest has sycamore, ironwood, oaks, and ferns. It ascends to cross a short footbridge at 0.4 mile. Then this skillfully constructed treadway gradually curves on ridges and coves with switchbacks and steps. At 1.8 miles is a rocky cove with wild roses, followed by a wall of boulders. Along the incline are occasional crossings and edges of the old wagon road, particularly noticeable at 2.1 miles. It intersects with the **MMET** at 2.4 miles. On the **MMET** left, north, it is 3.9 miles to its northern trailhead on SR 619, and south on the **MMET** it is 2.3 miles to **Sherman Gap Trail**. The **Shawl Gap Trail** descends east partly on old wagon road and on footpaths. After the last switchback the trail abruptly turns right (southeast) on a logging road to a small stream at 3.3 miles. It crosses a clear-cut for 0.1 mile on a seeded road, followed by a curve to the left and to gravel on the road at 3.9 miles. After a USFS gate there is a gravel parking area at 4.5 miles off SR 613. (This location is easy to miss, but if the weeds and brush are cleared from the gravel driveway, a USFS sign can be seen on a tree at the left edge of the entrance.) On SR 613 driving north it is 1.5 miles to the SR 619 juncture, where a left is 1.8 miles north to the northern trailhead of the **MMET**, left. (Ahead, north, on SR 619 it is 1.2 mi. to a juncture with SR 678 [Fort Valley Road].) Its eastern trailhead is at a parking area on SR 613, 1.5 miles south from a juncture with SR 619 (or 4.6 mi. from SR 678).

*Shawl Gap/Tuscarora
Trail, Lee Ranger District*

To begin the orange-blazed **MMET** from the SR 619 parking space, enter a
thicket of cedar and honeysuckle in a former farm field. Cross a stream at 0.2
mile to begin an ascent to a ridge. From here the trail follows a ridge before
dipping to a hollow at 0.4 mile for a climb north. At 1.8 miles the trail rounds the
nose of the mountain west of the Virginia Fish Cultural Station. Here is a scenic
view north toward the flat lands around the North Fork of the Shenandoah
River. Ascend steeply on Buzzard Rock ridge at 1.9 miles. At 2.2 miles is an
impressive view into the gorge of Passage Creek. Continue to follow the ridgeline among rocks and a forest of pines, chestnut oak, serviceberry, mountain
laurel, and rabbit pea. Descend to Shawl Gap at 3.9 miles. Cross **Shawl Gap
Trail** and continue on the **MMET/Tuscarora Trail**.

Ascend and descend on a rocky ridge with a narrow tread among hardwoods
and views east and west. Black walnut and hickory trees provide squirrel food
in this area. There are scenic peaks at 4.3 miles, 4.6 miles, and 5.2 miles. At 5.8 is
a rare flat area without rocks. Arrive at a juncture west with **Sherman Gap
Trail**, a former mountain road (pink blazed) at 6.1 miles. (This historic route

may have been constructed at the request of General Washington during the American Revolution.) After 0.1 mile the **Sherman Gap Trail** leaves to the east.

(The **Sherman Gap Trail** part that descends west at first descends steeply in loose rocks and among mountain laurel. At 0.4 mi. it levels out some among hardwoods and blueberries. It follows an up-and-down route over ridges and into deep hollows. Examples are at 1.2 mi., 1.8 mi., and 2.5 mi. At 2.7 mi. it makes a juncture with white-blazed **Botts Trail**, right. Here is a stone memorial sign in memory of R. Wayne Botts, a lifetime trail builder. [The 0.8-mi. **Botts Trail** passage parallels Passage Creek among verdant evergreens, ferns, and flowers, over and around rocks, and in mossy or wet places. After entering the Elizabeth Furnace Picnic Area, the trailhead is at the parking lot near the kiosk and rest rooms. Another 0.1 mi. is the western trailhead of **Shawl Gap Trail** at the Passage Creek bridge.] From the memorial sign the **Sherman Gap Trail** descends to a grove of white pines, crosses [wading necessary] Passage Creek, enters a dense and damp grove of trees, bushes, weeds, and grasses, to arrive at SR 678 at 3.1 mi. Cross the highway to a large gravel parking area and continue on the edge to follow old roads and trails over ravines and climb to the purple-blazed **Mudhole Gap Trail** at 3.5 mi., its western trailhead. [It is 0.1 mi. to the right on **Mudhole Gap Trail** to primitive campsites.])

(The **Sherman Gap Trail** part that descends east follows a well-designed group of seven switchbacks for 0.8 mi. It then follows an old road among hardwoods, pines, and blueberries on a ridge. After crossing a few tank traps it reaches a USFS boundary marker at 2.1 mi. It descends through private property to an easily missed trailhead on SR 613 at 2.2 mi. Only parking is on narrow roadside near a power pole and faint pink blaze on a hickory tree. A few yards left, north, on SR 613 is a private home postal box #3455. From the trailhead it is 1.2 mi. north to **Shawl Gap Trail**, left on SR 613.)

Continuing on the **MMET/Tuscarora Trail** the trail passes east of the ridge spine for 0.2 mile. After its return to the main ridge it reaches Little Crease Mountain at 6.6 miles where it moves more easterly for views of the South Fork of the Shenandoah River at 7.3 miles. After 0.1 mile there begins a right descent on switchbacks. It parallels the west side of Mill Run. On the northwest side of the hollow is Little Crease Mountain. At 9.6 miles the trail connects with yellow-blazed **Veach Gap Trail** from the right.

(The **Veach Gap Trail** continues ahead with the **MMET/Tuscarora Trail**, but in its right, west, direction, it descends on the old Morgan wagon road, mainly along the sometimes rocky and wet creekbed of Mill Run in a hemlock forest. After about half a mile it crosses the creekbed to a parking lot suitable for about eight vehicles at 1.3 mi., the trail's western trailhead. From here on SR 774 [Veach Gap Rd.] it is 0.7 mi. to SR 678 [Fort Valley Rd.]. North on SR 678 it is 6 mi. to Elizabeth Furnace Picnic Area, and south on SR 678 it is 1.6 mi. to Seven Fountains.)

Continuing on the **MMET/Tuscarora/Veach Gap Trail**, cross Mill Run and pass the Little Crease Shelter, 150 yards to the left at 9.7 miles. From here the trail ascends on a rocky road with legendary Revolutionary War history. (It is thought General Washington, who had surveyed the Massanutten Mountain in the 1750s, directed the road to be built in the 1780s for military redeployment if needed.) After 0.9 mile reach Veach Gap (1,800 ft.) at 10.6 miles. Here the **Tuscarora/Veach Gap Trail** leaves the **MMET** and descends east.

(On the eastern descent of the **Tuscarora/Veach Gap Trail** the steep and rough route makes two switchbacks before following a forest road to gate and parking lot at SR 613 (Panhandle Rd.) at 1.7 mi., the eastern trailhead of **Veach Gap Trail**. The parking lot has space for about eight vehicles. From here north it is 1.9 mi. to **Sherman Gap Trail**, left at power pole and pink blaze on a hickory tree [private property with trail entrance consent]. To the right, south, the **Tuscarora Trail** follows SR 613 to a low water cement bridge [Indian Hollow Bridge] over the scenic South Fork of the Shenandoah River at 1.3 mi. After another 2 mi. it crosses US 340. Then for a steep 7.6 mi., the trail intersects with the **AT**. After 0.4 mi. with the **AT** it reaches Hogback parking area on the Skyline Drive, milepost 21.1.)

On the **MMET** follow the ridge with successive ascents and descents on rocky conglomerate knolls. At 14.1 miles is Milford Gap and juncture with the white-blazed **Milford Gap Trail**.

(Here again is a trail across the Massanutten Mountain. Its beginning was a carriage road from the community of Detrick in Fort Valley, east through the gap, and down to the South Fork of the Shenandoah River. Today the west route is closed because of private property and the east side descends for 2.5 mi. to the abandoned Hazard Mill Campground and dead end. However, after 0.6 mi. on the **Milford Gap Trail**, there is a juncture with **Tolliver Trail**, forking right. It descends 1.8 mi. and ends at a turnaround area on FR 1186, which leads 0.3 mi. to SR 717 in Burners Bottom, and east of the fire warden's house. FR 1186 is not blazed; hikers using a vehicle will not see the orange blazes until the turn-around area.)

At 15.5 miles on the **MMET** is a juncture with **Indian Grave Ridge Trail** on the left. (The purple-blazed trail descends for 2.5 mi. through oaks and pines to a parking lot on SR 717, 3 mi. from SR 684 junction near Goods Mill Falls on the South Fork of the Shenandoah River. The trail received its name from legends of Native American burial sites.)

In Habron Gap (1,927 ft.) on the **MMET** at 18.8 miles, cross **Habron Gap Trail**. (The unblazed western side is closed because it descends into private property and would be a trespass. But the eastern side is blazed blue. It descends by Keyser Path for 1.4 mi. in locust and walnut groves to SR 684 near Fosters Landing of the South Fork of the Shenandoah River.)

The **MMET** continues on the ridge through numerous blueberry patches. At

21.7 miles it junctures with the yellow-blazed **Stephens Trail**, right, west. (The **Stephens Trail** descends on switchbacks for 0.8 mi. to join an old wagon road right. The treadway has sections of wet passage in the descending and ascending route. It exits at the north side of a parking lot at 4.6 mi. to access the **MMET** near SR 675 above Camp Roosevelt.)

There is a junction on the **MMET** with the **Kennedy Peak Trail** at 22.6 miles, left. (This 0.3-mi. white-blazed spur ascends to a former lookout tower [2,560 ft.] for an outstanding view of Page Valley.) There is an unblazed off-trail view of Fort Valley at 22.7 miles. The **MMET** skirts west of Kennedy Peak, then at 23.2 miles partially follows an old forest road to SR 675 (1,839 ft.) at 25 miles in Edith Gap. (On the road it is 6.5 mi. east to Luray and 1.4 mi. west on SR 675 to Camp Roosevelt.) The trail does not cross the road, but turns right to descend on steep switchbacks through old iron mines. At 25.8 miles it reaches the entrance road to a large parking lot to the right. At the parking area is the southern trailhead of **Stephens Trail**. The **MMET** turns left to SR 675 and after a few yards crosses the road to enter the northern trailhead of **Duncan Hollow Trail**, part of the **MMET**.

(The entrance to Camp Roosevelt is 0.1 mi. down SR 675. Historic Camp Roosevelt is the site of the first Civilian Conservation Corps [CCC] camp in the nation, operating April 4, 1933, through May 1942. A sign here recognizes Henry Rich, the first member. The fee campground has trailer and tent sites, picnic area, flush toilets, waste disposal, and internal trails. It is open from April 30 to September 30. From here on SR 675, down the road, it is 0.2 mi. to an intersection with FR 274 [Crisman Hollow Rd.], left, and SR 730 [Moreland Gap Rd.] straight ahead. On SR 675, right, the road leads to Kings Crossing and SR 678 [Fort Valley Rd.]. On FR 274, left, it is 0.9 mi. to **Lions Tale Trail**, a special interpretive facility with Braille. See description above.)

23    At 25.9 miles enter the graded orange-blazed **MMET/Duncan Hollow Trail** through an oak forest to Duncan Creek. Proceed 3 miles upstream on an old roadbed, often wet from seeps. Catback Mountain is west and Massanutten Mountain is east, both paralleling the hollow. At 29.2 miles is a junction, right and west, with blue-blazed **Gap Creek Trail**.

(The **Gap Creek Trail** ascends the east side of Middle Mountain on a steep, eroded, rocky, and rutted treadway with switchbacks. At 0.8 mi. it passes through flat Peach Orchard Gap. Old campsites are noticeable. To the north is a 0.2-mi. white-blazed spur trail that ascends to the base and a scramble up to the summit of Duncan Knob [2,803 ft.] on Catback Mountain. After a descent of 0.2 mi. it makes a juncture with yellow-blazed **Scothorn Gap Trail** to the left. [The **Scothorn Gap Trail** goes 1.6 mi. to an intersection with **MMET/Duncan Hollow Trail**. Along the way it has gentle ascents and descents, crosses intermittent small streams, passes through a grazing field, passes a spring left, and a pool right. From the juncture with the **MMET/Duncan Hollow Trail** it turns west and exits at FR 274 (Crisman Hollow Rd.), at 3 mi.] The **Gap Creek Trail** continues a descent on twelve steep switchbacks to cross a footbridge over Passage Creek and to FR 274 at 2.3 mi., its western trailhead. It is 1.6 mi. south on FR 274 to **Scothorn Gap Trail**.)

On the **MMET/Duncan Hollow Trail** a wet and sometimes muddy route continues for another mile on an old roadbed. It then climbs and curves around Middle Mountain at 31 miles. After turning north it descends along the west slope to connect with **Scothorn Gap Trail** at 31.9 miles. (A 6.5-mi. loop could be made here for a return to SR 675 at Camp Roosevelt by turning right on **Scothorn Gap Trail**.) (If following **Scothorn Gap Trail** to the left for its continuation and exit at FR 274, pass through a forest of tall trees and around a swamp/pond to cross a grazing field at 0.4 mi. For the next 1 mi. descend on an old road, steep in places, to rock-hop Passage Creek, and pass primitive campsites to exit at FR 274, the trail's western terminus. It is 5.2 mi. left, south, to US 211 near Massanutten Visitor Center, and 1.6 mi., right, north to **Gap Creek Trail**, right, and **Jawbone Trail**, left. Ahead, FR 274 goes 2.8 mi. to SR 675 and right to Camp Roosevelt.)

To continue on the **MMET/Duncan Hollow Trail**, south, follow an old wagon road and descend into the gorge of Big Run to cross the stream three times. At 34 miles connect with the white-blazed **Waterfall Mountain Trail**, right, the southern terminus of **Massanutten Mountain West Trail** (MMWT). (The **Waterfall Mountain Trail** [without a waterfall] ascends the mountain that bears its name, and ends at FR 274 [Crisman Hollow Rd.] after 1.2 mi. The **MMWT** crosses the road to Kerns Mountain and goes north.)

The **MMET/Duncan Hollow Trail** continues south and descends on two switchbacks to enter a former forest clear-cut and logging road. At 34.7 miles is a more recent forest road before repetitive stream crossings, open areas with new forest growth, and mature forest sections. There are views northeast of Strickler Knob. From the top of a hill descend to a USFS gate and exit to US 211, the southern terminus of **Duncan Hollow Trail** (9.9 mi.) and the **MMET** at 35.8 miles. Across US 211 is a parking lot in a barrow field, and the northern terminus of **Massanutten Mountain South Trail** (MMST). It is 2 miles up the highway to Massanutten Visitor Center; down the mountain and east is 8.4 miles to Luray.

USGS MAPS: Hamburg, Strasburg, Bentonville, Rileyville, Luray; USFS TRAIL NOS.: 404, 406, 405.1, 483, 483A, 484, 560, 560A, 567, 559, 458, 404A, 410, 409, 555A, 412

## MASSANUTTEN MOUNTAIN SOUTH AREA
*Page, Shenandoah, and Rockingham Counties*

### Massanutten Mountain South Trail (MMST)       24–32
LENGTH AND DIFFICULTY: 19.6 miles (31.4 km); moderate to strenuous
CONNECTING TRAILS: **Wildflower Trail** (0.5 mi.), **Bird Knob Trail** (2.2 mi.), **Roaring Run Trail** (4.3 mi.), **Pitt Spring Lookout Trail** (0.3 mi.), **Morgan Run Trail**

(1.4 mi.), **Fridley Gap Trail** (3.2 mi.), **Martin Bottom Trail** (0.9 mi.), **Second Mountain Trail** (1.9 mi.)

FEATURES: wildlife, anthills, spring, streams, isolation, scenic views, wildflowers

TRAILHEADS: The northern trailhead is at a parking lot across US 211 from the southern trailhead of the **Duncan Hollow Trail**, 2 miles east from the Massanutten Visitor Center, and 8.4 miles west of Luray. The southern trailhead is on SR 636 at a gate on FR 65 (Cub Run Rd.). Access is from a juncture of US 33A and SR 635 in Elkton. Go north 0.8 mile on SR 635 to SR 636 on the left, and follow it 1.5 miles to SR 603 (Bethel Church). Turn right, north, go 0.7 mile, and turn left on SR 636 (Runkles Gap Rd.). After 2.2 miles reach the gate area of FR 65. Parking is parallel along the side of FR 65 for 0.2 mile.

INTRODUCTION: Before you hike the **Massanutten Mountain South Trail**, visit the Massanutten Visitor Center at the New Market Gap on US 211. Books, maps, and directional assistance are available. At the south edge of the center's parking lot is an entrance to **Discovery Way**, a 0.2-mile trail with emphasis on history and biology. Backtrack. This section of the **Massanutten Mountain Trail** network has only one shelter and it is near the southern trailhead, but stream water is available within every 5 miles. The New Market Gap Picnic Area is near the northern trailhead. A number of trail sections follow fire roads. Spaces for primitive campsites are frequent.

DESCRIPTION: Descend from the parking lot on orange-blazed **Massanutten Mountain South Trail** (MMST) to cross small streams draining into Big Run. At 0.4 mile pass under a power line, follow an old woods road to the base of a spur ridge, and ascend an old skid road to 1.1 miles. After a clear-cut, cross an entrenched former turnpike, and join another old road to reach a forest road loop at the New Market Gap Picnic Area (1,572 ft.) at 1.7 miles. Bear left on the loop road to join the **Wildflower Trail**, a white-blazed interpretive trail (which ascends to the Massanutten Visitor Center after 0.3 mi.). At 1.9 miles leave the **Wildflower Trail** and ascend steeply to the ridge top of Massanutten Mountain at 2.3 miles. Follow the crest through hardwoods, scattered conifers, and berries. Pass a huge overhanging rock at 2.6 miles. On a rocky treadway reach an overlook at 2.8 miles. At 3 miles is a superb overlook of Shenandoah Valley and westward. At 3.8 miles in a level grassy area is a juncture with white-blazed **Bird Knob Trail** on the right. (This trail is a side loop that extends 2.2 mi. to FR 375 [Big Mountain Rd.] where it reconnects with the **MMST**. Along the way it goes through a forest wildlife clearing, after which it descends to cross a drainage from a spring-fed pond. Camping space is nearby. The trail does not go to 2,684 ft., wooded Bird Knob; instead it curves left and ascends to join the **MMST** on FR 375.)

The **MMST** bears left onto a woods road, where for 0.7 mile there are large anthills. Wet weather springs are along this stretch. Reach FR 375 (gated and locked to prevent vehicles on the woods road) at 5 miles. Bear right of gated road that protects wsva tv towers. Pass the reconnected **Bird Knob Trail** right at 5.5 miles and arrive at purple-blazed **Roaring Run Trail** on the left, east, at 6 miles.

(The rocky and usually brushy **Roaring Gap Trail** first ascends Big Mountain for 0.9 mi., then descends for 3.4 mi. to the site of Catherine Furnace on FR 65 [Cub Run Rd.] near SR 685 and 2.2 mi. out to US 340, southwest of Newport. Along the descent at 1.5 mi. is Roaring Run Gap. At 2.2 mi. is a pipeline and the beginning of an old road, and at 3 mi. there is a forest road crossing. The trail crosses a stream and turns right at 3.4 mi. It follows a wagon road on a steep bank to cross Roaring Run at 4.1 mi. Remains of the early 1800s furnace are mainly stone foundations and a chimney. Scattered on the level road is glassy green slag from the furnace. Near here was a CCC camp in the 1930s.)

On the **MMST** with FR 375, cross a pipeline at 6.8 miles and a power line crossing at 7.8 miles. At 8.7 miles is Pitt Spring. Here are campsites and the **MMST** crosses Pitt Spring Run on a wooden bridge, right, to leave FR 375 (FR 375 descends through Pitt Spring Gorge for 2 mi. to Catherine Furnace). The **MMST** follows an old road where a spring is just across the creek. At 9.5 miles is white-blazed **Pitt Spring Lookout Trail**. (It extends as a spur 0.3 mi. to good views of the South Fork of the Shenandoah River and Blue Ridge Mountains from an old lookout site.) There is a campsite left and off the road near a pond at 9.9 miles. At 12 miles the trail crosses Morgan Run and meets the yellow-blazed **Morgan Run Trail**, left.

(The **Morgan Run Trail** descends rapidly for 1.4 mi. into a scenic gorge. About halfway down is a grove of hemlocks. On wet and slippery rocks, the route is a scramble near rock overhangs, caves, pools, cascades, mosses, and ferns. There are five crossings of the stream; sometimes the route is in the streambed. At 1.3 mi. is a campsite, then tank traps on a wagon road to FR 65. Parking is on the roadside; it is 6.1 mi. south on FR 65 to the south terminus of **MMST**.)

Ahead the **MMST** crosses a number of streams frequented by wildlife for the next 2 miles. The treadway shifts from grassy to loose tread. It intersects the **Fridley Gap Trail** at 14.4 miles. (The purple-blazed **Fridley Gap Trail** ascends left on an exceptionally rocky and boulder-strewn mountainside to cross Third Mountain. It descends to Cub Run and an old forest road at 0.8 mi. left. [The old forest road is the 0.9 mi. blue-blazed **Martin Bottom Trail**, whose eastern terminus is at FR 65. It is 3.1 mi. south to the south terminus of **MMST**.] The **Fridley Gap Trail** continues south on an old forest road with an easy grade for 0.7 mi. to a grassy meadow and a juncture with the **MMST**, right. From here the **Fridley Gap Trail** goes east 1.6 mi. on an old road bordered with wild azalea, mountain laurel, and turkey beard [*Xerophyllum asphodeloides*]. It descends from Second Mountain on a steep, rocky treadway to FR 65 [Cub Run Rd.]. On the road, right, it is 1.7 mi. to Runkles Gap, the southern trailhead of the **MMST**.)

Continuing on the **MMST**, it is 130 yards ahead to the confluence of Fridley

Run and another stream in Fridley Gap. (To the right the **Fridley Gap Trail** descends in a hemlock grove to a large boulder field on the right and Mountain Run cascades on the left. It goes over large rocks to descend to a parking area at FR 1613, the trail's western trailhead. This point can be reached from I-81 by turning off at exit 257 on SR 608. After 3.1 mi., at Athlone, turn right on SR 620 [KOA entrance is here], and travel another 3.1 mi. to SR 722. Turn left, and left again on SR 868 [Airy Rd.]. After 0.2 mi. look for gravel FR 1613 and follow it to its end.)

The **MMST** in Fridley Gap goes upstream 60 feet, crosses the stream, and ascends steeply on the side of a sharp ridge of Fourth Mountain. From 15.1 miles to 15.4 miles are rock outcroppings with views toward Harrisonburg. At 15.9 miles the trail descends to make a horseshoe curve on a spur ridge before descending to Fridley Run. Here is a good campsite under hemlocks. The trail begins a gentle climb on the western side of Third Mountain, a dry area with trailing arbutus and blueberries, and impressive views of Fourth Mountain and the Shenandoah Valley. At 17.2 miles the trail crosses Third Mountain to follow a grassy old road; it makes a juncture with **Fridley Gap Trail** at 17.6 miles. Gypsy moth defoliation is substantial here. The **MMST** goes right to descend alongside Boone Run. Boone Run Shelter is on a spur trail, right, at 18.6 miles. The clean shelter with a nearby privy and a spring 60 yards beyond the shelter is maintained by the PATC. Descend to cross Boone Run at 18.7 miles and juncture with blue-blazed **Second Mountain Trail** to the south. (The 1.9-mi. **Second Mountain Trail** crosses Boone Run then climbs on switchbacks and a long rise along the ridge to a fork. The left fork, unblazed, climbs another 0.3 mi. to Kaylor Knob [2,960 ft.] with broad views to the south and east.) Continuing on the **MMST**, cross Boone Run four more times and reach FR 65 (Cub Run Rd.) right and left at 19.4 miles. It is 0.2 mile right, downstream, on FR 65 to the gate and SR 636. Parking is on the roadside.

USGS MAPS: Hamburg, 10th Legion, Elkton West, Stanley; USFS TRAIL NOS.: 645, 416B, 582, 584, 583, 419, 579, 580

## MASSANUTTEN MOUNTAIN WEST AREA
*Shenandoah and Page Counties*

33–46 **Massanutten Mountain West Trail (MMWT)**
LENGTH AND DIFFICULTY: 37.1 miles (59.36 km); moderate to strenuous
CONNECTING TRAILS: **Signal Knob Trail** (4.5 mi.), **Meneka Peak Trail** (1.2 mi.), **Tuscarora/Bear Wallow Trail** (4.6 mi.), **Tuscarora/Doll Ridge Trail** (5.8 mi.), **Mudhole Gap Trail** (4.6 mi.), **Mine Gap Trail** (0.9 mi.), **Wagon Road Trail** (0.7 mi.), **Woodstock Tower Trail** (0.2 mi.), **Lupton Trail** (0.5 mi.), **Seven Bar None Trail** (0.5 mi.), **Bear Trap Trail** (0.4 mi.), **Peters Mill Run**

Trail (8 mi.), **Jawbone Gap Trail** (1.6 mi.), **Waterfall Mountain Trail** (1.2 mi.), **MMET/Duncan Hollow Trail** (9.3 mi.)

FEATURES: Signal Knob, Woodstock Lookout, and other scenic views; outcrops, springs, wildlife, wildflowers

TRAILHEADS: The northern terminus is at **Signal Knob Trail** parking lot on SR 678 (Fort Valley Rd.) 3.4 miles south from the community of Waterlick on VA 55, and 0.6 mile north of Elizabeth Furnace Picnic Area. The southern terminus is at a juncture with **MMET/Duncan Hollow Trail**, 1.8 miles north on a gated USFS road from a parking area at US 211, 2 miles east of Massanutten Visitor Center. (Vehicular access along the **MMWT** from north to south is SR 758 on Woodstock Tower Rd., milepoint 13.9 mi.; SR 675 on Edinburg Gap Rd., milepoint 22.1; FR 374, milepoint 29.3; SR 730 on Moreland Gap Rd., milepoint 30.2; and FR 274 on Crisman Hollow Rd., milepoint 35.9.)

INTRODUCTION: This area of the **Massanutten Mountain Trail** system ascends and descends from a combination of ridgelines on Three Top Mountain, Powell Mountain, Short Mountain, Kerns Mountain, and Waterfall Mountain. Although mapping and trail titling show the **MMWT**'s north terminus starts from Signal Knob at **Signal Knob Trail**, the description here uses **Signal Knob Trail** as the essential access to and part of the **MMWT**. The plant life and wildlife are similar to that of the **MMET** and **MMST** areas, and again there are numerous lookouts, rocky terrain, and infrequent sources of water. A difference is the lack of a camping shelter, but more vehicular road crossings for shuttles, and passage through a section of ATV and ORV usage.

DESCRIPTION: From the north end of the north parking lot follow the yellow-blazed **Signal Knob Trail** on a graded tread through hardwoods, scattered conifers, azaleas, blueberries, filberts, and wildflowers. At 0.5 mile is a developed spring. Weave in and out of rocky coves to Buzzard Rock Overlook at 1.5 miles for an excellent view of Passage Creek Gorge. Turn left and ascend on exceptionally rocky tread for the next 2.5 miles. At 2.2 miles is Fort Valley Overlook. Arrive at white-blazed **Meneka Peak Trail**, left, at 3.4 miles. (Rocky **Meneka Peak Trail** is 1.2 mi. across Meneka Peak [2,393 ft.] with views east to Massanutten Mountain and Blue Ridge Mountains. It descends to intersect the **Tuscarora/Bear Wallow Trail**, where a left turn can make a 10.9-mi. circuit in a return from **Signal Knob Trail** to the parking lot.) At 4.4 miles pass a TV transmitting tower at the end of a road. This is not the end of the trail; stay on the yellow-blazed **Signal Knob Trail** to arrive at Signal Knob (2,106 ft.), a Confederate and Union Civil War lookout point. Views are of the North Fork of the Shenandoah River, Strasburg, Winchester, and Great North Mountain on the west and north horizon to West Virginia.

(There are three options for a return to the parking area. One is to backtrack for a total of 9 mi. A second option is to backtrack 1.1 mi. to **Meneka Peak Trail** and follow it as described above for 10.9 mi. The third option, as described below, is to descend on the orange-blazed **MMWT** south for 1.2 mi. to an intersection with, and a left turn on, the blue-blazed **Tuscarora/Bear Wallow Trail**. Following it makes a circuit distance of 10.6 mi.)

To continue on the orange-blazed **MMWT**, descend south on a USFS road toward the headwaters of Little Passage Creek. At 5.3 miles pass a spring and at 5.7 miles arrive at an intersection with **Tuscarora/Bear Wallow Trail**, left; **Tuscarora/Doll Ridge Trail**, right; and straight ahead on the **MMWT**.

(The **Tuscarora/Bear Wallow Trail** is 4.6 mi. down the mountain to SR 678 [Fort Valley Rd.]. On the way it crosses Green Mountain, and after 0.8 mi. it makes a juncture with the white-blazed **Meneka Trail**, left [that goes 1.2 mi. north to **Signal Knob Trail**]. After another 1.9 mi. it makes a connection with pink-blazed **Sidewinder Trail**, right [that goes 0.8 mi. to juncture with purple-blazed **Mudhole Gap Trail**]. Continuing to descend for another 0.9 mi., the **Tuscarora/Bear Wallow Trail** will pass white-blazed **Bear Wallow Spur Trail**, right [an easy trail that also leads 0.2 mi. to **Mudhole Gap Trail**]. For the next 0.8 mi. the **Tuscarora/Bear Wallow Trail** goes northeast, past old iron pits on the left and makes a connection with white-blazed **Tuscarora Spur Trail**, left. The spur goes 0.5 mi. to the large parking lot adjacent to the **Signal Knob Trail** parking area on SR 678. The **Tuscarora/Bear Wallow Trail** stays right, and after 0.2 mi. crosses SR 678 and connects with the **Shawl Gap Trail** at the Passage Creek bridge to the Elizabeth Furnace Picnic Area.)

(The **Tuscarora/Doll Ridge Trail** ascends southwest to the ridge top of Three Top Mountain and goes 3.5 mi. to an intersection with the **MMWT**. [See ahead.] This route is recommended by the PATC for the 71.1-mi. Massanutten Ring.)

Where the **MMWT** continued ahead at the **Tuscarora/Bear Wallow/Doll Ridge Trail** intersection, it follows a road southwest for 0.3 mile before skirting Strasburg Reservoir on a woods path. Below the dam the path gradually descends and rejoins the road after 0.6 mile. From here the trail gradually descends in its parallel with Little Passage Creek. At 6.8 miles is an abandoned manganese mine, left. Reach a locked gate across **MMWT** at 8.5 miles. At 8.6 miles is the gated northern entrance to the closed Powells Fort Camp, right. The purple-blazed **Mudhole Gap Trail** and parking space is left.

(The 4.6-mi. **Mudhole Gap Trail** descends on an old and rough wagon road among hemlocks in a gorge of Green Mountain. It crosses Little Passage Creek five times. At 1.1 mi. is a USFS road, which the trail follows in and out of coves. At 3.3 mi. is pink-blazed **Sidewinder Trail**, left [which goes 0.8 mi. to juncture with the **Tuscarora/Bear Wallow Trail**. On its ascent it crosses two small streams and follows switchbacks]. The **Mudhole Gap Trail** continues down the road to 4.3 mi. where white-blazed **Bear Wallow Spur Trail** is left. [It goes 0.2 mi. to juncture with **Tuscarora/Bear Wallow Trail**.] **Mudhole Gap Trail** continues on the road to pass a gate, pass the west terminus of **Sherman Gap Trail**, right, pass left on a primitive camping loop road, and exit at sr 678 [Fort Valley Rd.]. Across the road is the Elizabeth Furnace Campground entrance. [See **MMET** for description of 5.9-mi. **Sherman Gap Trail**.])

Continuing on the **MMWT**, leave the road, right, at the southern gated entrance to Powells Fort Camp at 9 miles. Ascend steeply to the top of Three Top Mountain (1,790 ft.) at 9.5 miles to juncture with **Tuscarora/Doll Ridge Trail** from the right and its 9.2 mileage. Both trails jointly follow left for a few yards before the **Tuscarora/Doll Ridge Trail** forks right and the **MMWT** continues left. (The **Tuscarora/Doll Ridge Trail** descends west on Doll Ridge to cross the North Fork of the Shenandoah River at 2.2 mi. and follow county roads to Shenandoah County Park at us 11 at the northeast of Maurertown and beyond.)

At 10.4 miles is a spur trail on the left, the purple-blazed **Mine Gap Trail**. (It descends 0.9 mi. east on a wagon road to FR 66 in Little Fort Valley.) Continue on the **MMWT** in a hardwood forest with shallow sags and scattered rocky knolls. There is evidence of some forest damage by the gypsy moth. Reach sr 758 and a parking area at Woodstock Gap at 13.9 miles. (For vehicular traffic it is 5.6 mi. west to Woodstock and us 11 on sr 758 and sr 665; and 3.9 mi. east on sr 758 to Detrick and sr 678 [Fort Valley Rd.].)

(For hikers who wish to ascend the pink-blazed trail to Woodstock Tower [1,893 ft.], ascend left on sr 758 from the **MMWT** parking area to another parking area, right. Ascend steps and meet white-blazed **Wagon Road Trail**, left. [It descends 0.7 mi. as a steep loop to Little Fork Recreation Area on sr 758 where there is a campground with water and rest rooms.] Reach the Woodstock Tower after 275 yd. from the parking area. There are grand views of seven bends of the North Fork of the Shenandoah River, west, and Woodstock Gap, east.)

Continuing on the **MMWT**, pass a hang glider launch site, right, at 14.1 miles. Juncture with purple-blazed **Lupton Trail**, left, at 15.7 miles. (It descends sharply 0.5 mi. to Peters Mill Run and FR 1702, the old **Powell Mountain Trail**, now an ATV and ORV route.) Pass a long rock pile. At 15 miles is a campsite, and at 17.2 miles is a juncture with blue-blazed **Seven Bar None Trail**. (It descends 0.4 mi. to Peters Mill Run and FR 1702.) Continue shifting from the ridgeline to the eastern side of rock formations and reach an excellent view of Edinburg and the Allegheny Mountains at 19.4 miles. (There is an unblazed spur trail to the right.) Here, as elsewhere on the trail, are brilliant fall colors from maple, black gum, sassafras, and blueberry. The 0.4-mile pink-blazed **Bear Trap Trail** is left at 19.9 miles. (It switchbacks to the headwaters of Peters Mill Run and FR 1702.) After another 0.2 mile the trail turns east to skirt Waonaze Peak (2,725 ft.) in dense rhododendron (the summit is forested). There is an overlook to the east at 20.5 miles, where switchbacks begin on a rocky eastern face of Waonaze Peak. Pass an intermittent spring at 21.3 miles. After a left switchback, descend to FR 1702 (**Peters Mill Run Trail** for ATVs and ORVs) in a curve at 21.5 miles. Turn right on the eroded road, pass a wildlife pond at 21.7 miles, and arrive at SR 675 (Edinburg Gap Rd.) in Edinburg Gap at 22.1 miles. Left, east, on SR 675 it is 1.9 miles to Kings Crossing and SR 678 (Fort Valley Rd.). Right, west, on SR 675 it is 4 miles to Edinburg.

Cross the road and bear left into an ATV parking area, where there are vault rest rooms. On the west of the parking area is orange-blazed **MMWT**, but it is used by ATVs and ORVs. An alternate route here is to follow and ascend FR 374 right, west. After 0.4 mile you can return to the **MMWT** route at 22.5 miles. Turn right and go north on a narrow trail among rock outcrops and to the north end of Short Mountain. Observe scenic views of Shenandoah Valley at 23.7 miles. Follow an undulating route on Short Mountain among rocky sections, a few campsites, switchbacks, and scenic views for 5.4 miles. Descend steeply to level off and reach FR 374 at 29.3 miles. To the left is a return to Edinburg Gap and to the right is SR 730. Cross FR 374 and after 0.9 mile arrive at SR 730 (Moreland Gap Rd.). To the right SR 730 goes 5.5 miles to US 11, south of Mount Jackson, and to the left, north, SR 730 goes 3.3 miles to SR 675 near Camp Roosevelt.

Cross the road and follow an easy old road until 0.3 mile where PATC crew workers have broken rock piles for a better treadway. Begin a series of ascending and leveling on the rocky west flank of Kerns Mountain to 31.5 miles, where a series of switchbacks complete the ascent to Jawbone Gap at 31.8 miles. A campsite is here, and to the left is a 0.1-mile white-blazed spur trail to a rock outcrop. (Ahead the blue-blazed **Jawbone Gap Trail** descends 1.2 mi. to FR 274 [Crisman Hollow Rd.]. After a descent on switchbacks and old logging roads there is a spring, left, at 0.8 mi.) In Jawbone Gap the orange-blazed **MMWT** turns right to follow the southwest crest line of Kerns Mountain. It leaves the ridge to turn east for a crossing of FR 274 at 35.9 miles. Right on FR 274 it is 0.9 mile to **Massanutten Story Trail**, and another 1.5 miles to US 211 and Massanutten Visitor Center. Left on FR 274 it is 2.1 miles to Scothorn Gap Trail and 4.7 miles beyond to SR 730 and SR 675 near Camp Roosevelt.

Continuing on the **MMWT** pass a wildlife field, cross an old road, and arrive at an overview on Waterfall Mountain at 0.3 mile. Turn left and among mountain laurel and pine follow the rim for another 0.3 mile. Turn sharply right and rapidly descend the mountain on short switchbacks with scree. Arrive at a juncture with the orange-blazed **MMET/Duncan Hollow Trail** at 37.1 miles, the terminus of **MMWT**. If continuing on the Massanutten Ring (Circle), turn left on the **MMET/Duncan Hollow Trail**. If taking an exit to US 211, turn right and go 1.8 miles to a parking area and the northern trailhead of the **MMST**, 2 miles east of Massanutten Visitor Center in New Market Gap. (See preceding description of the **MMET** and **MMST**.)

USGS MAPS: Strasburg, Edinburg, Rileyville, Toms Brook; USGS TRAIL NOS.: 408, 402, 427, 405.2, 405.3, 564, 550, 552, 552A, 449, 413, 455, 433, 409A, 412, 404, 410

*Shenandoah County, Virginia, and Hardy County, West Virginia*

**Mill Mountain Trail** (6 mi.), **Tuscarora Trail** (5.7 mi.)                 52, 5

LENGTH AND DIFFICULTY: 11.7 miles (18.7 km) combined; moderate to strenuous

CONNECTING TRAILS: **Big Schloss Trail** (0.3 mi.), **Big Schloss Cutoff Trail** (1.9    53–62
mi.), **Little Stony Creek Trail** (3.3 mi.), **Peer Trail** (2.9 mi.), **Little Sluice
Mountain Trail** (5.3 mi.), **Racer Camp Hollow Trail** (5.5 mi.), **White Rock
Trail** (0.3 mi.), **Old Mailpath Trail** (2.3 mi.), **Sulphur Springs Gap Trail** (2.9
mi.), **Cedar Creek Trail** (4.4 mi.)

FEATURES: scenic views, geological formations, springs, wildlife, wildflowers

TRAILHEADS: The southwestern trailhead for **Mill Mountain Trail** is at Wolf Gap
Recreation Area at the Virginia/West Virginia boundary on SR 675, 11.3 miles
west of I-81 exit 279 at Edinburg. For the northeastern trailhead to reach this
section of the **Tuscarora Tail**, exit 291 on I-81 west on SR 651 (Mt. Olive Rd.) 1.4
miles to SR 623 (Back Rd.) and turn left. Use SR 623 for 4.2 miles to SR 600
(Zepp Rd.) and turn right to go over Fetzer Gap 4.5 miles to SR 603 (Van Buren
Rd.). Turn left. At a fork with SR 713 stay left on SR 603. Pass the ruins of Van
Buren Furnace after 0.7 mile, and at 2.8 miles arrive at a parking area near two
gated USFS roads. The gravel road to the right, northwest (FR 1725), is also
**Sulphur Spring Gap Trail**, and the rocky road straight ahead (FR 1863) leads to
the **Tuscarora Trail** and **Cedar Creek Trail** after 0.4 mile.

INTRODUCTION: The **Mill Mountain Trail** is one of the district's most popular
trails because of Big Schloss with its panoramic views. The trail is a link between a network of trails to the southwest and a larger network of trails northeast. These trails follow ridges connected by hollows within the frame, saddles,
and fringes of Great North Mountain. The linear distance from the south near
VA/WV 259 at Fulks Run to Gore and US 50 north is about 50 miles. (Only the
Virginia trails are described here; the other trails are described in *West Virginia
Hiking Trails*, published by Appalachian Mountain Club Books.) There are a
number of partial and complete circuits and long distance options for vehicular
shuttles described ahead. The longest would be 30.7 miles on the **Tuscarora
Trail** from its connection with **Mill Mountain Trail** across the Shenandoah
Valley to Elizabeth Furnace Picnic Area at Massanutten Mountain. The com-
bination of **Mill Mountain Trail** and a section of the **Tuscarora Trail** will take
you into what is called the Big Schloss group of trails and ending the Wilson
Cove group of trails.

DESCRIPTION: Begin your hike from Wolf Gap Recreation Area at the West Vir-
ginia/Virginia border. There are nine campsites, a picnic area, and vault toilets.
From the parking area begin the orange-blazed **Mill Mountain Trail** near
campsite #9. Ascend on a wide woods road for 0.8 mile to the ridge crest,
where the trail becomes more of a rocky footpath. At 1.9 miles join the **Big**

**Schloss Trail**, right. It steeply ascends 0.3 mile on a white-blazed trail to a massive castle-like formation of sandstone (2,964 ft.) with panoramic views. To the east are views of Shenandoah Valley, Massanutten Mountain, and the Blue Ridge; north and northeast are ranges and peaks of the Great North Mountain; west includes West Virginia's Trout Run Valley and across mountain ridges to the Allegheny Mountains. Return to **Mill Mountain Trail**, turn right, and continue northeast. At 2.8 miles is a junction with blue-blazed **Big Schloss Cutoff Trail**.

(It descends 1.9 mi. east on switchbacks to FR 92. On a sometimes steep, but well-designed and scenic route the **Big Schloss Cutoff Trail** has seven switchbacks into a rocky hollow among large oaks at 0.9 mi., followed by a mountain laurel grove. At 1.3 mi. is a rocky area, then a ridge and final switchback at 1.5 mi. At FR 92 it is 0.5 mi. left to a parking area for yellow-blazed **Little Stony Creek Trail**. To the right it is 2.8 mi. to SR 675, where a right turn is 1.5 mi. to Wolf Gap.)

Continuing on the **Mill Mountain Trail** there are sections of wildflowers such as bleeding heart, white snake root, milkweed, and thistle among berry patches. At 4.6 miles is Sandstone Spring in a stand of hemlock. Ascend through an oak and mountain laurel forest to the site of a former airway beacon on Mill Mountain (3,293 ft.) at 5.5 miles. At 5.6 miles are patches of fly poison (*Amianthium muscaetoxicum*). From here the trail descends gradually and ends at 6 miles with its connection to **Tuscarora/Pond Run Trail**.

63

(Straight ahead into West Virginia the **Tuscarora Trail** descends 3.9 mi. to Waites Run Rd. [CO 5/1] and continues another 8.6 mi. along the state line to WV/VA 55. Branching off from the trail, after 1.4 mi. from **Mill Mountain Trail**, is **Halfmoon Trail** [3.2 mi.], left, and side trail **Halfmoon Lookout Trail** [0.8 mi.], right. **Halfmoon Trail** follows USFS 509 before its exit at Trout Run Rd. [CO 23/10], where a left, south, on the road is 5.5 mi. back to Wolf Gap.)

64–65

After leaving **Mill Mountain Trail** and turning right, east, on blue-blazed **Tuscarora/Pond Run Trail**, follow an old woods road 0.6 mile to a juncture with purple-blazed **Peer Trail** on the left in West Virginia, and the yellow-blazed **Little Stony Creek Trail** on the right in a saddle. Elevation at this point is 2,995 feet. (The 2.9-mi. **Peer Trail** is on private land with restrictions to users. For information contact the PATC [703-242-0693].)

(If you choose the **Little Stony Creek Trail** for a circuit, pass the locked Sugar Knob Cabin, owned and maintained by the PATC [user reservations are required]. Pass a spring here, and again at 1 mi. as the trail descends on the western slope of Stony Creek. Cross the stream twice, and pass a rock wall at 1.8 mi. With an easy treadway, the trail passes through hemlock, white pine, oak, maple, tulip poplar, and rhododendron. There are a number of good campsites along the trail. Arrive at FR 92 after 3.3 mi. to a parking area. Turn right and follow FR 92 for 0.5 mi. to blue-blazed **Big Schloss Cutoff Trail**, right. Leave FR

92 and ascend 1.9 mi. on switchbacks to **Mill Mountain Trail**. A turn left here will again pass **Big Schloss Trail** on the return to Wolf Gap Recreation Area at SR 675 for a circuit of 14.5 mi. If using the roads, continue on FR 92 from **Little Stony Creek Trail** 3.7 mi. and turn right to ascend SR 675 for 1.4 mi. to Wolf Gap Recreation Area.)

Staying on the **Tuscarora Trail** (which from this point for 2.9 mi. is also **Three Ponds Trail**) follow a broad ridge of Sugar Knob for 0.9 mi. and arrive at    66
an intersection with purple-blazed **Little Sluice Mountain Trail** (5.3 mi.) right, and orange-blazed **Racer Camp Hollow Trail** (5.5 mi.), left. Here is a saddle between Sugar Knob and Little Sluice Mountain, the most isolated area of this journey. (Both of these routes are used by hunters during hunting season; passage is with 4WDS. **Little Sluice Mountain Trail** follows a ridge south and descends to FR 92. For a return to Wolf Gap Recreation Area from here, turn right on FR 92 for 6.3 miles, and right on SR 675 for 1.4 miles. **Racer Camp Hollow Trail** descends north to Wilson Cove and gated FR 371.)

Continuing on the **Tuscarora/Three Ponds Trail,** begin to ascend Little Sluice    67
Mountain. Reach the ridge top at 1.2 miles and junction right at 1.5 miles with the blue-blazed **White Rock Trail**. The 0.3-mile spur trail leads to a large cliff that provides outstanding southeastern views of Little North Mountain, Cedar Creek, and Shenandoah Valley. At this point the journey has accumulated 9 miles. Descend, pass a spring, and at 9.5 miles arrive at pink-blazed **Old Mailpath Trail**    68
(2.3 mi.). (**Old Mailpath Trail**, a grassy road, goes to Wilson Cove. Halfway it crosses **Racer Camp Hollow Trail**.) For the remainder of this journey (2.2 mi.) the **Tuscarora Trail** becomes **Tuscarora/Little North Mountain Trail** and 6    69
miles beyond Cedar Creek to SR 600. At 9.7 miles meet purple-blazed **Sulphur Springs Gap Trail**, left. Here you have an option of a return to the northern trailhead of this hike. If following the **Tuscarora/Little North Mountain Trail**, descend steeply on sections of irregular treadway to a campsite at 11 miles, and cross a branch to join an old road. Arrive at yellow-blazed **Cedar Creek Trail** (4.4 mi.), a gated road, right and left at 11.7 miles. A turn left on the old road is 0.3 mile to a gate and parking lot. Another 130 feet goes to FR 1725. If completing the hike on **Sulphur Springs Gap Trail**, follow a narrow trail to a campsite at 10.2 miles, cross a stream, and enter a rocky gorge. Exit the rocky trail with large boulders to FR 1725 at 10.9 miles. Turn right and follow the scenic gravel road to the parking lot at 12.6 miles.

USGS MAPS: Wolf Gap, Woodstock; USFS TRAIL NOS.: 1004, 1004A, 415, 571, 401, 1036, 514, 1037, 414, 573; Tuscarora sections: 1013.2, 1013.1, 405.4

**Tibbet Knob Trail** (2.4 mi.), **North Mountain Trail** (6.5 mi.)    70–71
LENGTH AND DIFFICULTY: 8.9 miles (14.2 km) combined; strenuous    72–76
CONNECTING TRAILS: **Laurel Run Trail** (3.2 mi.), **Laurel Run Spur Trail** (5.5 mi.),
    **Stackrock Trail** (1.5 mi.), **Falls Ridge Trail** (2.6 mi.), **Fat Mountain Trail** (1.5 mi.)

FEATURES: scenic views, wildlife, wildflowers

TRAILHEADS: To reach the **Tibbet Knob Trail**, travel 11.3 miles west from Edinburg on SR 675 to Wolf Gap Recreation Area at the Virginia/West Virginia border. For its southern trailhead return east on SR 675 for 1.8 miles for a right turn on SR 789 (Sam Clark Rd.). After 0.3 mile turn right on SR 691 (Judge Rye Rd.). Ascend 1.6 miles to trailhead, right. Continuing on SR 691 it is 3.3 miles to the northern trailhead of **North Mountain Trail** and **Laurel Run Trail**, left, where SR 691 becomes CO 59 in West Virginia. For the southern trailhead of **North Mountain Trail** from Wolf Gap, return east 1.8 miles for a right turn on SR 789 (Sam Clark Rd.). After 0.3 mile turn left on SR 691 (Judge Rye Rd.). After 1 mile is FR 252 (Laurel Rd.), right at a large parking area. (This is a gated road to **Laurel Run Trail** and **Laurel Run Spur Trail** for connections with all the other trails in this group.) Continue 0.5 mile on SR 691 to Liberty Furnace and connection with SR 717. Turn right and follow SR 717, 2.2 miles to community of Jerome. (To the right is SR 701 [Dellinger Gap Rd.] to gated USFS road entrance to **Fat Mountain Trail** and **Falls Ridge Trail**.) Continue on SR 717, 2.7 miles to SR 720 (Crooked Run Rd.). Turn right on SR 720 and ascend 4.6 miles to top of mountain and the southern trailhead of **North Mountain Trail**.

INTRODUCTION: Trails described in this area are in Virginia or along the state line. The ridge trails are dry, but the other trails on the east side of the mountain have water sources. The entire area is popular with hunters and they frequent the campsites. Equestrians with trailers are served at Middle Mountain parking area located at FR 252 off SR 691 near Liberty Furnace. For hikers desiring loops, this group of trails provides choices initiated from either **North Mountain Trail** or **Laurel Run Spur Trail**.

DESCRIPTION: Begin at Wolf Gap Recreation Area parking, or across the road at a parking lot for the yellow-blazed **Tibbet Knob Trail**. Through large oaks and pines with an understory of sassafras, dogwood, azalea, and green striped maple, go 0.4 mile to a scenic overlook. After a steep climb reach Tibbet Knob (2,925 ft.) at 1.4 miles. Here is a splendid view of Trout Run, Long Mountain, and the straight and narrow ridge of Devils Hole Mountain, the route of SR 691 into West Virginia. You can also see Big Schloss to the northeast. Descend to SR 691 (Judge Rye Rd. in Virginia, which becomes Lost City Rd. in West Virginia) at 2.4 miles, the southern trailhead. (From here on SR 691 it is 1.5 mi. left, east, to SR 789, left, and to SR 675, for a 3.7-mi. vehicular return to the northern trailhead.) Turn right on SR 691 and hike, or drive, 3.4 miles to the northern trailhead of **North Mountain Trail** and **Laurel Run Trail**, both on the left side at ridge saddle.

(Yellow-blazed **Laurel Run Trail**, an old road, descends left for 3.2 mi. [of which only 2.2 mi. is necessary to intersect with **Laurel Run Spur Trail**, right, on FR 252]. On the descent there are hardwoods, pines, and hemlocks with understory sections of rosebay rhododendron. Pass campsites, wildlife ponds, and clearings, and cross a branch at 1.9 mi. Pass a gate before arriving at blue-blazed **Laurel Run Spur Trail** at 2.2 mi. [At this point **Laurel Run Trail** descends left for another 1 mi. to end at a crossing of Laurel Run and a USFS gate. Farther downstream it is 1.5 mi. on a gravel road to SR 691 large parking area and another 0.5 mi. to historic Liberty Furnace at SR 717.] **Laurel Run Spur Trail** goes southwest along FR 252 for 5.5 mi., ending at a buried gas pipeline right-of-way. Along the way **Laurel Run Spur Trail** connects with **Stack Rock Trail** and **Falls Ridge Trail** to the right, either of which could provide a loop or loops with the **North Mountain Trail**. Farther down the slope, **Laurel Run Spur Trail** makes a double juncture with **Fat Mountain Trail**, a circuit that would cross Falls Run.)

The orange-blazed **North Mountain Trail** ascends gradually for 0.8 mile to an overview of Massanutten and Blue Ridge Mountains across the Shenandoah Valley. At 2.2 miles reach purple-blazed **Stack Rock Trail**, left. (It descends 1.5 mi. to the **Laurel Run Spur Trail**. On the way it descends partly by an old telephone line. At 0.1 mi. it passes large rock formations and uses switchbacks at 0.8 mi.) Continuing on **North Mountain Trail** arrive at the western trailhead of **Falls Ridge Trail**, left, at 2.3 miles.

(The **Stack Rock Trail** and the **Falls Ridge Trail** could make an excellent circuit hike partly using the **Laurel Run Spur Trail** for a total of 5.4 mi. down and up to this point on the **North Mountain Trail**. On the **Falls Ridge Trail** there is a spring at 0.6 mi., followed by switchbacks. At 1.9 mi. it crosses **Laurel Run Spur Trail** to descend 0.5 mi. to meet **Fat Mountain Trail**, right. After another 0.1 mi. **Falls Ridge Trail** ends at a crossing of Fall Run and FR 1318. From here is a 2 mi. access by using SR 701 [Dellinger Rd.) to Jerome and SR 717.)

Continue ahead on the **North Mountain Trail**, sometimes on a steep and rocky treadway. The trail is lined with huckleberry, mountain laurel, hawthorn, and bear oak. Deer, turkey, grouse, and songbirds may be seen. At 2.7 miles, 3.9 miles, and 4.7 miles are rock outcrops for scenic views. At 5 miles the trail goes through a section of large, cone-shape anthills. Pass the site of an old homestead at 6 miles, and reach the southern trailhead in a parking lot at SR 720 at 6.5 miles. Although this is the official ending of the trail, there are hikers who would like to see it extended another 6 miles to connect with **Hunkerson Gap Trail** and Tomahawk Pond Recreation Area. Meanwhile there is another potential circuit by continuing south on the ridge for 0.2 mile, and pass a fenced-in communication facility to an east-west gas pipeline right-of-way. There are magnificent views in both directions. You will notice other hikers have followed an exceptionally steep grassy trail east to reach **Laurel Run Spur Trail**. The route crosses SR 720 and after about 1 mile you will notice a cairn and the blue blazes of **Laurel Run Spur Trail**. Farther beyond this point on the pipeline would be trespassing on private property. From here the circuit routing would connect with purple-blazed **Fat Mountain Trail** after 1.3 miles. Here is an option to follow the 1.5 miles on **Fat Mountain Trail** through reforested areas and cross Falls Run or stay on **Laurel Run Spur Trail**. If continuing on **Laurel Run Spur Trail**, pass **Falls Ridge Trail**, left at 2.8 miles, and **Stack Rock Trail**, left at 4.7 miles, and arrive at **Laurel Run Trail** at 5.5 miles, where a turn left and up the mountain to **North Mountain Trail** would be a loop of about 15.5 miles.

USGS MAPS: Wolf Gap, Orkney Springs, Lost City; USFS TRAIL NOS.: 578, 1009, 568, 568A, 572, 568B, 605

## Dry River Ranger District

The Dry River Ranger District is a compact, almost rectangular tract of 227,123 acres (of which 49,106 are in West Virginia). Its southwestern border adjoins the Deerfield Ranger District and Ramseys Draft Wilderness Area; its northeastern corner adjoins the Lee Ranger District. From one district boundary to the other, Shenandoah Mountain forms a singular range between the states. On the western side in West Virginia the creeks, runs, branches, and rivers drain to the South Branch of the Potomac River, and on the eastern side the drainage is to the forks of the Shenandoah River. On the high range are rugged and remote knobs with breathtaking scenery. Some windswept grassy knobs are Little Bald Knob, High Knob, and Flagpole Knob. The most dramatic is rocky Reddish Knob (4,397 ft.), with an asphalt parking area on top. From this range are views of North Fork Mountain in the Monongahela National Forest in West Virginia and the Shenandoah Valley and Blue Ridge Mountains in Virginia. The district's forest is mainly hardwoods, Virginia pine, and white pine, and on the higher elevations, red spruce. Rhododendron slicks occur throughout the district. Wildlife includes all the large and small game animals common to the Appalachian region. There is at least one rare animal, the Cow Knob salamander, known from near Reddish Knob. Native trout are in many of the streams and lakes. Examples of stocked lakes are Elkhorn Lake, Todd Lake, and Brandywine Lake. Among the streams are North River, Dry River, and the North Fork of the Shenandoah River.

Only one major east-west highway, US 33 between Harrisonburg and Brandywine, passes through the district. Some fantastic landscapes are viewed on the incline to High Knob. Comparable in scenic quality is the highway's forestry shroud alongside Dry River, at the base of Shenandoah Mountain. There is only one nongated access road from US 250 in the south. It is SR 715, which begins near Braley Pond Recreation Area in Deerfield Ranger District and goes north to become FR 96 at the Dry River Ranger District boundary. Campground and picnic areas with fee swimming facilities are Todd Lake (west of Stokesville on SR 718 and FR 95) in Virginia, and Brandywine (on US 33, 2 mi. east of Brandywine) in

West Virginia. Both are open from May 15 to September 30. Campgrounds open year round are Hone Quarry Campground (11 mi. west of Dayton on SR 257) in Virginia, and Camp Run (off WV 3 onto CO 3/1, northwest of Fort Seybert in West Virginia). Another campground and picnic area that has a smaller fee and fewer facilities is North River (west of Stokesville on SR 718, FR 95, FR 95B) in Virginia, open from March 1 to December 1. There is one picnic-only recreation area: Shenandoah Mountain (on rough FR 85 southwest of Reddish Knob).

The district's official trail inventory for 2001 listed 41 trails, one of which was 10-mile **Rocky Run** ATV Trail. Six trails were in West Virginia. In contrast, the *National Geographic* Map #791 listed and illustrated forty-seven trails. Of the USFS trails, twenty-seven showed a length change by use of GPS. With book and magazine authors privately measuring the trails, users should expect to see differences. In most cases the differences are minor. The district's longest trail is the 25.9-mile **Wild Oak Trail**; it makes a loop in the district's most southwestern section. A national recreation trail, it offers diversity of topography and flora and fauna, isolation, and backpacking challenge.

ADDRESS AND INFORMATION: Dry River Ranger District, 112 N. River Rd., Bridgewater, VA 22812; phone: 540-828-2591; from the junction of VA 257 and VA 42, go north 0.3 mile to North River Road and turn left. District maps and books are available.

## NORTH RIVER AREA
*Augusta County*

**Todd Lake Trail** (1 mi.), **Trimble Mountain Trail** (4 mi.)                                                   79–80

LENGTH AND DIFFICULTY: 5 miles (8 km) combined, round-trip; easy to moderate
FEATURES: lake, wildflowers, wildlife, scenic views, geological formations
TRAILHEAD: To reach Todd Lake Recreation Area from an intersection of VA 42 and
    SR 727 on the south side of the town of Bridgewater, travel west on SR 727, off VA
    42 (southern end of Dry River bridge) for 6 miles and turn left on SR 730. Follow
    SR 730 for 6 miles and turn right on SR 718 at Stokesville. After 1.3 miles, turn
    left on FR 95 and go 3.1 miles to FR 523 on the right, to lake and entrance. If
    coming from Staunton, travel west on US 250 for 7.9 miles. Turn right on VA 42
    and go 5 miles to a left on SR 760. After 3.3 miles reach SR 749, turn left, go 1
    mile, turn right, go 1.1 miles to SR 718 at Stokesville, and follow as above.
INTRODUCTION: Todd Lake Recreation Area is an excellent base camp for hikers in
    the North River Area. It has the best facilities on the Virginia side of the district.
    Activities include hiking, camping, fishing, and swimming. Facilities include
    camper and tent sites, flush toilets, warm showers, and waste disposal unit.
    There is no parking space for hiking the **Trimble Mountain Trail**, but there is a
    small space to park outside the campground gate, or at the old sewage facility
    on FR 95 below the dam.

DESCRIPTION: From the kiosk near the beach or outside the gate, follow the purple-blazed **Todd Lake Trail** sign counterclockwise to the dam in a grassy field. (To the right is yellow-blazed access to **Trimble Mountain Trail**.) Here are views of the lake and the mountains. American goldfinches frequent this area. Curve around the lake and at 0.7 mile descend steeply and cross a footbridge. Pass through a picnic and beech tree area for a return to trail origin. For the **Trimble Mountain Trail** follow the same route, but turn right before crossing the dam. Descend on an old road 0.1 mile to FR 95. Cross the paved road near the waste disposal unit to the sign for the **Trimble Mountain Trail**. After 0.2 mile the trail forks for a loop in a barrow area. Here are white and Virginia pine, and bristly locust (*Robinia hispida*). Turn right at the fork, ascend on an old road, and pass the site of a former sawmill at 0.3 mile. At 0.6 mile the trail levels off in an area of interest to birders. There are scenic views from a rock outcropping at 1.2 miles to see Broad Run and toward Elkhorn Mountain. Continue the circle through hardwoods and groves of mountain laurel around a slope to Trimble Mountain saddle. Here are more views, including views of the North River Campground area. At 2.1 miles reach the highest point on the trail (2,476 ft.; Trimble Mountain is 2,740 ft.). At 3 miles notice rocks along the trail with remnants of tree fossils. Gradually descend, and at 3.4 miles pass through a bed of maidenhair ferns in a hardwood cove. Return to a fork in the loop and exit at highway. (The trail was adopted for maintenance by BSA troop 145 of Dayton, Virginia, in 1984.)

USGS MAP: Stokesville; USFS TRAIL NOS.: 376, 375

81 **Wild Oak Trail**

LENGTH AND DIFFICULTY: 25.9 miles (41.4 km) round-trip; strenuous

82–87 CONNECTING TRAILS: **Grooms Ridge Trail** (4 mi.), **Hiner Spring Trail** (0.8 mi.), **Bald Ridge Trail** (8.3 mi.), **Dowells Draft Trail** (3.5 mi.), **White Oak Draft Trail** (2.5 mi.), **Bear Draft Trail** (1.3 mi.)

FEATURES: solitude, historic site, panoramic views, flora and fauna

TRAILHEAD: From Stokesville go north 1.3 miles on SR 718 to junction with FR 101 and FR 95. Turn left on FR 95 for 0.1 mile to parking area on the right.

INTRODUCTION: This trail was designated a national recreation trail in 1979. Its name represents the prominence of oak species on its circuit. When created, the **Wild Oak Trail** replaced such trails as the **Chestnut Ridge Trail**, the **Hankey Mountain Trail**, and the **Lookout Mountain Trail**. This is an excellent trail for backpacking and getting away from crowded campgrounds, but it is less remote during big-game hunting season from mid-October to the last of December. If you are hiking during that time, wear a blaze orange jacket and cap. Following mostly on ridge crests, trail elevation varies from 1,600 feet at its terminus to 4,351 feet on Little Bald Knob. Water sources are infrequent; hikers should plan accordingly. Passing through more than forty species of trees, including five kinds of pines, the trail is bordered with more than fifty species of wildflowers. Wildlife includes bears, deer, raccoons, turkeys, grouse, owls, hawks, foxes, rattlesnakes, chipmunks, and a wide range of songbirds. There are three points of entry: one is the northeastern trailhead listed on FR 95 near SR 718; a second is Camp Todd (not Lake Todd) on FR 95 in Horse Trough Hollow northwest; and a third is on FR 96, west of Hankey Mountain and north of US 250 on SR 715 in the south. For the purpose of making this a circuit hike, the three sections reached by means of these entry points are combined.

DESCRIPTION: From the FR 95 northeast (near SR 718) parking area and signboard, enter the forest to the left to follow the white-blazed spur trail for 0.2 mile. Ascend through hardwood forests, gradually reaching Grindstone Mountain. At 2.1 miles enter a stand of pitch pine with understory of mountain laurel. Pass a timber road, Little Skidmore, on the left at 2.4 miles. The trail now becomes steep and rocky to reach an overlook at 3.7 miles. At 4.2 miles is a junction with the **Grooms Ridge Trail**, also called the **Big Ridge Trail**, from the right. (It descends 4 mi. to FR 101, 1 mi. north of FR 95.) The main trail continues ahead on a wide trail, formerly the **Chestnut Ridge Trail**, and passes a steep and rocky section at 5.5 miles. It turns left at 6.9 miles to a junction with Bald Mountain Road. (Bald Mountain Rd. runs right for 5 mi. to FR 85, where the **Shenandoah Mountain Trail** intersects south of Reddish Knob. The western trailhead of **Buck Mountain Trail** is also on the Bald Mountain Rd., 2.5 mi. from the **Wild Oak Trail**.) At 7 miles is Little Bald Knob (4,351 ft.), the highest point on the trail. This area, particularly a few yards out on Bald Knob Road, provides magnificent views. Begin descent, sometimes on rocky terrain, to North River and Camp Todd on FR 95 at 10.2 miles. (This area is the site of a pioneer's cabin, fire guard station, and railroad tram for logging.)

After crossing the road near a Camp Todd historical marker, begin the exceptionally steep climb up Springhouse Ridge toward Big Bald Knob (4,100 ft.). At 11.5 miles pass a spring, and at 11.6 miles pass a junction with **Hiner Spring Trail**, right. (It goes 0.8 mi. to meet **Ramseys Draft Trail**, right and left, in Deerfield Ranger District. The **Ramseys Draft Trail** continues right 0.2 mi. to connect with 0.5-mi. **Hardscrabble Knob Trail** [4,282 ft.], left. Beyond, the **Ramseys Draft Trail** enters Dry River District to end at the southern trailhead of 3.2-mi. **Tearjacket Trail**.) Reach Big Bald Knob, a wide, flat wildlife clearing of mountain laurel, oaks, pitch pine, and blueberries at 12.4 miles. Pass a grassy open area at 12.6 miles and descend to a wildlife clearing with a pond at 13.1 miles. At 13.2 miles is a junction with the **Bald Ridge Trail** from the Deerfield Ranger District on the right. (It goes 8.3 mi. to Braley Pond off SR 715. Along the way it joins the **Bridge Hollow Trail** for a descent to the **Ramseys Draft Trail** and US 250.) Pass a stream in a rocky area at 13.8 miles, and at 15.4 miles reach

88

FR 96 (2,312 ft.). (To the right is SR 715, which descends 4 mi. to US 250. To the left FR 96 descends to a junction with FR 95, Elkhorn Lake, Todd Lake, and the northeast origin of the **Wild Oak Trail**.)

Cross the road and climb steeply through white pines and oaks. At 16.7 miles veer right from a side trail on the left. Join the **Dowells Draft Trail** on the right, at 17.5 miles. (It descends 3.4 mi. to near Braley Pond and to US 250 across the highway from the **Chimney Hollow Trail**, both in the Deerfield Ranger District.) Ascend to summit of Hankey Mountain (3,407 ft.) at 17.7 miles. Here is a wide, scenic area in a grassy field with wildflowers and scattered oaks. On the ridge crest pass two wildlife clearings and at 18.6 miles arrive at the second peak of Hankey Mountain (3,450 ft.). Here is a junction with an old forest road (FR 425) ahead, and the **White Oak Draft Trail** on the right. (It descends south to White Oak Draft and out to US 250, 3.5 mi. east of the **Dowells Draft Trail** on US 250 in the Deerfield Ranger District.) Leave the wildlife clearing and for the next 2 miles pass through five wildlife clearings. White oak and chestnut oak are prominent along the trail. At 20.4 miles is an overlook near a wildlife field. Oak, locust, and wildflowers are noticeable. Pass under a power line at 21.3 miles and reach another wildlife field at 21.6 miles. At 21.8 miles reach a junction with the **Bear Draft Trail** on the right, and a road to North River Campground on the left. (The **Bear Draft Trail** goes 1.1 mi. southeast to a gated forest road and SR 535 near Stribling Springs and east on SR 728 to VA 42. The road on the left that goes to North River Campground connects with the **North River Gorge Trail**.) Proceed ahead on what was formerly called the **Lookout Mountain Trail**. At 22.6 miles and 23.1 miles there are overlooks along the ridge that provide panoramic views. This is an area of table mountain pines, oaks, maples, and blueberries. Begin descent on switchbacks, at points steep and rocky. At 25 miles the trail passes a side trail on the right. (This trail leads to Girl Scout Camp May Flather and private property.) Turn left toward North River Gorge, turn right on a switchback to merge with an old riverside road downstream. Cross North River on a suspension footbridge to cross FR 95. At 25.7 miles connect with the spur trail, turn right and arrive at the parking area at 25.9 miles.

USGS MAPS: Stokesville, Reddish Knob, Palo Alto, West Augusta; USFS TRAIL NOS.: 716, 424, 447, 535 (only numbers for the Dry River Ranger District)

90 **North River Gorge Trail**

LENGTH AND DIFFICULTY: 4.6 miles (7.3 km); moderate

FEATURES: scenic river gorge, wildflowers, fishing

TRAILHEADS: To access the southern trailhead from the junction of FR 95 and FR 523 at Todd Lake, drive 1.5 miles south on FR 95 to FR 95B and turn left. Go 1 mile to the North River Campground across the bridge and park outside the campground in a small parking area immediately past the campground. For the northern trailhead, drive 1.6 miles east from Todd Lake on FR 95 to the gated trailhead, right, or 1.5 miles west on FR 95 from junction with FR 101. If parking space is a problem, park at the large parking area at the overlook parking, 0.3 mile east of the gate.

DESCRIPTION: Begin the hike downriver at a small parking area and the junction of FR 95B and 425 (Plankey Mountain Rd.). After 0.4 mile ford the river for the first of nine times. Descend through steep walls of Lookout Mountain and Trimble Mountain. Because the terrain is irregular and water depth uncertain, hikers should turn back if the crossings appear hazardous, particularly at rapids. Rocks can be slippery and mossy. Ford the river twice again by 0.7 mile. For the next 1.3 miles follow a large horseshoe curve on the northern side before fording again at 2.2 miles. Because of the mist and the moist earth, the vegetation is lush and dense with willow, alder, and rhododendron. Springtime wildflowers include orchids, coltsfoot, and stonecrop. Poplar, birch, oak, and maple are among the taller trees. Ford the river again at 2.5 miles, 2.8 miles, 3.1 miles, and 3.3 miles. On the right side of the river follow an old road to a crossing of the river at 4.1 miles. Cross, and follow road to a gate at FR 95 for 4.6 miles. (A loop can be made of this trail and part of the **Wild Oak Trail** for about 9 mi. As you approach the ninth crossing of North River, instead of crossing, continue on the old road downstream 0.2 mi. to the white-blazed **Wild Oak Trail**, right. Ascend and after 3.5 mi. to **Bear Draft Trail**, turn right on FR 425 (Plankey Mountain Rd.) and after a descent of about 1 mi. arrive at the parking lot for the **North River Gorge Trail**.)

USGS MAP: Stokesville; USFS TRAIL NO.: 538

## HEARTHSTONE LAKE AND REDDISH KNOB AREAS
*Augusta and Rockingham Counties*

**Timber Ridge Trail** (7.5 mi.), **Buck Mountain Trail** (5.7 mi.) 91–92

LENGTH AND DIFFICULTY: 13.2 miles (21.1 km) combined plus road contact (18.4 mi.); easy to strenuous

CONNECTING TRAILS: **Sand Spring Mountain Trail** (3.2 mi.), **Wolf Ridge Trail** 93–98 (4.7 mi.), **Narrowback Trail** (1 mi.), **Cookie Trail** (2.1 mi.), **Tillman Trail** (2 mi.), **Lynn Trail** (1.4 mi.)

FEATURES: panoramic views, flora and fauna, rock formations

TRAILHEADS: Hearthstone Lake, 3.6 miles south on FR 101 from connection with VA 257 (the only other road connection would be Reddish Knob on FR 85, 2.5 mi. south from SR 924 at the top of Shenandoah Mountain)

INTRODUCTION: This remarkable group of trails has the potential for at least five circuits with the help of short forest road connections. Some have a history of rocky roadbeds, timber or ore roads, ridge routes, and hunter single tracks. The youngest on inventory may be the **Cookie Trail**, but its location as a hunter's bushwhacking path has been there for many years. All of these trails access FR

101 (Tillman Rd.). The wilderness atmosphere offers much wildlife and copious wildflowers. Examples are starry campion, milkweed, yarrow, mountain mint, gold star, bellflower, black cohosh, flame azalea, rhododendron, trillium, laurel, and fetterbush. Most of the forests are hardwoods on dry ridges. Conifers include white pine and hemlock. Two of the trails ascend to the Reddish Knob area, the district's highest ridge. Water is available only at the low elevation; take adequate water with you.

The description begins with the longest and most challenging loop. It climbs to Reddish Knob on **Timber Ridge Trail** and descend on Buck Mountain. Either way your climb will be nearly 3,000 feet in elevation change. Park your vehicle at Hearthstone Lake, walk 0.7 mile back to FR 101, turn left, and follow FR 101 0.7 mile north to **Timber Ridge Trail**, left. Parking space is small here. (You may see a sign with the word Hearthstone.)

DESCRIPTION: Begin a steady ascent on the yellow-blazed **Timber Ridge Trail** to reach the ridgeline of Hearthstone Ridge at 1.3 miles. Arrive at a small knoll at 1.8 miles, gently descend to a saddle, and pass a wildlife pond at 2.2 miles. Ascend to a knoll (3,182 ft.) at 2.5 miles, and continue to ascend until reaching a slope and connection, right, with **Sand Spring Mountain Trail** on Sand Spring Mountain (3,720 ft.) at 4.2 miles.

(The **Sand Spring Mountain Trail** descends steeply on an old road beside or under a power line. There is a wildlife pond after 0.2 mi. and trailing arbutus on the road banks. At 2.3 mi. pass a wildlife pond, right, with frogs and butterflies. Ahead are large anthills and another wildlife pond on the left. Turn right off the road at 2.6 mi. and pass through a younger forest to FR 101 at 3.2 mi. [Across the road, east, is the western trailhead of **Narrowback Trail**.] To the right on FR 101 it is 1.1 mi. to **Timber Ridge Trail** for a loop of 8.8 mi.)

Continuing to ascend on **Timber Ridge Trail**, cross a saddle and reach a connection with **Wolf Ridge Trail** on a slope at 4.9 miles. (This trail descends on a ridge by the same name for 4.5 mi. After 0.4 mi. on a ridge, it connects with **Lynn Trail** [see description ahead]. The only semi-level areas are at 2.8 mi. and after crossing Wolf Run among rhododendron at 4.3 mi. At 4.5 mi. reach FR 101. If making a loop, turn right on FR 101, pass the **Sand Spring Mountain Trail** at 1.4 mi., and reach the **Timber Ridge Trail** for a loop of 11.9 mi.)

Staying on **Timber Ridge Trail** proceed through a saddle of two small knobs and ascend on a sharp ridge with occasional knolls. Arrive at the asphalt spur road to Reddish Knob from FR 85 at 7.5 miles. Turn left to access the asphalt parking lot at the top of Reddish Knob (4,397 ft.). Here is the western trailhead and shuttle point if the **Timber Ridge Trail** is to be your only trail. After a rest take a shortcut at the south side curve of the parking lot to avoid using the spur road to FR 85. The shortcut is the old access road to descend 0.2 mile to FR 85. Turn left on the road, descend, and after 1.4 miles turn left on gated FR 427. The

*Buck Mountain Trail,*
*Dry River Ranger District*

rocky roadbed has frequent hummocks; dense rhododendron and other ever-greens border sections of the route. After 2.2 miles on FR 427 enter a large grassy area. At its south end the yellow-blazed **Buck Mountain Trail** descends left away from FR 427.

Descend on **Buck Mountain Trail** through dense clusters of rhododendron and mountain fetterbush on a mossy treadway. A slightly level point is at 0.7 mile. At 1.2 miles on Buck Mountain Knob (3,665 ft.) is a wood sign indicating 4 miles to Hearthstone Lake. Sections of layered rock formation are at 2.4 miles. Follow an old road at 2.6 miles. Hardwoods include shagbark hickory in an open forest with scattered white pine and hemlock. Descend steeply to reach the North Fork of Little River at 3.4 miles. Cross and veer right. After about 0.2 mile the South Fork and North Fork make a confluence. For the remainder of the trail, crisscross and rock-hop rocky streambeds and sandbars, all reminders of flooding. A few smoother and scenic sections have groves of white pine and hemlock. There is a fire ring at 4.2 miles. Arrive at the Hearthstone Lake road at 5.7 miles for a circuit total of 18.4 miles.

For circuits using **Timber Ridge Trail**, park alongside the road at the **Tim-ber Ridge Trail**, 0.7 mile north on FR 101 from the Hearthstone Lake en-trance. Ascend as described above to join the **Sand Spring Mountain Trail** and return to make a loop by using FR 101 at 8.8 miles. The elevation change is about 1,870 feet. Another circuit, as described above, is with the **Timber Ridge Trail**, **Wolf Ridge Trail**, and FR 101 for a total of 11.9 miles. Elevation change is about 1,925 feet.

Other circuits could include the above on the western slopes of FR 101 (ex-cept the **Buck Mountain Trail**) for crossing FR 101 east to form loops with the **Narrowback Trail**, across the road from **Sand Spring Mountain Trail**, or the **Tillman Trail**, only 0.3 mile south of the **Timber Ridge Trail**. An example without any of the west slope trails is to begin the yellow-blazed **Narrowback Trail** at the FR 101 trailhead. Descend to cross a branch into a pine forest, cross another branch, and ascend through more pines and then hardwoods as you approach the ridge at 0.5 mile. (To the left the **Narrowback Trail** de-scends 0.5 mi. to its eastern terminus at FR 536.) To the right follow the yellow-blazed **Cookie Trail** in its ascent to the rocky ridge at 1.1 miles. Begin descent at 1.4 miles, undulate, pass a relay station, and follow a gravel road to a con-nection with the **Tillman Trail**, right, at 2.1 miles. (To the left and over the ridge, the **Tillman Trail** descends 1 mi. to its eastern terminus at FR 536. If desired, a loop could be made with 2.7 mi. on the crooked and narrow, but generally level, FR 536 to **Narrowback Trail**, left, and back to FR 101 for a total of 6.8 mi.) At the juncture with yellow-blazed **Tillman Trail** descend sharply on two switchbacks and enter a gap at 2.3 miles. Descend into a hollow among evergreens and rock-hop Big Run (usually low water). Exit at FR 101 for a combined total of the three trails. It is 1.9 miles north on FR 101 for a complete loop total of 5 miles.

In this group of trails there is **Lynn Trail** without a circuit option, but its beauty as a skillfully designed and constructed foot trail is worth a backtrack. As an appendage (listed above) off **Wolf Ridge Trail**, 4 miles up the ridge from FR 101, the **Lynn Trail** descends 1.4 miles to terminate at Briery Branch. If accessing it from the eastern trailhead of **Wolf Rock Trail** at FR 101, drive north on FR 101 (Tillman Rd.) 1 mile to SR 924/VA 257 and turn left, west, on SR 924 and drive 2.7 miles to a forest road, left, a few yards beyond a bridge (0.5 mi. up from Briery Branch Reservoir). Descend to a rough road and bear right in mud holes. Cross (no bridge) Briery Branch at 0.5 mile, and after another 0.3 mile notice red markers at a private property gate. (If parking here do not block the entrance.) Ascend at the yellow blazes where an old road becomes a footpath. After 0.1 mile is a campsite in a hemlock grove and near a branch. At 0.3 mile curve right on a well-graded switchback and then another, left at 0.4 mile to a ridge. Follow it on a scenic and open ridge to 0.7 mile. After three more switch-backs and carefully crafted water bars through dense laurel, fetterbush, and

trailing arbutus, connect with **Wolf Ridge Trail** at 1.4 miles. (Backtrack, or use
this route to connect with **Timber Ridge Trail**, described above.)

USGS MAPS: Palo Alto, Reddish Knob; USFS TRAIL NOS.: 431, 423, 378, 434, 432,
432A, 439, 436

## HONE QUARRY RECREATION AREA
*Rockingham County*

**Heartbreak Trail** (1.1 mi.), **Hone Quarry Ridge Trail** (5.9 mi.), **Big Hollow**    99–102
**Trail** (2 mi.), **Mines Run Trail** (2 mi.)

LENGTH AND DIFFICULTY: 4.5 miles (7.2 km) combined, partial round-trip; moderate to strenuous

FEATURES: geological formations, wildlife, wildflowers, scenic views

TRAILHEADS: To reach Hone Quarry Recreation Area from VA 42 in Dayton, take VA
257 west, and after Ottobine it is 4.8 miles to Hone Quarry Road on FR 62, right.
If going east from the intersection of FR 101 and VA 257, go east 0.6 mile to Hone
Quarry on FR 62, left.

INTRODUCTION: The Hone Quarry Recreation Area has three groups of trails, all
accessible from FR 62. The most southwestern group is listed above. A more
northern group and northeastern group are listed ahead. At the fee campground there are campsites, trailer sites, waste site, picnic area, rest rooms,
drinking water, and an upstream lake for fishing.

DESCRIPTION: From campsite #3 follow the yellow-blazed **Heartbreak Trail**
across Hone Quarry Run among boulders and hemlock to gradually ascend for
1.1 miles. Lichens and mosses are thick on the rocky terrain, and chunks of trailing arbutus grow between the rocks. Sounds of the creek, and from campers
and picnickers, rise from the left. Because of gypsy moth defoliation, there are a
few open spaces for views of Slate Springs Mountain and Hone Quarry Run. At
1.1 miles there is a junction with the **Hone Quarry Ridge Trail**, right and left.
(To the left the trail descends steeply 1 mi. to private homes. Do not take this
route.) Turn right on a wide jeep road used by ATVs and begin ascending the
ridge. There are young hardwoods, mountain laurel, blueberries, and rabbit
pea. Pass a flat knoll on the northern side at 2.1 miles, cross a narrow knoll, and
reach the **Big Hollow Trail** on the right at 3.1 miles on a knoll. (Either turn right
for a descent to the campground for a 4.5-mi. loop or continue left up the ridge
to complete the **Hone Quarry Ridge Trail**.) If continuing, arrive at **Mines Run
Trail**, left, at 3.3 miles. (The **Mines Run Trail** is frequented by mountain bikers.
The route descends steeply 2 mi. to SR 924, 0.3 mi. west of Briery Branch
Reservoir.) Ascend on the **Hone Quarry Ridge Trail** for 1.7 miles to FR 539.
Follow it for 2.1 miles to FR 85 on the top of Shenandoah Mountain. From gated
FR 539 it is 0.8 mile left, south, to SR 924 at Briery Branch Gap. If making a loop
on the **Big Hollow Trail**, descend rapidly on an old woods road through hard-

woods, rhododendrons, hemlocks, and pines. Exit in a hemlock grove on FR 62, turn right 50 yards to cross a low-water bridge, and return to the campground.

USGS MAP: Reddish Knob; USFS TRAIL NOS.: 435A, 435, 430, 435B

103–6 **Slate Springs Trail** (2.3 mi.), **Meadow Knob Trail** (3.3 mi.), **Pond Knob Trail** (2 mi.), **Cliff Trail** (3 mi.)

LENGTH AND DIFFICULTY: 6.7 miles or 11.2 miles (10.7 km or 17.9 km) combined, round-trip; strenuous

FEATURES: scenic views, remoteness, wildlife, wildflowers

TRAILHEADS: Trailheads for all four trails have forest road access. On FR 62 are the **Cliff Trail** across the road from the Hone Quarry Picnic Area, the **Pond Knob Trail** 2.5 miles farther upstream, and the **Slate Springs Trail** 0.3 mile farther upstream. The **Meadow Knob Trail** is accessed from FR 225B.

INTRODUCTION: An excellent circuit can be made with part of the **Slate Springs Trail**, all of the **Pond Knob Trail**, and 0.3 mile of FR 62 for a total of 6.7 miles. A longer and more scenic circuit can include 2.3 miles of the **Slate Springs Trail**, 1.4 miles on FR 225B, 1.7 miles on **Meadow Knob Trail**, all of the **Cliff Trail**, and 2.8 miles of FR 62 for a total of 11.2 miles. A two-car arrangement makes the latter circuit 7.4 miles. Hikers will see carsonite posts with multiple-use signs on these trails.

DESCRIPTION: At roadside parking on FR 62, begin the **Slate Springs Trail** in a hemlock grove and slope right of the ridge. Ascend on a steep, wide, and rocky treadway among a forest understory of dense mountain fetterbush (*Pieris floribunda*) and blueberry. Gold star and pungent pennyroyal are part of the ground cover. There is evidence of gypsy moth damage to the oaks. At 0.7 mile the ridge becomes more defined, and at 1.6 miles the ridge is narrow and rocky. Here are views left to Hone Quarry Ridge. Snakeskin and wrinkled shield lichens are on the trail boulders. After curving right from the ridge, ascend steeply in a damp area to a junction with FR 85A at 2.3 miles.

(To the left on the road it is 0.4 mi. to Flagpole Knob [4,302 ft.], and another 1.6 mi. to FR 85, where to the left it is 0.7 mi. to Hone Quarry Ridge, FR 539, and northwest access to the **Hone Quarry Ridge Trail**. Another 1 mi. leads to Briery Branch Gap and a junction with SR 924.)

Turn right on the road, and after 0.1 mile keep right at the road fork. (There is a spring after 0.1 mi. on the left fork road.) Descend and arrive at Meadow Knob (3,880 ft.) at 3.7 miles to connect with **Meadow Knob Trail**, right. Here is a large, flat, grassy bald with thistle, yarrow, and chickory. Locust, oak, and hemlock are at the forest edge. Scenic views are mainly north toward High Knob at the Virginia/West Virginia border. (At the eastern edge of the bald, a rough road follows the Slate Springs Mountain ridgeline 1.8 mi. east to FR 225 [ahead is 0.2 mi. to natural Maple Spring], which descends right to Black Run, makes a junction on the right with the **Blueberry Trail** and the **Mud Pond Gap**

Trail, and exits to SR 933. See **Blueberry Trail** description, ahead.) At the southeastern edge of the bald look for a yellow blaze and follow the trail for 0.7 mile to a small pond and grassy Pond Knob. Along the way are oaks and mountain fetterbush. At the junction the **Meadow Knob Trail** goes left and the **Pond Knob Trail** goes right. (**Pond Knob Trail** descends steeply on a ridge, but leaves it, left, on a switchback to a stream area among hemlocks to exit in a hollow at FR 62, 0.3 mi. downroad from the trailhead of the **Slate Springs Trail**. Loop is 6.7 mi.)

If continuing on the **Meadow Knob Trail**, descend from Pond Knob to a level area, and reach Oak Knob (3,500 ft.) after 1 mile. (The **Meadow Knob Trail** goes 1.4 mi. to intersect with the **Blueberry Trail** and **Mud Pond Trail**, which go to FR 225.) Turn right on the **Cliff Trail** and descend south on the western slope of the ridge for 3 miles to FR 62, a drop of 1,520 feet in elevation. On the descent, pass the headwaters of a stream at 0.5 mile, pass views of the valley at spur ridge curves, enter a rocky cove at 1.7 miles, and reach the major cliff overlook at 2.5 miles. Along the way are oaks, black birch, and mountain laurel. The unforgettable views from the cliff are of Hone Quarry Lake upstream to Shenandoah Mountain, the southern ridges of Slate Springs Mountain on the right, and Hone Quarry Ridge on the left and ahead. Continue descent on rocky switchbacks to FR 62, across the road from the picnic area of Hone Quarry Recreation Area, for a total of 7.4 miles. A return to the origin of the loop is 2.8 miles upstream on FR 62.

USGS MAPS: Reddish Knob, Brandywine; USFS TRAIL NOS.: 428–428B, 428A, 429

**Blueberry Trail** (1.7 mi.), **Mud Pond Gap Trail** (1.6 mi.), **Maple Spring Trail**  107–9
(5.2 mi.)

LENGTH AND DIFFICULTY: 3.3 miles (5.2 km) round-trip; moderate for first two trails; **Maple Spring Trail**, strenuous

FEATURES: wildlife, wildflowers, solitude

TRAILHEADS: The western trailhead is at the junction with the **Meadow Knob Trail**, and the eastern trailheads are on FR 225. Access is off VA 257 at Briery Branch on SR 731. Drive 1.6 miles to SR 742. Turn left, and drive 1.3 miles to SR 933. On SR 933 drive 1.3 miles to FR 225 (which is rocky in sections). It passes the site of the historic Union Spring mineral water health resort. After 1.8 miles on FR 225 is the **Mud Pond Gap Trail**, left. Another 0.7 mile up the road is the trailhead for the **Blueberry Trail**.

Another 5.4 miles on rocky and eroded FR 225 is **Maple Spring Trail**, right. After parking about 0.2 mile before reaching **Maple Spring Trail** or 0.2 mile beyond the access to **Maple Spring Trail**, descend abruptly on the yellow-blazed trail. As a foot trail, designed to remove it from private property farther west, it gradually descends in a hardwood forest. Enter a cove of the head-waters of Maple Spring Run at 0.5 mile and curve right to the flank of Chestnut

Ridge to an old forest road. Turn right and descend. At 3.2 miles curve right, climb over tank traps, and descend to another curve, left. Follow parallel to Maple Spring Run and intersect with another old road right and left. Turn right and after 90 yards cross Maple Spring Run. For the next 1.7 miles follow an inconsistent route of part road, part floodwater debris, streambeds, and rock layers to a final crossing at a gate and parking lot at 5.2 miles. (In 2003 the trail needed maintenance and blazing.) Access to the parking lot from Hinton on US 33 west is 5 miles to Rawley Spring. Watch for SR 846 (Rawley Springs Rd.), left, in a US 33 curve. Pass road connections, and turn right on an incline (may be a USFS sign here) and left to reach the parking lot after 0.7 mile.

DESCRIPTION: The first two trails can easily make a loop of 3.3 miles on the trails and 0.7 mile on FR 225. Begin at the **Blueberry Trail** because parking space is better at the ridge crest than it is for the **Mud Pond Gap Trail**. Ascend to two knobs through oak, locust, birch, and blueberries. Descend into Mud Pond Gap at 1.1 miles, and then ascend to grassy openings, Mud Pond, and the junction with the **Mud Pond Gap Trail**, left at 1.7 miles. Wildflowers and honeybees are here. Deer frequent the pond. From here **Meadow Knob Trail** extends west to Oak Knob and **Cliff Trail**. Continue the loop on the **Mud Pond Gap Trail**. Descend to a number of grassy spots with wildflowers and a more level area at 1.4 miles. Descend on a ridge slope where the trail meets a stream at 3.1 miles. In a damp area with hemlock, follow an old road to exit over hummocks at 3.3 miles. Turn left on FR 225 and ascend to point of origin at 4 miles.

USGS MAPS: Reddish Knob, Rawley Springs, Brandywine, Briery Branch; USFS TRAIL NOS.: 554A, 554, 490

## SLATE LICK BRANCH, RADAR MOUNTAIN, AND CLAY LICK HOLLOW AREAS
*Rockingham County*

These isolated and scenic areas are in the upper northwest corner of the district. In rugged backcountry the 3,000- to 4,000-foot-high Shenandoah Mountain range is to the west, and the less rugged VA 259 in the east provides access. On the approach to the gated USFS roads, the use of 4WDs is recommended. Where gates are unlocked during the hunting seasons, such vehicles may be even more essential. Some gates are not open at any time and you may need to walk some roads to the trailheads; other trails are the roads themselves. The major hunting season may be from early October through December. If there are questions about the season or gate policies, telephone the district office.

110–12    **Hog Pen Trail**, **Ant Hill Trail**, and **Slate Lick Branch Trail** travel through a special open valley and across forested mountainsides. It is a natural haven for hunters, fishermen, hikers, wildlife watchers, and tent campers. There is routing for disabled hunters, and from a parking area with a constructed platform visitors may watch wildlife in the nearby and faraway meadows. At the east entrance the forest road crosses (no bridge) Slate Lick Branch to a fork in the road. To the right is access to gated Slate Lick Lake. It is upstream from the lake that **Slate Lick Branch Trail** meanders 3.3 miles to crisscross the waters flowing from the east flank of Bald Knob (3,680 ft.). The trail ends at FR 240 (Gauley Ridge Rd.). The left fork of the entrance road enters lush meadow grasses and shrubbery among campsite sanctuaries. From this point the road dips to ford a stream and reaches a parking area on the hillside. It is from here that **Hog Pen Trail** ascends 0.6 mile on a pleasant road to curve right on a ridge. To the left and down the ridge is a grassy road 0.9 mile to Hog Pen Lake (reservoir), a desirable place for ducks and geese. Returning to the ridge, a left turn is on **Ant Hill Trail**. It is an old forest road among some tall hardwoods that ascends Trail Ridge. After 2.4 miles it connects with FR 240 (Gauley Ridge Rd.). You may either backtrack or turn right to follow FR 240 1.5 miles for a turn right on **Slate Lick Branch Trail**.

ACCESS: From the intersection of VA 42 and VA 259 in the town of Broadway, drive west 8.5 miles on VA 259 to the community of Fulks Run. Turn left, south, on SR 612 (Hopkins Gap Rd.). After 5.8 miles turn right on SR 817 (Genoa Rd.) to cross a bridge. Then travel 0.8 mile to a Slate Lick Field sign to turn left. It is 0.5 mile to a Watch Wildlife parking area, left. Descend and ford Slate Lick Branch as described above.

**Rader Mountain Trail** is listed in the district's inventory for the year 2001 as 4  113
miles long, but National Geographic map #791 has 1 mile at the tail end of a 2.4-mile usable and gated road. Both are incorrect, but the district distance is closest to a round-trip of 4.8 miles. The road (FR 597) has yellow blazes to its end. Along the way are a dozen wildlife fields spread over scenic sections of the high plateau. This area is popular with hunters. Evergreens, oaks, flame azaleas, and ferns provide natural boundaries. At the road/trail end is a tranquil and unblazed old jeep road. Its pathway gently descends 0.7 mile to a small freshwater pool. From this point the passageway is overgrown and shortly leads to a dead end on the east side of Laurel Run gorge. Backtrack.

ACCESS: From the intersection of VA 259 and VA 42 in the town of Broadway, drive west 8.5 miles from Broadway on VA 259 to pass through the community of Fulks Run. After another 1 mile turn left on SR 818 (Little Dry River Rd.) to parallel Little Dry River. Along the way SR 818 becomes FR 87. After 7.6 miles (from VA 259) rough FR 87 winds up the mountain to the crest and left to a juncture with FR 85 at 11.2 miles. Follow FR 85 on the ridge to 12.4 miles at the gate of FR 597, left, and yellow blazes. (Another access is from US 33 at the crest of the Shenandoah Mountain. Descending into West Virginia, FR 85 is immediately to the right. After 7.1 mi. on a very narrow rocky road, arrive at gated FR 597, right.)

**Clay Lick Trail** routing is a combination of gated grassy road, a short pathway,  114
and a mystical old jeep road. It lacks signs and blazes. A linear passage of 4.3 miles, a backtrack is necessary for 8.6 miles. The ancient part of the logging trail

once descended into a gorge all the way to SR 818 (Little Dry River Rd.), but private property became a restraint. Now it drops into Clay Lick Hollow between Stony Point Ridge to the west and Third Point and Middle Point peaks to converge with Seventy Buck Lick Run. The trail begins at a parking spot at a gate. It follows a seeded road, previously used for timbering, to a dead end on the side of Snake Hollow Mountain. Only a narrow path, more frequently used by deer than people, enters the forested embankment at 1 mile. After you come to the sunny side of the ridge you are likely to stop in surprise. In a wilderness atmosphere you see peaks, ridges, and chasms. Surrounding your position is a garden of mint, mullein, and white snakeroot among scattered pines and scrub oak. After a descent to the left the faint trail connects with the old logging road. Turn right and descend. At 2.1 miles pass the base of Third Point peak (3,071 ft.). Descend steadily along the headwaters of the hollow and pass the base of Middle Point (2,785 ft.) at 2.9 miles. Continue among hemlock, hardwoods, and laurel. At 4.1 miles the Clay Lick stream joins Seventy Buck Lick Run, 0.2 mile above the trail ending. Backtrack.

ACCESS: Drive 7.2 miles from Fulks Run on VA 259 north to SR 820, left. After 2.1 miles turn left in Bergton on SR 826 (Criders Rd.). After 3.8 miles pass through Criders (by store and post office), and after 0.6 mile turn left on SR 865 (German River Rd.) to cross bridge. At the next 0.6 mile watch for a narrow unsigned gravel road left up the side of a ridge. (If you cross a SR 865 bridge you have gone too far.) On the narrow USFS access road pass an unused poultry building to curve right around it to the forest road at 0.8 mile. Then drive 1.4 miles on a gradual ascent in the forest to a small parking space and gated road ahead. Begin your hike past the gate as described above.

USGS MAPS: Milam, Cow Knob, Fulks Run; USFS TRAIL NOS.: 593, 592, 422, 597, 594

## Deerfield Ranger District

The 164,183-acre Deerfield Ranger District is flanked on the southwest by the Warm Springs Ranger District and a smaller area of the James River Ranger District. On the northeast is the Dry River Ranger District. On the western side is Cowpasture River and Highland WMA, and on the eastern side is VA 42, west of Staunton, and Goshen and Little Mountain WMAS. As with the JNF districts, this district's mountain ranges run southwest to northeast. On the west is the Shenandoah Mountain Range, and on the east is the Great North Mountain Range. In between them is Deerfield Valley, a bucolic channel of country roads, churches, farmlands, hollows, and licks, drafts, and runs, with quaint stream names such as Danny Run, Body Lick, and Chair Draft feeding Calfpasture River. Walker Mountain, a narrow ridge in the valley's center, makes the valley the shape of a tuning fork. At the northern end of the valley, where US 250 cuts across the mountain passes, is Ramseys Draft Wilderness (6,519 acres), with a network of rugged trails.

Here is also Mountain House Picnic Area, 4.5 miles west on US 250 from West Augusta community. It is a historic site of a former wayside station. Other recreation facilities include a picnic area at Braley Pond, north of the junction of US 250 and SR 715. In addition to picnicking, it has a primitive campground, rest rooms, trails, and a stocked trout lake for fishing (see ahead). Another primitive campground is Shaws Fort, with rest rooms. It is accessed on SR 616, 1.5 miles south from US 250 at Head Waters. Across SR 616 from the campground is multiple-use yellow-blazed (3.5 mi.) **Shaws Fork Trail**, which ascends mainly on FR 396 and FR 1763. At the end of the latter forest road (which connects with the **Shenandoah Mountain Trail**), equestrians can follow FR 396 south to yellow-blazed (3.5 mi.) **Benson Run Trail**. At its end equestrians can continue south to FR 173 (Benson Run Rd.) and connect with yellow-blazed (4 mi.) **Holloway Draft Trail** (at the crossing of **Shenandoah Mountain Trail** [see ahead]), which descends east to SR 629 between West Augusta and Deerfield. The district does not have developed campgrounds or motorized trails.

The district has two educational facilities with interpretive trails for foot traffic only. One is Augusta Springs. Access from the district office at the west edge of Staunton is on SR 254 for 7 miles to Buffalo Gap, where a turn left on VA 42 is 7.6 miles to the large parking lot, right. You know there is something special about the **Augusta Springs Wetland Trail** when you begin a stroll through a tree-lined lane that is universally accessible. There are 11 interpretive points along a 0.6-mile circle that includes boardwalks. Information is provided about flora and fauna, and the history of former Augusta Springs Resort Hotel and Pendleton's spring water bottling plant. Between points 10 and 11 is the 1.1-mile **Augusta Springs Upland Trail**. It ascends a ridge and circles back to join the wetlands trail between points 8 and 9. The facility has rest rooms. The other educational facility is Confederate Breastworks on US 250 at the ridge top of Shenandoah Mountain. From the parking area the blue-blazed 0.5-mile **Confederate Breastworks Trail** ascends on steps to begin a circle. There is a series of interpretive plaques describing the area's history. Originally there was nearly 1 mile of trench works built by Brig. Gen. Edward "Allegheny" Johnson's troops in early April 1862. On May 8, 1862, General Johnson and Maj. Gen. Thomas J. "Stonewall" Jackson's Army of the Shenandoah sent the Union forces in full retreat at the Battle of McDowell, west at the present-day community of McDowell on US 250.

The district has two state champion size trees: a black birch (*Betula lenta*) on top of Gwin Mountain (6 mi. south of US 250 on FR 396), and an Eastern hemlock (*Tsuga canadensis*) in Ramseys Draft Wilderness (3 mi. upstream from US 250).S

Some trails in the district have become forest roads, and some forest roads have become trails. An example of the former is **Walker Mountain Trail** (13.7 mi.),

115–17

118–23

*Augusta Springs Wetland Trail,*
*Deerfield Ranger District*

now the gated FR 387, which is open during hunting seasons. You can reach it from Yost at the SR 640 and FR 61 junction. After 1.8 miles on FR 61, the southern roadhead is on the left. The northeastern access is at Bussard Hunter Access, off SR 600, 1.3 miles south from Deerfield. There are three trails, infrequently used, that access Walker Mountain from other roads. One is yellow-blazed **Back Draft Trail** (3 mi.); it crosses the mountain (9 mi. north from its southern roadhead) from SR 641 NW and FR 61 (Clayton Mill Creek Rd.) east at Marble Valley on SR 600. On the western junction with SR 641, the trail becomes the **Brushy Ridge Trail** (0.9 mi.) to SR 629, and from here it becomes **Short Ridge Trail** (0.9 mi., mainly used by equestrians) to FR 399 (Jerkemtight Creek Rd.), a former 4.2-mile trail. It is 4 miles south of Deerfield on SR 629. Another hunter access trail is the **Sam Ramsey Hunter Access Trail** (3 mi.). It is between FR 61 and SR 692, 4 miles south of Marble Valley. The **Falls Hollow Trail** (3 mi.) is a combination road (FR 347, 657, and 448) and footpath. It is on VA 42, 3.2 miles southwest from the junction with VA 254. A steep and rocky route, its chief attraction is Elliott Knob (4,463 ft.). The district's 2002 official trail inventory listed thirty-seven trails with a total of 137.5 miles, as listed on National Geographic Map #791. There are nine trails without blazes.

ADDRESS AND INFORMATION: Deerfield Ranger District, 148 Parkersburg Turnpike, Staunton, VA 24401; phone: 540-885-8028/8029; on VA 254 at the western edge of the city. Available are free brochures. Call about the purchase of books and maps.

## MILL MOUNTAIN AND SIDLING HILL AREA
*Bath, Rockbridge, and Augusta Counties*

### Mill Mountain Trail                                                                 124
LENGTH AND DIFFICULTY: 8.3 miles (13.2 km); strenuous
FEATURES: wildlife, scenic views
TRAILHEADS: To reach the southern trailhead, go west 1.7 miles on VA 39/42 from Goshen, and turn right on SR 600. After 1 mile turn left near a forest sign. To reach the northern trailhead, continue north on SR 600 for 10.2 miles and turn left (at Marble Valley) for 4.8 miles on FR 61 (Clayton's Mill Creek Rd.) to trailhead on the left.
DESCRIPTION: From the roadside parking at SR 600 the trail follows a forest road for 0.6 mile, where it becomes a yellow-blazed foot trail. It ascends and reaches the ridge of Mill Mountain for a right turn at 1.3 miles. For the next 1 mile there are excellent views from rock outcroppings. At 3.1 miles is a road junction: right leads down to scenic Ingram Draft; left leads to Panther Gap Draft. Continuing straight, the trail passes through former clear-cuts. At 3.8 miles it begins a steep climb and follows an old road to the top of Sidling Hill ridge. At 6 miles there is a footpath near the site of an old fire tower. At 6.7 miles it veers left at a fork. It then joins an old logging road from the left at 7.4 miles. Follow it in a descent to cross Little Mill Creek at FR 61 (Clayton's Mill Creek Rd.).
USGS MAPS: Green Valley, Craigsville; USFS TRAIL NO.: 492

## NORTH AND CRAWFORD MOUNTAINS AREA
*Augusta County*

### North Mountain Trail (North)                                                        125
LENGTH AND DIFFICULTY: 14.5 miles (23.2 km); strenuous
CONNECTING TRAILS: **Crawford Mountain Trail** (7.8 mi.), **Buffalo Spring Trail**   126–30
(0.2 mi.), **Falls Hollow Trail** (3 mi.), **Cold Spring Trail** (2.2 mi.), **Chestnut Flat Spring Trail** (0.3 mi.)
FEATURES: wildlife, scenic views, solitude
TRAILHEADS: To reach the northeastern trailhead, travel 7 miles west of Staunton on VA 254 to the junction with VA 42. Turn left on VA 42, go 0.7 mile, and turn right at Buffalo Gap Presbyterian Church on SR 688 (Dry Branch Rd.). Cross a picturesque bridge after 2.7 miles, and reach Dry Branch Gap after another 1.2 miles; there is a small parking area. For the southwestern trailhead, turn off VA 42, 2 miles southwest of Craigsville on SR 687 (Ramsey Draft Rd.) and go 3 miles to the ridge top. If coming from the west off SR 600, it is 1 mile up the mountain

to the trailhead. Another access to the trail is on FR 82, west from VA 42 at Miller Memorial Church (at Augusta Springs).

DESCRIPTION: Begin at the northeastern trailhead (it is also the southern trailhead for the **Crawford Mountain Trail**, which goes north to connect with the **Chimney Hollow Trail** [see ahead]). The gated, yellow-blazed **North Mountain Trail (North)** follows the ridge crest of Great North Mountain. Several springs are close to the trail, but overall the ridge is dry; water should be carried. For the first 1.2 miles the trail is on and off an old logging road. (At 1.8 mi. yellow-blazed **Buffalo Spring Trail** leads right 0.2 mi. to Buffalo Spring.) Following a rocky ridge, hikers will likely see grouse or turkey. Oak, white pine, birch, and locust are the predominant trees.

At 4.2 miles is the junction with FR 1448 (Elliott Knob Rd.); turn right. (On the left at 0.1 mi. is a spring and small pond among larch and red spruce—a fine campsite. Farther to the left the road descends east for 1 mi. where **Falls Hollow Trail** begins left. [The yellow-blazed 3.0-mi. trail goes north to Falls Hollow, turns east, and merges with FR 291. It descends to a gate at VA 42 in the community of North Mountain.] On FR 1448 it is 1.5 mi. to a gate at VA 42 south of North Mountain.) The **North Mountain Trail** ascends 0.2 mile to Elliott Knob (4,463 ft., the highest peak in the district). At the top, turn right and go 0.1 mile. Here is an outstanding panoramic view near the TV relay station and old fire tower. Continue south on the ridge through red spruce; at 4.5 miles the **Cold Spring Trail** is on the right at the junction. (The **Cold Spring Trail** descends into Deerfield Valley, with scenic rock outcroppings. On this trail, after 1.8 mi. there is a spring, then a creek. It passes over earth mounds, and at 2.2 mi. reaches a parking area near an old woods road on FR 77 [Cold Spring Rd]. Access to the parking area from the northern trailhead of **North Mountain Trail (North)** is 2 mi. west on SR 688 [Dry Branch Rd.]; turn left on FR 77 and drive 3.3 mi. to trailhead.)

The trail continues ahead on the crest of Hogback Ridge and passes a junction on the right with the **Chestnut Flat Spring Trail**, a 0.3-mile old woods road. At 8.1 miles the trail crosses FR 82 (Hite Hollow Rd.). It is 6.5 miles right (west) to SR 600, and 4.8 miles left (east) to VA 42. Hiking over a number of knobs, reach an old woods road at 10.1 miles, which leads to FR 38, left (east). The trail enters an old road (a favorite passage for deer hunters) at 12.5 miles and follows its descent for the next 2 miles to reach the trailhead at SR 687 (Ramsey Draft Rd.).

USGS MAPS: Elliott Knob, Deerfield, Craigsville; USFS TRAIL NOS.: 443, 445, 491

126, 131–32 **Crawford Mountain Trail** (2.6 mi.), **Chimney Hollow Trail** (3.5 mi.), **Crawford Knob Trail** (3.5 mi.)

LENGTH AND DIFFICULTY: 9.6 miles (15.4 km) combined; moderate to strenuous

FEATURES: springs, bear oak grove, wildlife, stream

TRAILHEADS: Directions to the southern trailhead of the **Crawford Mountain Trail** are the same as those given for the northern trailhead of **North Mountain Trail (North)** on SR 688, described above. For the **Chimney Hollow Trail**, go 9.5 miles west from Churchville on US 250; for the **Crawford Knob Trail**, go 2 miles west of Churchville on US 250 and turn south on SR 270 at Lone Fountain. After another 2 miles turn right on FR 1296.

DESCRIPTION: On the opposite side of the road from the northern trailhead of the **North Mountain Trail (North)**, the **Crawford Mountain Trail** ascends steeply over earth hummocks into a forest of oak, white pine, dogwood, haw, and sassafras. It reaches the top of Crawford Mountain ridgeline at 0.4 mile. After a gradual ascent, it reaches a junction with the **Chimney Hollow Trail** on the left. (The **Chimney Hollow Trail** leads 3.5 mi. north, passing over rock outcroppings, descending along a stream, entering stands of large white pine, and reaching its northern trailhead at a parking space on US 250. Across the road is the southern entrance to the **Dowells Draft Trail**. From here it is 9.5 mi. east on US 250 to Churchville.)

On the **Crawford Mountain Trail** it is 0.1 mile farther to a spur trail on the right (which leads 0.3 mi. through a wildlife clearing to a spring). At 2.6 miles is a junction with yellow-blazed **Crawford Knob Trail** on the right. (The **Crawford Knob Trail** enters a stand of bear oak, skirts the northern side of Crawford Knob [3,728 ft.], and descends on switchbacks. Along the way down the mountain are two springs. After following McKittrick's Branch and entering a timber regeneration area, it exits at FR 1296 [McKittrick's Rd.]. It is 0.4 mi. farther to SR 720 near Jerusalem Chapel.)

USGS MAPS: Elliott Knob, West Augusta, Stokesville; USFS TRAIL NOS.: 485, 489, 487


## DOWELLS DRAFT, BRALEY POND, AND BALD RIDGE AREA
*Augusta County*

**Dowells Draft Trail** (4 mi.), **White Oak Draft Trail** (2 mi.) 85–86

LENGTH AND DIFFICULTY: 6 miles (9.6 km) combined, partial round-trip; moderate

CONNECTING TRAIL: **Wild Oak Trail** (25.9 mi.)

FEATURES: wildflowers, wildlife, solitude

TRAILHEADS: The trailhead for the **Dowells Draft Trail** is across US 250 from the trailhead of the **Chimney Hollow Trail** (9.5 mi. west of Churchville on US 250). Its northern trailhead is at the **Wild Oak Trail** (see Dry River Ranger District).

To reach the **White Oak Draft Trail** from the roadside parking of the **Dowells Draft Trail**, go 3.5 miles east on US 250 to FR 466 on the left. (If arriving from Churchville, it is 0.5 mi. west of White's Store to FR 466 on the right [150 ft. from a small bridge on US 250]). Its northern trailhead is at the **Wild Oak Trail**.

DESCRIPTION: These two trails have trailheads on US 250, 3.5 miles apart, and they exit 1 mile apart on the **Wild Oak Trail** in the Dry River Ranger District. A loop of 7 miles can be made with two cars. The **Dowells Draft Trail** begins on an easy contour among young hardwoods, Indian pipe, and trailing arbutus. It enters a cove before descending to cross East Branch of Dowells Draft and a junction with FR 499 at 0.7 mile. After 0.2 mile to the right on the road, it leaves the road, on the left, and parallels Dowells Draft. At 2.1 miles it ascends away from the stream and gradually ascends to the **Wild Oak Trail** at 4 miles.

(To the left it is 2.1 mi. on the **Wild Oak Trail** to a crossing of FR 96 [FR 96 becomes SR 715 to the left in the Deerfield Ranger District, and to the right junctures with FR 95 near Elkhorn Lake in the Dry River Ranger District]. To the right on the **Wild Oak Trail** from the **Dowells Draft Trail** it is 0.2 mile to the first peak [3,407 ft.] and 0.8 mile to the second peak of Hankey Mountain. At the second peak it makes a junction with the **White Oak Draft Trail**. The **Wild Oak Trail** continues 3.4 mi. on old FR 425 to FR 95B at North River Campground.)

If hiking the **White Oak Draft Trail** from US 250, drive north on FR 466 to a parking space after 0.8 mile. From there follow the yellow-blazed trail to cross a stream at 0.2 mile, then leave the old road, left, at 0.4 mile. Ascend on a rocky area at 0.8 mile for views of Crawford Mountain. Reach the **Wild Oak Trail** at 2 miles.

USGS MAPS: West Augusta, Stokesville: USFS TRAIL NOS.: 650, 486

134, 84, 136  **Braley Pond Trail** (0.6 mi.), **Bald Ridge Trail** (8.3 mi.), **Johnson Draft Trail** (2.1 mi.)

LENGTH AND DIFFICULTY: 3.2 miles (5.1 km) combined, round-trip; easy; or 8.6 miles (13.7 km) one way; easy to strenuous (either option has trail overlaps)

CONNECTING TRAILS: **Bridge Hollow Trail** (1.8 mi.), **Wild Oak Trail** (25.9 mi.)

FEATURES: lake, rugged area, peaks, wilderness, wildlife, primitive campground

TRAILHEAD: From the junction of US 250 (0.2 mi. west from northern trailhead of the **Chimney Hollow Trail**) and SR 715 (with Elkhorn Lake sign), go 0.3 mile on SR 715 to FR 348-1 on the left, and go 0.6 mile.

DESCRIPTION: From the Braley Pond parking area the **Braley Pond Trail** crosses a footbridge to the dam. It circles the 5-acre lake among a young forest of pine, oak, huckleberry, birdsfoot violet, and false downy foxglove. Rainbow trout, sunfish, and largemouth bass are stocked in the lake. Halfway around the lake, counterclockwise at 0.3 mile, the trail meets the southern trailhead of the **Bald Ridge Trail**.

The **Bald Ridge Trail** (formerly called the **West Augusta Trail**) ascends nearly 2,000 feet in elevation. As a result, it passes through different terrain and hardwood and conifer species. Deer, turkey, grouse, and bear are among the wildlife. This is an excellent trail for birders. The yellow-blazed trail follows a beautiful forest road (FR 384A) through a forest of oak, hickory, and pine with streamlets. At 0.5 mile it turns left on FR 384 and the **Johnson Draft Trail** begins right.

(The yellow-blazed **Johnson Draft Trail** curves north and at 0.4 mi. passes another forest road left. At this point the trail curves southeast to parallel Braley Run. For the remainder of the easy treadway, the old road passes numerous grazing fields, clear-cuts, and lush damp areas with ferns and wildflowers. Complete the loop at a gate at 2.1 mi. and another 0.1 mi. to the kiosk.)

Continuing on the **Bald Ridge Trail** (which is also gated FR 348 that leads to US 250), turn off the road, right, at 1.1 miles. At 3.3 miles is an overview of Crawford Mountain and Elliott Knob, and at 3.6 miles it makes a junction with 1.8-mile **Bridge Hollow Trail**. (The **Bridge Hollow Trail** serves as a southern connector between the **Ramseys Draft Trail** and the **Bald Ridge Trail**.) From here to its end the trail stays on the high, rugged ridge. It crosses The Peak at 4.1 miles. It begins a climb near rock outcroppings at 5.5 miles and descends steeply at 6.1 miles to congested rock outcroppings. At 7.3 miles the trail starts its ascent of Gordons Peak on switchbacks and reaches the top (3,915 ft.) at 7.6 miles. After its descent on switchbacks, it passes through a laurel thicket and more outcrops to a junction with the **Wild Oak Trail**, right and left, at 8.3 miles.

Options here are to backtrack (a total of 16.6 mi.) or to extend the journey left (1.7 mi.) to the **Hiner Spring Trail** for a connection to the **Ramseys Draft Trail** and downstream to US 250 at Mountain House Picnic Area (a total of 17.8 mi.), or right on the **Wild Oak Trail** (2.2 mi.) to SR 715/FR 96 and 3.7 miles south on SR 715 to Braley Pond (a total of 15.2 mi.). A continuation of 2.1 miles on the **Wild Oak Trail** and 3.2 miles on the **Dowells Draft Trail** will create a total of 16.1 miles to FR 449. From FR 449 it is 1.3 miles to Braley Pond (right on FR 449 to SR 715, left on SR 715, and right on Braley Pond entrance road) for a 17.4-mile loop.

USGS MAP: West Augusta; USFS TRAIL NOS.: 653, 496, 491

## RAMSEYS DRAFT WILDERNESS AND SHENANDOAH MOUNTAIN AREA
*Augusta and Highland Counties*

### Ramseys Draft Trail                                                                   137
LENGTH AND DIFFICULTY: 7.3 miles (11.7 km); moderate to strenuous
CONNECTING TRAILS: **Bridge Hollow Trail** (1.8 mi.), **Road Hollow Trail** (2.4 mi.),   138–42
    **Jerry's Run Trail** (2 mi.), **Hiner Spring Trail** (0.8 mi.), **Hardscrabble Trail**
    (0.4 mi.), **Shenandoah Mountain Trail(North)** (7.1 mi.)
FEATURES: wilderness, historic site, wildlife, stream, hemlock forest
TRAILHEADS: From SR 715, which figures in the preceding trail description, it is
    5 miles west on US 250 to FR 68 and Mountain House Picnic Area, on the right,

for the southern trailhead. The northern trailhead is the junction with the **Shenandoah Mountain Trail (North)** (3 mi. to FR 95).

INTRODUCTION: Ramseys Draft is the district's most publicized and popular area for hikers and allied adventurers. It is surrounded by wilderness and ten high mountain knobs and peaks from 3,264 to 4,282 feet, except at a narrow southern opening at US 250. At this point is the historic site of Parkersburg Pike Lodge, now Mountain House Picnic Area, a way station for travelers between West Virginia and Virginia. Some of the appealing features of Ramseys Draft are its wildness; its history; its stands of tall virgin hemlock, white pine, and tulip poplar; its diverse moss and fern ground covers; and its wildlife habitat for bear, bobcat, deer, turkey, and species of warblers unique to this area. Other features are its deep-shaded coolness in the summer (the temperature is as much as 10° to 15° lower than outside the canyon), its excellent campsites, and its tumbling stream with native trout.

After the pioneer settlers the timbermen came and logged part of the area, but they spared the virgin hemlock forests in the Left Prong of Ramseys Draft between Hardscrabble Knob and Freezeland Flat. Other stands of hemlock were left on the slopes and up the Right Prong. In 1913 the USFS purchased the property and by 1935 began to treat the Left Prong as a wilderness. During the early 1930s the West Augusta CCC Camp was established outside the canyon. In 1934 it was vacated for troops of Company 5449 from Fort Oglethorpe, Georgia, to train there. Men of the CCC camp constructed the **Ramseys Draft Trail** and **Jerry's Run Trail** (and probably the **Shenandoah Mountain Trail [North]**). In the mid-1980s the canyon and up to its rims became the Ramseys Draft Wilderness. In 1985 there was a flash flood in adjoining West Virginia that brought death and destruction to riverside towns and farm country. In this area the canyon was flooded and long sections of the wide old road were destroyed. Because of its wilderness character, the trail route has been left to nature by the USFS. The result is that hikers have formed a zigzagging route over rock piles, debris, and remaining pieces of the road to increase the original trail distance with 0.8 mile. Four loop hikes can be made with the use of connecting trails, two of which (**Bridge Hollow Trail** and **Road Hollow Trail**) are outside the wilderness boundary. (For longer hikes these circuit options can include the **Shenandoah Mountain Trail** for a 30.7-mi. linear trail and the **Wild Oak Trail** for another 25.9-mi. loop [in the Dry River District].)

DESCRIPTION: From the parking area, pass the signboard on the **Ramseys Draft Trail** and after 135 feet reach a junction with the **Bridge Hollow Trail** on the right. (The **Bridge Hollow Trail** crosses a small creek to begin a steep ascent, at first parallel with US 250. It curves in and out of coves among mossy trail banks and laurel to skirt the northern side of Bridge Hollow. It reaches the **Bald Ridge Trail** at 1.8 mi. From here, on the left, it is 7.7 mi. to connect with the **Ramseys**

Draft Trail near its northern end—via the **Bald Ridge Trail**, the **Wild Oak Trail**, and the **Hiner Spring Trail**.)

Ahead on the **Ramseys Draft Trail** after 35 yards is the **Road Hollow Trail** on the left. (The **Road Hollow Trail** ascends around a spur ridge to a cove at 0.4 mi. The remaining 2.1 mi. are narrow and erratic ups and downs with slanted treadway for water diversion. Dipping into dry streambeds of Road Hollow, the trail leaves a final cove at 2.3 mi. to ascend the ridge and join the **Shenandoah Mountain Trail** at 2.5 mi. From there it is 5.8 mi. right to connect with the **Ramseys Draft Trail**. To the left it is 1.3 mi. to US 250.)

Continuing on the **Ramseys Draft Trail**, the treadway is over rock flats, rock piles, part of a creek bed, and part of a road. At 0.3 mile on the left is an abandoned USFS building, and at 0.6 mile the trail enters the wilderness boundary. At 2.4 miles is a deep ravine at the confluence of Jerry's Run and Ramseys Draft. After ascending an embankment there is a junction with **Jerry's Run Trail** on the left. (**Jerry's Run Trail** goes upstream in a narrow canyon. It hugs the stream among tall hemlock and oaks until about 1.6 mi., where it leaves the stream on a sloping ascent to a junction with the **Shenandoah Mountain Trail**. From there, on the right, it connects with the **Ramseys Draft Trail** after 4.7 mi.)

On the **Ramseys Draft Trail** the old road ends at 4.3 miles at the Left Prong and Right Prong, and the trail enters a laurel thicket to ascend the Right Prong. In a steady, almost straight ascent for 1.9 miles the trail is among moss-covered rocks, tall hemlocks and hardwoods, and a cascading stream. At 6.2 miles the trail junctions with the **Hiner Spring Trail** (formerly **Springhouse Ridge Trail**, followed by **Tearjacket Trail**) on the right. At the junction is an attractive camping area in a forest of maples, serviceberry, yellow birch, and fern beds. Ninety feet up the trail is Hiner Spring on the left. (The **Hiner Spring Trail** goes east on a descending grade in dense laurel to an open forest for a junction with the **Wild Oak Trail** [white-blazed]. If the **Wild Oak Trail** is followed to the right for 1.7 mi., it will connect with the **Bald Ridge Trail**. [See **Bald Ridge Trail**, previously described.])

Continue on the **Ramseys Draft Trail** for 0.2 mile to a ridge top where to the left the **Hardscrabble Trail** ascends 0.4 mile to a large boulder field at Hardscrabble Knob (4,282 ft.). (On the ascent is a continuous, dense bed of ferns. The best views of part of the canyon and peaks on the **Bald Ridge Trail** are from the southern edge of the boulders. Among the boulders are the remains of an old fire tower. Backtrack.) The **Ramseys Draft Trail** now makes a 0.9-mile graded descent with two cove curves and ends in a flat saddle among old-growth oaks. Backtrack, or choose one of the following options: (1) Continue northeast on the **Shenandoah Mountain Trail** for 3 miles to FR 95 (North River Rd.), accessible from Elkhorn Lake and farther south on FR 96 to SR 715 by vehicle; (2) backtrack to follow the **Hiner Spring Trail** to the **Wild Oak Trail**, the **Bald Ridge Trail**, and the **Bridge Hollow Trail** for a 17.9-mile circuit; or (3) follow the **Shenandoah Mountain Trail**, left, for a return on **Jerry's Run Trail** for a circuit of 16.4 miles, or via the **Road Hollow Trail** for a circuit of 15.6 miles.

USGS MAPS: West Augusta, McDowell, Palo Alto; USFS TRAIL NOS.: (only main trail and connectors) 440, 442, 448, 441, 716, 440A, 447, 446

## SHENANDOAH MOUNTAIN AREA
*Augusta, Highland, and Bath Counties*

143 **Shenandoah Mountain Trail (North)**

LENGTH AND DIFFICULTY: 7.1 miles (11.4 km); easy to moderate

144–47, 137   CONNECTING TRAILS: **Road Hollow Trail** (2.5 mi.), **Jerry's Run Trail** (2 mi.), **Sinclair Hollow Trail** (1.6 mi.), **Ramseys Draft Trail** (7.3 mi.), **Tearjacket Trail** (3.2 mi.)

FEATURES: wildlife, solitude, historic site, scenic view

TRAILHEADS: Access south is at the Confederate Breastworks on US 250, 2.1 miles west from Mountain House Picnic Area at Ramseys Draft. The northern trail-head for trail connections is at the **Ramseys Draft Trail**, but for road access it is 3 miles farther north to FR 95 (North River Rd.) in the Dry River Ranger District. FR 95 can be accessed from SR 718 at Stokesville.

DESCRIPTION: This beautiful trail weaves in and out of the Ramseys Draft Wilder-ness boundary on Shenandoah Mountain and around spur ridges in West Vir-ginia. Skillfully graded on a gentle ascent there are a number of views west to Shaws Ridge and Jack Mountain. It starts for the first 0.3 mile in the Civil War **Confederate Breastworks Interpretive Trail** in a forest of hardwoods, white pines, and hemlocks. At 1.3 miles the **Road Hollow Trail** makes a junction on the right. (It descends 2.5 mi. to connect with the **Ramseys Draft Trail** at its southern trailhead.) At 2.4 miles is **Jerry's Run Trail** on the right. (It descends 2 mi. to meet the **Ramseys Draft Trail**.) There is a thick hemlock grove at 3 miles. At 6 miles there is a grassy saddle with white snakeroot, white pines, and a junction with the **Sinclair Hollow Trail** on the left. (It descends 1.6 mi. to FR 64 [Shaws Fork Rd.] and SR 616, from which it is 6.9 mi. south to the village of Head Waters on US 250.) The main trail intersects with the **Ramseys Draft Trail** at 7.1 miles among old-growth oaks. (Here is a contact, left, with **Tear-jacket Trail** [3.2 mi. north in Dry River District].) Hiking options here are to backtrack, make a circuit with the **Ramseys Draft Trail**, or continue 3 miles ahead to FR 95 in the Dry River Ranger District (see preceding descriptions and distances).

USGS MAPS: McDowell, West Augusta, Palo Alto; USFS TRAIL NOS.: 447, 448, 441, 447D, 440, 447.1

**Shaws Ridge Trail** 148

LENGTH AND DIFFICULTY: 6.3 miles (10. km); moderate

FEATURES: solitude, wildlife

TRAILHEADS: To reach the southern trailhead, drive from the Confederate Breast-works parking area on US 250 west for 3.2 miles to the village of Head Waters and the junction with SR 616 on the right, to park at corner. To reach the northern trailhead, continue 1.8 miles farther west on US 250, where a turn right on SR 614 goes 5 miles to Jones Hunter Access and FR 501 on the right.

DESCRIPTION: This trail is mainly a hunter's trail, but it has potential for isolated camping, watching wildlife, and birding. Begin the trail in an ascent on the road embankment, and follow a yellow-blazed graded trail into a hollow with shag-bark hickory and banks of stonecrop. After arriving on the ridgeline, the trail passes through Virginia pine, maple, and witch hazel. It descends to pass Martins Draft headwaters at 2 miles. Deer frequent this area. The trail gradually ascends Shaws Ridge, and at the end it merges into gated FR 501. It is about 1.5 miles to exit at Jones Hunter Access.

USGS MAPS: McDowell, Doe Hill, Palo Alto; USFS TRAIL NO.: 652

## Shenandoah Mountain Trail (South) 149

LENGTH AND DIFFICULTY: 21.2 miles (33.9 km); strenuous

CONNECTING TRAILS: **Georgia Camp Trail** (4 mi.), **Shaw's Fork Trail** (3.5 mi.), 150–54 **Holloway Draft Trail** (4 mi.), **Nelson Draft Trail** (1 mi.), **Marshall Draft Trail** (1.3 mi.)

FEATURES: historic site, solitude, wildlife, scenic views

TRAILHEADS: The northern trailhead is on the southern side of US 250 at the Confederate Breastworks, 2.1 miles west from the Mountain House Picnic Area at Ramseys Draft. For the southern trailhead, take SR 627 (Scottstown Draft Rd.) 2.5 miles west from SR 629 (south of Deerfield), or 2.5 miles east from SR 678 (south of Williamsville).

INTRODUCTION: The trail was constructed by the CCC in the 1930s for isolated backcountry hiking. It follows the ridgeline of knobs and peaks between 3,000 and 3,900 feet in a forest of chestnut oak, maple, locust, pine, hemlock, rhodo-dendron, and laurel. A few springs are near the trail, and more than 50 streams flow from the mountainside, either west to Cowpasture River or east to Calf-pasture and Mill Creeks. The trail intersects with two forest roads and two short foot trails. There are options for exploring the Right Prong of Benson Run and historic points such as the Confederate Breastworks and Signal Corps Knob. Maps from the USFS may show the southern trailhead either ending at a private cabin on SR 678 at the Cowpasture River or dead-ending on a logging road between the cabin and SR 627. To avoid trespass, the USFS recommends the southern terminus be the ridge crossing of SR 627 (Scottstown Draft Rd.), thus making the trail distance 21.3 miles instead of 23.6 miles. Traffic volume is low on this trail, except during fall and spring hunting seasons.

DESCRIPTION: The trail begins at gated FR 396, 300 yards east of the Confederate Breastworks, and it follows the road on the ridgeline for the first 2.6 miles. Along the route it intersects with old logging roads, one at 0.9 mile, but at 1.4 miles **Georgia Camp Trail** descends to a gate at US 250, 1.5 miles east from Mountain House Picnic Area. (At 2.6 mi. there is an alternate route of 3.3 mi., which leaves the ridge on FR 396 and turns right on an old road for a descent to the Right Prong of Benson Run. It passes waterfalls and good campsites and meets the western end of FR 173 on the eastern side of the stream. The road ascends on switchbacks to cross the main trail. On this route is 3.5-mi. **Benson Run Trail**, used mainly by equestrians.) At 2.9 miles the trail is under a power line. At 3.1 miles the trail leaves the old road to skirt left of the ridge, but it returns to the top of the mountain at 3.9 miles. Here is one of a number of wildlife ponds found on the trail. For the next 3 miles are a few scenic views and rock outcroppings. At 7 miles there is a junction with FR 173. To the right is access to the alternate route (see above), and to the left it is 4.6 miles to SR 629. (The east side is now **Holloway Draft Trail**, mainly used by equestrians.) The main trail forks to the left at 7.1 miles. After 0.5 mile it reaches the ridgeline. Another 0.2 mile on the right is Phillips Spring, 300 yards down the hollow. The trail skirts west of The Bump (3,634 ft.) at 9.5 miles. Reach the junction with the **Nelson Draft Trail** at 11.3 miles. (It leads 1.3 mi. down the western side of the mountain to end at FR 394 [Sugar Tree Rd.]. The road goes northwest along Nelson Draft for 2.5 mi. to SR 614 near Patna and north of Williamsville.) From 11.6 miles to 13.8 miles are a number of views west to Bullpasture Mountain and east to Walker Mountain.

There is a major intersection at 17.5 miles. Rough Jerkemtight Road descends east for 5 miles to SR 629, using part of FR 399 along Jerkemtight Creek. Another old road runs south 0.4 mile up to Wallace Peak (3,795 ft.), site of a former fire tower. There is a spring on the southern side of the peak, accessed by a short trail from the eastern side. A few yards ahead on the main trail is a junction with the **Marshall Draft Trail** near a large black cherry tree. (An orange-blazed foot trail, it descends steeply for 1.3 mi. to FR 394 [Sugar Tree Rd.]. On a dry ridge it has chestnut oak, Virginia pine, and blueberry patches. See description under **Wallace Tract Trail** for use of **Marshall Draft Trail** and 2 mi. of FR 394 to provide an extended distance from the **Shenandoah Mountain Trail**.)

Continue on the **Shenandoah Mountain Trail** to ascend and skirt east of North Sister Knob at 19.1 miles. The trail then goes back to the western side of the ridge to South Sister Knob for views of Cowpasture and Jackson river valleys at 20.7 miles. After a descent the trail reaches its southern terminus at

155

SR 627 at 21.2 miles. (Across the road is the section of the **Shenandoah Mountain Trail** that has been abandoned because of private property near SR 678.)

USGS MAPS: McDowell, Deerfield, Williamsville, Green Valley; USFS TRAIL NOS.: 447, 113, 112, 110, 393, 547

**Wallace Tract Trail**                                                                          156

LENGTH AND DIFFICULTY: 2.5 miles (4 km); moderate

FEATURES: solitude, wildlife, wildflowers, swinging bridge

TRAILHEADS: The eastern trailhead is at a gated, signed, old logging road (FR 394-F) off FR 394 (Sugar Tree Rd.), 4.7 miles north from SR 627 (Scotchtown Draft Rd.), which is 0.6 mile east off SR 678, 3.4 miles south of Williamsville. The western trailhead is at the end of FR 282 (swinging footbridge over Cowpasture River), 0.8 mile off SR 678, 2.1 miles south of Williamsville.

DESCRIPTION: (This trail, plus 2 mi. of FR 394, north to 1.3-mi. **Marshall Draft Trail** is a 5.8-mi. route from the **Shenandoah Mountain Trail [South and West]** to Cowpasture River [see above]. If using this option, turn left [southwest] on FR 394 at the northern trailhead of the **Marshall Draft Trail**. Follow the scenic, infrequently used [except during hunting seasons] FR 394 for 2 mi. to the **Wallace Tract Trail**, right.) The **Wallace Tract Trail**, with sparse yellow blazes, descends gradually, first on the left slope of a ridge, then at 0.5 mile it switches to the right slope. With a grassy treadway it abruptly turns left on a side road at 1.1 miles among young pines and locust. It descends to a grove of locust and a damp, faint road to the left, where it crosses a stream (may be dry in the summer) at 1.5 miles. Enter a stand of large hemlocks and continue descent to exit from the forest into a hayfield at 1.9 miles. From there the trail may be unmarked; therefore, follow the right edge of the fertile hayfields of clover, lespedeza, and wildflowers such as bee balm and soapwort. The fields are woodchuck habitats. Pass a farm road that fords Cowpasture River, and turn right to the river edge before a break in the locust trees (which leads into another field). Continue downstream for 100 yards to the 170-foot-long swinging footbridge over Cowpasture River. Across the river is a grassy parking area, unless the gate 0.2 mile ahead on FR 282 is locked. Here is a parking area bordered with wildflowers, and it is 0.6 mile on FR 282 out to SR 678.

USGS MAP: Williamsville; USFS TRAIL NO.: 417

# Warm Springs Ranger District

This is the only GWNF district that completely borders the Monongahela National Forest in West Virginia. As a result it provides added depth to wild and scenic places for exploring, hunting, fishing, hiking, camping, and cross-country skiing in its 171,526 acres. The forest properties rise to join each other with communal trails and roads such as the **Allegheny Mountain Trail** between popular Lake Sherwood in West Virginia and Lake Moomaw in Virginia. A section of this high boundary is 25 miles of remote FR 55. Its lofty, scenic drive is known mainly to hunters, explorers, and foresters. On its serpentine route is Mad Tom (4,055 ft.) and High Top (3,640 ft.), where deer forage in fertile meadows above the clouds, and Paddy Knob (4,477 ft.), with tall asters and woodland sunflowers. At the northwestern corner of this long border is Locust Springs, a high plateau of northern hardwoods dappled with red spruce among bogs and beavers. There are more than 30 species of rare flora and fauna, rarely seen by humans except those adventuring into the web of trails. The district has more lake acreage than other GWNF districts. Lake Moomaw, for example, covers 2,530 acres and is a paradise for campers, fishermen, boaters, and hikers. It has a beach for swimming and a marina with thirty-six boat slips, luxuries in this backcountry free of expressways, malls, and billboards. Its streams are cold and fresh, and some are stocked with trout. Among them are Jackson River, Back Creek, Pads Creek, and Wilson Creek. It has one wilderness, Rough Mountain (9,300 acres), located in the southeastern corner, and it is close enough to the Rich Hole Wilderness in the James River Ranger District for improved turkey and bear habitat.

One of its surprisingly appealing and secluded camping areas is Blowing Springs, set in Back Creek Gorge on VA 39, 9.5 miles west of Warm Springs. It receives its name from a forceful spring that releases strong air currents from beneath the earth's surface. The grassy campground under the shade of scattered black walnut trees has fee camping facilities with trailer sites, picnic tables, drinking water, rest rooms, and fishing. Anglers find the stream good for bass and trout. The campground is open usually from March 15 to November 30. At the south end of the campground is **Back Creek Gorge Trail**. Among ferns and wildflowers it parallels the creek downstream on an enticing path that allows views of the creek and geological formations. Large trees include sycamore, beech, and hemlock. At 0.4 mile is a scenic pool and rapids with a more distinctive gorge atmosphere at 0.6 mile. At 1 mile there is a rock slide with tight passageway to the terminus at 1.3 miles. Backtrack. (If you are parking outside the campground gate, it is 0.3 mi. through the campground to the trailhead.) Access is 5.5 miles west on VA 39 from Hidden Valley Campground entrance, and 1.5 miles east on VA 39 from a juncture with SR 600.

Hidden Valley Campground access is 3.2 miles west on VA 39 from US 220 at Warm Springs to a turn north on SR 621 for 1 mile, then left on FR 241 for 1.5 miles. Its open season is the same as for Blowing Springs, mid-March through November, and camping fees are charged. Services and trail descriptions are ahead. With them is a description for Poor Farm primitive campground near **Jackson River Fishing Trail**.

Farther south and downstream from VA 39 are three other USFS campgrounds: McClintic Point, Bolar Mountain, and Greenwood Point at Lake Moomaw, and on the way to these is Bolar Flat Picnic Area. Access to all of these areas from the Hidden Valley entrance off VA 39 is east 0.4 mile on VA 39, for a right turn on SR 687 to historic Cowardin, then right on SR 603. (For visitors going north from Covington on US 220, turn west on VA 39 at Warm Springs and go 2.7 mi. to turn left on SR 687. For visitors coming east from West Virginia on VA 39, turn right on SR 600 after 1.5 mi. south of Mountain Grove.) McClintic Point Campground is on SR 603 on the western shore of Upper Lake Moomaw. After you cross the McClintic bridge the campground is on the left after a mile. Reservations are necessary for the use of group and primitive campsites (540-839-2521). There are vault toilets, hand water pump, grills, picnic tables, and an area for fishing (no electric hookups). Downstream for 2.5 miles on the left is Bolar Flat Picnic Area with vault toilets, drinking water, fishing, and boating. After crossing Mill Creek bridge you will arrive at the district's largest fee campground, Bolar Mountain Recreation Complex. At Bolar Mountain Campground #3 is a hike-in trail for free camping at Greenwood Point Campground. Services and trail systems for these campgrounds are described ahead. The district has two other picnic areas. Bubbling Springs has picnic tables, vault toilets, and trash cans, and is located south of Millboro on SR 665. Locust Spring has vault toilets and a network of trails. See descriptions ahead. Access is north of Thurmond, West Virginia, on WV 28 to FR 60/124, right, into Virginia.

The district has an inventory of fifty-three trails with 119.8 miles, mostly multiple-use, and two short ATV trails near Warwick Mansion at Hidden Valley. Recently added to the trail inventory is **Lost Run Trail** with two spurs in the Laurel Fork Area. They are described ahead. **Lick Block Trail** and **Polecat Hollow** 158–59 **Trail** are not blazed or maintained. Among a few restored trails is blue-blazed **Laurel Run Trail**. For the western access at the intersection of US 220 and VA 39, drive 7.2 miles north on US 220 to FR 124, right. After 3.5 miles park at scenic Duncan Knob Lookout (3,819 ft.). Hike north on a gated pastoral road for 0.3 mile to make a descent off the road, right, and gradually descend the slope of Jack Mountain through mountain laurel, oaks, and white pine. After crossing a small stream, the trail easily follows a ridge to its eastern terminus at SR 614 embankment at 3.1 miles. Parking is north around the curve near sanitary bins. North on SR 614 it is 1.6 miles to Burnsvillle, and south on SR 614 it is 7.2 miles to US 220.

(On your way from US 220 on FR 124 to Duncan Knob Lookout, you may wish to explore the western part of **Bear Rock Trail**. The trailhead is 0.7 mi. up the 160 mountain to a ridge after you enter FR 124. Enter right where hunters park, pass a gate at 82 yd., and follow an unblazed and unmaintained road. At 0.1 mi. keep left. Descend gradually through a hardwood forest to scattered white pines and a curve in the road at 1 mi. Enter a section of overgrowth and erosion to rock-hop Muddy Run at 1.6 mi. Easily ascend to SR 614 at 1.7 mi. Across the road is parking space for two cars. To the right and south it is 30 ft. to continue the **Bear Rock Trail**, left. The passage is through dense rhododendron and overgrowth without

*Lick Block Trail, Warm Springs Ranger District*

blazing or signage. It ascends steeply for 1.5 mi. to **Warm Springs Mountain Trail**. See description ahead.)

ADDRESS AND INFORMATION: Warm Springs Ranger District, Rt. 1, Box 30, Hot Springs, VA 24445; phone: 540-839-2521; on US 220, 1.8 miles south of Hot Springs. Available for free are brochures and flyers on Lake Moomaw, Locust Springs, Hidden Valley, campgrounds, and wilderness. There is a fee for topographical maps and a district map with trails.

## ROUGH MOUNTAIN WILDERNESS AREA
*Bath County*

161 **Crane Trail**

LENGTH AND DIFFICULTY: 3 miles (4.8 km); strenuous

FEATURES: isolation, rugged, wildlife

TRAILHEADS: From Millboro drive southeast on SR 633 to FR 129 and follow it 5 miles along the South Fork of Pads Creek to parking area and gate. The western trailhead is 8.8 miles north on VA 42 (right side) from I-64, exit 29.

DESCRIPTION: Follow an old road along the C&O Railroad bed for 1 mile and turn left at second small hollow to cross railroad and Pads Creek. Ascend steeply by a small stream in the Rough Mountain Wilderness to the ridge crest (2,600 ft.) at 1.3 miles. Explore the rocky cliffs and look west to Cowpasture River and Beards Mountain. To the east are views of Short Mountain and Mill Mountain. Descend on switchbacks to gate at VA 42 at 3 miles. Backtrack or use a second vehicle.

USGS MAP: Nimrod Hall; USFS TRAIL NO.: 454

## MIDDLE, LITTLE MARE, AND BEARDS MOUNTAINS AREA
*Bath County*

**Middle Mountain Trail** (5.5 mi.), **Brushy Ridge Trail** (3.9 mi.), **Salt Pond**     162–67
**Ridge Trail** (2.1 mi.), **Little Mare Mountain Trail** (6 mi.), **Gilliam Run Trail**
(2.3 mi.), **Beards Mountain Trail** (6.4 mi.)

LENGTH AND DIFFICULTY: 19.9 miles (31.8 km) combined, partial round-trip; moderate to strenuous

CONNECTING TRAILS: **Stony Run Trail** (4.5 mi.), **Blue Suck Trail** (3 mi.), **Sandy**     168–73
**Gap Trail** (3.4 mi.), **Little Mare Mountain Spur Trail** (0.7 mi.), **Beards Mountain Spur Trail** (1.7 mi.), **Salt Stump Trail** (2.5 mi.)

FEATURES: scenic views, outcrops, wildflowers, wildlife

TRAILHEADS: Use Douthat State Park Campground for base camp. From I-64, exit 27, drive north 5.5 miles on SR 629 to visitor center. **Sandy Gap Trail** trailhead: from US 220 at Valley View, drive 2.5 miles on SR 606 to junction with SR 703 and go 3.3 miles to trailhead on right. **Little Mare Mountain Trail** trailhead: from VA 39, near Bath Alum, go 0.8 mile south on SR 683 (or north 0.9 mi. from SR 629). **Gilliam Run Trail** trailhead: From northern entrance of Douthat State Park, drive 4.2 miles north on SR 629 to FR 361, right. **Beards Mountain Spur Trail** trailhead: from VA 39 at Millboro Springs, drive 5.2 miles south on VA 42 to SR 632 and turn right for 1 mile (also from I-64, exit 29, on VA 42, 10.5 mi. north to SR 632, left).

INTRODUCTION: With all the diversity of trails (ten in Warm Spring Ranger District and twenty-four in Douthat State Park), and base camp facilities for tired and hungry hikers in the park, this is a hiker's heaven. Although the 40 miles of park trails are for day hikes, they can be entrance trails to the 32 miles of linear trails in the forest for overnight camping. The nearest option for a circuit on the forest trails uses 2.3 miles on FR 194 and 1.7 miles on SR 629, explained below.

DESCRIPTION: Begin the hike in Douthat State Park (0.5 mi. south of the campground on SR 629) on orange-blazed **Stony Run Trail**. Ascend, and at 1.4 miles pass a junction with the **Locust Gap Trail** from the right. At 2.5 miles is Stony Run Falls on the left. For the next 2 miles ascend on switchbacks to a junction left with a short connector to the **Middle Mountain Trail** and right with yellow-blazed **Tuscarora Overlook Trail**. If not accessing the **Middle Mountain Trail** follow the **Tuscarora Overlook Trail** for scenic views to intersect on the ridge top with the blue-blazed **Blue Suck Trail** on the right, and the **Middle Mountain Trail** and the **Sandy Gap Trail** on the left after 0.9 mile.

(The **Blue Suck Trail** descends 3 mi. to just north of the visitor center in the park.) The **Middle Mountain Trail** goes 1.6 miles south to its end at the county line and district line, but its name is replaced by the continuing **Fore Mountain Trail** (see James River Ranger District).

(The **Sandy Gap Trail** descends for 0.6 mi. west to FR 125 [Smith Creek Rd.]. It then crosses Smith Creek at 0.8 mi., ascends to a large area of glacial rock slabs at 1.5 mi., and crosses a stream at 2.1 mi. Continuing, it ascends, crosses another stream near a spring at 2.4 mi., and reaches SR 703 [Homestead Skyline Dr.] through a channel of purple rhododendron at 3.4 mi. There is outstanding scenery with views west over the Jackson River. Flame azaleas, locust, and mountain laurel decorate the area. Bald Knob and Ingalls Airport are right, and SR 606 is 3.3 mi. left.)

Continue north on the ridge on the **Middle Mountain Trail**. Signs may show that the **Middle Mountain Trail** is also the **Salt Stump Trail** (which leads down the eastern side of Middle Mountain to SR 629 in the park). The main trail may have overgrowth, but it stays on the ridgeline, undulating among the oaks and sections of pitch pine. At 4.2 miles (on the **Middle Mountain Trail**) are excellent views. Begin to descend gradually along the ridge shoulder and reach FR 125 (Wilson Creek Rd.) at 5.5 miles. (To the right it is 1 mi. on FR 125 to SR 629 and Douthat State Park.) Turn left on FR 25 and go 0.3 mile to entrance of the **Brushy Ridge Trail** on the right. Begin by crossing tank traps on an old logging road, then cross a stream at 0.7 mile. Ascend gradually to a junction with the **Salt Pond Ridge Trail** on right at 2.5 miles.

(The **Salt Pond Ridge Trail** descends right to SR 629 and to Douthat State Park after 3.3 mi. In its descent it passes a number of large boulder outcroppings, streams, and tank traps to end at FR 194. [Some maps may show the trail continuing across the road and through private property to SR 629.] If attempting a loop, follow FR 194 for 2.3 mi. south to SR 629, turn left, and follow SR 629 for 1.7 mi. to the **Gilliam Run Trail** on the right at FR 361. After 2.3 mi. on the **Gilliam Run Trail**, reach the **Beards Mountain Trail**, where a right turn leads 2.2 mi. to the boundary of Douthat State Park. Here either the **Mountain Top Trail** or the **Mountain Side Trail** would lead to the **Brushy Ridge Trail** or the **Beards Mountain Gap Trail** for a return to the campground and a total of about 27 mi.)

At this point on the **Middle Mountain Trail** it is 12.5 miles from the beginning on the **Stony Run Trail**. Keep left at the fork on the **Brushy Ridge Trail** and reach a junction with a private road at 13.9 miles in Brushy Mountain Gap near Trappers Lodge. (Access here is from near the front entrance of The Homestead in Hot Springs. Permission from office officials is necessary for hiking access.)

Continue on forest property and begin the **Little Mare Mountain Trail**, northeast, on a downgrade on the ridgeline. At 16.9 miles is a junction with the **Little Mare Mountain Spur** (which descends 0.7 mi. to a road, formerly called the **Mare Run Trail**). Continue descending on the ridge in a hardwood forest and exit from an old road to SR 683 at 19.9 miles. It is 0.8 mile left to VA 39 and the Bath Alum community.

The nearest access to the **Beards Mountain Trail** from Douthat State Park is from the lake parking area. Cross the road, enter the **Buck Lick Interpretive Trail**, and turn left on the **Wilson Creek Trail**. Pass right of cabins, and at the last cabin (#50) turn right on the **Ross Camp Hollow Trail**. Turn left on the **Mountain Side Trail** and ascend to the corner of the park to a junction left with the **Mountain Top Trail** at 2 miles. Turn left on the **Beards Mountain Trail** and for the next 2.2 miles in a hardwood forest gradually descend over six low knolls. The farther from the park, the more likely the overgrowth. At a narrow point on the ridge, join the **Gilliam Run Trail**, left. (It descends steeply for the first 0.8 mi. to a junction with FR 361. Its other 1.5 mi. may be overgrown because it mainly parallels the forest road, which is easier to hike. Its northern trailhead is at gated FR 361 and SR 629, 4 mi. north of Douthat State Park.)

Continuing on the **Beards Mountain Trail**, there is a slight and easy decline to a junction with the **Walton Tract Trail** at 7 miles. To the left the **Beards Mountain Trail** descends in a low hollow to curve right at Hickman Draft. It dead-ends at the confluence with another stream at 5.8 miles. (The district plans to extend or connect the trail with FR 361.) The **Beards Mountain Spur Trail** follows a ridgeline before curving right at a bluff over Cowpasture River at 0.9 mile. It descends on the mountainside and crosses a high footbridge at an oxbow curve of the river at 1.5 miles. Canoe landings are on both sides of the access road. (See trailheads for access directions.)

USGS MAPS: Healing Spring, Warm Springs, Bath Alum, Nimrod Hall; USFS TRAIL NOS.: (forest trails only and in order of citing) 458 (Middle Mountain), 637 (Sandy Gap), 456 (Brushy Ridge), 620 (Salt Pond Ridge), 638 (Gilliam Run), 459 (Beards Mountain), 714 (Little Mare Mountain), 714A (Little Mare Mountain Spur), 459A (Beards Mountain Spur)


## PINEY MOUNTAIN AREA
*Bath County*

**Bear Rock Trail** (1.3 mi.), **Warm Springs Mountain Trail** (4.3 mi.), **Piney Mountain Trail** (7 mi.), **Tower Hill Mountain Trail** (1.3 mi.)

175–78

LENGTH AND DIFFICULTY: 13.9 miles (22 km) combined; strenuous

FEATURES: scenic views, wildlife, seclusion

TRAILHEADS: There are three accesses to the Piney Mountain trails. To reach the first, from the junction of VA 39 and SR 609 at Bath Alum, drive north on SR 609 for 2.7 miles to fork left. After another 3.3 miles turn left on FR 465. Park here if road is gated; otherwise, drive 1.3 miles to the **Bear Rock Trail**, right. The second access is on FR 358, off VA 39, 2.4 miles east from US 220 (down the eastern side of Warm Springs Mountain), and 4.2 miles west of the VA 39 and SR 609 junction in Bath Alum. On gated FR 358 it is 2.2 miles to the southern terminus of **Piney Mountain Trail (South)** on the right side of the road. To reach the third access, for the northern trailhead of the **Piney Mountain Trail (North)**, drive north of Warm Springs on US 220 from VA 39 for 4 miles and turn right on SR 614. After 0.9 mile look for trailhead on right. For the **Tower Hill Mountain Trail**, use the same route as for the **Bear Rock Trail**, except turn right at the fork of SR 609 on SR 624 and go 0.6 mile to trailhead on the left.

INTRODUCTION: All forest roads to these trails are gated except the northern end of the **Piney Mountain Trail** on SR 614 and the southern end of the **Tower Hill Mountain Trail** on SR 624, which does not connect with the other three trails. Gates are likely to be open during late fall and spring hunting seasons. The **Warm Springs Mountain Trail** dead-ends in the north; the **Piney Mountain Trail** dead-ends in the south; and the **Tower Hill Mountain Trail** dead-ends in the north. As a result of gates and dead ends, hikers can expect to hike more miles and might need a second vehicle. If all gates are closed and all trails with backtracking are hiked, the shortest additional distance is 10.2 miles with the use of two vehicles. Map users will notice the trail locations on the GWNF map are different from those on the district map.

DESCRIPTION: If entering on the **Bear Rock Trail**, go 1.3 miles from the gate on FR 465 to a rocky ravine. (To the left a connector trail descends 0.3 mi. to SR 609.) Ascend by a small stream to the ridgeline of the **Warms Springs Mountain Trail**, left and right, at 1.3 miles. If hiking left (south) follow an easy contour but ascend to House Rock (3,781 ft.) at 1.5 miles from the **Bear Rock Trail (East)**. Continue and junction with **Piney Mountain Trail (South)**, left at 2.4 miles. (If you take **Piney Mountain Trail [South]**, descend 1 mi. on switchbacks to cross FR 453. Ascend to the ridgeline of Piney Mountain, which has both white and yellow pines. Turn right, follow the ridge, descend, and switchback west to cross Jordan Run. Reach FR 453 at 4.2 mi., the trail's southern terminus. Options here are to hike left, south, 1.8 mi. to VA 39, backtrack, or follow the scenic and crooked FR 453, right, upstream for 2.5 mi. to rejoin the **Piney Mountain Trail [South]** and turn left. After ascending the switchbacks return to **Warm Springs Mountain Trail**, left and right, for a round-trip of 7.7 mi.)

If turning left follow the ridge 0.5 mile to junction, right, with **Piney Mountain Trail (North)**. Ahead is the summit of Bonner Mountain (3,690 ft.), the southern terminus of **Warm Springs Mountain Trail**. If following **Piney Mountain Trail (North)**, turn right and begin a descent of 2.1 miles on a slender ridge between small streams. Exit between two large white oaks at SR

614. About 175 yards, left and downstream, is space for roadside parking. Farther downstream it is 0.5 mile to US 220.

(If you plan more hiking in this network of trails, there are two northeast accesses on SR 614. The first is 1.7 mi. from the **Piney Mountain Trail [North]** exit to a small parking space, right, near a streamlet. Here is the crossing of **Bear Rock Trail [Central and West]**. [West of the road it goes 1.7 mi. on an old forest road on the side of Wilson Mountain to FR 124, the trail's western terminus.] On the east side of SR 614 and the south side of the streamlet, the central section of **Bear Rock Trail** goes upstream in dense rhododendron. A climb of 1.5 mi. on this trail will take you for an 8.6-mi. loop to **Warm Springs Mountain Trail**. The other access to the **Warm Springs Mountain Trail** is 3.6 mi. farther northeast on SR 614 to gated FR 1191, right, on the east side. From here an ascent of 1 mi. on the road connects you with the northern terminus of the **Warm Springs Mountain Trail**.)

If on your first arrival to **Warm Springs Mountain Trail** from **Bear Rock Trail (East)** you turned right, northeast, you would junction, left, with the continuing **Bear Rock Trail (Central)** after 0.2 mile. At first the **Bear Rock Trail (Central)** descends gradually on the mountainside, then descends steeply into a hollow to cross SR 614 at 1.5 miles, as described above. If not taking this exit, but staying on the **Warm Springs Mountain Trail**, continue on a generally pleasant contour in a hardwood forest with scattered pines, hemlocks, and rhododendron. Begin to gently descend at 0.8 mile from **Bear Rock Trail (East)** and increase the descent at 2.1 miles. Arrive at FR 1191A at 2.8 miles. Backtrack, or descend 1 mile on FR 1191A to exit at SR 614. From here it is 3.6 miles left and south on SR 614 to **Bear Rock Trail (Central and West)**. Another 2.2 miles is to US 220.

To hike the **Tower Hill Mountain Trail** follow the trailhead guide above and begin the ascent on a blue-blazed trail among oaks and white pines. After 0.5 mile is Chimney Rocks, with views of McClung Ridge. A turn right (northeast) leads to the forest boundary at 1.3 miles. (With the use of private property and USFS property this trail was formerly 14 mi. on Tower Hill Mountain to SR 614 near Williamsville.) Backtrack.

USGS MAPS: Warm Springs, Bath Alum, Burnsville; USFS TRAIL NOS.: 635, 451, 453, 452

## HIDDEN VALLEY AREA
*Bath County*

LENGTH AND DIFFICULTY: 20.8 miles (32.2 km) combined, partial circuit; easy to moderate

FEATURES: historic site, archaeological artifacts, fishing, wildlife

TRAILHEADS: From junction of US 220 and VA 39 in Warm Springs, drive 3.2 miles west on VA 39 to SR 621 and turn right. After 1 mile turn left on FR 241 and go 1.3 miles to crossing of the **Cobbler Mountain Trail**, and 0.2 mile farther to the campground, left. The western trailhead of the **Bogan Run Trail** is 3.3 miles north on SR 600 from Mountain Grove on VA 39, and the northern trailhead for **Hidden Valley Trail** is north on US 220, left on SR 623.

INTRODUCTION: The fee campground has trailer and tent sites, vault toilets, drinking water, and waste disposal unit in a white pine and hardwood forest. It has a double loop nature trail named to describe a campground worker who became lost nearby and was not found until the next day. Another nature trail is 1-mile **River Loop Trail**, accessible from the campground loop road. It is a good access for fishing in the Jackson River. The campground is usually open from March 15 to the end of November. A major feature of the valley is the Warwick House, built in 1848. It was the plantation home of Judge James W. Warwick. An example of Greek revival architecture, it was named to the National Register of Historic Places in 1973. In 1990 the GWNF signed a thirty-year adaptive rehabilitation agreement with Ron and Pam Stidham to restore and operate the building as a bed and breakfast facility. Previously the home was used as a hunt club, a farmhouse, or a school. During the renovation a USFS archaeologist discovered prehistoric components dating to 7000 B.C. In 1992 Hollywood came to Hidden Valley to film *Sommersby*, a post–Civil War saga starring Richard Gere and Jodie Foster. Judge Warwick's restored home suddenly became a mansion, and the plantation fields became old town props for a swarming cast.

DESCRIPTION: Circuit options range from 0.6 mile to 5.7 miles from the campground. If following the 5.7-mile loop, ascend from the **Lost Woman Trail (Lower)** trailhead, left, near campsite #28 in the campground. Stay left at the **Lost Woman Trail (Upper)**, and after 0.2 mile cross FR 241. Cross over a spur ridge of Cobbler Mountain and descend to cross a streamlet. At 1.7 miles pass right of a duck pond, and continue to cross a number of toe slopes of Cobbler Mountain. At 2.8 miles reach Muddy Run. (The **Muddy Run Trail** is a wide spur up a tributary where hemlock, pine, and birch form a canopy over cascades. Deer may be seen in the wildlife clearings and hawthorn thickets. It is 1 mi. to the end of government property.) Turn left and after 0.2 mile reach a junction with **Hidden Valley Trail**, right and left, at 3 miles. (A left turn downriver on a wide and easy passage would make a return to the campground for a 5.7-mi. loop.) Continuing upstream cross a bridge over Muddy Run and at 3.2 miles cross Jackson River suspension bridge to a junction with **Jackson River Gorge Trail**, left (formerly called the **Rock Shelter Trail**). (If turning left among evergreens and on the cliff side, follow the trail through some rough and damp sections, heavy undergrowth, and wet treadways among reeds and wildflowers. Arrive at FR 241 at 5 mi. Turn left, pass the **Hidden Valley Trail [West]** on the south side of the road, cross the Jackson River bridge, and pass the southern trailhead, left, of **Hidden Valley Trail**, on the north side of the road. Continue on the road to the campground at 5.8 mi. to complete the loop.)

If turning right, upstream, after crossing the suspension bridge, follow remnants of old roads washed away by past flooding, one of which was the great flood of 1985. It washed away the earlier footbridge. Parallel the river among sycamore, birch, hemlock, ironwood, and rhododendron. At 0.8 mile (3.1 mi. from the trail's southern trailhead at the FR 241 bridge) there are good views of a river bend. At 1.9 miles (4.2 mi.) are two river fords. At 2.4 miles (4.7 mi.) follow an old road away from the river, pass a beaver dam, and reach the northern trailhead at a parking area in a hawthorne grove at 2.5 miles (4.8 mi.). From here it is 3 miles on back roads to US 220. Access from the campground by vehicle is as follows: Leave the campground south on FR 241 and after 1.5 miles turn sharply left on SR 621. Follow it 1.9 miles to US 220 and turn left, north. Drive 7 miles to a left turn on SR 623 (Poor Farm Rd.). After 1.8 miles parallel the Jackson River bank and notice a sign indicating end of state maintenance. After 0.2 mile a left fork is to a camping area with a vault rest room. Here is also the 1.2-mile **Jackson River Fishing Trail**, known for its stocked-trout fishing. Follow the right fork 1 mile to pass gated forest roads and make a left to a parking area in a grove of hawthorne, the northern trailhead of the **Hidden Valley Trail**.

Another recommended trail for fishing is the 1-mile **Hidden Valley Trail (West)**. Its trailhead is west of the campground and Jackson River bridge on FR 241 to the left. Ahead on FR 241 is Warwick House. (This location is between the southern trailhead of **Jackson River Gorge Trail** and the bridge.) Trail users can park at the parking space on the east side of the bridge at **Hidden Valley Trail**. Originally the **Bogan Run Trail**'s eastern trailhead was here at the parking space for the **Hidden Valley Trail**. It followed FR 241 north across the Jackson River bridge, past the **Jackson River Gorge Trail** (former **Rock Shelter Trail**), past the Warwick House, spring, and cemetery, crossed Limekiln Run, and at 1.5 miles left FR 241, the current trailhead. The trail ascends the eastern slope of Back Creek Mountain in a hardwood forest. At 1.5 miles it begins switchbacks that bring the route to the Back Creek Mountain ridge top (3,400 ft.) at 2.5 miles, and a 1,500-foot change in elevation from the trailhead. Cross FR 121 (Back Creek Mountain Rd.) and begin a descent. Follow an old logging road where at 3.4 miles the road makes a scenic switchback on the nipple of a ridge. More switchbacks follow into Bogan Run hollow. Next is a southwestern turn across a slope to descend steeply at 5.3 miles. The exit at 5.5

miles was recently chosen to avoid private property. Here is a parking space on the east side of SR 600, 3.3 miles north from VA 39 at Mountain Grove community. Backtrack or arrange a support vehicle.

USGS MAP: Warm Springs; USFS TRAIL NOS.: 612, 613, 612A, 611, 481B, 481, 481D, 610, 603, 614

## BOLAR MOUNTAIN AREA
*Bath County*

189–96  **Fee Booth Spur Trail** (0.6 mi.), **Sugar Hollow Trail** (1.7 mi.), **Campground Spur Trail** (0.2 mi.), **Bolar Loop Trail** (2.1 mi.), **Island Overlook Spur Trail** (0.2 mi.), **Picnic Area Spur Trail** (0.1 mi.), **Roadside Trail** (1.5 mi.), **Greenwood Point Trail** (3.3 mi.)

LENGTH AND DIFFICULTY: 14.7 miles (23.6 km) combined, round-trip; easy to moderate

FEATURES: scenic views, lake, wildlife, fishing

TRAILHEADS: Access from Warm Springs on VA 39 west is 2.7 miles to SR 687, left. Drive 2.6 miles to SR 603. Turn right and follow SR 603 for 6.6 miles to Bolar Mountain Recreation Area entrance. From Hot Springs, drive west on SR 611 for 2.7 miles to a right turn on SR 687. After 2.8 miles turn left on SR 603 and go 6.6 miles. From the Gathright Dam of Lake Moomaw, drive north as follows: on SR 605, 3.8 miles; on SR 687, 6.4 miles; turn left on SR 603 and continue 6.6 miles. If coming from West Virginia on VA 39, turn right on SR 600 and go 7 miles.

INTRODUCTION: Bolar Mountain Recreation Area is the largest fee campground in the district. There are ninety nonreserved campsites and trailer sites with twenty-seven having electric and water hookups in two of the three campgrounds. All have flush toilets. Facilities and services include trailer dump sites, picnic areas, rest rooms, drinking water, and areas for fishing, swimming, and boating with ramp and marina. At Bolar Flats is a wheelchair-accessible fishing pier. There are also group camps and picnic shelters for rent. Usually the open season is from Memorial Day to Labor Day or later into October or November for some facilities, such as boating and hiking. All the trails except the **Greenwood Point Trail** are in a compact unit near the facilities. Backtracking is necessary for the **Greenwood Point Trail**.

DESCRIPTION: For short hikes, park at the swimming area, cross the road to the trail sign, and choose a starting trail. All trails connect at different levels of the mountainside in a forest of oaks, maples, and Virginia and white pines. The 1.7-mile **Sugar Hollow Trail** goes over the mountain ridge to follow a small stream, and the 2.1-mile **Bolar Loop Trail** is a central connector for all the mountainside trails. There are scenic views of the lake from some of the trails, particularly the **Island Overlook Spur Trail**. The 1.5-mile **Roadside Trail** parallels FR 1736 to connect with **Greenwood Point Trail** at the cul-de-sac of campground #3. Between campgrounds #2 and #3 is a short and scenic interpretive trail loop constructed by Eagle Scouts. If hiking the **Greenwood Point Trail** cross the stream and ascend on switchbacks to a dry spur ridge in a thick forest. At 0.8 mile descend from a scenic view of the lake to a cove. At 1.7 miles reach a knoll, descend to a hollow, and ascend to a ridge. From this ridge the trail descends to Greenwood Point Campground at 3.3 miles. There is a vault toilet but no drinking water. Lake reflections at sunrise or sunset and the sounds of waterfowl add to the excitement of camping here. Backtrack, or arrange to be picked up by boat.

USGS MAP: Falling Spring; USFS TRAIL NOS.: 723, 721, 727, 722, 726, 725, 724, 720

## LAUREL FORK AREA
*Highland County*

Buck Run Trail (3.3 mi.), Locust Spring Run Trail (3.1 mi.), Laurel Fork Trail    197–210
(6.5 mi.), **Cold Springs Run Trail** (1.3 mi.), **Middle Mountain Trail** (1.6 mi.), **Christian Run Trail** (1.3 mi.), **Buck Run Spur Trail** (0.7 mi.), **Slabcamp Run Trail** (3 mi.), **Locust Spring Run Spur Trail** (1.5 mi.), **Bearwallow Run Trail** (2.7 mi.), **Lost Run Trail** (2.8 mi.), **Lost Run Spur Trail** (0.8 mi.), **Lost Run Spur Trail (North)** (0.4 mi.), **Straight Fork Trail** (1.2 mi.)

LENGTH AND DIFFICULTY: 30.2 miles (48.3 km) combined, multiple circuits; easy to moderate

FEATURES: historic site, rare flora and fauna, high plateau, seclusion

TRAILHEADS: From Bartow, West Virginia, drive northeast on WV 28 for 8.9 miles to FR 60/142 and turn right. From Monterey, Virginia, drive west on US 250 to junction with WV 28, turn north on WV 28, and after 6.7 miles turn right on FR 60/142. From US 33 at junction of WV 28, turn south on WV 28 and drive 16 miles to FR 60/142 and turn left. Another access is reached from the junction of US 220 in Virginia and Forks of Water, SR 642. Drive 10.3 miles on SR 642 (passing through Blue Grass community at 4.3 mi.) to FR 457 (Middle Mountain Rd.), right. Drive 0.8 mile to 1.2-mile **Straight Fork Trail**, right, and gated road left to connect with **Christian Run Trail**. Another 1.5 miles on SR 642 descends to a curve and the southern trailhead of **Laurel Fork Trail**, right. (If following SR 642 farther up the mountain, it will connect right with FR 106, the road that winds north to connect with western trailheads, Locust Springs Picnic Area, and WV 28.)

INTRODUCTION: Laurel Fork, in the headwaters of the Potomac River, is an isolated high area, elevation 2,600 to 4,100 feet. The steep slopes in the area are circumvented by a network of easy, graded, and abandoned railroad beds, logging roads, and other trails. It is an ideal area for day hikes and overnight backpacking for nature study. The **Laurel Fork Trail** extends southwest to northeast somewhat centrally through the entire area, and six trails branch from it.

To fully experience this beautiful forest where regenerative power is demonstrated, multiple circuit hikes are recommended. Because of the high elevation there are red spruces and northern hardwoods. Orchids and ferns are trailside, and more than thirty species of rare flora and fauna thrive here. Among the animals are the snowshoe hare, the fisher, and the northern flying squirrel.

DESCRIPTION: From the parking area of the Locust Springs Picnic Area, begin on the **Buck Run Trail**, east (or the **Locust Spring Run Trail**, southeast for 3.1 mi.), to the central trail, the **Laurel Fork Trail**. (The **Buck Run Spur Trail** goes off to the right from the **Buck Run Trail** for 0.6 mi. to connect with the **Locust Spring Run Trail**.) Pass a beaver pond and meadows, and stay on the southern side of the tributary along Buck Run, descending along the stream stocked with brook trout. Wood sorrel provides sections of ground cover. Reach the **Laurel Fork Trail** at 3.3 miles; continue several miles on it, or take either of two options.

One option at this point is to turn left, cross a stream, and go 0.6 mile to the **Cold Springs Run Trail** on the right; follow it south for 1.3 miles, where it becomes the **Middle Mountain Trail**. At 2.9 miles is the **Christian Run Trail**, right. (Ahead on Middle Mountain Rd. it is 1.7 mi. to a gate and left to the western trailhead of **Straight Fork Trail**. It descends on switchbacks for 1.2 mi. to Straight Fork, where an access road, right, leads to SR 642.) Follow it for a 1.5-mile hike looping back to the **Laurel Fork Trail** and a total of 8.3 miles. A right turn down the **Laurel Fork Trail** for 0.7 mile will connect with the **Buck Run Trail** or the **Locust Spring Run Trail** on the left. A return on either trail to the parking area would total 12.3 miles for the circuit.

Another option from the **Laurel Fork Trail** begins at the junction of the **Buck Run Trail**. Turn right, going upstream by Laurel Fork. At 3.6 miles (from the beginning at the parking area) reach the junction with the **Slabcamp Run Trail** on the right. This trail leads up the tributary for 3 miles to a junction with the **Locust Spring Run Spur Trail**, then continues 1.5 miles to the **Locust Spring Run Trail** (on which is a stand of red spruce and red pine) on the left for 1.5 miles and a return to parking area for a total circuit of 9.6 miles.

If continuing upstream on the **Laurel Fork Trail**, pass the **Christian Run Trail** on the left at 4 miles. Birch, oak, cherry, maple, beech, hemlock, and red spruce are on the trail. Wildflowers, ferns, and mosses are abundant. Animals in the area are bear, deer, turkey, grouse, raccoon, mink, and beaver. At 6.5 miles reach the **Bearwallow Run Trail** on the right. (Continuing up the stream for 1.4 mi. leads to SR 642 and limited parking space.) Bear right on scenic **Bearwallow Run Trail**, viewing beaver ponds and meadows, and after 2.7 miles on this trail reach FR 106 at 9.2 miles. Take a right on FR 106 to a junction with the **Locust Spring Run Spur Trail** at 11.2 miles. Go right on the **Locust Spring Run Spur Trail** for 1.5 miles to a junction with the **Locust Spring Run Trail**, bear left, and return to the parking and picnic area for a circuit total of 14.2 miles.

The trio of Lost Run trails provides a refreshing ridge top hike to keep your feet dry, in contrast to the numerous wet sections of trails on or near **Laurel Fork Trail**. As a logging road the treadway is smoother than the ripples on old railroad beds in the hollows. Access to the trailhead from wv 28 (Locust Springs Picnic Area) is on FR 106 for 3.1 miles. Parking is on the left, east, roadside in a curve. (Another access is reached by turning off wv 28 on FR 57 [0.2 mi. south of Island Campground entrance] and ascending 3.2 mi. to FR 106. Turn left and after 0.9 mi. the trailhead is right.) The trailhead is unsigned and unblazed. After 100 yards on the road, pass a gate, enter a rhododendron grove, and ascend four switchbacks among Eastern hemlock, red spruce, and banks of ground pine. On the main ridge in open hardwoods and at 0.7 mile is a footpath, right. (The **Lost Run Spur Trail** turns west, but after 0.3 mi. it begins to curve left and descends through evergreens to the upper hollow of Lost Run. At 0.8 mi. it dead-ends. Backtrack.) Continuing on the main ridgeline begin a descent at 0.9 mile. Gradually curve right and left until a low knoll, after which turn left to another small knoll at 2.1 miles. (To the left the 0.4-mi. **Lost Run Spur [North]** descends on a side ridge to dead-end. Backtrack.) The **Lost Run Trail** turns sharply right and for the next 0.7 mile descends to the main ridge center to dead-end. Backtrack.

USGS MAPS: Thornwood, Snowy Mountain, Hightown; USFS TRAIL NOS.: 598, 633, 450, 634A, 634, 599, 598A, 600, 623A, 601, 632, 632A, 632B, 604

## James River Ranger District

The 164,260-acre James River Ranger District is bordered by West Virginia and partly by the Monongahela National Forest on the west, the New Castle Ranger District in the JNF on the south, the Glenwood Ranger District in the JNF on the east, and the Warm Springs Range District of the GWNF on the north, where Douthat State Park is at the district border. The longest contiguous forest properties are North Mountain in the northeast, which adjoins the 9,200-acre Rich Hole Wilderness; Fore Mountain in the center; and Potts Mountain in the south, where 20 acres of the 5,700-acre Barbours Creek Wilderness and 95 acres of the 3,665-acre Shawvers Run Wilderness are at the district line with the New Castle Ranger District. The James River begins here, from the confluence of Jackson River and Cowpasture River. Trout streams in the district are Jackson River, Smith Creek, and Jerry's Run. In the northwestern corner is a section of Lake Moomaw, a popular recreation area. Forest vascular plants include southern hardwoods, and conifers such as hemlock and white pine in the lower elevations and red spruce on the high peaks and ridges.

The district has a 19.6-mile Highlands Scenic Tour under the guidelines of the 211–14 USFS Byways Program. The circuit is composed of two segments: 11.3 miles of FR

*Cock's Comb Trail on North Mountain, James River Ranger District*

447, named Top Drive, and sr 700 (Collierstown Rd.) on the western side of North Mountain; and 8.3 miles of sr 850 (formerly us 60, named North Mountain Rd.). The loop crosses i-64 at interchanges 35 (sr 269-850) and 43 (sr 780). Trail connections are on the first 6.8 miles of usfs 447 (Top Dr.). Access is exit 43 off i-64, south. After 0.1 mile on usfs 447 is stop #1, right, at a Highlands Scenic Tour information board, where you can obtain a brochure/map. At 2.5 miles, stop #3, is **Rhododendron Trail**, a short, 90-yard path to see 100-year-old rhododendrons and views of Rich Hole Wilderness. At 3 miles, stop #4, is **Knoll Wayside Trail**, a 0.3-mile loop for a walk in the forest. At 4.3 miles, stop #5 is **Cock's Comb Trail and Overlook**, a steep 0.4-mile round-trip trail for wide views of Rich Hole Wilderness. At 5.9 miles is stop #6 at **North Mountain Overlook Trail**. Here is a large parking area with a 0.2-mile easy trail suitable for wheelchair users. The scenery is exceptional with eastern views of Shenandoah Valley and Big House and Little House mountains. At 6.8 miles is stop #7. Here is the end of FR 447 and an intersection with SR 700 (Collierstown Rd.), right and left. (The 8.6-mile **North Mountain Trail** from Longdale ends here. See description ahead.) The Highlands Scenic Tour descends west on steep, narrow, and crooked SR 700 to continue its loop.

Through the center of the district (east to west) is I-64, with ten access points to 215–17 other main arteries for the backcountry. Many of the state roads and forest roads remain unchanged from past years and retain their tranquil character. On these routes visitors drive to the recreation areas, the largest of which is Morris Hill Recreation Area. It has campground and picnic facilities near Gathright Dam at Lake Moomaw. One access is exit 10 off I-64 to Callaghan, and then proceeding north on SR 600 to SR 666 and SR 605 following the signs. The Morris Hill campground is open from May 1 through October, and it is located high on a ridge in a hardwood forest, where it receives a cool breeze from the lake. It has trailer and tent sites, waste disposal units, rest rooms, and warm showers. Access to 3.1-mile white-blazed **Fortney Loop Trail** is between campsites #32 and #33. The trail has a spur trail off the south side for switchbacks to Fortney Boat Ramp, and on the north side of the loop is 0.3-mile **Cove Trail** for scenic views of the lake and across to Coles Point. There is also 1.0-mile **Morris Hill Bike Route** on the west side of the campground, which can be assessed opposite campsite #21. The camping fee includes use of the beach at Coles Point and boat ramp charge at Fortney Boat Ramp.

Nearby is Coles Point Picnic Area on the northern side of the dam. Continue 218–20 north from the campground, and pass or stop for a visit to the Corps of Engineers visitor center and parking area. It serves as an educational source for the history of the area, and for the dam's functions. Drive across the dam and keep left to the Coles Point Picnic Area. Here are group picnic shelters, a swimming beach, and a bathhouse. There is also 1.8-mile **Coles Trail**, a nature trail loop near the side of the lake. From Coles Point parking area is access to **Kelly Bridge Trail**. It is 0.2 mile round-trip to a pier, and is constructed with cement to benefit users with wheelchairs. Construction was by USFS personnel and the Covington Kiwanis Club. Also from the parking area is 0.1-mile **Beach Trail**. It is mainly a curve through hardwoods with periwinkle and grassy places with borders of redbud. On your way back to the campground and after crossing the dam, count off 0.6 mile to an unnamed trail on the left. Park here and walk 0.1 mile through laurel and rhododendron to an outstanding view of the base of the dam.

Another recreation area is nearby at the southernmost end of the lake and accessed north from the corner of SR 600 and SR 666. It is Fortney Branch with a large parking area, boat ramp, fishing, rest rooms, and drinking water. The district's other recreational facility is Longdale. Access is exit 35 off I-64 at Longdale Furnace west 2.2 miles on US 60. Services are picnic areas, rest rooms, drinking water, fishing, and swimming with cold showers. It is open from May 15 to September 15. Trails here (see descriptions ahead) are open all seasons.

221    The **Allegheny Trail** is the district's longest (15.5 mi.) trail. **Black Run Trail** is a new unsigned and unblazed, but easy loop added to the district's inventory. Access is from I-64, exit 43 north, then left on SR 850 (US 60) for 0.8 mile to SR 780 (Brattons Run Rd.) for a turn right. Follow it through the intersection known as California and at 3 miles make a sharp left. After crossing Brattons Run stay right to find a parking space before gate. The trail crosses Black Run, follows a USFS road for 0.7 mile, turns left on another USFS road, passes wildlife clearings, and in a hollow at 2.4 miles leaves the road left to cross tank traps. From here the trail is on an old road that parallels Black Run. The route is a sensitive plant life environment because of damp and wet areas. Complete the loop at 4 miles. It comes into the district south of Smith Knob on the Allegheny Mountain and descends to Jerry's Run at exit 1 on I-64. (Its proposed southern route would include part of the **McAllister Fields Trail** [2.5 mi.], a hunters' trail on Brushy Mountain.) (See description ahead.)

ADDRESS AND INFORMATION: James River Ranger District, 810-A Madison Ave., Covington, VA 24426; phone: 540-962-2214; access is exit 24 from I-64 to Madison Ave., west of the Holiday Inn. Available are district map with trails, and brochures or flyers on recreation areas.

## LONGDALE AREA
*Alleghany, Botetourt, and Rockbridge Counties*

222    **North Mountain Trail (Central)**
LENGTH AND DIFFICULTY: 8.6 miles (13.8 km); strenuous
CONNECTING TRAIL: **YACCer's Run Trail** (3 mi.)
TRAILHEADS: The western trailhead is accessible from Longdale Recreation Area. From the junction of I-81 and I-64 at Lexington, go west on I-64 for 21 miles to exit 35, and drive west on SR 850 for 2.2 miles to Longdale Recreation Area on the left. Trailhead is at the picnic parking area, to the left. To reach the northern trailhead, turn off I-64, exit 43 at the Goshen sign, on SR 780 and follow it south to FR 477 (Top Dr., Highlands Scenic Tour) for 7 miles to the junction with SR 770. Trailhead is a few yards left on SR 770.
DESCRIPTION: Elevation change is 2,055 feet. For the first 0.3 mile the **North Mountain Trail (Central)** and the **YACCer's Run Trail** are together, after which the **North Mountain Trail (Central)** goes straight and crosses FR 271 (Tri-County Rd.) at 0.4 mile. (To the right is a parking area for hunters and hikers.) Follow the orange-blazed trail over tank traps and ascend left of Downy

Branch. At 2.6 miles is a primitive campsite and access to FR 333 (Simmon's Rd.), left, which is not maintained. The forest has both northern and southern hardwoods, white pine, and rhododendron. The ascent becomes steeper for the next 1.6 miles to the top of North Mountain. Turn left (northeast) on the crest and shift back and forth on the boundary of the JNF and the GWNF. Expansive views are from rock outcroppings at 6 miles, 7.5 miles, and 7.7 miles. Evergreens are dense in some sections of the trail, and the updraft from Longdale Valley is usually strong. At 8 miles skirt right of a knob (3,244 ft.), and exit at SR 770 (Collierstown Rd.) and parking area at 8.6 miles. To the left is a junction with FR 447 (Top Dr.). (SR 770 descends east on a narrow, crooked road to Colliers-town, and west 3.8 mi. to Longdale on an equally challenging road.) (Ahead on FR 447 [Top Dr.] it is 6.8 mi. to I-64, exit 43.)

USGS MAP: Longdale; USFS TRAIL NOS.: 658, 467, 465

YACCer's Run Trail (3 mi.), Blue Suck Trail (2 mi.), Anthony Knobs Trail (2.9 mi.) 223–25

LENGTH AND DIFFICULTY: 7.9 miles (12.6 km) combined, round-trip; moderate
CONNECTING TRAIL: **North Mountain Trail (Central)** (8.6 mi.)
FEATURES: streams, wildlife, scenic views
TRAILHEAD: Longdale Recreation Area parking lot (see directions for **North Mountain Trail [Central]**, above).
DESCRIPTION: These trails connect and form two loops, one of 3 miles on the **YACCer's Run Trail**; the other two trails form another 4.9-mile loop. Turkey, deer, and grouse are often seen by quiet hikers on these loops. Begin on the **North Mountain Trail (Central)** up the steps from the parking lot, and after 0.3 mile leave the **North Mountain Trail (Central)** by turning right on the gray-blazed **YACCer's Run Trail**. Cross Downy Branch, and ascend on a north-ern slope of the ridge to a clearing with silverberry. Make a sharp right at 0.2 mile, cross a small stream at 0.4 mile, and reach a knoll at 1 mile. Descend, and cross a ravine and Blue Suck Branch to a junction with an old road, the **Blue Suck Trail**, left and right, at 1.5 miles. (The road right leads back to the picnic area, but the **Blue Suck Trail** follows upstream for 1.7 mi. to FR 271 and a junction with the **Anthony Knobs Trail**.) At 1.8 miles the **YACCer's Run Trail** goes right and the **Anthony Knobs Trail** goes left. (If hiking back to the parking area at this point, follow right on a ridge of oaks and pines to scenic views at 2 mi. and 2.3 mi. At 2.7 mi. begin a descent, and at 3 mi. reach paved FR 172, 0.1 mi. from the parking lot, on the right.) If hiking the **Anthony Knobs Trail**, ascend and follow the ridge up and down knolls, but stay left of old woods roads. At 1.8 miles turn left, descend, cross Sinking Creek, and reach FR 271 and junction with the **Blue Suck Trail** at 2.9 miles. Return to other trails by ascend-ing slightly and descending to a tributary of Blue Suck Branch.

USGS MAP: Longdale Furnace; USFS TRAIL NOS.: 467, 704, 666, 460

226–27   **Rich Hole Trail** (5.9 mi.), **White Rock Tower Trail** (6 mi.)

LENGTH AND DIFFICULTY: 11.9 miles (19 km) combined; strenuous

FEATURES: wilderness, scenic views, stream, wildlife, wildflowers

TRAILHEADS: To reach the northern trailhead for the **Rich Hole Trail**, get off I-64
(west of Lexington) at exit 43 onto SR 850 and go west 2.8 miles to parking area
on the right. (From I-64, exit 35 in Longdale, take SR 850 east for 5 mi. to parking
area on the left.) For the southern trailhead of the **Rich Hole Trail** and the
northern trailhead of the **White Rock Tower Trail**, take exit 35 off I-64 and
drive northeast on SR 850 for 1.3 miles. Turn left on narrow FR 108 and drive 1.3
miles to parking area. To reach the southern trailhead of the **White Rock
Tower Trail**, drive southwest on SR 770, across the bridge from SR 850 at the
northern side of I-64, exit 35. After 0.6 mile SR 770 becomes FR 333; follow it for
3.1 miles to parking area where trail is on the northern side.

INTRODUCTION: These contrasting trails can be hiked separately or as a single unit.
In either choice a two-car arrangement is needed. There is an elevation change
of 2,080 feet on the **Rich Hole Trail** and about 2,870 feet on the **White Rock
Tower Trail**. The wilderness is covered with about 90 percent second growth
mixed hardwoods and pitch and table mountain pines. There are a few old-
growth stands of northern red oak, basswood, and sugar maple. Hikers will notice damage to the dogwoods from anthracnose and to the hemlock by woolly
adelgid. Rocky outcroppings are on both Brushy and Mill Mountains. Deer and
grouse are frequently seen.

DESCRIPTION: Beginning at the northern trailhead of the **Rich Hole Trail** there is
a good view to the south after 0.5 mile on Brushy Mountain. At 0.8 mile the
grade is steep and rocky until a saddle is reached on Mill Mountain near a large
cliff at 1.2 miles. Dense laurel, rhododendron, azalea, blueberry, and fetterbush
are common on the ridgeline. (To the north are the headwaters of Alum Creek,
the site of most of the old-growth hardwoods in the wilderness.) Turn left at the
saddle and begin a long, graded descent into North Branch Hollow. At 1.8 miles
North Branch begins among fern beds in rich, moist soil. At 2.3 miles make the
first of thirteen crossings of North Branch. The trail widens to an old road at 4.4
miles, and at 5.9 miles arrives at the junction with the **White Rock Tower Trail**.
Here, at the edge of the wilderness, is a parking area on FR 108.

To continue the hike on unmarked and unblazed **White Rock Tower Trail**,
turn right up rocky and curvy FR 108 to a gate. Beyond the steep climb the road
ends at 2.3 miles at White Rock on Mill Mountain (3,055 ft.). Along the old road
is evidence of the popularity of deer hunting. White Rock is the site of former
White Rock fire tower. A few red spruce and fragrant mountain mint are here.
Views west are of Cowpasture Valley and beyond to Beards Mountain. From
here follow the trail on the western slope of the ridge to a panoramic view at 2.8
miles. Pass other rock outcroppings among chestnut oak and laurel. (An occasional orange blaze may be seen.) At 4.8 miles curve left around the ridge and

descend on switchbacks to an old road and timber cut at 5.3 miles. Leave the road and ridge and reach the cul-de-sac of FR 333 at 5.6 miles (1,761 ft.).

USGS MAP: Longdale Furnace; USFS TRAIL NOS.: 464, 466


## POTTS VALLEY AREA
*Alleghany County*

**Children's Forest Trail** (0.3 mi.), **Children's Forest Long Loop Trail** (2.6 mi.),    228–30
**Children's Forest Horse Trail** (3.2 mi.)

LENGTH AND DIFFICULTY: 6.1 miles (9.7 km) round-trip; easy to moderate
FEATURES: forest restoration, historic site, wildflowers
TRAILHEAD: From Covington go south on VA 18 for 11.7 miles to SR 613 on the left. Go 3 miles on SR 613 to FR 351 on the right. After 0.8 mile is the parking area on the right.
DESCRIPTION: The **Children's Forest Trail** is a unique trail. It is a loop nature trail in a young forest with wildflowers. It was created to honor more than 1,000 children from Virginia, West Virginia, Maryland, and Pennsylvania who re-forested 177 acres with shortleaf pine after a Potts Mountain forest fire in 1971. The trail, with a stone monument and the names of the children in a time capsule to be opened in 2072, was dedicated in April 1972. From the parking area are excellent views of Potts Valley and Peters Mountain range. (This area is close to and northeast of Barbours Creek and Shawvers Run wildernesses in the New Castle Ranger District of the JNF. See Chapter 2.)

To hike the **Children's Forest Long Loop Trail**, leave monument counter-clockwise and after 0.1 mile turn right. After 0.6 mile merge into a hardwood forest from a pine forest. Ascend to an old road with trailing arbutus and turn left at 0.8 mile. (The old road is part of the **Children's Forest Horse Trail**.) At 1.5 miles leave the road left, pass a stream at 1.9 miles, and after crossing ridges return to the west side of the **Children's Forest Trail**. (The 3.2-mi. **Children's Forest Horse Trail** makes a loop on roads around the other two trails, and uses the large parking area.)

USGS MAP: Gordon Mines; USFS TRAIL NOS.: 626, 627, 628


## POND FLAT AREA
*Alleghany County*

**Pond Flat Trail** (4.3 mi.), **Laurel Branch Trail** (2.1 mi.)    231–32

LENGTH AND DIFFICULTY: 6.3 miles (10.08 km) round-trip; easy to moderate
FEATURES: streams, scenic ridge, wildlife, historic sites
TRAILHEADS: From Covington at US 220/60/18, drive south on VA 16 for 7.2 miles to a parking place, right, for the east trailhead of **Pond Flat Trail**. Drive farther south 2 miles to turn right on SR 614 and follow it 2.8 miles to an intersection

right and left with SR 600. (Ahead, left on SR 600, it is 0.5 mi. to a narrow road entrance and parking space for **Morning Knob Trail**. The trail is unblazed, but ascends steeply on a timber road with two major switchbacks to a former forest fire lookout tower at 1.6 mi. All scenic views have vanished with new forest growth. Remains are a few artifacts and a lonely outhouse.) On SR 600, right, ascend 0.5 mile to a curve and gate on the ridge, right, for the west trailhead of **Pond Flat Trail**. (Continuing ahead on SR 600 it is 0.7 mi. to the west trailhead of FR 456, **Laurel Branch Trail**.)

DESCRIPTION: (These trails are not blazed.) If beginning at the west trailhead walk past the gated road east on the ridge where the road has hummocks of shale. On the ridge, curve around a hollow, then curve left. Beginning at 0.5 mile, pass through or near six wildlife fields, meadows, and plateaus for 1 mile. Along the way at 0.8 mile and 1 mile are switchbacks with a beautiful 180-degree view. At 1.6 miles stay right at a fork and at 1.7 miles stay left of a fork. Stay right at a junction with FR 456 (Laurel Branch Rd.), left at 2 miles. (The **Laurel Branch Trail** is a road that descends 0.7 mi. north to cross Laurel Branch. After the crossing the road ascends on a ridge between Laurel Branch south and Rams Hollow Creek north. There are eleven curves for 1.4 mi. to reach a gate at SR 600. If making a loop, a left turn, south, on SR 600 is 0.7 mi. to west trailhead of **Pond Flat Trail**, a total distance of 4.8 mi.)

Continuing east on **Pond Flat Trail** follow the south side of the ridge on a good roadway and dip to a gap at 2.4 miles. Ascend and descend to reach a shift from the south side to the north side of the ridge at 3.3 miles. At 3.5 miles cross a stream, hummocks, and junction with an old road left. Stay right and pass lake and wildlife field on the right. Pass through a grove of white pine. Descend steeply to a switchback at 4.2 miles and reach a damp area with ferns, coltsfoot, ragwort, and other wildflowers. Cross a small stream on a grassy road and arrive at the parking area at 4.3 miles.

USGS MAP: Jordan Mines; USFS TRAIL NOS.: 355, 356

## FORE MOUNTAIN AREA
*Alleghany County*

### 234 Fore Mountain Trail
LENGTH AND DIFFICULTY: 13.3 miles (21.3 km); strenuous
CONNECTING TRAILS: **Dry Run Trail** (7.8 mi.), **Middle Mountain Trail** (8.8 mi.)
FEATURES: scenic views, wildlife, wildflowers, trout stream
TRAILHEADS: For the southwestern trailhead, turn off I-64, exit 16, north at inter-
section and traffic lights of US 60/220 (Madison St.) and SR 1104 (Valley Ridge
Rd.). (District office is left on Madison St., 0.1 mi. to sign on right.) Descend
right on Valley Ridge Road for 0.2 mile to sign for Dolly Ann Work Center. Turn
left between a motel and a restaurant and go 0.3 mile to parking area on the

left. The northeastern trailhead is actually in Douthat State Park, bordering the Warm Springs Ranger District, but parking is on sr 606, 4.3 miles north from the junction of va 188 and us 60/220 in downtown Clifton Forge. (No I-64 exit here; take exit 27 from east or exit 24 from west to va 188 in Clifton Forge.) To reach sr 606 from Covington, turn off us 60/220 (0.7 mi. west of district office) on sr 625 (Dolly Ann Dr.), which becomes fr 125, and follow fr 125 for 8.4 miles to sr 606. Turn right and go 1.1 miles to trail crossing.

INTRODUCTION: This trail is the district's longest and most publicized. It is multiple use, with the Bordernier Riding Club maintaining parts of the route. Because the northern trailhead is inaccessible to vehicular traffic, it is necessary to backtrack the 3.1 miles from the top of Middle Mountain to sr 606 at Smith Creek, or hike out in Douthat State Park. The trail is vulnerable to ATVs and 4WDs for at least 5 miles on Fore Mountain. **Dry Run Trail** is a road, partially  235
gated, heavily used by 4WDs, and eroded in places.

DESCRIPTION: From the parking area at Dolly Ann Work Center, begin at the trail sign on a foot trail. One major switchback is at 1 mile in a forest of oak, hickory, and maple. At 1.3 miles is a view of Covington. Reach the top of the mountain at 2 miles to follow a grassy timber road bordered with white snakeroot and azaleas. At 4 miles is a view to the east of Low Moor Valley and Rich Patch Mountains. In a grazing field at 6 miles is a junction on the left with the **Dry Run Trail**.

(The **Dry Run Trail** descends on fr 448 for 0.5 mi. to cross fr 125. Along the way are chinquapin, mountain laurel, and Deptford pink. It descends from fr 125 to a wide saddle with a field of wildflowers and space to park. A gated timber road is on the right, but the **Dry Run Trail** ascends on an open and eroded road. At 2.6 mi. it reaches a view of Bald Knob to the right, and another view at 3.4 mi. of Big Knob [4,072 ft.]. After crossing Peters Ridge at 5 mi., the trail descends to Dry Run at 5.9 mi., where it parallels the stream to gated fr 339 at 7.8 mi. Space for parking is small. Access here is 0.3 mi. on Cypress Street from us 220 [N. Alleghany Ave.] in Covington, and 2.7 mi. west of district office.)

To continue on the **Fore Mountain Trail** (less used than the first 6 mi.), follow the mountain ridgeline. At 7.1 miles are views east to Clifton Forge. There are rock outcrops at 9 miles (2,823 ft.), after which the trail descends steeply to two major switchbacks. At 9.5 miles is a junction with fr 337 (it is an ungated dead-end road on the right, but 0.7 mi. to the left is sr 606). The trail descends 0.7 mile into a hardwood forest with beds of wintergreen to cross sr 606 (McGraw Gap Rd.) at 10.2 miles. Rock-hop or wade Smith Creek, a stocked trout stream, at 10.3 miles to begin an ascent of Pine Spur Ridge. After 1 mile there are views of Clifton Forge and Smith Creek Valley. Reach the ridge top at 13.3 miles, the end of the trail in the district but the beginning of the **Middle Mountain Trail** in Warm Springs Ranger District (in this chapter) and a trail network in Douthat State Park. Backtrack for equestrians; for hikers, an extended hike can be another 8.8 miles (see Chapter 11).

USGS MAPS: Clifton Forge, Covington, Healing Springs; USFS TRAIL NOS.: 473, 471

## JERRY'S RUN AREA
*Alleghany County*

236–37 **Jerry's Run Trail** (2.4 mi.), **Batlick Mountain Trail** (2.3 mi.)

LENGTH AND DIFFICULTY: 9.4 miles (15 km) round-trip; easy to moderate

FEATURES: trout stream, cascades, wildlife, seclusion

TRAILHEAD: Access is 12 miles west of Covington and 2 miles east of the state line on I-64, exit 2; travel south on FR 198 for 0.6 mile, where the road becomes FR 69. The parking area is 0.4 mile ahead on the left.

DESCRIPTION: These two trails dead-end. **Jerry's Run Trail** has a high traffic volume, but the volume on the **Batlick Mountain Trail** is exceptionally low. Cross the road at the parking area to a 4WD road for **Jerry's Run Trail** and descend into a forest of white pine and hemlock to rock-hop Jerry's Run, a stocked trout stream, at 0.4 mile. At 0.5 mile on the right, at a white oak, is the **Batlick Mountain Trail** trailhead.

The **Batlick Mountain Trail** ascends at the base of a ridge and makes eleven switchbacks—all skillfully designed—in an open forest to the top of the mountain at 0.9 mile. After a turn left on the ridge there is a weathered bench at 1.1 miles. The trail now curves right, follows a flat ridge, makes a curve left, and halts at 2.3 miles near a USFS boundary marker (which may not be easy to detect). Here is the Virginia/West Virginia state line. Beyond the otherwise unmarked trail is private property. This is a good place for meditation. Backtrack.

To continue on **Jerry's Run Trail**, follow the 4WD road through a grand forest of beech, maple, oak, and hemlock with rhododendron undercover. Rock-hop Jerry's Run eight times among cascades, rock piles, and pools to a dead end at 2.4 miles. Beyond is heavily posted private property. Backtrack.

USGS MAP: Jerry's Run; USFS TRAIL NOS.: 659, 641

## ALLEGHENY MOUNTAIN AREA
*Alleghany County, Virginia, and Greenbrier County, West Virginia*

238 **Allegheny Trail**

LENGTH AND DIFFICULTY: 15.5 miles (24.8 km); strenuous

FEATURES: scenic views, wildlife, isolation

TRAILHEADS: From I-64, take exit 1 (12 mi. west of Covington); at Jerry's Run sign, turn north 0.2 mile to dead-end road and parking space for southern trailhead. For northern trailhead, from I-64, exit 7 (7.5 mi. west of Covington), at SR 661, turn north 10.4 miles on SR 661 and SR 781 to Rucker Gap and enter West Virginia.

Descend 0.8 mile on CO 14 to Lake Sherwood Road, turn left, and proceed 1.3 miles to parking area on the left. (It is 2.5 mi. farther to Neola and WV 92.)

INTRODUCTION: The 300-mile **Allegheny Trail** is a foot trail from the Pennsylvania state line through West Virginia to north of Pearisburg, Virginia. Coming south, at milepost 253, it enters Virginia in this section, with 10.5 miles in the James River Ranger District. On its way it passes through pieces of private property. The other 5 miles are in the Monongahela National Forest in West Virginia. Constructed by the West Virginia Scenic Trails Association, the trail will be about 330 miles when completed. (The trail is an ongoing project and probably will cross Brushy Mountain from Jerry's Run, south of I-64, on its way to Peters Mountain. From there it will connect with its most southern section south of Paint Bank. Although the district maps show the **Allegheny Trail** south of I-64 connecting with **McAllister Fields Trail**, the district has reported that no action 239 has been taken at this writing. The delays are in a right-of-way across Chesapeake and Ohio Railroad property and passage through Westvaco property. See JNF, Chapter 2.)

DESCRIPTION: Begin at the southern trailhead and follow the yellow-blazed trail in a hardwood forest to the top of a ridge. Descend, cross a stream in Fox's Hollow at 0.9 mile, and pass left of a logging road at 1.1 miles. Ascend on a ridge spine to overlooks at 2.3 miles and 2.4 miles. Views southeast are of Brushy Mountain and Jerry's Run hollow (locally called Doe Lick), and north to Smith Knob. Follow the boundary between Virginia and West Virginia on an old woods road, but turn left onto private property and another road at 3.3 miles. Turn right at 3.7 miles. Cross a stream at 4.3 miles, and ascend on switchbacks. Leave private property at 4.6 miles. After following the ridge in and out of private property and USFS property, reach Smith Knob (3,400 ft.) at 8.1 miles. From a grassy bald there are outstanding views north to Laurel Run Valley and southeast to Panther Ridge. Descend in a rough area to junction with CO 15/3 (White's Draft Rd., which descends 5.2 mi. down the mountain in West Virginia to WV 92) at 9.7 miles. Curve around a ridge of Allegheny Mountain, leave Virginia, and descend on switchbacks to Laurel Run at 11.1 miles. For the next 4.4 miles the trail crosses Laurel Run six times, and passes by and through wildlife fields and forests of white pine, hemlock, hardwoods, and rhododendron to a parking area at CO 14 (Lake Sherwood Rd.). Along the way are excellent campsites.

USGS MAPS: Jerry's Run, Alvon, Rucker Gap; USFS TRAIL NO.: 701

## OLIVER MOUNTAIN AREA
*Alleghany and Bath Counties*

### Oliver Mountain Trail 240
LENGTH AND DIFFICULTY: 8 miles or 9.6 miles (12.8 km or 15.4 km) round-trip; moderate to strenuous

241–43    CONNECTING TRAILS: **Brushy Lick Trail** (6.1 mi.), **Medden Hollow Trail** (1.8 mi.),
**Jackson Trail** (1 mi.)

FEATURES: lake, scenic area, wildlife, seclusion

TRAILHEADS: From Covington at the junction of US 60/220, go north on US 220 for 3.7 miles to SR 687 and turn left. Go 3.3 miles to SR 641 and turn left. After 0.5 mile turn right on SR 666 and follow it 4.2 miles to its end and a junction with SR 600. At this junction it is 0.3 mile right to the northern trailhead at Lake Moomaw Fortney Branch Boat Ramp and parking area. To the left it is 0.7 mile on SR 600 to FR 192. It ascends 3.1 miles to the western trailhead.

INTRODUCTION: Topographical maps show the **Oliver Mountain Trail** to be approximately 10 miles, 3 miles of which are on private land. The trailheads would be from Lake Moomaw to Rucker Gap on SR 781 at the Virginia/West Virginia state line. In 1982 the USFS listed the trail as 7.5 miles, and in 1992 as 3.4 miles. Actually, the first 4.8 miles, from Lake Moomaw to Oliver Mountain, are on USFS property and can be easily followed. Because a backtrack of 3.2 miles is necessary to the FR 192 trailhead, the distance has been added for round-trip plans. For a period of years the USFS had permission for the entire distance through private property.

DESCRIPTION: A fee of $2 is required to park at the Lake Moomaw Fortney Branch Boat Ramp and parking area between May 1 and September 30. At the parking area's ramp edge, there is 0.3-mile **Fishing Access Trail** that hugs the mountainside to make a scenic route into a cove and exposed ridge. To begin the yellow-blazed **Oliver Mountain Trail** from the parking area, walk up the road 385 feet and climb over the right guardrail. Descend an embankment to a small stream. Ascend on a shale treadway with deer moss, turkey oak, and mountain laurel. At 0.7 mile is a wide cove and at 0.8 mile are views of the high parking area for the end of FR 192. After four other coves the trail reaches the ridge crest at 1.5 miles. Ahead it is 0.1 mile to the small parking area at the end of FR 192. To the right is the **Brushy Lick Trail**.

(The **Brushy Lick Trail** is orange-blazed; it follows a dry ridge of hardwoods and Virginia pine, north. At 0.4 mi. is a junction, right, with the **Medden Hollow Trail**. [It is unmarked and unmaintained. It descends on a spur ridge for 0.8 mi. with views of Lake Moomaw. It then drops steeply into a hollow to follow an old logging road. It skirts the northern side of the ridge but curves around it at 1.3 mi. From here it descends into Medden Hollow, a narrow cove of Lake Moomaw at 1.8 mi. Backtrack.] Continuing on the **Brushy Lick Trail**, there are steep knobs, but at 1 mi. there is a saddle where the trail divides for a loop ahead and to the left. Ahead the trail ascends its steepest knob to 1.2 mi. It descends steeply and after a drop over some lesser knobs for 1,000 vertical ft. it reaches Hughes Draft. Here are the cove waters of Lake Moomaw at 2.6 mi. Turn left and follow a 4WD road upstream. [Abandoned tents and dead trees from beaver dams offer a ghostly hollow.] Rock-hop the stream [which may be dry in summer] four times, and turn left on a grassy old road at 3.7 mi. Follow upstream of shallow Brushy Lick, crossing it twice. At 4.6 mi. stay left among a few old apple trees near a campsite. Ascend steeply up a hollow to the saddle for rejoining the trail at 5.2 mi. Turn right and ascend on knobs to **Oliver Mountain Trail** at 6.1 mi.)

On the **Oliver Mountain Trail**, cross the parking space of FR 192 (considered the western trailhead because of the trail's dead end). Ascend on a narrow ridge, and stay close to the ridge's eastern edge for the next 0.8 mile. At 3.2 miles is a junction with the **Jackson Trail** on the left. (It descends steeply on a ridge to end after 1 mi. at a large parking area for FR 192. This space is useful if the other parking space is crowded or the gate to it is locked.) The **Oliver Mountain Trail** continues 0.2 mile to a low saddle on Oliver Mountain. For the next 1.4 miles to the private property boundary are four knolls on an average of 3,100 feet in elevation. The forest is open hardwood with trees such as oak, locust, ash, and hickory. Backtrack to FR 192, or to Lake Moomaw if only one vehicle is available.

USGS MAPS: Rucker Gap, Falling Spring: USFS TRAIL NOS.: 438, 469, 502, 510, 469A

# Glenwood/Pedlar Ranger District

Of its 144,906 acres, the Pedlar Ranger District has more territory east of the BRP than any of the state's districts. As with Glenwood Ranger District in the JNF, which adjoins the Pedlar Ranger District on the south, it is separated from the more western districts by the Shenandoah Valley. (Both districts are now administratively combined.) On its eastern boundary is the state's piedmont, and the northern area extends almost to Waynesboro and Shenandoah National Park. The Maury River joins the James River on the district's southwestern corner, but the northwestern corner of the district drains into the South River, which flows into the North Fork of the Shenandoah River. Some of the state's most majestic mountain peaks are here: The Priest (4,063 ft.), Mt. Pleasant (4,071 ft.), and Cold Mountain (4,023 ft.). The district has the state's highest cascading waterfall, 1,200-vertical-foot Crabtree Falls in the South Fork of the Tye River gorge. On the western side of the district and east of Steeles Tavern is the 10,900-acre St. Mary's Wilderness, which ascends east to the BRP. Additionally, in 2000 the 5,903-acre Priest Wilderness, east and south of Crabtree Falls, and 4,608-acre Three Ridges Wilderness, north of VA 56 and south of the BRP, were designated. Northern and southern hardwoods, hemlock, and Virginia pine are the district's dominant trees. Thousands of acres, particularly of oaks, have been defoliated by the gypsy moth. Of interest to anglers are the stocked streams of the North Fork of the Tye River, Irish Creek, the South Fork of the Piney River, and Pedlar River.

Among the man-made attractions in the district is Sherando Lake Recreation Area, a compound for camping, fishing, hiking, boating, and swimming. Showers for campers are available at the lake's bathhouse and two recently reconstructed camping bathrooms. It is open from April 1 to October 30. Group camping reservations are arranged by the district office. The district's trail system has excellent options for day hikes or long backpacking circuits. Many of the forest trails connect with 56.9 miles of the **AT**, which tracks the entire length of the district, a distinction shared by three other districts of the state's eleven. The majority of the trails are color-blazed, particularly the horse trails with orange or yellow diamonds, and 23 miles of ATV trails (some with blue blazes) off VA 130 on the west side of the BRP overpass. Maintenance of the **AT** is provided by the Appalachian Trail clubs: Old Dominion, Tidewater, and Natural Bridge. Of the thirty-four trails listed in the district's TIS inventory, thirteen connect with the **AT** or the BRP. A few

244 trails are isolated. An example is 0.4-mile **Panther Falls Trail** on Pedlar River. Access is from US 60, 0.1 mile east of the BRP underpass, at FR 315 on the right. The crooked road descends 3.2 miles to a small parking area on the left. At a signboard a trail descends 0.1 mile to the upper level of Panther Falls. To reach the other access trail, which is more scenic, continue on FR 315 for 0.3 miles and turn left on FR 315A. After 0.5 mile is a large parking area. Walk down an old gated forest road for 0.2 mile and turn left in a meadow of wildflowers by Pedlar River. After 0.2 mile reach the falls, which begin in a flume, swirl into a deep pool (which has a deadly undertow), and foam in a sculptured hole before falling again into a pool. Other trails are short dead ends near mainstream traffic. An example is the **Mine**

245 **Bank Mountain Trail**, a 0.6-mile walk from the BRP, mp 23.5 (the highest point, 3,333 ft., north of the James River on the BRP).

There are a number of gated or tank trap road-trails whose mysterious appearance invites browsing. Such a road is FR 42 and its side roads, 2.6 miles north on SR 664 from Sherando Lake Recreation Area. If followed its entire length, the road goes to a western entrance of St. Mary's Wilderness, but the first 4.9 miles have the hiking options, all on the left. After 0.5 mile there is a gated road (FR 1237), the former **Turkey Pen Ridge Trail**, which follows flat terrain to the **Mills Creek Trail** for 1.3 miles by Orebank Creek. At 1.5 miles on FR 42 is FR 1234 (Mills Creek Rd.), gated for traffic to Mill Creek Reservoir. A few yards ahead is a parking area on the left, where a 360-foot, blue-blazed spur trail leads to the road. Another 1.4 miles on FR 42 is Kennedy Creek and off-road campsites. One mile

246 farther on FR 42 is the **Kennedy Ridge Trail**. It goes over a tank trap to ascend steeply on an old and rocky road for 3.1 miles, where it joins FR 162B, an access to St. Mary's Wilderness. Travel 0.2 mile farther on FR 42 for a gated road and a short walk to Coles Run Reservoir. As a finale, continue another 0.8 mile (passing the junction with FR 52 out to Stuarts Draft), and hike the dead-end 1.4-mile **Johns**

247 **Run Trail**/Road. Its mysteries are revealed in a deep, wet gorge.

ADDRESS AND INFORMATION: Glenwood/Pedlar Ranger District, P.O. Box 10, Natural Bridge Station, VA 24579; phone: 540-291-2188. Available are district map with trails, Sherando Lake brochure, wilderness map.

## ROCKY ROW AREA
*Rockbridge and Amherst Counties*

**Saddle Gap Trail** (2.5 mi.), **Little Rocky Row Run Trail** (2.7 mi.), **AT** (6.2 mi.)  248–49, 489
LENGTH AND DIFFICULTY: 8.9 miles (14.2 km) combined; strenuous
FEATURES: rock outcrops, scenic views, wildlife, wildflowers
TRAILHEADS: For the **Little Rocky Row Run Trail** drive from US 501 and VA 130
   junction (east of Glasgow) east 2.5 miles to parking area at James River Overlook at Rockbridge and Amherst county line. (Trail is 150 yd. back [west] on
   northern bank of US 501.) To reach the **Saddle Gap Trail**, leave US 501/VA 130
   (west of Snowden) on SR 812 and fork right on FR 36 to drive 2.8 miles to trail
   sign on left. For the **AT** follow the same route on FR 36, but stop 0.9 mile after
   leaving US 501/VA 130.
DESCRIPTION: **Little Rocky Row Run** and **Saddle Gap** trails are all blue-blazed
   and ascend to the **AT** within a 3.7-mile section. To avoid walking on busy
   highways, hikers should start north on the **AT** at FR 36 and after 5 miles turn
   right to descend on the **Saddle Gap Trail**. A hike downstream to the **AT** origin
   on FR 36 is a 9.4-mile circuit. An advantage of this loop is the **AT** shelter, Johns
   Hollow, 0.6 mile after leaving north on FR 36. (All other combinations need a
   two-car arrangement unless backtracking.) The most impressive feature on this
   section of the **AT** is Fullers Rocks (2,480 ft.), 0.1 mile north of its junction with
   the **Little Rocky Row Run Trail**. Here is a spectacular view of James River
   Gorge and James River Face Wilderness.
   If ascending on the **Saddle Gap Trail** from FR 36, climb over a large tank
   trap into a forest of hemlocks and hardwoods near a stream. Leave the stream
   at 0.5 mile and follow switchbacks to the junction with the **AT**. When hiking
   the **Little Rocky Row Run Trail** from US 501/VA 130, look for a hiker's sign
   150 yards west of the Rockbridge and Amherst county line. Ascend on switchbacks to the ridge crest. The trail is festooned with azalea, fern, and chinquapin. Rocks are laced with lichens and mosses. Pass under a power line at 0.6
   mile where there are magnificent views of James River Gorge. Ascend switchbacks and follow ridge to a junction with the **AT** at 2.7 miles. To the left it is 0.1
   mile to Fullers Rocks; to the right it is 1.9 miles to Johns Hollow Shelter, and
   another 0.6 mile to FR 36. From here it is 0.9 mile to US 501/VA 130 and 3.9 miles
   on the highway to the overlook and point of origin for the **Little Rocky Row
   Run Trail**.
USGS MAPS: Buena Vista, Glasgow, Snowden; USFS TRAIL NOS.: 703, 512, 1

250–52, 489    **Henry Lanum Trail** (6.2 mi.), **Mt. Pleasant Trail** (0.5 mi.), **Old Hotel Trail** (3 mi.), **AT** (2.1 mi.)

LENGTH AND DIFFICULTY: 12.3 miles (19.7 km) combined, round-trip; moderate to strenuous

FEATURES: scenic views, wildflowers, stream, balds, historic site

TRAILHEAD: From junction of US 60 and SR 634 (1 mi. west of Long Mountain Wayside; 16.9 mi. west of Amherst and 4 mi. east of BRP on US 60), drive north on SR 634 (Coffey Town Rd.) 1.7 miles. Turn right on SR 755, which becomes FR 48 after 1.4 miles, and follow it 1.3 miles to a parking area at Hog Camp Gap. There is also parking for these trails just beyond Hog Camp Gap. Take a short spur road to the right. An information board is there also. Here is the intersection with the **AT**.

INTRODUCTION: These combined trails make two loops. The **Henry Lanum Trail** and the **Mt. Pleasant Trail** make a circuit of 7.2 miles; the **Old Hotel Trail** and the **AT** section provide a loop of 5.7 miles (to include a 0.6-mi. spur to the shelter). Formerly the **Pompey and Mt. Pleasant Loop Trail**, the trail was renamed by the USFS in honor of Henry (Hank) Lanum Jr. in 1991. For many years Lanum was active in maintaining the **AT** for the Natural Bridge Appalachian Trail Club. The trail area is within the 5,900-acre Mt. Pleasant National Scenic Area. The **Old Hotel Trail** received its name from a Richerson family whose large home was the scene of social events and a hospitable respite for overnight guests. In a tract of about 700 acres the family kept slaves and raised cattle, sheep, and swine.

DESCRIPTION: From the parking area at Hog Camp Gap, FR 48 continues 0.3 mile to FR 51 and a parking area, but the Hog Camp Gap gate may be closed (particularly in the winter), and the road should be walked on the blue-blazed side. Begin on the blue-blazed **Henry Lanum Trail** and ascend on a wide treadway in a hardwood forest. Indian pipe (*Monotropa uniflora*) and starry campion (*Silene stellata*) are among the wildflowers. Reach a knoll at 1.5 miles; follow a more rocky and narrow footpath through mountain laurel and rhododendron; tiger lily and wild hydrangea are among the August flowers. At 2 miles arrive at Pompey Mountain (4,032 ft.) in a wooded area. From here the trail descends 0.7 mile to a wide saddle where flowers and filberts grow tall in moist and rich soil. To the right the **Henry Lanum Trail** continues, and to the left a 0.5-mile spur trail ascends to Mt. Pleasant. Also on the left is a spring, 125 yards from the spur. Ascend steeply to a rocky plateau (4,071 ft.) with magnificent scenery. Sweeping views are of Buffalo River drainage, Cold Mountain, Chestnut Ridge, and toward the east, Tye River Valley. In rock pockets and crevices are dense growths of mosses, sedum, blueberries, and scattered mountain ash (*Sorbus* *americana*). After returning to the **Henry Lanum Trail**, descend on a rocky road past a spring on the right at 3.3 miles, and another at 3.4 miles on the left. In a rocky area, cross a stream at 3.9 miles. Then gradually ascend in a forest of yellow birch for a return to the parking area and signboard at 5.2 miles (plus 1 mi. for the **Mt. Pleasant Trail**).

From the parking area at the **Henry Lanum Trail** cross the stile and enter blue-blazed **Old Hotel Trail**. Descend gradually in the forest. At 0.8 mile is a clearing with an eastern view of the North Fork of the Buffalo River Valley and Mt. Pleasant. There are thick patches of blueberries at 1.1 miles. At 1.5 miles is an ideal campsite in a grassy area with large white oaks. (Near, but east of here, is the site of the former Richerson home.) This area is also good for birding. Cross Little Cove Creek at 2.9 miles, ascend, and reach a junction at 3 miles with a left spur trail to the **AT**. Across the creek is Cow Camp Gap Shelter, maintained by the Natural Bridge Appalachian Trail Club. Ascend steeply for 0.6 mile to the **AT**. (To the left it is 3.8 mi. to US 60 and Long Mountain Wayside.) Turn right, ascend steeply, cross a rock wall, and reach the summit of Cold Mountain (4,022 ft.) at 4.4 miles. Here is a supreme panoramic view from a grassy and granite bald, excellent for stargazing. Reach the northern summit of Cold Mountain at 4.7 miles, beyond which the trail descends to the Hog Camp Gap parking area at 5.7 miles.

USGS MAPS: Montebello, Fork of Buffalo; USFS TRAIL NOS.: 702, 701, 515, 1

## LOVINGSTON SPRING AREA

*Amherst, Rockbridge, and Nelson Counties*

**Lovingston Spring Trail** (3.1 mi.), **AT** (3.9 mi.)                          253, 489
LENGTH AND DIFFICULTY: 7 miles (11.2 km) combined, round-trip; moderate
FEATURES: springs, historic site, wildflowers, wildlife, isolation
TRAILHEAD: From junction of US 60 and SR 634 (described above for Mt. Pleasant area), drive 4.9 miles on SR 634 to where it becomes FR 63. Ascend 2 miles on FR 63 to Salt Log Gap and turn left on FR 1176. After a 1-mile ascent, turn right at fork on FR 246 for a few yards and park in a level area opposite an old road, FR 1176A (Greasy Spring Rd.).
DESCRIPTION: This delightful double circuit has ridges and vales, lush vegetation, natural springs, remoteness, and a shelter. If hiking clockwise, descend on the rough road 0.2 mile to a junction with the **AT**. (Ahead on the road it is 0.2 mi. to Greasy Spring.) Turn left and ascend on blue-blazed **Lovingston Spring Trail** 0.6 mile to crest of the ridge, and near a parking area for 4WDS. (To the left it is 150 yd. to FR 1176, where a 0.2-mi. ascent reaches Rocky Mountain radio towers [4,072 ft.] and scenic views.) On the trail (formerly the **AT**), descend through tall dense ferns, spikemoss, clubmoss, and white snakeroot (*Eupatorium perfoliatum*) to Lovingston Spring at 0.9 mile. Past the spring there is an old road

that forks right. (It descends 0.4 mi. past two cottage ruins and a small pond to a junction with the **AT** and the North Fork of the Piney River. A turn right on the **AT** makes a return circuit of 3.1 mi.)

To continue on the **Lovingston Spring Trail**, follow the old road (FR 1176B) among hardwoods, hemlocks, and rhododendrons to the crest of Elk Pond Mountain. After a slight descent among woodland sunflowers, reach Twin Springs on the **AT** at 3.1 miles. Here the **AT** passes between two natural springs. (Ahead on the **AT** it is 2.4 mi. to Spy Rock, noted for its supreme scenery.) To complete the circuit, turn right and follow the **AT**. At 3.5 miles is Seeley Woodworth Shelter on the left, with a capped spring. At 5.2 miles cross pioneer's road and rock-hop the North Fork of the Piney River. Deer and raccoon frequent this area. Ascend, and at 6.1 miles pass Wolf Rocks, which offers a view of Rocky Mountain and The Priest. Descend and complete circuit at 7 miles.

USGS MAP: Montebello; USFS TRAIL NOS.: 731, I

## TYE RIVER AREA
*Nelson County*

254 **Crabtree Falls Trail**

LENGTH AND DIFFICULTY: 2.9 miles (4.6 km); strenuous

FEATURES: cascading falls, scenic views, mosses

TRAILHEADS: To reach the northern trailhead from the west, drive from the BRP (Tye River Gap, mp 27.2) on VA 56 east 6.6 miles to Crabtree Falls parking lot. From the east, at the junction with US 29 take VA 56 west to Massies Mill and about 12 miles to the parking lot. To reach the upper (southern) trailhead, use a 4WD or a high-axle vehicle on SR 826 (Crabtree Meadows Rd.). It is 2.7 miles west on VA 56 from the Crabtree Falls parking area. Turn left on SR 826 and go 3.7 miles to a large parking lot.

INTRODUCTION: This is the district's most visited trail and also the most dangerous; more lives are lost here than in all the other districts in the GWNF. To be safe while experiencing its beauty, stay on the trail. The USFS has constructed a graded trail with sections of steps, overlooks, platforms, and guardrails for the first 2 miles. The trail features five major cascades and a number of smaller ones for 1,200 feet. (While in the Crabtree Falls area, hikers may find it worthwhile to visit Montebello State Fish Hatchery, which has excellent picnic facilities, 3 mi. west on VA 56 from the falls, and the scenic **AT** suspension bridge over the Tye River 4.5 mi. east from the falls on VA 56.)

DESCRIPTION: From the northern trailhead, pass the signboard and cross the arched bridge over the South Fork of the Tye River. The first constructed overlook is at 0.3 mile. Among switchbacks there are other rock or wood platforms for viewing. Ferns, wildflowers, and mosses are prominent. At 0.8 mile is a

*Crabtree Falls Trail, Glenwood/Pedlar Ranger District (Photograph by David Wagner, U.S. Forest Service)*

small cave, a favorite spot for children. Pass some memorial signs and at 1.7 miles reach the upper falls. Here is a rock wall for an overlook of Crabtree Creek and into the Tye River Valley. From here the remainder of the trail is on a wide woods road, parallel to Crabtree Creek, to the parking lot on SR 826 (Crabtree

Meadows Rd.). Camping is not allowed here, but a short walk to the left from the parking area at Crabtree Meadows will lead visitors to some available space for dispersed primitive camping.

255 (To reach the **AT** from here, hike the Crabtree Meadows Rd. 0.5 mi. east to a junction. Ahead [south] is the **Shoe Creek Trail**, which descends 3.5 mi. to SR 827, an access west of Massies Mill. To the left on the **AT** it is 1.2 mi. to The Priest [4,063 ft.], a forested massif with outcrops for exceptional views. To the right on the **AT** it is 3.3 mi. west to Spy Rock for views of The Priest, Mt. Pleasant, Cold Mountain, Whetstone Ridge, and other summits.)

USGS MAPS: Montebello, Massies Mill; USFS TRAIL NO.: 526


## WHETSTONE RIDGE AND SOUTH MOUNTAIN AREA
*Rockbridge County*

256 **Whetstone Ridge Trail**

LENGTH AND DIFFICULTY: 11.4 miles (17.2 km); moderate to strenuous

FEATURES: scenic views, isolation, wildflowers, wildlife

TRAILHEADS: Access north is at the parking area on the BRP, mp 29.1. Access to the southern trailhead is on SR 603 (Irish Creek Rd.), 2.5 miles east of the junction with SR 608 at Cornwall (north of Buena Vista), and 12 miles from the northern trailhead (across the BRP to SR 813, right, and 0.4 mi. to underpass of BRP for a descent on SR 603 to the parking area).

DESCRIPTION: This old trail has been restored with relocations and maintenance to make it the longest trail in the district, and one of the finest for viewing autumn colors. From the BRP parking lot, go north to enter the woods and parallel the BRP for 0.2 mile to Whetstone Ridge (3,080 ft.) and turn left. The easy treadway is through chestnut oak, striped maple, black gum, mountain laurel, flame azalea, and occasional white pine. Patches of blueberries are in sunny spots. Half of the first 2 miles of trail has been relocated, which opens new spaces for mosses and mushrooms. For a short section after 2.5 miles the trail switches back and forth on a woods road. At 4.4 miles the trail turns abruptly right on a different ridgeline. Rock outcroppings and overlooks are at 5 miles and 5.5 miles for views of Irish Creek Valley, The Priest, Rocky Mountain, and other summits. At the latter overlook is Adams Peak (2,976 ft.) to the northwest. Two other overlooks are at 6.3 miles (2,551 ft.). After 0.4 mile the trail skirts a flat knob to begin the remainder of the route on South Mountain. It undulates on five knolls, one as high as 2,800 feet, for the next 1.6 miles. After a descent from the last knoll, the footpath becomes a woods road. On an easy treadway follow the ridgeline to 9.9 miles. From here begin a rapid descent, first on the mountain's western slope and later to the eastern slope, on a grassy and rocky road. Reach the parking area across SR 603 (near Irish Creek) at 11.4 miles.

USGS MAPS: Montebello, Cornwall; USFS TRAIL NO.: 523

## SHERANDO LAKE AREA
*Augusta County*

**Slacks Overlook Trail** (2.6 mi.), **White Rock Falls Trail** (2.6 mi.), **White Rock Gap Trail** (2.5 mi.)

257–59

LENGTH AND DIFFICULTY: 4.8 miles (7.7 km) combined, round-trip; moderate

FEATURES: waterfall, scenic overlook, historic site

TRAILHEAD: Slacks Overlook, BRP, mp 19.9

INTRODUCTION: This circuit arrangement is one of at least five day options at or near Sherando Lake Recreation Area. All of the **White Rock Falls Trail** (see BRP, Chapter 4) is used in this circuit and connecting parts of the other two trails. Additionally, there are connecting trails in this area to the St. Mary's Wilderness.

DESCRIPTION: At the northwestern corner of the Slacks Overlook parking lot (2,787 ft.) on the BRP, descend 85 yards to the orange-blazed **Slacks Overlook Trail**. (To the left it goes 0.8 mi. to end at the **Torry Ridge Trail**.) Turn right, and follow an even contour in a forest of chestnut oak (greatly defoliated by the gypsy moth) and blueberries. At 1 mile curve to a cove for another ridge and then descend to a junction with the orange-blazed **White Rock Gap Trail** at 1.8 miles. (To the left the **White Rock Gap Trail** descends easily 2.2 mi. to FR 91 in the Sherando Lake campground.) From here the loop goes right on the **White Rock Gap Trail**, passes an old homesite, and crosses the BRP (mp 18.5) at 2.2 miles. Across the BRP the loop continues on orange-blazed **White Rock Falls Trail**. Descend gradually, and follow an old woods road with switchbacks. At 3.9 miles reach the falls, right, and a rocky area of cascades and pools. (Here in the gorge is evidence of damage to the hemlocks by the woolly adelgid.) Ascend steeply among boulders and overlooks at 4.2 miles for views of The Priest and other mountains. Cross White Rock Creek at 4.5 miles and return to the BRP parking area at 4.8 miles.

USGS MAP: Big Levels; USFS TRAIL NOS.: 480A, (**White Rock Falls Trail** is mainly on BRP property), 480

**White Rock Gap Trail** (2.5 mi.), **Slacks Overlook Trail** (2.6 mi.), **Torry Ridge Trail** (6 mi.), **Blue Loop Water Trail** (0.9 mi.)

259, 257, 260–61

LENGTH AND DIFFICULTY: 8.5 miles (13.6 km) combined, round-trip; moderate

FEATURES: rock outcrop, scenic views, wildflowers, stream

TRAILHEADS: At parking area near group camp in Sherando Lake Recreation Area. To reach Sherando Lake from the BRP, mp 16, travel 4.3 miles northeast on SR 814 and SR 664 to entrance, left. Drive 2 miles. (Access to this circuit is also at the Slacks Overlook, BRP, mp 19.9.)

DESCRIPTION: This circuit uses most of the **White Rock Gap Trail**, all of the **Slacks Overlook Trail**, part of the **Torry Ridge Trail**, and part of the **Blue Loop Water Trail**. Begin the hike at the sign near the parking area at the group camp. Pass north of the Upper Sherando Lake, follow upstream, and cross a tributary to the North Fork of Back Creek at 0.9 mile. Ascend gradually in a more narrow hollow, and at 2.2 miles turn right on orange-blazed **Slacks Overlook Trail**. Reach the overlook at 4 miles. From here the trail continues on the eastern slope of Torry Ridge, where gypsy moth damage has destroyed most of the oaks. At 4.8 miles meet the yellow-blazed **Torry Ridge Trail**. (To the left it goes 1 mi. to Bald Mountain [3,587 ft.], accessible on FR 162 from Bald Mountain Overlook, BRP, mp 22.2.) Turn right and follow a narrow ridge through small oaks, serviceberry, mountain laurel, blueberries, wildflowers, grasses, and gray-green lichens on rocks and trees. At 6.7 miles turn right at a junction with blue-blazed **Blue Loop Water Trail**. Pass junction on the left with 0.3-mile **Dam Trail**. (It descends steeply to dam and parking area.) Here is a lookout. After a descent of another 0.4 mile, the trail passes a water tower and meets campsite #7-A in White Oak Campground. From here it is 0.9 mile through the campgrounds west to point of origin for a circuit of 8.5 miles.

263      (If a longer hike is desired, include the **Blue Loop Parking Trail**: continue on the rocky **Torry Ridge Trail**, which now shows both yellow and blue blazes, for 1 mi. to trail junction, and right on the **Blue Loop Parking Trail**. Descend 0.8 mi. to exit at the junction of FR 91 and FR 91B [fisherman's access road] at the bridge. On FR 91 it is 1.6 mi. to point of origin for a circuit of 10.1 mi.)

264–65      (There are two short and scenic trails at the lake. The **Lakeside Trail** circles the lake for 1 mi., and 0.7-mi. **Cliff Trail** switchbacks on the eastern slope of the lake from and to the **Lakeside Trail**.)

USGS MAP: Big Levels; USFS TRAIL NOS.: 480, 480A, 506, 507, 507A, 507B, 300, 302

261, 260, 266    **Blue Loop Water Trail** (0.9 mi.), **Torry Ridge Trail** (6 mi.), **Mills Creek Trail** (7 mi.)

LENGTH AND DIFFICULTY: 15.3 miles (24.5 km) combined, round-trip; strenuous

CONNECTING TRAILS: **Blue Loop Parking Trail** (0.8 mi.), **Slacks Overlook Trail** (2.6 mi.)

FEATURES: rock outcrops, stream, isolation, wildlife, wildflowers

TRAILHEAD: Near campsite #7-A in White Oak Campground at Sherando Lake

DESCRIPTION: This circuit follows all but 1 mile of the **Torry Ridge Trail** and all of the multi-use **Mills Creek Trail**, the latter being the best choice for campsites and overnight backpacking trips. Ascend on the **Blue Loop Water Trail** past the water tower and overlook in an ascent to the **Torry Ridge Trail** at 0.9 mile. Turn right, and pass rock formations and a junction with the **Blue Loop Parking Trail** at 1.9 miles. Ascend a long wide ridge to the summit of Torry Mountain (2,781 ft.) at 2.9 miles. Pass large boulders, descend, pass blueberry patches, and at 4.1 miles meet the **Mills Creek Trail**, left. (To the right the remainder of the **Torry Ridge Trail** descends on multi-use switchbacks to Mount Torry Furnace on SR 664, 1.3 mi. north of the entrance to Sherando Lake.) Follow the **Mills Creek Trail** on a narrow treadway through blueberries and mountain laurels to a hollow and a junction with a woods road at 4.8 miles. Turn left, cross a stream, and reach Mills Creek at 5.6 miles. Cross Orebank Creek, turn left, and follow FR 1237 (Turkey Pen Ridge Rd.). After 0.6 mile, ascend and descend to cross Mills Creek at 6.9 miles. (To the right a spur trail of **Mills Creek Trail** follows downstream to Mills Creek Reservoir at 0.8 mi.) The main trail turns left to follow a long, generally flat hollow. Occasionally crossing the stream, it passes through tall hardwoods and hemlocks. Rhododendrons and ferns are prominent near good campsites. At 9.9 miles the trail begins a steep ascent with switchbacks (about 1,000 ft. vertical gain in 1 mi.) to reach FR 162 (3,437 ft.) at 11.1 miles. (To the right, FR 162 descends on the ridge along the St. Mary's Wilderness border, 2.5 mi. to Green Pond and the western trailhead of the **St. Mary's Trail**.) Turn left, ascend, reach a junction with FR 162C at 11.4 miles, and turn left on it for about 0.1 mile to the summit of Bald Mountain (3,587 ft.). Turn left on the **Torry Ridge Trail** and follow it 2.9 miles to a junction with the **Blue Loop Water Trail**. Turn right, descend, pass the **Dam Trail** and the lookout, which has views of the lake area, and return to point of origin at 15.3 miles.

USGS MAPS: Big Levels, Sherando; USFS TRAIL NOS.: 507A, 507, 518

## St. Mary's Trail

LENGTH AND DIFFICULTY: 6.5 miles (10.4 km); moderate to strenuous

CONNECTING TRAILS: **St. Mary's Gorge Trail** (0.5 mi.), **Mine Bank Creek Trail** (2 mi.)

FEATURES: wilderness, river, waterfall, old mines, natural lake

TRAILHEADS: From I-81, exit 205, drive east on VA 56 through Steeles Tavern for 2.5 miles. Turn left on SR 608 and go 3 miles (passing under railroad bridge) to FR 41 on right. Go 1.5 miles to parking area and gate. The northeastern trailhead is accessible on FR 162 near Green Pond, 3.8 miles down the mountain from BRP, mp 22.2, Bald Mountain Overlook. (Entrance gate to FR 162 may be closed.)

DESCRIPTION: These are unmaintained and unblazed wilderness trails with a potential circuit of 17.8 miles when forest roads outside the wilderness boundary are used. Begin the hike up the left side of St. Mary's River in an area of wildflowers, sumacs, ferns, hardwoods and pines. At 1.2 miles wade or rock-hop the river. (Crossing may be dangerous or impossible after heavy rain.) Near the confluence with Sugar Tree Branch, the **St. Mary's Trail** turns right and the **St. Mary's Gorge Trail** turns left. (It dead-ends after 0.5 mi. at the base of the gorge and at the beautiful St. Mary's Waterfall.) On the main trail, pass cascades and fern beds at 1.5 miles. Leave Sugar Tree Branch at 1.7 miles. For the next 6.5 miles the trail passes through relics of past manganese mining and near quartzite rock slides. At 3.7 miles reach a junction with the **Mine Bank Creek Trail**, right.

(The **Mine Bank Creek Trail** ascends in Mine Bank gorge under tall hardwoods and hemlocks, parallel with the stream. At 1.6 mi. the trail leaves the stream and ascends steeply to the BRP, mp 23, opposite Fork Mountain Overlook. To the left [northeast] it is 0.2 mi. to the western trailhead of the **Bald Mountain Trail**, which curves around the spur ridges for 2.2 mi. to exit at FR 162. Along the way at 1.2 mi. is a good campsite with a water source in a grove of rhododendron. Ascend to another campsite at 1.5 mi., cross a ravine to continue on a rocky trail with moss and ferns. At 1.7 mi. is a switchback followed by a sign and exit to FR 162. Gypsy moth damage to the hardwoods is noticeable on the trail. If making a loop for the **St. Mary's Trail**, turn left on FR 162. Pass access to the **Torry Ridge Trail**, right, at 0.1 mi. and the **Mills Creek Trail**, right, at 0.4 mi., and descend to Green Pond and a junction with the **St. Mary's Trail** at 2.9 mi. If not making a loop with the **St. Mary's Trail**, you can make a loop by turning right on FR 162 and hiking 0.7 mi. out to the BRP. Turn right and follow the BRP road shoulder 0.8 mi. to Fork Mountain Overlook and beyond to the right at a road and parking space to rejoin **Mine Bank Creek Trail** for a loop of 3.7 mi. A backtrack on **Mine Bank Creek Trail** to **St. Mary's Trail** is another 2 mi.)

Continuing on the **St. Mary's Trail**, at 3.7 miles cross small streams, and arrive at good campsites at 3.9 miles. At 4.9 miles the trail crosses St. Mary's River for the last time, but crosses other small streams, one near a forest of pitch pine at 5.3 miles. The trail ascends to a level area (Big Levels), passes old FR 162 and Green Pond, and ends at FR 162 opposite FR 162B (Kennedy Ridge Rd.) at 6.5 miles. (If making a circuit south on FR 162, as described above, it is 17.8 mi.)

USGS MAPS: Vesuvius, Big Levels; USFS TRAIL NOS.: 500, 500B, 500C, 500E

271–72 **Cellar Mountain Trail** (2.9 mi.), **Cold Spring Trail** (1.3 mi.)

LENGTH AND DIFFICULTY: 8.4 miles (13.4 km) round-trip; strenuous

FEATURES: rugged wilderness, spring, wildlife

TRAILHEAD: From FR 42, go 1.2 miles north of FR 41 to small parking area (see **St. Mary's Trail** access directions to FR 41).

DESCRIPTION: These trails join near the dead end of FR 162A outside the northern edge of St. Mary's Wilderness. (A circuit of 14.2 mi. could be made by omitting the **Cold Spring Trail**, following FR 162A for 2.8 mi., and returning on the **St. Mary's Trail** to FR 41 and FR 42.) Begin on an old woods road and ascend on switchbacks in a mixed forest. The understory has chinquapins, berries, mountain laurels, and azaleas. Pass large anthills. At 1.7 miles reach the top of Cellar Mountain (3,640 ft.), and remain on the ridge to a junction with the **Cold Spring Trail** and FR 162A. (The **Cold Spring Trail** descends 1 mi. on switchbacks to a convergence of streams and springs. It ends 0.3 mi. farther at the wilderness boundary and private property.) Backtrack.

USGS MAPS: Vesuvius, Big Levels; USFS TRAIL NOS.: 501, 524

*The woods are made for the hunters of dreams,*
*The brooks for the fishers of song.*
SAM WALTER FOSS (1858–1911)

# 2. Jefferson National Forest

The Jefferson National Forest (JNF) was created by Congress in 1936. It received part of the Natural Bridge National Forest, which had been absorbed by the GWNF in 1933. The two forests cover 1.7 million acres. The JNF has 704,231 acres in four ranger districts (New Castle, New River Valley [including former Wythe Ranger District], Clinch, the Glenwood part of the Glenwood/Pedlar), and one national recreation area, Mount Rogers.

Located in the Appalachian geological fold belt of ridges and valleys in southwestern Virginia, southeastern West Virginia, and southeastern Kentucky, the JNF extends 220 miles southwest from Glasgow to Pennington Gap. It includes portions of twenty-two counties in Virginia; Letcher and Pike Counties (961 acres) in Kentucky; and Monroe County (18,526 acres) in West Virginia. The forest boundaries touch Tennessee and North Carolina in the southwest, where Mount Rogers, the state's highest peak, rises 5,729 feet. The New River Valley, New Castle, and Glenwood part of the Glenwood/Pedlar Districts border the GWNF, but the Glenwood is the only one through which the BRP passes. The JNF has eleven wilderness areas: Beartown, Kimberling Creek, Lewis Fork, Little Dry Run, Little Wilson Creek, Mountain Lake, Peters Mountain, James River Face, Thunder Ridge, Barbours Creek, and Shawvers Run, totaling 58,047 acres. There are 500 miles of trout streams, 1,132 miles of forest roads, and 2,350 miles of boundary lines in the entire forest.

The JNF is in three physiographic provinces. The most western rock strata are plateaus with flat-topped ridges and narrow valleys. Soils are derived from sedimentary rocks. Coal seams occur mainly in Dickenson, Lee, Wise, and Scott Counties. In the Ridge and Valley Province, which is most of the forest, the ridges are sandstone and the valleys are underlain with shales and carbonates. Many of the rock formations are heavily faulted. There is natural gas throughout this province; about 2 percent of the JNF is under federal lease for oil or natural gas. In the most eastern province, the Blue Ridge Mountains consist mainly metamorphic and igneous rock. Numerous ridgelines, coves, and toe slopes have rich soil as a result.

In plans to protect or provide additional habitat for wildlife, the U.S. Forest Service has implemented management programs to increase the areas for grass and forb and browse acreage, to retain den tree clumps and hard mast for terrestrial and arboreal wildlife, and to emphasize the featured species system. Another emphasis is placed on special management areas of the Recreation Opportunity Spectrum for a total of 7,275 acres in the districts. Roaring Branch, in the Clinch District, has a clear, cascading stream and rock outcrops. Hipes Branch, in the New Castle District, contains a cascading trout stream and remote slopes to rocky cliffs for bear, deer, and turkey habitat. Rush Creek includes old-growth hemlock, Whitetop Laurel Gorge and rock walls by a trout stream (protecting sixteen species of salamanders on Whitetop Mountain), and old-growth hardwoods in Little Laurel Creek, all within Mount Rogers National Recreation Area. Apple Orchard Falls has falls and old-growth hemlock in the Glenwood District; Mill Creek contains a wilderness-type area with Angel's Rest in the New River Valley District; and Little Wolf Creek has an isolated area for wildlife observation in the New River Valley District. On the endangered, threatened, and sensitive species list in the 1985 *Land and Resource Management Plan*, there are thirty-nine animal and twenty-three plant species. The two endangered plants are the Virginia round-leaf birch (*Betula uber*) and the small-whorled pogonia (*Isotria medeoloides*). Endangered animal species are the Virginia big-eared bat (*Plecotus townsendi virginianus*), the gray bat (*Myotis grisescens*), and the Indiana bat (*Myotis sodalis*). The bald eagle (*Haliaetus leucocephalus*) is no longer endangered, but threatened.

The JNF has 35 recreational areas in which 25 have developed campgrounds. Mount Rogers National Recreation Area has 5, with a total of 277 campsites; all the other districts together have 328 campsites. Fishing, hiking, and picnicking are the most popular activities associated with the campgrounds. Other sports are boating, swimming, cross-country skiing, bicycling, horseback riding, and hunting. For ATVs there are more than 15 miles of roads available. Unless marked otherwise, such as the **AT**, or trails for the disabled, all trails are open to bikers. The JNF has not forgotten people with disabilities. One of the finest examples of outdoor facilities for the disabled is the Fenwick Mines area of the New Castle Ranger District.

There are more than 1,000 miles of trails in the forest, with the **AT** being the longest (300 mi.) and the most famous. Trail descriptions below will show frequent connections with it and other trails. Other long-distance trails are two equestrian trails: the **Virginia Highlands Horse Trail** (82 mi.) in the Mount Rogers National Recreation Area and the **Glenwood Horse Trail** (65 mi.) in the Glenwood/Pedlar Ranger District. Another long trail is the **Iron Mountain Trail** (57 mi.) in the Mount Rogers area, which also has the most trails (127), but nearly 50 percent are not maintained or up to USFS standards. During the 1980s almost all trail systems in the JNF received inadequate attention due to limited funding and staffing. Volunteers, particularly the Appalachian Trail clubs, worked to fill the void. The projected recreation demand table of the 1985 *Final Environmental Impact Statement* of the JNF showed a need for more campsites, hiking trails, and ATV accommodation in the 1990s and beyond.

ADDRESS AND INFORMATION: George Washington and Jefferson National Forests, 5162 Valleypointe Parkway, Roanoke, VA 24019; phone: 540-265-5100. Available for free are JNF newsletter, JNF map with recreation locations, wilderness brochures, and campground and dispersed camping brochures and flyers. JNF map, sportsman district maps, AT maps, topographical maps, and Mount Rogers map have small fees.

## Glenwood/Pedlar Ranger District

The most northeastern district of the JNF is the 72,300-acre Glenwood Ranger District. It is on the Blue Ridge Mountains, northeast of Troutville to the James River between Glasgow and Big Island, where it borders the Pedlar Ranger District of the GWNF. With the administration combined for the George Washington and Jefferson National Forests, the Glenwood and Pedlar Districts were combined also. Geographical boundaries remain the same in their respective forests. For the first 13 miles the forest is a corridor, mainly on the northern side, along the BRP. At Bearwallow Gap the forest boundaries expand north to the James River near Buchanan and south to the Peaks of Otter in the BRP (see Chapter 4). The width is about the same for the remainder of the distance. Major natural attractions are the wilderness areas and the high peaks of the northeast, and the man-made attractions are the AT and the BRP, which parallel each other through the district.

There are two wilderness areas: James River Face (8,886 acres), Virginia's first, made possible by the Congressional Wilderness Act of 1975; and adjoining Thunder Ridge (2,344 acres). Both represent some of the most geologically rugged and botanically diverse areas in the state. The more adverse terrain is on the steep river face of the gorge, where dense vegetation discourages exploration. Impressive views of the gorge, river, and mountain are from the overlooks on US 501/VA 130 southeast of Glasgow. Access into the interior of the preserve is by the AT, the **Sulphur Spring Trail**, the **Piney Ridge Trail**, the **Belfast Trail**, the **Gunter Ridge Trail**, and the **Balcony Falls Trail**.

(A special property in the district is the 378-acre Locher Tract, purchased in 1970 with Land and Water Conservation Fund monies. Once a family farm, the property has 1 mile of riverfront. **Locher Tract Trail** is a 0.6-mi. grassy labyrinthine loop around a lake and by a bubbling spring. There are beaver, wood ducks, deer, wild turkey, pileated woodpecker, and American goldfinch. Near a gravel road is a stable chimney of one of the Locher family houses, surrounded by periwinkle groundcover. Nearby is access to **Balcony Falls Trail**, which ascends into the James River Face Wilderness and to the AT. Access to the Locher Tract is from VA 130, near Natural Bridge Station, south on SR 759 [Arnold Valley Rd.] for 0.9 mi. to a left on VA 782 [James River Rd.]. Parking is at the end of the road after 1.7 mi.)

273

Cave Mountain Lake Campground (with access from VA 130 near Natural Bridge Station across the James River on SR 759 and SR 781) is the largest and most used of the district's campgrounds. A fee area, it has flush toilets, family and group campsites, trailer sites, picnic area, trailer waste disposal station, and showers at the bathhouse near the lake and beach. The **Wildcat Mountain Trail**, a 4.8-mile loop trail, was developed primarily for the use of campers at the campground. (See description ahead.)

The North Creek Campground (with access from I-81, exit 168, near Buchanan on SR 614 to Arcadia and FR 59) is more primitive. It has a hand pump, vault toilets, and trailer waste disposal unit. It also has a loop trail, the **Whitetail Trail** (2.6 mi.), primarily developed for users of the campground. The yellow-blazed trail is easy to moderate, with a short loop of 0.9 miles within the longer loop. On the longer route is a wildlife waterhole and wildlife clearing, an excellent spot for birdwatchers. Another district camp is Hopper Creek Group Camp, where reservations are necessary from the district office. Access is off SR 759 from Natural Bridge Station. In addition to the picnic area at Cave Mountain Lake, there is Middle Creek Picnic Area on SR 614, south of Arcadia. The district's rainbow trout streams are North Creek, Middle Creek, and Jenning's Creek—all flowing toward Arcadia to become Jenning's Creek. On the eastern side of the district is Hunting Creek near VA 122.

Outstanding projects in the district during the 1990s were the North Creek Special Management Plan, east of Arcadia, and the 65-mile **Glenwood Horse Trail**, which runs the entire length of the district. The North Creek project is special because the emphasis is decidedly in favor of preservation and recreation instead of timber harvesting in the 7,400-acre holding. Significant characteristics are the preservation of 1,825 acres in the Apple Orchard Falls area, an emphasis on songbirds as the featured wildlife species, protection of wildlife habitat waterholes, erosion prevention in the trout streams, and increased trail mileage.

The district's **Glenwood Horse Trail** is the finest equestrian trail in central Virginia. Its existence is the work of the USFS, horsemen's associations, and riding clubs. There are four trailheads. The southern trailhead is at Day Creek parking lot near Camp Virginia Jaycee. From the junction of US 460/221 and SR 697 (1.5 mi. between Villamont and Montvale west of Bedford), drive north on SR 697 for 0.6 mile and turn left on FR 186 for 0.4 mile to FR 3082. At this trailhead there is a spur, which goes west on FR 3082. The main trail goes north (right), and an alternate trail loop through Blackhorse Gap goes north on FR 186. The Buchanan trailhead is off VA 43. Take exit 162 (or 167 if coming from the north) on I-81 to US 11 in Buchanan. Take VA 43 south 1.7 miles and turn right on SR 625 for 0.3 miles. The Hunting Creek trailhead is west of Big Island. Off US 501, stay on VA 122 for 3 miles south. Turn right on SR 602, and after 0.5 mile fork left to continue 3.4 miles to the parking lot on the left. (If coming from Roanoke, turn north on VA 122 in Bedford.) The northern trailhead, Hellgate Creek, is south of Natural Bridge

Station. From I-81 take exit 175 or 180 to US 11 at Natural Bridge; follow VA 130 for 3.2 miles. Turn right on SR 759, go 0.7 mile, and turn left on SR 702. After 1 mile turn right on SR 815 for 0.3 mile to the parking lot. It is recommended that riders unfamiliar with the orange-blazed main trail (and brown for alternate routes) request information from the district office.

The longest hiking trail only in the district is 51.5 miles of the **AT**, and the second longest is 6.5-mile **St. Mary's Trail**. The **AT**'s highest elevation is on Apple Orchard Mountain (4,225 ft.), and its lowest point is at the James River bridge (660 ft.). In the Apple Orchard Mountain area are a number of rare plants and animals. Examples are the oak fern (*Gymnocarpium dryopteris*) and the giant snail-eating ground beetle (*Scaphinotus webbi*). Some trails are not blazed; others are blue, orange, or yellow. Most of the trails form networks; 12 connect with the **AT**. Three separate trails, rarely used, are on the southwestern corridor of the BRP and the **AT**. On the wilderness trails, look for the Carolina hemlock (*Tsuga caroliniana*) at its most northern range limit and the paper birch (*Betula papyrifera*) at its most southern range limit.

ADDRESS AND INFORMATION: Glenwood/Pedlar Ranger District, P.O. Box 10, Natural Bridge Station, VA 24579; phone: 540-291-2188; on VA 130, 0.5 mile west of Natural Bridge Station. Available are district map with trails; brochures on recreation opportunities and Glenwood horse trails; flyers on hiking, camping, and wilderness areas.

## WILDCAT MOUNTAIN AREA
*Rockbridge and Botetourt Counties*

**Wildcat Mountain Trail** (4.8 mi.), **Panther Knob Nature Trail** (1 mi.), **Cave Mountain Lake Trail** (0.8 mi.)               276–78

LENGTH AND DIFFICULTY: 6.6 miles (10.6 km) combined; easy to strenuous
FEATURES: natural arboretum, trout lake, wildlife, scenic areas
TRAILHEADS: These three loop trails are located in the Cave Mountain Lake Recreation Area. (See recreation information in introduction of this section.) Access is off VA 130 near Natural Bridge Station on SR 759 (Arnold Valley Rd.) south. Cross the James River Bridge and follow SR 759 to an intersection at 3.2 miles. Turn right on SR 781 (Cave Mountain Rd.) and go 1.6 miles to the lake's entrance, left. After 1.1 miles arrive at the intersection with the campground area ahead and the lake area to the right. In the campground locate the **Wildcat Mountain Trail** entrance between campsites #29 and #31. For the other two trails the loops begin at the parking area for the lake beach and picnic shelter.
DESCRIPTION: If choosing the orange-blazed **Wildcat Mountain Trail**, ascend in a hollow and cross a branch six times in the first 0.4 mile within a forest of hardwoods and pines. Wildflowers are part of the ground cover. At 0.7 mile arrive at FR 3744 with crown vetch on its banks. Turn right and after 60 feet turn

left off the road. Ascend a ridge among an old and new growth forest with undergrowth of sassafras, raspberry, snakeroot, and asters. Reach the top of a ridge at 1 mile and descend slightly into a white pine grove. For the next 0.9 mile ascend and occasionally descend to shallow gaps in a forest badly damaged by Hurricane Hugo. Be alert to erratic routings by hikers off the original trail. Reach the crest of a ridge and bear right. There are views to the east here, particularly in the wintertime. At 2.5 miles leave a ridge by turning right to descend onto an old road. From here the trail will cross or follow old roads for most of the way back to the campground. In the process the trail will swing around ridges and cross small headwater streamlets of Back Run mainly in Bear Hollow. Some water veins are large enough for rock-hopping, such as at 3.6 miles. At 4 miles is a grove of dying hemlock (from aphid blight), but within 0.3 mile downstream are healthy carpets of running cedar. Rock-hop the creek again at 4.5 miles. At 4.7 miles exit at campsite #41 and return to the trail's sign at 4.8 miles.

From the entrance road and campground junction descend to the beach and picnic area parking lot. Begin the **Panther Knob Nature Trail** and the **Cave Mountain Lake Trail** counterclockwise from the picnic shelter and Panther Knob sign. After 0.2 mile the **Panther Knob Nature Trail** turns right to ascend and make multiple curves. There is a descent into a hollow before completing the loop at 0.8 mile. Return to the parking lot at 1 mile. (All of the trail's markers are missing and some maintenance is needed, but you could make your own list of how many trees and flowers you can identify.) On the lake's loop trail, continue along the lake to fishing sites, descend to cross Back Run below the dam, then ascend to a natural rock dam. From this scenic point and fishing sites, turn right to a grassy road where a left turn is a return to the beach, bathhouse, and parking area after 0.8 mile.

USGS MAP: Arnold Valley; USFS TRAIL NOS.: 326, 3005


## CURRY CREEK AND HAMMOND HOLLOW AREAS
*Botetourt County*

279–81, 489    **Curry Creek Trail** (0.7 mi.), **Spec Mines Trail** (2.8 mi.), **Hammond Hollow Trail** (3.3 mi.), **AT** (10 mi.)

LENGTH AND DIFFICULTY: 6.2 miles to 11.4 miles (9.9 km to 18.2 km) combined, round-trip; moderate to strenuous

FEATURES: scenic views, wildlife, wildflowers, streams

TRAILHEADS: The most southern terminus is on the **AT** at Salt Pond (1.1 mi. west from gated FR 191 at BRP mp 101.5). The most northern is at Bobblets Gap (BRP mp 93.2 and FR 4008). Other accesses are described below.

INTRODUCTION: All three of the spur trails run northwest off the **AT** and descend separately and end separately, but they are connected by the **AT**, which parallels the BRP at the top of the mountain, and by FR 634, which is a comparable parallel farther down the mountainside. By using the **AT** and the roads, multiple circuits can be made. Except for the first 3.5 miles on FR 634, all other roadway is part of the **Glenwood Horse Trail** system. Wildlife in the areas includes deer, turkeys, grouse, raccoons, squirrels, owls, hawks, songbirds, and snakes, including the timber rattlesnake. Vascular plants are mainly southern hardwoods, pines, rhododendron, mountain laurel, wildflowers, and ferns. There are more than ten different stream crossings and six scenic overlooks.

DESCRIPTION: If hiking northeast on the **AT** at Curry Creek, a 11.4-mile loop can be made by descending on the blue-blazed **Curry Creek Trail** for 0.7 mile to right on FR 634-1 for 3.5 miles to FR 186 and joining the **Glenwood Horse Trail** (FR 186 becomes SR 606 out to US 11, north of Troutville). Turn right and ascend FR 186 for 2.2 miles to the **AT** at Black Horse Gap at 6.4 miles. Return right on the **AT** for 5 miles, passing Wilson Creek Shelter, to point of origin.

Another 8-mile circuit on the **AT** is at Iron Mine Hollow Overlook at the BRP. Descend on the **Spec Mines Trail** (planned yellow blazing) 2.1 miles and turn left on FR 634. (The trail continues another 0.7 mi. to SR 645, which accesses SR 640 to US 11.) Follow FR 634 2.4 miles to FR 186, turn left, and ascend 2.2 miles on FR 186 to the **AT** at Black Horse Gap. Turn left on the **AT** for 1.3 miles to point of origin at Iron Mine Hollow Overlook, and Taylors Mountain Overlook along the way. (The **Spec Mines Trail** can also be used to turn right on FR 634-2 for 3 mi. to a right turn on the **Hammond Hollow Trail**. Ascend 1.4 mi. to the **AT** at 6.8 mi. Turn right on the **AT** for 2.8 mi. for a return to Iron Mine Hollow Overlook at 9.6 mi. Along the **AT** is Harveys Knob Overlook.)

For an additional use of the **Hammond Hollow Trail**, after the 1.4-mile descent from the **AT** to FR 634-3, turn right (which is both the **Hammond Hollow Trail** and the **Glenwood Horse Trail**) for 1.9 miles. Turn right for 0.1 mile and turn right again on FR 4008 at 3.4 miles. (At FR 4008 junction with SR 617, there is an access north on SR 617 to SR 625 and US 11 south of Buchanan.) Ascend on FR 4008 1 mile to main route of the **Glenwood Horse Trail**, and another 1 mile up to the **AT** and the BRP at Bobblets Gap. A return right on the **AT** passes Bobblets Gap Shelter en route to the **Hammond Hollow Trail** for 0.8 mile and a total of 6.2 miles.

USGS MAPS: Villamont, Montvale; USFS TRAIL NOS.: 20, 28, 27, 1

## JENNINGS CREEK AND NORTH CREEK AREAS
*Botetourt County*

**Buchanan Trail** (1.5 mi.), **Cove Mountain Trail** (1.8 mi.)  282–83

LENGTH AND DIFFICULTY: 3.3 miles (5.3 km) combined, round-trip; easy to moderate

FEATURES: scenic views, wildlife, spring

TRAILHEADS: For the **Buchanan Trail**, go east 1.2 miles on VA 43 from Buchanan, turn left on Quarry Road, and after 1 mile look for trail on right. For the **Cove Mountain Trail**, take I-81, exit 168, follow SR 614 to Arcadia, turn right on SR 622 at Arcadia Store, and go 0.1 mile for parking.

DESCRIPTION: These trails have different entrances into the forest but meet 100 yards down the slope from the **AT**. The **Buchanan Trail** ascends from an old quarry to a logging road at 0.8 mile. At 1.3 miles is a spring. The **Cove Mountain Trail** ascends steeply to an old logging road. At 0.9 mile and 1.4 miles are wildlife waterholes. Dappled with sunlight, the wide trail is exceptionally scenic with autumn colors. At 1.8 miles it joins the **Buchanan Trail**. (A loop of 7.9 mi. can be made by hiking the **AT** southwest 3 mi. [Cove Mountain Shelter is at 1.7 mi.] to blue-blazed **Little Cove Mountain Trail**. Turn left sharply, descend, and follow the trail 2.8 mi. to Jennings Creek and SR 614. Turn left on SR 614 and after 0.7 mi. make a junction with the **AT** at a parking area, where a left on the **AT** provides a return to Cove Mountain and Buchanan trails after 1.4 mi.) (The **Glenwood Horse Trail** partially follows the **Buchanan Trail** and the **Cove Mountain Trail**.)

USGS MAPS: Arnold Valley, Buchanan; USFS TRAIL NOS.: 24, 23

284, 489    **Little Cove Mountain Trail** (2.8 mi.), **AT** (1.7 mi.)

LENGTH AND DIFFICULTY: 4.5 miles (7.2 km) combined; moderate

FEATURES: wildlife, stream, scenic views

TRAILHEAD: From I-81, exit 168, take SR 614 through Arcadia (see **Cove Mountain Trail**, above, for connection options), past junctions with FR 59 (North Creek Rd.) and SR 618 (Middle Creek Rd.), and after 0.5 mile on SR 614 park at trail sign by Jennings Creek, on the right.

DESCRIPTION: The trail crosses Jennings Creek on a footbridge and three times on Little Cove Creek. It ascends and reaches a ridge at 1 mile. It crosses two forest roads, the **Glenwood Horse Trail**, and reaches the **AT** at 2.8 miles. Here are views of Purgatory Mountain and Buchanan. Backtrack or continue left on the **AT** for 1.7 miles to mp 90.9 at the BRP for a support vehicle at VA 43, or turn right on the **AT** and follow it back to SR 614 at Jennings Creek for a 7.9-mile loop.

USGS MAPS: Buchanan, Montvale; USFS TRAIL NO.: 25

285–86, 489    **Apple Orchard Falls Trail (West)** (3.4 mi.), **Cornelius Creek Trail** (2.9 mi.), **AT** (1.2 mi.)

LENGTH AND DIFFICULTY: 6.8 miles or 7.3 miles (10.9 km or 11.7 km) combined, round-trip; strenuous

FEATURES: wildflowers, wildlife, waterfall, scenic views

TRAILHEADS: From I-81, north of Buchanan, exit 168, follow SR 614 for 3.3 miles, past Arcadia, and turn left on FR 59, which leads to North Creek Campground. Pass the camp and reach road's end and parking area after 7.5 miles from I-81. Access is also from mp 78.7 on the BRP, Sunset Field Overlook. See Chapter 4 for **Apple Orchard Falls Trail (East)**.

DESCRIPTION: Both trails begin at the end of FR 59 for the northern trailheads, the **Apple Orchard Falls Trail** left and the **Cornelius Creek Trail** right. They both join the **AT** 1.2 miles apart, and their elevation change is about the same, 2,000 feet. Backtracking is 6.8 miles round-trip on the **Apple Orchard Falls Trail**, or making a loop with the **Cornelius Creek Trail** and the **AT** is 7.3 miles. On the blue-blazed **Apple Orchard Falls Trail** there are steep sections and a number of stream crossings. At 2 miles it reaches the spectacular 200-foot Apple Orchard Falls. Ascend to a large overhanging rock at 2.3 miles. Continue the steep ascent to 2.6 miles where a seeded forest road is right. (The old road is 1.1 mi. to **Cornelius Creek Trail** for a shortcut loop of 6 mi.) Cross the **AT** at 3.2 miles, where a 0.2-mile spur connects to the BRP at 3.4 miles. The **Cornelius Creek Trail** follows Cornelius Creek and up the western side of Backbone Ridge on old logging roads. It makes a sharp left to ascend Backbone Ridge, then a sharp right on the ridge where at 2.3 miles it passes the seeded forest road for a shortcut connection to **Apple Orchard Falls Trail**. At 2.9 miles it connects with the **AT**. Backtrack, or turn left and go 1.2 miles on the **AT** to connect with the **Apple Orchard Falls Trail**.

USGS MAP: Arnold Valley; USFS TRAIL NOS.: 17, 18, 1

## THUNDER RIDGE AND TERRAPIN MOUNTAIN AREA
*Bedford County*

### Hunting Creek Trail 287

LENGTH AND DIFFICULTY: 1 mile (1.6 km); moderate to strenuous

FEATURES: scenic views, wildflowers, stream

TRAILHEADS: The western trailhead is at mp 74.9 of the BRP where the **AT** crosses. To reach the eastern trailhead, from the Big Island junction of US 501 and VA 122 go 3 miles on VA 122. Turn right on SR 602 for 1.5 miles, where it becomes FR 45. Drive 3.5 miles to an extreme left curve; trailhead is on the right.

DESCRIPTION: This deluxe leg-stretcher is blue-blazed, short, and switchy, dropping 1,000 feet out of the sky at Thunder Ridge (3,485 ft.) to riparian fern beds and the headwaters of trout-stocked Hunting Creek. Its eastern trailhead at FR 45 is also a junction with the **Glenwood Horse Trail**.

USGS MAP: Snowden; USFS TRAIL NO.: 3

### Terrapin Mountain Trail (3.3 mi.), Reed Creek Trail (5.6 mi.) (The latter trail 288–89 may not be on the official USFS trail inventory.)

LENGTH AND DIFFICULTY: 8.9 miles (14.2 km) combined; moderate to strenuous

FEATURES: scenic views, cascading stream, wildflowers, wildlife

TRAILHEADS: To access the western trailhead of **Terrapin Mountain Trail** from the junction of US 501 and VA 122 near Big Island (and 1.5 mi. east of BRP junction) drive south 2.9 miles on VA 122 to turn right on SR 602 (Hunting Creek

Rd.). After 0.4 mile stay left at fork. (Ahead is Goff Mountain Rd., which ascends to the BRP at James River Valley Overlook.) The state road becomes FR 45 at 1.5 miles. At 2.2 miles the 65-mile **Glenwood Horse Trail** enters FR 45 from the right to follow FR 45 ahead and beyond the **Terrapin Mountain Trail** western trailhead. (See **Glenwood Horse Trail** information in introduction of this section.) At 3.5 miles in a sharp curve left is the eastern trailhead for **Hunting Creek Trail** described above. After another 1.1 miles is Camping Gap and **Terrapin Mountain Trail** western trailhead, left. To access the eastern trailhead continue south on VA 122 for 0.7 mile for a turn right on Terrapin Mountain Lane at the corner of the Church of God. After 0.8 mile arrive at a parking area and gated USFS road.

If choosing to hike the **Terrapin Mountain Trail** down the mountain from the western trailhead, ascend on a yellow-blazed road/trail and after 50 yards bear left on a foot trail away from a horse trail. On a steep ascent pass through chestnut oak, rhododendron, witch hazel, wild cherry, and golden ragwort to where the trail divides at 0.5 mile. (To the left the trail passes the north side of the knob to rejoin the trail on the right.) Ascend to the right; notice views to the left. At 0.7 mile is a spur path right. (It is first on a ridge then slightly descends to a magnificent view southwest to Onion Mountain, and south-southeast to mountain ranges between Bedford and Lynchburg. Backtrack.) Descend northeast and junction with the shortcut from the left at 0.9 mile in a shallow gap. After two switchbacks, ascend briefly. Descend among hickory and oaks. The trail undulates before reaching scenic views to the left. Descend on more switchbacks and at 2.1 miles arrive at a spectacular view of Hunting Creek Valley and the Blue Ridge Mountains. After seven more switchbacks turn right on an old road at 2.5 miles. After a few yards the trail abruptly turns left off the road because of a rock slide. Steeply descend on a rocky surface, likely without blazes. Reach a junction with the yellow-blazed **Reed Creek Trail**, right, at 3.1 miles. Continue to descend 0.2 mile on an old road to the USFS gate and parking area. Backtrack, or arrange a shuttle, or follow **Reed Creek Trail** back to Camping Gap for an 8.9-mile loop.

If choosing a loop follow **Reed Creek Trail** on an easy and pleasant old road for 3 miles. In a hardwood forest the road gently weaves in and out of eleven hollows where seepage or small headwaters provide fern and golden ragwort beds. This and other wildflowers are scenic in the springtime, and the colorful forest leaves are brilliant in autumn. In a hollow at 2 miles to the right is a cliff with a thin waterfall. At 3.3 miles cross rocky and cascading Reed Creek, followed by hummocks. Turn right upstream on a hunter's road. The tumbling creek has waterfall tiers at 3.7 miles. Cross the creek again at 4.1 miles in a scenic curve to the left. (Another old road is to the right.) Continue ascent and at 4.6 miles in a cove pass through an acre of golden ragwort, then a grove of black walnut and yellow poplar trees. After passing through scattered white

*Reed Creek on Terrapin Mountain Trail loop, Glenwood/Pedlar Ranger District*

pines at 5.5 miles arrive at FR 45 (Hunting Creek Rd.), right and left. Stay right and after 50 yards return to the center of the parking area at Camping Gap at 5.6 miles for a loop of 8.9 miles.

USGS MAP: Snowden; USFS TRAIL NOS.: 5 and FR 3009

## JAMES RIVER FACE WILDERNESS AREA
*Rockbridge County*

**Balcony Falls Trail** (4.1 mi.), **Sulphur Spring Trail** (6.6 mi.)  290–91
LENGTH AND DIFFICULTY: 10.7 miles (17.1 km) combined; strenuous
FEATURES: wilderness, scenic views, wildlife, wildflowers, sulphur spring
TRAILHEADS: From junction of VA 130 and SR 759 near Natural Bridge Station, take
    SR 759 for 0.9 mile, turn east on paved SR 782, pass James River Recreation
    Area, and continue straight on gravel road to FR 3093 for 1.5 miles to northern
    trailhead parking area for the Locher Tract. To reach the southern trailhead,
    continue on SR 759 for 2.3 miles, then turn east on SR 781 (which becomes FR 35)
    for 3.2 miles to the parking area at Sulphur Spring Hollow.

DESCRIPTION: These trails connect with other trails in the James River Face and Thunder Ridge wilderness areas, but the arms go in such opposite directions it is difficult to form circuits. These trails are also used for horse traffic. Begin the **Balcony Falls Trail** on a gradual contour for the first 1.6 miles, after which the trail ascends steeply on switchbacks into the James River Face Wilderness. At 2.5 miles is a major scenic view of the James River Gorge and the town of Glasgow. (Balcony Falls is a rapids in the James River near the confluence of Maury River.) Following a former old fire road the trail becomes the **Sulphur Spring Trail** at 4.1 miles, with an altitude gain of 1,450 feet.

Continuing ahead the trail skirts west of the main ridge, then returns to the main ridge for a junction with the **AT** at 5.5 miles. (A turn right on the **AT** is 0.5 mi. from a junction with the **Belfast Trail**.) Cross the **AT**, follow an easy grade, and at 5.7 miles there is an excellent view of James River Gorge. At 7.8 miles join the **Piney Ridge Trail** on the left. (The **Piney Ridge Trail** descends 3.7 mi. south to FR 54.) After 70 yards the trail crosses the **AT** and begins its descent to Sulphur Spring Hollow. Pass Sulphur Spring on the right at 10.4 miles and reach the southern trailhead on FR 35 at 10.7 miles. Total elevation change is 1,175 feet.

USGS MAP: Snowden; USFS TRAIL NOS.: 7, 3001

292–93 **Belfast Trail** (2.8 mi.), **Gunter Ridge Trail** (4.7 mi.)

LENGTH AND DIFFICULTY: 7.5 miles (12 km) combined; strenuous

FEATURES: geological formations, scenic views, wildlife, stream

TRAILHEADS: The northwestern trailheads are separate. The southeastern trailhead is a merge with the **AT**. To access the northwestern trailheads from VA 130 near Natural Bridge Station drive southwest on SR 759 for 1.5 miles to the **Gunter Ridge Trail** across the Elk Creek bridge on the left. Continue ahead on SR 759 for 1.7 miles, turn left on SR 781, and reach the **Belfast Trail** trailhead after another 1.3 miles.

DESCRIPTION: If beginning with the **Belfast Trail**, cross a footbridge over Elk Creek, meet the **Glenwood Horse Trail**, pass the site of a former Boy Scout Camp, and begin to ascend on the northern side of Belfast Creek. At 0.6 mile enter the James River Face Wilderness. Leave the creek and at 1.4 miles arrive at Devil's Marbleyard, a unique pile of blocky rubble of sandstone, part of a fold that happened about 200 million years ago. Holes in the blocks were bored by worms, known as *Skolithus*, when the rocks were sand, according to geologist Edgar Spencer of Washington and Lee University. Reach a ridge crest at 2 miles, join the **Gunter Ridge Trail** on the left at 2.4 miles, and join the **AT** at 2.8 miles. Backtrack, or follow the **Gunter Ridge Trail**. (Make a loop by turning right on the **AT** and following it 1.8 mi. Turn right and descend on the **Sulphur Spring Trail** for 2.8 mi. to FR 35. Turn right on FR 35 and follow it 1.9 mi. to the **Belfast Trail** for a circuit of 9.2 mi.)

On the blue-blazed **Gunter Ridge Trail** from the **Belfast Trail**, stay in the slight hollow to a saddle and follow it out to a knoll at 0.9 mile on Gunter Ridge. Begin a descent in hardwoods with mountain laurel and blueberries as an understory. Follow 20 switchbacks to the leaving edge of the wilderness at Little Hellgate Creek. Cross the **Glenwood Horse Trail** at 3.8 miles on FR 3015. (To the right on FR 3015 its is 1.3 mi. to **Glenwood Horse Trail** trailhead at Big Hellgate Creek.) Leave the forest and follow a road to exit at SR 759 at 4.7 miles.
USGS MAP: Snowden; USFS TRAIL NOS.: 9, 8 (no number for **Glenwood Horse Trail**)

## Piney Ridge Trail

294

LENGTH AND DIFFICULTY: 3.7 miles (5.9 km) one way; strenuous
FEATURES: wilderness, wildlife, wildflowers
TRAILHEADS: To reach the southern trailhead from the BRP, go west on US 501 for 1.8 miles to FR 54 on the left. Drive 0.6 mile on a narrow road past Big Island Hunt and Fish Club to park near the trailhead on the right. The northern trailhead is at the **AT** (2.9 mi. north on the **AT** from Petites Gap on the BRP, mp 71).
DESCRIPTION: At the southern trailhead by yucca, follow Piney Ridge between Snow Creek and Peters Creek among hardwoods, Virginia pine, and mountain laurel. Enter the James River Face Wilderness at 1.5 miles. Reach the junction with the **Sulphur Spring Trail** 70 yards north of the **AT** at 3.7 miles. Backtrack. (If planning for a potential loop, turn right on the **AT**, follow it through Hickory Stand, down the mountain to Matts Creek Shelter, by super scenic views of the James River Gorge, and to US 501 at the James River bridge for 7.6 mi. Turn right on US 501, hike 1.3 mi. to FR 54, turn right, and go 0.6 mi. to southern trailhead of the **Piney Ridge Trail** for a total of 13.2 mi.) Elevation gain, 1,550 feet.
USGS MAP: Snowden; USFS TRAIL NO.: 2

# New Castle Ranger District

The New Castle Ranger District is northwest of the city of Roanoke. It is bordered on the southwest by the New River Valley Ranger District in the JNF, and on the north by the James River Ranger District in the GWNF. The western boundary is the state line of West Virginia, except a section of West Virginia between Peters and Potts mountain ranges in Monroe County. The mountain ranges are, as with the New River Valley Ranger District, formed in a southwest to northeast direction. Johns Creek, the central drainage, flows northeast into Craig Creek, whose confluence is at the James River at Eagle Point.

The district has 42,000 acres in which are two wilderness areas. Both are north

*Hanging Rock Trail,*
*New Castle Ranger District*

295

296–97

of New Castle, border the GWNF, and are rugged and remote. In Shawvers Run Wilderness Area (3,665 acres) the highest peak is Hanging Rock (3,800 ft.), a unique geological formation with panoramic views. The 0.7-mile **Hanging Rock Trail** accesses the outcropping. From there you can see west to Potts and Little Mountain ranges in Virginia and beyond to Peters Mountain range in West Virginia. Access to the trail from New Castle is west on VA 311 for 10.3 miles to FR 177-1, right. Go north on Potts Mountain Road for 3.3 miles to parking lot, left. In the center of Barbours Creek Wilderness Area (5,700 acres) is the **Lipes Branch Trail** (2.3 mi.). It ascends to the eastern Potts Mountain ridgeline from The Pines, a campground on SR 617, 12 miles northeast from New Castle. **Cove Branch Trail** (1.7 mi.) connects the two wilderness areas from FR 275 in an ascent to FR 177-1, 1.8 miles north of Hanging Rock. This wilderness, as with Shawvers, has an abundance of wildlife.

The district has five recreational sites open all year and without fees. Craig Creek Recreation Area has 130 acres in Botetourt County and has a picnic area, fishing and canoeing at Craig Creek, and space for hiking and horseback riding. Access is from New Castle: drive north on SR 615 for 11 miles to SR 817 in Oriskany. Turn right on SR 817 and arrive at the recreation area after 0.5 mile. Fenwick Mines Recreation Area is in Craig County and has large family or group picnic facilities, historic mining sites, and trails. It has rest rooms but no potable water. From New

Castle drive north on SR 615 for 5 miles to SR 611 and turn left. Drive 0.5 mile to SR 685 and turn right to the recreation area. Roaring Run Recreation Area is in Botetourt County and provides picnic units, vault rest rooms, but no potable water. Trout fishing is at Roaring Run. Attractions are historic sites of iron ore mining. From the junction of US 220 and SR 615 in the Eagle Rock community, drive 6 miles northwest on SR 615 to SR 621 and go right 0.9 miles to the recreation area. Steel Bridge Recreation Area is in Craig County and has a family camping area with a central hand pump for water, and rest rooms. There are also picnic sites and fishing in the stream. From New Castle drive west on VA 311 to Paint Bank. Turn right on VA 18 and go 3.5 miles to campground on Potts Creek. The Pines Recreation Area is in Craig County. It has a family camping area with hand-pumped water and rest rooms. There is also group camping and trails for equestrians. Other recreation is fishing and hiking trails. From New Castle drive north on SR 615 for 2.5 miles. Turn left on SR 609 for 2 miles to SR 611. Turn left on SR 611 and drive to SR 617. Turn right on SR 617 for 5.5 miles to the campground entrance, left.

This district has a diversity of trails. Of the thirty-eight trails officially listed, twenty-four are multiple-use for hikers, bicyclists, and equestrians. On Patterson Mountain there is a network (thirteen or more routes) of nearly 16 miles for ORV usage. **Lees Creek Trail**, a 2.8-mile equestrian trail, is accessible off SR 666 on FR 5061, west of Woodville Spring. The **Appalachian Trail** (hiking only) has 32.4 miles passing through the district. Twenty-six of the thirty-eight trails were not blazed in 2003, but the district staff stated that plans were to increase both blazing and maintenance in the future, and to use a GPS method for confirming the trail distances. All blazes are yellow or orange except the **Dragon's Tooth Trail** (1.2 mi.), which is blue. (The **Dragon's Tooth Trail** is an access trail to the **Appalachian Trail** from a parking area off VA 311 about 2.5 mi. west of the community of Catawba. The trail receives its name from a rock formation and overlook. Also from the parking area is **Boy Scout Trail** [0.4 mi.], a shorter access, and farther north, to the **AT**.) During the 1990s the district provided a model project in phases to serve people with disabilities: the Fenwick Mines Recreation Area with specialized trails.

ADDRESS AND INFORMATION: New Castle Ranger District, P.O. Box 246, New Castle, VA 24127; phone: 540-864-5195; fax: 540-864-6969; on SR 615, 1.5 miles east of New Castle. Available are district recreational flyers.

## SEVENMILE MOUNTAIN AREA
*Craig County*

### Sevenmile Mountain Trail

LENGTH AND DIFFICULTY: 5.2 miles (8.3 km); easy to strenuous
FEATURES: historic site, wildlife, autumn colors, isolation
TRAILHEADS: From New Castle drive west on VA 311 and turn left on SR 658 at sign

to Craig Springs. Drive 4.6 miles to fork. (It is 3.4 mi. left on SR 632 to eastern trailhead, right.) Continue on SR 658 for 5.1 miles to a parking lot, left. (Opposite the parking lot is FR 279.)

DESCRIPTION: Follow the sign and yellow blazes in the forest to a curve right of a large sink hole. Enter the first of four hollows and ridges among mixed hardwood and scattered rhododendron for 0.9 mile. Ascend steeply but level out at 1.1 miles. Ascend again on switchbacks, the last of which is at an old stone fence at 1.4 miles. After another 50 yards arrive at an old wildlife field, right. The remains of a stone chimney mark a heritage homesite. Follow an old road north among hardwoods with brilliant autumn colors, as elsewhere on the trail. The trail easily levels off along the ridgeline, and becomes wide at 2.1 miles. At 2.7 miles is a boundary and geological marker. As the trail begins a descent it is most notable at 4.1 miles. Continue descent and cross an old forest road at 5 miles. After a switchback near the trailhead, descend on steps and to a small parking lot.

USGS MAP: Looney; USFS TRAIL NO.: 5015

## PETERS MOUNTAIN AREA
*Monroe County, West Virginia*

238 **Allegheny Trail**

LENGTH AND DIFFICULTY: 8.3 miles (13.3 km); easy to moderate

FEATURES: wildlife, wide grassy trail

TRAILHEADS: To reach the southwestern trailhead from Waiteville, travel 0.8 mile northeast on CO 17 to CO 15 (Gap Mills Rd.) for 3.5 miles to the parking area on top of Peters Mountain. (Access here is also on CO 15, 5.4 mi. southwest from the village of Mills Gap at WV 3.) The northeastern trailhead is in the community of Laurel Branch; go 5.1 miles northeast to CO 20 (Crowder Rd.) on CO 17 from the junction of CO 15, and 5.5 miles southwest on SR 600 (which becomes CO 17 at the state line) from Paint Bank in Virginia.

INTRODUCTION: The **Allegheny Trail** is a 300-mile hiking trail from its junction with the **AT** in the New River Valley Ranger District to the West Virginia/Pennsylvania state line, near Bruceton Mills. It is administered by the West Virginia Scenic Trails Association. Divided into four sections, this part is in section IV (from the **AT** to Meadow Creek on Lake Sherwood Rd. near Neola, W.Va.), with nearly 30 miles finished and another 25 miles planned or under construction. The area to be completed extends from Laurel Branch north to Jerry's Run junction with I-64 in the GWNF. The part north of there, 15 miles, is now open for an ascent to the state line and a descent to follow Laurel Run in the Monongahela National Forest. (See **Allegheny Trail** in the New River Valley Ranger District in this chapter, in the James River Ranger District in Chapter 1, and in the index.)

DESCRIPTION: From the parking area on Gap Mills Road, CO 15, the trail passes a gate and descends south to parallel the road for 0.2 mile. It makes a sharp left onto a grassy forest fire road, FR 5057. On a gentle contour the trail descends from about 3,330 feet to 2,870 feet in more than 5 miles. At 2.3 miles the trail passes an open area near the crest of Peters Mountain. Although there are not any outcrops for views, this trail is most beautiful during mid-October, when leaf colors are at their peak. After curving around a few spur ridges and crossing tributaries that flow to Potts Creek, the trail reaches the end of FR 5057 at 5.6 miles. Here is a junction with abandoned Crowder Road, CO 20 (a former access road between Laurel Branch and Gap Mills). The trail turns right on Crowder Road and after 2.7 miles reaches a parking area near a gravel quarry, 0.2 mile before the road intersects with CO 17.

USGS MAP: Ronceverte; USFS TRAIL NO.: 701

## NORTH MOUNTAIN AND LICK BRANCH AREA

*Botetourt, Craig, and Roanoke Counties*

### North Mountain Trail (South)                                       302

LENGTH AND DIFFICULTY: 13.5 miles (21.6 km); moderate to strenuous

CONNECTING TRAILS: **Dragon's Tooth Trail** (1.2 mi.), **Deer Trail** (1.6 mi.), **Grouse**    299, 303–7
**Trail** (1.5 mi.), **Turkey Trail** (1.7 mi.), **Lick Branch Trail** (4.4 mi.), which connects with **Ferrier Trail** (2.3 mi.)

FEATURES: wildlife, solitude, wildflowers

TRAILHEADS: The southwestern trailhead is 2.5 miles west of Catawba on the northern side of VA 311, halfway between the SR 624 junction and the **Dragon's Tooth Trail** parking area (and 0.1 mi. west of Catawba Grocery Store). To reach the northeastern trailhead, go 6.3 miles farther north on VA 311 to the junction with SR 618 at Broad Run Trading Post. Turn right on SR 618, which becomes FR 183, and cross rocky Broad Run, sans bridges, ten times (or more during rainy season). After 7.6 miles there is roadside parking only at Stone Coal Gap near a private property road entrance sign. Another access to this point from the southeast is 2.8 miles from SR 600 (1 mi. on SR 748 and 1.8 mi. on FR 183). There may be a state road sign indicating that SR 748 is the end of the road, but it is only the end of state maintenance; FR 183 is in good condition. The SR 748 junction with SR 600 is 0.2 mile west of its junction with SR 665 (1.5 mi. south to Haymakertown), and 10.9 miles west on SR 600 and SR 799 to VA 311 at Catawba.

INTRODUCTION: During the years of litigation for secure passageway of the **AT** on Catawba Mountain, the **North Mountain Trail** became a significant alternate route. Never had its knobby ridge had such foot traffic or been so well maintained—that is, the southwestern 9 miles before it left the ridge to cross Catawba Valley. The other 4.5 miles northeast to Stone Coal Gap remained secluded. Consequently it lost its identity, and when hikers heard of the **North**

**Mountain Trail**, it was the 13.2-mile **AT** alternate, not the 13.5 miles entirely on top of North Mountain. (The former **AT** alternate is closed here. Instead, hikers wishing access to Tinker Cliffs on the **AT** can use **Andy Lane Trail** [2 mi.] described ahead.) For the purpose of distinction, this **North Mountain Trail** has "South" in its title because it is the most southwestern of five trails in the state by the same name. The trail is high and dry, and water sources are unreliable. It has at least thirty knobs, some around the side and some over the top, and a few outcrops. In a diverse hardwood forest there are patches of huckleberries, mountain laurel, wildflowers, and families of Carolina towhee, grouse, and turkey.

DESCRIPTION: From the parking area on VA 311 near the trail sign, ascend switchbacks to an outcrop for views of Sinking Creek Mountain at 1.3 miles. At 2.4 miles is the **Deer Trail**, the first of three graded side trails that descend left (north) to FR 224. (The yellow-blazed **Deer Trail** descends 1.6 mi. to a parking area on FR 224, 1.7 mi. from VA 311 and 7.1 mi. southwest from SR 618.) At 3.4 miles is a junction with the **Grouse Trail**, on the left. (It descends on a yellow-blazed trail for 1.5 mi. to FR 224, 3.5 mi. from VA 311 and 5.4 mi. southwest from SR 618.) At 6.2 miles is a junction with the **Turkey Trail**, on the left. (It descends on a yellow-blazed trail for 1.7 mi. to FR 224, 7.2 mi. from VA 311 and 1.7 mi. southwest from SR 618.) (The FR 224 entrance from VA 311 is 2.1 mi. north on VA 311 from the **North Mountain Trail** southwestern trailhead and parking area.) On the **North Mountain Trail** between the **Grouse Trail** and the **Turkey Trail**, at 5.4 miles, is the trail's highest knob (3,062 ft.). At 7.4 miles on the right is a sign pointing to an intermittent spring about 200 yards down the mountainside.

308–9   (A former alternate route, the **Catawba Creek Trail**, went east and down the mountain from here. Hikers wishing to use part of the route, now named **Andy Lane Trail**, can begin from a parking lot on SR 779 [9 mi. west from Daleville, or 8.3 mi. northeast of Catawba]. The trail enters the forest and crosses Little Catawba Creek and Catawba Creek, 0.3 mi. apart, to enter a meadow. At 1 mi. the trail leaves the valley and begins its ascent in a hollow, occasionally crossing a stream. Under the northern shadow of Tinker Cliffs Overlook, the trail steeply ascends to Scorched Earth Gap and a junction with the **AT**.)

Continuing on the **North Mountain Trail**, which becomes more overgrown with summer foliage, the trail passes under a power line at 9.9 miles. On the ridgeline the sound of a cement plant can be heard to the south. The faint yellow-blazed trail passes through groves of mountain laurel, patches of lily-of-the-valley (at 11.8 mi.), and continuous stands of blueberries. At 12.3 miles the trail veers left on a mossy area to begin the descent on two switchbacks to FR 183 at Stone Coal Gap. Exit is on an embankment, and there may not be any signs. This is the northeastern trailhead (2,118 ft.).

Across the road and 100 feet right, a bearing tree on the left is the eastern trailhead of the **Lick Branch Trail**. Follow it under a power line past a private property sign on the left to enter a hardwood forest. Ascend through a huckleberry patch. At 0.7 mile reach the ridgeline of Broad Run Mountain. Turn left at a cairn on a faint trail and faint blazes. (To the right is the **Price/Broad Mountain Trail**, which follows the ridge northeast to SR 606 and the northern section of the **Price/Broad Mountain Trail**. See Patterson and Price Mountains Area, ahead.) The **Lick Branch Trail** curves right, away from the main ridge, at 1.1 miles to descend on a spur ridge. At 1.6 miles it curves left (southwest) to the headwaters of Lick Branch and makes a junction with the **Ferrier Trail** on the right.

(The 2.3-mi. **Ferrier Trail** ascends on a slope to the thin ridgeline of Lick Mountain and follows it 1.3 mi. to a right curve on a spur ridge, parallel to Rolands Run Branch. It soon descends left and follows a grassy road to a locked gate, the end of the trail at FR 5026. A turn left here on FR 5026 will, after 1.1 mi., connect with the western trailhead of the **Lick Branch Trail**. Otherwise, a turn right on FR 5026 leads out 2.3 mi. to New Castle at the junction of SR 615/616.)

Continuing on the **Lick Branch Trail**, descend gradually for 2.8 miles and at least twenty-six rock-hoppings of the stream. There are tall hardwoods and hemlocks, rhododendron, ferns, and wildflowers such as goldstar and wild geranium. Although the gorge is narrow, there are a number of desirable flat areas for campsites. At 4.4 miles the trail ends at FR 5026 cul-de-sac, immediately after crossing the branch and passing a locked gate. It is 1.1 miles on FR 5026 to the western terminus of the **Ferrier Trail** on the right. To reach these points from New Castle by vehicle, leave the junction of SR 615 and SR 616 at First National Bank in downtown New Castle and go 1.2 miles on SR 616; turn right on SR 690, and after 0.4 mile it becomes FR 182. It is 0.5 mile farther to FR 5026, on the right.

USGS MAPS: Looney, Catawba, New Castle: USFS TRAIL NOS.: 263, 5009, 186, 188, 187, (**Andy Lane Trail**, unnumbered), 262, 189

## FENWICK MINES AREA
*Craig County*

**Fenwick Nature Walk** (1 mi.), **Fenwick Wetlands Trail** (0.8 mi.)                    310–11
LENGTH AND DIFFICULTY: 1.8 miles (2.9 km) combined, partial round-trip; easy
FEATURES: geological formations, facilities for physically disabled, history
TRAILHEAD: From the ranger station in New Castle go northeast on SR 615 for 3 miles to SR 611 (Barbours Creek Rd.) and turn left. Go 0.2 mile and turn right on SR 685, which leads into FR 181 and continues 1.8 miles on FR 181 to parking area. (Fenwick Mines Picnic Area is 0.5 mi. ahead on the right.)
INTRODUCTION: The Fenwick Mines Recreation Complex is another example of progressive leadership in the JNF not only to provide facilities to accommodate people with disabilities, but to include the general public also. The complex has a picnic area and a horse loading ramp. Overnight camping is not allowed. A

model trail/picnic area with specific tables and rest rooms for the handicapped is provided.

DESCRIPTION: From the parking area walk left on the **Fenwick Wetlands Trail**, cross Mill Creek on a bridge shaded by hemlock, and advance to a grassy open area. Ahead, the 5-foot-wide trail of wood and crushed limestone winds around a stocked fishing pond, past an observation desk, and through a marsh for 0.8 miles to a picnic area. Sweet pepperbush, cattails, wild phlox, and Joe-Pye-weed (*Eupatorium fistulosum*) are near the trail. (In folk legend, Joe Pye was a Native American who taught the colonists the healing use of the plant for fevers.) Sounds of frogs and songbirds are prominent in the spring and summer.

To the right of the parking area the self-guiding **Fenwick Nature Walk** crosses Mill Creek on a bridge and follows an old railroad grade. (From 1892 to 1923 the Low Moor Iron Company moved 938,000 tons of iron on the railroad to area furnaces.) After turning on the loop to descend, return along Mill Creek with its unique rock formations with slants, steps, flumes, and cascades. The exceptionally attractive area is shaded with tall oak, cherry, birch, and hemlock.

USGS MAP: New Castle; USFS TRAIL NOS.: 5003, 5003A, 5003B, 5007

## PATTERSON AND PRICE MOUNTAINS AREA
*Botetourt and Craig Counties*

312–19    **Patterson Mountain Trail** (5.7 mi.), **Tucker Trail** (1 mi.), **Helms Trail** (1.3 mi.), **Loop Trail** (1.3 mi.), **Elmore Trail** (1.6 mi.), **Price/Broad Mountain Trail** (10.2 mi.), **Kelly Trail** (2 mi.), **Sulphur Ridge Trail** (2.8 mi.)

LENGTH AND DIFFICULTY: 25.9 miles (41.4 km) combined; easy to strenuous

FEATURES: wildlife, wildflowers, solitude

TRAILHEADS: There is access to three southwestern trailheads: For the **Patterson Mountain Trail**, take SR 606, 9 miles west from US 220 in Fincastle, to SR 614; go 0.7 mile and turn left on SR 612. After 0.3 mile turn right on FR 184. For the **Price/Broad Mountain Trail** the trailhead is 7 miles west from US 220 in Fincastle on SR 606 at the top of a ridge with a parking area. From New Castle ranger station, go northeast on SR 615 for 4.1 miles and turn right on SR 606. Go 1.7 miles to SR 614 and turn left. Go 0.7 mile and turn left on SR 612; turn right after 0.3 mile on FR 184 to the **Patterson Mountain Trail**. The other access is at the connection with **Lick Branch Trail** as described above for North Mountain and Lick Branch.

The northeastern trailheads are accessed from US 220 near Eagle Rock at the James River. Turn west from US 220 on SR 615 for 0.9 mile to SR 685. Follow it 0.5 mile to the junction with SR 818, and follow SR 818 6.6 miles (on old railroad grade) to FR 5020 on the left. After 3.3 miles be alert for space on the side of the road to park in a slight cove. To the right about 30 feet into the woods, ascending, is the nonmaintained **Patterson Mountain Trail**. Immediately to the right is its end, cut off with a steep road embankment. Ahead, 0.7 mile, is a parking space on the left. To the right is a clear-cut and the **Elmore Trail**. There is not a sign by the USFS as to where FR 5020 ends and FR 184 begins, but follow the road another 6.5 miles to approach the southwestern trailhead of the **Patterson Mountain Trail**.

INTRODUCTION: There are eight potential loops, from 5 miles to 15 miles, and as many roadside trailheads in this network of trails when sections of FR 184 are used. The two main trails are on high mountain ridges with side trails descending into Patterson Valley, where there are frequent streams and hollows. Nearly all of the trails are signless, or signs are decayed. (In 2002 only **Sulphur Ridge Trail** was blazed yellow.) Current blazes are faint yellow. Trail usage in this area is rated low. However, this charming and diverse area of hardwoods, scattered conifers, mountain laurel (in bloom the last two weeks of May), serviceberry, blueberry, and delicate trailing phlox on the steep slopes has an appeal to hikers, birders, and hunters. Deer, turkeys, owls, and songbirds are prominent. The elevation range is from 1,250 to 2,200 feet.

DESCRIPTION: Begin at the southwestern trailhead of the **Patterson Mountain Trail** (parking space is limited to the roadside). After 1.2 miles the trail is on a more gradual grade and on the right slope of the ridge. Hardwoods dominate, but mountain laurel and white and Virginia pine offer a contrast. At 2.6 miles is a junction with the **Tucker Trail** on the right. (It leads down the ridge, steeply at first, for 1 mi. to gated FR 5015 at FR 184.) Continue ahead on the **Patterson Mountain Trail** for another 0.9 mile across a ridge spine to the **Helms Trail**, on the right, in a shallow sag.

(The **Helms Trail** descends on a scenic steep slope with well-graded switchbacks for 0.9 mi. to a junction with the **Loop Trail**. From here it continues 0.4 mi. to FR 184 at Patterson Creek. The **Loop Trail** goes east on a faint trail marked by faint yellow blazes for 0.1 mi. to a logging road. It goes downstream, and at a road fork it turns left. At a wildlife clearing it turns right on an old logging road at 0.7 mi. But after 50 ft. it turns left into blueberry bushes and a faint trail. It descends into a small gorge and follows right downstream. It then turns left up another ravine, but soon turns right to follow down another gorge to a junction with the **Elmore Trail** at 1.3 mi. To the right the **Elmore Trail** goes 0.4 mi. downstream to Patterson Creek, where it would have to be forded to reach FR 184 across the trailhead for the **Price/Broad Mountain Trail**. To the left the **Elmore Trail** ascends on the eastern slope of the gorge for 0.3 mi. to a large pine tree at FR 184. [To the right on the road it is 1.1 mi. down the mountain to the **Elmore Trail** trailhead at Patterson Creek.] After 0.1 mi. up the road, left, it leaves the road at the edge of a clear-cut [parking area is to the right] into the forest for its ascent of 0.7 mi. to the **Patterson Mountain Trail**.)

Continuing on the **Patterson Mountain Trail** from the junction with the **Helms Trail**, it is 1.5 miles on the ridge of open forest to the **Elmore Trail**. There are occasional glimpses through the foliage in the summertime of the Craig Creek Valley and Richpatch Mountains on the left (north) and Price Mountain to the right (south). In a low saddle the **Elmore Trail** is down the mountain on switchbacks to FR 184 (described above). The **Patterson Mountain Trail**, abandoned, continues on the ridge before descending on a slope to end at FR 5020/ 184 (also described above) at 5.7 miles.

If hiking the **Price/Broad Mountain Trail** from its northeastern trailhead, begin at the Patterson Creek Road. Here is a hiking logo but in 2003 no blazes or other signs. It is across the road from the **Elmore Trail**'s southern trailhead, and is 4.8 miles east of the western trailhead of the **Patterson Mountain Trail** on FR 184. (There are two streams on this road: Little Patterson Creek, which flows west after about 1.5 mi.; and Patterson Creek, which flows east for the remainder of the road in the valley.) Follow the **Price/Broad Mountain Trail** into the forest on a road to a wildlife clearing, but turn right before the clearing on a mossy road. Follow the road about 250 yards, and after crossing a small gully be alert for a footpath on the left up the slope. (An old sign to beware of the bears may be here.) Ascend to the ridgeline. After 3.1 miles is the junction with the **Kelly Trail**, on the right. (This trail descends 1.6 mi. down a steep slope to Patterson Creek. Rock-hop and pass through a flat area of tall trees to the road for 100 yd. There is neither parking space nor a sign. It is 2.4 mi. west to the trailhead of the **Patterson Mountain Trail**. It is also 0.3 mi. west of the **Tucker Trail** trailhead.)

Continuing on the **Price/Broad Mountain Trail**, the ridge crest has oak, locust, birch, and blueberry. At 4.6 miles reach a junction on the right with the **Sulphur Ridge Trail**. (At first it follows an old woods road in a 1.8-mi. descent to Sulphur Springs Branch. It then turns left, heads upstream [but may be dry in the summer], and then for 1 mi. follows another old road with banks of blueberries and scrub pine to join the trail termini with the **Price/Broad Mountain Trail** at SR 606 parking area.) From the first connection with the **Sulphur Ridge Trail**, the **Price/Broad Mountain Trail** continues another 1.2 miles before reaching SR 606, as described above for the North Mountain and Lick Branch Area. The trail now continues southwest to connect with **Lick Branch Trail**.

USGS MAPS: Oriskany, New Castle, Catawba; USFS TRAIL NOS.: 148, 191, 181, 153, 151, 334, 182, 149

## ROARING RUN AND STONY RUN AREA
*Botetourt County*

320–22  **Roaring Run Falls and Loop Trail** (1.5 mi.), **Iron Ore Trail** (2.4 mi.), **Hoop Hole Trail** (9 mi.)

LENGTH AND DIFFICULTY: 12.9 miles (20.6 km) combined, partial round-trip; easy to strenuous

FEATURES: waterfall, iron furnace ruins, wildlife, solitude

TRAILHEADS: From the junction of US 220 and SR 615 at Eagle Rock by the James River, take SR 615 northwest along Craig Creek for 6 miles to SR 621. Proceed right on SR 621 for 0.9 miles to Roaring Run Furnace Recreation Area on the left, and 0.3 miles farther to a parking area for northeastern trailheads. From Low Moor at I-64/US 60/220 (between Covington and Clifton Forge), go south 5.8 miles on SR 616 and 3.3 miles on SR 621 to the parking area. For the southern trailhead, go 3.7 miles southwest from the Roaring Run parking area to Stony Run parking area on SR 621 and SR 615.

DESCRIPTION: All these trails are listed as national recreation trails. The **Roaring Run Falls and Loop Trail** makes a loop upstream with bridge crossings from the picnic area to cascades and an umbrella waterfall. There is a heavy canopy of hardwoods and hemlock, and the stream is stocked with trout. Across the creek from the picnic area are ruins of an iron furnace. Camping is not allowed on this trail.

The yellow-blazed **Iron Ore Trail** ascends from the **Roaring Run Falls and Loop Trail** southwest on an old wagon road. It passes between Iron Ore Knob and Shoemaker Knob. After passing under a power line at 0.4 mile it turns left at 0.8 mile at an old road junction. It crosses beneath a power line again at 0.9 mile in an area of young hardwoods and pines. Fragrant trailing arbutus (*Epigaea repens*) and white-pink mountain laurel border the old roadbed. At 1.4 miles it reaches a ridge crest to enter a stand of large oaks. It ascends to another ridge at 1.8 miles and bears sharply left. (There are good campsites here.) The trail ascends steeply in a rocky section to a summit where a forest fire has destroyed most of the mature trees. At 2.2 miles a descent begins, and a junction with the **Hoop Hole Trail** is reached at 2.4 miles. Backtrack or take the **Hoop Hole Trail** loop right or left to join a shorter loop at the southern end, where it ends at SR 615.

If hiking left, follow a steep and brushy slope for 0.7 mile to a spring. At 1.6 miles are tall trees with sparse understory. Cross a headwater stream of Crawford Branch and Stony Run before reaching a junction with the double loop at 2.2 miles. To the left the trail crosses the stream near excellent campsites. It then continues downstream along Stony Run by a treacherous ravine and towering hemlocks. After crossing the stream again, it reaches a display sign and a parking area near SR 615.

If hiking the larger loop, right from the **Iron Ore Trail**, the route is more strenuous, reclusive, and rarely maintained. It ascends and descends a knob to the eastern side of a sag and then climbs to Pine Mountain at 1 mile. On a rocky isolated ridge it ascends another knob (3,341 ft.) and at 2 miles curves to the southern side of a peak on Rich Patch Mountain. In a steep descent it veers west of Bald Knob to rapidly descend into the headwaters gorge of Hipes Branch. Rhododendron, hemlock, ferns, and wildflowers are here at 3.1 miles. After crossing the stream the trail turns east across the shoe of Bald Knob to a junction left and right at 3.8 miles with the shorter loop. A turn left is 0.3 mile east across a fork of Stony Run to complete the longer loop. To continue on the western side of the shorter loop, the trail parallels a fork and then the main stream of Hipes Run in a narrow gorge for nearly 1 mile. Abruptly it changes to a northeastern direction and slight ascent on its mountainside route to complete the loop at Stony Run and the parking area. There is a signboard 0.1 mile before the parking area.

USGS MAP: Strom; USFS TRAIL NOS.: 264, 264A, 5004, 5001

323 **Craig Creek Trail**

LENGTH AND DIFFICULTY: 2.1 miles (3.4 km) round-trip; easy

FEATURES: fishing, wildflowers

TRAILHEAD: Craig Creek Recreation Area is 9 miles northeast of Fenwick Mines and 10.6 miles southwest of Roaring Run on SR 615. From the junction of SR 615 and SR 817 in Oriskany it is 0.4 mile on SR 817 to FR 5075 for a right turn.

DESCRIPTION: This nonblazed trail is within an oxbow of Craig Creek at the northern base of Patterson Mountain. Its termini are at the first trail sign and at the Craig Creek picnic area. On the left side of the slope the trail ascends in a young hardwood forest with a ravine to the ridge top at 0.2 mile where the trail loop divides. There are mountain laurel, woodmint, and huckleberry. Turn right to reach a grassy and scenic field at 1 mile, where deer and woodchuck are among sundrops and other wildflowers. At the parking area, follow the creek downstream to an old woods road. Turn left and ascend to a ridge and to the trail origin.

USGS MAP: Oriskany; USFS TRAIL NO.: 5006

## New River Valley Ranger District

*(Former Blacksburg and Wythe Ranger Districts)*

The former Blacksburg and Wythe Ranger Districts are now administratively merged to form the New River Valley Ranger District. For clarity of trail location, the trails are grouped separately according to the former district boundaries, beginning with Blacksburg. Although the district is geographically segmented into three areas, the **AT** connects them by crossing the New River between Narrows and Pearisburg and Sinking Creek Valley east of Newport. Within the geographical segments are eight recreational/activity sites described below.

The district's southwestern section, southwest of Pearisburg, extends from Brushy Mountain north to Wolf Creek Mountain and includes two nonfee campgrounds near each other by Dismal Creek: Walnut Flats and White Pine Horse Camp. These camping areas provide camping and trailer sites, rest rooms, and

*Falls of Dismal Creek Trail, New River Valley Ranger District*

drinking water. Fishing is available at White Pine Horse Camp. At the campgrounds are accesses to six connecting trails for hikers and equestrians on 15.2 miles plus USFS gated roads. The trails range in distance for short loops in the Dismal Creek Valley to the ridgeline of Flat Top Mountain. They are **Hoof and Hill** **Trail** (1.7 mi.), orange blazed; **Little Horse Trail** (5.3 mi.), nonblazed; **Pearis Thompson Trail** (3.4 mi.), orange blazed; **Pebble Loop Trail** (0.7 mi.), non-

324–26

327–28　blazed; **Standrock Branch Trail** (1.3 mi.), nonblazed; and **Ribble Trail** (2.8 mi.), nonblazed. Access from Crandon on VA 42 east is 3.8 miles to SR 606, left. After 0.4 mile on SR 606 is a crossing of the **AT**, at which is Trents Grocery Store (276-928-1349) with its services to both **AT** hikers and users of the campgrounds. At 1 mile on SR 606 turn right on SR 671 (may be SR 201 on maps) and follow it to a USFS road. After 1.7 miles arrive at the camping area. Along the way (0.9 mi. from

329　SR 606), right, is roadside parking for the steep 100-yard **Dismal Falls Trail**. It has a scenic multilayered fall and pool.

Peters Mountain, the boundary between Virginia and West Virginia, plus a southwestern corner of Monroe County in West Virginia, and south to Hohn Creek Mountain comprise the northern section of the district. In this section is fee-required White Rock Campground. It has forty-nine camping and trailer units with a dump station, grills, rest rooms, drinking water, fishing, and wildlife view-

330　ing. At the campground is **Virginia's Walk**, a 1.3-mile nonblazed trail. You can begin the loop at the upper camping driveway. The trail crosses tributaries of White Rock Branch and twice crosses the Virginia/West Virginia state line in and out of the Mountain Lake Wilderness Area. Vascular plants include oak, maple, birch, hemlock, haw, orchid, wild phlox, and itchweed (*Lygodium palmatum*). The poisonous roots of the latter can be made commercially into an insecticide powder. You may see deer, raccoons, birds, and salamanders along the trail. Access is from US 460 southeast of Pearisburg, and across the New River bridge, to turn north on SR 635 for 16 miles to Kire intersection. Turn right on SR 613 for 0.8 mile, and turn left on FR 645 to the campground. On your way from US 460 you passed two other small recreation sites. The first is Interior Picnic Area, 10.8 miles on SR 635 from US 460. On a grassy site under some white pines are picnic tables, grills, and hand pump for water. Fishing is nearby at Big Stony Creek. Proceeding

331　east for 0.6 mile is Cherokee Flats, left. The site has **Cherokee Trail**, constructed for the mobility impaired. On grated bridges the trail is through hemlock, rhododendron, and hardwoods for 0.2 mile to Big Stony Creek for wildlife observation. A scenic fisherman's trail continues upstream on a less maintained route for 0.4 mile. (Near Cherokee Flats is a parking area and kiosk for **AT** hikers crossing SR 635.) A fourth recreation site in this general area is fee-required Cascades Recreation Area. Access is from US 460 in Pembroke north on SR 623 for 4 miles. It has picnic units with tables and grills, flush toilets, and water fountains all accessible to mobility-impaired users. (Trails at this location are described ahead.) This part of the district has two wilderness areas: Peters Mountain Wilderness (3,325 acres) on the southeastern slope of Peters Mountain, and Mountain Lake Wilderness (11,311 acres) on a highland plateau of the Eastern Continental Divide north of Johns Creek to Little Mountain. The **AT** passes through both wildernesses.

Forming the southeastern section of the district, near Blacksburg, is a long strip of Brush Mountain and Sinking Creek Mountain. Between them is Poverty Creek west and Craig Creek east. As with the northern section this part of the district adjoins the New Castle Ranger District in the northeast. There are two recreation areas in this section. One is Pandapas Pond Recreation Area. Access is 3 miles north of Blacksburg on US 460 from the north intersection of US 460 and downtown US 460 Bus. The area has two large parking lots, one near the entrance mainly for equestrians, and another closer to the lake for hikers and mountain bikers. Camping is not allowed. Provided are picnic tables, rest rooms, and fishing. There are four trails used for hiking only. Access them from the end of the parking lot near the lake. Descend 0.2 mile on a well-designed trail to the rest room and lake. Turn right or left on the 0.7-mile **Pandapas Pond Trail**. If going right pass 332–48 the **Poverty Creek Connector Trail** (0.2 mi.) near the dam at 0.1 mile. At 0.2 mile pass a cove with azaleas, asters, thistles, hardwoods, and evergreens. Enter another cove, after which you come to an intersection at 0.4 mile. Turn left to cross the lake on a boardwalk and complete the loop at 0.7 mile. (If going ahead at the intersection you will connect with **Ladyslipper Trail** [0.3 mi.], a nonblazed foot trail, which connects with **Larkspur Trail** [0.3 mi.], nonblazed. See below.) Farther up the lake is connecting **Wetland Boardwalk Trail** for a 0.2-mile loop. Here are waterlilies, willows, and tag alders. Thirteen multi-use trails are listed here, with a total mileage of 21.3 miles, plus forest roads. The trails connect and make multiple loops downstream and up and down the mountainsides: **Horse Nettle Trail** (3 mi.), blazed orange; **Indian Pipe Trail** (0.5 mi.), nonblazed; **Jacob's Ladder Trail** (1.3 mi.), blazed orange; **Joe Pye Trail** (1.2 mi.), blazed orange; **Pebble Loop Trail** (0.7 mi.), nonblazed; **Larkspur Trail** (0.3 mi.), nonblazed; **Poverty Creek Trail** (7.2 mi.), blazed orange; **Powerline Trail** (1 mi.), blazed orange; **Prickley Pear Trail** (0.8 mi.), nonblazed; **Queen Anne Trail** (1.2 mi.), blazed orange; **Skullcap Trail** (1.6 mi.), nonblazed; **Snake Root Trail** (2.1 mi.), nonblazed; and **Trillium Trail** (1.1 mi.), nonblazed.

The other recreation area is Caldwell Fields, a group of three fields for group activities. Addison field is open to the public for day use only without fee. The other two fields require fee reservation and may be used for overnight groups up to 120 users and forty cars per field. There is a vault toilet but no drinking water. Nearby is Craig Creek, a stocked trout stream. Access is from US 460, opposite the highway from the Pandapas Pond entrance, on SR 621 (Craig Creek Rd.) for 8.6 miles. At the fields FR 630 goes north 0.7 mile to a roadside parking area for **Sarver Trail** (1.1 mi.). Park under the power line and ascend under it to a curve 349 right into the forest at 0.1 mile. Ascend steeply through hardwoods, yellow pine, and patches of trailing arbutus. At 0.8 mile arrive at a pioneer homesite. A spring is nearby. After another 0.3 mile intersect with the **AT**.

All sections of the district have large and small game animals, and the best trout streams are Big Stony Creek, Craig Creek, and Dismal Creek. The district has 176 miles of forest roads. Through the 110,100-acre district pass 83.2 miles of the **AT**. It enters from the west at SR 608 (the former Wythe Ranger District border) northeast of Crandon, and from the east of SR 620 (the New Castle Ranger District border) west of Catawba (see Chapter 3). Other than the **AT** there are 47 trails (of which 15 are blazed and 22 are multi-use) with a total of 72 miles. In the Mountain Lake Wilderness area there is not a trail to Mann's Bogg, and the usfs discourages unscientific usage of this and other sensitive environments. Near the wilderness area and off sr 613 are trails at the University of Virginia Biological Station. They are not open to the public except by advance permission. Private Mountain Lake resort trails, also on sr 613 and near the station, require permission from the management at the time of visitation.

ADDRESSES AND INFORMATION: New River Valley Ranger District (Blacksburg Office), 110 Southpark Dr., Blacksburg, va 24060; phone: 540-552-4641; Wytheville Office, 155 Sherwood Forest Rd., Wytheville, va 24382; phone: 540-228-5551.

## CASCADES RECREATION AREA
*Giles County*

350–52 **Cascades Trail** (3.8 mi.), **Conservancy Trail** (3.6 mi.), **Barney's Wall Trail** (0.4 mi.)

LENGTH AND DIFFICULTY: 7.8 miles (12.5 km) combined, round-trip; moderate to strenuous

FEATURES: waterfall, cliffs, trout stream, scenic views

TRAILHEAD: In Pembroke on us 460 take sr 623 north for 3.5 miles to the parking lot at Cascades Recreation Area, a day-use facility.

INTRODUCTION: At the parking lot are rest rooms, a picnic ground, a host's cabin, and short trails to the creek for mobility- impaired populations. The major attraction here is the Cascades. The **Cascades Trail** (1.9 mi. one way) is a national recreation trail, designated in 1979. Popular and spectacular, the Cascades has a claim to being one of Virginia's most photographed waterfalls. Making a dramatic 66-foot drop into an oval pool, it is one of two major falls on Little Stony Creek. Its headwaters are 7 miles upstream in a red spruce bog near Lone Pine Peak in the Mountain Lake Wilderness Area and are fed by eight other significant streams from Big and Butt Mountains. (Although the **Conservancy Trail**'s western trailhead can be reached by vehicle on sr 714, it is included as a backtracking trail here because sr 714 may be rough and muddy in inclement weather. Also, the eastern trailhead is not on sr 714 but makes an easy connection with the **Cascades Trail**.)

DESCRIPTION: From the parking area the inviting trail goes 0.2 mile to a junction. Take the right route, cross the footbridge over Little Stony Creek (which is stocked with rainbow and brook trout). The trail ascends over rocks and webs of tree roots by rare wildflowers. Cross another footbridge at 1.6 miles, turn right, and reach the Cascades at 1.9 miles. On the western wall is an observation deck. (Climbing the side walls in the gorge is prohibited.) Backtrack, but for a different return do not cross the footbridge after 0.2 mile. Instead take the first right from the waterfalls, ascend 100 yards to an old wagon road, and turn left to follow its descent to the parking lot.

At the junction with the wagon road the **Conservancy Trail** (1.8 mi. one way) begins. It goes up the old road in an archway of rhododendron for 0.6 mile to a fork; turn left. (The jeep road on the right descends to the Upper Cascades.) Immediately after this fork is a second fork. The wagon road goes ahead, but the **Conservancy Trail** turns left up the ridge on an older road and through hardwoods. After another 0.3 mile cross a stream in a rhododendron and hemlock thicket, and continue the ascent. Along the way **Barney's Wall Trail** goes left for 0.2 mile to a precipitous outcropping with magnificent vistas of the gorge and beyond to the New River Valley. (For an extended hike, you may turn left on the road after reaching SR 714. The road continues west, first near the rim, then in a cove, and finally onto a plateau with a field and views from large cliffs at Butt Mountain. A closed fire tower is nearby, but it can be reached on a short hike behind the gate. Panoramic views are of Pearis Mountain in Virginia and the Peters Mountain range on the Virginia/West Virginia boundary. Backtrack.) (On SR 714 it is 6.4 mi. to SR 613, 1.2 mi. southwest of Mountain Lake Resort.)

USGS MAP: Eggleston; USFS TRAIL NOS.: 70, 7013, 7013A

## PETERS MOUNTAIN AREA
*Giles County, Virginia, and Monroe County, West Virginia*

### Allegheny Trail 238
LENGTH AND DIFFICULTY: 12.7 miles (20.3 km); moderate to strenuous
FEATURES: Hanging Rock, wildlife, wildflowers
TRAILHEADS. Access to the northeastern trailhead from Waiteville, West Virginia, is 0.8 mile on WV 17 northeast to CO 636 (Gap Mills Rd.), where it is 3.5 miles left (north) to a parking area on the left at the top of Peters Mountain. (Access here from the northern side of Peters Mountain is on CO 15, 5.4 mi. southwest from Gap Mills at WV 3). The southwestern trailhead can be reached via the **AT** from SR 635 in Virginia. From US 460, southeast of Pearisburg, it is 10 miles on SR 635 to Stony Creek bridge (1 mi. west of Interior Picnic Area). From a small parking space it is 40 yards to the **AT** and a left turn. Pass Pine Swamp Branch Shelter at 0.4 mile and ascend steeply to the top of Peters Mountain, where at 1.9 miles is a blue-blazed 0.2-mile connector to the **Allegheny Trail**. (Or continue on the **AT** for 0.2 mi. to the yellow-blazed **Allegheny Trail** on the right.) The southwestern access from West Virginia is from Sugar Camp Farm parking area. It is accessible from the junction of US 219 and Painters Run Road (CO 219/21) 2.4 miles southwest of Lindside on US 219. After 1.2 miles on Painters Run Road turn left at the junction with Green Valley Road (CO 219/24) and proceed 0.5 mile to the parking area. Access from the parking area is on 1.8-mile blue-blazed

353 **Groundhog Trail**, which ascends the northern side of Peters Mountain with switchbacks to junction with the **AT**. It is 3.3 miles northeast on the **AT** to the **Allegheny Trail**.

INTRODUCTION: The **Allegheny Trail** in this district is the southwestern terminus of a 300-mile footpath that extends from here to the West Virginia/Pennsylvania state line, near Bruceton Mills. Administrative management is by the West Virginia Scenic Trails Association, and the trail is divided into four corridor sections. This part of the trail is in Section IV; at least 50 miles are planned to connect with Section III at Meadow Creek on Lake Sherwood Road near Neola, West Virginia. Planning and construction are under way to complete the trail through Alleghany County, Virginia, south from Jerry's Run at I-64, and into the northeastern area of Craig County near Paint Bank in Virginia. (See New Castle Ranger District in this chapter.)

DESCRIPTION: In an open hardwood forest the trail begins as a footpath, but after 0.7 mile it becomes a forest road for 4WDS, used mainly by hunters. Here and throughout the traverse you are likely to see or hear deer, turkeys, grouse, hawks, and chipmunks. The trail passes a private cottage on the northern side and a dirt road that descends on private property on the northern side. At 4.3 miles the old road becomes a foot trail. To the left is a private grassy field with apple trees and deer blinds. There is a scenic rock formation at 5.6 miles, after which the foot trail becomes an old road again in a hardwood forest. White snakeroot and fern patches are frequent. At 8.1 miles the trail crosses from Virginia into West Virginia. After 9.3 miles there is a gradual descent on a scenic old road to a damp area among mountain laurel. At 10.1 miles, on the right is a locked gated road near a spring. Soon the trail becomes a path to a field with dewberries and shooting stars (*Dodecatheon meadia*). The trail leaves the leeward side and crosses to a rocky area at 11.5 miles in its approach to Hanging Rock Raptor Migration Observatory (3,812 ft.). Formerly a fire tower, it has a railed deck for a 360° view of Peters Mountain and the valleys below in both states. The descent continues to the parking area at Mill Gap Rd (CO 15). The area is good for bird-watching.

USGS MAPS: Interior, Waiteville; USFS TRAIL NOS.: 65, 701

## HUCKLEBERRY RIDGE AREA
*Giles County*

354 **Flat Peter Loop Trail**

LENGTH AND DIFFICULTY: 8 miles (12.8 km); moderate

FEATURES: old-growth hemlock, wildlife

TRAILHEAD: From US 460, southeast of Pearisburg, travel on SR 635 for 13.5 miles to FR 772 on the left. After 0.2 mile is a parking area for gated Kelly Flats Road (FR 942).

DESCRIPTION: Also called the **Huckleberry Loop Trail**, it is an excellent loop for the study of flora and fauna and Peters Mountain tributaries to Stony Creek. From the gate the yellow-blazed trail continues up the road and after 0.5 mile leaves the road on the right in a young hardwood forest. It rock-hops North Fork Creek, follows upstream for 1 mile to a clearing, crosses the creek again to the former **Dixon Branch Trail** north of Huckleberry Ridge to rock-hop 1.7 miles 355–56 upstream. At the headwaters is a virgin stand of hemlock. At 3.3 miles the trail crosses a saddle on Huckleberry Ridge for a left turn on former **Dismal Branch Trail**. (The trail enters Peters Mountain Wilderness Area after it crosses the saddle and is difficult to follow from here to Kelly Flats Rd. Future work is planned on this portion to make it easier to follow.) It proceeds downstream, sometimes in the middle of the creek bed, among rhododendron slicks. Its junction with old Kelly Flats logging road, FR 10400, is at 5.5 miles. A turn left followed by crossing Laurel Branch at 6.5 miles brings the hiker to a field of wildflowers, birds, butterflies, and, occasionally, grazing deer. The loop is completed at a gate near the parking area.

USGS MAP: Interior; USFS TRAIL NO.: 52

## MOUNTAIN LAKE WILDERNESS AREA
*Giles County*

**War Spur Loop Trail** (1.7 mi.), **War Spur Connector Trail** (1.1 mi.), **War Spur**   357–59
**Overlook Trail** (0.1 mi.)

LENGTH AND DIFFICULTY: 3.3 miles (5.3 km) combined, round-trip; easy
FEATURES: overlook, old-growth hemlock, wilderness
TRAILHEAD: From US 460 at Hodges Chapel, west of Newport, travel on SR 613 for 7.2 miles (along the way is Mountain Lake Resort and a junction with SR 700 at 4.8 mi., and University of Virginia Biological Station at 5.7 mi.). Access from SR 635, coming south on SR 613, is 5.2 miles.
INTRODUCTION: Salt Pond Mountain, on the Eastern Continental Divide, may be the district's most diverse and significant natural environment. For nearly 7 miles from Bald Knob (4,363 ft.) near Mountain Lake in the southwest, to Wind Rock (4,128 ft.) and Potts Mountain in the northeast, the mountain plateau is a master field trip for biologists and geologists. There are cliffs and jumbled mounds of Tuscarora sandstone, swales, bogs, virgin forests, rare plants and animals, and a 25-acre natural lake (3,875 ft., the highest in the state). More than twenty streams have their headwaters in this natural showplace. One stream, Little Stony Creek, with its headwaters in a red spruce bog, is the source of Cascade Falls. In 1960 the USFS set aside a 1,583-acre tract for preservation. It became part of the 6,900 acres included in the Wilderness Study Area in 1975. In 1984 and 1988 Congress approved the Mountain Lake Wilderness with 11,113 acres, 2,500 of which are in West Virginia.

DESCRIPTION: From the parking area the **War Spur Loop Trail** goes to the right through a mixed forest with an understory of striped maples, azaleas, ferns, and carpets of wintergreen. At its junction with the **War Spur Overlook Trail** there is a short side trail to an overlook (3,650 ft.) with impressive views of War Spur Hollow, Johns Creek Valley, and other parts of the wilderness area. The **War Spur Loop Trail** descends to War Spur Branch and a stand of virgin hemlock and red spruce at 1.8 miles. After an ascent and junction with the **War Spur Connector Trail**, it is 0.9 mile right on a grassy treadway to the **AT**. Backtrack to the parking area on the connector. (A loop of 6.2 mi. can be made by hiking the **AT** north and west [past Wind Rock] to SR 613 for a return on the road, right, to the parking area.)

USGS MAPS: Eggleston, Interior, Waiteville; USFS TRAIL NOS.: 68, 68A, 69

## JOHNS CREEK AND MOUNTAIN AREA
*Giles and Craig Counties*

360 **Johns Creek Mountain Trail**

LENGTH AND DIFFICULTY: 2.9 miles (4.6 km); moderate

FEATURE: rock outcrops

TRAILHEADS: From Newport go east on VA 42 for 1.1 miles, turning left on SR 601 for 6 miles to Rocky Gap parking area. The eastern trailhead is on Maggie Road (SR 658), 1.5 miles south to VA 24 near Simmonsville, and 2.7 miles north to SR 632 near Maggie.

DESCRIPTION: From the parking area the 0.5 mile is a southeastern access route on the **AT** up the old Kelly Knob fire tower road. On the way are views of Salt Pond Mountain, Potts Mountain, and Johns Creek Valley. The trail turns left from the **AT** on the ridge crest. At 0.6 mile the trail crosses a forest road, and again at 2.2 miles. There are rock outcrops and other scenic spots along the ridge in an oak/hickory forest. Views from the ridge include Sinking Creek and Sinking Creek Mountain to the south.

USGS MAPS: Waiteville, Newport; USFS TRAIL NO.: 57

361 **Sartain Trail**

LENGTH AND DIFFICULTY: 8.4 miles (13.4 km) round-trip; moderate

FEATURES: walnut grove, wildflowers, wildlife

TRAILHEAD: From Newport go east on VA 42 for 1.1 miles, turning left on SR 601 for 8.1 miles to SR 632. After a turn left on SR 632 (becomes FR 156) proceed 0.8 mile to the parking area. Going west on VA 42, turn right on SR 658, past Simmonsville, and drive 4.1 miles to SR 632, where a left turn is 4.9 miles from the parking area.

DESCRIPTION: Formerly the **Johns Creek Trail**, the new name is from Sartain Branch, one of a number of Salt Pond Mountain drains that cross the trail. The trail is in the Mountain Lake Wilderness Area, and the trailhead is near the **AT** crossing of FR 156. At first the trail goes north to skirt an inholding, but after 1 mile it returns to the old Johns Creek wagon road where gold star (*Hypoxis hirsuta*) flowers are prominent. After nine stream crossings there is a campsite at 2.5 miles near a double white oak and the mouth of Sartain Branch. At 3.2 miles is an open black walnut grove with some trees more than 9 feet in circumference. The trail ends at patches of blackberries and flame azaleas under a power line at 4.2 miles. Views of the cliffs on Salt Pond Mountain are of the northwest. Backtrack.

USGS MAPS: Waiteville, Newport; USFS TRAIL NO.: 1068

## Former Wythe Ranger District

The 170,000-acre former Wythe Ranger District is now part of the New River Valley Ranger District. It has long, wide strips of mountain ranges. The two longest are Brushy and Walker Mountains in a northeast-southwest direction. Flowing between them are the North Fork of the Holston River, which flows southwest from the center of the district, and Walker Creek to the northeast. In the most southwestern corner of the district are shorter mountain ranges of Pond and Glade Mountains. Between them is the Mount Rogers National Recreation Area and I-81. The northeastern corner of the district adjoins former Blacksburg Ranger District. On the district's edges are towns such as Tazewell, Marion, Wytheville, and Pulaski. Hungry Mother State Park, which adjoins the district, is 3 miles north of Marion. On the Brushy Mountain range are two wilderness areas: Beartown (5,109 acres), west of Burke's Garden; and Kimberling Creek (5,542 acres), northeast of the community of Bastian. Burke's Garden is an enormous, craterlike agricultural bowl whose ellipsoidal rim is district property. It reaches an elevation of 4,710 feet at the eastern edge of Beartown Mountain. On the southern rim are 8 miles of the **AT**. The garden was a Shawnee Indian hunting ground when Englishman James Burke discovered it in the 1750s. The easiest entrance route is on SR 623, from VA 61, east of Tazewell. Kimberling Creek Wilderness Area's main feature is its wildness with little evidence of human habitation. South of the major mountain ranges is I-81, which runs through the Great Valley, and north through the center is I-77, which passes through a 1-mile tunnel in Big Walker Mountain.

There are four recreational areas: Stony Fork Campground is on SR 717, 4 miles west from I-77, exit 9, and 8 miles north on US 52 from I-81, exit 21. In a forest of hardwoods and rhododendron, this model facility has single and double units, flush toilets, showers, and trailer waste disposal station. From a nature trail is the western trailhead of the **Seven Sisters Trail**. The other three recreational areas are picnic areas at Dark Horse Hollow, 5.5 miles north of Wytheville on US 52; Big

Bend, 12 miles farther north on US 52 and east on FR 206; and Wolf Creek, 3.5 miles west from I-77, exit 58 and access US 52 and west on SR 614.

Stocked trout streams include the East Fork of Stony Fork (see Stony Fork Campground, above); Reed Creek (see **Crawfish Horse Trail**, formerly **Channel Rock Trail**, ahead); the South Fork of the Holston River, west of Sugar Grove; and Wolf Creek (see **Wolf Creek Trail**, ahead).

There are two special points of interest in the former district. In Groseclose there is the 180-acre Settlers Museum of Southwest Virginia, a joint project with the USFS and Charles Phillippi, for a planned living history farm. The **AT** passes through it. The other unique feature is the Big Walker Mountain Scenic Byway. For 16.2 miles, beginning at the junction of I-77, exit 47 on SR 717, the leisure motor route goes west, past the Stony Creek Campground, and ascends and descends Big Walker Mountain on US 52/21 to VA 42. There are stops along the way for observing wildflowers (and sometimes wildlife), history markers, an observation tower, and at the crest of Big Walker Mountain is a 1-mile trail on the former **AT** to Monster Rock. (Also on the former **AT** is now yellow-blazed **Walker Mountain Horse Trail** for 12.3 mi. It joins the orange-blazed **Crawfish Horse Trail** on Brushy Mountain.)

The former district has 61 miles of the **AT** from the boundary of the Mount Rogers National Recreation Area near I-81 to Crandon at the boundary of the former Blacksburg Ranger District. In addition to the **AT** there are 55 miles of other trails, a variety of blue-blazed spur trails from the **AT**, and a 10-mile horse trail. Two blue-blazed alternates on the **AT** are the **Boss Trail** (2 mi.) (named in honor of Keith Smith of Virginia Tech Outing Club) and the **High Water Trail** (2.7 mi.) (used when Little Wolf Creek floods) at SR 615, off VA 42, west of Bland. The **Roaring Fork Trail** (2.3 mi.) is an unmaintained route to the confluence of Roaring Fork and Cove Branch gorge in remote Beartown Wilderness (accessible from FR 631 and FR 222 from SR 625, north of VA 42 at Ceres). **Wolf Creek Trail** and **Wolf Creek Nature Trail** are now combined for 2.4 miles, 3.5 miles west of I-77, exit 58, on SR 614; and four trails at Peak Creek Opportunity Area (near Gatewood Reservoir west of Pulaski). (The latter trails are on the district's inventory, but are not blazed, signed, or maintained. They are **Beaver Hut Trail** [0.4 mi.], **Blue Gill Trail** [0.2 mi.], **Citation Trail** [0.2 mi.], and **Ridge Trail** [1 mi.].) There are some other unblazed and unsigned trails. The 1.2-mile dead-end **Round Mountain Trail** is described by Robert Tennison as a "troad" (trail road). On the north side of Round Mountain it is accessible off US 52, 1.1 miles north of Bastian, then west on FR 688 for 0.5 mile, right. The 2-mile **Lynn Camp Trail** is another "troad" that is used by maintenance crews to access the Knot Maul shelter **AT** area. Access is off VA 42, at Ceres, north on SR 625 for 1.6 miles to FR 632, left. **Lick Creek Trail** has 2.3 miles to a dead end as "troad" on an old logging road. Access is off VA 42 at Sharon Springs, north over Brushy Mountain on SR 623 for 2.6 miles to the creek,

362

363–65

366–67

368–72

373

374

left. All trails in the district have low traffic volume, except the **Stony Fork Nature Trail**, which is moderate. The **Crawfish Horse Trail** (10 mi.) is an orange-blazed  375 equestrian loop. It parallels Reed Creek in Crawfish Valley, crosses the Tennessee Valley Divide on Walker Mountain, follows part of Bear Creek and high ridges of Brushy Mountain, and passes through a gorge of Channel Rock Hollow. Access from I-81, exit 60, is north on SR 617 to Blacklick, left on SR 625, which becomes FR 727, and to a gate and parking lot.

ADDRESS AND INFORMATION: Wytheville Office: 155 Sherwood Forest Rd., Wytheville, VA 24382; phone: 276-228-5551. Available are district trail maps, camping and scenic byway flyers, and wilderness areas brochure with maps.

## STONY FORK AREA
*Wythe County*

**Stony Fork Nature Trail** (1 mi.), **Seven Sisters Trail** (4.8 mi.)  376–77
LENGTH AND DIFFICULTY: 5.8 miles (9.3 km) combined, partial round-trip; easy to
  moderate
FEATURES: nature study, trout stream, wildlife
TRAILHEADS: From I-77, exit 47, on SR 717, go 1.3 miles to eastern trailhead, and 2.6
  miles farther on SR 717 to Stony Fork Campground and western trailhead.
DESCRIPTION: Begin at campsite #32 and follow a yellow blaze through locust, Virginia pine, hemlock, and oak with understory of striped green maple and laurel
  in a loop. The **Stony Fork Nature Trail** continues right at 0.4 mile for a return to
  the campground; the **Seven Sisters Trail** begins on the left. It ascends on a ridge
  to curve in a hollow at 0.6 mile. Here the forest is filled with black cohosh, laurel,
  and maple. At 0.9 mile the trail enters another hollow with fragmented shale
  and continues on a ridge among chestnut oak. It reaches the crest of Little
  Walker Mountain at 1.1 miles, where it follows the ridgeline with oak, maple,
  wintergreen, and galax. At 1.7 miles is the highest peak (3,310 ft.) on the trail.
  From here the trail descends to other peaks at 2.5 miles and 2.9 miles. It reaches
  an old forest road at 3.8 miles, turns left to follow a wide mossy treadway, and
  descends to the base of the mountain at East Fork at 4.7 miles. Here are tall white
  pines and dense rhododendron. It is 90 yards to the parking area at SR 717.
USGS MAPS: Big Bend, Crockett; USFS TRAIL NOS.: 6502, 6509

## TRACK FORK AREA
*Wythe and Pulaski Counties*

**Track Fork Trail** (4 mi.), **Polecat Trail** (1.4 mi.)  378–79
LENGTH AND DIFFICULTY: 5.4 miles (8.6 km) combined; easy to moderate
FEATURES: stream, wildlife, historic site

TRAILHEADS: There are three vehicular access routes to the *Track Fork Trail* and two to the **Polecat Trail**. The northern route from I-77, exit 47, begins on SR 717 (east from Stony Fork Campground) and goes east 2 miles to a junction with SR 601 and 603. Continue east on SR 601 for 10.1 miles and turn right (south) on SR 600. After 2.5 miles, reach the crest of Little Walker Mountain and the western trailhead on the left. This point can also be reached by turning right on SR 603 (from SR 717 described above) for 4.6 miles to the junction on the left with SR 600. Follow SR 600 through beautiful Crockett Cove Valley, pass FR 707 after 6.9 miles, and ascend to the trailhead after another 1.3 miles. (From the FR 707 junction, it is 2.8 mi. east to the **Polecat Trail** trailhead.) Another access to SR 600 is from I-77 in Wytheville. After turning north from I-81, turn right on the first ramp, exit 41, to SR 610 (Peppers Ferry Rd.) and turn right again. Cross I-77, go under I-81, and after 0.3 miles turn right on SR 603 (Cove Rd.). Cross over I-81 and follow SR 603 for 4.2 miles to SR 600 on the right. (If coming east on I-81, take exit 72 and follow above directions.) To approach the eastern trailhead from I-81 take exit 94 onto VA 99 north through Pulaski where it becomes SR 738 (Robinson Tract Rd.). After 4 miles turn left on SR 641 (Cox Hollow Rd.). Follow it and FR 692 for 3.8 miles to the parking area and trailhead. The south approach to the **Polecat Trail** is from I-81/77 at Fort Chiswell. Drive 3 miles north on VA 121 and SR 610 through Max Meadows to the junction with SR 712. Follow SR 712 for 6 miles to FR 707 on the left; ascend and descend for 1.8 miles to roadside parking on the left and trailhead on the right.

DESCRIPTION: These remote trails are frequented with turkeys, deer, raccoons, skunks, and songbirds. If entering **Track Fork Trail** from the eastern trailhead, proceed upstream on a wide old wagon road near a timber cut. The forest contains white pines, hemlocks, rhododendrons, hardwoods, and wildflowers among ferns. Near one of the Track Fork crossings at 1 mile is a junction with the **Polecat Trail** on the left. (It goes 1.4 mi. to FR 707.) At 1.3 miles the trail crosses into Wythe County from Pulaski County and ascends to a ridge saddle at 2.5 miles. Here is a sunny, grassy area for a good campsite. An old wagon road used by pioneers veers from the trail. From here the trail ascends on the southern slope of Little Walker Mountain, passes an old road, on the left, at 3.6 miles, and reaches SR 600 at 4 miles.

If entering the **Polecat Trail** from FR 707, follow an old railroad grade to cross a tributary of Peak Creek at 0.6 mile. Cross the stream again at 0.8 mile. There are excellent campsites in this area of tall hardwoods and rhododendron patches. The trail abruptly climbs a ridge at 1 mile, then descends to cross a tributary of Track Fork. Among rhododendron and witch hazel the trail reaches the **Track Fork Trail** at 1.4 miles. (It is 1 mi. right to the parking area of FR 692, and 3 mi. left to SR 600.)

USGS MAP: Long Spur; USFS TRAIL NOS.: 6516, 6517

# Mount Rogers National Recreation Area

Virginia's highest and most spectacular land mass is a 60-mile series of mountain ranges from Damascus to the New River. Easily a star attraction, it is between the Great Valley on the north and North Carolina on the south. It is Mount Rogers National Recreation Area, Virginia's unique national forest district. It is unique because its scenic beauty and potential for varied recreation prompted Congress to designate this natural wonder a national recreation area in 1966. Like a diamond in Mount Rogers's crown of jewels is Grayson Highlands State Park, centrally adjoining on the southern side. Within the Mount Rogers NRA's 117,000 acres are seven family campgrounds, of which all except one have spaces for RV camping. There are four horse camps. A large new horse camp is planned on the south side of SR 603 across from the Fox Creek Horse Camp. There are three wildernesses, four special management areas, and a vast network of trails. Although the Mount Rogers area is particularly scenic throughout, what most significantly sets it apart from other Virginia mountain areas is the boreal crest zone. The zone frames Whitetop Mountain (5,530 ft.) in the west, Mount Rogers (5,729 ft.) in the center, and the three peaks of Pine Mountain (4,859 ft.) in the east. Inside are extensive alpine mountain balds, dense red spruce (*Picea rubens*), oleoresin fragrant Fraser's fir (*Abies franseri*), dazzling displays of purple rhododendron, and matchless views from rocky crags. The weather is typically cool and moist, but it can change suddenly into fierce thunderstorms in the summer and blizzards in the winter. These storms and the more frequent whiteouts from fog in any season can be a dangerous risk for hikers unprepared and inexperienced.

Habitat for wildlife varies widely because of the low valleys and remote coves in comparison with high, open, windswept plateaus, a 3,700-foot elevation change. At least 156 species of birds have been sighted, some of which may be seen in any season: sparrow hawk, ruffed grouse, downy woodpecker, white-breasted nuthatch, junco, song sparrow, and more. Among the most common mammals are deer, fox, raccoon, gray squirrel, woodchuck, and chipmunk. The bear population, once hunted to near extinction, is being restocked by the state's Department of Game and Inland Fisheries. Deer hunting is popular, and its season is usually mid-November to early December. Classified as sensitive on the endangered and threatened species list are the sharp-shinned hawk (*Falco peregrinus anatum*) and the golden pigmy salamander (*Desmognathus wrighti*). Populations of pintos, paints, bays, and other kinds of ponies have been introduced as grazing animals to keep the high meadows open. They are most noticeable between Grayson Highlands State Park and Rhododendron Gap, or as far east as the peaks of Pine Mountain. Fishing is permitted in the national recreation area's trout-stocked lakes and streams. There are also four streams capable of maintaining a trout population without artificial stocking. They are Big Wilson Creek, Whitetop Laurel Creek, Fox Creek, and Helton Creek.

Wilderness areas are designated to maintain some of the natural regions. They are Lewis Fork (5,618 acres), Little Wilson Creek (3,613 acres), and Little Dry Run (2,858 acres). The first two are in the central area of the district, but Little Dry Run is in the northeast, south of Speedwell on US 21. In addition to the wilderness areas are four special management areas, part of the USFS's Recreation Opportunity Spectrum. The purpose of the special management areas is to "protect and maintain the qualities that make [the special areas] stand out." They are Whitetop Mountain (1,115 acres), Rush Creek (85 acres), Whitetop Laurel Creek (800 acres), and Little Laurel Creek (200 acres).

The district's human history, after the Native Americans, included first the hunter, trapper, and pioneer settlers with herdsmen. With the growth of railroads and the timber industry at the turn of the century, towns such as Troutdale and Konnarock developed. Timber harvesting stripped the valleys and high mountainsides of prime hardwoods and conifers. Until 1883 Mount Rogers had been called Balsam Mountain, rich with large spruce and fir forests, but Virginia's legislature memorialized its first state geologist, William Barton Rogers, by renaming the mountain. Since 1966 the USFS, new steward of the area, has built forest roads, lakes, and recreational facilities to serve the public.

None of this development outshines the trail system. The Mount Rogers NRA's official Transportation Inventory System (TIS) shows 116 trails (12 of which are segments of the same trail, the 81.1-mi. **Virginia Highlands Horse Trail**). Total trail mileage is 356 miles, of which 55 trails are not blazed. The other 49 trails are blazed yellow, orange, white, and light blue. Blazes usually are not used in the Wilderness Areas. (Severely eroded or overgrown trails could be removed from the inventory and maps unless repaired, and those abandoned for many years could also be taken off the maps to prevent user confusion. An example of the latter is the 2.5-mi. **Mullins Branch Trail**.) Plans are to phase out dark blue and raspberry blazes. Some blazes are yellow squares, or diamonds, or triangles. Orange diamond blazes are on the multiple-use **Virginia Highlands Horse Trail**. Two of its sections allow motorcycles, hikers, and bicyclists for a total of 27.2 miles. Its western trailhead is at Elk Garden at SR 600 to the eastern trailhead at New River Trail State Park on SR 737, north of Fries. The second longest is 71.6 miles of the **Appalachian Trail** with white blazes. Its maintenance is chiefly by Piedmont Appalachian Trail Hikers, Mount Rogers AT Club, and the Appalachian Trail Conference's Konnarock Crew stationed in Sugar Grove. In addition to the 81.8 miles, horseback riding is allowed on 170.3 miles of 56 other trails, 5 of which allow motorcycles. Mountain bicyclists are allowed on 47 trails.

Trails listed for foot traffic account for only 30.6 miles, not counting the **Appalachian Trail**. Most of these hiking trails are short spurs or interpretive trails where groups would be slow and giving attention to the environment or using wheelchairs. (All multiple-use trails are open to hikers.) Two interpretive trails are **Two Ponds Trail** (0.5 mi.) at the Mount Rogers NRA Headquarters, and **Whisper-**

ing Waters Trail (0.6 mi.) at Grindstone Campground. The longest trail with foot traffic only and high usage is **Mount Rogers Trail** (4 mi.) from Grindstone Campground to the top of Mount Rogers and **Mount Rogers Spur Trail** (0.5 mi.). Other foot trails of high usage are (including the **AT**) **Beartree Lake Trail** (1 mi.), **Hale Lake Trail** (0.7 mi.), **Pine Mountain Trail** (1.9 mi.), **Raven Cliff Furnace Trail** (0.5 mi.), and **Wilburn Ridge Trail** (1 mi.).

Multiple-use trails with high usage include **Crest Trail** (3.4 mi.), **Fairwood Valley Trail** (2 mi.), **Virginia Highlands Horse Trail** (14.9 mi., from Elk Garden east to SR 603), **Rhododendron Gap Trail** (1.4 mi.), **Scales Trail** (1.3 mi.), **Virginia Creeper Trail** (18.5 mi., North Carolina state line to Damascus), and **Wilson Creek Trail** (0.7 mi.). For detailed mapping of these and other trails with ratings of low, medium, and high visitor use, consult either the Mount Rogers NRA Headquarter staff, or use National Geographic map #786.

Because some of the trails are of great distances and there are a number of options in making loop trails, I have divided the park into three geographical sections: Western Section, Central Section, and Eastern Section. The trail descriptions will also locate the nearest campgrounds. Campgrounds are usually open from April 15 to December 1. Only the Raccoon Branch Campground is open year round. The Western Section includes the area from the town of Damascus east on US 58 and SR 603 to SR 600, a north-south route. The campground with the most services in this section is fee-required Beartree Recreation Area on FR 837 off SR 603. It has family and group camping for tents, and family and group camping with RVs (no hookups). There is an RV dump station, picnic area, rest rooms, showers, drinking water, fishing, swimming, and boating. Reservations can be made. A network of bicycle trails can begin here. North is a connection to Iron Mountains horse trails, and south across SR 603 is a connection to the **AT**, which connects with the **Virginia Creeper Trail**. On the **AT** are two shelters: Saunders southwest and Lost Mountain southeast.

The Central Section includes the area from SR 600 east on SR 603 to VA 16, a north-south route. Along the south border of the forest is access from US 58 and from Grayson Highlands State Park on SR 362. Through the center is the largest concentration of facilities and recreation. There are five campgrounds: two are equestrian camps and three are general family camps. The farthest west is fee-required Grindstone Campground with family tent and RV camping. It has a RV dump station, picnic area, rest rooms, showers, and drinking water. Reservations can be made. There are trail accesses from here north to **Iron Mountain Trail**, and south for an ascent to Mount Rogers on a hiking trail. **Whispering Waters Trail**, an interpretive loop, has an access from the campground. Farther east on SR 603 it is 1.7 miles to Fairwood Picnic Area, and between it and the nearby Fox Creek Horse Camp is a crossing of the **AT**, north-south. Not only is Fox Creek Horse Camp crowded, but so is nearby Old Virginia Horse Camp. (It is near this area that the USFS has plans for establishing a larger camp for equestrians.) To access the other two campgrounds continue east 4 miles on SR 603 to Troutdale and turn left on VA 16. After 2.3 miles turn left on SR 650 to fee-required Hurricane Campground. It has family tent and RV camping, rest rooms, showers, drinking water, and fishing. There is access here to horse trails, and to hiking-only trails such as the **AT** and a 1.1-mile loop on **Hurricane Knob Trail**. Back on VA 16 it is 3.1 miles north to fee-required Raccoon Branch Campground. It has family tent and RV camping, RV dump station, rest rooms, drinking water, and fishing. The Central Section also has the Mount Rogers NRA headquarters, 5.5 miles north on VA 16. It has hiking only on **Two Ponds Trail** and the **AT**, which passes through the parking area and across VA 16.

All of the above campgrounds are in the north Mount Rogers NRA valley areas, but outside on the south boundary is high and scenic Grayson Highlands State Park. Access to it from SR 16 in Volney is west 7.7 miles on US 58 to a right turn on SR 362. It has a family tent, RV, and group camping facilities with picnic areas. There is also a family horse camp. In addition to a dump station, there are rest rooms, drinking water, and showers. Reservations can be made. There are trails within the park, including part of the **AT** with accesses on **Rhododendron Trail** and **Appalachian Spur Trail** to the **AT**.

In the Eastern Section only two trails cross VA 16 east. They are the **AT** from the Mount Rogers NRA Headquarters (where it soon turns north), and the **Virginia Highlands Horse Trail** which crosses VA 16 from the entrance of the road to Raccoon Branch. From there the horse trail goes 50.5 miles to SR 737, 1 mile north of the fee-required New River Recreational Area at Buck Reservoir. It has family tent and RV camping facilities with RV dump station, rest rooms, drinking water, and fishing. Here is also a connection with the **New River Trail** that goes north from Fries and Galax to Pulaski. (See ahead for a description of the entire 55.3-mile trail.)

(Along the way on this section of the **Virginia Highlands Horse Trail**, from west to east, is access to fee-required Comers Rock Recreation Area. It has family tent camping, picnic area, rest rooms, and drinking water. Two hiking-only trails are here: **Comers Rock Trail** [0.4 mi.] and **Unaka Trail** [1 mi.]. Nearby to the west is hiking-only **Hale Lake Trail** [0.7 mi.]. After crossing US 21 [3 mi. south of Speedwell] the **Virginia Highlands Horse Trail** follows FR 14 where three allied trails go to or near fee-required Hussy Mountain Horse Camp. Facilities there are family camping, rest rooms, and drinking water.) (See a description ahead of the **Iron Mountain Trail [East]**.)

Continuing east on the **Virginia Highlands Horse Trail**, you will reach Ewing Mountain. From it there is difficult **Ewing Mountain Trail** (2 mi.) north to easier **Raven Cliff Horse Trail** (1.2 mi.) into fee-required Raven Cliff Recreation Area. Facilities are family tent and RV camping, picnic area, rest rooms, drinking water, and fishing. Where the above two trails meet at SR 643, the fee-required Collins Cove Horse Camp is nearby. It has family and group horse camping, and rest rooms. Highway access to these campgrounds is west from VA 94 at Porters Cross-roads on SR 619 for 3.3 miles to Huddle for a turn left, then right for Collins Cove, or 5.7 miles to Raven Cliff Campground, left.

The Mount Rogers NRA also provides a tour called Mount Rogers Scenic Byway. It extends from Troutdale west to Konnarock for 13.2 miles on SR 603, and from Damascus to Volney for 32.5 miles on US 58. Points of interest are farms, forests, stores, schools, mountain history, and arts and crafts. The Mount Rogers Interpretive Association publishes a free brochure/map titled "Ridges and Rivers Route." It describes briefly a 132-mile adventure from Abingdon to Pulaski on the **Virginia Creeper Trail**, **Beech Grove Trail**, **Iron Mountain Trail**, **Virginia Highlands Horse Trail**, and the **New River Trail**. (Along the way are a few short sections where bicyclists and equestrians must make detours.)

The trail descriptions ahead are from west to east, beginning with the **Virginia Creeper Trail** and followed by trails on or near the southwestern area of Iron Mountain for the Western Section of the NRA. In the Central Section the descriptions are for trails in the Lewis Fork and Little Wilson Creek Wilderness Areas, and more on the Iron Mountain Area. The ending coverage of the NRA trails is on the most eastern section of Iron Mountain, Little Dry Run Wilderness, and Raven Cliff.

ACCESS: For location of the Mount Rogers NRA headquarters, take exit 45 from I-81 in Marion, follow VA 16 for 7 miles south.

ADDRESS AND INFORMATION: Mount Rogers National Recreation Area, 3714 Hwy. 16, Marion, VA 24354; phone: 276-783-5196; fax: 276-783-5504; web: <www.southernregion.fs.fed.us/gwj>; report wild game violations: 800-831-1174. Call 800-628-7202 or 276-783-5196 for information about reservations for Mount Rogers NRA campgrounds. For Grayson Highlands State Park call 800-933-7175. For questions about outdoor skills and ethics of forest "Leave No Trace" policy, call 800-332-4100. Mount Rogers Interpretive Association: 800-628-7202. The headquarters office is also a museum and visitor center. Available are maps of Mount Rogers and wilderness areas, books, **AT** map—all for purchase. Free material includes general flyers and brochures about some trails such as the **Virginia Creeper Trail** and campground facilities.

## Western Section

The Western Section of Mount Rogers NRA has a high concentration of trails near the Beartree recreational facilities. It is from this area that some combinations of the trails can be used from a central campground. North of it is the western section of **Iron Mountain Trail**, a trail that originates in Tennessee and arrives in Virginia for 1.4 miles to Damascus. From Damascus the trail follows Iron Mountain for 13.4 miles north of Beartree Recreation Area to Skulls Gap at SR 600 North. At the south edge of the Beartree facilities are the long, winding, and partially parallel US 58, **AT**, and **Virginia Creeper Trail**.

In addition to the long trails and the connecting trails that loop near the Beartree area, there are several others. The farthest west is **Tennessee Trail**, a 1.1-mile multiple-use trail along Pond Ridge from the **AT** to FR 32 west of Damascus. Multiple-use trails down the north side of Iron Mountain are yellow-triangle-blazed **Buzzard Den Trail** (1.6 mi.), nonblazed **Clark Mountain Trail** (3.7 mi.), yellow-diamond-blazed **Sawmill Trail** (2.8 mi.), and **Skulls Gap Trail** (1 mi.), which drops to Horseshoe Bend. Among mountain-biking trails (where motorcycle and equestrian use is not permitted) are blue-blazed **Taylor's Valley Trail** (2.6 mi.), an alternative route on the south side of the **Virginia Creeper Trail**, and **Saunders Trail** (2.1 mi.), which parallels (and runs between) the **AT** and US 58. Additional mountain-biking trails are near the Beartree facilities. They are **Beartree Gap Trail** (3.3 mi.), **Yancy Trail** (0.3 mi.), and **Shaw Gap Trail** (1 mi.). One of the most isolated trails is hikers-only **Lover's Leap Trail** (0.5 mi.) on top of panoramic Whitetop Mountain (5,520 ft.). Access to it is from US 58 on SR 600 for 1.7 miles to FR 89. Also off SR 600 up the mountain at Elk Garden is multiple-use **Elk Garden Trail** (1.5 mi.), which drops 1,000 feet in elevation to end at SR 600. The only trails continuing east from SR 600 to the Central Section are the **AT** and **Iron Mountain Trail**.

## WHITETOP LAUREL CREEK AREA
*Washington and Grayson Counties*

### Virginia Creeper Trail

LENGTH AND DIFFICULTY: 34.1 miles (54.6 km); easy

FEATURES: waterfalls, trout and bass streams, historic sites, trestles, farmland, wildlife, wildflowers

TRAILHEADS: To reach the eastern trailhead, travel 15.2 miles on US 58 from the junction with VA 91 in Damascus. Take SR 726 for 1.7 miles to the visitor center at Whitetop Station parking area. The western trailhead is near the corner of Green Springs Road and A Street (one block south on Pecan St. from Main St.) in Abingdon.

INTRODUCTION: The most southwestern area of the Mount Rogers National Recreation Area is at the Tennessee state line, adjoining Cherokee National Forest. At the western corner, and at the foot of Iron Mountain, is the town of Damascus, known nationally for its hospitality. From the town and east to the base of Whitetop Mountain is the **AT**, US 58, Whitetop Laurel Creek, and Green Cove Creek, all winding and twisting and partially parallel to each other. Even Straight Branch is not straight. Following the creeks is the curving **Virginia Creeper Trail**, straighter than the **AT** and the roads because its design is based on an old railroad bed. There are points of brilliant fusion when streams, trails, and roads converge, intersect, or simply tease one another by proximity. In this setting of natural and human history are options for weeks of multiple back-

*Virginia Creeper Trail, Mount Rogers NRA*

packing circuits combining the **AT**, the **Virginia Creeper Trail**, and the **Iron Mountain Trail**. Although separate from these routes, the **Daniel Boone Auto Trail** touches this area. The area is also part of the Mount Rogers Scenic Byway, with 32.5 miles of US 58 from Damascus east to Volney. The nearest developed campground is Beartree Recreation Area on FR 837, 3 miles west on US 58 from its junction with SR 603, and 6.6 miles east on US 58 from its junction with VA 91.

The **Virginia Creeper Trail**, a national recreation trail, extends from the Virginia/North Carolina state line, in the community of Whitetop, northwest to Abingdon. The first 16.5 miles are in the Mount Rogers National Recreation Area. The remaining mileage is supervised by the Washington County Park Authority but is described here for continuity. (An extension of the trail into North Carolina is being studied by North Carolina Rails-Trails, Inc.) Its history is as exciting as its recreational opportunities. Hundreds of years ago the route was a Native American trace from North Carolina to the Ohio Valley. Daniel Boone used part of the trace on his westward explorations. In 1887 a railroad company was chartered, first to haul iron ore and later to transport timber. It became the Virginia-Carolina Railroad by 1900 and the Norfolk & Western Railroad by 1918, with a 75-mile route from Abingdon to Elkland, North Carolina. Usage and distance declined after the Great Depression, but supply and passenger services continued until the final run March 31, 1977, from West Jefferson, North Carolina, to Abingdon. Called the V-C railroad, it acquired the sobriquet of Virginia Creeper. According to one legend, the name comes from the five-leafed, red (in autumn), high climbing woody vine (*Parthenocisus quin-*

*quefolia*) common in the area. According to another legend, the slow speed on the gorge curves and the incline of 1,650 feet in elevation from Damascus to Whitetop Station gave the railroad (and later the trail) its name.

Users of the trail will cross many trestles and bridges, pass waterfalls, follow stocked fishing streams, go through farmlands and residential areas, and may see a diversity of mammals, birds (at least 50 species), wildflowers (at least 170 species), and historic sites. The USFS ranks traffic volume on the trail as high. On a typical weekend are equestrians (sometimes as many as twenty-five in a convoy), bicyclists, walkers, joggers, strollers (particularly near Abingdon), and backpackers. All vehicular traffic (except bicycles) is prohibited. Campsites are infrequent outside the forest property. (The USFS recommends camping 100 ft. from streams.) Guidelines for bikers require a warning passing bell, and bikers as well as equestrians must dismount for trestle crossings. Both food supplies and restaurants can be found in Damascus and Abingdon. For anglers a Virginia fishing license is necessary. Shuttle service is provided by Blue Blaze Shuttle Service, P.O. Box 982, Damascus, VA 24235; phone: 276-475-5095; web: <www.Blueblaze.NAXS.com>.

DESCRIPTION: If beginning at the eastern trailhead, look for the visitor center at Whitetop Station sign at the junction of US 58 and SR 726 (15.2 mi. from US 58 and VA 91 junction at Damascus, and 9.6 mi. west on US 58 from Grayson Highlands State Park). (There is another SR 726, 2.2 mi. farther west on US 58, which leads to Taylors Valley.) Follow SR 726 for 1.7 miles to parking area at Whitetop Station. This is 1 mile northwest of the Virginia/North Carolina state line. (If beginning at the state line, the nearest road access can be reached by continuing 0.8 mi. farther on SR 726 to a left turn on SR 753 and crossing Big Horse Creek. To the right it is 0.3 mi. to the state line, from which backtracking is necessary.) At 0.7 mile is the first bridge, near a beaver dam and with excellent views of Whitetop Mountain. The Whitetop Station parking area is reached at 1 mile, and at 1.1 miles the trail crosses SR 755/726, the trail's highest elevation (3,577 ft.). From here it begins a gentle descent for the next 24 miles. The trail passes by a commercial Christmas tree farm at 1.7 miles and over a 270-foot-long trestle at 1.9 miles. Green Cove Station is reached at 3.9 miles. Access here is on SR 600, 1 mile off US 58 (13.7 mi. east from VA 91). After two more bridges the trail enters an area of hemlock, old apple trees, and patches of wildflowers. At 5 miles cross gravel road, SR 726. Pass a cattle pasture on rolling hills with ferns and blackberries at 5.6 miles. More bridges and cascades follow in the Green Cove Creek gorge. At 6.3 miles SR 859 crosses the trail. Access is 2 miles off US 58 (9.2 mi. east from VA 91). There are good campsites in this vicinity. From 7.2 miles to 7.4 miles is an exceptionally scenic place. The **AT** joins the trail to cross the 540-foot-long Luther Hassinger Memorial Bridge (trestle). Underneath is the confluence of Whitetop Laurel Creek and Green Cove Creek. At 7.9 miles is a parking area for the **AT** and the **Virginia Creeper Trail** at historic railroad site of Creek Junction. Access is 1.3 miles off US 58 on SR 728 (8.8 mi. east from VA 91). The **AT** leaves the **Virginia Creeper Trail** at 8 miles. For the next 3.3 miles there are ten bridges and trestles, waterfalls, hardwoods and rhododendron, and a section with 1,000-foot-high rock walls on the northern side of the gorge. There are good campsites at 9.1 miles. At 11.2 miles the trail passes through private property and a cattle farm to reach the village of Taylors Valley at 11.7 miles. Access is on SR 725, 2.6 miles out to TN 91 in Tennessee (2.3 mi. south of the US 58 and VA 91 junction). The **Virginia Creeper Trail** remains east of the creek to a parking area and to a gate. Near the gate is a 0.4-mile spur trail up Straight Mountain to the **AT**. (A right turn on the **AT** is an ascent to the crest of Straight Mountain for scenic views of area mountains and the Whitetop Laurel gorge at 1.8 mi. Saunders Shelter is 0.3 mi. farther.) At 13.9 miles, at Straight Branch, is a signboard about Mount Rogers National Recreation Area. Beyond is an access to a parking area, picnic tables, fireplaces, the **AT**, and US 58 (3 mi. east of junction with VA 91). There is a good campsite at 14.1 miles. For the next 2.7 miles the trail parallels US 58; passes waterfalls, bluffs, and rhododendron thickets; and crosses four bridges. The last of the latter is Iron Bridge in sight of US 58. After crossing VA 91 at 16.8 miles the trail joins the **AT** at 17.2 miles; there is a spring on the northern side of US 58. At 17.6 miles the **AT** stays with US 58, and the **Virginia Creeper Trail** forks left to cross bridges over Laurel Creek and Beaverdam Creek in Damascus. The **Virginia Creeper Trail** reaches the corner of Laurel and Beaverdam avenues at 18.2 miles. Here is an information display and caboose near a parking area. (Damascus has restaurants, a post office, grocery stores, campsites, and an **AT** hostel.)

For the next 3.4 miles the trail runs parallel between US 58 and Laurel Creek, whose mouth is at the South Fork of the Holston River. Along the way are residential houses, an abandoned warehouse, and crossings of SR 718, SR 715, and SR 1230. The trail goes under a US 58 bridge at 21.6 miles and parallels South Fork through cow pastures and gates to reach SR 712 at 23.6 miles. (It is 93 yd. left to SR 711, accessible from US 58 on SR 907.) Access from US 58 on SR 712 is 1.2 miles (6.5 mi. from I-81, exit 19, in Abingdon). More pastures and a bridge over Rockhouse Run lead to Alvarado Bible Church on SR 710 at 25.4 miles. Access to US 58 is 2.8 miles east on SR 710 and SR 722 (5 mi. south from I-81). After three farm gates the trail crosses a long curved bridge (618 ft.) over South Holston Lake at the confluence of South Fork and Middle Fork at 26.7 miles. Views are outstanding of the South Holston Lake and rivers. More gates, bridges, and trestles follow up the Middle Fork gorge in a forest of large oaks, poplars, and hemlocks. At 28.2 miles is the trail's longest trestle (645 ft.). After passing through River Knobs and leaving the Middle Fork the trail crosses SR 677 (near Watauga Station) at a parking area at 30.3 miles. Access is 2.1 miles off US 58 on SR 677 (1.5 mi. south of I-81).

The character of the **Virginia Creeper Trail** changes for the final 3.8 miles.

Horse traffic is prohibited, bicycle traffic increases, and urban views appear. Following three trestles through the Great Knobs, the trail crosses a golf cause-walk at 32.5 miles in the Winterham golf community. At 32.6 miles is the beginning (or end) of a 1.5-mile self-guided nature walk. Along the **Virginia Creeper Trail** are numbered markers to match a brochure on the plant species. Two historic markers indicate an old sawmill site and train turnaround. Pass under I-81, and at 34 miles is probably the largest white oak on the entire **Virginia Creeper Trail**. The final trestle (253 ft. long), over Town Creek, is at the trailhead on Green Springs Road. Across the street is a parking lot, and in this area is the site of pre–Revolutionary War Black's Fort. Now there is a small museum and information center with sheltered v-c Locomotive #433, a symbol of why this trail exists.

USGS MAPS: Abingdon, Damascus, Grayson, Konnarock, Park; USFS TRAIL NOS.: 4575, 1

## IRON MOUNTAIN AREA (WEST)
*Washington and Smyth Counties*

397–402, 489, 403 **Straight Branch Trail** (1.7 mi.), **Lum Trail** (1 mi.), **Iron Mountain Trail** (11.1 mi.), **Shaw Gap Trail** (1 mi.), **Beartree Gap Trail** (3.3 mi.), **Beartree Lake Trail** (1 mi.), **AT** (2 mi.), **Feathercamp Branch Trail** (1.9 mi.)

LENGTH AND DIFFICULTY: 20.8 miles (33.4 km) combined, circuit; moderate

404–8 CONNECTING TRAILS: **Chestnut Ridge Trail** (1.8 mi.), **Rush Trail** (1.8 mi.), **Feathercamp Ridge Trail** (0.7 mi.), **Wright Hollow Trail** (3 mi.), **Beech Grove Trail** (3.3 mi.)

FEATURES: geology, historic site, wildlife, wildflowers

TRAILHEADS: Access to Beartree Recreation Area is off US 58 on FR 837 at Beartree Gap (6.6 mi. east from US 58 and VA 91 junction at Damascus, or 3 mi. west from US 58 and SR 603 junction). Drive 1.5 miles on FR 837 to group campground, and another 2.3 miles to the family campground.

INTRODUCTION: The Iron Mountain area west of the Mount Rogers National Recreation Area includes the southwestern range from Damascus northeast to Skulls Gap on Iron Mountain at SR 600. The area is bordered on the southern side by US 58 and the Whitetop Laurel Creek area and extends upstream to the Konnarock vicinity. The base camp is Beartree campgrounds, which have rest rooms, warm showers, and waste disposal stations. The picnic area has twenty picnic pavilions, a grassy area for sports, and a lake with a 300-foot swimming beach and bathhouse. Beartree Lake is stocked with trout, and there is a fishing pier for the disabled. The group campground is open all year, but reservations are necessary from the district office. The family campground is usually open from April to late November (and during deer season in late November and early December). For the purpose of grouping trails for circuits near campgrounds, the descriptions are divided into three sections of the **Iron Mountain Trail** (west, central, and east). Three circuits are described here, but hikers will find other options with district maps.

DESCRIPTION: The first loop is 5.4 miles, the second option is 14.3 miles, and the third is 20.8 miles. Begin the first loop counterclockwise on the **Straight Branch Trail**, near the gate of Chipmunk Circle at the family campground. It follows the old gated road 1.7 miles to SR 600. Along the way are stands of wild orchids at the gravel pits and wildlife among the hardwoods and hemlock. Turn left on SR 600 and ascend 1 mile to the **Iron Mountain Trail** at Skulls Gap. (Notice new SR 600 alignment here, but **Iron Mountain Trail** is on old SR 600 near Skulls Gap.) Keep left here on both road and trail for 0.7 mile to leave SR 600 and follow the **Iron Mountain Trail** on the left. Reach Straight Branch Shelter and spring at 4.4 miles. To the left is yellow-diamond-blazed **Lum Trail**. Descend on it through rhododendron and black birch along Straight Branch for a return to the campground at 5.4 miles.

The second loop begins at Chipmunk Circle at the campground on the **Lum Trail**. Follow it up to Straight Branch Shelter and turn left on the **Iron Mountain Trail**. Descend easily and follow a level ridgeline before a slight descent to Shaw Gap at a clearing at 4.3 miles. En route there are views of Mount Rogers and Whitetop Mountain. At Shaw Gap, the yellow-square-blazed **Shaw Gap Trail** and the yellow-diamond-blazed **Beartree Gap Trail** descend left. To the right is unmaintained yellow-triangle-blazed **Chestnut Ridge Trail**. (It goes 1.8 mi. to FR 615, which after 2.5 mi. reaches SR 730.) The **Iron Mountain Trail** stays on the ridgeline. For the second loop, turn left on the **Shaw Gap Trail**, which immediately forks left of yellow-diamond-blazed **Beartree Gap Trail**.

If choosing the **Beartree Gap Trail**, descend gradually to switchbacks, pass through a gap, pass right of a small lake, and cross a stream after 2.1 miles. Descend alongside the stream to cross campground entrance road after another 0.7 mile. Intersect with the **Beartree Lake Trail** near the dam. (The **Beartree Lake Trail** circles the lake for 1 mi.) Turn right at the dam, cross US 58 and intersect with the **AT** after 0.2 mile for a total of 7.6 miles since leaving the campground. (To the right on the **AT** it is 8.2 mi. to the junction with the **Iron Mountain Trail**. To the left on the **AT** it is 31.3 mi. to the northern junction with the **Iron Mountain Trail**.) Backtrack to the lake, take either side upstream, pass through the picnic areas, and arrive at the group campground off FR 837 at 9 miles. Go to the end of group tent camping for the trailhead of the **Shaw Gap Trail**. Follow the dark blue-blazed trail upstream through rhododendron and on a mossy treadway to Shaw Gap at 10 miles. Turn right on the **Iron Mountain Trail** and backtrack to Straight Branch Shelter for a return on the yellow-diamond-blazed **Lum Trail**, a distance of 14.3 miles.

For the third and longest loop, continue on the **Iron Mountain Trail** from Shaw Gap. Reach a grassy summit with panoramic views at 4.7 miles. At 5.9 miles reach a junction with FR 90. (On the left FR 90 descends 1.3 mi. to US 58, and on the right it ascends 1.4 mi. to former Feathercamp Mountain fire tower. The yellow-square-blazed **Rush Trail** is also right for 1.8 mi. off FR 90.) At 6.1 miles the circuit reaches a spring and Sandy Flats Shelter. From here cross Feathercamp Branch and intersect with blue-blazed **Feathercamp Branch Trail** on the left. (It descends 2 mi. to US 58.) Skirt southern slope of Feathercamp Mountain. (The yellow-triangle-blazed **Feathercamp Ridge Trail** ascends right for 0.2 mi. to FR 90 and the site of a former fire tower with scenic views.) Also from the **Iron Mountain Trail** at this point the yellow-square-blazed **Wright Hollow Trail** is on the right. (It is 3 mi. to Sawmill Rd. and Creasy Hollow.) Continue ahead on the **Iron Mountain Trail** and descend gradually to cross the yellow-diamond-blazed **Beech Grove Trail** at 9.4 miles. (The **Beech Grove Trail**, also for motorcycles, goes right for 2.4 mi. to SR 605 and 1 mi. left to US 58.) Ascending, the **Iron Mountain Trail** continues ahead to 10.6 miles and a junction with the **AT**. (To the right the **AT** goes 3.5 mi. to downtown Damascus.) Turn left on the graded **AT** and descend. At 12.1 miles cross the **Beech Grove Trail**, and at 12.6 miles intersect with blue-blazed **Feathercamp Branch Trail** on the left. (The **AT** continues ahead to cross US 58 after 0.1 mi. and reach the **Beartree Gap Trail** after another 6.1 mi.) Turn left on the **Feathercamp Branch Trail** and follow upstream through rhododendron, hemlock, and maple. At 13.1 miles cross old logging road, and at 14.5 miles intersect with the **Iron Mountain Trail**. Turn right and return to the campground on the **Iron Mountain Trail** and the **Lum Trail** for a total of 20.8 miles.

USGS MAPS: Damascus, Konnarock, Whitetop Mountain; USFS TRAIL NOS.: 168, 4544, 301-6, 4545, 4551, 4563, 1, 169

## Central Section

Mount Rogers, Virginia's highest mountain (5,729 ft.), is the major point of interest in this section. It is within Lewis Fork Wilderness with its steep and deep hollows, and upland evergreens. To the southeast of this section is Grayson Highlands State Park and Little Wilson Creek Wilderness. North of these high mountains and running the center of this section in a valley is SR 603 with Big Locust Creek running west, and Fox Creek running east. Beyond the valley, north, on a parallel range is Iron Mountain with its sub-mountains, ridges, and knobs. Farther north with more ridges and streams, the north side of the central section is close to I-81 at the city of Marion. In this section are five campgrounds (described in the introduction to the Mount Rogers NRA section of this chapter), and the NRA headquarters on VA 16. The trail loops described ahead have been chosen where possible to originate from campgrounds. Some trails are isolated with only road access, and others connect with major linear trails such as the **Virginia Highlands Horse Trail** with 31.3 miles and the **Appalachian Trail** with 40 miles. Among the unconnected trails are **Grassy Branch Trail** (3.2 mi.), a nonblazed horse trail that ascends from SR 603 southwest to SR 600; orange-blazed **Currin Valley Horse Trail** (5.2 mi.) off VA 16 on SR 671 west of the NRA Headquarters; and nonblazed **Little Wilson Creek Trail** (3.2 mi. round-trip) with its scenic views of cascades stocked with rainbow and brook trout. To reach the latter from the junction of US 58 and VA 16 at Volney, travel west on US 58 for 4.5 miles; turn right on SR 817 and stay left for 1.1 miles. (Care is requested in parking because of private property. Please respect the wilderness area by not attempting to create new and unofficial trails.) 409–11

The Central Section of the Mount Rogers NRA is a maze of fifty-four trails for hikers, bicyclists, equestrians, and one solitary 1.6-mile trail for motorcyclists across Bear Mountain. In a swirl of trails that crisscross up and down peaks and ridges, and across streams and plateaus, there is a trail for everyone.

## LEWIS FORK WILDERNESS AREA
*Smyth and Grayson Counties*

**Mount Rogers Trail** (4 mi.), AT (2.9 mi.), **Pine Mountain Trail** (2 mi.), 412, 489,
**Cliffside Trail** (1.4 mi.), **Lewis Fork Trail** (5.5 mi.) 413–15
LENGTH AND DIFFICULTY: 12.3 miles (19.7 km) combined, circuit; strenuous
CONNECTING TRAILS: **Flattop Trail** (1.7 mi.), **Mount Rogers Spur Trail** (0.5 mi.) 416–17
FEATURES: wilderness, scenic views, Mount Rogers summit, wildflowers, wildlife
TRAILHEAD: Mount Rogers trailhead parking area is 0.4 mile east of Grindstone
  Campground on SR 603, 5.9 miles west of Troutdale, and VA 16, or on a 0.3-mile
  spur trail in the campground.
INTRODUCTION: The 5,730-acre Lewis Fork Wilderness is between the Grindstone
  Campground on SR 603 (part of Mount Rogers Scenic Byway) in the north and
  Grayson Highlands State Park in the southeast. It rises 2,450 feet in elevation
  from near Big Laurel Creek to the summit of Mount Rogers (5,729 ft.), the
  state's highest point. The wilderness extends west to SR 600 near Elk Garden
  and east to Pine Mountain. In the northeast it is near Fox Creek parking area. A
  forest within a forest, its diversity of plant and animal life is part of its allure.
  Other appeals are its wild hollows with tucked away bubbling streams, open,
  high, flowery meadows, dense spruce and fir stands, and awesome views of the
  area's vastness. In the highest areas of the wilderness it is uncommonly wet—
  fog, mist, and rain in summer and snow, sleet, ice, and rime in winter—an
  overture to hypothermia and disorientation.
DESCRIPTION: Blue-blazed **Mount Rogers Trail**, a national recreation trail since

1979, receives heavy use. (The Mount Rogers NRA staff have indicated they are phasing out all blazes in the wilderness areas except the **AT**.) Begin either at the Mount Rogers trailhead parking area on SR 603 or from **Mount Rogers Tie Trail** (0.3 mi.) in Grindstone Campground. Ascend on switchbacks for 1.1 miles and reach the top of Broad Ridge, where the trail is flat and straight. At 2.3 miles intersect with **Lewis Fork Spur Trail** on the left. (It descends 0.4 mi. to connect with **Lewis Fork Trail**, which ascends to **Pine Mountain Trail** and descends to exit at SR 603.) Along the way it intersects with **Cliffside Trail** and other connecting trails east to both the **Virginia Highlands Horse Trail** and the **AT**.) Continue the ascent, pass a large outcrop, and enter a red spruce and yellow birch stand at 3.3 miles. Meet with white-blazed **AT** at 4 miles. (To the right the **AT** descends 2.1 mi. to a parking lot at SR 600, Elk Garden Gap.) Turn left on the **AT**, follow an easy grade to an open meadow with views at 4.9 miles. Begin a slight ascent into stands of Fraser fir to the **Mount Rogers Spur Trail** at 5.7 miles. (The spur trail goes left 0.5 mi. one way, in dense and dark fir and spruce to the summit of aromatic Mount Rogers.) Continue on the **AT**, leave the wilderness at 6 miles, and pass Thomas Knob Shelter. Arrive at Rhododendron Gap with views to the left from the cliffs at 6.9 miles. (Here the **AT** turns right and parallels the **Wilburn Ridge Trail** for outstanding views into North Carolina and Tennessee. Rhododendron patches provide a colorful garden in June. After 1.4 mi. the **AT** enters Grayson Highlands State Park, where there are more banks of rhododendron, grassy plateaus with lichen-covered boulders, and grazing ponies in alpine meadows. From here the **AT** continues into Little Wilson Creek Wilderness, crosses Pine Mountain [East], and descends to SR 603, after 10.5 mi. from the state park.)

For a continuation of the **Mount Rogers Trail** circuit, go straight ahead at Rhododendron Gap on blue-blazed **Pine Mountain Trail** (the former **AT**). After 0.8 mile (total of 7.7 mi. on the loop) arrive at an intersection with the moderately used and nonblazed equestrian **Lewis Fork Trail**, right and left; turn left. (To the right the **Lewis Fork Trail** ends in a few yards outside the wilderness area boundary at the multiple-use, highly used, and nonblazed **Crest Trail** [3.4 mi.], right and left. The **Crest Trail** is a shortcut for the **Virginia Highlands Horse Trail** from Cabin Ridge in the west to The Scales—an intersection of five trails in the east. The **Crest Trail** also serves as a connection to busy **Rhododendron Gap Trail** [1.4 mi.] for horses to or from Grayson Highlands State Park and **Lewis Fork Trail**.) The **Pine Mountain Trail** continues straight, past a spring, and ends after 1.1 mi. at the **AT**.

On the **Lewis Fork Trail** pass left of **Cliffside Trail** at 7.9 miles. (The difficult **Cliffside Trail** descends steeply, crosses **Lewis Fork Trail**, and ends at a switchback with the **Lewis Fork Trail** in Lewis Fork hollow after 1.5 mi.) Continuing on the **Lewis Fork Trail**, gradually descend and make a long curve at the headwaters of Lewis Fork. At 9.3 miles in a sharp right curve, take **Lewis Fork**

Spur Trail left for an ascent of 0.5 mile to rejoin **Mount Rogers Trail**. (The **Lewis Fork Trail** descends to cross Lewis Fork, then across **Cliffside Trail**, and after a juncture with **Old Orchard Trail** descends to SR 603 to end at **Fairwood Valley Trail** after 3.9 mi.) After rejoining **Mount Rogers Trail**, turn right and backtrack to the fork near Grindstone Recreation Area at 11.6 miles. If turning left on **Mount Rogers Tie Trail**, exit in the campground at 11.9 miles. If at the fork you stay right, arrive at SR 603 and the parking area at 12.1 miles. Here is a connection with **Flattop Trail**, left, and **Fairwood Valley Trail**, right. 423–24

An option for making a loop on the **Mount Rogers Trail** is to descend entirely from the **Pine Mountain Trail** on the **Lewis Fork Trail** as outlined above and after contact with the **Fairwood Valley Trail**, right and left, at a total of 13.2 miles. Turn left for 1 mile to arrive at the **Mount Rogers Trail** parking area at 14.2 miles. Another option with emphasis on hiking only is to follow the scenic **Pine Mountain Trail** 1.1 miles to the **Appalachian Trail**, turn left, and descend on it for 3.4 miles to cross SR 603 and meet **Fairwood Valley Trail**. Turn left and after 1.7 miles arrive at the **Mount Rogers Trail** parking area at 13.9 miles.

USGS MAP: Whitetop Mountain; USFS TRAIL NOS.: 166, 1, 4595, 4533.2, 4533

**Sugar Maple Trail** (2.3 mi.), **Helton Creek Trail** (3.5 mi.), **Helton Creek Spur Trail** (1.2 mi.), **Virginia Highlands Horse Trail** (0.8 mi.) 425–27, 380

LENGTH AND DIFFICULTY: 4.7 miles or 6.5 miles (7.5 km or 10.4 km) combined, circuit; moderate

FEATURES: wilderness, wildlife, wildflowers, stream, historic site

TRAILHEAD: From US 58 (6 mi. west of Grayson Highlands State Park, and 1.5 mi. east of SR 600) turn on SR 783 and go 1.5 miles to where road becomes FR 4032 at parking lot.

DESCRIPTION: Park in a meadow where camping is allowed. Begin on the **Sugar Maple Trail** on the right, at first gate near old cement trough; ascend and pass sites of old houses. At 0.3 mile turn right through fields of asters and goldenrod; pass another gate, and at 0.8 mile enter woods. Ascend on switchbacks to a contour grade. Reach junction with the **Helton Creek Trail** at 2.3 miles, the end of the **Sugar Maple Trail**. (An option here for a loop of 4.7 mi. is a left turn on the **Helton Creek Trail** for a descent to Helton Creek and a return to the parking lot.) Continue ahead on a gentle grade of an old tram road for 1.1 miles to the **Virginia Highlands Horse Trail** beyond the headwaters of Helton Creek. Turn left on the horse trail and after 0.8 mile arrive at a field where the **Helton Creek Spur Trail** turns left. (The **Virginia Highlands Horse Trail** continues ahead 0.5 mi. to its western trailhead at SR 600 at the gap of Elk Garden.) Descend on the spur trail, an old logging road, cross Helton Creek, and intersect with the **Helton Creek Trail**. Turn right and parallel the creek to the point of origin for a loop of 6.5 miles.

USGS MAP: Whitetop Mountain; USFS TRAIL NOS.: 4572, 4538, 4538A

## LITTLE WILSON CREEK WILDERNESS AREA
*Grayson County*

428–33 **Wilson Creek Trail** (1.8 mi.), **Wilson Creek Horse Trail** (4.8 mi.), **Scales Trail** (1.3 mi.), **First Peak Trail** (3.2 mi.), **Kabel Trail** (2.1 mi.), **Big Wilson Creek Trail** (2.1 mi.)

LENGTH AND DIFFICULTY: 11.5 miles (18.4 km) circuit; moderate to strenuous

380, 489, 421, 434–36 CONNECTING TRAILS: **Virginia Highlands Horse Trail** (junction), **AT** (junction), **Crest Trail** (3.4 mi.), **Third Peak Trail** (1.6 mi.), **Jackie Street Trail** (2.5 mi.), **Hightree Rock Trail** (4.7 mi.)

FEATURES: cascades, balds, wildflowers, wilderness

TRAILHEAD: The circuit begins in the Grayson Highlands State Park, the closest access to the wilderness, at the Highlands Campground. Access is off US 58 at the park sign 7.7 miles west from Volney and VA 16 junction. (A rough and primitive route for 4WDS is on FR 613, off SR 603, 2.6 mi. west from VA 16 in Troutdale. The road is closed in winter, has turnaround problems, and is 4 mi. from SR 603 to gate or summit of Pine Mountain.)

INTRODUCTION: High on the open balds of Pine Mountain and down the slopes to cascading Big Wilson and Little Wilson Creeks is the 3,855-acre Little Wilson Creek Wilderness. It is adjacent to Grayson Highlands State Park on the west, where Big Wilson Creek is the boundary, and extends east to the mountainside of Hightree Rock. From the wilderness headwaters are two Little Wilson Creeks, one on each side of First Peak. Both streams drain separately to Big Wilson, whose mouth is at the New River by US 58. Big Wilson is a native trout stream. Stands of red spruce and Fraser fir grow in the higher elevations, and the heath balds have hawthorne, white yarrow, and loosestrife. Old trails and roads and new trails provide loops within loops and make enough connections to go anywhere in the recreation area. The Grayson Highlands Campground is the ideal location for a base camp. It has all facilities, including hot showers. (See Grayson Highlands State Park, Chapter 11.)

DESCRIPTION: On entrance to the campground's grassy field, look for the **Wilson Creek Trail** sign on the left. The trail descends to Big Wilson Creek, where there are waterfalls and cascades in dense rhododendron at 1 mile. At 1.2 miles the trail returns to a primitive road, which also serves as the **Wilson Creek Horse Trail**. After a right turn, cross Quebec Branch, pass a meadow, and reach the park boundary at 1.8 miles. The old road now becomes the **Scales Trail**. Continue and after 0.1 mile cross the **AT** where a bridge crosses over Big Wilson Creek. (To the right the **AT** makes a crescent and returns to the old road at the crest of Pine Mountain after 2.5 mi.) Continue ascent to The Scales, a wide saddle whose name comes from a former weighing and loading dock for summer-grazing cattle at 3.1 miles. Today there is a corral, mainly for horses. Here is also an intersection where the **AT**, the **Virginia Highlands Horse Trail**, and the

**Scales Trail** cross one another. Approaching from the west is the **Crest Trail**, which ends here; the **First Peak Trail** ends here from the east.

Continuing the circuit, take the **First Peak Trail**, ascend a bald slope with blueberries, gooseberries, ferns, and wildflowers, and observe the Big Wilson Creek Valley. Scattered hardwoods are sugar maple and beech. At 4 miles is a junction on the left with the **Third Peak Trail**. (It descends 1.6 mi. to rough FR 613.) After 0.4 mile farther, reach the flat summit of Third Peak (4,920 ft.). Enter Little Wilson Creek Wilderness at 4.7 miles, ascend gently to Second Peak (4,857 ft.) at 5 miles. Descend to a junction with the **Jackie Street Trail** on the left. (The **Jackie Street Trail** descends steeply 2.5 mi. to a forest road and follows it 1 mi. to a gate and exit at SR 739 [Rocky Hollow Rd.]. Turn left for 1 mi. to SR 603, where a right turn on SR 603 is 1.2 mi. to Troutdale and VA 16.)

Pass over forested First Peak (about 4,600 ft.) and descend on rocky tread-way to a junction on the left (east) with the **Hightree Rock Trail** (also called the **Mill Creek Trail**) at 6.3 miles. (It is partially relocated, has switchbacks, crosses the headwaters of the other Little Wilson Creek, and skirts the cliffs of Hightree Rock. It descends to a hollow, crosses Mill Creek, and enters Rocky Hollow for its eastern trailhead on SR 739. It is 2.4 mi. left [north] on SR 739 to SR 603, where a right is 1.2 mi. from Troutdale and VA 16.)

On the circuit, turn right on the **Kabel Trail** to follow an old railroad grade. After curving north from Bearpen Ridge, cross a small stream that flows into Little Wilson Creek. At 8 miles the trail leaves the old railroad grade for a steep and rocky route. At 8.4 miles the **Kabel Trail** ends at a junction with the **Big Wilson Creek Trail**. Descend ahead on a rough passage, partially eroded, to the wilderness boundary at 9.2 miles and Big Wilson Creek at 9.5 miles. Rock-hop or wade the creek and arrive at a primitive road (**Upchurch Road Trail**), usable for horses and 4WDs in Grayson Highlands State Park. (Downstream the road is gated at SR 817, which leads to SR 806 out to US 58.) Turn right and ascend steeply on switchbacks; at 10.7 miles is a large cascade, the site of a former footbridge over the creek. The road turns left and reaches the junction with the state park's **Wilson Creek Trail** at 11.3 miles. If ascending left here, it is 0.2 mile to the campground; if continuing to the horse trail on the left, it is 0.9 mile to the campground.

USGS MAP: Troutdale; USFS TRAIL NOS.: (first two trails in state park; no USFS trail numbers), 4523, 4524, 4606, 4607

## IRON MOUNTAIN AREA (CENTRAL)

*Smyth and Grayson Counties*

**Dickey Gap Trail** (0.4 mi.), **AT** (5.9 mi.), **Hurricane Creek Trail** (0.5 mi.), **Iron Mountain Trail** (4.4 mi.), **Comers Creek Fall Trail** (0.3 mi.), **Comers Creek Trail** (0.7 mi.), **Virginia Highlands Horse Trail** (3.8 mi.)

LENGTH AND DIFFICULTY: 11.8 miles (18.9 km) combined, circuit; moderate

FEATURES: fishing, waterfall, wildflowers, scenic views

TRAILHEAD: Access to Hurricane Campground is from VA 16, 2.3 miles north of Troutdale, to SR 650. On SR 650 go 1.5 miles to FR 84, turn left, and go 0.3 mile to campground entrance.

INTRODUCTION: Exciting circuit hikes are possible in the central area of Iron Mountain by using only trails, trails and forest roads, or only forest roads. These combinations are listed as having low traffic volume by the USFS. Described below are circuit options for 5.6 miles, 5.7 miles, 11.8 miles, 5.9 miles, and 8.3 miles. A good base camp for these hikes is Hurricane Campground. (For the Raccoon Branch trails, Raccoon Campground is a good base camp.) The Hurricane Campground has trailer and tent campsites, warm showers, flush toilets, and waste disposal. Attractions include trout fishing in Hurricane and Comers Creeks, and nature study. The **Hurricane Knob Trail** is a scenic 1-mile loop entirely within the campground. Access to the trail is across the road from the bulletin board at the left side of the rest rooms or by a large white pine tree near campsite #5. The fee campground may be open from mid-April to mid-November.

DESCRIPTION: From the campground entrance, at junction of FR 84 bridge (confluence of Comers and Hurricane Creeks), take the blue-blazed **Dickey Gap Trail** through hemlock, birch, maple, and rhododendron for 0.4 mile to junction with the **AT**. Turn right, follow the **AT**, and at 2.1 miles cross a stream. At 2.9 miles meet an old logging road on the right and left. (To the right the **Hurricane Creek Trail** descends 0.5 mi. to intersect with FR 84 [Hurricane Creek Rd.], where a right turn leads 2.2 mi. downstream by picturesque Hurricane Creek to the campground for a loop of 5.6 mi.) Continue on the **AT**, ascend on switchbacks near a stream, and reach Chestnut Flats at 4.4 miles. Here is a junction with yellow-blazed **Iron Mountain Trail (Central)**, left and right.

(The **AT** follows left on the **Iron Mountain Trail** for a few yards, then turns right, south, to ascend and descend Iron Mountain 2.3 mi. to Fox Creek trailhead parking area at SR 603. It is 3.9 mi. east on SR 603 to Troutdale and a store on VA 16.) (To the left on the **Iron Mountain Trail** follow a ridgeline with a steep mountain drop on the northern side for 2.4 mi. Begin a descent to reach Comers Creek at 2.8 mi., and intersect with the **Comers Creek Fall Trail** on the left. [The **Iron Mountain Trail** goes another 0.5 mi. to its eastern terminus at VA 16, near FR 741, and 1.8 mi. north of Troutdale.] Follow the **Comers Creek Fall Trail** 0.3 mi. to the falls and a junction with the **AT**. From here complete the circuit of 5.7 mi. by following the **Comers Creek Trail** 0.7 mi. to the campground.)

Continue right on the **Iron Mountain Trail** for the longest circuit, and arrive at the crest of Flat Top Mountain (4,451 ft.) at 5.4 miles from the campground. Descend to a dirt road, turn right, and after 0.1 mile turn left into the forest. At 6 miles reach a junction with primitive FR 828, Flat Top Gap. (Ahead is Cherry Tree Shelter and spring on the **Iron Mountain Trail** after 0.3 mi.) (To the left FR 828 descends for 3.2 mi. to SR 603 near Grindstone Campground. Along the way is 1-mi. **Flattop Trail**, which descends to Mount Rogers trailhead parking area at SR 603.) Leave the **Iron Mountain Trail** at the junction with FR 828, turn right, and follow the **Virginia Highlands Horse Trail**. After 1.8 miles reach Hurricane Gap and intersection with FR 84. Turn right on FR 84 and for 4 miles follow alongside Hurricane Creek to the campground for a total of 11.8 miles.

Another moderate, shorter loop follows the **Dickey Gap Trail** as described above to the **AT**. But take the left this time, and pass Comers Creek fall and cascades at 1.3 miles. Enter a thicket of rhododendron and then a stand of open hardwoods. Reach SR 650/VA 16 junction at 2.5 miles. Cross SR 650 and after 0.8 mile on the **AT** reach a junction with the **Virginia Highlands Horse Trail**. Turn left and follow the horse trail for 2 miles to SR 650. Turn left on SR 650 for 0.1 mile to FR 84. Turn right and go 0.3 mile to entrance of the campground for a total of 5.7 miles. For a scenic forest roadway circuit that is particularly beautiful with autumn leaf colors, follow nonblazed **Comers Creek Trail** downstream. Tall trees, mosses, ferns, and wildflowers make this an excellent nature study walk. At the junction with FR 643, after 0.7 mile, turn left on the road away from the creek. Follow the gravel road around Bear Ridge for 2.3 miles to Barton Branch. Go upstream for 1 mile to a junction with FR 870. Turn left on FR 870, go 1.8 miles between Seng Mountain and Bear Ridge to FR 84. Turn left again, and after 2 miles return to the campground for a total of 8.3 miles.

USGS MAPS: Troutdale, Whitetop Mountain; USFS TRAIL NOS.: 4518, 1, 4530, 301, 4576, 4526, 337

## Dickey Knob Trail (2.3 mi.), Raccoon Branch Nature Trail (0.2 mi.) 444–45

LENGTH AND DIFFICULTY: 4.8 miles (7.7 km) combined, round-trip; easy to strenuous

FEATURES: fishing, wildlife, scenic overlook

TRAILHEAD: The trailhead is in Raccoon Branch Campground on VA 16, 2.3 miles south of Sugar Grove (and 11 mi. south of I-81, exit 45).

INTRODUCTION: This combination of two very different trails allows for a walk in the woods to a challenging climb. The longer route is also more isolated, though the campground is near a busy highway. Raccoon Branch Campground has trailer and tent sites, flush toilets (no showers), and waste disposal station. Interesting attractions include trout fishing at Dickey Creek and Raccoon Branch and backcountry exploring. The fee campground is open year round.

DESCRIPTION: At Raccoon Branch Campground, the **Dickey Knob Trail** and the **Raccoon Branch Nature Trail** begin between campsites #4 and #6 to cross a wooden footbridge at the confluence of Dickey Creek and Raccoon Branch.

Turn right to hike the 4.6-mile round-trip **Dickey Knob Trail**. The trail ascends gradually at first, then becomes steeper. Near the top of the knob is an excellent view east of the Sugar Grove Area. At elevation 3,649 feet arrive at the site of a former fire tower. Backtrack. Walk upstream for the nature trail among shady evergreens.

USGS MAPS: Troutdale, Atkins; USFS TRAIL NOS.: 346, 4610

## Eastern Section

For 50.5 miles the Eastern Section route of the orange-diamond-blazed **Virginia Highlands Horse Trail** goes east from VA 16 (2.1 mi. south of Sugar Grove across the road from the entrance to Raccoon Branch Campground) to Buck Reservoir 1 mile north of New River Campground. This section of Mount Rogers NRA has fewer users and is more isolated than the western and central sections. (It is suggested that hikers carry a map of this section for long-distance hiking, camping, and where a shuttle vehicle can be arranged. Contact the headquarters office for conditions of the trail and map options [276-783-5196]. The office has a free brochure on the Horse Heaven–Iron Mountain Loop area, but you may need National Geographic map #786 or other maps for more geographical detail.) Hiking and equestrian usage are allowed on the entire distance, bicycles on 41.9 miles, and motorcycles (from October 1 to April 1) on 27.2 miles. The trail crosses roads and highways as follows: SR 601 after the first 3.9 miles; US 21 after the next 24.8 miles; SR 602 after the next 10.7 miles; VA 94 after the next 7.1 miles; and to the end at SR 737 after 4 miles. Connecting trails along the way (none of which

446–54  have blazes) include **Kirk Hollow Trail** (0.8 mi.) north to SR 675; **Little Dry Run Trail** (4.4 mi.) south 1.3 miles to Comers Rock Campground and north 3.1 miles through Little Dry Run Wilderness to US 21; **Dry Run Gap Trail** (1 mi.) south to **Iron Mountain Trail (East)**; **Henley Hollow Trail** (1.6 mi.) north to US 21; **East Fork Trail** (2.7 mi.) east on FR 14; **Divide Trail** (0.7 mi.) south to **Iron Mountain Trail (East)**; **Mike's Gap Trail** (2.8 mi.) northwest to SR 6702 and southeast to FR 690A; and **Ewing Mountain Trail** (2 mi.) north to Collins Cove Horse Camp at SR 643. (Here it is 1.2 miles west on multi-use **Raven Cliff Trail** to Raven Cliff Campground [family and groups]). On the **Virginia Highlands Horse Trail**, one mile before reaching VA 94, is Sunrise Cabin (reservations only: 800-628-7207).

## IRON MOUNTAIN AREA (EAST)
*Wythe and Grayson Counties*

455–57  **Iron Mountain Trail (East)** (2.5 mi.), **Hale Lake Trail** (0.6 mi.), **Unaka Nature Trail** (1 mi.)
LENGTH AND DIFFICULTY: 6.6 miles (10.6 km) combined, round-trip; moderate
FEATURES: scenic views, fishing, solitude, wildlife, endangered species

TRAILHEAD: On US 21, 17 miles south of US 11 in Wytheville (5 mi. south of Speedwell included), turn right on FR 57 and follow it for 3.5 miles to Comers Rock Recreation Area.

INTRODUCTION: This area is more remote and less used than other sections of the national recreation area. The potential for solitude is great. There are two lengthy trails that carry over from the southwestern sections of the Iron Mountain Area. Some portions of the **Iron Mountain Trail** are unmarked, overgrown, and unmaintained, and other sections are on private land. The equestrian trail is more up to standard. A few of the short side trails and singular trails are maintained. Examples are the **Henley Hollow Trail**, the **Little Dry Run Trail**, the **Divide Trail**, and the **Hale Lake Trail**. In this area is an endangered tree species, the round-leaf birch (*Betula uber*), found nowhere else in the world. It is protected by both state and federal laws. In a primitive environment the campgrounds are generally primitive. Comers Rock has nine campsites, vault toilets, and a hand water pump. Camping is on a breezy, dry ridge with an observation stand. Nearby is Hale Lake for trout fishing. Another campground is Raven Cliff on Cripple Creek. It has twenty campsites, picnic shelters for groups, and flush toilets. Cripple Creek is noted for its smallmouth bass and redeye fishing. The remains of Raven Cliff Iron Furnace are accessible from the campground on 0.5-mile **Raven Cliff Furnace Trail**. To reach it from Comers Rock Campground, go 5 miles north on US 21 to Speedwell, where a right turn (northeast) on SR 619 is 6 miles from a sign on the right. Both campgrounds require fees for campers and are open year round. 458

DESCRIPTION: At Comers Rock, begin at campsite #7 and go 100 yards to an **Iron Mountain Trail** sign. Turn left on the **Comers Rock Trail**. (The trail on the right, **Little Dry Run Trail** [4.4 mi.], descends a slope to the West Fork of Dry Run and a junction with the **Virginia Highlands Horse Trail** at 1.2 mi. and beyond to Little Dry Run Wilderness and US 21.) After 0.5 mile, reach the panoramic views of Iron Mountain Range, Point Lookout Mountain, and Comers Rock Valley. Thick understories of striped green maple and witch hazel are on the trail. Backtrack to the trail junction near the campsite and take a left turn on the yellow-blazed **Iron Mountain Trail**. Hike through oak, white pine, hemlock, and rhododendron for 2.2 miles. Cross FR 57-B and descend to Hale Lake at 2.5 miles. Circle the lake on the **Hale Lake Trail** for 0.6 mile through pine, black gum, and tall sweet pepperbush. Backtrack for a total of 5.6 miles. The 1-mile **Unaka Nature Trail** begins right facing the picnic shelter in the campground and forms a loop through an outstanding range of botanical species. 459

A circuit could be made by taking the right fork at the campground and proceeding 1.2 miles on the **Little Dry Run Trail** to the orange-blazed **Virginia Highlands Horse Trail**. Then proceed right on an old wagon road for 3 miles to US 21. If not using another car for support, hike 1.2 miles right on US 21 to FR 57 to intersect the **North Mountain Trail (East)**, and right on FR 57 back to camp for 3.6 miles. For a longer circuit and less road walking, follow the above, except at the junction with the **Virginia Highlands Horse Trail** at the West Fork of Dry Run take the **Little Dry Run Trail** for 3.1 miles to US 21. Cross the highway and enter **Henley Hollow Trail**. Ascend for 1.6 miles to the **Horse Heaven Trail**. Take a left, go 2 miles, turn right on FR 4009, hike 1.3 miles to a gate, cross FR 14 (unmaintained **Clark Mountain Trail**), and take the **Divide Trail** for 0.7 mile to a junction with the yellow-blazed **Iron Mountain Trail (East)**. Take a right, and after 3 miles, exit at Dry Run Gap on US 21 across the road from FR 57. If a second car is waiting here, the hike would be 12.7 miles. Otherwise hike FR 57 back to camp for 16.3 miles.

460–61

USGS MAPS: Speedwell, Cedar Springs; USFS TRAIL NOS.: 301-2 (Iron Mountain), 337, 342, 4571, 305, 306, 307, 309, 4638, 4549, 301-1 (Iron Mountain)

## Clinch Ranger District

The Clinch is the JNF's most western ranger district. Its 90,000 acres are in three major sections. The largest section is south of the towns of Big Stone Gap, Norton, and Coeburn to the Clinch River Valley. It has two campgrounds, Bark Camp (4.1 mi. south of the junction with US 58A in Tacoma on SR 706, and left on SR 699 for 0.3 mi. to SR 822 for 1.7 mi.) and High Knob (3.5 mi. south of Norton on VA 619, and left on FR 238 for 1.6 mi.). The smallest section is scenic, windswept Stone Mountain, west of Big Stone Gap and Appalachia between the northern fork of the Powell River Valley and the Powell River. Cave Springs Recreation Area is near the western end of the section (off US 58A west of Big Stone Gap on SR 621 for 6.6 mi.). The most northern section extends from the Pound River Valley up to the high boundary line of Kentucky and Virginia. To the northeast of this section is Breaks Interstate Park and to the southwest in Kentucky is a tract with the headwaters of the famous Cumberland River. Nearby is Cane Patch Campground (6.5 mi. west of Pound on SR 671). The district's forest is mainly southern and northern hardwoods with a mixture of white pine, hemlock, and other pines. Because of a geological environment different from the other JNF districts, the Clinch is unique in mineral development. Although coal is not mined on its properties, it does have 100 gas wells, some of which are pumping into an interstate system. An additional 30 wells may be drilled in the future.

A major highway runs through the district: US 58A follows the **Trail of the Lonesome Pine**, a pioneer route to Kentucky. The route was made famous by John Fox Jr.'s 1908 classic novel of the same name about mountain railroads and feuding families. It was made into a movie in 1915 and in 1936 was the first outdoor technicolor film, starring Sylvia Sidney and Henry Fonda. In Big Stone Gap at the June Tolliver Playhouse the story is presented as an outdoor drama from June to September.

But the centerpiece of each section in this rugged mountain area is a long backpacking trail of physical challenge and natural beauty. Other trails have unique distinctions also. An example is the district's only Kentucky trail, the remote 4.7-mile **Mayking Loop Trail** west of Cane Patch on SR 671 to the state   462 border, or east from Oven Fork, Kentucky, on CO 932. Another trail, the **Little Stony Creek Trail**, is the district's only national recreation trail. It passes the district's highest waterfalls. A unique trail in the district is **Pound Lake Trail**, a   463 5-mile interpretive canoe trail accessible at Pound or Wise boat launches.

In 2003 a new trail, **Pickem Mountain Trail**, was under construction for 3.3   464 miles between High Knob Tower and Flag Rock Recreation Area. It would extend the **Chief Benge Scout Trail** for a total linear distance of 19 miles. Going west the trail follows existing USFS roads 238, 238B, and 238C to Pickem Mountain roads 2420 and 2420E. From there the trail would descend west to cross a bridge over Lost Creek. A new parking area would be constructed at the new trailhead facility at Flag Rock. Access from Norton from US 58A is south on SR 619 to sign on left. The new trail is a joint project by the USFS and the city of Norton.

ADDRESS AND INFORMATION: Clinch Ranger District, 9416 Darden Dr., Wise, VA 24293; phone: 276-328-2931. Available are district map with trails, recreation flyers, and hunting and fishing brochures.

## PINE MOUNTAIN AREA
*Wise and Dickenson Counties*

### Pine Mountain Trail             465
LENGTH AND DIFFICULTY: 26.2 miles (41.9 km); moderate to strenuous
CONNECTING TRAILS: **Austin Gap Trail** (4.1 mi.), **Bob Gap Trail** (1.5 mi.), **Counts**   466–68
**Cabin Trail** (1.8 mi.)
FEATURES: solitude, scenic rock outcrops, wildlife
TRAILHEADS: The southwestern trailhead is at US 23 in Pound Gap on the Virginia side of the state line (4.5 mi. northwest of the town of Pound in Virginia and 3 mi. south of the town of Jenkins in Kentucky). All of the real estate, except US 23 and its boundaries, at this trailhead is on private property. Traditionally, it was understood by the private landowners, USFS, and **Pine Mountain Trail** users that the 1-mile narrow road from US 23 northeast to the WIFX radio tower and USFS boundary line was a trailhead access. At the publication of this book, the unwritten agreement remained in effect, but the following changes should be known to trail users. One is the construction of State Line Foodmart on the south side of Pound Gap and Mountain Stop Market on the north side of the gap. In addition there is the Apostolic Church and School constructed up the ridge, northeast, where now a paved access road connects with a gravel road to the USFS boundary. Another change is that the new **Pine Mountain Trail Ex-**   469 **tension** (under construction in 2003) continues south from the State Line Food-

mart into the woods and to USFS property. Trail users should receive permission from any of the private landowners for parking. Otherwise, the USFS recommends the following: From the State Line Foodmart drive 0.4 mile east on US 23 to SR 667 (Old US 23) junction and park. Or drive a 4WD up the paved Apostolic Church Drive at Mountain Stop Market to the gravel road (where there is a yellow blaze) and follow it to the WIFX radio tower and USFS boundary. It is at this point some guidebook distances begin the actual **Pine Mountain Trail**. The northeastern trailhead is at the Elkhorn City police station in Kentucky. It is on the left immediately after crossing Russell Fork bridge, 6.5 miles west on KY/VA 80 from Breaks Interstate Park.

INTRODUCTION: The **Pine Mountain Trail** (formerly the **Cumberland Mountain Trail**) is listed by the USFS as a multi-use trail for hikers, bikers, and equestrians; but there are steep, narrow sections with many rock outcrops that are difficult for bikers and impassable for horses. (An easier route for equestrians in both directions is about halfway on the trail at Mullins Rd., FR 616, off SR 611 between Isom and Blowing Rock on the Virginia side.) The trail is exceptionally challenging and adventurous along a wild and dry crest of Pine Mountain. Its mileage and routing remain subject to change. There are at least fifteen major gaps and many minor ones involving frequent undulations. Large rock formations and cliffs have outstanding views. Some of the rocky and dense forest areas are challenging, and the rocks are slippery when wet. Trail elevation is usually between 2,500 and 3,000 feet. After ascending from Skegg Gap going north, the trail descends to its terminus with a 1,900-foot drop. Some trail sections become overgrown with weeds, briars, and vines in the summer. Other sections may be difficult to follow due to recent logging. Water sources may be infrequent or almost nonexistent during a drought. The USFS owns about 60 percent of the property on which the trail passes, and at least 2.5 miles of the trail pass through Breaks Interstate Park. You will notice a number of signs, mainly on the Kentucky side, warning users not to trespass on private land.

Wildlife is prominent with about thirty-five species identified among mammals. Among the thirteen reptiles known from the trail area, only the timber rattler and northern copperhead are poisonous. Nearly fifty species of birds are known to inhabit or be migratory on the mountain. Wildflower species are more than 110 and about 15 species of ferns. Among a dozen or more shrubs are the rosebay rhododendron, whose delicate pink blossoms in late June and early July make a special showcase of color. You will pass through about thirty-five species of trees, of which five are evergreens. Oaks, hickories, and maples are prominent. You are likely to see evidence that pioneer settlers and some hardy families as late as the 1940s have lived on the harsh mountain ridges and gaps with livestock, meager farmland, log cabins, moonshine stills, and burial sites.

In addition to obtaining information from the USFS Clinch Ranger District office (see address above), you may contact a private volunteer group, the Pine Mountain Trail Conference (PMTC), P.O. Box 784, Whiteburg, KY 41858; phone: 606-633-2362. One of the goals of the PMTC is to have a 120-mile foot trail along the Virginia/Kentucky border from Cumberland Gap National Historical Park northeast to Breaks Interstate Park.

DESCRIPTION: If you are choosing to hike or backpack northeast from US 23 in Pound Gap, use the options described under "Trailheads" above. From the radio towers at 1 mile and satellite dishes at 1.1 miles enter the USFS property at a yellow blaze. At 1.5 miles is Raven's Nest (elev. 2,961 ft.), and in open spaces are wildflowers, such as beds of loosestrife that bloom in July. Here is a large sandstone rock outcropping with outstanding views of Letcher County in Kentucky and Wise County in Virginia. Northeastern views are of the long Pine Mountain ridgeline. Descend on switchbacks to Austin Gap at 1.8 miles on the Virginia side. (To the right is blue-blazed **Austin Gap Trail**. It divides to have two routes of descent, but reconnects on a spur ridge for a singular descent of 1 mi. to SR 630, 4 mi. east of US 23 in Pound. The 4-mi. loop crosses Bad Creek twice and follows a beautiful level ridge through rhododendron and witch hazel.)

After 0.1 mile on **Pine Mountain Trail** pass a short spur trail to Skyview Rockshelter. Below the shelter may be a source of water. Arrive at Mullins Rock at 2.6 miles and at Tucker Gap at 2.9 miles. Descend on old roads to a more level area at 3.3 miles. Ascend and descend to reach Bryant Gap at 4 miles. After another 0.3 mile there may be water at a thick rhododendron ravine known as 4-Springs Bog. Enter private property and at 5.6 miles in the Doubles cross an undependable stream near a dry bog on the east side of the ridge. Enter Dickenson County on the Virginia side. In Kentucky is Pike County. For the next 1.7 miles on private property are some dirt roads from former logging and pipeline right-of-way clearing. Watch closely for trail blazes and trail routing. After Osburn Gap ascend 0.5 mile to reenter the USFS property, but leave the USFS line again after 1 mile. Pass Big Lick Gap at 8 miles and Cantrell Gap at 9.1 miles. Arrive at Bob Gap at 10 miles. (To the right is blue-blazed multi-use **Bob Gap Trail**. It descends on a ridge 1.5 mi. to SR 622 at Cutler Creek. From here the road descends 1.4 mi. to SR 631; a left turn is 1.8 mi. to the community of Isom.)

At 11.6 miles the trail connects with FR 616 where there is horse and mountain bike traffic. (It is 1.6 mi. down the mountain on the Virginia side of SR 611, where a right turn is 2.3 mi. to the community of Isom.) After 0.1 mile is a side road to Mullins Pond, right. Unless it is dry weather, there is a spring above the pond. Stay on **Pine Mountain Trail** which follows northeast on FR 616 to 12.4 miles, where you leave the road, left, to Birch Knob. Follow an old woods road to Dutton Gap, then Blowing Rock Gap and to Potter Gap at 13.4 miles. Another 0.3 mile is **Count Cabin Trail**, right. (The blue-blazed and steep horse trail descends 1.8 mi. to a parking area with signage at SR 611, 1 mi. east of the community of Blowing Rock.)

Pass under a power line at 16.3 miles and by Flag Rock at 17.1 miles where views are east into Virginia. For the next 4 miles the trail meanders near the state line and ridge top to pass Horse Head Ledge for a possible water source at 18.9 miles, Gold Fish Pond as a possible water source at 19.7 miles, and Skegg Gap at 21 miles. Unique to this area (though there is a cemetery at 20.4 mi.) is that topographic maps list this section as so remote that the state boundary lines are not known. After Skegg Gap ascend right on a foot trail east of a knob to approach an old forest road and follow it 200 feet to an ATV route at 21.5 miles. To the left the ATV route steeply ascends 0.1 mile to the top of a knob for a campsite and dead end. To the right ATV traffic uses the **Pine Mountain Trail** to its northeast terminus.

Continue on the old road and at 21.6 miles on the left are rock piles from pioneer farming, and at 21.7 miles are rosebay rhododendron thickets. Indian Council Cave is left (50 yd.) at 22 miles. In this area you are entering the boundary of Breaks Interstate Park and beginning a descent of about 1,900 feet in elevation to the riverbanks of Russell Fork. Pass under a power line at 22.5 miles for a descent into a hollow that sometimes is a source of water. At 23.2 miles it is 65 yards left to spectacular views at Elkhorn City Overlook. Continue on the old road with the yellow blazes and cross a small stream at 25.2 miles. Turn right and parallel the stream to a gravel road at the riverside at 25.4 miles. Turn left and arrive at the Elkhorn City Police Station at 26.2 miles.

USGS MAPS: Jenkins East and West, Clintwood, Hellier, Elkhorn City; USFS TRAIL NOS.: 201, 201A, 201B, 201C. (The USGS topo maps are out of date. Recommended is National Geographic Clinch Ranger District map #793.)

470 **Red Fox Trail**

LENGTH AND DIFFICULTY: 2.2 miles (3.5 km) round-trip; moderate

FEATURE: historic site

TRAILHEAD: From northern Pound on US 23, go west on SR 667 (old US 23) and ascend 0.6 mile to a parking area and trail sign.

DESCRIPTION: The trail begins at a gate near an old railroad grade. It turns left and after 0.3 mile turns right into the forest and begins an ascent on the original wagon road to Pound Gap. Along the way and at the end of the 1.1-mile trail, Killing Rock, are interpretive markers. (Killing Rock is where Marshall Taylor "Red Fox," preacher and U.S. marshal, and his cohorts ambushed a wagon carrying the Ira Mullins family, May 14, 1892. Five in the wagon were killed, but two escaped. Red Fox was hanged October 27, 1893, at the Wise County Courthouse in Wise.) Backtrack.

USGS MAP: Jenkins West; USFS TRAIL NO.: 205

## Laurel Fork Trail 471

LENGTH AND DIFFICULTY: 3 miles (4.8 km) round-trip; moderate

FEATURE: primitive lakeside camping

TRAILHEAD: On US 23 in Pound, near western junction with US 23B, turn at signed entrance to the North Fork of Pound Reservoir. After 0.6 mile is a parking lot and a boat ramp.

INTRODUCTION: The 4,500-acre land area was authorized by Congress in 1960 to be constructed by the U.S. Army Corps of Engineers; it became operational in 1966. Operated for flood control, it also offers many recreational activities— fishing and boating at the 154-acre lake, picnicking, hiking, camping, and nature study—originally in nine locations. One attraction is to explore the old roads and logging trams on the mountainside of Pine Mountain. There are two areas that have trails: Laurel Fork and Phillips Creek. (Across the dam is the 0.5-mi. **Lakeside Trail**, a short walk to an overlook of the lake. It is maintained by 472 the Corps of Engineers.)

DESCRIPTION: The trail begins on the western slope of the ridge near the rest rooms. At 0.7 mile it ascends through a weedy old field with poison ivy to a ridge crossing at 1 mile. Among dogwood, hickory, and hemlock it descends to cross a small stream and enter a large grassy meadow at the lake and boat ramp at 1.5 miles. Backtrack.

USGS MAPS: Flat Gap, Jenkins West; USFS TRAIL NO.: 206

## Phillips Creek Trail 473

LENGTH AND DIFFICULTY: 1 mile (1.6 km) round-trip; easy

FEATURE: historic site

TRAILHEAD: In Pound, from US 23, go west 5.7 miles on SR 671 to entrance, right, on SR 834 for the Cane Patch Campground.

DESCRIPTION: A former day-use facility, the area is now a campground with showers and a bathhouse and is near Phillips Creek swimming area. The interpretive trail begins at the end of the camping area and makes a 1-mile loop through a wildlife food plot and continues by an old homesite, a whiskey-still site, waterfalls, an Indian history area, and a narrow-gauge railroad bed.

USGS MAP: Flat Gap; USFS TRAIL NO.: 202

## STONE MOUNTAIN AND WALLEN RIDGE AREA

*Lee and Wise Counties*

## Stone Mountain Trail 474

LENGTH AND DIFFICULTY: 13.5 miles (21.6 km); strenuous

CONNECTING TRAILS: **Olinger Gap Trail** (1.1 mi.), **Lake Keokee Loop Trail** (3.7 475–77 mi.), **Payne Branch Trail** (2.3 mi.)

FEATURES: outstanding views, wildlife, cascades, rock formations, old-growth hemlock

TRAILHEADS: Reach the southwestern trailhead at Cave Springs Recreation Area from the junction of US 58A and US 23 in downtown Big Stone Gap. It is 4.1 miles west on US 58A to SR 621; turn right. Follow SR 621 along Powell River for 6.6 miles to FR 845. A right turn leads 0.3 mile to the campground entrance. Another route is from US 58A at Ely. Turn north on SR 676, go 1 mile to SR 621 and turn right; then go 4.4 miles to turn left on FR 845. The northeastern trailhead is on US 23 on the western side of Roaring Branch bridge, 1.4 miles north of downtown US 58A in Big Stone Gap, and 1.3 miles south of the VA 68/160 junction in Appalachia. Park 0.2 miles north of the trailhead on US 23 at a dumpster and flea market site.

INTRODUCTION: The **Stone Mountain Trail** is the district's third longest trail and equals or surpasses the scenic quality of the **Pine Mountain Trail**. One of its appeals is Cave Springs Recreation Area, where vehicles can be safely parked for an extended backpacking trip. Other factors are the beauty of Roaring Run, the magnificent views of Black Mountain in Kentucky and mountain ridges in southwestern Virginia, and fishing in Lake Keokee from a short connector trail. Because of the deep, damp gorge and the dry rock outcroppings, there is a wide range of trees, flowers, ferns, mosses, and lichens. Among the wildlife are deer, turkeys, raccoons, owls, and hawks. The peak of fall color for maple, sassafras, blueberry, and black gum is in mid-October. The unique masonry at Cave Springs was constructed by the USFS in the 1960s, and the many stone steps in Roaring Run were installed by the CCC in the 1930s.

DESCRIPTION: If beginning at the Roaring Branch trailhead, ascend the moss-covered stone steps parallel to the cascading stream for 0.6 mile to rock-hop the branch. Towering old-growth hemlock, some over 300 years old, and dense rhododendron keep the gorge deeply shaded. After crossing the branch twice more, follow the ascending trail through hardwoods and mountain laurel to a ridge crest and knoll at 3 miles. At 4 miles is High Butte (3,050 ft.), with superb views of Powell River Valley, Powell Mountain, Wallen Ridge South, and the North Fork of the Powell River Valley North. The Black Mountain range in Kentucky is to the northwest. The trail descends, passes a sheer rock formation, and undulates over knolls for the next 1.9 miles for a gentle descent to Olinger Gap.

(Here the blue-blazed **Olinger Gap Trail** descends north to join the **Lake Keokee Loop Trail**. To the right is 2.5 mi. and to the left is 1.2 mi. to the parking area and boat ramp of Lake Keokee Recreation Area. The 92-acre lake is stocked with bass, sunfish, and muskie. Camping is prohibited, but there are picnic tables and rest rooms. In a hardwood forest with mountain laurel, wintergreen, galax, wild orchids, and ferns, the trail passage is easy to moderate. Access by highway is 8 mi. southwest from Appalachia [4.6 mi. on VA 68 from the junction with US 23; 1.9 mi. on SR 606; 0.6 mi. south on SR 623; and 0.9 mi. south on SR 876].)

From Olinger Gap the **Stone Mountain Trail** ascends and passes right of an old cabin at 6.3 miles and left of a clear-cut at 7 miles, undulates for 1 mile before reaching a dangerous cliff overlook at 8 miles, and makes a steep descent to Low Gap at 8.4 miles. After the sag, the trail ascends through an expansive mountainside of ferns and reaches the crest of the ridge at an old fire tower site at 10 miles. After 0.2 mile on the old road, the trail turns left on a footpath.

(Ahead on the old road is the blue-blazed **Payne Branch Trail**. It descends on a remote, rocky, and hydric passage to parallel Payne Branch in rhododendron slicks and groves of fetterbush and sweet pepperbush. A small parking area is near a large oak tree, opposite a white and green house trailer in the community of Sigma. It is 1.3 mi. out on SR 625 to SR 606, where northeast on SR 606 it is 4.6 mi. to SR 623, the access route to Lake Keokee.)

At 10.8 miles the **Stone Mountain Trail** leaves the high ridge, passes beside a spectacular rock wall and overhangs, and begins a long descent. After twenty-six switchbacks in an open hardwood forest, the trail reaches an overlook above the subterranean stream of Cave Springs at 13.3 miles. The remaining 0.2 mile leads to the campground or parking area by a small lake fed by the springs.

USGS MAPS: Appalachia, Big Stone Gap, Keokee; USFS TRAIL NOS.: 207, 327, 402, 213

## Wallen Ridge Trail

478

LENGTH AND DIFFICULTY: 6.6 miles (10.6 km); easy to moderate

FEATURES: wildlife, wildflowers

TRAILHEADS: From west on US 58A in Dryden, turn south on SR 737 (or SR 629) for a few yards; turn left on SR 619 and follow it 1.6 miles to SR 642. Turn left on SR 642 for 0.2 mile and turn right on SR 619, Lovelady Road. It is 2.6 miles to Lovelady Gap, a parking area for four vehicles and the western trailhead. (Access is also from US 23 in Jasper, 3.9 mi. west on SR 611 to SR 619 and right 1.1 mi. to Lovelady Gap.) The eastern trailhead is on FR 641, 6.5 miles northeast from SR 611, and 3.1 miles southwest from US 23 (opposite SR 844, Wildcat Rd.) and 2.1 miles south on US 23 from the US 58A junction in Big Stone Gap.

DESCRIPTION: Hiking east on the yellow-blazed trail, follow the forest boundary on pleasant Wallen Ridge, which has an average elevation of 2,800 feet. Turkeys and squirrels may be seen in an open hardwood forest of mainly maple, oak, and hickory. Dense patches of sweet cicely (*Osmorhiza claytonii*) are prominent. Other wildflowers are black cohosh, puttyroot, and jewelweed. Views of Stone Mountain (NW), Powell and Jasper Mountains (SE), and the valleys in between are visible in the winter. At 1 mile is a large tree growing in a rock formation, and at 4.9 miles is a saddle where a blue-blazed spur trail descends steeply for 0.4 mile to FR 641 (5.1 mi. from SR 611 east and 1.4 mi. west from the main trailhead). The trail ascends a knob before dropping to Turkey Cove Gap at 5.4 miles. After 1 mile it crosses a small stream and joins a rocky road for its final 0.2-mile descent to FR 641.

USGS MAPS: Big Stone Gap, Keokee; USFS TRAIL NO.: 329

### 479 Appalachia Trail

LENGTH AND DIFFICULTY: 2.2 miles (3.5 km) round-trip; moderate

FEATURES: rhododendron slicks, outcrop

TRAILHEAD: Access is from the junction of US 23 (W. Main St.) and Inman Street (opposite VA 68/160) in Appalachia. Follow Inman Street across the bridge 0.2 mile to Spruce Street, turn left, then right on Roberts Street, which becomes Cold Springs Drive for 0.7 mile to a dead end. There is space for parking one or two cars at the USFS gate. Parking is also available at the Municipal Building at the entrance to Cold Spring Drive.

DESCRIPTION: The yellow-blazed trail follows an old forest road through a cool and dark channel of rhododendron and hemlock to a fork at 0.6 mile. It turns right to follow a power line on the left before switching to another power line. The trail ends at 1.1 miles beside an outcropping with impressive views of Stone Mountain and Powell River. Backtrack.

USGS MAP: Appalachia; USFS TRAIL NO.: 214

## HIGH KNOB AND LITTLE STONY CREEK AREA
*Wise and Scott Counties*

### 480 Chief Benge Scout Trail

LENGTH AND DIFFICULTY: 16.4 miles (26.2 km); moderate to strenuous

481–84 CONNECTING TRAILS: **High Knob Lake Shore Trail** (1 mi.), **Bark Camp Lake Trail** (3.5 mi.), **Kitchen Rock Trail** (0.6 mi.), **Little Stony Creek Trail** (2.9 mi.)

FEATURES: panoramic High Knob, lakes, wildlife, wildflowers, waterfalls

TRAILHEADS: The western trailhead is at the parking lot of High Knob Tower (4,162 ft.). From US 58A and SR 619 in Norton, travel on SR 619 for 4.5 miles to junction with FR 238 on the left. After 0.6 mile, turn right to High Knob Tower parking area. To reach the eastern trailhead from Coeburn, go 3.2 miles south on VA 72 to SR 664, 1.1 miles west on SR 664, 1.3 miles south on FR 700, and 0.9 mile south on FR 701 to Falls of Little Stony parking area. (Central access points are described below.)

INTRODUCTION: The **Chief Benge Scout Trail** is partly new and partly the former **Mountain Fork Trail** and **High Knob Trail**. It passes through two campgrounds: High Knob Recreation Area with camping, picnicking, swimming (with bathhouse and warm showers May 1 to October 31), and fishing facilities; and Bark Camp Recreation Area with camping (with electric hookups and showers), picnicking, and fishing (electric motors only). Excellent for backpacking the entire distance, the trail also allows convenient day hikes from three road crossings. It follows sections of stream sides, old railroad grades, and logging roads through a botanical display of rosebay rhododendron, mountain laurel, gentian, orchids, and beds of fern, galax, and wintergreen. Wildlife includes deer, turkeys, raccoons, beavers, and owls.

DESCRIPTION: If beginning at High Knob Tower parking area, views include Tennessee, Kentucky, and a vast expanse of southwestern Virginia. The yellow-blazed trail descends 1.3 miles to High Knob campground, joins the **High Knob Lake Shore Trail** loop near the bathhouse, and crosses Mountain Fork footbridge. It passes large rock formations before reaching FR 704 at 3.9 miles. From here the trail curves on a spur ridge, crosses Bark Camp Branch, and ascends on an old road to a beautiful grazing field at 6.8 miles. (Deer and turkey frequent the area.) At the end of the field the trail turns sharply left and follows an old road in a hardwood forest to Edith Gap, where it crosses SR 706 at 7.5 miles. (Access on SR 706 is 0.7 mi. north to FR 704, and right to FR 238, which leads left to High Knob.) The trail begins a descent to cross the headwaters of Little Stony Creek. It follows the northeastern side of the creek until it makes a junction with the **Bark Camp Lake Trail** at 9.6 miles. It continues on the southern side of the lake and across the dam at 11.3 miles.

(The **Bark Camp Lake Trail** circles the lake. It provides a tranquil walk on a well-designed path where hemlock is frequent and fragrant. Beds of ferns and running cedar are prominent. Wood ducks fly over a lake that has bass, sunfish, and muskies. The campground has a paved trail from the parking area to a fishing deck for the physically handicapped. Also, on the northern side of the parking area is the **Kitchen Rock Trail**, a 0.5-mile loop in a hardwood forest. One access to the camp is from the junction of US 58A and SR 706 in Tacoma [halfway between Norton and Coeburn]. Drive south 4 miles to SR 699, turn left for 0.2 mile on SR 699, and turn right on SR 822. It is 1.6 miles on SR 822 to FR 933 on the right, the entrance road to the campground.)

From the dam the **Chief Benge Scout Trail** descends on the northern side of the stream to SR 822, where it crosses at 11.8 miles. For the next 4.6 miles the trail follows sections of an old railroad grade, rock-hops Little Stony Creek a number of times, and passes through tulip poplar and rhododendron groves. It exits to the eastern trailhead at the Falls of Little Stony parking area at 16.4 miles on SR 701.

(At the end of the parking area the yellow-blazed **Little Stony Creek Trail** [a national recreation trail] descends through a deep gorge with spectacular scenery. Three falls [25, 12, and 30 ft.] are within the first 0.5 mi. Two high footbridges and a spur trail to the first fall also offer exciting views. The stone steps at the falls are skillfully designed. The trail serves as a 2.9-mi. extension of the **Chief Benge Scout Trail** to Hanging Rock Picnic Area on FR 805, off a curve from VA 72, 2.1 mi. north of Dungannon and 9.2 mi. south of Coeburn.)

USGS MAPS: Coeburn, Dungannon, Fort Blackmore, Wise, Norton; USFS TRAIL NOS.: 401, 401A, 211, 209, 331

## DEVIL'S FORK AREA
*Scott County*

485  **Devil's Fork Loop Trail**
LENGTH AND DIFFICULTY: 7.3 miles (11.7 km) round-trip; strenuous
486  CONNECTING TRAIL: **Straight Fork Ridge Trail** (1.8 mi.)
FEATURES: cascades, pools, old-growth hemlock
TRAILHEAD: From VA 72 (0.3 mi. north of Dungannon), go 8.9 miles west on SR 653 to SR 619. Turn right on SR 619, and after 1.1 miles turn left on FR 619 in a curve (beside a fenced-in white house). (Also, from VA 72/65 in Fort Blackmore, it is 2.9 mi. north on paved SR 619 to junction with SR 653.) From High Knob it is a continuous 7.4-mile descent on SR 619 to FR 619, right at the white house.
DESCRIPTION: From the parking area the trail goes 0.3 mile to Y Bottom, the junction of Straight Fork, right, and Devil's Fork, left, the beginning of the loop. If hiking left, the trail follows an old railroad grade (difficult to recognize in some rough areas) beside cascades, flumes, and pools. At 1.6 miles is a pool sculpted by rushing water to form the Devil's Bathtub. With the shade of old-growth hemlocks, the treadway is rocky, mossy, and damp. After 2.4 miles and eleven stream crossings, the trail turns north at Three Forks to ascend on a narrow ridge between Deep and Corder Hollows. For the next 3 miles the trail is in a hardwood forest, crossing spur ridges of Little Mountain, and dipping into hollows with small streams. At 5 miles is a good campsite, and at 5.7 miles is the junction on the left with the **Straight Fork Ridge Trail**. (The **Straight Fork Ridge Trail** ascends steeply 1.8 mi. to FR 237. Access at the top of the mountain is 3.9 mi. from SR 619 at High Knob.) The trail loop turns right and descends on an old and steep road to the parking area at 7.3 miles.
USGS MAPS: East Stone Gap, Fort Blackmore; USFS TRAIL NOS.: 212, 204

## GUEST RIVER GORGE AREA
*Wise County*

487  **Guest River Gorge Trail**
LENGTH AND DIFFICULTY: 5.8 miles (9.3 km) one way; easy
488  CONNECTING TRAIL: **Heart of Appalachia Bike Route (and Scenic Drive)**, (128 mi.) (phone: 888-798-2386
FEATURES: historic sites, tunnel, waterfalls and cascades, railroad trestles, cliffs
TRAILHEAD: From US 58A in Coeburn take VA 72 south 2.3 miles to entrance, left (across from the Flatwoods Group Picnic Area), and descend 1.4 miles to parking area.

*Guest River Gorge Trail,*
*Clinch Ranger District*

INTRODUCTION: In 1994 this former section of the Norfolk-Southern Railway was dedicated for hiking and bicycling (and the first 1.4 mi. for physically handi- capped usage). The railroad route had been constructed in 1922, and in the process cuts were made through Pennsylvania sandstone (formed about 300 million years ago). Except for the tunnel area in the gorge, the trail is on the northeast side of the Guest River. The sound of the cascading whitewater echoes against the cliff walls. The river has smallmouth bass, sunfish, and catfish. Canoeing and kayaking are allowed. Almost completely in a hardwood forest, only Virginia pine may be seen on the cliff tops and hemlock between the trail and river. Wildflowers include white snakeroot, asters, and jewelweed. Mountain laurel and devil's walking stick are also visible.

DESCRIPTION: From the southwest corner of the parking area descend 150 yards on a paved access to the trail entrance sign and a fine gravel surface. On the way is a large kiosk with information about the Guest River Gorge, resting benches, and a rest room. After 0.3 mile enter the 300-foot Swede Tunnel, from which you cross a high trestle with scenic views of the Guest River Gorge. Crossing the 150-foot bridge, you will notice the beginning of numerous sections of rugged rock walls through the gorge. At 1 mile there is an example of how small trees, flowers, and vines survive on the multiple cliffs. At 1.3 miles is a side trail, left, to a small waterfall, and nearby the main trail's fine gravel ends at a 30-foot bridge. The river is closer to the trail at 1.5 miles. Near the 2-mile signpost is a high cliff overhang and again at 2.1 miles. The latter high cliff has small Virginia pines clinging at the top. Other spectacular rock walls are at 2.4 miles, 2.7 miles, and 2.8 miles. At 2.9 miles is a scenic view of the river. At 3.5 miles is Lick Log Branch Waterfall, left. After another 2.2 miles, pass the entrance, left, of the **Heart of Appalachia Bike Route**. Immediately ahead is the 153-foot trestle over the Guest River, where you can see the confluence of Guest River and Clinch River. Here is also the active Clinchfield Railroad. Backtrack.

USGS MAP: Coeburn; USFS TRAIL NO.: 216

# PART II. National Park System Trails

# 3. Appalachian National Scenic Trail

The **Appalachian Trail** (AT) is the world's most famous hiking trail. Its history    489
of challenge and adventure, its natural beauty, and its astonishing length have
played a part in the idealization of the first of America's national scenic trails.

Many individuals dream of completing the trail's 2,168 miles as a through-hiker
in one season; others are satisfied to finish sections as part of a long-term goal. Of
the millions whose feet have touched its pathway at fleeting stops in parks and
forests, only a few, less than 2,000, have taken the more than 5 million foot-
steps from Maine to Georgia. Some follow this continuous footpath through fourteen states for physical endurance, spiritual achievement, educational encounters, therapeutic experiences, or a combination of reasons. Earl Shaffer, from
York, Pennsylvania, in 1948 the first through-hiker, said he made the journey from
Georgia to Maine to fulfill the wish and plans that he and his hiking friend, Walter
Winemiller, had made to hike the entire **AT**. Then came World War II, and both
men were in combat zones of the Pacific. Winemiller was killed on Iwo Jima. In
1965 Shaffer was also the first to traverse the **AT** in the opposite direction. In 1998
he walked the **AT** again from Georgia to Maine. At least one known hiker, Mary
Kilpatrick of Philadelphia, had completed the **AT** in sections of unflagged and
unblazed routes ten years earlier. But the first woman through-hiker was Emma
Gatewood ("Grandma Gatewood") of Ohio, in 1955. The first person to document
the distance of the **AT** with a measuring wheel was Myron Avery, first president of
the PATC, founded in Washington, D.C., in 1927, and chairman of the Appalachian
Trail Conference from 1930 to 1952.

Since the days of the early explorers, the challenge and magnetic appeal have
intensified among the young and the elderly, among the star athletes and the
physically disabled, and among scientists to catalog the **AT**'s geology and biology.
Setting a record for twelve completions of the AT (seven through-hikes and five
sectional hikes) is Warren Doyle of Hayes, North Carolina. His first hike was in
1973, and he plans to complete his thirteenth in 2005. For each hiker who has
completed the **AT**, there is a different personal story of pain and pleasure, failure
and fulfillment, and the kinetic drive to go back again. In Shaffer's *Walking with
Spring* he wrote, "I knew that many times I would want to be back again . . . on the

cloud-high hills where the whole world lies below and far away[,] . . . by the windworn cairn where admiring eyes first welcome newborn day."

The concept and name of the **AT** belong to Benton MacKaye, a forester and author from Shirley Center, Massachusetts. He has said that his thoughts of such a trail came early in the century, before the **Long Trail** in Vermont was begun in 1910. Among others who had long trail concepts was Allen Chamberlain, a Boston newspaper columnist and early president of the Appalachian Mountain Club (formed in 1876). By 1921, trail leaders in New England and in the Palisades Trail Conference (which later became part of the New York–New Jersey Trail Conference) planned connecting trails. An example of their efforts was the first and original section opened October 7, 1923, in the Harriman–Bear Mountain section of the Palisades Interstate Park. After 1926 the leadership of Arthur Perkins of Hartford, Connecticut, translated MacKaye's dream into reality; but it was Myron H. Avery of Lubec, Maine, who more than any other individual was instrumental in implementing and coordinating the agreements with government agencies (such as the ccc) and with volunteers to complete the **AT**.

The entire **AT** routing design was initially completed August 15, 1937, but considerable relocations were to follow. Trail mapping and maintenance nearly came to a standstill during World War II, and even when Shaffer began his journey, many sections of the **AT** were unblazed. A number of the Appalachian Trail Conference leaders considered his mission impossible. Today the **AT** is secure, with only a few miles unprotected or yet to be purchased as part of the National Park Service (NPS). Protection came by the National Trails System Act of 1968, to which supplemental amendments were made in 1970, 1978, and several times since. The trail's maintenance, however, depends on thirty-two organized clubs (and hundreds of volunteer workers in those clubs), whose chief purpose is assisting the Appalachian Trail Conference in planning and maintaining sections of the **AT**.

One-fourth (544.6 mi.) of the total **AT** mileage is in Virginia (including about 22 mi. that zigzag along the West Virginia state line in Jefferson and Monroe Counties). The highest point for the trail in Virginia is Mount Rogers (5,729 ft.), and the lowest is at the James River bridge (660 ft.). It passes through the JNF, the GWNF, part of the BRP, and almost all of the Shenandoah National Park. Ten volunteer clubs jointly assist the USFS and the NPS in planning and maintaining the **AT**. The Tennessee Eastman Hiking Club maintains 3.5 miles in Virginia (another 127.3 mi. are in Tennessee and North Carolina) from the state line to Damascus; Mount Rogers Appalachian Trail Club, 55.8 miles from Damascus to SR 670; Piedmont Appalachian Trail Hikers, 57 miles from SR 670 to SR 623 and SR 615 to I-77; Outdoor Club at Virginia Tech, 35.9 miles from US 460 bridge at Pearisburg to Pine Swamp Branch Shelter and SR 615 at Laurel Creek to SR 623, permanent assignment (additional temporary assignment from SR 611 to SR 612, 8.1 mi.); Roanoke Appalachian Trail Club, 118.9 miles from Pine Swamp Branch Shelter to Black-

*Appalachian Trail bridge over the James River*

horse Gap (FR 186) and SR 608 to New River (US 460), permanent assignment
(additional long-term temporary assignment from SR 611 to SR 608); Natural
Bridge Appalachian Trail Club, 90.2 miles from Blackhorse Gap (FR 186) to Tye
River (VA 56); Tidewater Appalachian Trail Club, 10.5 miles from Tye River (VA 56)
to Reeds Gap (SR 664); Old Dominion Appalachian Trail Club, 26.4 miles from

Reeds Gap (SR 664) to Rockfish Gap (I-64); Potomac Appalachian Trail Club, about 159 miles (another 80.1 mi. in West Virginia, Maryland, and Pennsylvania). Because of relocations, the above mileages are subject to change.

The condensed listing of milepoints in this chapter is meant to emphasize major points of interest such as shelters, post offices, scenic views, highway crossings, food, amenities, and some trail connections. It is recommended the hiker acquire the guidebooks listed below. A number of trails that include parts of the AT are described in Chapters 1, 2, 4, and 5. The USFS number for the AT is 1, the blaze is white, and side trails (leading to views, shelter, and water) are blue-blazed.

ADDRESSES AND INFORMATION: Appalachian Trail Conference, P.O. Box 807, Harpers Ferry, WV 25425; phone: 304-535-6331; e-mail: <info@atconf.org>; web: <www.appalachiantrail.org>; office is located at the corner of Washington and Jackson Streets. Available are free brochure and general information about the AT. If the following books and maps are not available at bookstores and outfitters, order from the Appalachian Trail Conference: *Appalachian Trail Guide, Maryland and Northern Virginia* (and map); *Shenandoah National Park* (and map); *Central and Southwest Virginia* (and map). For information about huts and cabins rented by the PATC in the Shenandoah National Park, contact PATC, 118 Park St., SE, Vienna, VA 22180; phone: 703-242-0315 (for hikes, 703-242-0965).

## Appalachian Trail
Milepoint 550.1 to milepoint 0.0

| MILEPOINT | | |
|---|---|---|
| FROM N | FROM S | LOCATION AND DESCRIPTION |
| 550.1 | 0.0 | Tennessee/Virginia state boundary (3,200 ft.), 11.3 mi. N of US 421 |
| 546.6 | 3.5 | Damascus, Virginia (1,928 ft.), US 58; lodging, groceries, restaurant, stores, post office 24236 |
| 543.1 | 7.0 | Feathercamp Ridge, yellow-blazed **Iron Mtn. Trail** (extends 16.8 mi. to Chester Flats [4,320 ft.] junction with **AT**) |
| 541.0 | 9.1 | Crossing of US 58, second time since Damascus |
| 537.2 | 12.9 | Saunders Shelter; water |
| 532.6 | 17.5 | Joint crossing with **Virginia Creeper Trail** on 0.1-mi. railroad trestle |
| 530.8 | 19.3 | Lost Mtn. Shelter; water |
| 529.7 | 20.4 | Eastern crossing of US 58, near Summit Cut (3,160 ft.); groceries (2 mi. E and W) |
| 526.0 | 24.1 | Buzzard Rock (5,080 ft.); scenic |
| 522.8 | 27.3 | Cross SR 600, Elk Garden (4,434 ft.); groceries, restaurant 3.5 mi. W; Whitetop, VA post office 24292, groceries 3.4 mi. E |

| FROM N | FROM S | LOCATION AND DESCRIPTION |
|--------|--------|--------------------------|
| 519.0 | 31.1 | Access trail to Mount Rogers (0.5 mi.), highest peak in Virginia (5,729 ft.); no scenic views |
| 518.6 | 31.5 | Thomas Knob Shelter; water |
| 513.4 | 36.7 | Wise Shelter; water (side trail 0.5 mi. to Grayson Highlands State Park parking area and 1.2 mi. E to campground) |
| 507.6 | 42.5 | Old Orchard Shelter; water |
| 505.9 | 44.2 | Cross SR 603, Fox Creek (3,480 ft.), campground w |
| 499.5 | 50.6 | Side trail to Hurricane Campground (0.5 mi. w) |
| 497.4 | 52.7 | Cross SR 650 (near VA 16), Dickey Gap (3,313 ft.); Troutdale, groceries, restaurant, post office 24378 (2.6 mi. SE on VA 16) |
| 495.9 | 54.2 | Raccoon Branch Shelter; water |
| 493.4 | 56.7 | Trimpi Shelter; water |
| 490.8 | 59.3 | Cross SR 670 (4.7 mi. E to VA 16 and Sugar Grove) |
| 482.9 | 67.2 | Partnership Shelter; water |
| 482.8 | 67.3 | Mt. Rogers National Recreation Area visitor center and district ranger office, cross VA 16 (3,220 ft.); Sugar Grove, post office 24375, groceries, restaurant (2.6 mi. SE on VA 16) |
| 475.8 | 74.3 | Louise Chatfield Shelter; water |
| 471.3 | 78.8 | Groseclose, motel, restaurant, groceries at junction of US 11/I-81/SR 683; Atkins, post office 24311, laundry, groceries (3.2 mi. w on US 11) |
| 468.6 | 81.5 | Davis Path Shelter; no water |
| 459.1 | 91.0 | Cross VA 42; Ceres, post office 24318 (5.2 mi. E) |
| 457.0 | 93.1 | Knot Maul Branch Shelter; spring (0.2 mi. N) |
| 448.0 | 102.1 | Chestnut Knob Shelter (4,410 ft.); no water, rim of Burkes Garden |
| 440.9 | 109.2 | Davis Farm Campsite; water (0.5 mi. w) |
| 438.2 | 111.9 | Jenkins Shelter (2,470 ft.); water |
| 433.4 | 116.7 | Cross Little Wolf Creek and eleven other crossings within 2.5 mi. (**AT High Water Trail**, 2.7 mi., is N) |
| 426.2 | 123.9 | Cross US 52 to SR 612; Bastian, groceries, meals, post office 24314 (1.8 mi. N); Bland, groceries, motel, meals, laundry, post office 24315 (2.5 mi. s) |
| 425.6 | 124.5 | Cross I-77 overpass |
| 423.9 | 126.2 | Helveys Mill Shelter (0.3 mi. s off **AT**); water |
| 414.1 | 136.0 | Jenny Knob Shelter (0.2 mi. sw off **AT**); water |
| 412.9 | 137.2 | Cross SR 608, Lickskillet Hollow (2,200 ft.) (0.8 mi. N of VA 42 and Crandon); groceries (0.8 mi. E) |

| FROM N | FROM S | LOCATION AND DESCRIPTION |
|--------|--------|--------------------------|
| 407.6 | 142.5 | Cross SR 606; groceries, restaurant (0.8 mi. w) |
| 406.3 | 143.8 | Side trail (0.3 mi.) to Dismal Creek Falls |
| 400.5 | 149.6 | Wapiti Shelter (near Dismal Creek); water |
| 392.1 | 158.0 | Doc's Knob Shelter; water |
| 386.8 | 163.3 | Campsite, spring, on Pearis Mtn. |
| 386.3 | 163.8 | Angels Rest (3,550 ft.), Pearis Mtn.; scenic views |
| 384.3 | 165.8 | Pearisburg, VA 100 and US 460 junction; groceries, restaurants, post office 24134, laundry (1 mi. SE on VA 100), lodging (0.2 mi. SE) |
| 383.8 | 166.3 | Cross Shumate Bridge (US 460) over New River |
| 377.0 | 173.1 | Rice Field Shelter; water (0.5 mi. E) |
| 371.1 | 179.0 | Juncture with **Groundhog Trail** (N), the southernmost in West Virginia to the state's **Allegheny Trail** (**Groundhog Trail** is 2 mi. to West Virginia county road 219/24) |
| 367.2 | 182.9 | Juncture with **Allegheny Trail** (NE) in Peters Mtn. Wilderness (3,920 ft.) |
| 364.7 | 185.4 | Pine Swamp Branch Shelter (2,530 ft.); water |
| 362.3 | 187.8 | Cross SR 635 and Stony Creek |
| 360.8 | 189.3 | Bailey Gap Shelter; water (seasonal) |
| 352.0 | 198.1 | War Spur Shelter; water |
| 346.2 | 203.9 | Laurel Creek Shelter; water |
| 343.8 | 206.3 | Sinking Creek Valley, cross VA 42; groceries (1.6 mi. w) |
| 339.8 | 210.3 | Sarver Cabin; water (0.3 mi. E) |
| 333.8 | 216.3 | Niday Shelter; water |
| 328.7 | 221.4 | Audie Murphy Monument |
| 324.9 | 225.2 | Cross SR 620 from New River Ranger District into New Castle Ranger District |
| 323.9 | 226.2 | Pickle Branch Shelter; water (0.5 mi. E) |
| 320.4 | 229.7 | Dragons Tooth (rock formation on Cove Mtn. [3,050 ft.]); scenic |
| 312.0 | 238.1 | Cross VA 311; Catawba, groceries, restaurant, post office 24070 (1 mi. w) |
| 311.0 | 239.1 | Boy Scout Shelter; water (seasonal) |
| 310.1 | 240.0 | Catawba Mtn. Shelter; water |
| 308.5 | 241.6 | McAfee Knob (3,197 ft.); cliffs, scenic views |
| 307.8 | 242.3 | Campbell Shelter; water |
| 302.9 | 247.2 | Big Tinker Cliffs (2,980 ft.); scenic views |
| 302.4 | 247.7 | **Andy Layne Trail** (descends N 2 mi. to SR 600) |
| 301.8 | 248.3 | Lamberts Meadow Shelter; water |
| 296.4 | 253.7 | Hay Rock, Tinker Ridge; scenic views |

| FROM N | FROM S | LOCATION AND DESCRIPTION |
|--------|--------|--------------------------|
| 292.4 | 257.7 | Junction of US 220 and SR 816; Cloverdale, groceries, lodging, stores, restaurant, laundry, post office 24077 (2.3 mi. E); Daleville, post office 24083 (1.2 mi. w), groceries, lodging, restaurant on the **AT** |
| 290.9 | 259.2 | Cross under I-81 on SR 779 and across US 11; Troutville, post office 24175, groceries, lodging (1 mi. N on US 11) |
| 287.4 | 262.7 | Fullhardt Knob Shelter (2,676 ft.); water (cistern) |
| 281.2 | 268.9 | Wilson Creek Shelter; water |
| 278.8 | 271.3 | Cross Black Horse Gap Rd., FR 186, near BRP mp 97.7 |
| 273.9 | 276.2 | Bobblets Gap Shelter; water (0.2 mi. w) |
| 270.7 | 279.4 | Bearwallow Gap (2,238 ft.), BRP mp 90.9, and junction with VA 43/SR 695; Buchanan, post office 24066, groceries, restaurant, lodging (5 mi. NW) |
| 267.5 | 282.6 | Cove Mtn. Shelter; no water |
| 264.3 | 285.8 | Cross SR 614, Jennings Creek Rd.; groceries, lodging (1.4 mi. E) |
| 255.6 | 294.5 | Cornelius Creek Shelter; water |
| 254.6 | 295.5 | Black Rock; scenic views |
| 252.9 | 297.2 | Parkers Gap Rd. (3,380 ft.), FR 812, BRP mp 78.4 |
| 251.1 | 299.0 | Thunder Hill Shelter; water (seasonal) |
| 243.4 | 306.7 | Marble Spring; camping and water |
| 237.9 | 312.2 | Matts Creek Shelter; water |
| 235.9 | 314.2 | Cross James River Foot Bridge (678 ft.) |
| 235.8 | 314.3 | US 501/VA 130; Big Island is SE on US 501 (5.1 mi.) for groceries, restaurant, post office 24526; Glasgow is NW on US 501/VA 130 (5.9 mi.) for groceries, lodging, restaurant, post office 24555 |
| 234.1 | 316.0 | Johns Hollow Shelter; water |
| 232.0 | 318.1 | Fullers Rocks (2,472 ft.); scenic views |
| 225.3 | 324.8 | Punchbowl Shelter; water (0.2 mi. w) |
| 220.6 | 329.5 | Pedlar Dam |
| 216.5 | 333.6 | Brown Mtn. Creek Shelter; water |
| 214.7 | 335.4 | Cross US 60 at Long Mtn. Wayside (2,026 ft.); groceries (1 mi. w at junction with SR 634); Buena Vista, groceries, lodging, restaurant, post office 24416 (9.3 mi. w on US 60) |
| 211.9 | 338.2 | Bald Knob (4,059 ft.); scenic views |
| 210.9 | 339.2 | Cow Camp Gap Shelter; water (0.6 mi. SE on **Hotel Trail**) |
| 209.7 | 340.4 | Cole Mtn. (4,022 ft.); bald, scenic views |
| 208.4 | 341.7 | Hog Camp Gap, FR 48; parking area, water at Wiggins Spring (0.5 mi. w) |

| FROM N | FROM S | LOCATION AND DESCRIPTION |
|---|---|---|
| 206.2 | 343.9 | Salt Log Gap (3,247 ft.), FR 63 (extension of SR 634), and junction with FR 48 |
| 200.7 | 349.4 | Seeley-Woodworth Shelter; water |
| 199.6 | 350.5 | Twin Springs; water and campsites |
| 198.4 | 351.7 | Fish Hatchery Rd.; Montebello, groceries, restaurant, commercial campground, post office 24464 (1.9 mi. W, including SR 600 and VA 56) |
| 197.9 | 352.2 | Spy Rock; scenic views (0.1 mi. E) |
| 197.6 | 352.5 | Maintop Mtn. (4,040 ft.); summit forested, but view on side trail (0.1 mi. S) |
| 194.7 | 355.4 | Crabtree Farm Rd., SR 826, campsites (0.5 mi. W), 3.7 mi. farther W to VA 56 |
| 193.8 | 356.3 | The Priest Shelter; water |
| 193.3 | 356.8 | The Priest (4,063 ft.); scenic views |
| 189.0 | 361.1 | Cross VA 56 and Tye River suspension footbridge; groceries (1.1 mi. W) |
| 186.4 | 363.7 | Harpers Creek Shelter; water |
| 182.2 | 367.9 | Hanging Rock; scenic views |
| 180.2 | 369.9 | Maupin Field Shelter; water |
| 177.9 | 372.2 | Three Ridges Parking Overlook, BRP mp 13.1 |
| 169.7 | 380.4 | Humpback Mtn.; side trail to Humpback Rocks, scenic views |
| 164.0 | 386.0 | Paul Wolfe Shelter; water |
| 159.1 | 391.0 | Rockfish Gap (1,902 ft.), end of BRP and beginning of Skyline Drive; lodging and restaurant; Waynesboro, lodging, groceries, restaurants, laundry, stores, post office 22980 (4.5 mi. W), cross overpass of US 250 and I-64 to continue N |
| 158.3 | 391.8 | Self-registration for hiking permits; side trail (0.2 mi. W) to Skyline Drive entrance station |
| 154.1 | 396.0 | Bear Den Mtn. (2,885 ft.); scenic views |
| 152.1 | 398.0 | Calf Mtn. Shelter (maintained by PATC); water (0.2 mi. W) |
| 139.1 | 411.0 | Blackrock Hut (for long-distance AT hikers only); water (0.2 mi. E) |
| 138.5 | 411.6 | Blackrock (3,092 ft.); scenic views |
| 133.8 | 416.3 | Doyles River Cabin (advance reservations required from PATC); water |
| 131.7 | 418.4 | Loft Mtn. Campground, Skyline Drive mp 79.5; groceries, restaurant, camping, laundry, May through October |
| 125.9 | 424.2 | Pinefield Hut (for long-distance AT hikers only); water |
| 117.7 | 432.4 | Hightop Hut (for long-distance AT hikers only); water (0.2 mi. W) |

| FROM N | FROM S | LOCATION AND DESCRIPTION |
|---|---|---|
| 111.3 | 438.8 | South River Picnic Grounds; water |
| 108.0 | 442.1 | Pocosin Cabin (locked and advance reservations required from PATC); water |
| 106.0 | 444.1 | Lewis Mtn. Campground, Skyline Drive mp 57.6; water (seasonal), camping, groceries, lodging (0.1 mi. w) |
| 105.3 | 444.8 | Bearfence Mtn. Hut (for long-distance AT hikers only); water unreliable |
| 101.8 | 448.3 | Hazeltop (3,816 ft.), highest point of AT in Shenandoah National Park |
| 98.2 | 451.9 | Big Meadows Wayside and Harry Byrd Visitor Center; open all year |
| 97.3 | 452.8 | Big Meadows (3,500 ft.); camping, lodging, restaurant (0.1 mi. E) |
| 93.8 | 456.3 | Rock Spring Cabin (locked and advance reservations required from PATC); water, Rock Spring Hut (for long-distance AT hikers only) |
| 93.5 | 456.6 | Spur trail (0.9 mi. E) to Hawksbill Mtn. (4,050 ft.); highest peak in Shenandoah National Park; Byrd's Nest #2 Picnic Shelter |
| 92.1 | 458.0 | Crescent Rock (0.1 mi. E); scenic views |
| 90.0 | 460.1 | South service road to Skyland Lodge |
| 89.2 | 460.9 | North service road to Skyland Lodge (0.3 mi. w); lodging and restaurant |
| 87.2 | 460.9 | Stony Man Mtn. Overlook (3,097 ft.), Skyline Drive mp 38.6; water |
| 85.0 | 465.1 | Pinnacles Picnic Ground, Skyline Drive mp 36.7; water |
| 81.6 | 468.5 | Mary's Rock (3,514 ft.); panoramic views (0.1-mi. side trail to summit) |
| 79.7 | 470.4 | Thornton Gap (2,307 ft.), US 211, Skyline Drive mp 31.5; restaurant |
| 78.5 | 471.6 | Pass Mtn. Hut (for long-distance AT hikers only); water (0.2 mi. E) |
| 71.1 | 479.0 | Elkwater Gap, Skyline Drive mp 23.9; groceries, restaurant (0.1 mi. E) |
| 70.3 | 479.8 | Range View Cabin (locked and advance reservations required from PATC); water |
| 69.6 | 480.5 | Rattlesnake Point Overlook, Skyline Drive mp 23.9; Mathews Arm Campground (1 mi. w) |
| 69.0 | 481.1 | Junction with **Tuscarora Trail** (a 230-mi. trail into West Virginia and Maryland to rejoin the AT at Dean's Gap, Pennsylvania) |

| FROM N | FROM S | LOCATION AND DESCRIPTION |
|--------|--------|--------------------------|
| 65.4 | 484.7 | Gravel Springs Hut (for long-distance **AT** hikers only); water |
| 64.1 | 486.0 | South Marshall Mtn. (3,212 ft.); scenic views; North Marshall Mtn. (3,368 ft.) 1.2 mi. apart; scenic views |
| 58.8 | 491.3 | Compton Springs; water |
| 55.6 | 494.5 | Possum's Rest; outcropping, N boundary of Shenandoah National Park |
| 54.9 | 495.2 | Tom Floyd Wayside (primitive camping for long-distance **AT** hikers only); self-registration camping permits; water, no open fires |
| 52.0 | 498.1 | Cross US 522; Front Royal, groceries, restaurants, lodging, laundry, stores, post office 22630 (3.2 mi. to 4.2 mi. W) |
| 46.8 | 503.3 | Denton Shelter; water |
| 43.8 | 506.3 | Manassas Gap; cross VA 55 to SR 725 and under I-66; Linden, groceries, post office 22642 (1 mi. W on VA 55) |
| 41.3 | 508.8 | Manassas Gap Shelter; water |
| 36.9 | 513.2 | Dick's Dome Shelter; water (0.2 mi. E) |
| 34.6 | 515.5 | Sky Meadows State Park; steep side trail 1.3 mi. to fee campsites and shelter, water |
| 28.5 | 518.6 | Ashby Gap, US 50; Paris, restaurant (0.1 mi. E), post office 22130 (0.8 mi. E), restaurant and lodging (1.2 mi. E) |
| 27.9 | 522.2 | Rod Hollow Shelter; water |
| 21.0 | 529.1 | Sam Moore Shelter; water |
| 18.0 | 532.1 | Bear Den Rocks; scenic views (Bear Den Hostel lodging 0.2 mi. E) |
| 17.4 | 532.7 | Snickers Gap (1,060 ft.), junction of SR 679 and VA 7; Bluemont, restaurant and groceries (0.3 mi. to 1 mi. W), post office (1.7 mi. E) |
| 10.1 | 540.0 | Blackburn Trail Center; camping, water, shelter (0.3 mi. E), campsites (0.1 mi. E) |
| 6.9 | 543.2 | Lesser Memorial Shelter (0.1 mi. E); water (0.3 mi. E) |
| 3.9 | 546.2 | Keys Gap; WV/VA 9, groceries, restaurant (0.3 mi. W and 0.3 mi. E) |
| 0.0 | 550.1 | Loudoun Heights, West Virginia/Virginia state line (1,200 ft.), and juncture with 3.2-mi., blue-blazed **Loudoun Heights Trail**; N on the **AT** is a 1.4-mi. descent in West Virginia to US 340 and crossing of Shenandoah River Bridge; lodging (0.1 mi. W), camping (1.2 mi. W); farther N 0.3 mi. on **AT** into Harpers Ferry is side trail (0.2 mi.) to Appalachian Trail Conference headquarters; town has lodging, groceries, stores, laundry, restaurants, post office 25425; farther N 0.7 mi. on **AT** is crossing of Potomac River on Bryon Memorial Footbridge into Maryland. |

**490**

*The mountains through which the Parkway runs are*
*considered to be among the oldest in the world.*
HARLEY E. JOLLEY (1920– )

# 4. Blue Ridge Parkway

America's most scenic highway, the Blue Ridge Parkway (BRP) traverses the ridge-line of the Southern Appalachians from Shenandoah National Park to the Great Smoky Mountains National Park. Initial funding for construction of the 469-mile ribbon of natural beauty was allocated by Congress in 1933 under the authority of the National Industrial Recovery Act. Three years later a bill introduced by North Carolina congressman Robert Lee Doughton authorized the administration and maintenance of the highway by the NPS. Many members of Congress opposed the bill on the belief that the federal government could not afford this luxury during the Great Depression. After a close favorable vote in the Senate, President Frank-lin D. Roosevelt signed the bill on June 22, 1936. Although most of the parkway was completed in the 1930s, its final 6.5 miles at Grandfather Mountain were not dedicated until September 11, 1987.

Credit for the BRP idea goes mainly to Harry F. Byrd, a U.S. senator from Virginia, but Theodore E. Straus of Maryland, a member of the Public Works Administration, gives himself credit. Senator Byrd accompanied President Roose-velt on an inspection tour of the CCC camps in the Shenandoah National Park in August 1933. At this occasion the president expressed his satisfaction with the CCC's work and its potential. When Senator Byrd suggested the Skyline Drive be extended to the Great Smokies, the president replied that he liked the idea and that perhaps it should also include a route to New England. He instructed the senator to discuss the idea with Harold L. Ickes, Roosevelt's secretary of the interior. They later worked out a right-of-way. Initially the plans for the route were to include Tennessee, but political controversy, routing problems, and the influ-ence of North Carolina ambassador Josephus Daniels, a close friend of Secretary Ickes, omitted the state. (Governors in the Northeast were contacted by Secretary Ickes, but the governors were not interested in the project.) Land purchases, over a narrow corridor in most places, included 81,536 acres in North Carolina and 30,887 in Virginia. Designed and engineered for leisure travel at no more than 45 mph, there are scores of overlooks, waysides, and parking areas for recreational purposes. Commercial vehicles are not allowed. (For information on partner orga-nizations focused on protection of Parkway viewing areas, call the BRP office in Asheville, N.C., at 828-271-4779, ext. 201.)

Flora on the parkway is diverse because of the elevation range from 646 feet at the James River (mp 63.2) to 3,950 feet at Apple Orchard Mountain (mp 76.7). Among the most common flowering plants are rosebay and catawba rhododendron, mountain laurel, flame azalea, black-eyed Susan, aster, trillium, and wild geranium. Less common, but of exceptional fragrance, is rose azalea (*Rhododendron roseum*), usually in blossom in late May or early June. The hardwoods on the BRP are those common to the Southern Appalachians, and the conifers are hemlock, pine, and in high elevations, red spruce and Fraser fir. The gypsy moth on hardwoods and the sap-sucking woolly adelgid on hemlocks have caused damage or defoliation to hundreds of acres along the BRP. At best, because of the difficulty and expense of treatment, the NPS is trying to protect the immediate corridor of the BRP. At the visitor centers there is a free information brochure that lists the peak flowering species and the location of more than 345 wildflowers. Motorists, and particularly hikers, will see wildlife on the parkway and trails. More common species are chipmunk, woodchuck, opossum, raccoon, deer, and gray squirrel. Less likely to be seen are fox, bobcat, and black bear. At least 100 species of birds, including the spring migrators, have been identified.

The chief recreational areas in Virginia are at Humpback Rock, Otter Creek, Peaks of Otter, Roanoke Mountain, Smart View, Rocky Knob, and Mabry Mill. A popular tourist attraction, the BRP draws more than 21.5 million visitors annually, with the peak attendance in October, because of the kaleidoscope of forest colors, and in July. Activities include camping, fishing, bicycling, hiking, horseback riding, picnicking, cross-country skiing, and nature study. Hotel-type lodging is offered only at Peaks of Otter Lodge, open year round (and with special winter rates from the end of November to the end of March) at mp 84–87. Cabins (open June 1 through Labor Day) are available at Rock Castle Gap (mp 174), which is part of the Rocky Knob recreational area. Reservations are advised for either location (see Addresses and Information, below).

In addition to outdoor activities and lodging, there are historic exhibits, museums, cultural displays, arts and crafts shops, visitor centers, and restaurants. Food service is available at Otter Creek (mp 68.8), Peaks of Otter (mp 85.6), and Mabry Mill (mp 176.2). Gasoline is available at Peaks of Otter. The nearest towns and cities along the parkway for support services and amenities are Waynesboro, Buena Vista, Roanoke, Floyd, Meadows of Dan, and Fancy Gap.

With such popularity and density of visitors, the NPS has a number of important regulations designed to protect the natural environment. Camping is allowed only at designated campgrounds. Fires are permitted only in campgrounds and picnic areas. All plants and animals are protected by law. Hunting and the carrying of firearms are prohibited. Pets must be on a leash or under physical control. Littering is prohibited. Quiet hours in campgrounds must be observed from 10 P.M. to 6 A.M. No swimming is allowed.

In Virginia the NPS lists thirty-eight individual trails and seven short strips of the

AT that connect to parking areas. Three trails, such as the **White Rock Falls Trail**, are mainly in a national forest but are accessible via the BRP. Although the NPS claims 18.5 miles for the **Roanoke Valley Horse Trail**, only 10.8 miles (from mp 110.6 to mp 121.4 at US 220) are defined. Crossing the Roanoke River is a major problem. Hikers may find the multiple-use **Chestnut Ridge Trail**, which connects with the **Roanoke Valley Horse Trail**, to be the most desirable. The longest foot trail is 10.8-mile **Rock Castle Gorge Trail** (mp 167.1), and the shortest are 0.1-mile round-trip trails such as **The Priest Overlook Trail** (mp 6) and the **Boston Knob Trail** (mp 10).

Topographically paralleling the parkway are 126.4 miles of the AT from Waynesboro at I-64/US 250 to near Troutville at SR 653. Sections of the AT farthest away in the parallel are The Priest and Bald Knob in the Pedlar Ranger District of the GWNF and Cove Mountain in the Glenwood Ranger District of the JNF. (Both districts are now combined with the George Washington and Jefferson National Forests.)

The NPS advises hikers to leave information with a ranger when vehicles are left away from campgrounds overnight. Be prepared for any sudden change in weather. Do not drink from the streams or springs unless the water is purified. Camp only at designated sites. Do not climb rocks at road cuts. Do not carry firearms. Do not damage or feed wildlife, or damage any flowering plants. For fishing, a state license is necessary for people 16 years or older.

ADDRESSES AND INFORMATION: Blue Ridge Parkway, 199 Hemphill Knob Rd., Asheville, NC 28803; phone: 828-298-0398 for recorded information and other telephone numbers; 828-271-4779 for road and weather conditions; 828-271-4744 for administration; and 800-727-5928 for accidents, fire, or other emergencies (callers with cellular telephone do not call CH). For ranger offices near the BRP, the districts and addresses are as follows: Ridge District (mp 0–106), Montebello Office, 133 Whetstone Ridge Rd., Vesuvius, VA 24483, phone: 540-377-2377, fax: 276-377-6758; Big Island Office, P.O. Box 345, Big Island, VA 24526, phone: 804-299-5941; Peaks of Otter Office, Rt. 2, Box 163, Bedford, VA 24523, phone: 540-586-4357. Plateau District (mp 106–216), 1670 Blue Ridge Parkway, Floyd, VA 24091; Vinton Office, 2551 Mountain View Rd., Vinton, VA 24179, phone: 540-857-2490; Rocky Knob Office, phone: 540-745-9681, fax: 540-745-9665; Fancy Gap Office, Rt. 2, Box 3, Fancy Gap, VA 24328, phone: 276-728-4511. Reservations for Peaks of Otter, phone: 540-586-1081 (800-542-5927 toll free in Virginia). For Rocky Knob Cabins, phone: 540-593-3503. Available for free are BRP brochure with map, BRP Virginia trails list, special locality trail maps, and flyers for services, campgrounds, lodge, and general information.

### Mountain Farm Trail (mp 5.9) 491

An easy, 0.4-mile round-trip, self-guiding trail from Humpback Rocks Visitor Center, past pioneer Carter family homestead, to "kissin' gate."

**492  Humpback Rock Trail (AT) (mp 6)**

From Humpback Gap (2,360 ft.) parking area east to the **AT** is a strenuous ascent south for 0.8 mile to excellent views north and west. Continuing south, it is 1 mile to the northern crest of Humpback Mountain, with good views north and east, and to the south at the summit (3,650 ft.). Descend 1.7 miles to 0.3-mile, blue-blazed spur trail, right, to large Humpback Rock Picnic Area (mp 8.4). (The trail from Humpback Gap to the Humpback Rock and north to the **AT** are now entirely blue blazed since the **AT** has been relocated farther away from the Parkway to the east.)

**493  Cotoctin Trail (mp 8.4)**

From the farthest circle of Humpback Rock Picnic Area, this easy, 0.3-mile round-trip, unblazed path leads to a rock outcrop with sedum and a view of Rockfish Valley.

**494  Greenstone Trail (mp 8.8)**

From Greenstone parking area east, follow an easy, 0.2-mile round-trip, self-guiding trail around green volcanic chlorite and epidote of the northern Blue Ridge Mountains.

**495  The Priest Overlook Trail (mp 17.6)**

This is an easy, 0.1-mile round-trip walk for a southeastern view of The Priest (4,065 ft.).

**258  White Rock Falls Trail (mp 18.5)**

From a grassy parking area (west), cross the BRP to a moderately difficult GWNF orange-blazed trail. Follow it for 1.4 miles to beautiful cascades. Ahead are strenuous 1.3 miles to Slacks Overlook (mp 19.9). (Described in Chapter 1.)

**259  White Rock Gap Trail (mp 18.5)**

On the western side of the BRP. This is a moderate walk for 0.4 miles to a junction on the left with the **Slacks Overlook Trail**, partly in the GWNF. (Described in Chapter 1.)

**496  Big Spy Mountain Trail (mp 26.3)**

This grassy, easy trail extends 0.1 mile to a panoramic view (3,185 ft.) of the Shenandoah Valley, west, and Tye River Valley, east. The knoll has butter-and-eggs, lavender, bee balm, clover, and other wildflowers.

**497  Yankee Horse Trail (mp 34.4)**

An easy, 0.2-mile trail on the site of an old narrow-gauge logging railroad, where timber was harvested in the 1920s. Wigwam Falls is in a hemlock grove (2,140 ft.).

**498  Boston Knob Trail (mp 38.8)**

A graded, easy 0.1-mile trail under black birch and dogwood to a scenic view (2,523 ft.).

**Indian Gap Trail** (mp 47.5)                                                      499

Within an easy, 0.3-mile loop trail are large balancing rocks, oaks, and mountain laurel (2,098 ft.).

**White Oak Flats Trail** (mp 55.2)                                                 500

From the picnic table at White Oak Flats parking area (1,460 ft.), go south for an easy, 0.1-mile round-trip in open forest by a small stream.

## OTTER CREEK/JAMES RIVER RECREATION AREA

This recreation area extends along Otter Creek from a parking overlook with picnic tables (mp 58.2) to a visitor center at the James River bridge (mp 63.6). In between is a campground with a restaurant and gift shop (mp 60.8) (phone: 434-299-5862). The area is bordered on both sides by the GWNF and is accessible from VA 130 on the northern side and from US 501 on the southern side of the James River, upriver from Lynchburg. One of the area's most popular activities is fishing in Otter Creek. The sixty-seven-unit campground has trailer and tent sites, flush rest rooms, and waste disposal system. Both the restaurant and the campground receive a high volume of visitors. The area has four trails.

**Otter Creek Trail** (3.4 mi.), **Otter Lake Trail** (0.8 mi.) (mp 60.8 to 63.6)      501–2
LENGTH AND DIFFICULTY: 4.2 miles (6.7 km) combined; easy
FEATURES: cascades, fishing, wildlife, wildflowers, historic sites
TRAILHEADS: The northern trailhead is at Otter Creek restaurant parking lot, and
  the southern trailhead is at the visitor center.
DESCRIPTION: Follow downstream on the trout-stocked Otter Creek through a
  forest of oak, beech, hemlock, hornbeam, rhododendron, and mountain laurel.
  At 0.6 mile pass Terrapin Hill Overlook and go under the BRP and VA 130,
  crossing Otter Creek twice. Pass Lower Otter Creek Overlook at 1.9 miles and
  reach a junction with the **Otter Lake Trail** at 2.4 miles. (The **Otter Lake Trail**
  ascends left to switchbacks on the hillside. After 0.3 mi. there is a bench for
  resting and for viewing the lake below. At 0.8 mi. the trail descends to steps
  below the dam to a junction with the **Otter Creek Trail**.) Continuing on the
  **Otter Creek Trail**, pass the 0.2-mile Otter Lake parking area to descend below
  the dam at 2.7 miles. After following part of an old railroad grade, arrive at the
  visitor center parking area at 3.4 miles.
USGS MAP: Big Island

**James River Trail** (0.2 mi.), **Trail of Trees** (0.5 mi.) (mp 63.6)              503–4
LENGTH AND DIFFICULTY: 0.9 miles (1.5 km) combined, round-trip; easy
FEATURES: elevated footbridge, canal lock, botanical tour, scenic view
TRAILHEAD: Otter Creek Visitor Center parking area
DESCRIPTION: From the visitor center at the northern end of the James River

*James River Trail,*
*Blue Ridge Parkway*

Bridge, descend to a junction of trails under the bridge. Walk on a unique elevated footbridge under the James River Bridge for scenic river views. Descend on steps to an island at Battery Creek Lock in a grassy area with information exhibits at 0.2 mile. Here is the lowest point in elevation (about 600 ft.) of any trail on the BRP. Backtrack to the **Trail of Trees**, left, on a self-guiding botanical tour, which loops back to the visitor center.

USGS MAP: Big Island

505  **Thunder Ridge Trail** (AT) (mp 74.7)

An easy, 0.1-mile walk on the **AT** to views of Arnold Valley, west.

285  **Apple Orchard Falls Trail** (mp 78.7)

The access to the falls from Sunset Field Overlook (3,474 ft.) is in 0.2 mile of BRP property to the JNF, where the strenuous hike descends 1.2 miles. Backtrack. See Chapter 2 for details.

506  **Onion Mountain Loop Trail** (mp 79.7)

A short, easy, 0.2-mile trail in a deciduous forest with rhododendron and mountain laurel over lichen-covered rocks (3,195 ft.).

## PEAKS OF OTTER RECREATION AREA

*(mp 82.5 to 87.6)*

The Peaks of Otter is a 4,200-acre recreational park on the BRP. There are no otters here. Three peaks (Flat Top, Sharp Top, and Harkening Hill) form a triangle, however, and a lake and visitor center are in the center of the triangle. Facilities include a trail system of 15 miles for viewing magnificent scenery and studying at least fifty-five species of trees and shrubs. Among them are tree-of-heaven, Carolina hemlock, minnie bush (*Menziesia pilosa*), mountain ash, and fragrant thimbleberry. At least sixty species of wildflowers have been found here as well as more than forty-five species of birds and other wildlife. The park has a visitor center, a picnic area, a 24-acre lake stocked with brown and rainbow trout, and a large, 141-site campground (without hookups). A concessioner operates the fifty-eight-room Peaks of Otter Lodge and Restaurant, open all year. (Address for the lodge is Virginia Peaks of Otter Co., P.O. Box 489, Bedford, VA 24523; phone: 540-586-1081; visitor center phone: 540-586-9263.)

**Fallingwater Cascades Trail** (1.6 mi.), **Flat Top Trail** (4.4 mi.), **Cross Rock Trail** (0.1 mi.) (mp 83.1 to 83.5)    507–9

LENGTH AND DIFFICULTY: 6.1 miles (9.8 km) combined, partial round-trip; moderate to strenuous

FEATURES: cascades, scenic views, geological formations

TRAILHEADS: Fallingwater Cascades parking area, or Peaks of Otter picnic area

DESCRIPTION: The **Fallingwater Cascades Trail** and the **Flat Top Trail** were designated national recreation trails in 1982. Together they offer the scenic splendor of cascades in a gorge and of panoramic views from a high rocky peak. From Fallingwater Cascades parking area follow signs a few feet to the trail and turn right. Descend for 0.4 mile to the cascades, where hemlock, striped maple, and rosebay rhododendron form a partial cover. Cross the falls four times, using care on slippery rocks in a flume area. After 0.3 mile by the cascades ascend to a junction with an access to the **Flat Top Trail**, right. Either turn left for completion of the **Fallingwater Cascades Trail**, or stay right to cross the BRP and reach the Flat Top parking area.

For the **Flat Top Trail** enter a forest of tall poplars and parallel the BRP to the first switchback. Here begins a 1,492-foot increase in elevation by switchbacks to Flat Top Mountain (4,001 ft.). On the way there is a steep, short, spur trail, **Cross Rock Trail**, to the left, at 2.2 miles. Pass The Pinnacle rock formation and reach Flat Top at 2.8 miles for panoramic views of the area. Southwest is a spectacular view of Sharp Top. Descend on switchbacks to the Peaks of Otter picnic area on VA 43, 0.6 mile east from the visitor center. Backtrack or use a second vehicle.

USGS MAP: Arnold Valley

**Sharp Top Trail** (1.5 mi.), **Elk Run Trail** (0.8 mi.), **Harkening Hill Trail** (3.3 mi.), **Johnson Farm Loop Trail** (2.1 mi.) (mp 85.7 to 86)    510–13

LENGTH AND DIFFICULTY: 10.7 miles (17.1 km) combined, round-trip; easy to strenuous

FEATURES: scenic views, wildflowers, wildlife, historic sites, geological formations

TRAILHEADS: The **Sharp Top Trail** begins at the camp store and bus station across the BRP from the visitor center; all other trails begin at the visitor center.

DESCRIPTION: The **Sharp Top Trail** (3 mi. round-trip) is the area's most popular trail peak. A strenuous ascent by foot, it can also be accessed by a BRP shuttle bus. At the top (3,875 ft.) are views of Bedford and the piedmont to the east, the Shenandoah Valley to the west, and the Blue Ridge Mountains north and south. Southwest on Sharp Top is a 0.4-mile spur trail among boulders to Buzzards Roost, also a site for scenic sights.

Another popular trail is the **Elk Run Trail**, an easy, 0.8-mile self-guiding loop nature trail near a stream. Its entrance is from the northern side of the parking area at the visitor center. (A brochure is available.) A much longer moderate to strenuous loop is the **Harkening Hill Trail**. It begins behind the visitor center near the amphitheater and ascends west on switchbacks to a ridgeline. The summit of Harkening Hill (3,364 ft.) is 1.8 miles. Descend and after 0.1 mile pass the Balanced Rock on a short side trail to the right. At 2.3 miles are views of former farmland and the current Johnson Farm trail area. After another 0.3 mile is a junction with the **Johnson Farm Loop Trail** on the left. Continue for 0.7 mile on the right for a return past an access trail to the lodge and on to the visitor center, or follow the **Johnson Farm Loop Trail** to leave the forest and enter the Johnson Farm area. There is a restored farmhouse and barn, outbuildings, and a garden. Follow the trail right, partially on an old road, cross a stream, and at 1.8 miles reach a junction with the **Harkening Hill Trail**, which returns to the parking lot at the visitor center. (There is also an easy, 1-mi. trail that circles Abbott Lake to the east of the visitor center and in front of Peaks of Otter Lodge.)

(Five miles south of the visitor center on the BRP begin a number of moderately difficult trails either on or connected by the **AT**. They range from 0.6 mi. to 2.9 mi. Hikers should look for these connections at mp 90.9, 92.5, 95.4, 95.9, 96.0, and 97.0, with a spur trail to Bobblets Gap lean-to from mp 93.1. See Glenwood/Pedlar Ranger District in Chapter 2.)

USGS MAP: Peaks of Otter

514 **Stewarts Knob Trail** (mp 110.7)

At the far end of the parking lot (1,275 ft.) is a 0.1-mile path, one way, leading up the embankment among oak, hickory, and sweet cicely. Keep right on all turns to a pedestrian overlook with a bench. Here is a magnificent view of the city of Roanoke.

515 **Roanoke River Trail** (mp 114.9)

From the parking area, the main trail leads to series of trails. One is a 0.6-mile loop beyond and underpassing the high bridge of the BRP. It passes through large stands of hemlock and wildflowers such as dwarf iris. A linear 0.1-mile trail, one way, descends to a river overlook. Other linear short trails (made by fishermen and explorers) descend to the river rocks and sandbars.

### Roanoke Mountain Summit Trail (mp 120.4)  516

Access is on a winding, narrow loop road from the BRP to a parking lot at the summit of Roanoke Mountain. The access is 3.7 miles round-trip and restricted to vehicles without trailers. The 0.3-mile rocky trail offers good views of Roanoke Valley. (Beginning in 2002 the BRP closes the road to vehicular traffic from November 30 through March 15. At all other times usage is from sunrise to sunset only.)

## ROANOKE MOUNTAIN CAMPGROUND
*(mp 120.5)*

Leave the BRP and drive 1.1 miles on Mill Mountain Spur Road to Chestnut Ridge Overlook. The Roanoke Mountain Campground is 0.2 mile ahead. The campground has trailer and tent campsites (no hookups), flush rest rooms, and a waste disposal system. The **Chestnut Ridge Trail** makes a loop around the campground. The campground is open all year. One mile beyond the campground is Roanoke's Mill Mountain Zoological Park (phone: 276-343-3241). The campground is closed from October 1 until May.

### Chestnut Ridge Trail (mp 120.5)  517
LENGTH AND DIFFICULTY: 5.4 miles (8.6 km), round-trip; moderate
FEATURES: historic site, wildflowers
TRAILHEAD: Chestnut Ridge Overlook
DESCRIPTION: This trail is part of the **Roanoke Valley Horse Trail** system; hikers  518
may find the trail rough, though well graded. It has gentle and moderate ascents and descents in a hardwood forest with mountain laurels and blueberries. Patches of galax, cat's claw, and woodland sunflowers are frequent. From the Mill Mountain Spur Road at Chestnut Ridge Overlook parking area follow the red-blazed trail left for 1.5 miles to SR 699 (Yellow Mountain Rd.). An access side trail to cross Mill Mountain Spur Road is on the left; otherwise cross under the bridge left and continue south through the woods. At 2.1 miles is a junction with a trail loop, left, around the campground, and again at 3.1 miles. At 4.5 miles reach SR 672. Across the road is a short access trail to the **Roanoke Valley Horse Trail**. It divides near Gum Spring Overlook. (From there it runs parallel to the BRP south to US 220 and north to cross SR 668.) Turn left on SR 672 and pass under the Mill Mountain Spur Road. Begin an ascent at 4.7 miles and reach the point of origin at 5.4 miles.
USGS MAP: Garden City

519 **Buck Mountain Trail** (mp 123.2)

From Buck Mountain Parking Overlook ascend moderately 0.5 mile through hardwoods, scattered pine, and mountain laurel to the summit of Buck Mountain. Here are scenic views of southern Roanoke Valley. Backtrack.

520 **Smart View Loop Trail** (mp 154.5)

The **Smart View Loop Trail** begins at the parking lot near the picnic entrance. Follow the sign across a field to picnic area access at 0.3 mile. Continue through cattle pasture to south of Smart View Parking Overlook and then descend to stream. Large deciduous trees, abundant wildflowers, and elderberry grace the trail. Cross Rennet Bag Branch, pass a dead-end spur trail on the right, and follow slope to eastern edge of park maintenance area. Complete the loop at 2.6 miles.


## ROCKY KNOB RECREATION AREA
*(mp 167–174)*

The Rocky Knob Recreation Area has 4,200 acres, mainly east of the BRP; Rock Castle Gorge is its primary geographic feature. Major activities are camping, picnicking, hiking, fishing, and nature study. It has more than 150 species of birds, and among the mammals are deer, bear, bobcat, raccoon, and fox. Reptiles include rattlesnake and copperhead. Seasonal changes may vary as much as three weeks because of the altitude difference from the low country at the gorge. Heavily wooded with the usual Appalachian species, this area also has a large section of Carolina hemlock on the northern slopes of the gorge. Early settlers named the gorge from the octagon-shaped quartz crystals with pyramid tips.

Facilities at the recreation area include a visitor center, picnic grounds (with a 1.3-mi. yellow-blazed loop trail around the picnic area), housekeeping cabins, Rocky Knob Campground, and backcountry camping in Rock Castle Gorge. The developed campground is at mp 167. It has ninety-two trailer and tent sites (no hookups), flush rest rooms, and waste disposal system. Firewood is for sale. It is open usually from May 1 through October. At mp 169 is a picnic area and ballfield, and between the picnic area and the campground is an access trail to scenic Saddle Parking Overlook, mp 168. A spur trail also goes to the summit of Rocky Knob (3,572 ft.), with its twin knobs. The housekeeping cabins, at mp 174, are operated by the concessioner who operates the restaurant and gift shop at the popular Mabry Mill, mp 176. Backcountry camping is allowed only in the gorge, and no-fee permits from the ranger are necessary.

521 **Rock Castle Gorge Trail** (mp 167.1)

LENGTH AND DIFFICULTY: 10.6 miles (16.9 km) round-trip; strenuous

522–24 CONNECTING TRAILS: **Woodland Trail** (0.8 mi.), **Black Ridge Trail** (3 mi.), **Hardwood Cove Trail** (0.8 mi.)

FEATURES: scenic views, waterfalls, homesite history, fishing

TRAILHEADS: Rocky Knob Campground, mp 167.1. (There is also vehicular access to the lowest level of the trail's descent near the end of SR 605, which is 0.7 mi. from VA 8, north of the Rock Castle Creek bridge.)

DESCRIPTION: This is a popular trail with diversity in plant and animal life, temperature, and terrain. It was designated a national recreation trail in 1982. From Rocky Knob Campground entrance, cross BRP to fence stile and begin to ascend on a grassy bald. Follow white blazes for 0.6 mile to Saddle Parking Overlook. The trail continues up the edge of the mountain, and the red-blazed, 0.8-mile **Woodland Trail** goes right to the parking lot and shelter in the picnic area. Ascend steeply and reach the summit of Rocky Knob at 0.8 mile. Here is a log shelter constructed by the CCC in the 1930s. The superb views are of Rock Castle Valley, VA 8, and on to Woolwine. At 1.2 miles is a junction with the **Woodland Trail**, which descends 0.3 mile to a picnic area across the parkway. Arrive at the Rock Castle Gorge Overlook (3,195 ft.) (mp 168.7) at 1.7 miles. Parallel the BRP in and out of woods and open grassy spaces. At 1.9 miles join the **Black Ridge Trail**, right. (It slightly ascends to the visitor center after 0.1 mi. From the visitor center the 3-mi., blue-blazed **Black Ridge Trail** follows moderately through forest and open pasture balds. It passes a scenic rock formation at 2 mi. and descends in an open pastoral setting. It loops back to the visitor center.)

Continuing on the **Rock Castle Gorge Trail**, pass a number of resting benches and arrive at Grassy Knoll (3,480 ft.) at 3.4 miles. Begin descent into a deep defile with a cascading stream. The forest canopy is composed of large sugar maples, oaks, and virgin tulip poplar. After a number of switchbacks, reach the **Hardwood Cove Trail** at 4.3 miles. (It is a 0.8-mi. self-guiding nature trail that runs jointly with the **Rock Castle Gorge Trail**. Markers and brochures explain the geology and biology of the area.) Enter an enormous 12-acre jumble of boulders known locally as the Bear Rocks, a haven for wildlife. At the end of the nature trail, cross Rock Castle Creek at 4.9 miles. Turn left on the old Rock Castle Pike, a pioneer road for wagons and carriages transporting people and supplies from the foothills to the Great Valley through Rock Castle Gap (2,970 ft.). Descend among borders of rosebay rhododendron, cascades and flumes in the stream, and mossy treadway. Cross the creek a couple of times, pass a large vacant two-story clapboard house with an old-fashioned springhouse, and cross the creek again at 7.1 miles. At 7.4 miles reach a primitive campground (1,720 ft.), the site of a former CCC camp. (A permit from the ranger is necessary to camp here.) Continue on the old road to where the trail turns sharply left up a slope at 7.6 miles. (Ahead 100 yd. is a parking area and gate for access to VA 8. See Trailheads, above.) From here the trail ascends gradually in and out of coves from Little Rock Castle Creek. In a mixed forest there are ferns, bloodroot, and trillium. Pass a number of resting benches, and at 9.5 miles the climb becomes more moderate. Enter a field and return to the fence stile at the point of origin at 10.6 miles.

USGS MAP: Woolwine

525  **Mountain Industry Trail** (mp 176.2)

This 0.4-mile round-trip walk passes through a reconstructed community show-ing mountain use of waterpower. E. B. Mabry's Mill (originally operated from 1910 to 1935) is probably the most photographed view of human history on the BRP. In addition to other buildings there is a modern restaurant and gift shop at the parking area. A highlight of the year is the arts and crafts festival in October.

526  **Round Meadow Creek Trail** (mp 179.2)

From the Round Meadow Parking Overlook (2,800 ft.) descend steeply on a 0.5-mile loop trail into a gorge of rhododendron and tall hemlock.

527  **Blue Ridge Music Center Trail** (mp 213)

This outdoor amphitheater is the site of weekend concerts during the summer. Work began on a new trail from the parking lot in 2002.

*Shenandoah, like our other National Parks, is a museum.*
*Its exhibits are scenery, wildlife and flowers.*
HENRY HEATWOLE (1915–1989)

# 5. Shenandoah National Park

The 196,000-acre Shenandoah National Park is on the northern Blue Ridge Mountains from Front Royal south to Waynesboro, where it connects with the BRP at Rockfish Gap. Its ragged dimensions (it varies from 2 to 13 mi. wide) represent the piecing together of about 3,870 tracts acquired from private landowners in the 1920s and early 1930s. Winding through the park's full length is the famous 105-mile Skyline Drive, an engineering work of art. In its gentle weave along the ridgeline, the scenic highway encounters sixty peaks that range from 2,000 feet to 4,000 feet in elevation. Almost halfway in the park, near Skyland, is Hawksbill (4,051 ft.), the park's highest point, and to its east is the notable Old Rag (3,268 ft.), a singular, granite-topped mountain. Paralleling the drive is 101 miles of the **AT**, to which the **Tuscarora Trail** connects west of Mathews Arm Campground. In addition, there are more than 400 miles of other trails in the park. Gracing the hollows and canyons are sixteen waterfalls with a range in height of 28 to 93 feet. For spectacular views, visitors may choose among seventy-five overlooks to the historic Shenandoah Valley, the south fork of the Shenandoah River, Massanutten Mountain range to the west, and rolling piedmont to the east.

The park is easily accessible from I-66 at the northern end, I-64 at the southern end, I-81 on the western side, and US 29 and US 522 on the eastern side. Two major highways cross the park and divide it into three parts: North District from Front Royal to US 211 in Thornton Gap, Central District from US 211 to US 33 in Swift Run Gap, and South District to US 250/I-64 in Rockfish Gap.

Congress authorized the park in May 1926, after which the state purchased through condemnation 280 square miles of land from private citizens. From state legislative appropriations and private gifts the land was donated to the federal government—a gift from Virginians to the nation. In December 1935 the park was fully established, and the Skyline Drive, begun in 1931, was completed in 1939. Congress set aside 80,000 acres for wilderness areas in 1976.

Nearly 95 percent forested, mainly with hardwoods, the park contains more than 100 species of trees. But vast areas of the forests were defoliated by the gypsy moth in the late 1980s and early 1990s. Springtime is the season to see many of the 1,200 species of flowering plants, some of which are trillium, wild orchid, pink azalea, and mountain laurel. But October (middle two weeks) is the month of the

*Hazel Mountain Overlook,*
*Shenandoah National Park*

most brilliant colors, when the maples and poplars of the coves turn orange and yellow, and the black gums and oaks on the mountain tops are burgundy red and rust. Of the 2 million annual visitors, more come in October than any other month. (July is the second most popular month.)

A sanctuary for wildlife, the park is home to 200 species of birds, of which 35 are warblers. Bear, deer, turkey, grouse, raccoon, squirrel, and chipmunk are the animals most likely seen. Timber rattlesnakes and copperheads are the only two poisonous snakes, and neither is likely to be seen from November through March. It is illegal to kill, harm, feed, or even frighten any wildlife in the park.

Visitor centers are at Dickey Ridge, 5 miles south from Front Royal; Big Meadows, halfway through the park; and Loft Mountain Information Center at mile 79.5 in the southern part of the park. There are four campgrounds: Mathews Arm (mile 22.2), Big Meadows (mile 51.2), Lewis Mountain (mile 57.5), and Loft Mountain (mile 79.5). Electricity and water hookups are not available. (Big Meadows is usually open from early April through November; Mathews Arm and Lewis Mountain mid-May through October; and Loft Mountain early May to end of October.) Overnight lodging and restaurants are at Skyland Lodge (mile 41–43) and Big Meadows Lodge (mile 51.2). One or both may be open from early April to November. Cabins may be rented at Lewis Mountain (mile 57.5). Additionally, the PATC has six backcountry trail cabins for rent. (For information on location and fees, see PATC address, below.) There are seven picnic areas along the highway. Gasoline and groceries are available at Elkwallow (mile 24.1), Big Meadows (mile 51.0), and Loft Mountain (mile 79.5).

Backcountry campers must obtain a free permit to camp. Campers are encouraged to use Leave No Trace camping and hiking practices. Regulations are provided upon obtaining the permit. Pets must be restrained, and except for seeing-eye dogs, none are allowed in public buildings or on some of the trails, such as the top section of Old Rag Mountain. Forbidden on the trails are ATVs, snowmobiles, and bicycles, but snow skiing is allowed on any roads or trails. Horseback riding is confined to equestrian trails. The usual speed limit for autos in the park is 35 mph.

Foot trails and equestrian trails form a network throughout the park. There are at least forty-three designated short- and long-circuit hikes, but hikers with park maps, or observing any of the Skyline Drive's thirty trail-access signboards, can create more. Some of the trails with high traffic volume are **Whiteoak Canyon** (5 mi.), **Cedar Run** (3.5 mi.), **Dark Hollow Falls** (0.7 mi.), **South River Falls** (1.3 mi.), **Doyles River** (4.7 mi.), **Jeremys Run** (5.3 mi.), and **Old Rag** (3.1 mi.). Some basic information is provided in the pages ahead. Hikers with extensive plans are advised to have park trail maps and PATC's books and maps on the **AT** side trails and circuit trails. Because Old Rag Mountain is distinct from the main ridgeline of the park, its trails are described here in more detail.

There are two access roads and two access trails to the summit of Old Rag Mountain. Only day hikes are permitted. To avoid the crowds, go on a weekday. If accessing the northern side from Skyline Drive at Thornton Gap, drive 8 miles east on US 211 to Sperryville. Turn right on US 522, and after 0.7 mile turn right on VA 231. Drive 8.1 miles to SR 601 at Hughes River bridge. Turn right, upstream, and continue for 3.4 miles (SR 602 becomes SR 707 and then SR 600) to a large overflow parking area on the left. Ahead it is 0.5 mile to the **Nicholson Hollow Trail**, right, and another 0.5 mile to a small parking area for the **Ridge Trail**.  528 (Ahead is gated, yellow-blazed **Weakley Hollow Fire Road**.) Begin the 2,160-foot-in-elevation climb of the **Ridge Trail** at the trail sign. After 1.5 miles reach the ridge where the forest is less dense but the rock scramble becomes more intense. Crawl over, pass around, and twist through the granite fissures to reach the summit (3,268 ft.) at 2.7 miles. The panoramic views are of Berry and Weakley Hollows and Hawksbill (4,050 ft.) to the west; to the northwest is Stony Man Mountain (4,011 ft.); and to the east the horizon fades into piedmont farms and sky. Autumn is the most colorful season to visit. Among the boulders are sumac, goldenrod, maple, chestnut oak, and sassafras. The **Ridge Trail** ends 0.4 mile down the western side of the summit to join the **Saddle Trail**. Backtrack or follow the **Saddle Trail** on switchbacks 1.1 miles to the **Weakley Hollow Fire Road**. Turn right and follow its easy passageway of 2.5 miles to the **Ridge Trail** trailhead and point of origin.

The shorter and easier access to the summit is from Berry Hollow parking area. From the northern access trailhead, drive back to VA 231, turn right (south), and proceed 1.7 miles to Etlan. Turn right on SR 643 and drive 4.2 miles to a junction with SR 600. Turn right and continue upstream by Robinson River for 4.9 miles to end-of-road parking. Hike up the yellow-blazed **Berry Hollow Fire Road** for 0.9 mile to a junction with the **Weakley Hollow Fire Road** and the **Old Rag Fire Road**. Turn right, go 0.4 mile to Old Rag Shelter and spring to begin the **Saddle Trail**. Ascend on switchbacks and pass Byrd's Nest Shelter #1 on the right. (Camping is not permitted in or near the shelter or on the Old Rag summit.) From here follow the **Ridge Trail** 0.4 mile to the summit. Backtrack or use a two-car shuttle. Hikers arriving from downtown Madison at US 29 should take VA 231 west 5.3 miles to Banco, where SR 670 goes left (VA 231 forks right to Etlan and SR 602 for the **Ridge Trail** access as described above). Follow SR 670 3.5 miles to Syria, turn right and stay on SR 643 for 0.3 mile, then turn left onto SR 600 for 4.1 miles to Whiteoak Canyon Falls access area, and another 1 mile to the **Saddle Trail** access parking area.

ADDRESSES AND INFORMATION: Shenandoah National Park, 3655 US Hwy. 211E, Luray, VA 22835; phone: 540-999-3500; on US 211, 4 miles west of Skyline Drive, and 5 miles east of Luray. Available are brochures and maps of the park, and recreation, accommodations, and trail information brochures and flyers. Books and maps may be ordered from the PATC, 118 Park St. SE, Vienna, VA 22180-4609; phone: 703-242-0693, or from the Appalachian Trail Conference, P.O. Box 807, Harpers Ferry, WV 25425; phone: 304-535-6331. Visitor centers on the Skyline Drive carry many of the publications and maps in stock and sold by the Shenandoah National Park Association.

Trail listings below are from north to south and include the following information: current trail name; distance in nearest 0.1 mile, one way; trailhead parking (P); direction (E if on eastern side and W if on the western side of the Skyline Drive); difficulty—easy, moderate, or strenuous, determined for the general public and not horse traffic; some major or unique features; connections with other trails (and some circuit options); and park boundary access (avoiding private property). Trail blazes are blue for foot trails and yellow for horse/foot trails (marked with an [h] at horse trail mileage).

The park has 522.2 miles in its trail system (142.2 mi. in the North District, 240.8 mi. in the Central District, and 139.5 mi. in the South District), of which 101 miles are the **AT**. The total includes all the short trails to huts, shelters, waysides, campgrounds, overlooks, walking paths in developed areas, and work centers. Most of these are unnamed and are not described below. Wilderness mileage is 175.3, and volunteers help to maintain 282.7 miles.

## North District

529–69

Front Royal to US 211, beginning mile to mile 31.5

| MILE | TRAIL NAME | MILEAGE | TERMINI AND BRIEF DESCRIPTION |
|------|------------|---------|-------------------------------|
| 0.1 | Dickey Ridge Trail | 9.2 | Dickey Ridge to visitor center and **AT** at Compton Gap; easy to moderate; historic homesite |
| 4.6 | Fox Hollow Nature Trail | 1.0 | **Dickey Ridge trailhead (P)** connects with **Dickey Ridge Trail** near visitor center; easy; self-guiding to old farm |
| 5.1 | Snead Farm Loop Trail | 0.8 | From Skyline Drive with use of **Dickey Ridge Trail**; easy; near visitor center, homesite |
| 9.2 | Lands Run Gap Trail | 2.0(h) | **Lands Run Gap trailhead (P)** from Skyline Drive to park boundary (W), gated at SR 622; moderate; cascades, falls; connects with **Dickey Ridge Trail** (E) to Fort Windham Rocks (lava flow 8 million years old), Springhouse Rd., and **Hickerson Hollow Trail** (E) |
| 9.2 | Hickerson Hollow Trail | 1.0(h) | **Lands Run Gap trailhead (P)** from Skyline Drive to park boundary (E); easy; historic homesite |
| 10.4 | Compton Peak Trails | 0.4 | **Compton Gap trailhead (P)** at **AT** crossing of Skyline Drive N is 2.1 mi. to 0.2-mi. Possums Rest, s is 0.8 mi. to two scenic spur trails (E and W) of Compton Peak (E trail has columnar basalt); easy to moderate |

| MILE | TRAIL NAME | MILEAGE | TERMINI AND BRIEF DESCRIPTION |
|---|---|---|---|
| 10.4 | Compton Gap Fire Rd. | 2.2(h) | Compton Gap fire road goes from Skyline Drive to Springhouse Rd., then it is the **AT** to **Compton Gap Trail**, then to park boundary; easy |
| 12.3 | Jenkins Gap Trail | 0.8(h) | From Skyline Drive to park boundary (W) to SR 634, has parking at Skyline Drive and **AT** access; moderate |
| 12.3 | Bluff Trail | 3.4(h) | Access (E) to **Mt. Marshall Trail** and to Gravel Springs Gap at 17.5 m; moderate; 0.4-mi. in wilderness |
| 12.6 | Mt. Marshall Trail | 5.4(h) | From Skyline Drive to park boundary (E); strenuous; 3.9 mi. in wilderness, access to The Peak (2,925 ft.) |
| 17.6 | Big Devils Stairs Trail | 1.6 | **Gravel Springs Gap trailhead (P)** at **AT** crossing of Skyline Drive, access on **Bluff Trail** to park boundary (E); moderate; canyon cascades; **Bluff Trail** connects with **Mt. Marshall Trail**, which connects with **Jordan River Trail**(h); **Harris Hollow Trail**(h) descends (E) from Gravel Springs Hut to park boundary for 1 mi.; moderate |
| 17.6 | Browntown Trail | 2.3(h) | From Skyline Drive to park boundary (W); strenuous |
| 19.4 | Keyser Run Trail | 4.4(h) | **Keyser Run trailhead (P)** from Skyline Drive to park boundary (E); moderate; connects with **Little Devils Stairs Trail** for access to SR 614 (E) and **Hull School Trail** (S) |
| 19.4 | Piney Branch Trail | 4.2 | **Keyser Run trailhead (P)** accessed from **Keyser Run Trail** to **Pole Bridge Link Trail**, descends to **Hull School Trail**; strenuous; waterfalls, 2.2 mi. in wilderness, historic homesite |

| MILE | TRAIL NAME | MILEAGE | TERMINI AND BRIEF DESCRIPTION |
|---|---|---|---|
| 19.4 | Little Devils Stairs Trail | 2.0 | **Keyser Run trailhead (P)** from Skyline Drive (E) on **Keyser Run Trail** to left turn and descent into canyon; strenuous; cascades, 1.5 mi. in wilderness; across Skyline Drive is access to **AT** and Little Hogback Mtn. |
| 20.4 | Hogback Spur Trail | 0.3 | From Skyline Drive (W) to **AT** to Hogback Mtn. (3,474 ft.); easy; scenic |
| 20.8 | Sugarloaf Trail | 1.4 | From **AT** (near Hogback Mtn. Overlook on Skyline Drive) to **Pole Bridge Link Trail**; moderate; stream |
| 21.1 | Tuscarora Trail | 6.2 | From **AT** parking lot (W 0.4 mi. on **AT**) near Hogback Overlook on Skyline Drive to park boundary (W); moderate; streams, cascades, 3.9 mi. in wilderness |
| 21.1 | Thompson Hollow Trail | 0.4 | From **Tuscarora Trail** to park boundary (W); easy; 0.3 mi. in wilderness |
| 21.1 | Overall Run Trail | 0.7 | At junction of **Tuscarora Trail** and **Thompson Hollow Trail** (W) downstream to **Overall Run/Beecher Ridge Trail**; easy; stream, 0.7 mi. in wilderness |
| 22.1 | Piney Ridge Trail | 3.2 | From **AT** at Range View Cabin (E) to **Piney Branch Trail**; strenuous; historic homesite, waterfalls, 2.3 mi. in wilderness |
| 22.1 | Fork Mtn. Trail | 1.1 | From **Piney Ridge Trail** to **Hull School Trail** (E); moderate; 1.1 mi. in wilderness |
| 22.2 | Traces Nature Trail | 1.7 | Mathews Arm Campground Loop; easy; historic homesite |
| 22.2 | Elkwallow Trail | 2.0 | From Mathews Arm Campground to Elkwallow Wayside; easy; parallels Skyline Drive on w side |

| MILE | TRAIL NAME | MILEAGE | TERMINI AND BRIEF DESCRIPTION |
|------|-----------|---------|-------------------------------|
| 22.2 | Beecher Ridge Trail | 3.1(h) | From **Mathews Arm Trail** to **Heiskell Hollow Trail** (W); moderate; ends at connector trail to Overall Run |
| 22.2 | Mathews Arm Trail | 4.7(h) | From Mathews Arm Campground to park boundary (W); moderate; 3.2 mi. in wilderness, gated at road off SR 630 E of Bentonville |
| 22.2 | Heiskell Hollow Trail | 3.3(h) | **Knob Mtn. Trail** to park boundary (W); strenuous; extends on private land to SR 697, 3.1 mi. in wilderness |
| 22.2 | Knob Mtn. Trail | 7.1(h) | Mathews Arm Campground to **Jeremys Run Trail**; moderate; 6.6 mi. in wilderness; from s junction with **Knob Mtn. Trail**, **Jeremys Run Trail** is 0.8 mi. to park boundary (W); cascades |
| 22.2 | Weddlewood Trail | 1.3(h) | **Mathews Arm Trail** to **Heiskell Hollow Trail**; easy; 0.6 mi. in wilderness |
| 24.1 | Jeremys Run Trail | 5.3 | From **AT** at Elkwallow to **Knob Mtn. Trail** (W); strenuous; stream, waterfalls, 5.2 mi. in wilderness, wildlife |
| 24.1 | Knob Mtn. Cutoff Trail | 0.5 | From **Knob Mtn. Trail** to **Jeremys Run Trail** (W); easy; 0.5 mi. in wilderness |
| 25.5 | Thornton River Trail | 2.5 | From Skyline Drive parking area (E) to **Hull School Trail**; moderate; springs, wildflowers, stream, 2.2 mi. in wilderness; connects with 1.5-mi. **Thornton Hollow Trail**(h) to SR 612; on w side of Skyline Drive is connection to **AT** |
| 28.1 | Hull School Trail | 4.4(h) | From Skyline Drive to Keyser Run Rd. (E); moderate; crosses North Fork of Thornton River and Piney River, wildlife, partly on fire roads, crosses streams and ridges, 4.1 mi. in wilderness |

| MILE | TRAIL NAME | MILEAGE | TERMINI AND BRIEF DESCRIPTION |
|---|---|---|---|
| 28.1 | Rocky Branch Trail | 3.0(h) | From Skyline Drive parking area and from **Hull School Trail**, crosses **AT**, then Skyline Drive and ends w at gate to SR 666; moderate; borders wilderness |
| 28.1 | Neighbor Mtn. Trail | 6.6(h) | From Skyline Drive parking area follow access road to Byrd's Nest #4 (W) and cross **AT** on ridgeline; strenuous; scenic; terminus with **Jeremys Run Trail**, then out Jeremys to SR 611 near Vaughn, 6.2 mi. in wilderness |
| 28.5 | Pass Mtn. Trail | 2.7 | From Skyline Drive at Beahms Gap parking overlook follow spur trail 0.1 mi. to **AT** and follow it s 2.1 mi. to Pass Mtn. Hut, descend E; strenuous; wilderness; exit is on US 211, 2.5 mi. E of Skyline Drive |
| 30.2 | Pass Mtn. Overlook Trail | 0.1 | On Skyline Drive at Pass Mtn. Overlook; easy, leg-stretcher loop in forest and to rocky bluff |

## Central District

570–652

From US 211 to US 33, mile 31.5 to mile 65.5

| MILE | TRAIL NAME | MILEAGE | TERMINI AND BRIEF DESCRIPTION |
|---|---|---|---|
| 33.5 | Buck Hollow Trail | 3.0 | From Skyline Drive Meadow Spring parking area to US 211 (2.6 mi. E of Skyline Drive); easy; stream, 1.9 mi. in wilderness; access to **AT** (W) of Skyline Drive |
| 33.5 | Hazel Mtn. Trail | 4.6(h) | From Skyline Drive (E) to **Pine Hill Gap Trail** and park boundary with exit to SR 681; moderate; 4.3 mi. in wilderness; connects with **Buck Ridge Trail**, **White Rocks Trail**(h), **Hazel River Trail**(h), **Pine Hill Gap Trail**(h) |

| MILE | TRAIL NAME | MILEAGE | TERMINI AND BRIEF DESCRIPTION |
|------|-----------|---------|-------------------------------|
| 33.5 | Buck Ridge Trail | 2.4 | From Skyline Drive on **Hazel Mtn. Trail** to **Buck Hollow Trail**; moderate; potential loop, 2.1 mi. in wilderness |
| 33.5 | White Rocks Trail | 2.8(h) | From Skyline Drive on **Hazel Mtn. Trail** to Hazel River; moderate; waterfall, cave, 2.8 mi. in wilderness |
| 33.5 | Hazel River Trail | 3.1(h) | From Skyline Drive on **Hazel Mtn. Trail** to park boundary (E); moderate; 2.6 mi. in wilderness, access to SR 600 |
| 33.5 | Sams Ridge Trail | 2.0 | From Skyline Drive on **Hazel Mtn. Trail** and **Broad Hollow Trail** to park boundary (E); strenuous; exit to SR 681; access to **Catlett Spur Trail** and **Catlett Mtn. Trail** |
| 33.5 | Meadow Spring Trail | 0.5 | From Skyline Drive Meadow Spring parking (W) to **AT**; easy; **AT** (N) 0.7 mi. to spectacular views from Mary's Rock (3,514 ft.) and 1-billion-year-old granodiorite stone |
| 35.1 | Hannah Run Trail | 3.7 | At Pinnacle Overlook on Skyline Drive (E) to **Nicholson Hollow Trail**, junction with **Catlett Spur Trail** (1.1 mi.) and **Catlett Mtn. Trail** (1.2 mi.); moderate; historic homesite, stream, 3.4 mi. in wilderness |
| 35.1 | Hot Mtn./Short Mtn. Trail | 2.2 | From Skyline Drive at Pinnacle Overlook descend (E) to **Hazel Mtn. Trail** and hike between two peaks to **Nicholson Hollow Trail**; moderate; stream, 2.2 mi. in wilderness |
| 35.1 | Pine Hill Gap Trail | 1.9(h) | From **Hazel Mtn. Trail** to park boundary (E); moderate; 1.6 mi. in wilderness, access to SR 681 or SR 707 |

| MILE | TRAIL NAME | MILEAGE | TERMINI AND BRIEF DESCRIPTION |
|---|---|---|---|
| 36.4 | Leading Ridge Trail | 1.5 | From Skyline Drive at Jewell Hollow Overlook N on **AT**, 0.3 mi. NW to trail; strenuous; dead end, secluded |
| 37.8 | Corbin Cabin Cutoff Trail | 1.4 | From Skyline Drive W parking to **AT**, but E to Corbin Cabin and **Nicholson Hollow Trail** (E); moderate; 1.3 mi. in wilderness |
| 38.3 | Nicholson Hollow Trail | 5.5 | From Skyline Drive and **AT** (E) to Corbin Cabin and park boundary; moderate; stream, cascades, wildflowers, 4.9 mi. in wilderness, access to SR 600 and Old Rag Mtn., circuit potential |
| 38.3 | Crusher Ridge Trail | 1.8 | From Skyline Drive (W) (N from Stony Man Overlook near **Nicholson Hollow Trail**); crosses **AT** after 0.1 mi.; follows NW on Crusher Ridge; descends on switchbacks to Shavers Hollow (no public access from SR 699); strenuous, secluded |
| 39.1 | Little Stony Man Trail | 1.0 | **Little Stony Man trailhead (P)** S on **AT** 0.3 mi. to trailhead for ascent to peak (3,011 ft.); easy; scenic geology, connects to 1-mi. **Stony Man Nature Trail** for cliffs, views |
| 39.1 | Passamaquoddy Trail | 1.3 | **Little Stony Man trailhead (P)** S on **AT** 0.3 mi. to right fork; easy; scenic, cliffs, and to Skyland developed area |
| 41.7 | Stony Man Horse Trail | 0.9(h) | Near Stony Man parking area to Stony Man Mtn.; easy; parallels scenic nature trail |
| 41.7 | Skyland/Big Meadows Horse Trail | 11.2(h) | Skyland stables to Big Meadows stables at 51.2 m; strenuous; crosses **White Oak Canyon Trail**, **Cedar Run Trail**, and Rose River fire road (E) |

| MILE | TRAIL NAME | MILEAGE | TERMINI AND BRIEF DESCRIPTION |
|---|---|---|---|
| 41.7 | Skyland Trail (also Skyland Fire Rd.) | 3.2(h) | From Skyland to park boundary (W); strenuous; access to SR 672, crosses **AT** at Furnace Spring, connects with **Furnace Spring Horse Trail** (0.4 mi.) to picnic area; easy |
| 41.7 | Skyland/Big Meadows Horse Trail | 1.8(h) | From stables at Skyland s to cross Skyline Drive and to Old Rag Fire Rd.; easy |
| 42.6 | Whiteoak Canyon Trail | 5.0 | **Whiteoak Canyon trailhead (P)** (near entrance s of Skyland) to park boundary (E); moderate; outstanding scenery, waterfalls upper and lower, high traffic; access to SR 600 in Berry Hollow, circuit potential |
| 42.6 | Millers Head Trail | 0.8 | In Skyland from **AT** to Millers Head; easy; scenic views |
| 43.0 | Limberlost Trail (ADA accessible) | 1.3 | **Limberlost trailhead (P)** off E side of Skyline Drive on **Old Rag Fire Rd.**; easy; old-growth hemlocks, wildflowers, stream (for disabled: hard-packed crushed greenstone surface. Ideal for people with mobility limitations and families with young children in strollers. Benches every 400 ft.), loop, no pets, connects with **Crescent Rocks Trail** and **Whiteoak Canyon Trail** |
| 43.0 | Old Rag Fire Rd. | 5.1(h) | **Limberlost trailhead (P)** descends E; strenuous; scenic, 3.3 mi. in wilderness (see above for Old Rag Mtn. trails); connects with **Limberlost Nature Trail** (1.3 mi.), **Whiteoak Canyon Trail** (5 mi.), **White Oak Canyon Horse Trail**(h) (1.8 mi.), **Corbin Mtn. Trail** (3.8 mi.) which connects with **Indian Run Trail** (2.3 mi.), |

| --- | --- | --- | --- |
| | | | **Corbin Hollow Trail** (2 mi.), **Robertson Mtn. Trail** (2.4 mi.) (latter two trails are scenic routes to **Weakley Hollow Fire Rd.**[h], 2.3 mi.), **Saddle Trail** (1.1 mi.), **Berry Hollow Fire Rd.**(h) (0.8 mi.), circuit potential |
| 44.4 | Crescent Rocks Trail | 1.1 | Crescent Rock Overlook on Skyline Drive to **Limberlost Trail**; easy; hemlock grove; across Skyline Drive (N) is 0.4-mi. spur to **Bettys Rock Trail** for scenic views w |
| 45.6 | Cedar Run Trail | 3.1 | **Hawksbill Gap trailhead (P)** crosses E over **Big Meadows Horse Trail**, descends to **White Oak Canyon trailhead** at SR 600; strenuous; waterfall, wildflowers, 2.1 mi. wilderness, circuit potential (0.9-mi. Cedar Run Link is a connector near SR 600) |
| 45.6 | Hawksbill Trail | 1.8 | **Hawksbill Gap trailhead (P)** from Skyline Drive at 45.6 m; w to Upper Hawksbill parking at 46.7 m; moderate; summit of Hawksbill (4,050 ft.) observation deck, spectacular views, red spruce and balsam fir |
| 46.7 | Salamander Trail | 0.7 | From **Upper Hawksbill trailhead (P)** follow NW to **Hawksbill Trail**, left to **AT**, and left to near Rock Spring Hut (formerly **Nakedtop Trail**); moderate; rare Shenandoah salamander in area; access also from 47.8 m |
| 49.3 | Rose River Fire Rd. | 6.5(h) | From Skyline Drive to park boundary (E); strenuous; former Gordonsville Pike, access to SR 670; scenic, wildlife; connects with **Skyland/Big Meadows Horse Trail** (11.2 mi.), **Rose River Loop** |

| MILE | TRAIL NAME | MILEAGE | TERMINI AND BRIEF DESCRIPTION |
|------|-----------|---------|-------------------------------|
| | | | **Trail** (2.7 mi.), and **Stony Mtn. Trail**(h) (1.1 mi.), which goes to Rapidan Rd.; **Upper Dark Hollow Trail**(h) (2 mi.) can make a loop with following **Stony Mtn. Trail** with **Rose River Fire Rd.** |
| 49.3 | Red Gate Fire Rd. | 4.8(h) | Across Skyline Drive from **Rose River Fire Rd.** to park boundary (W); moderate; portion of old Gordonsville Pike, gated near SR 611 |
| 50.7 | Dark Hollow Falls Trail | 0.8 | **Dark Hollow Falls trailhead (P)** to falls at Hogcamp Branch; easy; falls, access to **Rose River Fire Rd.** and Rose River falls, circuit potential |
| 51.1 | Lewis Spring Falls Trail | 1.8 | From Skyline Drive near Byrd Visitor Center to parking area at Big Meadows Lodge, near **AT**; moderate; waterfall, return on **AT** for loop; **Black Rock Trail** (0.2 mi.) is w of lodge to **AT** for scenic views; **Forest Trail** (1 mi.) between visitor center and lodge/campground, forest succession |
| 51.1 | Rapidan Fire Rd. | 7.4(h) | From Skyline Drive to park boundary (E); long, strenuous; wildlife, headwaters of Rapidan River; connects with **Mill Prong Horse Trail** (1.6 mi.), **Stony Mtn. Trail**(h) (1.1 mi.), **Upper Dark Hollow Trail**(h) (2 mi.), **Charlie Thomas Trail** (unblazed in Rapidan WMA), **Camp Hoover Rd.**(h) (1 mi.), circuit options N to **Rose River Fire Rd.** and s to **Fork Mtn. Horse Trail**(h) (0.6 mi.) and **Laurel Prong Trail** (2.3 mi.) |
| 51.1 | Tanners Ridge Horse Trail | 0.8(h) | Big Meadows stables for connectors to Tanners Ridge; easy; crosses Lewis Spring Rd. |

| MILE | TRAIL NAME | MILEAGE | TERMINI AND BRIEF DESCRIPTION |
|------|-----------|---------|-------------------------------|
| 51.6 | Tanners Ridge Rd. | 1.4(h) | On Skyline Drive near Tanners Ridge Overlook to park boundary (W); easy; access to SR 682 |
| 52.8 | Mill Prong Trail | 1.2 | Milam Gap (P) at Milam Gap **AT** crossing to **Mill Prong Horse Trail**; moderate; Big Rock Falls; connects N with **Camp Hoover Trail**(h) (1 mi.) to **Rapidan Fire Rd.**; **Laurel Prong Trail**(h) S 0.6 mi. as horse trail to **Fork Mtn. Trail**(h) (1.3 mi.), which descends to **Staunton River Trail** (part horse and foot for 0.8 mi. and foot 3.9 mi. to Rapidan River access to SR 622); from Fork Mtn. Rd. is **Jones Mtn. Trail** (5.5 mi.), which leads to PATC cabin (locked) and **Staunton River Trail**, where **McDaniel Hollow Trail** (0.4 mi.) is second connector; circuit options |
| 52.8 | Fork Mtn. Fire Rd. | 2.8(h) | **Rapidan Fire Rd.** to **Fork Mtn. Trail**; moderate; 2 mi. in Rapidan WMA; connections with Lower Rapidan Fire Rd. (h) (1.8 mi.), which joins **Graves Mill Horse Trail**(h) (2.1 mi.) and access (E) to SR 649 (W of Criglersville) or SR 662 from Graves Mill (S) |
| 54.4 | Powell Mtn. Trail | 3.6 | From Skyline Drive at Hazeltop Ridge Overlook (SW) to park boundary; strenuous; scenic ridge trail; access at SR 759, NE of Jollett |
| 55.1 | Conway River Fire Rd. | 1.4(h) | At parking lot and **AT** crossing at Bootens Gap on Skyline Drive (E) to park boundary; moderate; connects to roads in Rapidan WMA and to SR 615; on **AT** (N) 0.4 mi. is S end of **Laurel Prong Trail**, which |

| MILE | TRAIL NAME | MILEAGE | TERMINI AND BRIEF DESCRIPTION |
|---|---|---|---|
| | | | leads to **Cat Knob Trail** (0.5 mi.) and **Jones Mtn. Trail** (5.5 mi.) and Bear Church Rock with views |
| 56.4 | Bearfence Loop Trail | 0.8 | **Bearfence Mtn. trailhead (P)** s on **AT**; easy; geology, rock scramble (catoctin basalt), scenic |
| 56.8 | Meadow School Trail | 1.5(h) | From Skyline Drive parking (W) to park boundary; moderate; access to SR 759 E of Jollett |
| 56.8 | Slaughter Trail | 4.2(h) | From Skyline Drive parking (E) to park boundary; strenuous; cross **AT**, wildlife, wildflowers; access to SR 66, NW of Standardsville |
| 57.5 | Lewis Mtn. Trail | 0.8 | From s end of Lewis Mtn. Campground on Skyline Drive to top of mountain and old farm site; easy; backtrack |
| 59.5 | Pocosin Hollow Fire Rd. | 2.6(h) | From Skyline Drive parking (small) E to **Pocosin Horse Trail** (1.3 mi.) and **Pocosin Hollow Trail** (2.8 mi.); moderate; remnants of old homesites, cascading stream, **AT** spring; circuit options by using South River Rd. to **AT** |
| 62.8 | South River Falls Trail | 1.6 | **South River Falls trailhead (P)** from picnic area to park boundary; moderate; waterfall; return on South River Fire Rd.(h) (2.3 mi.) (sw), road N is (1.4 mi.) through Rapidan WMA to **Pocosin Horse Trail** |
| 62.8 | Dry Run Falls Rd. | 2.0(h) | From Skyline Drive gated road w to park boundary; easy; access to SR 625, N of Elkton |
| 62.8 | Saddleback Mtn. Trail | 1.4 | **South River Falls trailhead (P)**, from picnic area follow **AT** s 0.5 mi.; easy; loop of 3.5 mi. with **AT** |

From US 33 to US 250/I-64, mile 65.5 to mile 105

| MILE | TRAIL NAME | MILEAGE | TERMINI AND BRIEF DESCRIPTION |
| --- | --- | --- | --- |
| 68.6 | Smith Roach Gap Trail | 1.3(h) | From Skyline Drive to park boundary (E); easy; gated SR 626 |
| 73.2 | Simmons Gap Fire Rd. | 3.7(h) | From Skyline Drive both (E) and (W) to park boundaries (also called Beldor Rd.); easy; gated at SR 628 |
| 76.1 | Rocky Mount Trail | 5.4 | From Skyline Drive (near Two-Mile Run Overlook) (W) to **Gap Run Trail**; strenuous; geology, stream, peak (2,741 ft.); combine with **Gap Run Trail** (2.3 mi.) for 10-mi. loop; 5.2 mi. in wilderness |
| 76.2 | One Mile Run Trail | 3.7 | From Skyline Drive (park at Two-Mile Run Overlook, w, and hike s 0.1 mi. to trailhead) to park boundary; moderate; stream, 2.7 mi. in wilderness, secluded, ends at private road |
| 76.9 | Brown Mtn. Trail | 5.3 | From Skyline Drive at Brown Mtn. Overlook (W) to Big Run bridge; strenuous; scenic ridgeline, 5.2 mi. in wilderness, fossilized sandstone; can be loop with 1.3 mi. of **Big Run Portal Trail**(h) and **Rocky Mtn. Run Trail** (2.7 mi.) for 11 mi. |
| 76.9 | Rockytop Trail | 5.7 | From end of **Brown Mtn. Trail** (also called **Rocky Mtn.–Brown Mtn. Trail**) and **Big Run Portal Trail**(h) to **Big Run Loop Trail**; strenuous; splendid views, turkey beard, fossils; circuit option with **Brown Mtn. Trail, Big Run Loop Trail, Big Run Portal Trail**, and **Rocky Mtn. Run Trail** is about 18 mi. |

| MILE | TRAIL NAME | MILEAGE | TERMINI AND BRIEF DESCRIPTION |
|---|---|---|---|
| 79.4 | Patterson Ridge Trail | 3.1(h) | From Skyline Drive on Loft Mtn. (W) to **Big Run Portal Trail**; moderate; follows sandstone ridgeline, 2.9 mi. in wilderness |
| 79.4 | Big Run Portal Trail | 4.2(h) | From **Big Run Loop Trail** to **Brown Mtn. Trail** and **Rockytop Trail** (NW); easy to moderate; popular trail for hikers; wildlife, wildflowers, 3.9 mi. in wilderness; no public access at NW end, but SW from **Patterson Ridge Trail** (mile 79.4), or Brown's Gap (mile 82.9) on **Madison Run Fire Rd.** |
| 79.5 | Frazier Discovery Trail | 1.3 | **Loft Mtn. trailhead (P)** at Loft Mtn. Wayside (gas and restaurant in summer); easy to moderate; elevation to peak (3,325 ft.) (E), partly on **AT**, loop can be made to Loft Mtn. Campground |
| 81.1 | Doyles River/Jones Run Trail | 4.7 | **Doyles River trailhead (P)** (200 ft. N of Big Run Overlook) (S) to Skyline Drive mile 83.8; moderate to strenuous; waterfalls, tall trees, crosses **Brown's Gap Fire Rd.**; (**Doyles River Trail**, 2.2 mi., **Jones Run Trail**, 2.5 mi.); circuit with **AT** 8 mi.; popular |
| 81.1 | Big Run Loop Trail | 4.2 | **Big Run trailhead (P)** (W) (trail in three parts); moderate; 2.2 mi. to **Big Run Portal Trail**(h) (right), turn left on second part, horse and foot 1.3 mi. to **Rockytop Trail** (right), turn left on third part, 0.7 mi. to **AT**, turn left, after 1.6 mi. to **Doyles River trailhead (P)**; circuit of 5.8 mi.; popular |
| 82.9 | Madison Run Fire Rd. | 5.6(h) | Brown's Gap on Skyline Drive to park boundary (W) at SR 663, E of Grottoes; moderate; graded road with switchbacks, accesses **Austin** |

| MILE | TRAIL NAME | MILEAGE | TERMINI AND BRIEF DESCRIPTION |
|------|-----------|---------|-------------------------------|
| | | | **Mtn. Trail** and **Furnace Mtn. Trail**; from SR 663 to junction with SR 659, left, is Stull Run Fire Rd.(h) (2.1 mi.) to dead end |
| 82.9 | Brown's Gap Fire Rd. | 3.5(h) | Brown's Gap on Skyline Drive to park boundary (E); strenuous; crosses **Doyles River Trail**, waterfalls, scenic, wildlife |
| 82.9 | Austin Mtn. Trail | 3.2 | Brown's Gap on fire road to spur right at **Rockytop (W) Trail**, first left, exit to **Madison Run Fire Rd.**; moderate; loop if hiking back on fire road |
| 82.9 | Lewis Peak Trail | 2.6 | Brown's Gap on Skyline Drive (W) to **Rockytop Trail**, after 1.8 mi. turn left to park boundary (no public access); strenuous; 0.3 mi. to peak, scenic views, 2.5 mi. in wilderness |
| 84.1 | Doyles River/Jones Run Trail | 4.7 | **Jones Run trailhead (P)** s end from 81.1 m; (see **Doyles River trailhead [P]** above) |
| 84.7 | Furnace Mtn. Trail | 3.4 | Blackrock summit parking on Skyline Drive to **Trayfoot Mtn. Trail**, right, after 1.4 mi. straight ahead to end at Madison Run Fire Rd.; moderate; **Furnace Mtn. Summit Trail** (0.5 m) (2,657 ft.); scenic views; w access is SR 663 E of Grottoes; 3.3 mi. in wilderness |
| 84.7 | Trayfoot Mtn. Trail | 5.4 | Blackrock summit parking on Skyline Drive to Blackrock, past junction of **Furnace Mtn. Trail** to **Paine Run Trail**(h) (3.7 mi.); strenuous; Blackrock scenic views, rock outcrops; use of **Paine Run Trail** and **AT** is circuit of 10 mi. |
| 87.4 | Paine Run Trail | 3.7(h) | **Blackrock Gap trailhead (P)** on Skyline Drive (W) to park boundary; moderate; stream, |

| MILE | TRAIL NAME | MILEAGE | TERMINI AND BRIEF DESCRIPTION |
|---|---|---|---|
| | | | spring, 3.6 mi. in wilderness (W); best access is on sr 663, e of Harriston |
| 87.4 | Moormans River Fire Rd. | 6.9(h) | **Blackrock Gap trailhead (P)** (E) on Skyline Drive (North Fork and South Fork) to Jarman Gap on Skyline Drive 96.8 m; moderate to strenuous; stream, wildlife |
| 90.0 | Riprap Trail | 4.4 | **Riprap trailhead (P)** on Skyline Drive (W) to park boundary; moderate to strenuous; scenic, stream, wildflowers, 4.2 mi. in wilderness; 0.4 mi. on **AT** to trailhead, Calvary Rocks, Chimney Rock; junction with **Wildcat Ridge Trail** (2.5 mi.) for return to Wildcat Ridge parking Skyline Drive 92.1 m, loop of 7.1 mi. with **AT** to origin 9.8 mi. |
| 92.1 | Wildcat Ridge Trail | 2.5 | Wildcat Ridge parking area on Skyline Drive (W) to **Riprap Trail**; strenuous; views, 2.3 mi. in wilderness (see connection with **Riprap Trail** and **AT**, above) |
| 94.1 | Turk Mtn. Trail | 0.9 | From Turk Gap parking area on Skyline Drive (0.2 mi. s on **AT**) to summit of Turk Mtn. (2,981 ft.); easy; wildflowers, superb view, geology, 0.9 mi. in wilderness |
| 94.1 | Turk Gap Trail | 1.6(h) | From Turk Gap parking area on Skyline Drive (W) to park boundary; moderate; old manganese mine, 1.4 mi. in wilderness |
| 94.1 | Turk Branch Trail | 2.5(h) | From Turk Gap parking area on Skyline Drive (E) to South Fork of **Moormans River Fire Rd.**; moderate; 1.7 mi. in wilderness; circuit can be made s on fire road to Jarman Gap (mile 96.7) and return on the **AT**, 7.5 mi. |

*More than an end to war, we want
an end to the beginnings of all wars.*
FRANKLIN D. ROOSEVELT (1882–1945)

# 6. National Battlefield Parks

## Colonial-Era Trails

### COLONIAL NATIONAL HISTORIC PARK
*York and James City Counties*

Yorktown is best known for the Yorktown Battlefield, the location of the last major battle of the American Revolution. It was on October 19, 1781, in the home of Augustine Moore, near the banks of the York River, that peace commissioners ratified the terms by which Lord Cornwallis surrendered to Washington's allied French and American forces. Jamestown Island is best known as the location of the first permanent English settlement, founded in 1607. Both of these historic sites, plus a 23-mile parkway connecting them through Colonial Williamsburg and the Cape Henry Memorial, are components of the 9,833-acre Colonial National Historic Park. The park was designated by an act of Congress in 1930. Since then two historic trails in the park have been established, sponsored in part by the Peninsula Council of Boy Scouts. These are the **Yorktown Battlefield Trail** and the **Jamestown Colony Trail**.

ACCESS: To reach Yorktown Battlefield, turn off US 17 onto the Colonial Parkway and go 0.6 mile to the visitor center parking area. To reach Jamestown, follow the Colonial Parkway west from Yorktown for 23 miles. Otherwise, turn off I-64, exit 242, on VA 199 (west) to VA 31 and follow the signs to Jamestown.

**Yorktown Battlefield Trail**                                                          683
LENGTH AND DIFFICULTY: 12.5 miles (20 km); easy
FEATURES: battlefield history, museum, bicycling
TRAILHEAD: Yorktown Battlefield Visitor Center
DESCRIPTION: At the visitor center examine the exhibits and request a trail map
    from the information desk. (The trail can be hiked or cycled with or without the
    3.5-mi. French Artillery Park Loop.) When leaving the visitor center look for the
    sign "Hornwork," the main British defense line, on the left, and follow over the
    earthworks to a five-point road junction. Cross the road, turn left, and continue
    walking on VA 238 east until reaching Surrender Road, SR 704, junction. Turn

right and go 0.2 mile to yellow-marked Goosley Road. Proceed on Goosley Road to W. Tour Road; turn left and reach reconstructed redoubt, an outer line of defense, at 1.2 miles. Continue ahead to the French Loop, marked by a brown sign, right, at 2.9 miles. (The French Artillery Park Loop through the French encampment is 3.5 mi.) On returning, continue ahead to Washington's Head-quarters area at 7.9 miles. From there, follow the road over Beaver Dam Creek bridge, cross under US 17, and reach Surrender Field Pavilion at 10.2 miles. Here swords were formally exchanged by General O'Hara and General Benjamin Lincoln to signify the end of the war. From the parking lot follow the red-arrow tour across the road and through a wooded area; go to junction at SR 704. Cross road to Grand French Battery. From here, cross through the Second Siege line (and cross VA 238) to redoubts of the British line #9 and #10. Visitor center is ahead, left, at 12.5 miles.

684  **Jamestown Colony Trail**

LENGTH AND DIFFICULTY: 5.0 miles (8.0 km); easy

FEATURE: colonial history

TRAILHEAD: Jamestown Visitor Center

DESCRIPTION: Visit the visitor center before beginning the hike, and acquire a brochure with a trail map. Go to the tercentenary monument behind the center and follow interconnecting loops to historic sites for 1.5 miles. To visit additional historic sites, drive or hike the Island Loop Drive for 3.5 miles. If hiking, stay on the grassy shoulder facing traffic, examining the exhibits along the way. Subjects include colonial shipbuilding, agriculture, Indian trade, winemaking, medicine, household supplies, and brick making. There is an admission fee to Jamestown.

USGS MAP: Surry

ADDRESS AND INFORMATION: Colonial National Historic Park, P.O. Box 210, York-town, VA 23690; phone: 757-898-3400 (in Yorktown) and 757-229-1282 (in Jamestown). Available for free are brochures and other handouts; books are on sale.

## Civil War–Era Trails

There are seven Civil War battlefield parks in Virginia, at least twenty-eight his-toric attractions, and more than 250 sites designated by state historical markers along the highways. They commemorate four years (July 21, 1861–April 12, 1865) of tragedy in 1,000 battles, engagements, skirmishes, and encounters; 60 percent of the war was fought in Virginia. (During the Civil War the number of men in battle was 4,137,304—1 in 8 of the population—and more than 617,000 died. In contrast, more than 120,000 died in World War I and 400,000 in World War II.) To hike the trails in these battlefields is to retrace and recount the heroic bravery and valor of the Confederate and Union soldiers. Choosing to hike during the season of the year in which the battles were fought enhances the experience.

## MANASSAS NATIONAL BATTLEFIELD PARK
*Prince William County*

The First Battle of Manassas was fought here on July 21, 1861, when Union general Irvin McDowell attacked a strategic east-to-west railroad junction over a stream called Bull Run. During this famous battle on Henry Hill, Confederate general Barnard Bee of South Carolina, in an attempt to rally his Third Brigade, used Gen. Thomas J. Jackson's brigade as an anchor. "Form, form," said General Bee, "there stands Jackson like a stone wall, rally behind the Virginians." A few minutes later General Bee was killed by Union gunfire. The battle ended in a rout for General McDowell's troops and a Confederate victory. The Second Battle of Manassas, August 28–30, 1862, secured a place in history for Gen. Robert E. Lee as he defeated the 75,000 Union troops with his 48,327 Confederates. In the two battles the South lost 11,456 men and the North 17,170. These battles are commemorated in the 3,200-acre Manassas National Battlefield Park. There are 50 miles of walking routes, including a 20-mile bridle trail in the park. It is recommended that hikers stop at the visitor center before their tours.

ACCESS: From I-66, exit 47, turn on VA 234 (north) (Sudley-Manassas Rd.), and go 0.6 mile to park entrance and visitor center on right. From US 29 turn on VA 234 (south) and go 0.4 mile to park entrance on left.

**Henry Hill Trail** (1.2 mi.), **Stone Bridge Trail** (5.5 mi.), **Deep Cut Trail** (6.5 mi.)     685–87
LENGTH AND DIFFICULTY: 13.2 miles (21.1 km); easy
FEATURE: battlefield history
TRAILHEADS: At parking space at visitor center; or at parking lot on US 29 at Prince
   William and Fairfax county line, 1.3 miles east of VA 234 junction with US 29; or
   from parking lot on SR 622, 0.9 mile from US 29 and 1.4 miles east on US 29 from
   junction of VA 234.
DESCRIPTION: From the visitor center begin on the 1.2-mile **Henry Hill Trail**. It has
   interpretive signs, artillery positions, and four push-button stations explaining
   in detail the fight to control the hill in the First Battle of Manassas. For a more
   detailed look at the First Battle of Manassas, take the blue-blazed **Stone Bridge
   Trail** from either of two access points on the **Henry Hill Trail**. If turning at the
   first right (east), pass Jackson's Guns and the site of the Van Pelt House; cross
   the Stone Bridge (the first was destroyed by the Confederates, the second was
   built about 1870); reach the Farm Ford across Bull Run; and pass the Carter
   House ruins and the Stovall Marker. At marker #7 is Matthews Hill, a slope
   facing Henry Hill, where the armies clashed and General McDowell thought the

Union forces had won the war. Parallel the Sudley Road and arrive at the Stone House, a Union field hospital after the fighting was over. Cross US 29 to marker #9, the Henry House, a significant point because the battle here left the Union forces in retreat. Return to the **Henry Hill Trail** and to the visitor center.

If hiking the **Deep Cut Trail**, which has two spur routes of 2.3 and 2.5 miles, hikers can save distance by crossing the Sudley Road highway after Matthews Hill. Follow the green (X) markers to a picnic area. This tour focuses on the third and last day of the Second Battle of Manassas, August 30, 1862. At stop B there is an unfinished railroad where General Jackson deployed his wing of troops in an excellent defensive position. (Here is a parking lot on SR 622 [Featherbed Lane] and a 2.3-mi. side trail, right, on the railroad bed to Sudley Church, Sudley Rd., and Bull Run.) At stop C is Groveton Monument. (Here a loop side trail for 2.5 mi. circles Battery Heights and the Brawner Farm.) Cross Featherbed Lane and parallel it to the historic Dogan House at stop D. Here is the Groveton Confederate Cemetery, where repose two known and between 250 and 500 unknown Confederate soldiers. Cross the highway, US 29, to monuments honoring the 5th and 10th New York Infantry. Union troops were driven off the ridge at the battle for Chinn Ridge at stop F. Before the trail crosses Chinn Branch, there is a monument to Col. Fletcher Webster, who was killed here. (He was the only son of U.S. senator Daniel Webster.) Following the retreat from the ridge, the Union forces clustered at Sudley Road (near stop G) bank for protection (bank is barely visible today). It rained during the night and all the next day, and during the darkness the Union troops retreated across Bull Run; the battle was over. Major General John Pope's army suffered 10,000 killed and wounded, and 4,000 missing. General Robert E. Lee's army suffered about 8,500 killed and wounded and only a few missing.

USGS MAPS: Manassas, Gainesville

ADDRESS AND INFORMATION: Manassas National Battlefield Park, 12521 Lee Hwy., Manassas, VA 22110; phone: 703-361-1339. Available for free are brochure and flyers; trail guide and books are on sale.


## FREDERICKSBURG AND SPOTSYLVANIA
## NATIONAL MILITARY PARK

*Spotsylvania and Orange Counties, City of Fredericksburg*

This military park comprises 5,644 acres and seven major historic sites, including four major battlegrounds: Fredericksburg (December 11–13, 1862); Chancellorsville (April 27–May 6, 1863); Wilderness (May 5–6, 1864); and Spotsylvania Court House (May 8–21, 1864). No other theater of war in America has had such fierce fighting and slaughter. The Union army lost more than 65,000 men, and the South lost at least 35,000.

The Fredericksburg Visitor Center and the Chancellorsville Visitor Center have exhibits, slide shows, and displays to acquaint the visitor with the history of the Civil War action. Hikers should stop at these centers before taking the hikes. Two interpretive trails at the visitor center in Fredericksburg are the **Sunken Road** 688–89 **Trail** and the **Lee Drive Trail**. The 0.2-mile **Sunken Road Trail** begins behind the visitor center and parallels Sunken Road (Telegraph Rd.) to six markers, the last being at the Kirkland Monument. Confederates were entrenched behind this wall. By darkness on December 13, 1862, more than 7,500 Federal troops lay dead or wounded on the open space between the wall and the river. During the night, Sgt. Richard Kirkland from South Carolina responded to the anguished pleas for water from the wounded Union soldiers. His humanitarian act of distributing water at the risk of his life gave him the title "Angel of Marye's Heights." A walk from the visitor center accesses Marye's Heights and the Fredericksburg National Cemetery. Here are graves for 15,243 men, of which 12,770 are unknown. The verses of Theodore O'Hara's "The Bivouac of the Dead" (written to honor Kentuckians in the Mexican War) are on metal plaques here.

The dark blue-blazed 5.2-mile **Lee Drive Trail** is an easy route to Prospect Hill, with information markers along the way. It can be an auto route or a walking route. Two vehicles are necessary unless you backtrack. To reach the trail from the visitor center, take US 1 south for 0.6 mile and turn left into Battlefield Park. At 0.2 mile farther is a paved foot trail, 350 yards right, to General Lee's command post. From here go 0.4 mile to Howison Hill parking area and exhibit; the trail begins behind the artillery site. At 0.5 mile pass behind the park maintenance area; cross Lee Drive and reach a picnic area at 1.2 miles. Cross the road again, following the well-graded trail through oaks and scattered pines with holly and dogwood forming a light understory. Cross Deep Run at 1.7 miles, ascend on a gentle terrain to a road, and follow the shoulder to Lansdowne Valley Road, SR 638. Reenter the woods, right, at 2.9 miles and arrive at Prospect Hill exhibit area near General Lee's defense line at 5.2 miles.

USGS MAPS: Fredericksburg, Guinea

ACCESS TO FREDERICKSBURG VISITOR CENTER: On US 1, Lafayette Boulevard between Sunken Road and Willis Street, or from US 1A, take VA 3, William Street, east for 0.3 mile to Hanover Street. After another 0.8 mile turn right at Littlepage Street and continue 0.3 mile to Lafayette Boulevard. Turn right and go 0.1 mile to parking area.

## Chancellorsville Battlefield

The next major battle after Fredericksburg occurred the following spring, April 27–May 6, 1863, 11 miles west on the Orange Turnpike (now VA 3) at Chancellorsville crossroads. Some historians claim General Lee achieved his greatest military victory here. This battle is also where he lost General "Stonewall" Jackson, who General Lee claimed was a "right arm" military leader. There are three trails here for a comprehensive tour of what happened in dozens of square miles of forest thickets. The **Jackson Trail** (east and west) is a 10.9-mile hike or auto tour. The **Chancellorsville History Trail** is a 4-mile loop from the Chancellorsville Visitor Center on the northern side of the turnpike, and the 1-mile **Hazel Grove Fairview Trail** leads to the battle sites on the southern side of the turnpike.

For the **Jackson Trail**, prepare by examining the exhibits and audiovisuals at the Chancellorsville Visitor Center. If hiking, a second vehicle should be at the Jackson flank attack marker west on VA 3. Otherwise, for the vehicle route, drive north from the visitor center on Bullock Road for 0.8 mile to the apex of General Hooker's last line at Ely's Ford Road, SR 610. Turn right and go 0.7 mile to Chancellorsville Inn ruins, an area captured from General Hooker in an incredible victory by the Confederates on May 3, 1863. Cross VA 3, and go 1.1 miles on SR 610 to the Lee-Jackson Bivouac. Here, on the night of May 1, 1863, the Confederate leaders planned the battle of Chancellorsville. General Lee would never see Jackson again. From here the hiker, history buff or not, can hike or ride the road following General Jackson's famous and risky flank march along Furnace Road. Reach Catharine Furnace remains at 1.4 miles, turn left on **Jackson Trail** (east), and reach Brock Road, SR 613, at 4.2 miles. (Here Jackson turned south as part of the plan to deceive Gen. Joseph Hooker's scouts.) After 0.3 mile turn right on **Jackson Trail** (west). Cross the small stream, a significant spot to pause and imagine what this trail in the wilderness must have been like with a 7-mile column of thirsty horses and men stopping for water. Rejoin SR 613 at 6.7 miles, cross Orange Plank Road, SR 621, at 7.9 miles, and reach VA 3 at 9.4 miles. Turn east on VA 3 for 1.5 miles to the site where on May 2 General Jackson surprised the Union army with a flank attack. The victorious march ended in tragedy for General Jackson when that night he was mistakenly shot by his own troops. He died of pneumonia eight days later at Chandler Plantation at Guinea Station, south of Fredericksburg. Taking General Jackson's place was cavalry officer J. E. B. Stuart, who on the morning of May 3 proved his leadership ability at the decisive battle at Fairview. Access to this point is by trail or vehicle from Stuart Drive south of the visitor center.

USGS MAPS: Chancellorsville, Brokenburg

ACCESS TO CHANCELLORSVILLE VISITOR CENTER: From I-95, exit 130, in Fredericksburg, drive west on VA 3 for 8 miles.

### Wilderness Battlefield

A year almost to the day after Chancellorsville, the premier Civil War leaders, Confederate general Robert E. Lee and Union lieutenant general Ulysses S. Grant, led in their first battle with each other, May 5–6, 1864. Fought in a dense thicket of scrubby trees known as the Wilderness, the battle was a draw; but Union casualties numbered more than 17,000, and Confederate losses were about 11,000. General Grant broke the stalemate by repositioning at Spotsylvania Court House to the southeast. There is a 2-mile foot trail loop, the **Jordan Flank Attack Trail**, at an exhibit shelter.

ACCESS TO THE WILDERNESS BATTLEFIELD: From Chancellorsville Visitor Center drive west 4.3 miles on VA 3 and turn left on VA 20. Continue for 2 miles to trailhead, right.

## Spotsylvania Court House Battlefield

Two days after the Wilderness battle, there were two weeks of battle northwest of Spotsylvania Court House that ended without a decisive victory for either side. More than 25,000 soldiers fell during May 8–21, 1864. But the loss to General Lee is considered greater because he had fewer men in reserve. General Grant's battle plan was to push on to Richmond, 50 miles south, but the Confederates stopped the effort on May 8, 1864.

The **Spotsylvania Battlefield Trail** is 7 miles long. Begin the hike at Sedgwick    694–97
Monument and exhibit shelter on SR 613. The blue-blazed loop trail goes north and parallels Grant Drive. Cross the road at 0.6 mile along Upton's trace, and turn left over Doles' Salient at 0.9 mile. Cross Bloody Angle Drive to McCoull Spring and to the McCoull House ruins at 1.6 miles. Turn left here through woods, and parallel Gordon Drive left to Bloody Angle Drive. Here is the **Bloody Angle Loop Trail** at 2.5 miles. On May 12 this area was the scene of the most intense and desperate hand-to-hand combat of the war in 20 hours of rain, mud, and blood. After hiking the short, blue-blazed **Bloody Angle Loop Trail**, return to the Mc-Coull House ruins at 4.2 miles. From here the red-blazed **McCoull/Harrison Loop Trail** goes 1.5 miles and passes the Harrison House ruins on its southern approach to crossing Gordon Drive again. Reach SR 613 at 5.5 miles. Here a connecting trail, the white-blazed **Laurel Hill Loop Trail**, goes to Hancock Road after passing the Maryland Monument. Cross Hancock Road and return to the exhibit shelter at 7 miles. The trail is a national recreation trail.

USGS MAPS: Spotsylvania, Brokenburg, Chancellorsville
ACCESS TO SPOTSYLVANIA COURT HOUSE BATTLEFIELD: From the Wilderness area at VA 3, drive southeast 10 miles on Brock Road, SR 613, to Spotsylvania Exhibit Shelter. From Fredericksburg drive south on US 1 for 3 miles and turn right on VA 208 for 6 miles to Spotsylvania Court House. Turn right on SR 613 for 2 miles.

ADDRESS AND INFORMATION: Fredericksburg and Spotsylvania National Military Park, 120 Chatham Lane, Fredericksburg, VA 22405; phone: 540-373-4461.


## RICHMOND NATIONAL BATTLEFIELD PARK
*Chesterfield, Hanover, and Henrico Counties*

An area of 763 acres, the Richmond National Battlefield Park commemorates battlegrounds and other sites in the drive to capture the Confederate capital during the Civil War. Six sites were associated with Gen. George McClellan's campaign in 1862 (Chickahominy Bluff, Beaver Dam Creek, Gaines's Mill, Glendale Malvern Hill, and Drewry's Bluff). In 1864 Gen. Ulysses Grant led campaigns at Cold Harbor, Fort Harrison, and Parker's Battery. Other nearby battlefields, such as Fair Oaks, White Oak Swamp, and Savage Station, are not within the park system but were part of McClellan's campaigns. A loop drive of 100 miles from the Chimborazo Visitor Center is necessary to visit all the historic battle areas, restored houses, cemeteries, and other park facilities scattered in a three-county area. Five designated hiking trails are in the park, a total of 3.6 miles. Before visiting or hiking, go to the Chimborazo Visitor Center in Richmond for historical information and detailed maps on the motor routes. Also, each major battlefield has interpretive facilities, and both Cold Harbor and Fort Harrison have visitor centers.

ACCESS: Southbound on I-95 in downtown Richmond, take exit 74B to Franklin Street (west); go one block to 14th Street and turn left. At the first traffic light turn right on East Broad; Chimborazo Visitor Center is at 3215 E. Broad Street. Northbound I-95 traffic should take exit 74C (east) to E. Broad Street and follow directions as above.

698–702    **Cold Harbor Trail** (1.1 mi.), **Breakthrough Point Trail** (0.2 mi.), **Fort Harrison Trail** (0.1 mi.), **Fort Brady Trail** (0.4 mi.), **Fort Darling Trail** (0.5 mi.)

LENGTH AND DIFFICULTY: 2.3 miles (3.7 km); easy

FEATURES: battlefield history, James River overlook

TRAILHEADS: See information at each trail.

DESCRIPTION: The **Cold Harbor Trail** is 1.1 miles, a loop trail through Confederate and Federal earthworks involved in the battle of Cold Harbor, May 31–June 13, 1864. The battle cost the Federal army thousands of casualties in a few hours and was Gen. Robert E. Lee's last major victory. (Cold Harbor is on VA 156 northeast of I-295 and SR 615 junction.) **Breakthrough Point Trail**, a short loop trail of 0.2 mile, is near the Watt House. It follows a portion of the Seven Days Battle line to the point where Confederate forces broke through Federal defenses at the Battle of Gaines's Mill, June 27, 1862. (Access via a spur road from VA 156 at Cold Harbor.)

The **Fort Harrison Trail** is 0.1 mile, a loop with exhibits describing construction techniques and soldier life at Civil War field fortifications. The **Fort Brady Trail** is farther downriver on the park road to Fort Brady. (Access is off VA 5 [New Market Rd.] south of Richmond at Battlefield Park Rd.)

Across the James River (west) at Drewry's Bluff is the site of Fort Darling and the Confederate Naval/Marine Training Center. The **Fort Darling Trail** loops 0.5 mile to an overlook of the James River where Confederate artillery stopped a Federal fleet, including the ironclad **Monitor**, from steaming upstream to attack Richmond. (Access from the James River Bridge in Richmond on I-95 south to 64A and the junction with SR 613 [Willis Rd.]. Go right [north] at junction with US 301/1 for 0.8 mi. to Bellwood Rd., SR 656, on right. After taking SR 656, go under I-95 and make a sharp left on Fort Darling Rd.)

ADDRESS AND INFORMATION: Richmond National Battlefield Park, 3215 E. Broad St., Richmond, VA 23223; phone: 804-226-1981. Available are brochures and flyers.

## NEW MARKET BATTLEFIELD HISTORICAL PARK
*City of New Market*

The 280-acre New Market Battlefield Park and Hall of Valor is a registered national historic landmark. It is administered by Virginia Military Institute as a nonprofit educational facility and was made possible by a gift from VMI alumnus George Randall Collins. The area honors the 257 teenage cadets under the command of Gen. John C. Breckinridge, who with other batteries and companies on May 15, 1864, courageously forced the Federal units to retreat. Before hiking the **New Market Battlefield Trail**, visit the park museum for information and audio- 703 visuals. The 1-mile loop trail from the parking lot at the Hall of Valor leads to the historic Bushong Farm, where Confederate wounded were treated after the battle. Among the forty-three Confederates killed, ten were VMI cadets. Pass exhibit markers around the "field of lost shoes" to Federal lines and scenic overlooks 200 feet above the North Fork of the Shenandoah River. Return along the cliffs through a border of cedar and redbud.

ACCESS: From I-81, exit 264, junction of VA 211, follow signs. (Open daily 9–5.)

ADDRESS AND INFORMATION: New Market Battlefield Historical Park, New Market, VA 22844; phone: 540-740-3102.

## PETERSBURG NATIONAL BATTLEFIELD
*Prince George County and City of Petersburg*

Established as a national military park in 1926, the site of the Petersburg siege was designated a national battlefield in 1962. Its 2,700 acres extend to Fort Lee on the east, to US 460 and VA 109 on the south, and to US 301 on the west, with VA 36 running through the northern edge. A 16-mile auto tour of the siege lines around Petersburg begins at the junction of US 301, Crater Road, and the park's Siege Road. The route includes four of the major forts General Lee maintained during the ten-month siege, June 15, 1864, to April 2, 1865.

After General Lee's army defeated General Grant's army at Cold Harbor on June 3, 1864, Grant said that the key to taking Richmond was Petersburg; but a series of Union fumbles on June 15 and 18 cost him 10,000 men and a long delay in the capture of the city. The delay became ten months, the longest siege in American warfare. More than 70,000 soldiers died. During this time General Grant's Army of the Potomac, with 100,000 men, was well armed and supplied from the City Point (Hopewell) Military Railroad, on which 500,000 tons of material were transported. In contrast, General Lee's army of 60,000 men was far less well equipped for the battle of Fort Stedman. Finally, with his defenses crumbling, General Lee evacuated Petersburg on the night of April 2, 1865.

Besides the siege lines, the auto tour at the Petersburg National Battlefield includes Poplar Grove National Cemetery, a tract of 8.7 acres southwest of Fort Wadsworth. From early June to late August the park has a living history program of artillery demonstrations and live exhibitions of soldier life of the Civil War. Comprehensive displays and audiovisuals are at the visitor center. There are 14 miles of trails, including spurs and paved interpretive routes, of which 10.3 miles are part of the *Petersburg Battlefield National Recreation Trail*.

ACCESS: From I-95 in Petersburg, turn at signs on VA 36 east, E. Washington Street (and US 301 south and US 460 east), and go 1.8 miles to park entrance on right.

704 **Petersburg Battlefield National Recreation Trail**

LENGTH AND DIFFICULTY: 7 miles (11.2 km) combined, round-trip; easy

FEATURE: battlefield history

TRAILHEAD: At parking area on VA 109, Mahone Avenue junction with A Avenue, 1.2 miles south from VA 36, and 1.6 miles northeast from junction of US 460 and VA 109.

DESCRIPTION: Designated a national recreation trail in 1981, this loop trail has two optional spurs. The wide trail is exceptionally well designed and marked. Its surface is chiefly beds of pine needles, with spots of blacktop or gravel. The first major historic stop is at Meade Station, one of the key supply points for Grant's military railroad. At 0.5 mile turn left on Jordon Point Road, go 125 yards, and

705-7 turn right on the **Branch Trail** to Siege Road at 1.1 miles. (On the right is the **Battery 5 Spur Trail**, which proceeds right along the multi-use lane to the visitor center and to the site of the famous 17,000-pound Union mortar, the "Dictator." Backtrack for a round-trip total of 1.7 mi. Along the way, near the park entrance from VA 36, is the **Battery 7 Trail**, a round-trip side trail of 1.3 mi.)

After returning to **Branch Trail** follow it across Siege Road to Fort Friend and

708 the **Friend Trail**. Cross Harrison Creek and reach a junction, left, with Fort Stedman at 2.7 miles from the beginning of the **Petersburg Battlefield Trail**.

709-11 (At this point those who wish to hike the **Short Loop Trail** should bear left to Fort Stedman exhibit, cross Siege Rd., and go to the **Encampment Trail**; turn right. After 50 yd. turn left, cross Harrison Creek, and follow the **Harrison Creek Trail** for 0.6 mi. to Attack Rd. Turn left, and reach Union Camp at Siege Rd. Turn right on old Prince George Courthouse Rd., returning to parking area for a total of 4.7 mi.)

Continue on the **Petersburg Battlefield Trail** to Colquitt's Salient and to Fort Haskell at 3.9 miles. Here is an excellent example of the well-preserved fortifications. Cross and parallel Siege Road past the Taylor House site to the railroad at 4.5 miles. (Here the **Crater Spur Trail** continues across the railroad 712 to the site of the ironic and incredible plans of the 48th Pennsylvania Infantry to tunnel under the Confederate line. After a loop of 1.3 mi. return to the **Petersburg Battlefield Trail**.) Follow the **Petersburg Battlefield Trail** east to the **Encampment Trail**, cross Taylors Creek, pass the junction with the **Short Loop Trail** at 5.6 miles, and return to trailhead and parking area for a total of 7 miles. (If spur trails are hiked the total round-trip is 11.3 mi.)

ADDRESS AND INFORMATION: Petersburg National Battlefield, P.O. Box 549, Petersburg, VA 23804; phone: 804-732-3531.

## APPOMATTOX COURT HOUSE NATIONAL HISTORICAL PARK
*Appomattox County*

After the Federal victory on April 1, 1865, at Five Forks, southwest of Petersburg, General Lee realized the siege of Petersburg was over. The next day both Petersburg and Richmond were evacuated, and a western retreat began. Lee made a skillful withdrawal but counted on supplies arriving at Amelia for his tired and starving army. The supplies never came, and valuable time was lost foraging for food. Furthermore, 8,000 of his men, one-fourth of his army, were wounded, killed, or captured on April 6 in the swampy bottom of Sayler's Creek (now Sailor's Creek Battlefield Historical Park on SR 617, 2 mi. north of VA 307 near Rice. The park has an auto tour to designated stops identifying the sequence of the battle.) General Lee set up his headquarters about 1 mile east of the Appomattox River on the old Richmond-Lynchburg Stage Road. (The trail described next follows General Lee's route from his headquarters to other significant points in the final days of the Confederacy.)

After the end of the Civil War, the Appomattox Court House village was neglected for sixty-five years—the former McLean House was dismantled, the courthouse burned in 1892, and other buildings were in decay. Even the bill passed by Congress in 1930 to build a monument was never honored. Finally, in 1934 the NPS recommended complete restoration of the village, and in 1935 Congress passed a bill authorizing it as a national historical monument. In 1954 it was also designated a national historical park. The park has 1,323 acres and thirteen major buildings that have been meticulously restored.

ACCESS: From the town of Appomattox go east on VA 24 for 3 miles to entrance on left. From US 60 at Mt. Rush, go west on VA 24 for 17 miles to entrance on right.

### Appomattox History Trail
713
LENGTH AND DIFFICULTY: 6 miles (9.6 km); easy
FEATURES: battlefield history, McLean House
TRAILHEAD: visitor center
DESCRIPTION: A recommended beginning point for the hike is the visitor center at

Appomattox Court House, following east by the jail to Surrender Triangle on the Old Richmond–Lynchburg Road, where approximately 22,000 Confederates laid down their arms on April 12, four years to the day after the first shots were fired at Fort Sumter. Descend on a grassy ridge following trail arrow sign to the Appomattox River Wayside at 0.6 mile. Cross a bridge by the marker honoring Joel Walker Sweeney, the inventor of the five-string banjo, and reach the site of the Apple Tree. Here, General Lee waited on April 9 for a response from General Grant to Lee's offer of surrender. Pass the **Appomattox National Environmental Study Area Trail** on the right and follow VA 24 to the site of General Lee's last field headquarters at 1.5 miles. Here General Lee held his last council of war on the night of April 8. From this point follow the trail onto a woods road at 1.8 miles, enter a Virginia pine stand for 0.2 miles, and reach an open field at Alexander Sweeney's Prizery. Again enter the woods, cross the Appomattox River at 2.4 miles, and follow it upriver for 0.4 mile to a sharp left uphill. Reach Prince Edward Court House Road, SR 627, at 3.8 miles. Cross the road and continue through a hardwood forest with mountain laurel and huckleberry.

At 5 miles reach the North Carolina Monument honoring troops who distinguished themselves in three major battles—Big Bethel, Gettysburg, and Chickamauga—and who fired the final Confederate shots at Appomattox. Go 0.2 mile to VA 24. (A spur of 0.5 mi. on the left along the highway leads to the site of General Grant's headquarters.) Turn right to a Confederate cemetery at 0.3 mile and follow the old coach route to McLean House. Here, at 1:30 P.M. on Palm Sunday, April 9, General Lee met with General Grant to surrender in dignity and honor the Army of Northern Virginia. (When General Lee mounted his horse "Traveller" to return to his men, General Grant and his officers lifted their hats to him in respect. General Grant immediately ordered rations issued for the hungry men in gray and ordered paroles to be printed.) Complete the hike to the visitor center at 6 miles.

USGS MAPS: Appomattox, Vera

ADDRESSES AND INFORMATION: Appomattox Court House National Historical Park, P.O. Box 218, Appomattox, VA 24522; phone: 540-352-8987. (For Boy Scout credit on history trails, contact Blue Ridge Mtn. Council, Boy Scouts of America, 2131 Valley View Blvd., Roanoke, VA 24012; phone: 540-265-0656.) Available for free are brochures and flyers; books are on sale.

*The history of every country begins*
*in the heart of a man or a woman.*
WILLA CATHER (1876–1974)

# 7. National Historical Parks

## CUMBERLAND GAP NATIONAL HISTORICAL PARK

*Lee County, Virginia; Bell County, Kentucky; and Claiborne County, Tennessee*

Before the American Indians made use of it along the "Warrior's Path," Cumberland Gap had been the pass for buffalo and deer that roamed across it in large herds seeking new pastures. It was the main pass on the wilderness trail that became the Wilderness Road, marked by Daniel Boone from Virginia to Kentucky in 1775. By 1792 more than 100,000 pioneers had crossed the gap for Kentucky and beyond. Subsequently the route became a significant artery of migration, trade, and transportation to the West. In both the American Revolution and the Civil War it was an important military objective. Its rich history prompted Congress in 1940 to designate 20,270 acres (of which 7,526 are in Virginia) as the Cumberland Gap National Historical Park. During the twentieth century the gap became a capacity traffic channel for US 58 in Virginia and US 25E in Tennessee and Kentucky. To solve the transportation congestion the famous gap underwent a major change in the 1990s, when to the south the nearly 1-mile Cumberland Gap Tunnel was constructed for four-lane traffic. With this change there are plans to restore the gap to some of its original conditions as a wilderness road/trail.

The park's headquarters and visitor center are on the Kentucky side of the gap, near the west end of the tunnel and at the east edge of the town of Middlesboro. The town of Cumberland Gap is in Tennessee, and the Wilderness Road Campground is in Virginia. At the visitor center is the 1.5-mile **Fitness Trail**, which makes a south loop. Across US 25E from the visitor center is SR 988. After 0.7 mile it reaches a parking lot for access to some old and new trails. Also from the visitor center and parallel to SR 988 is **Thomas Walker Trail**. At the parking lot it connects with the **Thomas Walker Connector Trail** east for 0.9 mile, and 1.1 miles if making a loop. On two points of the loop it connects with the 2-mile **Boone Trail/Wilderness Road Trail** that is partly on the old US 25E route. With circuitous methods all other trails in the park's system can be accessed. At the parking lot SR 988 goes north and the Pinnacle Road forks east for 3.3 miles on a winding vehicular ascent to a dead end at Pinnacle Overlook (2,440 ft.). Here are panoramic views, the southwestern trailhead of the 16.6-mile **Ridge Trail** (see

715

716–18

719     ahead), the eastern trailhead of 0.8-mile **Fort McCook Trail**, and a 0.1-mile access to Fort Lyon.

(If desiring to access the **Ridge Trail** on the **Sugar Run Trail** use SR 988 [Sugar Run Rd.] north from the **Thomas Walker Trail** parking area. It goes 2.5 mi. to a picnic area with moss-covered rocks, dense hemlocks, and access to the 2.2-mi. **Sugar Run Trail** by cascading Sugar Run.)

With interpretive help from the visitor center a motor route can be planned to Cubbage, Kentucky, for penetrating Brush Mountain to the Hensley Settlement. Once a high and hardy pioneer community, it was abandoned in the early 1950s, but the NPS has restored a few buildings. It is easily accessible by foot from the remote **Ridge Trail**.

To access Tri-State Peak (1,990 ft.) from Wilderness Road Campground, travel west on US 58 for 1.3 miles to turn right on North Cumberland Drive. (If arriving from the west or south, turn east on US 58 and after 0.5 mi. turn left on North

720–21     Cumberland Dr.) After 0.8 mile is a parking area. Follow the signs on the **Wilderness Road Trail** to the historic Iron Furnace site, near the CSX Railroad tunnel under the gap. Continue ahead for 0.6 mile to a connection with the **Tri-State Trail**, left and right. (To the right, ahead, the **Tri-State Trail** goes 0.1 mi. to Fort Foote and a connection with the **Boone Trail/Wilderness Road Trail**, where with circuitous routing all other trails in the park's system could be accessed.) On the left the **Tri-State Trail** goes 0.6 mile to the Tri-State Pavilion and exhibit.

722     Backtrack. (To the south is the long **Cumberland Trail** into Tennessee.) Within the park is the large Wilderness Road Campground on US 58, 1.8 miles east of the US 58/25E junction. It has trailer and tent sites (some with full hookups), comfort stations, waste disposal unit, picnic area, amphitheater, and nature trails. The

723–26     **Greenleaf Nature Trail**, 0.7 mile, begins at the amphitheater. To the left the trail dips into a valley with tall hardwoods. It makes a figure eight in combination with 1.1-mile **Honey Tree Trail**, which loops on a slope. After 0.5 mile from the US 58 entrance to the campground is a parking area, right, for the **Boone Trail** and the **Colson Trail**. The 2-mile **Boone Trail** goes to Cudjo Cave and into the gap for joining the **Wilderness Road Trail** for an exit at SR 988. The 0.5-mile **Colson Trail** connects the **Boone Trail** and the **Gibson Gap Trail** (see ahead). Other trails that access the campground are described below. The campground is open year round.

727     **Ridge Trail**

LENGTH AND DIFFICULTY: 16.6 miles (26.6 km); strenuous

728–33     CONNECTING TRAILS: **Sugar Run Trail** (2.2 mi.), **Lewis Hollow Trail** (1.8 mi.), **Gibson Gap Trail** (4.8 mi.), **Hensley Trail** (0.4 mi.), **Chadwell Gap Trail** (2.1 mi.), **Ewing Trail** (2.4 mi.)

FEATURES: scenic outcrops, historic site, caves, wildlife, wildflowers

TRAILHEADS: The southwestern trailhead is at the Pinnacle Overlook. For the northeastern trailhead, take SR 724 from US 58 at Ewing and go 1 mile to Civic

Park for parking. This is the southern trailhead of 2.4-mile **Ewing Trail**, an access trail to 16.6-mile **Ridge Trail** for a hiking total of 19 miles.

DESCRIPTION: If overnight camping is planned, first secure a backcountry use permit from the park office. Begin the hike at the Pinnacle parking area, ascend to the ridge, and follow an old fire road on the crest. Occasional rock outcroppings provide views into Kentucky and Virginia. The **Ridge Trail**'s forest cover is chiefly oak, hickory, black locust, and black birch with an understory of mountain laurel, dogwood, chestnut sprouts, and buckberry. Frequent patches of woodland sunflower, purple phlox, red fire pink, and blue Virginia spiderwort provide colorful trail borders. Wildlife is less abundant, but deer, grouse, squirrel, chipmunk, black bear, and rattlesnake may be sighted. At 1.7 miles is a junction with the **Lewis Hollow Trail** (also called the **Skylight Cave Trail**), right, and the **Sugar Run Trail**, left. (The **Lewis Hollow Trail**, with high traffic volume, descends 0.5 mi. to Skylight Cave. [A flashlight is necessary to examine the ceiling.] The trail divides at 0.8 mi. with a 0.2-mi. trail left to the Wilderness Road Campground Picnic Area. The right fork continues parallel with Lewis Hollow to end at 1.8 mi. inside the campground entrance station.) (The **Sugar Run Trail** descends southwest to the headwaters of Sugar Run, and at 1.5 mi. provides a fork at the confluence of Sugar Run and a tributary. To the right is a descent to Sugar Run Picnic Area; to the left the trail descends to SR 988, 0.9 mi. south of the picnic area.)

On the **Ridge Trail** at 5.1 miles approach a primitive campsite and a junction with the **Gibson Gap Trail**, right. (It descends to a long, sweeping switchback before crossing Station Creek at 2.3 mi. It then stays on the mountainside for a number of coves, descends on switchbacks, and crosses Station Creek twice more before reaching the campground. Also used as a horse trail, it provides access to a parking area at US 58 near the campground. Along the way it makes a contact west with **Honey Tree Trail**, a 0.1-mi. spur to **Greenleaf Nature Trail**, a 0.1-mi. spur to the campground, and a contact with the east end of 0.5-mi. multi-use **Colson Trail**.) Continuing on the **Ridge Trail** at 10.5 miles is Indian Rock, with good views. At 11 miles and 11.7 miles are short, steep trails on the left to Hensley Settlement, and at 1.4 miles is Chadwell Gap (3,385 ft.), with a primitive campsite. Reach another side trail at 12.6 miles that leads 0.2 mile left to Martins Fork campsite with water. The **Ridge Trail** meets the **Chadwell Gap Trail** on the right at 12.8 miles. (The beautiful 2.1-mi. **Chadwell Gap Trail** with its scenic switchbacks and caves is currently closed because of private property access. Contact the visitor center for information on its potential reopening.)

The **Ridge Trail** makes a junction with the **Ewing Trail**, right, at 15.6 miles. This connection has high horse traffic, but ahead, at 16.4 miles, there is a foot trail, right, to the **Ewing Trail**. At this junction is White Rocks primitive campground 0.2 mile down the steep mountain on the Kentucky side. Ahead the **Ridge Trail** reaches its northeastern terminus at 16.6 miles at White Rocks.

Here is a spectacular view of the three states from rock formations bordered with huckleberries. On the **Ewing Trail** descend steeply on switchbacks for 0.5 mile on a footpath to the old road with horse traffic. Follow it on switchbacks for 1.9 miles to Civic Park (which has a stream and a shelter). From here it is 1 mile on SR 724 to Ewing on US 58, 14.9 miles east of the Wilderness Road Campground. (West from SR 724 for 0.3 mi. is a state historical marker near the junction of US 58 and SR 684. It cites that near there in October 1773, Boone was leading his own family and several other families to Kentucky, but the pioneer attempt failed when his teenage son, James, and five other youths were tortured and murdered by Shawnee Indians at Indian Creek.)

USGS MAPS: Middlesboro South and North, Varilla, Ewing

ADDRESS AND INFORMATION: Cumberland Gap National Historical Park, Box 1848, Middlesboro, KY 40965; phone: 606-248-2817; headquarters is off US 25E west of Cumberland Gap Tunnel at the eastern edge of town. Available for free are a brochure and map of the park, and flyers for campground and backcountry camping; books are on sale at the visitor center.

*There is where the birds warble sweet in the springtime . . .*

JAMES A. BLAND (1854–1911)

# 8. National Wildlife Refuges

Under the U.S. Fish and Wildlife Service of the Department of Interior is the National Wildlife Refuge System; its purpose is to manage the preservation of wildlife. The system was established in 1903 when President Theodore Roosevelt authorized the first refuge on Pelican Island, Florida. By the 1990s the nation had set aside more than 500 refuges with more than 90 million acres of lands and waters for this purpose. Emphasis is on management benefits of waterfowl, but protection for all species is provided. Where compatible with wildlife management plans, recreational use is allowed. Examples are hunting, fishing, hiking, bicycling, picnicking, boating, swimming, and nature study.

Of the fourteen refuge locations in Virginia, seven provide partial to more advanced recreational activities. Hours of usage or days of closure may vary according to seasons. Telephoning in advance is recommended. Because of budgetary limitations two NWR complexes have been established to manage three refuges each. Of those refuges with recreational activities, Mason Neck and Occoquon Bay are in the Potomac River NWR Complex, and Rappahannock River Valley NWR is in Eastern Virginia Rivers NWR Complex. Also described is Eastern Shore of Virginia NWR. Because the above NWRs have smaller (or singular) trail systems than the other refuges, they are described here first. Back Bay NWR, Chincoteague NWR, and Great Dismal Swamp NWR are described in more detail. (The scenic and intriguing Presque Isle NWR, established in 1952, has been closed because of ferry safety precautions. Call Eastern Virginia Rivers NWR Complex at 804-333-1410 for an update.)

Rappahannock River Valley NWR, in Richmond County, was established in 1996 and has 4,842 acres. Its recreational services are fishing, hiking, photography, and bird-watching, all at freshwater Wilna Pond. The refuge offers environmental studies, and plans are to have multiple bird-watching sites.

USGS MAPS: Champlain, Montross

ACCESS: From intersection of US 17/360 in Rappahannock take US 360 east across the Rappahannock River bridge. From the bridge's east end it is 2 miles to SR 624 (Newland Rd.), left and north. (It is 2.6 miles east on US 360 to Warsaw.) Follow SR 624 for 4.2 miles and turn left on Strangeway Road. After 0.3 mile take right on Sandy Lane. After 1.1 miles is refuge entrance and access to multi-use route to Wilna Pond.

ADDRESS AND INFORMATION: Rappahannock NWR, P.O. Box 1030 (336 Wilna Rd.), Warsaw, VA 22572; phone: 804-333-1470; fax: 804-333-3396.

Mason Neck NWR was established in 1996 and has 2,276 acres in Fairfax County. Only 18 miles south of Washington, D.C., it has upland forests, bogs, and Potomac riverfront marsh where large beds of yellow pond lilies and rose mallow flourish. More than 211 bird species have been identified. The refuge has a high traffic volume on the 3-mile **Woodmarsh Trail**, which forks after 0.8 mile.

735

USGS MAP: Fort Belvoir

ACCESS: From US 1 travel east on VA 242 (Gunston Rd., east of Lorton) for 4.1 miles to High Point Road, right. (Straight ahead here on SR 600 [Gunston Rd.]

736 leads 1.5 miles, right, to **Garthan Great Marsh Trail**, a 0.6-mile paved trail to an observation deck. The trail is wheelchair accessible.) On High Point Road go 0.7 mile to the **Woodmarsh Trail** parking area, left.

ADDRESS AND INFORMATION: Mason Neck NWR, 14416 Jefferson Davis Hwy., Woodbridge, VA 22191; phone: 703-490-4979. There is a trail brochure guide at the parking area.

Occoquon Bay NWR was established in 1998 and has 643 acres in Fairfax County. In addition to its forests and marshes, it has large undeveloped grassland areas and is within the Atlantic flyway for migrating birds. Refuge activities include hunting, fishing, hiking, and environmental education sites. For hiking there are 4 miles of old roads (used previously by the U.S. Army) for a network of foot trails. They retain the army names of Lake, Deephole Point, Fox, Locust Bayview, Easy, Charlie, and Bravo. There are 2 miles of road for vehicles and bicycles. Domestic pets are not allowed on the refuge. Neither is swimming, boating, jogging, picnicking, or camping. Visiting hours may be only from Thursday through Sunday. (Telephone for hours and changes.)

USGS MAP: Fort Belvoir

ACCESS: From US 1 in Woodbridge drive east 0.7 mile on Dawson Beach Road to parking area, right.

ADDRESS AND INFORMATION: Occoquon Bay NWR, 14344 Jefferson Davis Hwy., Woodbridge, VA 22191; phone: 703-490-4979.

The 651-acre Eastern Shore of Virginia NWR is in Northampton County. It has a 0.5-

737 mile loop **Eastern Shore Nature Trail** with an observation deck for viewing waterfowl in Megathy Bay. From here the islands of Skidmore and Smith can be seen in the Atlantic Ocean.

USGS MAP: Townsend

ACCESS: If crossing the Chesapeake Bay Bridge-Tunnel on US 13, drive to the community of Kiptopeke and turn right on SR 600 to the visitor center. If driving south on US 13 from Maryland, turn left on SR 600.

ADDRESS AND INFORMATION: Eastern Shore of Virginia NWR, 5003 Hallet Circle, Cape Charles, VA 23434; phone: 757-331-2760.

## BACK BAY NATIONAL WILDLIFE REFUGE
*City of Virginia Beach*

Established in 1938, the 5,568-acre Back Bay NWR has been set aside primarily to protect the habitat of migrating waterfowl on the Atlantic flyway. It is located between Little Island Park in Sandbridge and False Cape State Park. On the east is Atlantic Ocean frontage, on the west is a marginal section of mainland, and in the center are many islands, including Long Island and Ragged Island in the bay. The refuge does not allow camping but does permit hiking and biking through the refuge to enter False Cape State Park, which does allow camping. Camping permits are required, and applications must be made in person at Seashore State Park in northern Virginia Beach. (See Addresses and Information, below, and Seashore State Park and Natural Area in Chapter 11.)

The refuge and the park share a number of natural environment management policies, but they differ in some of the recreational opportunities. An agreement between them allows for highly restricted use of the refuge dike road (**Back Bay Dike Trail**) by motorized vehicles. As a result hikers may see vehicles transporting nature study groups through the refuge to the park's Environmental Education Center. A day-use area only, the refuge charges an entrance fee and requires all vehicles left overnight for backpacking into the park to be parked at Little Island Park, a Virginia Beach facility outside the refuge's entrance gate.

Nearly 300 avian species have been recorded in the refuge, including 30 species of waterfowl such as geese, ducks, and swans. The peak of fall migration is in December, and the migratory peak for songbirds and shorebirds is in the spring. There are three endangered species in the refuge: bald eagle, loggerhead sea turtle, and peregrine falcon. Among the regular mammals are deer, raccoon, gray fox, mink, and otter. Turtles include the eastern mud, red-bellied, and snapping. In addition to water and black rat snakes there is the poisonous cottonmouth moccasin. The feral swine are from domesticated stock and are considered trespassers. Some of the common vascular plants are coastal gaillardia (*Gaillardia pulchella*), marsh mallow, meadow beauty, spikerushes, beach holly, yaupon, wax myrtle, maple, live oak, pine, and red cedar.

**Bay Trail** (0.4 mi.), **Seaside Trail** (0.2 mi.), **Dune Trail** (0.2 mi.), **Back Bay Dike Trail** (3.8 mi.), **Outdoor Classroom Trail** (0.1 mi.)
LENGTH AND DIFFICULTY: 9.3 miles (14.9 km) combined, round-trip; easy
CONNECTING TRAIL: **Barbour Hill Interpretive Trail** (2.4 mi.)

738–42

743

FEATURES: wildlife, wild plants, refuge, beach, waterfowl, historic site

TRAILHEAD: At the refuge visitor center in the daytime, or if parked overnight, 1.5 miles north at Little Island Park near the refuge entrance gate.

INTRODUCTION: The trails provide an exciting coastal experience for hiking and biking. The experience is enhanced when the trails in False Cape State Park are used for an extended retreat to the coastal backcountry. Planning for either or both requires different schedules and equipment, but it is essential to bring water to both refuge and park, neither of which has a supply. All water must be carried in, and one gallon per day per person is recommended. In addition, insect repellent and sun lotion should be taken. The most comfortable seasons and the best times to see wildlife are spring, fall, and winter. Summer is unpleasant because of humidity and insects. The refuge is closed (and so is the park) from the first to the second Saturday in October for hunting. Also, the refuge may have other seasonal closings to protect waterfowl. (Call in advance if planning long trips.)

DIRECTIONS: Begin from the visitor center on the **Dike Trail** (road) at the trail network signboard. To the right is the **Bay Trail**, which follows a wide trail 0.4 mile among yaupon, wax myrtle, live oak, and cordgrass to an observation deck at Buck Island Bay. A side feature is Sunset Point, part of a boardwalk trail called **Outdoors Classroom**. It also has an observation deck to encounter bay-edge biological habitats. It connects with an access to the visitor center parking area. To the left of the **Dike Trail** is the short **Seaside Trail**, an all-sand treadway to the ocean. (The first 2.7 mi. of the **Dike Trail** are without shade trees.) After 280 yards the trail forks left to follow the East Dike. At 0.3 mile is the **Dune Trail**, a boardwalk trail, left, to the ocean. (A loop can be made by turning left on the beach to turn left again on the **Seaside Trail** for a return of 1 mi.)

Continuing on the **Dike Trail** pass closed crossover dikes of the impoundments at 0.6 mile, 1.5 miles, and 1.7 miles on the right. At 2.2 miles turn right on a crossover dike between the freshwater lakes; enter a forest at 2.7 miles and reach a junction with the West Dike road. Turn left in a grove of maple, willow, and pine. Exit the forest at 3.3 miles, and reach a junction on the right with the western side of the False Cape State Park's **Barbour Hill Interpretive Trail** (road) at 3.5 miles. (There may not be a trail sign here.) Continue ahead and turn right at the entrance to False Cape State Park at 3.8 miles. Backtrack. (The **Barbour Hill Interpretive Trail** continues on the right into the park. Proceed first to an observation deck on the left to view waterfowl, and continue 0.7 mile farther to the park's contact station. Another 0.7 mile, right, leads to a campsite. Return to the **Dike Trail** [described above] after a loop of 2.1 mi. to make a day's round-trip back to the visitor center at 9.7 mi.)

USGS MAPS: North Bay, Knotts Island

ACCESS: From the southern end of US 60 (Pacific Ave.) at the beach in Virginia Beach, cross the bridge and drive south 4.7 miles on General Booth Boulevard.

Turn left on SR 615 (Princess Anne Rd.), go 0.8 mile and turn left on Sandbridge Road. After 5.4 miles turn right on Sandpiper Road and continue 3.7 miles to Little Island Park. Access to Back Bay NWR entrance is 0.2 mile, and it is another 1.3 miles to the visitor center and parking area. If coming from I-64 in western Virginia Beach, take VA 407, exit 286 (Indian River Rd.) southeast to cross Princess Anne Road at Pungo at 12 miles. Cross the road, and after 1.1 miles turn left on New Bridge Road and follow it 1.2 miles to Sandbridge Road. Follow it 3.1 miles to Sandpiper Road and turn right. Follow it as described above.

ADDRESSES AND INFORMATION: Back Bay NWR, 4005 Sandpiper Rd., Virginia Beach, VA 23456; phone: 757-721-2412. Available are information brochures and bird list. False Cape State Park (mailing address only), 4001 Sandpiper Rd., Virginia Beach, VA 23456; phone: 757-426-7128. Available are brochures with maps and permit and camping information. Seashore State Park and Natural Area (for False Cape camping permits), 2500 Shore Dr., Virginia Beach, VA 23451; phone: 757-481-2131; Little Island Park (a city park near refuge entrance), phone: 757-426-7200.

## CHINCOTEAGUE NATIONAL WILDLIFE REFUGE
*Accomack County*

The northernmost of Virginia's barrier islands is also one of the most fascinating. Assateague Island, 37 miles long and spanning the Maryland/Virginia line, was designated a national seashore in 1965. The Virginia portion consists of Chincoteague NWR and a small NPS facility near the southern tip of the island. As part of an interagency agreement, the NPS administers, as an agent of the Fish and Wildlife Service, a portion of the beach for surfing, swimming, and fishing. Established in 1943, the refuge area is managed for migratory birds, endangered species, and other native animals. Over 300 species of birds use the refuge for at least a portion of the year, including geese, ducks, swans, herons, hawks, egrets, ibises, gulls, and terns. The wild ponies have made the island nationally famous with the "Pony Swim" and auction the last Wednesday in July. During Thanksgiving week the refuge holds "Waterfowl Week" for observing the waterfowl at their peak in numbers. This is the only time the gated 7.5-mile Service Road is open to private vehicles. The refuge has another road, the 3.2-mile Wildlife Loop, which is used by hikers, bikers, and birders around freshwater Snow Goose Pool. From 3 P.M. to dusk motor vehicles are allowed on the road. To begin, take the first left turn on the Service Road behind the refuge visitor center. After 1 mile the loop turns right and crosses the pool on a dike to enter a wooded area. At 1.9 miles is a junction on the left with 1.2-mile **Swan Cove Trail**. (It is a side trail for walking and bicycling 744 from Toms Cove visitor center of the NPS.) The loop route turns west and then north to pass right of other freshwater impoundments before returning to the refuge visitor center.

*Woodland Trail, Chincoteague National Wildlife Refuge*

745–47    Another trail is the **Lighthouse Trail**, a short (less than 0.3 mi.) walk to the 124-foot-tall Assateague Lighthouse, an active facility of the U.S. Coast Guard. It is diagonally west across Beach Road from the refuge visitor center. The most popular walk in the refuge is the 1.6-mile **Woodland Trail** (formerly the **Pony Trail**). It is a hiking and biking loop from a parking area on Beach Road between the refuge and the NPS visitor center. Through pine and water oak the trail passes an open area and observation deck near a marsh. Here the ponies frequently graze. The area is also known for the Sika elk and white-tailed deer roaming freely in the refuge. Additionally, the endangered Delmarva fox squirrel (*Sciurus niger cinereus*) nests and feeds here. At the beach, across from the NPS amphitheater, is 0.6-mile **Toms Cove Nature Trail**, an interpretive trail about coastal wildlife and such flora as glasswort and sea oxeye.

The refuge's most remote and challenging walk is the 7.5-mile (15 miles round-trip) Service Road from the visitor center to a cul-de-sac at Wash Flats. Among dunes, wetlands, and marshes the road was created from a dike when freshwater impoundments were made. The road provides an excellent opportunity to observe waterfowl. To reach it from the visitor center, go north on the Wildlife Loop for 1 mile to the road's gate. Camping or straying from the road is not allowed. Although the road is not a trail, backpackers may hike the 25 miles between Toms Cove north to Oceanside Campground or nearby Assateague State Park in Maryland. Because camping is not allowed in the Virginia section, backpackers must plan to hike 13.5 miles to the first campsite 1 mile over the state line. Beyond that point there are other campsites on the beach and on the bayside at campsites shared with canoeists. All drinking water must be carried in. Permits and reservations are necessary and may be acquired from the visitor center at either

Toms Cove in the south or Barrier Island in the north. (See Addresses and Information, below.)

USGS MAPS: Chincoteague East and West, Boxiron

ACCESS: From US 13 junction with VA 175, go 10.5 miles east on VA 175 to Chincoteague. Turn left on N. Main Street and continue four blocks, then turn right on Maddox Boulevard and go 2.2 miles to refuge visitor center, left. For Toms Cove Visitor Center (NPS), continue another 2 miles to the beach. In Maryland for Barrier Island Visitor Center (NPS), take MD 376 for 4.2 miles east of Berlin, turn right on MD 611, and go 3 miles, right.

ADDRESSES AND INFORMATION: Chincoteague NWR, P.O. Box 62 (8231 Beach Rd.), Chincoteague VA, 23336; phone: 757-336-6122. Assateague Island National Seashore, P.O. Box 38 (8586 Beach Rd.), Chincoteague, VA 23336; phone: 757-336-6577. In Maryland, Assateague State Park, 7307 Steven Decatur Highway, Berlin, MD 21811; phone: 410-641-2120. Assateague Island National Seashore headquarters, 7206 National Seashore Lane, Berlin, MD 21811; phone: 410-641-1441. Available are brochure with maps, bird list, information flyers on camping permits for NPS, and other materials.


## GREAT DISMAL SWAMP NATIONAL WILDLIFE REFUGE
*Cities of Suffolk and Chesapeake*

Few places in Virginia invoke such legends and mystery as the Great Dismal Swamp. George Washington once owned a share of it, calling it a "glorious paradise." Colonel William Byrd II cursed it as a "vast body of dirt and nastiness." He is said to have given the swamp its name, having nearly lost his life surveying the state line through it in 1728. Earlier, in 1664, William Drummond, a governor of North Carolina, had discovered the lake that bears his name, but made no claim for it. In 1763 George Washington organized a draining and logging company, and one of the ditches bears his name. Eventually all the timber was cut from the vast swamp, and 140 miles of roads were created for access, thus leaving the ditches. The result was the destruction of the swamp's natural hydrology and the decline of plant and animal diversity. In 1973, climaxing years of efforts by conservationists to preserve the swamp, the Union Camp Corporation donated 49,100 acres of land to The Nature Conservancy. This land was then conveyed to the Department of the Interior, and the refuge was officially established through the Dismal Swamp Act of 1974. The refuge currently covers 131,770 acres, 82,150 of which are in Virginia, and 49,620 are in North Carolina.

Lake Drummond, in the heart of the swamp, is a 3,100-acre circular natural lake kept pure by the tannic acid from the cypress and juniper trees. Its average depth is 5 feet. The swamp is unique because it is not a depressed marshland. Instead it is a "perched bog," with the lake at its highest point and streams slowly draining from it. Peat bogs near the lake and elsewhere may be as deep as 18 feet. Access to the lake by boat is from Feeder Ditch off US 17, 3.5 miles north of the North Carolina state line. The U.S. Army Corps of Engineers maintains a campground on this route. (For information, call 757-421-7401.) Hiking and biking access is on Washington Ditch. Among the flora and fauna are 8 species of turtles, 14 species of frogs, 15 species of snakes (including copperhead, canebreak rattlesnake, and cottonmouth moccasin), 48 species of trees, 29 species of shrubs, 20 species of vines, and 209 species of birds. Bear, bobcat, and deer inhabit the swamp, and crappie and perch are in the lake. Birding is best in the spring during migration and when the flowers are in bloom. This is also the best time for hiking because the insects are less troublesome. Some of the wildflowers to look for are dwarf trillium, silky camellia, climbing hydrangea, swamp azalea, sheep laurel, and swamp rose. A rare fern is the log fern, found in the swamp more than elsewhere.

The refuge is open to hiking, biking, nature study, fishing, and boating year round during daylight hours. Because the refuge is meant to protect and manage the swamp's unique ecosystem, portions of the refuge are closed to public use. Some of the ditch roads are maintained; others have become impassable. The best two hiking routes are described below.

748–50   **Jericho Ditch Trail** (5.9 mi.), **Dismal Town Boardwalk Trail** (0.9 mi.), **Washington Ditch Trail** (4.5 mi.)

LENGTH AND DIFFICULTY: 20.7 miles (32.4 km) combined, round-trip; easy
FEATURES: swamp, Lake Drummond, wildlife, wildflowers, historic site
TRAILHEADS: See Access, below.
DESCRIPTION: The **Jericho Ditch Trail** (road) is the longest and most exploratory toward the center of the swamp. At 1.8 miles it intersects with Hudnell Ditch (east) at Five Points. To the immediate right (south) is Lynn Ditch, and to the southeast is Jericho Ditch. At 5.3 miles (after making the only turn in the long straight trail) the trail turns more to the south, passes Camp Ditch, left, and at 5.9 miles reaches Middle Ditch, right. Beyond this point the **Jericho Ditch Trail** is not passable. Backtrack, or use Middle Ditch and Lynn Ditch for a loop of 14.7 miles to SR 642 via Jericho Lane to point of origin.

At the parking entrance to the **Washington Ditch Trail** is the **Dismal Town Boardwalk Trail** and a directional signboard. The first 0.8 mile on the loop nature trail are on an elaborate elevated boardwalk. Side trails extend to observation points in a forest of red maple, swamp black gum, elm, and ash. Parts or all of the swamp may be dry, depending on the season of the year. The trail returns to the signed **Washington Ditch Trail**. To the left the **Washington Ditch Trail** goes straight for 4.5 miles to Lake Drummond; to the right it is 0.1 mile to the parking area. Hikers to Lake Drummond should carry drinking water and insect repellent and wear strong, protective footwear. Round-trip is 9 miles.

USGS MAPS: Suffolk, Corapeake, Lake Drummond, Lake Drummond NW

ACCESS: For access to the **Jericho Ditch Trail**, begin at junction of US 13/VA 32/VA 337 in downtown Suffolk. Drive east 0.7 mile on US 13/VA 337 to right fork on SR 642 (White Marsh Rd.). Follow it south for 0.8 mile to Jericho Ditch Lane on the left. (The other two trails can be accessed 4.5 mi. farther south on SR 642; make a left turn to the parking area.) Another access is from the courthouse in downtown Suffolk on US 13/VA 32 south for 3.4 miles to fork. Follow signs on VA 32 (Carolina Rd.) for 4.4 miles to SR 675 (Cypress Chapel Rd.). Turn left for 0.5 mile to SR 642 (White Marsh Rd.). After 1.8 miles reach a junction with SR 604 (Desert Rd.), where to the right is the refuge office (closed on weekends), and straight ahead (northeast) 1 mile is the Washington Ditch entrance road, right.

ADDRESS AND INFORMATION: Dismal Swamp NWR, (3100 Desert Rd.) P.O. Box 349, Suffolk, VA 23439; phone: 757-986-3705; fax: 757-986-2353; web: <www.great dismalswamp.fws.gov>. Available are brochure of bird species, brochure of Dismal Swamp with map outline, and leaflets on flora and fauna.

*Little drops of water*
*Little grains of sand,*
*Make the mighty ocean*
*And the pleasant land.*
JULIA A. F. CARNEY (1823–1908)

# 9. Other Trails in the National Park System

## ASSATEAGUE ISLAND NATIONAL SEASHORE
*Accomack County, Virginia, and Worcester County, Maryland*

With 39,630 acres, the 37-mile Assateague barrier island is a haven for migratory waterfowl, wild ponies, and students of nature. Of the island's total acreage, 17,377 acres are federal property, with 6,897 in Maryland and 10,479 in Virginia. For hiking opportunities, see (in Chapter 8) Chincoteague NWR.

ACCESS: From the town of Chincoteague at junction of VA 175 and SR 2113, follow SR 2113 for 2.2 miles to Refuge Information Center.

ADDRESS AND INFORMATION: Assateague Island National Seashore, 7206 National Seashore Lane, Berlin, MD 21811; phone: 410-641-1441.

## BOOKER T. WASHINGTON NATIONAL MONUMENT
*Franklin County*

This national monument honors Booker T. Washington (1856–1915), who was born a slave on the James and Elizabeth Burroughs plantation. The story of his life, in *Up From Slavery*, is one of childhood poverty and illiteracy and an adulthood that included graduation from Hampton Institute, the founding of the Tuskegee Institute, and distinction as an American educator whose advice was sought by Presidents William McKinley, Theodore Roosevelt, and William H. Taft. The monument area has a visitor center, living historical farm, picnic area, and hiking trails. The set of trails was designated a national recreation trail in 1981. The park is open year round.

751–52    The 0.5-mile **Plantation Trail** begins at the parking area of the visitor center and follows a wide trail to the reconstructed kitchen cabin, tobacco barn, pigpen, hen house, and horse barn. After this loop, return to the junction with the **Jack-O-Lantern Branch Trail** south of the tobacco barn. For 1.5 miles the trail has interpretive markers and makes a loop. For the first 0.8 mile it follows Jack-O-Lantern Branch among wildflowers such as orchid, soapwort, and mandrake. Some of the trees are Virginia pine, black walnut, and sycamore. After turning right near Gill Creek the trail passes a small cemetery on its return to the tobacco barn. It is believed the Jack-O-Lantern Branch received its name from foxfire, an eerie phosphorescent light caused by a luminous fungus in decaying wood. It is visible along the stream at night.

ACCESS: From Rocky Mount junction of US 220 Bypass and VA 40, go 1.1 miles east on VA 40 to VA 122. Turn left on VA 122 and go 12.3 miles to entrance of the monument on the right.

ADDRESS AND INFORMATION: Booker T. Washington National Monument, Rt. 3, Box 310, Hardy, VA 24101; phone: 540-721-2094. Available are brochure with map, trail guide, and information flyers.

## GEORGE WASHINGTON BIRTHPLACE NATIONAL MONUMENT
*Westmoreland County*

Pope's Creek Plantation, which the Washington family acquired in 1718, was the first home of George Washington, who was born there February 22, 1732. After 3 ½ years his father, Augustine, and his mother, Mary Ball, moved the family to the Little Hunting Creek Plantation—later named Mount Vernon. Four years later they moved near Fredericksburg. George was eleven when his father died. His half-brother, Augustine II, inherited Pope's Creek Plantation, but young George frequently returned for stays at his birthplace.

In 1858 the commonwealth acquired the area, but the Civil War delayed restoration. With the assistance of the Wakefield National Memorial Association in 1923 and John D. Rockefeller in 1931, the commonwealth was able in 1932, the 200th anniversary of Washington's birth, to officially transfer the 394 acres with buildings to the federal government. It is open daily, except December 25 and January 1. (To reach Monroe Hall, the birthplace of James Monroe, drive west 2.8 mi. on VA 3 to Oak Grove, then take VA 205 to the historic site.)

There are two significant trails of interest to the visitor. From the visitor center take the easy, 1-mile **Washington Historic Trail** on a gravel path along the edge of the cliffs to the birthplace site. On the way pass through an exceptionally large grove of aging cedars. Circle by the kitchen house, memorial house, barn, and farm area to complete the loop. The 1-mile **Washington Nature Trail** is at the picnic area, accessible by driving back to the granite monument and turning right. Follow the trail signs in a loop to interpretive plaques about the trees, shrubs, flowers, animal life, and history of the area.

753–54

USGS MAP: Colonial Beach South

ACCESS: From US 301 junction with VA 3 (36 mi. from I-95 in Fredericksburg), go east 12.5 miles on VA 3 to left turn on VA 204.

ADDRESS AND INFORMATION: George Washington Birthplace National Monument, 1732 Popes Creek Rd., Colonial Beach, VA 22443; phone: 804-224-1732; fax: 804-224-2142; web: <www.nps.gov/gewa>. Available for free are brochures and flyers; books are on sale at the visitor center.

## GEORGE WASHINGTON MEMORIAL PARKWAY

*Arlington and Halifax Counties and City of Alexandria in Virginia*

Established in 1930, the George Washington Memorial Parkway administers 7,142 acres on the Potomac shores in Virginia and Maryland. On the Virginia side is the 28-mile, landscaped riverfront, limited-access parkway from Mount Vernon to the American Legion Memorial Bridge (I-495); Fort Hunt; Jones Point Lighthouse; Arlington House, Roosevelt Island; Turkey Run Park; and Great Falls National Park. In addition there are other recreational, natural, and historical facilities. (Mount Vernon, the colonial mansion and estate of George and Mary Washington, is not part of the NPS. It has been owned and maintained by the Mount Vernon Ladies' Association since 1858.) Of particular interest for recreation are the 18-mile **Mount Vernon Trail** and 10.1-mile **Potomac Heritage Trail**, both of which parallel the parkway and the river, and the 13 miles of trail network in Great Falls National Park.

ACCESS TO MOUNT VERNON TRAIL: Parking area at Mount Vernon and parking area at Roosevelt Island.

755 **Mount Vernon Trail**

LENGTH AND DIFFICULTY: 18 miles (28.8 km); easy

756–58 CONNECTING TRAILS: **Dyke Marsh Trail** (1 mi.), **Jones Point Trail** (0.5 mi.), **Potomac Heritage Trail** (10.1 mi.)

FEATURES: hike and bike paved trail, scenic views, historic site, urban adventure, waterfowl

TRAILHEADS: parking lot at Mount Vernon for south on VA 235 (Mount Vernon Hwy.); parking lot for north at Roosevelt Island by parkway

DESCRIPTION: This limited-access trail for bikers, hikers, joggers, and strollers begins at the last parking lot for recreational vehicles at Mount Vernon. Descend in a forest to Little Hunting Creek at 1 mile. Here is Riverside Park, a place to fish and picnic. At 2.9 miles cross the parkway; on the left is a trail diversion to Forest Hunt Park for picnic area, rest rooms, drinking water, and telephone. Continue on the left side of the parkway 5 miles to Alexandria Avenue and cross over to the riverside. Enter the 240-acre Dyke Marsh at 5.6 miles, where 250 species of birds have been seen. Water and rest rooms are available at Belle Haven, another picnic area, at 7.2 miles. From here the **Dyke Marsh Trail** goes 1 mile on a road to the Dyke Marsh shoreline. Cross Hunting Creek bridge and go under I-95 on South Street. (To the right is the **Jones Point Trail**, which goes 0.5 mi. round-trip partly through woods and a meadow to Jones Point Lighthouse, named in honor of a fur trader whose cabin was here in 1692.)

At 8.9 miles leave the wooded area and enter the historic city of Alexandria (with a citywide network of bike trails). Continue to 11.4 miles, where the 107-acre Daingerfield Island begins. Picnicking, sailing, fishing, and a restaurant are 759 here. After crossing Four-Mile Run there is a junction, left, with the **Four Mile**

*Mount Vernon Trail, National Park System (Courtesy Virginia Tourism Corporation)*

Run Trail (hike and bike). (It follows 2.2 mi. upstream to Shirlington Road [past I-395] to join the **Washington and Old Dominion (W&OD) Railroad Trail** [hike and bike]; see Chapter 14.) Pass by the western side of the National Airport from 12.6 miles to 14.3 miles. Reach Gravelly Point at 14.5 miles for an excellent view of the nation's capitol. Follow along the edge of the Potomac past hardwoods, shrubs, and white pines to the Lyndon B. Johnson Memorial Grove at 15.9 miles. Food, water, rest rooms, and telephone are here. At 16.5 miles is Memorial Bridge. (To the right across the river is Lincoln Memorial and upstream from there is the **Rock Creek Trail**. It connects with the **C and O Canal Trail**, which follows the Potomac River to the **AT** in Harpers Ferry, West Virginia.) Continue along the parkway, pass under the Theodore Roosevelt Memorial Bridge, and reach the parking area and causeway to Roosevelt Island at 17.6 miles. At 18 miles the trail ends but connects with the **Custis Trail** (hike and bike), left. (It parallels I-66 to Bon Air Park, where it connects with the **Four Mile Run Trail** and the **W&OD Railroad Trail** ahead and to the left. See Chapter 10.) At the parkway, where the **Mount Vernon Trail** ends, is the southern trailhead of the **Potomac Heritage Trail** for foot travel only.
USGS MAPS: Mount Vernon, Alexandria, Washington West

760–61

762

### Turkey Run Park

The George Washington Memorial Parkway's headquarters is at Turkey Run Park, a developed and landscaped area between the parkway and the Potomac River near I-495. A day-use area, it also has a visitor center, three picnic areas, rest

763  rooms, telephone, and four short trails. On the eastern side is 75-yard **River Trail** from parking and picnic area A to the **Potomac Heritage Trail**. From this picnic
764–66  area west is 0.7-mile **Woods Trail**, which parallels the park road to picnic area C. From here a loop is made with the **Big Switchback Trail** (110 yd.), the **Turkey Run Trail** (0.5 mi.), and a few yards of the **Potomac Heritage Trail**. The 10-mile, blue-blazed **Potomac Heritage Trail** is a foot trail only, and no camping is allowed. It meanders between the parkway and the Potomac River through a hardwood forest of river birch, sycamore, beech, oak, and witch hazel. Spots of the terrain are rocky high bluffs, floodplains, and slippery creek crossings. A national scenic trail, it is maintained by the PATC and is part of a long trail proposed through three states and the District of Columbia by the Potomac Heritage Trail Association.

At the stream crossing of Turkey Run the **Potomac Heritage Trail** goes 1.6 miles through floodplain sections northwest to its trailhead at I-495, and 8.4 miles southeast to Roosevelt Island. Access to the northwestern trailhead is from I-495 (Capital Beltway), exit 13, on VA 193 (Georgetown Pike) east at Balls Hill Road north. At the fourth block, turn left (over I-495) on Live Oak Drive to its cul-de-sac and trailhead. Downriver from Turkey Run follow the trail 0.7 mile to a rocky area and at 0.9 mile to a concrete tower for river gauging and yellow-blazed **River Trail**, an access to picnic area C. Continue downriver, pass under VA 123 bridge
767–70  and over ramps to arrive at Marcy Park at 3.6 miles. Follow the **Battery Trail** briefly to the parking area and then follow an old road. Cross rocky Pimmit Run and under Chain Bridge at 4.2 miles. Cross the **Gulf Branch Nature Trail** in a steep damp area at 4.8 miles and **Donaldson Run Trail** at 5.3 miles. Cross the **Windy Run Trail** at 6.7 miles (see Arlington County in Chapter 12 for details on the latter three trail crossings). Continuing between the parkway and the river, pass through a forested floodplain in sections, cross Spout Run, pass under Key Bridge, and reach a junction with the **Custis Trail** (hike and bike) at a grassy area at 8.2 miles. After 0.2 mile is the southeastern trailhead at Roosevelt Island parking area and pedestrian bridge. Here is the northern trailhead of the **Mount Vernon Trail**.

USGS MAPS: Falls Church, Washington West

ACCESS: From I-495, exit 14 (Capital Beltway), on the George Washington Memorial Parkway southeast 2 miles. From 14th Street Bridge (Memorial Bridge) on the parkway northwest 7 miles.

ADDRESS AND INFORMATION: George Washington Memorial Parkway, NPS, Turkey Run Park, McLean, VA 22101; phone: 703-289-2500/2510; fax: 703-289-2598. Available are brochures and maps of Turkey Run Park and other properties the park service administers.

## GREAT FALLS NATIONAL PARK
*Fairfax County*

The Great Falls National Park on the shore of the Potomac River is the most northern of the George Washington Memorial Parkway properties. It is northeast of Reston and is bordered on the north by Riverbend Park, a Fairfax County recreational park. Formed from the clear cascades high in the West Virginia mountains, the Potomac River puts on its dramatic finale of thundering white water here, a feature that gives the park its name. This spectacular natural area had a trading post on its riverbanks for Native Americans and early colonists, and later it was a shipping point to pioneers moving upriver. In 1784 the Patowmack Company was formed to navigate the falls with canals and locks, which were completed in 1802. During this time the town of Matildaville (now in ruins) developed as a central trading post. In 1828 the Chesapeake and Ohio Canal Company purchased the Patowmack Company but constructed the new canal and locks on the Maryland side of the river.

Park facilities include a visitor center, picnic areas, a snack bar, and trails (including a short access trail for the physically disabled to a river overlook) for hiking, biking, and horseback riding. Rock climbing and fishing are allowed, but camping is not. There is no boat access. Visitors are warned to stay away from the slippery edges of the jagged rocks along the shoreline. (Each year there are fatalities from falls or hazardous water sports in the park.)

ACCESS: From I-495 (Capital Beltway), exit 13, take VA 193 west (Georgetown Pike) for 3.9 miles to junction with SR 738, and turn right into the park.

**River Trail** (1.5 mi.), **Patowmack Canal Trail** (1.3 mi.), **Ridge Trail** (1.5 mi.), 763, 771–74
**Old Carriage Road Trail** (1.6 mi.), **Swamp Trail** (0.9 mi.)
LENGTH AND DIFFICULTY: 5.1 miles (8.2 km) combined, round-trip; easy
CONNECTING TRAILS: **Matildaville Trail** (1.1 mi.), **Mine Run Trail** (0.5 mi.), **River-** 775–80
    **bend Equestrian Trail** (0.4 mi.), **Heritage Trail** (1.7 mi.), **Upland Trail** (2 mi.),
    **Difficult Run Trail** (3.1 mi.) (the latter three trails are in adjoining parks in
    Fairfax County)
FEATURES: scenic views, waterfalls, historic site, canal ruins
TRAILHEAD: visitor center
INTRODUCTION: Combined distance of one-way trails, including spurs, is about 13
    miles, but round-trips can double the distance of some trails. The **River Trail**, the
    **Patowmack Canal Trail**, and the **Swamp Trail** are foot trails only. The **Matil-**
    **daville Trail** is foot and horse only. If planning a long trip, a park trail map is
    recommended. Also, the park offers guided tours. Described below is an exam-
    ple of a loop using a combination of multiple-use trails and hiking trails only.
DESCRIPTION: At the parking area at the visitor center examine the trail diagram
    board. If beginning on the blue-blazed **River Trail**, turn left or right. (To the left

it is 0.7 mi. to the boundary with Riverbend Park and its 1.7-mi. **Heritage Trail**.) Turn right and cross Patowmack Canal site to scenic overlooks of waterfalls and Falls Island. Pass through a picnic area and connector trails to the canal near Mather Gorge among walnut, oak, and sycamore. Pass spur to Sandy Landing and arrive at Cow Hoof Rock, a scenic area, at 1.4 miles. Ahead the foot trail ends at the **Ridge Trail**, left or right, which is a hike, bike, and horse trail at 1.6 miles. (To the right it is 0.3 mi. to a connection with the **Old Carriage Road Trail** and a return to the visitor center for a loop of 3 mi.) Continue left in a forest of oak, ash, river birch, and elm; pass a picnic area and at 2.2 miles reach a junction with the **Difficult Run Trail**. (It goes right to Difficult Run Park in Fairfax County.) Turn left and continue 0.2 mile to a river view, and backtrack. Also backtrack to the junction with the **River Trail** at 3.2 miles. Turn left, and after 0.3 mile reach a junction with the **Matildaville Trail**, right, and the **Old Carriage Road Trail**, right, both of which lead back to the visitor center. Continue left, then right on the **Ridge Trail** for 0.2 mile to a right turn on the **Swamp Trail** at 3.7 miles. (The **Ridge Trail** continues northwest for 0.4 mi. to the park road.) The 0.9-mile foot trail is through a forested, flat, low area with markers about wildlife and wild plants. At 4.6 miles is a junction with the **Old Carriage Road Trail**, right and left. Turn left, and after 0.2 mile there is a connector, right, with the **Matildaville Trail** to the town ruins. Continue north on the **Old Carriage Road Trail** to the visitor center at 5.1 miles. (If continuing on the **Old Carriage Road Trail**, cross the park road, and near Clay Pond connect with the **Mine Run Trail**, the **River Trail**, the **Upland Trail**, and the **Riverbend Equestrian Trail** for a total round-trip of 3.4 mi.)

USGS MAPS: Seneca, Vienna, Falls Church, Rockville

ADDRESS AND INFORMATION: Great Falls National Park, NPS, 9200 Old Dominion Drive, McLean, VA 22102; phone: 703-285-2964; fax:703-285-2231; web: <www.nps.gov/gwmp/grfa>. Available are park brochure and trail map.


## PRINCE WILLIAM FOREST PARK
*Prince William County*

A forested watershed of Quantico Creek, the 18,571-acre park is shaped like a sweet birch leaf with the tip near the town of Independent Hill and the stem base at the town of Triangle. In the southeastern corner of the county, the park is bordered on the south and southwest by SR 619 (Joplin Rd.), on the south by Quantico Marine Corps Base, on the north by VA 234 (Dumfries Rd.), and on the east by I-95 and the town of Dumfries. The park is rapidly becoming a prized oasis of woodland in a metropolitan environment 32 miles south of Washington, D.C., and 23 miles north of Fredericksburg. A significant feature of the park is the physiographic divide of the Piedmont Plateau with its hilly ridges in the west, and a drop at the fall line to the Coastal Plain Province in the east. Granite, schist, and quartzite are part of its geology, and Catoctin greenstone (also found in high elevations of the Blue Ridge Mountains) is at the confluence of Quantico Creek and its South Fork. Pyrite was mined here in the early part of the twentieth century. The park's unconsolidated soils were subjected to severe erosion during the two centuries the park was farmland.

Its terrestrial community of ninety-five plant species is dominated by hardwoods and scattered Virginia pines. Its plant diversity is enhanced by the transition from northern to southern climate ranges and the eastern and western physiographic provinces. Some plants are rare; for example, the whorled pogonia (*Isotria verticillata*), a yellow-green wild orchid, can be seen here. With diverse topography there is diverse wildlife. Deer, turkey, grouse, fox, beaver, raccoon, and squirrel are most common. There are 152 species of birds, including the great horned owl, cuckoo, brown creeper, and scarlet tanager. The lakes have trout, bass, bluegill, and perch.

Archaeological research traces the area's cultural resources to as early as 4500 B.C. Potomac Indians may have had villages in the park area as early as A.D. 700. English settlement and tobacco plantations were here after 1650, and by 1731 Prince William County was formed. Between 1899 and 1920 pyrite mining was a major industry. In the meantime, the soil was so depleted the farmers had difficulty maintaining a livelihood. The U.S. government purchased the area, with closed mines and poor farms, for reclamation and recreation under the National Industrial Recovery Act. It was named the Chopawamsic Recreation Demonstration Area. Visitors today will notice part of that history in the cabin camps, lakes, and trails constructed by the CCC from 1934 to 1940. During World War II the U.S. Army used the park for a top secret military installation, and in 1948 the park was returned to the NPS and renamed Prince William Forest Park. The park area also played significant roles in other wars. During the Revolutionary War local militia repaired Telegraph Road for Gen. George Washington's troops to pass through on their way to defeat the British at Yorktown in 1781. There are thirty-five cemeteries in the park where men of both sides of the Civil War are buried. In World War I the pyrite mines produced ingredients used in gunpowder.

Public facilities today include five cabin camps for groups, two tent camps (Turkey Run Ridge and Oak Ridge), a concessionaire campground with hookups for trailers and recreational vehicles (Travel Trailer Village on VA 234), a primitive backcountry campground (Chopawamsic, which requires a permit), ponds for fishing, picnic areas, visitor center, and 35 miles of trails. Bicycling is allowed on the paved roads and some of the fire roads. Hunting is prohibited. Among the sixteen trails three are interpretive. The shortest and easiest is 0.2-mile **Pine** **Grove Forest Trail** at the visitor center. It is popular with children and is easy for the physically impaired. The **Geology Trail** is a 2-mile loop that uses other trails such as the **Quantico Falls Trail**, part of the **North Valley Trail**, all of the **Cabin Branch Mine Trail**, part of Pyrite Mine Road, and a short piece of the Scenic

781–86

Road. Access is from parking lots D or E. The other trail about natural science is the **Farms to Forest Trail**, a double-loop in which the first loop is 1.1 miles long. Yellow-blazed, it is keyed to markers about trees, birds, and topography. Halfway around the loop a 1.7-mile extension begins. It goes deeper into the forest and passes by a tributary to Quantico Creek. Active or former beaver ponds are prominent on this trail. Access is at Oak Ridge Campground entrance.

There are a number of short loop options. The most popular is the **Laurel Trail**. It is a 1.3-mile, yellow-blazed loop north of the visitor center, which partly uses the

787      **Birch Bluff Trail** on the eastern side of the loop. At the northwestern corner of the trail is an access bridge over South Fork to the **South Valley Trail**. (Because there is no bridge at the northern end of the **Birch Bluff Trail**, it is not recommended

788      for a loop to the pyrite mine site.) Another short loop is the **Little Run Trail**, a 0.7-mile, yellow-blazed loop at Turkey Run Ridge Campground, off Park Central Drive.

A loop of 2 miles can be made to the pyrite mine site. Begin at parking lot D on Park Central Drive and follow Pyrite Mine Road to a junction with orange-blazed

789      **Cabin Branch Mine Trail**. Turn left, and after 0.3 mile turn right on the **North Valley Trail** to the mine site. Continue downstream and make another right to return on the Pyrite Mine Road.

790–92      Another 2-mile loop is **Chopawamsic Trail**. Formerly called the **Deer Ridge Trail** and the **Bobcat Ridge Trail**, it circles the campsites in a 430-acre tract reserved for backpack camping. All water must be carried in; trash must be carried out; and no pets are allowed. A permit is necessary for camping in this area, and during the winter hunting season the area is closed. Access is 2.1 miles west on SR 619 from the visitor center. Turn left on Breckenridge Road and go 0.7 mile to the parking lot.

Below is a description of the park's longest trail, the **South Valley Trail**, with its options for shorter or longer loops. It, as with all other trails in the park's main area, are for day use only.

ACCESS: From I-95, exit 150, at SR 619, turn west to the park entrance road on the right near I-95 ramps.

793–94      **Laurel Trail** (1.3 mi.), **South Valley Trail** (9.7 mi.)

LENGTH AND DIFFICULTY: 9.2 miles (14.7 km) combined; easy to moderate

795–97, 786      CONNECTING TRAILS: **Turkey Run Ridge Trail** (1.4 mi.), **High Meadows Trail** (2.1 mi.), **Oak Ridge Trail** (1.6 mi.), **Farms to Forest Trail** (2.8 mi.)

FEATURES: historic site, stream, lake, wildflowers, wildlife

TRAILHEADS: visitor center or Oak Ridge Campground

DESCRIPTION: Begin at the visitor center on the western side of the yellow-blazed **Laurel Trail** loop. After 0.4 mile intersect with Orenda Road, and cross the bridge over South Fork to white-blazed **South Valley Trail**, right and left. (To the right it goes 0.9 mi. to Pyrite Mine Rd. and the **North Valley Trail**.) Turn left, leave the road, and continue upstream. (On Orenda Rd. north it is 1 mi. to Park Central Dr. and parking area D for a junction with Pyrite Mine Rd.) Cross Mary Bird Branch and at 1.4 miles reach a junction with the **Turkey Run Ridge Trail** coming from the right. (It goes north 1.4 mi. to Turkey Run Ridge Campground and connects with 0.5-mi. **Mary Bird Branch Trail** and 2.1-mi. **High Meadows Trail**.) At 1.6 miles cross Park Central Drive near parking lots A and B. Ahead, in an oxbow of the creek, is a 0.1-mile spur to parking lot C of Park Central Drive. Intersect with Park Central Drive again at 3 miles, meet Taylor Farm Road on the right, and cross Park Central Drive near parking lot I. (The Taylor Farm Rd. goes 0.6 mi. north to intersect with the **High Meadows Trail** and Turkey Run Ridge Campground.) The main trail parallels the stream, passes gneiss rocks, and continues through a forest of tall hardwoods.

At 5 miles reach a junction with the **High Meadows Trail**, right. (It goes 2.1 mi. to Turkey Run Ridge Campground.) A few yards beyond, the trail crosses the creek, but there may not be a bridge. Farther upstream, on the approach to Lake #5, is an arched bridge over the creek. Cross the stream at the intersection with Mawavi Road at 6.7 miles. (The road goes 0.5 mi. left to Camp #2 and right 0.4 mi. to Park Central Dr. and parking lot G.) Continue ahead through a forest of oak, poplar, birch, and wild azalea to the last crossing of South Fork (where there may not be a bridge). The trail then skirts close enough to SR 619 to allow traffic to be heard, but it soon veers northeast to reach a junction with the **Oak Ridge Trail** at 9 miles.

(To make a loop back to the visitor center, turn right on yellow-blazed **Oak Ridge Trail**, hike 0.5 mi., cross Mawavi Rd., and at 1.6 mi. reach Black Top Rd. Turn right, cross Taylor Farm Rd. at 2.4 mi., and arrive at Turkey Run Ridge Campground at 3.3 mi. From there hike on the **Turkey Run Ridge Trail** for 1.4 mi. to the **South Valley Trail** for a return to the visitor center at 6.2 mi., a round-trip total of 15.2 mi.) Continue ahead 0.2 mile to Old Ridge Road, Oak Ridge Campground on the left, and the **Farms to Forest Trail** at 9.2 miles.

USGS MAPS: Joplin, Quantico

ADDRESS AND INFORMATION: Prince William Forest Park, P.O. Box 209, Triangle, VA 22172; phone: 703-221-7183; fax: 703-221-3258; web: <www.nps.gov/prwi>. Available are free brochures with park map.

# PART III. State Managed Trails

*The woods are made for the hunters of drama,*
*The brooks for the fishers of song.*
SAM WALTER FOSS (1858–1911)

# 10. Wildlife Management Areas

Of Virginia's 25.5 million acres of land, 4 million acres are public lands, and this includes 176,102 acres in twenty-nine wildlife management areas (WMAS). The following WMA descriptions primarily emphasize trail usage, though some other facilities are listed as well. Only the WMAS with named or specifically designated trails are described in this chapter, and those with a network of trails are described in more detail. The Virginia agency responsible for developing and preserving these public hunting lands is the Department of Game and Inland Fisheries. From the mountains to the sea, the state has lands of diversity for both game and nongame wildlife. The areas are a source of pleasure and education to hunters, anglers, naturalists, hikers, campers, birders, and others who love the outdoors. Primitive camping, unless otherwise posted, is permitted for a maximum of seven days, with no more than three camp units for a group. Camping is prohibited within 100 yards of boat ramps or fishing lakes. Hiking and camping are not recommended during hunting season, and hikers must wear a blaze orange cap and jacket. If poaching is observed, report the violation to 800-237-5712. Because facilities and regulations vary at each WMA, it is recommended that hikers call in advance about hunting seasons and potential campsites. A few of the WMAS have given special attention to singular trails; they are collectively described in this introduction. Gated roads are open from the first Saturday in October to the second Saturday in February, and from the second Saturday in April to the third Saturday in May.

The Gathright WMA is a showplace of conservation and recreation in the rugged Alleghany Highlands bordering West Virginia. Three government agencies have been responsible for the management of the area since Congress authorized the Gathright Dam on the Jackson River in 1947. Finally in 1965 the U.S. Corps of Engineers began construction; the dam was completed in 1981, and recreational use began in 1982. In 1978 Congress renamed the 2,530-acre lake in honor of Benjamin Moomaw, an area citizen whose efforts made the project possible. The WMA's original 18,000 acres became 13,428 when the GWNF became responsible for the lake and its shoreline. Gathright's 2-mile **Sweet Acorn Trail** follows an old 799 woods road, spot bordered with scenic wildlife grazing fields, on the spine of Bolar Mountain. (No camping is allowed.) Access is 3 miles north of the entrance

273

800 to Lake Moomaw Campground on sr 600 to gated **Bolar Ridge Fire Trail**, right. It is 1.5 miles up a steep, scenic road to the trailhead, right. For more information: Gathright wma, P.O. Box 996, Verona, va 24482; phone: 540-248-9360.

Ragged Island wma has 1,537 acres in Isle of Wight County. It has three canoe trails into one of the largest undisturbed brackish marshes remaining on the James River. One of the state's 300 watchable wildlife areas, it has 220 species of 801 birds and 38 species of fish. The 0.5-mile, round-trip **Ragged Island Trail** is a path from a parking area at the southwestern end of James River Bridge on us 17/us 258/va 32 (northeast of Bartlett). The surprisingly pleasant and worthwhile walk with a 400-yard boardwalk goes through loblolly pine, cordgrass, saltgrass, and sea lavender to an observation deck at the river. (No camping is allowed.) For more information: Ragged Island wma, 5806 Mooretown Rd., Williamsburg, va 23188; phone: 757-253-4180.

Formerly known as Apple Manor wma, reflecting the orchard on the property and other nearby orchards, the G. Richard Thompson wma has 4,160 acres on the Blue Ridge Mountains. It is the only wma with the **AT** weaving through its boundaries. East of Front Royal it is between i-66 north to the border of Sky Meadows State Park and us 50. Access near Linden from va 55 is on sr 638, which has a number of gated access routes to the **AT**, and at the first access to the **Ted Lake** 802 **Trail**. The **Ted Lake Trail** can also be accessed from sr 688, 1.2 miles north from va 55 near Markham. If accessing the blue-blazed trail from sr 638, follow it 1 mile to its intersection with the **AT** at a spring and Manassas Gap Shelter. It then descends on a ridge to sr 688. The wma has a lake stocked with bass and sunfish on sr 688, and its moist, rich hollows have especially large zones of trillium. For more information: Thompson wma, 1320 Belman Rd., Fredericksburg, va 22401; phone: 540-899-4169.

ADDRESS AND INFORMATION: Virginia Department of Game and Inland Fisheries, 4010 W. Broad St. (Box 11104), Richmond, va 23230; phone: 804-367-1000; website: <www.dgif.state.va.us/>. Available for free are *Virginia Wildlife Watcher's Guide*, a tabloid about all the places to observe wildlife; *Virginia Hunting Guide*, a tabloid about all the wmas, hunting and fishing seasons, and map sources; and leaflets and brochures on bird lists and endangered species. A fee is charged for *Virginia Wildlife*, an excellent subscription journal dedicated to the conservation of Virginia's wildlife and natural resources.

## AMELIA WILDLIFE MANAGEMENT AREA

*Amelia County*

With more than 3 miles of frontage along the Appomattox River, ponds, and considerable diversity of vegetation, the Amelia wma is an excellent wildlife habitat. The adjoining lands of Westvaco and Chesapeake Corp. significantly expand its recreational opportunities. The 2,217 acres of state land, purchased in 1967,

include 100 acres of water and 850 acres of fields. Anglers can expect bass, blue-gill, crappie, and walleye pike. All of its trails are easy. The **Woodcock Trail** is 4   803–6
miles round-trip and follows an old winding trail partly along a small stream to the Appomattox River for backtracking. Its access is at the entrance parking lot on SR 652. Access to 2.5-mile **Lake Trail** is at the boat ramp parking area, off SR 652 and under huge oaks. The 2.5-mile loop may not be maintained at all points, but at the beginning take a left, and follow the lake boundary south. After 1.4 miles cross the **Bunny Trail**, which goes 0.7 mile left, to SR 692. This is a serene environment. Follow the lake boundary to the dam and return through the woods to the parking area. The **Marsh Point Trail** is a 1-mile ridge route that splits at 0.7 mile. Both legs then lead down the hill to the bottomland and the banks of the Appomattox River. Backtrack to its start, which was at the main parking area on the ridge of SR 652.

USGS MAP: Chula

ACCESS: From US 360 east of Amelia, take SR 604 north and go 7 miles to Masons Corner. Turn left on SR 616; continue 1.5 miles and turn right on SR 652 to the WMA entrance.

ADDRESS AND INFORMATION: Amelia WMA, 910 Thomas Jefferson Rd., Forest, VA 24551; phone: 434-525-7522.

## CLINCH MOUNTAIN WILDLIFE MANAGEMENT AREA
*Smyth, Russell, Tazewell, and Washington Counties*

The 25,477-acre Clinch Mountain WMA, the state's second largest, is scenic, remote, high, and rugged. Laurel Bed Lake, a 330-acre man-made lake, is excellent for trout fishing. Adjacent to the lake is a unique stand of black cherry that has been designated a natural area by the Society of American Foresters. The trees in the cove are more than 3 feet in diameter and more than 85 feet high. Big Tumbling Creek, heavily stocked with trout, forms falls and pools through deep gorges to the North Fork of the Holston River, west of Saltville. Activities include picnicking, horseback riding, boating, canoeing, birding, hiking, and berry picking. Camping is allowed at the designated site on Little Tumbling Creek. It is open from the third Saturday in March to Labor Day. The campground has water, fireplace, firewood, and vault rest rooms (and is part of the Division of State Parks).

The WMA has several administrative access roads that are developed, gated, and closed to vehicles. They make two exciting hiking routes in Twin Hollows and Short Mountain (4,020 ft.). Both are 3 miles each and are accessed from the main entrance road. Also, hunters have made a 3-mile loop that ascends from Jackson Gap above the campground to White Rocks, right, along the ridge top to Panther Lick Cove, and descends to follow Brian Cove Creek back to the campground. To access the lake and campground, follow the same directions as under trailhead for the *Clinch Mountain Trail,* below.

807 **Clinch Mountain Trail**

LENGTH AND DIFFICULTY: 2.4 miles (3.8 km); strenuous

FEATURES: scenery, wildlife, black cherry grove, ruggedness

TRAILHEAD: To reach the WMA from I-81 at VA 91 (Glade Spring, exit 29) go north on VA 91 for 5.2 miles into Saltville. In the center of Saltville take SR 634 on the left; cross the Holston River bridge and proceed to the junction with SR 613. Turn left on SR 613, drive 4 miles to SR 747, and turn right up Tumbling Creek Road and continue 2 miles to entrance to the WMA.

DESCRIPTION: Cross below the dam from the parking area to the trail junction. Continue ahead up the mountain at the edge of the Black Cherry Natural Area. (The right and left trails follow the Laurel Bed Creek.) Ascend steeply for 1 mile to ridge crest (3,800 ft.), then descend on switchbacks to Little Tumbling Creek and the campground road at 2.4 miles. Backtrack, or have a car waiting. It is 1.5 miles, left, on the road to the campground.

USGS MAP: Saltville

808 **Red Branch Trail**

LENGTH AND DIFFICULTY: 8.4 miles (13.4 km) round-trip; moderate to strenuous

FEATURES: wildlife, scenic wildflowers, seclusion

TRAILHEAD: After entering the WMA on SR 747, park at the trout holding pond.

DESCRIPTION: Begin on the western side of the road and follow up the hollow. Ascend gradually, then enter the Red Branch Hollow at 2.6 miles. Follow Red Branch, steep in places, for another 1.6 miles to the edge of the WMA boundary. Directly west is the top of Beartown Mountain (4,700 ft.). Remote and rugged, hikers may wish to hike to the top of the mountain to see a number of plant species, including red spruce, normally found much farther north or on higher elevations. Backtrack.

USGS MAP: Saltville

ADDRESS AND INFORMATION: Clinch Mountain WMA, Rt. 1, Box 107, Marion, VA 24354; phone: 276-782-9051.

## GOSHEN/LITTLE NORTH MOUNTAIN WILDLIFE MANAGEMENT AREA
*Rockbridge and Augusta Counties*

The Goshen WMA to the south, the Little North Mountain WMA to the north, and Goshen Pass Natural Area in between form a 33,697-acre tract, largest of state-owned land stretching 35 miles from White Rock Mountain west of Lexington to Buffalo Gap west of Staunton. A scenic area of sandstone and limestone, rugged mountain terrain, and an abundant variety of flora and fauna, this large forest offers hikers alluring trails and roads for solitude and scenic views. Some trails are unnamed. An example is a trail network across the Goshen Pass swinging footbridge. Trails meander to an overlook of the river and outside the Goshen Pass Natural Area to a BSA camp at Lake Merriweather and up to the ridge top of Little North Mountain WMA. There are at least eight campsites on the named trails. (See introduction to this chapter for information on camping and opening of gated roads.) In addition to hunting in the WMAs, there is fishing, canoeing, and kayaking in the white water of the Maury River.

ACCESS TO GOSHEN PASS AREA: From I-81, exit 195, at junction of US 11 north of Lexington, take US 11 north for 1 mile to junction with SR 716 west, and turn left. Go under I-81 on SR 716 and proceed 3.5 miles to VA 39. Turn right on VA 39 and go 6.4 miles to Laurel Run Picnic Area in Goshen Pass by the Maury River. (Goshen Pass swinging bridge is 1.7 mi. farther upriver on the right.)

ACCESS TO LITTLE NORTH MOUNTAIN AREA: See trailhead access below.

## Laurel Run Trail                                                           809

LENGTH AND DIFFICULTY: 4.2 miles (6.7 km) round-trip; moderate
FEATURES: cascades, rhododendron groves
TRAILHEAD: In Goshen Pass at the junction of the stream, Laurel Run, and VA 39, a
   few yards downriver from the picnic area.
DESCRIPTION: After parking at the Laurel Run Picnic Area, cross the road and walk
   downriver to a gated hunter's 4WD road on the right by the stream. Ascend on
   the road by a tumbling creek in a channel of rosebay rhododendron, oaks,
   maples, hemlock, and witch hazel to the end of the road at 2.1 miles. Backtrack.
USGS MAP: Goshen

## Guy's Run Trail (4.2 mi.), Piney Mountain Trail (2 mi.), Meadow Ground Trail   810–12
(2.1 mi.)

LENGTH AND DIFFICULTY: 23.6 miles (37.6 km) combined, round-trip; moderate to
   strenuous
FEATURES: streams, scenic views, wildlife, seclusion
TRAILHEAD: From Laurel Run Picnic Area drive upriver on VA 39 for 3.3 miles to
   Guy's Run Access Road and entrance gate on the left (0.6 mi. beyond junction
   with SR 601). (The gated small roads across the road from a parking area at SR
   601 are not on WMA property.)
DESCRIPTION: If camping on this potentially long hike, use care that vehicles do
   not block access roads. Begin **Guy's Run Trail** at the gated road from the
   parking area. At 2 miles an old road extends left. (It crosses the stream, traverses Forge Mountain, and crosses other tributaries for about 1.5 mi. to the
   bluffs over the Maury River and Goshen Pass. Backtrack to **Guy's Run Trail**.)
   Continue upstream among hardwoods, hemlock, and rhododendron. At 2.3
   miles meet the **Piney Mountain Trail** on the right. (It leads steeply right of
   Piney Branch for 2 mi. to the top of Bratton Mountain [3,000 ft.].) Backtrack to
   **Guy's Run Trail** and continue upstream along Guy's Run. Ford the stream
   several times and observe the potential campsites on the way. At 4.2 miles the

**Meadow Ground Trail** and a campsite are on the right at a trail fork. The right fork leads 2.1 miles to the top of a beautiful mountain gap called the Mohla Loop, 6.3 miles from VA 39. Backtrack. The left fork steadily ascends east on ridges, makes a junction with SR 627 on the southern side of Coopers Knob, and ascends steeply to Big Butt (4,400 ft.). Here is the site of a former fire tower. Backtrack 7.8 miles to VA 39 (except during the seasons when the gates are open).

USGS MAPS: Goshen, Millboro

813 **Little North Mountain Trail**

LENGTH AND DIFFICULTY: 12.8 miles (20.5 km); moderate

FEATURES: wildlife, scenic views, geological formations, wildflowers

TRAILHEADS: To reach the southern trailhead from Guy's Run access area on VA 39, drive northeast on SR 601 across the bridge of Calfpasture River. Follow SR 601 for 11.2 miles to a junction with SR 682 and turn right. Ascend on SR 682 for another 3.8 miles to TV/radio relay towers and trailhead. If approaching from Augusta Springs, turn off VA 42 on SR 811, go 0.3 mile, and turn left on SR 601. Follow SR 601 3.9 miles to SR 682.

For the northern trailhead on VA 42, drive southeast 2.2 miles from the junction of VA 254 and VA 42 in Buffalo Springs (9 mi. west of Staunton on VA 254). On the left of the highway is a trail sign; on the right side of the highway is roadside parking. (It is 6 mi. southwest on VA 42 to Augusta Springs.)

DESCRIPTION: (It is recommended that this trail be hiked from southwest to northeast. Contact the WMA office before hiking and inquire about any changes, trail route closures, or relocations.) Wildlife on the mountain includes bear, deer, grouse, and turkey. From near the TV/radio relay towers, go north 450 feet to an old woods road on the left and follow the ridge. (There may or may not be white blazes, and the trail may be overgrown in sections.) West are views of Little Calfpasture River and Elliott Knob on the Great North Mountain range. Views to the east are of dairy farms in the Shenandoah Valley and the Blue Ridge Mountains farther east. (Blazes may disappear after about 2 mi.) Descend to cross SR 603 after a forest gate at Pond Gap (and near the wildlife boundary) at 4.8 miles.

Pass under a power line and descend to Jackson Hunter Access Road at 5.5 miles. Turn right and ascend to Pig Path Gap, a scenic area. Continue ascending on the road and turn right on a foot trail at 8.1 miles. At 8.7 miles is a trickling stream (which may be dry in the summer). Ascend, follow the ridge, and descend to King Mountain Gap at 10 miles. (Ignore white or colored blazes to the left or right.) Ascend on a fire road and follow it for 1.7 miles to an overgrown foot trail on the left. Descend steeply and cross a small stream at 12.2 miles. Reach the C&O Railroad at 12.4 miles at a signal box. (Some of the trains that pass through here have retained those lonesome steam-whistle type sounds, fitting for the backcountry.) Turn left on the railroad track and follow it to an old woods road on the right. Turn right and descend about 150 yards to the trailhead sign at 12.8 miles. Backtrack, or have a second vehicle waiting.

USGS MAPS: Goshen, Augusta Springs, Churchville

ADDRESS AND INFORMATION: Goshen/Little North Mountain WMA, 50 Lori Lane, Churchville, VA 24421; phone: 540-248-9360.


## HIDDEN VALLEY WILDLIFE MANAGEMENT AREA
*Washington County*

Hidden Valley WMA is a scenic, high mountain area, excellent for hiking. It has a 60-acre lake nestled in the headwaters of Brumley Creek (3,600 ft.) and filled with trout. Except during hunting season, few people are seen on the trails. Camping is permitted around the lake. The lake has a boat ramp.

**Brumley Creek Trail** (3 mi.), **Long Arm Hollow Trail** (2.5 mi.), **Brumley Rim**      814–16
**Trail** (4.7 mi.)

LENGTH AND DIFFICULTY: 9.5 miles (15.2 km) combined, round-trip; easy to strenuous

FEATURES: lake, stream, wildlife, serenity

TRAILHEAD: In Abingdon take US 19/58A northwest for 10.3 miles to SR 690, right, and go 2 miles up a steep but paved road to Hidden Valley and lake parking area.

DESCRIPTION: If hiking the **Brumley Creek Trail** from the parking area by the lake, follow the trail to the end of the lake, pass the dam, and take the trail to the left at the fork. (The **Long Arm Hollow Trail** goes right.) Follow downstream through oak, hickory, maple, birch, locust, cherry, and hemlock to a junction at 2.3 miles, right, with the **Brumley Rim Trail**. Continue ahead to a connection with Little Brumley Creek at 3 miles, and a picturesque waterfall on the left. Backtrack to the lake or take the **Brumley Rim Trail** for a loop.

For the **Long Arm Hollow Trail**, from the parking lot follow the trail to the dam and take the right fork below the dam. Ascend, following the creek, for 2.5 miles to the ridge top. Several trails converge. (The trail to the right runs to an FAA tower at 0.5 mi. Farther ahead the trail descends for another 1.3 mi. to the entrance road, and from there it takes a right and goes 1 mi. back to the parking area.) The **Brumley Rim Trail** turns left, following the ridge for 3 miles. Turn left at trail junction and descend to Stagger Hollow for 1.7 miles. When you reach the **Brumley Creek Trail**, turn left and, after another 2.3 miles, return to the parking area. (A number of other unnamed trails descend from the **Brumley Rim Trail** toward Poor Valley; if hikers are unfamiliar with the area, topographical maps are advised.)

USGS MAP: Brumley

ADDRESS AND INFORMATION: Hidden Valley WMA, Rt. 1, Box 107, Marion, VA 24354; phone: 276-782-9051.

## HIGHLAND WILDLIFE MANAGEMENT AREA
*Bath and Highland Counties*

The Highland WMA encompasses some of the best high mountain land in this remote corner of the state. The 14,284 acres are divided into two large tracts, plus a smaller one. The largest tract lies on Jack Mountain and includes 4,400-foot Sounding Knob, the best-known landmark in the county. The mountaintop includes a grazed open area, maintaining a bald appearance. The other large tract is scenic Bullpasture Mountain, bordering the edge of Bath County and the Bullpasture Gorge.

ACCESS TO SOUNDING KNOB: From Staunton take US 250 west to McDowell, and after 2 miles turn left on SR 615. Continue on SR 615 to the **CCC Fire Trail** shortly beyond Davis Run.

ACCESS TO BULLPASTURE MOUNTAIN: Take US 250 to McDowell and turn left on SR 678 to the Bullpasture Gorge parking area. From the south, take VA 39 from I-81 north of Lexington; from VA 39 take SR 625 to Williamsville, then SR 678 through Bullpasture Gorge to the parking area.

817 **CCC Fire Trail**
LENGTH AND DIFFICULTY: 10 miles (16 km) round-trip; strenuous
FEATURES: Sounding Knob, scenic views, wildlife
TRAILHEAD: See above for Sounding Knob.
DESCRIPTION: This fire road is open to motor traffic only during hunting seasons, but it is open to hikers year round. Follow on left of Davis Run for 1 mile. (At this point a 2-mi. exceptionally steep trail leads left, ascending to the western slope of Buck Hill and into remote Jack Mountain.) Continue on the road to a gap in the ridge; turn right, following the ridge (a private road comes in from the left side of the mountain), and go north to Sounding Knob. As the road skirts the knob, take a side trail to the left at 1 mile from the gap, ascending steeply to the knob. Return and continue to WMA boundary at 5 miles. Backtrack.
USGS MAPS: Monterey Southeast, Williamsville

818 **Bullpasture Mountain Trail**
LENGTH AND DIFFICULTY: 7 miles (11.2 km) round-trip; moderate
FEATURES: wildlife, stream, seclusion
TRAILHEAD: See above for Bullpasture Mountain.
DESCRIPTION: In the Bullpasture Gorge explore this area by crossing the river from the parking area and following the gated trail along the river and up the mountain. At 2 miles an optional trail to the right leads up a hollow to the top of Bullpasture Mountain and, at approximately 2 miles, to SR 614 on the other side.

Back on the **Bullpasture Mountain Trail**, at 3.5 miles another trail on the left leads across the mountain, also connecting with SR 614. It roughly parallels the other trail for approximately 2.5 miles. Backtrack (unless crossing the mountain for vehicle shuttle at SR 612, 613, or 614).

USGS MAPS: Monterey Southeast, Williamsville

ADDRESS AND INFORMATION: Highland WMA, P.O. Box 996, Verona, VA 24482; phone: 540-248-9360.


## HOG ISLAND WILDLIFE REFUGE
*Surry and Isle of Wight Counties*

Acquired in 1953, the 3,200 acres of Hog Island have become one of the prime waterfowl areas along the James River. In recent years some 10,000 Canada geese and 15,000 ducks have been on the refuge at peak times, plus herons, egrets, and dozens of other species. The waterfowl benefit from an intensive management program of the Virginia Game Commission. The controlled ponds are drained in the spring, and millet is grown through the summer. As the fall waterfowl migration starts, the areas are flooded. The spectacle of birds coming in to feed in the refuge is impressive. Woodlands in the area are chiefly loblolly pine. Hiking in this area is allowed only during the daytime; no camping.

ACCESS: From VA 10 at Bacon's Castle, take SR 650 to entrance gate, having passed VEPCO's Surry nuclear power plant and the Carlisle Tract on the right.

There are at least four loop trails, with parking areas at the beginning of each. The first trail reached on the refuge road leads a short distance—0.3 mile— into the woods. The loops are 1.7 miles, 3 miles, 4.2 miles, and 3.2 miles, in combinations of trails around the lakes. Also, at the refuge headquarters, a 0.6-mile trail extends northwest to the edge of the James River. All the trails are unnamed.

ADDRESS AND INFORMATION: Hog Island WMA, 5806 Mooretown Rd., Williamsburg, VA 23188; phone: 757-253-4180.


## POWHATAN WILDLIFE MANAGEMENT AREA
*Powhatan County*

This 4,415-acre tract 30 miles west of Richmond, on the rolling central Piedmont Plateau, is ideal for the hiker. Dispersion is easy with thirteen trails dipping into copses, winding around lazy brooks, and rising on gentle ridge crests. The area is 75 percent forest, with fields near the six stocked lakes. Hunting for turkey, dove, and quail is popular. Bluegill, bass, and catfish are in the lakes. Powhatan Lakes, two of the WMA's largest, are north of US 60 with entry on SR 625. Around the perimeter of the southern tract, between US 60 and VA 13, are seven access points at which to park and begin the trails. Short to long circuits can be made on the trails. A few need to be backtracked. The combination described below includes all the trails.

ACCESS: For main access point drive 1.5 miles south of US 60 on SR 627 (4 mi. west of US 60/522 junction), then turn left and go 0.5 mile to parking area on Deer Lane, SR 622.

819–31 **Fescue Trail** (2.1 mi.), **Squirrel Ridge Trail** (0.4 mi.), **Nature Trail** (0.6 mi.), **Arrowhead Trail** (2.8 mi.), **Holly Trail** (0.7 mi.), **Pine Trail** (1.1 mi.), **CCC Trail** (1.5 mi.), **Dogwood Trail** (1.5 mi.), **Franklin Trail** (0.6 mi.), **Redbud Trail** (0.4 mi.), **White Oak Trail** (0.7 mi.), **Red Oak Trail** (0.6 mi.), **Power Line Trail** (0.8 mi.)

LENGTH AND DIFFICULTY: 15.6 miles (25 km) combined, partial round-trip; easy
FEATURES: wildlife, stream, wildflowers
TRAILHEAD: See main entrance to WMA at end of description.
DESCRIPTION: No trails are blazed, and some are not marked by signs. The **Fescue Trail** trailhead is on the left, 0.25 mile after entry on SR 622, Deer Lane. This trail runs 0.7 mile to a crossing of Sallee Creek, making a junction at 1.7 miles with the **CCC Trail** and ending at Salmon Creek at 2.1 miles. Backtrack, or turn left on the return at the **CCC Trail** for connections to other trails in making a loop. Begin this labyrinth of trails by descending from the parking area between the two lakes, right. Follow grassy open space to a stand of large oaks on a knoll on the left. (Grassy road to right goes 0.5 mi. to parking area across the road, SR 627, from the Cozy Acres Campground.) From the knoll on the **Squirrel Ridge Trail** descend and ascend through open area to forest road. Here is part of the **Nature Trail**. After 0.4 mile meet the **Arrowhead Trail** and take the left on a wide avenue, partially open, bordered with a magnificent display of redbud. At 1.2 miles is a junction with the **Holly Trail**, which goes right.

At the junction of the **Arrowhead** and the **Holly** trails, there are three options. The shortest is to go left on the **Arrowhead**, bearing left at the clearing near Sunfish Pond; cross the dam at 1.4 miles among fennel, sumac, and alder; and follow the **Pine Trail** to parking area for a loop of 2.1 miles.

Option two is to follow the **Arrowhead Trail** east, without taking the shortcut to the lake. This route will cross Sallee Creek, reach a junction with the **CCC Trail** at 1 mile, and offer two choices of a loop back to the parking area. If turning right on the **CCC Trail**, go 0.5 mile to the **Dogwood Trail**, take another right for 0.8 mile, and turn right again at the junction with the **Holly Trail**. From this junction go another 0.8 mile back to the **Arrowhead**, follow the directions across the dam, and return to the parking area for a total of 5.2 miles. Or, if turning left on the **CCC Trail**, the hiker can follow for 1.1 miles to a junction of the **Fescue Trail**. Turn left here and return to parking area on the **Fescue Trail** for a total of 5.5 miles.

For the third option for routes from the junction of the **Holly Trail** and the

Arrowhead Trail, bear right on the Holly Trail, and go 0.8 mile to a junction with the Dogwood Trail. Turn left, cross Sallee Creek, pass the Franklin Trail on the right, and reach a fire road after another 0.8 mile. (To the right is an access road and the game-manager residence, and to the left is access to the CCC Trail and the short Redbud Trail.) Continue straight ahead across the fire road, entering on the White Oak Trail, which after 0.7 mile becomes the Red Oak Trail. Follow the Red Oak Trail for 0.6 mile to another fire road, and turn left on the Arrowhead Trail. Follow the Arrowhead Trail straight west to its original junction with the Holly Trail (crossing only the CCC Trail) for 1.8 miles. Backtrack, or go right across the Sunfish Pond and turn left on the Pine Trail to the parking area at the original trailhead. Total loop is 6 miles. (The Power Line Trail extends from a parking area on SR 601, 0.5 mi. from the junction of US 60 and SR 684.) Combined mileage of all options is 15.6 miles. Camping is not allowed on these trails.

ACCESS: For the main access point, drive 1.5 miles south of US 60 on SR 627 (4 mi. west of US 60/522 junction), then turn left and go 0.5 mile to parking area on SR 622 (Deer Lane).

ADDRESS AND INFORMATION: Powhatan WMA, 1320 Belman Rd., Fredericksburg, VA 22401; phone: 540-899-4169.


## RAPIDAN WILDLIFE MANAGEMENT AREA
*Greene and Madison Counties*

The 10,327-acre Rapidan WMA has eight separate tracts, chiefly in Madison County north of Standardsville and approximately 25 miles southwest of Culpeper. Four of the parcels are mortised into the Shenandoah National Park, with Fork, Doubletop, and Bluff Mountains being the most popular for hiking. It is a scenic, rugged, and forested area, and the Rapidan River cascades between two parcels of the WMA. Near its beginning is the confluence of Mill Prong and Laurel Prong. The major trails originate in the Shenandoah National Park. (For descriptions of the Staunton River Trail, the Jones Mountain Trail, the Laurel Prong Trail, the Doubletop Mountain Trail, and fire roads, consult the *Shenandoah National Park Appalachian Trail Guide*, published by the PATC, 118 Park St., SE, Vienna, VA 22180-4609; phone: 703-242-0315; e-mail: <publications@patc.net>; web: <www.patc.net>.) Also, see Chapter 5 in this guide. Other recreation in the WMA is fishing for brook trout and hunting for bear, deer, and wild turkey.

ACCESS TO THE RAPIDAN RIVER AREA: From Criglersville take SR 670 1 mile to SR 649, turning left. Go for 3 miles to Shenandoah National Park boundary, and continue to a junction with SR 622; turn right, following SR 622 up the river.

ADDRESS AND INFORMATION: Rapidan WMA, 1320 Belman Rd., Fredericksburg, VA 22401; phone: 540-899-4169.

*Saponi Trail, White Oak Mountain* WMA

## WHITE OAK WILDLIFE MANAGEMENT AREA
*Pittsylvania County*

The White Oak WMA has 2,712 acres of which about two-thirds are forested with oaks, hickory, beech, and Virginia and loblolly pines. Its west frontage is the quietly flowing Banister River for 4.5 miles. There are 12 ponds on the WMA, and five of them are available to fishing. Pete's Pond, the largest, has largemouth bass, bluegill, redear sunfish, and channel catfish. Open fields have a wide variety of birds for bird-watching. Among the wildlife are deer, turkey, quail, and squirrel. There are back roads for equestrians, and there are two hiking trails. The 0.9-mile **Hiawatha Nature Trail** is at the north edge of the area. Access to it from Spring Garden Road (SR 640) northwest on Motleys Mill Road (SR 649) is 1.3 miles to a dirt parking area on the right. If coming from Chatham (and off US 29 Bypass) drive east on Halifax Road (SR 832) 3.9 miles to Motleys Mill Road (SR 649) and turn right. It is 1.3 miles on the left. Look carefully for a trail sign at the northwest corner of the parking area, or simply walk 80 yards down the road to a gated road, left. A white blaze is on the right before the gate. Follow the white blaze off the forest road through old and new growth for 0.5 mile to the bank of Banister River. Here are trout lilies, wild ginger, and ironwood. Duck houses are nearby. Ascend steeply from the river through mountain laurel and to a scenic overlook at 0.7 mile. From here exit to a field and turn right. Here is a handsome display of yellow and orange cross vine (*Anisostichus capreolata*) shrouding the trees. Such a view is well worth a hike through any forest. Ahead is a small lake where the trail turns left on a road to complete the loop back to the parking lot.

The 2.1-mile **Saponi Trail** is at the south edge of the area. Access to it is from the Spring Garden community on Spring Garden Road (SR 640) west on either SR 707 or SR 706. Make a sharp turn at a WMA sign, left if SR 707, and right if from SR 706. Follow Shotgun Road. Drive past the WMA manager's residence and to the **Saponi Trail** sign at Pete's Pond, a dead-end road. This desirable and educational path was created in 1997 by the Dan River Trail Association and the Virginia Department of Game and Fish. Follow through a hardwood and pine forest to descend and cross a small stream coming from the lake. Pass under a power line and cross the stream again near the confluence of another stream from the right at 0.6 mile. Cross the stream twice more. At 0.9 mile is a rocky area with cliff overhangs on the south side of the creek. Along the creekside is an abundance of wildflowers and flowering shrubs. Some are bloodroot, dwarf iris, mountain lettuce, ninebark, spicebush, and rattlesnake orchids. At 1 mile curve left from the creek to ascend among open areas for wildlife grazing. Follow a road through pine forest management sections. At 1.5 miles be alert to a footpath leaving the road, left. Follow it through sections of dense forest and pass under the power line to complete the loop at 2.1 miles.

USGS MAP: Spring Garden

ACCESS: In addition to accesses described above, another route north from Danville is to turn off US 29 onto Spring Garden Road (SR 640), right. Follow it about 5.5 miles to turn left on SR 707, and go 7.8 miles to turn left on SR 649.

ADDRESS AND INFORMATION: White Oak WMA, 1037 Shotgun Rd., Chatham, VA 24531; phone: 434-432-1377.

What we experience of Nature is in models,
and all . . . are so beautiful.
RICHARD BUCKMINSTER FULLER (1895–1983)

# 11. Parklands, Natural Area Preserves, and Forests

Virginia's park system was created in 1936 for the purpose of managing and protecting diverse land and water resources and cultural history, and to offer the public a natural environment for outdoor recreation. From the original six to the nearly seventy parks, historic sites, and natural areas of today, the natural legacy remains strong. Virginians voted their approval of the park system in 1993 when they passed a $93 million bond referendum to acquire four more parks and ten natural areas. In addition, existing parks are slated to receive renovations and improvement of facilities in the future. The 65,000-acre park system is administered by the Division of State Parks, which has four division branches: information, administration and management, maintenance and operation, and design and construction. As a unit it is part of the Department of Conservation and Recreation.

To catalog the parks geographically, the division lists them as occurring in Blue Ridge Highlands, Shenandoah, Central, Northern Virginia, and Tidewater and Eastern Shore. In this chapter, I combine the park descriptions near or west of the mountains (Blue Ridge and Shenandoah) in a Mountains category; parks that are in central and northern Virginia are combined in a Central category; and parks that are in the lowlands east of central Virginia, near bays, and on the eastern shore are grouped together as Coastal. They are described alphabetically.

In 2002 the state had 36 state parks, 34 natural area preserves, and 11 forests. All parks with trails are described below, and six of the preserves open to the public with trails are described as well. For the parks there are more than 1,400 campsites, 180 cabins, and more than 300 miles of trails. One major state forest with trails is described and four others have state parks within them. Additionally, the state's Board of Historic Resources has a protective program for 250 Virginia historic landmarks. Many of these landmarks overlap or connect with federal, state, regional, and local properties described throughout this book. One historic site owned by the state, but not described elsewhere, is Gunston Hall in Fairfax County. It is the colonial home and plantation of George Mason (1725–1792), the "Father of the Bill of Rights." The house with its splendid architectural beauty, other buildings, and 556 acres were deeded to the commonwealth by Mr. and Mrs. Louis Hertle. The facility is managed by the National Society of the Colonial 834 Dames of America. There is a nature trail, the 0.4-mile **Barn Wharf Trail**, and a walk to the Potomac River for a round-trip of up to 1.7 miles. Access is from us 1 east on va 242 (near Lorton) and 3.5 miles to Gunston Hall, left. Address: Gunston Hall, 10709 Gunston Road, Mason Neck, va 22079; phone: 703-550-9220.

Because of the diverse locations of the parklands, hikers can choose parks with trail networks at high elevations, such as Grayson Highlands, or near sea level, such as First Landing State Park and Natural Area. Among primitive and remote areas are Clinch Mountain, deep in the Appalachian range, and False Cape, at the Atlantic Ocean. Trail features and other facilities are described here, but some details about fees for campgrounds; swimming pools; boat, horse, or bicycle rentals; and picnic shelter or cabin reservations are not listed because of unpredictable changes. All fees are low or moderate, with cabin rentals being the most expensive. For cabin and campground reservation applications and fee information, call park headquarters or campgrounds for a brochure titled "Reservations and Fees Guide." Wheelchair users should request an "Accessibility List." The park system has used Ticketron or Ticketmaster for reservations, but in the future each park may be responsible for its own rentals. If in doubt, call the park office.

Here are a few introductory facts about the parks. Camping rates are nightly, and cabin rates are usually weekly and a minimum of two nights. The cabin facilities include central heating and air conditioning, microwave oven, coffee maker, linens, dinnerware and flatware, and pots and pans. Park usage fees are charged. A small fee is also charged for pets that are kept in cabins and campgrounds, and they must be on a leash or in an enclosed area at all times. Pets are not allowed at any state park lodge, or at the cabins at Chippokes Plantation State Park. Firearms or alcohol are not allowed. No hunting is allowed except at special parks (Hungry Mother, Grayson Highlands, Occoneechee, and Pocahontas). Fishing permits, according to state law, are required for individuals over age sixteen. Some parks rent canoes, paddle boats, hydrobikes and rowboats; annual boat launch passes are available for frequent visitors. In addition there are senior citizens' discounts and special discounts for annual passes for parking and swimming. No wildlife or plant life can be removed from the parks.

Lodges are at Breaks Interstate, Douthat, and Belle Isle; cabins are at Claytor Lake, Hungry Mother, Douthat, Fairy Stone, Smith Mountain, Staunton River, Twin Lakes, Belle Isle, Chippokes Plantation, First Landing, and Westmoreland. Parks with electrical and water hookups at campgrounds are Claytor Lake, Grayson Highlands, Hungry Mother, Natural Tunnel, Douthat, Bear Creek Lake, Fairy Stone, Holliday Lake, Occoneechee, Pocahontas, Smith Mountain Lake, Staunton River, Twin Lakes, Chippokes Plantation, Kiptopeke, and Westmoreland. Environmental education centers are located at Hungry Mother, Natural Tunnel, Pocahontas, Lake Anna, Leesylvania, Mason Neck, Caledon, False Cape, and First Landing. Three parks have restaurants: Breaks Interstate, Hungry Mother, and Douthat. Groceries are available at Grayson Highlands, Douthat, Leesylvania, First Landing, Kiptopeke, Westmoreland, and York.

Almost all parks have a foot trail system. Those with bridle trails are Breaks Interstate, Grayson Highlands, New River (has horse rentals), Wilderness Road, Shenandoah River (has horse rentals), Sky Meadows, Bear Creek Lake, Fairy Stone, Holliday Lake, James River, Occoneechee, Pocahontas, Staunton River, Twin Lakes, Lake Anna, Belle Isle, Chippokes Plantation, and York River.

ADDRESS AND INFORMATION: Virginia State Parks, 203 Governor St., Suite 306, Richmond, VA 23219; phone: 804-786-1712. Available are brochures, leaflets, and a booklet, *Virginia State Parks*. For Division of Planning and Recreation Resources, phone: 804-786-2556. For camping and cabin reservations, phone: 800-933-PARK; web: <www.dcr.state.va.us>.

# Mountain Division

## BREAKS INTERSTATE PARK
*Dickenson County*

In 1954 the 4,500-acre Breaks Interstate Park was created by joint action of the Kentucky and Virginia legislatures to protect controlled areas of natural beauty and to open them for recreational use. An allotment of land with legend, history, and spectacular scenery, the park also has complete facilities. Among them are an Olympic-size swimming pool; forest campsites with full services; grounds designated for picnicking, hiking, and bridle trails; cabins; a motor lodge; a restaurant; a visitor center with exhibits; and a playground. One area is for horseback riding. Other activities include fishing and nature studies. Some of the facilities and activities are open year round, but the regular schedule is from Memorial Day to Labor Day. The Russell Fork River has carved out what is often called the "Grand Canyon of the South," a 1,600-foot-deep gorge extending 5 miles, leaving the "Towers"--natural sandstone skyscrapers. All trails are marked and blazed. The forest is chiefly hardwoods, with abundant wildflowers, ferns, lichens, and mosses on the forest floor. (South of Russell Fork River, 2.5 miles of the 26.2-mile **Pine Mountain Trail** of the Jefferson National Forest passes through Breaks Interstate Park. The trail does not connect with any of the trails described below. See Clinch Ranger District, Chapter 2.)

ACCESS: From Haysi in Virginia take VA 80 north for 8 miles and turn left to entrance. From Elkhorn in Kentucky take KY 15, then VA 80 for 7 miles to entrance on right.

835–40 **Ridge Trail** (0.5 mi.), **Geological Trail** (0.4 mi.), **Grassy Overlook Trail** (0.5 mi.), **Overlook Trail** (0.7 mi.), **Towers Trail** (0.2 mi.), **Tower Tunnel Trail** (0.2 mi.)
LENGTH AND DIFFICULTY: 5.2 miles (8.3 km) combined, round-trip; easy
TRAILHEAD: any of the overlook parking areas

DESCRIPTION: All of these are blazed rim trails designed to provide scenic views of the canyon's river, rock formations, faults, and vegetation. They can be interconnected among themselves and with the following two sets of trails. Some of the trails must be backtracked. For an educational tour make a ridge loop with the **Geological Trail**, which provides information about trees, shrubs, wildflowers, rock outcrops, caves, fossils, rock faults, and rock formations.
USGS MAP: Elkhorn City

**Center Creek Trail** (0.4 mi.), **Grassy Creek Trail** (0.5 mi.), **Laurel Branch Trail**   841–46
(1.3 mi.), **Loop Trail** (0.4 mi.), **Prospectors Trail** (1.5 mi.), **River Trail** (1 mi.)
LENGTH AND DIFFICULTY: 9.1 miles (14.6 km) combined, round-trip; moderate to strenuous
TRAILHEADS: At the visitor center, or Stateline Overlook parking areas, or at Tower Tunnel parking.
DESCRIPTION: Each of the three trailheads offers connection to any of these trails. It is recommended the hiker secure a trail map from the visitor center. On descent, parts of the trails are steep; exceptions are part of the **Laurel Branch Trail** and the **Loop Trail**. The following is a challenging loop trail arrangement: Park at the Stateline Overlook, hike the **Ridge Trail** for 0.5 mile to the Notches, descend for a few yards to the **Prospectors Trail**, make a left turn on it and go another 0.8 mile. Turn right on the exceptionally steep **River Trail**, and descend for another 0.3 mile. Turn right, following the riverbank for 0.3 mile to the confluence of the Russell River and Grassy Creek. Turn right, ascend slightly, and reach the **Laurel Branch Trail** 0.4 mile farther. (The **Center Creek Trail** turns left here to the Center Creek Picnic Area.) Turn right; ascend steeply for 0.5 mile to the Notches. From here turn right on the **Geological Trail** for 0.4 mile to the Stateline Overlook for a total loop of 3.2 miles. Distance for all trails combined is 9.1 miles.
USGS MAP: Elkhorn City

**Lake Trail** (0.5 mi.), **Cold Spring Trail** (0.4 mi.)   847–48
LENGTH AND DIFFICULTY: 2 miles (3.2 km) combined, round-trip; easy
TRAILHEAD: visitor center parking area
DESCRIPTION: These trails connect and provide entry to the Laurel Lake area, which has a swimming pool, or connect via the **Laurel Branch Trail** with the other trails in the two preceding entries. The **Cold Spring Trail** may be wet and rocky.
USGS MAP: Elkhorn City

**Deer Trail** (0.4 mi.), **Beaver Trail** (0.3 mi.)   849–50
LENGTH AND DIFFICULTY: 1.1 miles (2.7 km) combined, round-trip; easy
TRAILHEAD: parking area near cottages

DESCRIPTION: Begin on the **Deer Trail** at the grassy shoulder of the parking lot. Descend into the forest of hardwoods, filberts, and running cedar. Join the **Beaver Trail** at the lake for a circuit and backtrack.

USGS MAP: Elkhorn City

ADDRESS AND INFORMATION: Breaks Interstate Park, Breaks, VA 24607; phone: 540-865-4413.

## CLAYTOR LAKE STATE PARK
*Pulaski County*

Claytor Lake State Park, established in 1948, has 472 acres, of which 350 acres are wooded. The park is located on a portion of the 4,500-acre Claytor Lake. Activities and facilities include boating, waterskiing, and fishing from a modern marina; swimming at a sand beach with bathhouse; and camping with full services, or in vacation cabins. There is a handicapped-accessible fishing pier and 0.3-mile walkway at picnic area #1. Other activities include nature study, horseback riding, picnicking, and hiking.

ACCESS: From exit 101 on I-81 between the towns of Radford and Dublin, take SR 660 southeast for 2 miles to the park entrance.

851–52 **Claytor Lake Trail, Bent Tree Trail**

LENGTH AND DIFFICULTY: 1.6 miles and 0.7 mile (3.7 km); easy

TRAILHEADS: marina parking area, campgrounds C and D and cabin area

DESCRIPTION: The blue-blazed **Claytor Lake Trail** begins at the woods line across the road from the marina parking lot. Look for the trailhead display. The trail passes through a mixed hardwood and pine forest and offers several views of Claytor Lake. Return to the starting point through a portion of the campground. White-blazed **Bent Tree Trail** connects and circles inside **Claytor Lake Trail**. Vegetation includes pine, sycamore, yellow poplar, locust, oak, and hickory. Pets must be kept on a leash.

USGS MAP: Dublin

853 **Shady Ridge Trail**

LENGTH AND DIFFICULTY: 0.6 mile (0.9 km); easy

TRAILHEAD: picnic area parking lot

DESCRIPTION: This is a self-guiding, interpretive trail with eight posts keyed to the brochure found in a rack at the beginning of the trail. Ascend steeply at first; after forking for a loop at the ridge crest, the wide trail is easy. You will find good exposure to the history of the area, ecology, flora and fauna, and lichens and mosses. Among the birds is the eastern phoebe.

USGS MAP: Dublin

ADDRESS AND INFORMATION: Claytor Lake State Park, 4400 State Park Rd., Dublin,

VA 24084; phone: 540-643-2500; fax: 540-643-2502. Available are brochures of the park and of the **Shady Ridge Trail**.

## DOUTHAT STATE PARK
*Bath and Alleghany Counties*

Deep in the Allegheny Mountains, Douthat State Park has 4,493 acres of scenic high ridges, more miles of hiking trails than any of the state's other parks, and a 50-acre lake stocked with trout. Its facilities include a visitor center with exhibits, a restaurant, a camp store, vacation cabins, and a swimming beach with bath-house. Activities include boating, fishing, picnicking, camping, nature study, and hiking. Trails are color coded and generally in good condition. A hiking map from the park office is recommended for long hikes. The campgrounds are open from the Monday nearest April 1 to the Monday nearest December 1.

There are twenty-four trails, ranging in length from 0.3 mile to 4.5 miles, in the park system. Most of these are clustered near Douthat Lake, where they connect for circuits. For example, use 1 mile of the **YCC Trail** (which parallels the highway and lake) and a spur across the road to include 1.2 miles of the **Wilson Creek Trail** for a loop of 2.4 miles to the park office and back. Or make a circuit from camp-ground A or B with the **Backway Hollow Trail** to join the **Huffs Trail** at 0.4 mile or 0.7 mile. Then swing onto the mountainside with the **Laurel View Trail** to include a slice of the **Blue Suck Trail** for a loop of 4.5 miles or 5.2 miles, depending on which campground was the starting point. This could be extended by using the **Middle Hollow Trail** and the **Pine Tree Trail**. A short walk on the **Heron Run Trail** for about 0.7 mile is popular for views of the western side of the lake. Another short trail, the 0.3-mile **Buck Lick Interpretive Trail**, is on the eastern side of the lake near the restaurant. It has markers about geology, forest succession, and flora and fauna. Whether choosing a single trail or a combination, hikers will find the park's network to be scenic and worthwhile. Described below are two circuit hikes that extend to the most remote and challenging areas of the park. For hikers who seek backpacking excursions into the adjoining GWNF from these circuits, see Warm Springs Ranger District in Chapter 1.

ACCESS: From Clifton Forge at the junction of I-64/US 60 and SR 629, go north 5.5 miles on SR 629 to the park office.

854

855

856–59

Stony Run Trail (4.5 mi.), **Tuscarora Overlook Trail** (0.9 mi.), **Middle Mountain Trail** (2 mi.), **Salt Stump Trail** (2.5 mi.), **Backway Hollow Trail** (0.9 mi.), **Huffs Trail** (1.2 mi.), **Blue Suck Trail** (3 mi.)

168, 174, 162, 173, 861–62, 169

LENGTH AND DIFFICULTY: 15 miles (24 km) combined, round-trip; moderate to strenuous
FEATURES: wildlife, scenic views, geological formations

TRAILHEAD: park office

DESCRIPTION: These trails are on the western side of Wilson Creek, forming a connecting system for a long loop that ascends to Middle Mountain Ridge (and a network of trails in the GWNF) and descends in the northern end of the park, where connecting trails south provide a return to the campgrounds and park office.

863–64

Begin from the park office, hiking down the road 0.5 mile to the trailhead for orange-blazed **Stony Run Trail** on the right. (Or take the **Beards Gap (Hollow) Trail**, which is closer to the park office.) Ascend; at 1.4 miles pass a junction with the **Locust Gap Trail** on the right. Continue ahead for another 1.1 miles to Stony Run Falls on the left. For the next 2 miles ascend on switchbacks to a junction with the **Middle Mountain Trail** and the yellow-blazed **Tuscarora Overlook Trail** at 4.5 miles. Take the right fork on the **Tuscarora Overlook Trail** to a scenic view at 5 miles. At 5.9 miles make a sharp left turn, and after a few yards make a sharp turn right to be on the white-blazed **Middle Mountain Trail**. (A right turn at the 5.9-mi. junction, on the **Blue Suck Trail**, leads down the mountain for 3 mi. to the park office.)

Follow the ridge trail to the edge of the park boundary at 7.7 miles to begin the **Salt Stump Trail**. Descend, passing the **Pine Tree Trail** on the right at 8.7 miles, and reach the **Backway Hollow Trail** on the right at 10.3 miles. (A second vehicle could be arranged near here at the campground.) Follow the **Backway Hollow Trail** for 0.7 mile to the junction on the right with the **Huffs Trail**. Take the **Huffs Trail**, passing the **Laurel View Trail** on the right and then the **Middle Hollow Trail** intersection, and reach the **Blue Suck Trail** at 12.2

865

miles. Turn left on the **Blue Suck Trail**, pass the **Tobacco House Ridge Trail** on the right and then the group camping area, and return to the park office at 13.1 miles. Forest cover along the trails is chiefly hemlock, oak, Virginia pine, white pine, poplar, maple, beech, and birch. Some of the understory is redbud, dogwood, sassafras, mountain laurel, rhododendron, buckberry, and sourwood. Wildflowers and berries are plentiful.

USGS MAP: Healing Spring


866–69    **Brushy Hollow Trail** (3.5 mi.), **Mountain Top Trail** (2.3 mi.), **Ross Camp Hollow Trail** (0.8 mi.), **Wilson Creek Trail** (1.4 mi.)

LENGTH AND DIFFICULTY: 8 miles (12.8 km) combined, round-trip; easy to strenuous

FEATURES: stream, scenic views, wildlife, wildflowers

TRAILHEAD: park office area

DESCRIPTION: These trail combinations are on the eastern side of Wilson Creek. Use a vehicle to the trailhead for the **Brushy Hollow Trail** near Wilson Creek. Inquire of trail adviser at the park office for the best area in which to park, as space is limited. Hikers must ford the creek (actually a river; if the water is high, a better route would be to take the **Beards Gap Trail** from the park office).

Begin the trail across Wilson Creek, and after 1 mile begin a long series of switchbacks northeast and north extending to a junction with the **Beards Gap Trail** on the left at 3.2 miles. (The **Beards Gap Trail** descends steeply for 1.1 mi. to the visitor center.) Continue ahead, passing excellent overlooks west into the Wilson Creek valley. At 3.5 miles pass a junction on the left with the **Buck Hollow Trail**, which has an outstanding overlook 0.5 mile west on its 1-mile descent to the **Wilson Creek Trail**. Continue ahead a few yards to a junction with the **Mountain Side Trail** on the left and the **Mountain Top Trail** on the right. (The **Mountain Side Trail** goes 1.4 mi. north on the western side of the 870 slope to rejoin the **Mountain Top Trail**.) Turn right on the **Mountain Top Trail**, ascending switchbacks, and pass scenic views at 5.2 miles. Turn sharply left at park boundary and from the junction of the **Beards Mountain Trail** in the GWNF. Descend and pass a junction with the **Mountain Side Trail** on the left at 5.8 miles. At 6.6 miles, near the last rental cabin, veer right and take either the **Guest Lodge Trail** or the **Ross Camp Hollow Trail** to the **Wilson Creek Trail**. 871 Continue on the **Wilson Creek Trail**, paralleling the park road (SR 629) and passing a picnic area and, on the right at 7.5 miles, a junction with the **Buck Lick Interpretive Trail**. Immediately beyond the junction is the **Buck Hollow** 872 **Trail** on the left, mentioned previously. Continue ahead on the **Wilson Creek Trail** to the park office at 8 miles.

USGS MAP: Healing Spring

ADDRESS AND INFORMATION: Douthat State Park, Rt. 1, Box 212, Millboro, VA 24460; phone: 540-862-8100; fax: 540-862-8104.


## GOSHEN PASS NATURAL AREA
*Rockbridge County*

At one of Virginia's most scenic spots for white water, the turbulent Maury River 873–74 twists and cuts its way through Goshen Pass in North Mountain. Highway 39 turns with the river, providing exciting views. Picnicking is allowed, but parking space is along the highway, and limited. At the **Laurel Run Trail** site where Laurel Run joins the Maury River, for example, vehicles should be parked so as not to block the trail or the road. The **Laurel Run Trail** is 4 miles round-trip and easy to follow. (See Goshen Wildlife Management Area, Chapter 10.) At the western end of the gorge a 150-foot suspension bridge for pedestrians crosses the Maury River on **Goshen Pass Trail** so hikers can explore the Round Mountain area. With the natural area and the WMA the state has a total of 33,000 acres in the Little North Mountain range. Adjoining national forest land adds more recreational opportunities.

The Maury River was named after the famous oceanographer Matthew Fontaine Maury, the first man to chart the seas of the world. He retired in Lexington, and upon his death his body was carried through Goshen Pass before burial, as he had requested, by VMI cadets.

ACCESS: From the junction of VA 39 and VA 252 (9 mi. north of Lexington), go west on VA 39 for 5.5 miles to Goshen Pass.

ADDRESS AND INFORMATION: Virginia State Parks, 203 Governor St., Suite 306, Richmond, VA 23219; phone: 804-786-1712.

## GRAYSON HIGHLANDS STATE PARK
*Grayson County*

Virginia's highest state park (5,090 ft.) is a 4,935-acre preserve amid rugged peaks of igneous rock, alpine meadows, waterfalls, and spruce-fir forests. An area of mountain grandeur, it borders the crest zone of Mount Rogers, whose mile-high peak is the center of attraction for both the state park and the adjacent Mount Rogers National Recreation Area (see Chapter 2). Solitude is easy to find in this park. Facilities include campgrounds with electrical and water hookups, some facilities for the disabled, primitive campground, groceries, rest rooms and hot showers, horse trails, hiking trails, and a visitor center with exhibits. Activities include mountain biking, freshwater fishing, hiking, hunting, horseback riding, picnicking, and nature study.

875–77    There are three loop trails at separate locations in the park. The **Rock House Ridge Trail** (1.8 mi.) is an easy route from the picnic area to an example of a pioneer homestead and cemetery. The trail follows a low saddle around a knoll and receives its name from a huge leaning shelter-type rock formation. The **Cabin Creek Trail** can be accessed from Massie Gap near the entrance to the equestrian campground. Moderate in difficulty, it descends 0.6 mile to Cabin Creek, named for pioneers who settled in the hollow. Near the base are big-toothed aspens, whose leaves are known for quivering in the breeze. At 1 mile is a 25-foot waterfall. The trail is completed on an old railroad grade after 1.9 miles. Another moderate loop is accessed from the parking area at the visitor center at the end of the highest road. The **Listening Rock Trail** descends from the parking area to Buzzard Rock and Listening Rock for views of the valley below. To complete the 1.8-mile route, return to the road and make a right to the parking area. At the parking area entrance, right, is a 200-foot trail to Wildcat Overlook (4,935 ft.), a jumble of boulders with a magnificent view of North Carolina and Tennessee. Described below is a combination of trails, including a scenic section of the **AT**, for a remarkable diversity of topography.

ACCESS: On US 58 7.7 miles west from Volney and 25 miles east from Damascus to park entrance on VA 362

**Wilson Creek Trail** (1.8 mi.), **AT** (4.6 mi.), **Rhododendron Trail** (0.5 mi.), **Big**    878, 489,
**Pinnacle Trail** (0.4 mi.), **Twin Pinnacles Trail** (1.6 mi.), **Stampers Branch Trail**    879–82
(1.7 mi.)

LENGTH AND DIFFICULTY: 10.6 miles (17 km) combined, round-trip; easy to
strenuous

FEATURES: waterfall, grazing fields, scenic views, rock formations, wildlife,
wildflowers

TRAILHEADS: campground or Massie Gap parking area

DESCRIPTION: This connecting-trail arrangement is recommended for a hike of a
full day; take a day pack with lunch, a camera, and rain gear. Park regulations
require all hikers to be off the trails at sundown.

From the campground follow the **Wilson Creek Trail** sign, descending to
Wilson Creek in a forest of red maple, beech, and yellow and black birch, with
an understory of striped maple and ferns at 0.6 mile. Follow upstream with
cascades on right, and reach a 25-foot waterfall at 1 mile. Ash and rhododendron decorate the area. At road junction turn sharply right, follow old logging
road, and cross Quebec Branch at 1.3 miles. Pass through open meadow, reaching the **AT** near Wilson Creek at 1.7 miles. Turn left, cross stile, and follow
white-blazed **AT** through thick grass spotted with flame azalea, mountain laurel, and large sweet blueberry bushes. Cross Quebec Branch again at 2.7 miles
and ascend to rocky ridge crest at 3.4 miles. At 3.9 miles is a sign on the left to
the Massie Gap parking area. Continue ahead, following an old open cattle
road; cattle and ponies may be grazing nearby.

Cross stile at 4.4 miles, leaving Grayson Highlands State Park. Follow the **AT**,
veering left at fork with blue-blazed **Rhododendron Trail** at 4.5 miles. After 1.1
miles more, come to a junction with the **Rhododendron Trail** again on a huge
rocky peak of Wilburn Ridge. (From here it is 2 mi. on the **AT** to the summit of
Mount Rogers [5,729 ft.], Virginia's highest mountain. The summit has no view
and is covered with the only spruce-fir forest in the state. Fog often surrounds
its green and fragrant beauty.) Follow the blue-blazed trail right to an enormous array of boulders with a 360° view at 5.9 miles. Vegetation, stunted by
strong winds, is rhododendron, mountain ash, azalea, and conifer. Descend to a
junction with the **AT** at 6.8 miles, and follow the **Rhododendron Trail** to the
Massie Gap sign at 7.2 miles. Continue the descent to the Massie Gap parking
area at 7.7 miles.

Cross the parking area and begin the steep climb—gaining 400 feet in elevation—on the **Big Pinnacle Trail** to the summit of Big Pinnacle (5,068 ft.) at 8.1
miles. Views are spectacular, the sights including Mount Rogers and White Top
Mountain (Virginia's second highest peak) and the valleys of Virginia, North
Carolina, and Tennessee. Wildflowers, ferns, and lichens are abundant. From
here continue through dense grass, scattered spruce, and hawthorn bushes on

the **Twin Pinnacles Trail** to Little Pinnacle (5,089 ft.) for more scenic views at 8.6 miles. Descend to a junction with the **Stampers Branch Trail** at 8.9 miles and turn left, but not before a visit to the visitor center nearby. Continue descent on the **Stampers Branch Trail**, crossing main road, Stampers Branch, and Wilburn Branch, and reaching a log cabin near the campground for a complete loop of 10.6 miles.

USGS MAPS: Whitetop Mountain, Troutdale, Park, Grassy Creek

ADDRESS AND INFORMATION: Grayson Highlands State Park, 829 Grayson Highlands Lane, Mouth of Wilson, VA 24363; phone: 276-579-7092; fax: 276-579-2374. Available for free are park brochure of information with map and leaflets; there is a fee for detailed map, "Mount Rogers High Country and Wildernesses."

## HUNGRY MOTHER STATE PARK
*Smyth County*

Excellent mountain scenery, a picturesque lake, and well-planned trails make the 2,180-acre Hungry Mother State Park a popular recreation area. More than 12 miles of trails make hiking very pleasurable. The paths were largely established by the CCC in the 1930s. Most of the park is a designated natural area. Facilities include campgrounds, vacation cabins, a visitor center, and a restaurant. Hiking, horseback riding, picnicking, swimming, paddleboating, fishing, and nature study are popular activities. There is a 0.7-mile handicapped-accessible trail from parking lot #6 to the beach. The park's name honors Molly Marley, who, according to legend, escaped with her child from Indian capture. Molly collapsed, but the child wandered downstream to a pioneer home, where the child said the mother was hungry. The search party found Molly had died.

883–84    In addition to the longer combination of trails described below, there is a double loop with the **Raider's Run Trail** (1.5 mi.) and scenic **Old Shawnee Trail** (1 mi.). Access is from the parking area between the information center and the store.

ACCESS: Take I-81 at VA 16 into Marion. Follow the signs and proceed 3 miles north of Marion on VA 16 to the park entrance.

885–90    **Molly's Pioneer Trail** (0.6 mi.), **Molly's Knob Trail** (1.6 mi.), **CCC Trail** (1 mi.), **Lake Trail** (3.1 mi.), **Middle Ridge Trail** (1.1 mi.), **Ridge Trail** (0.7 mi.)

LENGTH AND DIFFICULTY: 10.5 miles (16 km) combined, round-trip; easy to moderate

FEATURES: scenic views, historic site, wildlife, wildflowers

TRAILHEAD: parking area near visitor information beyond the rental cabins

DESCRIPTION: All these trails connect, but backtracking is necessary to connect one to another in order to form loops. **Molly's Pioneer Trail** is a short loop of 0.6 mile, red blazed and interpretive in nature, to educate about the wild animals, trees, shrubs, and flowers. Halfway around this trail **Molly's Knob Trail** (1.6 mi.) begins. Follow **Molly's Knob Trail** to the summit (3,270 ft.) for views of Marion, Mount Rogers, and White Top Mountain to the southwest. Backtrack, or descend to a junction with the **CCC Trail**, orange blazed, for 1.1 miles to Campground D. This route requires vehicle shuttle. Another route from **Molly's Knob Trail** can be made by taking the **CCC Trail** to a junction with the **Lake Trail** (3.1 mi.) and looping back to the visitor center. Or, to make yet another loop, take the **Middle Ridge Trail** (1.1 mi.) from **Molly's Knob Trail** to the **Lake Trail**. A shorter route from Molly's Knob can be taken by picking up the **Ridge Trail** (0.7 mi.), on the left 0.8 mile from the knob, and then connecting with the **Lake Trail**. Whatever the loop arrangements, a trail map from the visitor center will assist in planning and can prevent extra climbing or unexpected, long connections. Signs are posted at the intersections. Wildlife in the area includes deer, raccoon, fox, squirrel, grouse, and wild turkey. Flora includes pines—Virginia, pitch, shortleaf, and white—and the usual southern Appalachian hardwoods, with banks of wintergreen and trailing arbutus, wildflowers, ferns, and Indian pipe amid the forest-floor duff.

USGS MAPS: Marion, Chatham Hill

ADDRESS AND INFORMATION: Hungry Mother State Park, 2854 Park Blvd., Marion, VA 24354; phone: 276-781-7400; fax: 276-781-7402.

## NATURAL TUNNEL STATE PARK
*Scott County*

This 850-acre park has a natural tunnel that William Jennings Bryan declared the eighth (natural) wonder of the world. Probably originating during the early Pleistocene epoch of at least 1 million years ago, the enormous cave was the result of groundwater carrying carbonic acid that dissolved the section of limestone and dolomitic bedrock in Hunter Valley. Since then Stock Creek has flowed through to join the Clinch River. Paralleling the creek, with room to share in the tunnel, is the Norfolk-Southern Railroad line, first constructed in 1882 by Southern, Ohio, and Atlantic Railroad companies. It is reported that Daniel Boone, in 1769, was the first white man to explore this immense karst formation. The park has a visitor center with railroad artifacts, a chairlift, the 0.3-mile **Tunnel Trail** to the gorge and tunnel, a modern swimming complex, a picnic area, a campground with hot showers, rim trails, the 0.2-mile **Spring Hollow Trail**, and the Cove Ridge Outdoor Education Center.

ACCESS: On US 23 at Clinchport go north for 2 miles, turn right on SR 871, and go 0.6 mile to the park entrance.

**Lover's Leap Trail** (0.4 mi.), **Tunnel Hill Trail** (0.7 mi.), **Center Trail** (0.2 mi.), **Gorge Ridge Trail** (0.3 mi.), **Purchase Ridge Trail** (1.1 mi.)

LENGTH AND DIFFICULTY: 2.8 miles (4.5 km) combined, round-trip; moderate

FEATURES: scenic views, wildflowers, lichens, geological formations

TRAILHEAD: visitor center

DESCRIPTION: Begin the **Lover's Leap Trail** at the visitor center. Honor all signs about extreme danger. (After 0.2 mi. the **Tunnel Hill Trail** begins left for 0.7 mi. to the swimming pool and picnic parking area.) At 0.4 mile is Lover's Leap overlook. Here are views of the gigantic chasm with a rim of about 3,000 feet and a depth of 400 feet. (After the overlook, the **Center Trail** is on the left and connects with the **Tunnel Hill Trail**.) Continue on the **Gorge Ridge Trail**, which goes to the campground, but after 0.2 mile the **Purchase Ridge Trail** goes right. It follows the chasm rim 1.1 miles through hardwoods of oak, dogwood, and ash, with black cohosh and may apples on the forest floor, to a knoll. Backtrack to the visitor center for a total of 2.8 miles.

On the banks of the steep **Tunnel Hill Trail** are ash, walnut, poplar, columbine, and ladies' tresses. From the base chairlift there is a 500-foot boardwalk upstream to an observation deck at the tunnel's mouth. Entrance into the tunnel is prohibited. Backtrack, or take the chairlift to the visitor center.

USGS MAP: Clinchport

ADDRESS AND INFORMATION: Natural Tunnel State Park, Rt. 3, Box 250, Duffield, VA 24244; phone: 276-940-2674; fax: 276-940-2029. Available are park brochure and map.

## SHOT TOWER AND NEW RIVER TRAIL STATE PARK
*Carroll, Grayson, Pulaski, and Wythe Counties*

This is Virginia's longest state park. It is unique in mineralogy, topography, and human history. Except for the Shot Tower tract and former railroad stations, the park's width averages 80 feet for its 57.3 miles. In December 1986 Norfolk Southern Corporation donated the railroad corridor to the Division of State Parks. As a result the way opened for developing a rails-to-trails avenue, the **New River Trail**, from termini in the south at Galax and Fries to a northern terminus in Pulaski. It parallels 39 miles of the spectacular New River, which geologists claim to be one of the oldest rivers (350 million years) in the world. It has carved its riverbed from a much higher plateau during the millenia and has exposed rich deposits of iron ore, lead, zinc, and limestone.

The New River Valley's archaeological history reveals that Native Americans were here about 10,000 B.C., more as transients than long-term settlers. Shawnee and Cherokee had settlements in the area at the time European explorers and pioneers came after the mid-eighteenth century. European family names frequently became the names of the villages, industries for the natural resources,

*New River Trail,*
*New River Trail State Park*

streams, and mountains. Some industries have lasted 200 years, indicating how the railroad was part of their marketing success. As each new town developed upriver, a new railroad branch was extended from the main line. Now that most of the industries have closed and the rails and ties have been removed, this historic railroad continues to serve the public in a way never imagined by the immigrant laborers. They would be less surprised about use of the river. Never navigable for industrial use, the river today is popular for the white-water sports of canoeing, kayaking, and rafting. Concentrated rapids are near Fries, the Shot Tower, and Bertha, and class 3–4 rapids are at Foster Falls, downriver from the Shot Tower.

The park's most southern trailhead is in the town of Galax, north of US 58 at Chestnut Creek. After 12 miles the trail meets a 5.5-mile branch from the other southern trailhead in the town of Fries by the New River. After joining, the trail follows the railroad bed north to the eastern edge of Pulaski. Because the northern trailhead is at mile marker #2, the actual combined hiking distance is 55.2 miles. Along the route are 29 trestles, 3 bridges, 2 tunnels, 2 dams, a lake, and stretches of white water. In addition to the 3 trailheads, there are 10 major access points for parking. They are Cliffview, Gambetta, Chestnut Yard, Byllesby, Ivanhoe, Austinville, Shot Tower, Foster Falls, Allisonia/Hiwassee, and Draper. Since some of the trestles have been renovated and a smooth passageway has been constructed on all trestles, the trail accommodates horseback riding, hiking, bicycling, cross-country skiing, jogging, and parents with baby carriages. Electric wheelchairs are allowed, and the park allows, without charge, the use of its three-wheel electric vehicle; its range is 25 miles. (Call for more information.)

The Shot Tower section of the park was formerly Shot Tower Historical State Park, opened to the public in 1968 after extensive renovation. The property was a gift to the commonwealth by the Lead Mines Ruritan Club in 1964. Its early history began in 1807 when Thomas Jackson, a joint owner of a lead mining company in Austinville, constructed a 75-foot-high stone tower with a 75-foot-deep shaft in the earth where an access was from the bank side of the New River. The tower was constructed for the purpose of making lead bullets. At the tower

896 are picnic tables, rest rooms, the park headquarters, and 0.7-mile **Shot Tower Historical Trail** on the northern side of the tower. A fee is charged for climbing the tower, and tours may be arranged with the park rangers.

ACCESS TO PARK HEADQUARTERS: At exit 24, I-77, turn east at Poplar Camp on VA 69 to US 52. Turn left and drive 1.5 miles to park entrance, left.

ACCESS TO GALAX TRAILHEAD: From I-77, exit 14, on US 58 west, drive 10.5 miles to parking area right (across the bridge) at junction of East Stuart Street and Railroad Drive.

ACCESS TO FRIES TRAILHEAD: From I-77, exit 14, on US 58 west, drive 9.5 miles, turn right on Hanes Road, and follow signs to Cliffview and SR 721. From Cliffview follow SR 721 (and old SR 606) 5.8 miles to Fries. From I-81, exit 80, at Fort Chiswell, turn south on US 52. After 1.3 miles, turn right on VA 94. (If coming from the Shot Tower, cross the New River bridge on US 52 north and take the first left [SR 619] to Porters Crossroads. Turn left on VA 94.)

ACCESS TO PULASKI TRAILHEAD: From I-81, exit 94, north on VA 99, drive 2 miles to Xaloy Drive, right.

897 **New River Trail**

LENGTH AND DIFFICULTY: 55.2 miles (88.3 km); easy to moderate

FEATURES: scenic views, geological formations, historic site, wildlife, wildflowers, trestles, riverside, multiple uses

TRAILHEADS: See directions above.

INTRODUCTION: The trail is described from Galax to Pulaski in mile points, but the 5.5 miles from Fries to Fries Junction are included as linear distance. For the first 45.5 miles the route is downriver, but after crossing Claytor Lake the trail soon begins an ascent to Pulaski. Hikers will notice the original mile markers begin from Pulaski. Where intact, the markers can serve for distance counting for hikers going southwest. Unless backtracking, two cars will be needed. If planning a through-hike, advance arrangements will be necessary for camping. A few private campgrounds exist near the trail. Information about them can be obtained from the park office. Because there are so many historic sites to visit and scenic areas to observe, through-hikers may wish to allow 3–4 days. Topographical maps may help to enhance the trail's intrigue.

The park has a few regulations designed to benefit all trail users. No motor vehicles are allowed, and no parking is permitted in front of gates. There is to be no trespassing on private property, no littering, no firearms, and no alcohol. Pets must be leashed. All group excursions must have a permit. Equestrians and bicyclists must follow the courtesy and safety rules regarding passing, speed, and dismounting.

Nearby convenience stores are located in Galax, Fries, Ivanhoe, Austinville, and Draper. Water fountains are at Cliffside and Shot Tower, and rest rooms are at Cliffside, Fries, near Byllesby Dam, Shot Tower, Foster Falls, and Draper. Accommodations for the physically impaired are at Ivanhoe and Cliffside.

DESCRIPTION: From the parking lot and trail information sign in Galax, follow the trail downstream, cross two bridges, and at 0.7 mile notice original railroad mile marker 51. Reach Cliffview at 2.3 miles. Here is a parking area, a substation office for a ranger, a picnic area, rest rooms, and across SR 721 the Cliffview Trading Post. It provides camping (no hookups), bicycle rentals, and trail supplies. To the northwest is "Cliffside," a mansion built in 1902 by state senator Thomas Felts. (For highway access here from US 58, see access directions above to Fries. For access to the next parking area, Chestnut Yard, follow SR 721 north to junction with SR 607, right, and follow it to Chestnut Creek. To reach the Gambetta parking area go 1 mi. on SR 607 from the SR 721 junction and turn left on SR 793.)

Continue from Cliffside into a forest with white pine, hardwoods, wild rose, and filberts. At 5.4 miles is Chestnut Creek waterfalls with a large pool. Ahead are banks of rhododendron. After a gate there is a bike rack and horse tie-up at the Chestnut Yard parking area at 6.4 miles. Ahead at 6.7 miles is a clearing where the Chestnut Yard railroad turntable was used to switch engine direction. There are pastures at 6.9 miles and a 190-foot trestle at 8.3 miles. Reach Gambetta parking area, left, at SR 793, at 9.5 miles. At 10.5 miles is an oxbow turn between Toby Knob (west) and Bald Rock (east) in an isolated area. Chestnut Tunnel, 193 feet long, is at 11.3 miles. The trail crosses its longest bridge, 1,089 feet, over the New River at Fries Junction, where at 12 miles it joins the Fries trail section. (From the Fries trailhead there is a Norfolk & Western Railroad caboose that serves as a town information center, with rest rooms, water, and a telephone.) Hiking downstream, cross trestles at 0.6 mile, 1.5 miles, 2 miles, 2.5 miles, 3.7 miles, and 4.8 miles. Wood ducks and Canada geese may be near the river islands, and from 2.6 miles to 4.7 miles are continuous river rapids on the New River.

After Fries Junction the trail crosses a trestle at Brush Creek, which flows from Mount Rogers National Recreation Area of the JNF. At 13.2 miles is the site of an old health spa, now a rest stop with a picnic table and rest room. Arrive at Byllesby Dam and SR 602 at 14.5 miles. The access road ascends 3.7 miles to VA 94, where it goes right to Ivanhoe and left to Fries. At 17.1 miles is Buck Dam, which, as with Byllesby, was constructed in the early years of the century for electrical energy. Between the dams are rapids. Waterfowl and songbirds are frequently seen here. Cross Big Branch trestle and arrive at the parking lot in Ivanhoe at 19 miles. Here is a store, a telephone, and water. (Access from VA 94 is on SR 639 in the town.) At 20.2 miles is the remains of an enormous rock crusher, a 1901 model used for early industries in Ivanhoe. After the quarry area the trail leaves the riverside, turns left, and cuts more directly to cross the river on a 670-foot-long bridge. Reach the historic Austinville Lead Mines at 22.8 miles. Although closed in 1981, it served the area's industrial life for nearly 200 years. Cross SR 636 in the community of Austinville at 23 miles. (Access here is right on SR 636, which becomes VA 69 and goes 4.5 mi. east to I-77, exit 24.) The famous Austin family homestead is at 24.1 miles, the birthplace of Stephen Austin, founder of Texas, and son of Moses Austin, who owned the local lead mines. For the next 2 miles are a few old abandoned buildings on the right and a 135-foot-long tunnel. Soon the gentle sounds of the river rapids are replaced by the rumble of I-77 traffic high on the New River Bridge. After passing under the bridge, there is a side trail to the Shot Tower (described above) at 26.2 miles. Picnic tables and a rest room are near the tower.

Continuing on the trail, cross a high bridge over US 52, Shorts Creek, and an access road to a parking area near the river. This area has scenic views of the two bridges over the New River and the surrounding area. The trail is near the river at 27.1 miles, and high rock formations are on the right. There is a picnic area and rest room at 27.3 miles. Arrive at the entrance to Foster Falls Recreation Area at 27.6 miles. Here is Millrace Campground (primitive tent sites only), canoe launch and portage, picnic area, livery stables, rest rooms, children's playground, sports field, outdoor performance stage, historic railroad station and museum, and administrative offices for the New River Trail State Park. (Before entering the area's gate, you will see the historic Foster Falls Hotel, built in 1888, which for twenty-five years served as a hotel, commissary, post office, and boardinghouse in a village of 100 people. The hotel later served as a boarding school.)

Access to Foster Falls from US 52 (near the south side of Jackson Bridge) is east on SR 608 for 1.8 miles to the entrance, left. (Ahead on SR 608 is 5 mi. to Barren Springs Station at VA 100, where north are two accesses to the trail.) From near the railroad station continue on the trail northeast to pass Baker Island and rapids in the New River at 28.4 miles. The scenery has hardwoods, high rock formations, and ribbons of wildflowers such as yellow flax, asters, and jewelweed. Wildlife includes deer, raccoon, wild turkey, opossum, squirrel, and multiple species of songbirds. Pass an old house on the right near a natural spring at 31.3 miles. Between here and the river are swamp poplar (*Populus heterophylla*) and boxelder. There is a cave and rock wall at 31.8 miles. Arrive at a gate and the north end of FR 622 (Lone Ash Rd.) at 32.4 miles. (The public road ascends and then descends for 1.3 mi. to VA 100, 0.5 mi. north of the Barren Springs crossroads and country store.)

After 2 more miles on the trail and around a long curve, access Depot Road right, a narrow passage that goes 0.4 mile to Lone Ash Road and VA 100. Pass under the VA 100 bridge where it crosses the New River at 34.7 miles. After a chain gate follow a sweeping curve among hardwoods with an understory of redbuds. On the banks and among the rocks are large patches of maidenhair fern. At 36.5 miles is a shelter with seats, near a crossing from private property to a meadow by the river. For the next mile the river has sections of rapids and pools favored by ducks and geese. Cross scenic Big Reed Creek on a 651-foot trestle at 38.5 miles. (Here is milepoint 13.2, one of many official markers from northeast to southwest with measurements from the 2.0 milepost marker in Pulaski.) Pass an old cable crossing of the New River at 38.7 miles and by a chain gate to arrive at a crossing of SR 693 in Allisonia at 39.3 miles. To the right is a parking area, rest room, and sheltered picnic table provided without charge by Pulaski County and local citizens. Inquire at a parking area store about lodging in the Allisonia community. (For a road return to VA 100, take SR 693 south 1 mi., turn right on Boone Furnace Rd. on SR 607 for 4.1 mi. to Barren Springs at VA 100.) Historic Allisonia has a number of buildings with turn-of-the-last-century architecture; the train depot is also preserved. Continue northeast, pass a parking area for boat launching in the New River, and at 41.3 miles cross SR 693 again.

Cross the 970-foot-long bridge, which offers great views of the river/lake, and enter a forested canopy of ash, locust, and maple. At 42.6 miles (1 mi. from the bridge) is a side trail, left, to Horseshoe Campground and General Store. The trail ascends slightly through groves of redbud and offers splendid views of the lake area. Cross 420-foot-long Delton Trestle at 42.7 miles, where nearby is a foundation for a former railroad engine water tank. Cross two other long trestles and leave the forest and enter farmland. At 45.6 miles is Draper parking area. Here are picnic tables, a rest room, a telephone, a signboard, and Bryson Store across the road. (For egress to I-81, go northwest by a few historic buildings on SR 658 to VA 76, and turn left for 1 mi. to exit 24. If returning to Allisonia, turn right on VA 76 [Possum Hollow Rd.] to SR 672 [Lowmans Ferry Rd.], turn right, and cross Claytor Lake, reach a junction with SR 693 [Julia Simpkins Rd.], turn right, and go to Hiwassee and Allisonia, a distance of 12.6 mi.)

The scenery now changes to rolling farm hills, cattle, and patches of yellow stalk. To the northwest is cone-shaped Draper Mountain. At 48 miles the trail crosses VA 76 on a trestle. The hum of I-81 traffic is heard. Pass under I-81 at 48.1 miles. As if a sign for the trail to end, there is a lone original railroad crossing signal, right, at 49.3 miles. Cross a 476-foot-long trestle over Peak Creek, and arrive at Dora Junction, the northern trailhead parking area at 49.7 miles. This whistle stop is named for an iron furnace and Pulaski Iron Company. Ahead it is 2 miles on the closed railroad grade to the Pulaski depot. Access here is on Xaloy Way, off VA 99, and 2 miles south to I-81, exit 94. If returning to Draper, drive under I-81 to VA 76 (Possum Hollow Rd.) and turn right.

USGS MAPS: Galax, Austinville, Max Meadows, Fosters Falls, Hiwassee, Duplin, Pulaski

ADDRESSES AND INFORMATION: Shot Tower and New River Trail State Park, 176 Orphanage Dr., Foster Falls, VA 24360; phone: 276-699-6778; fax: 276-699-1423 (Cliffview substation: 276-236-8889); Cliffview Trading Post, 442 Cliffview Rd., Galax, VA 24333; phone: 276-238-1530. Available are brochures, flyers, and map of the trail and shot tower.

## SHENANDOAH RIVER STATE PARK
*Warren County*

One of the state's newest parks (1,604 acres) opened in 1999 and is still in the process of development. In 2003 it had four large picnic shelters near the edge of the South Fork of the Shenandoah River, and launch areas for anglers and canoeists. Its River Right Campground has ten spacious and primitive sites (tents only) with potable water for individuals and groups (full service is planned in the future). Reservations are required for camp sites (800-933-PARK). The park's trail system provides options for multi-use or trails for walking only. The park has Indian Hollow Stables, open every day except Wednesdays from April 1 through October 31. For a fee there are guided trail rides up to two hours that can include lunch. Interpretive rides are available on request. (Visitors may see the name of Raymond R. "Andy" Guest Jr. associated with the park's name. The state legislature honored him because of his influence and leadership in making the park possible.)

ACCESS: If arriving from the south, drive north from Luray on US 340 for 11 miles to Bentonville, where at the post office it is 0.1 mile ahead to park entrance, left. Ascend. If arriving from the north on US 340, drive 7.6 miles south from the Skyline Drive access road and town limit sign of Front Royal, and turn right for the park entrance. It is 1.9 miles to the campground parking area.

898–912 **Allen's Mountain Trail** (1.2 mi.), **AJ's Drop Trail** (1.3 mi.), **Bluebell Loop Trail** (1.3 mi.), **Campbell's Jump Trail** (0.5 mi.), **Cassidy Point Trail** (0.7 mi.), **Clean Sweep Trail** (0.2 mi.), **Cook's Trail** (0.5 mi.), **Culler's Trail** (2.8 mi.), **Paw Paw Trail** (1 mi.), **Point Trail** (1 mi.), **Redtail Ridge Trail** (0.5 mi.), **Sawmill Hollow Trail** (0.5 mi.), **Tater Patch Trail** (1.3 mi.), **Turkey Roost Trail** (0.2 mi.), **Wildcat Ledge Trail** (0.4 mi.)

*Shenandoah River State Park*

LENGTH AND DIFFICULTY: 13.4 miles (21.4 km) combined; easy to moderate
FEATURES: river rapids, scenic ledges, fishing, wildlife, wildflowers
TRAILHEADS: equestrian parking area, picnic areas and campground
DESCRIPTION: The trail system is an interconnecting maze for a variety of uses.
The longest multi-use trail for equestrians (hikers and bicyclists may also use it) is orange-blazed **Culler's Trail**. Its trailhead is at a parking area on the left after

passing the contact station. (If there are questions about the conditions of trails or new trails inquire at the contact station or telephone in advance.) The other four equestrian trails are blue-blazed **Tater Patch Trail**, gray-blazed **Sawmill Hollow Trail**, green-blazed **Cassidy Point Trail** (all easy), and teal-blazed **AJ's Drop Trail** (more challenging). These trails pass through a mixed hardwood and Virginia pine forest with understory growth of rhododendron, mountain laurel, and cedar. There are five pedestrian trails described ahead; the other trails are multi-use for hikers and bicyclists.

From the far end of the campground parking area begin the dark-blue-blazed **Bluebell Loop Trail** on a pea gravel base among locust, cedar, and persimmon. Leave the campground at 0.1 mile and at 0.3 mile make a juncture with beige-blazed (pedestrian only) **Wildcat Ledge Trail**, right. If choosing it, ascend steeply on a dry and shaley ridge. Pass a bench and arrive at a scenic and rocky overlook. Among the lichens and wildflowers are wild pink (*Silene pensylvanica*), a low and brilliant pink flower that blooms in April/May. Backtrack. Continue right on the **Bluebell Loop Trail**. After 0.3 mile is a fork for a loop. Take either route in this grassy floodplain. Flora consists of bluebell, fruitful papaw, and purple flowering raspberry. After backtracking return to the parking area for a total of 2.4 miles.

Also at the parking lot, opposite the campground, is gold-blazed **Point Trail**. It ascends a ridge, but before it becomes steep the green-blazed (pedestrian only) **Campbell's Jump Trail** is right. Ascend on **Point Trail** for 1 mile among hardwoods and pine. Backtrack. At the entrance to the campground parking area (but opposite the campground) is silver-blazed **Allen's Mountain Trail**. It begins on an old road near a small stream. After 0.1 mile there is a juncture with **Campbell's Jump Trail**. Here you can continue on the **Allen's Mountain Trail** upstream among ferns and mountain laurel. Leave the stream and ascend to a ridge where a curve is made in a hollow. At 0.6 mile is the top of a hill. Complete the curve and descend to the parking area at 1.2 miles. If choosing the **Campbell's Jump Trail**, cross the small stream and ascend steeply. After 110 yards make a juncture with yellow-blazed (pedestrian only) **Turkey Roost Trail**, ahead. (It continues an ascent to Highpoint Picnic Area and parking lot across the entrance road after 0.2 mi.) Continuing right on the **Campbell's Jump Trail** cross the entrance road at 0.2 mile. Briefly in the forest follow its edge in a cleared grassy area, south of picnic shelters #1 and #2. At 0.3 mile juncture left with white-blazed (pedestrian only) **Cook's Trail**. (It ascends 0.2 mi. to juncture with **Clean Sweep Trail** before ending at Highpoint Picnic Area and parking lot at 0.5 mi.). Staying on **Campbell's Jump Trail** for another 0.1 mile, arrive at a juncture with purple-blazed (pedestrian only) **Clean Sweep Trail**, left. To the right is black-blazed **Paw Paw Trail**, which goes left and right. To the right is the parking area for picnic shelter #1.

If you choose to continue hiking on the **Clean Sweep Trail**, ascend on a scenic dry, open forest ridge where there are beds of rocks from a prehistoric river. Juncture with the **Cook's Trail** at 0.2 mile, then follow a well-designed route that crosses two ravine bridges. Ascend to Highpoint Picnic Area and parking at 0.5 mile. If returning to the campground on the **Turkey Roost Trail**, you will have made a loop of 1.4 miles. If you choose to hike the 1-mile **Paw Paw Trail**, this will be the trail (and old road) for the most scenic views of the river and beautiful forest with large sycamore and a dense understory of papaw, spicebush, and alder. You may see deer, red fox, wild turkey, and other wildlife. Waterfowl and songbirds are prominent.

USGS MAP: Bentonville

ADDRESS AND INFORMATION: Shenandoah River State Park, P.O. Box 235, Bentonville, VA 22610; phone: 540-622-6840; fax: 540-622-6841; e-mail: <shenandoahriver@dcr.state>. Brochures available.

## SKY MEADOWS STATE PARK
*Clarke and Fauquier Counties*

This historic property is part of a 7,883-acre tract purchased by Capt. James Ball from Lord Fairfax in 1713. Successive owners sold and divided the property until in 1966 a housing development was plotted for this farm of mountain and valley meadows. But Paul Mellon prevented the development from materializing and gave 1,132 acres to Virginia State Parks in 1975. The park opened in 1983. In 1987 another 248 acres were added that contain 3.6 miles of the AT. In 1991 Mellon gave an additional 462 acres. Hikers do not have to go far on this preserve to appreciate the donor's generosity. The stone house on a hilltop was constructed by Isaac Settle about 1835. He gave it to his son Abner, who named it Mount Bleak. From this house visitors receive information on the park. The park has a lake for fishing; the **Lost Mountain Bridle Trail** (6 mi.) (with a staging area); a picnic area; farm buildings; a primitive hike-in campground; and trails. 913

ACCESS: From US 50, drive south on US 17 for 1.2 miles to park entrance on SR 710. From I-66, exit 23, drive north on US 17 for 6.4 miles.

**Piedmont Overlook Trail** (0.7 mi.), **North Ridge Trail** (1.7 mi.), **Gap Run Trail** 914–18 (1.2 mi.), **South Ridge Trail** (1.6 mi.), **Snowden Trail** (1.1 mi.)

LENGTH AND DIFFICULTY: 5.3 miles (8.5 km) combined, round-trip; moderate to strenuous

CONNECTING TRAIL: AT (3.6 mi.) 489

FEATURES: scenic views, historic site, wildflowers

TRAILHEAD: From the visitor center at west end of parking lot

DESCRIPTION: Short and long loops can be made on these connecting trails. The longest loop is described here. At the service road ascend on the **Piedmont Overlook Trail** in a field of clover and wildflowers. Views are of Lost Mountain and Gap Run Valley toward the east. At 0.5 mile join the **North Ridge Trail** and reach a junction with the **Gap Run Trail** at Gap Run at 1 mile. Here is a rocky area with papaw, spicebush, and jack-in-the-pulpit. (The trail descends to the primitive campground.) Continue uphill on the **North Ridge Trail** to a junction with the **South Ridge Trail** at 1.6 miles. (To the right is a spur trail that ascends steeply for 0.4 mi. to the **AT**, where a resting bench is appreciated. The **AT** goes left to Thompson WMA and 1-66, and right to Ashby Gap and US 50. Backtrack.) The **South Ridge Trail** follows an old woods road and at 2.6 miles goes through a stile to grassy pastures and scenic views. The **Gap Run Trail** is left at 2.9 miles. (It is 0.6 mi. to the shelter and campsites.) To the right on the gravel road is access to the **Snowden Trail**, a 1.1-mile loop in a forest with interpretive signs. Return 0.6 mile on the service road for a loop of 5.3 miles (not counting the **Gap Run Trail** or side trails).

USGS MAP: Upperville

ADDRESS AND INFORMATION: Sky Meadows State Park, 11012 Edmonds Lane, Delaplane, VA 20144; phone: 540-592-3556; fax: 540-592-3617; e-mail: <skymeadows@der.state.va.us>. Available are brochures and flyers on history and trail outline.


## WILDERNESS ROAD STATE PARK
*Lee County*

This park represents 200 acres that the state purchased in 1993. The property includes a section of the Daniel Boone Wilderness route into Kentucky. On the property is an 1870s mansion used now for special activities such as meetings and weddings. There is a regional gift outpost and seasonal programs on the history of the early frontier. Two trails are planned. One is 1-mile **Indian Ridge Trail**, an easy loop from a parking lot and kiosk to Indian Creek Overlook. The other multiuse trail is on an old railroad bed from Martin's Section west to a campground in Cumberland Gap National Historical Park. Contact the state park for an update on trail progress.

USGS MAPS: Middlesboro, Varilla, Ewing

ACCESS: From the community of Ewing drive west 5 miles to turn right on SR 923 and follow signs to SR 690.

ADDRESS AND INFORMATION: Wilderness Road State Park, Rt. 2, Box 115, Ewing, VA 24248; phone: 276-445-3065; fax: 276-445-3066. Brochure available.

919

# Piedmont Division

## BEAR CREEK LAKE STATE PARK
*Cumberland County*

Centered in the heart of the Cumberland State Forest, this peaceful and serene 326-acre park was established in 1938. Activities include boating (boat rentals are available), fishing (for blue gill, largemouth bass, and crappie), picnicking (reservations are available if desired), hiking (around the lake and side trails), swimming (in the lake near beach and bathhouse), and camping (with electrical and water hookups; reservations are highly recommended). The nearby 15.2-mile **Willis River Trail** can be accessed from SR 666, the park entrance road, near the campground and beach. (See Cumberland State Forest at the end of this chapter.)

ACCESS: From the town of Cumberland drive east 0.5 mile on US 60 and turn left on SR 622. Drive 3.3 miles to SR 629 and turn left; turn left again on SR 666.

**Lakeside Trail** (0.8 mi.), **Running Cedar Trail** (0.2 mi.), **Lost Barr Trail** (1.5 mi.), **Circumferential Trail** (1.5 mi.), **Pine Knob Trail** (0.5 mi.)          920–24

LENGTH AND DIFFICULTY: 4.5 miles (7.2 km) combined, round-trip; easy

FEATURES: lake, wildflowers, fishing, wildlife

TRAILHEAD: parking loop in picnic area

DESCRIPTION: From the picnic area hike downstream (northwest) on the orange-blazed **Lakeside Trail**. After 0.3 mile reach a junction with blue-blazed **Running Cedar Trail**, right, which connects to Campground C. (It passes through beds of running cedar [clubmoss] and under tall tulip poplars.) Pass other side trails to Campground A and reach the lake's dam at 0.8 mile. Around the dam to the other side of the lake is the **Lost Barr (Bear) Trail**. It is an interpretive, self-guiding loop trail with ten stations with descriptive signage. At 0.8 mile at a road bridge it connects with white-blazed **Circumferential Trail**. Follow it to cross Bear Creek Road bridge, pass through lowlands, and cross Little Bear Creek footbridge to rejoin the **Lakeside Trail** at 3 miles. (To the right is an access trail to the **Willis River Trail**.) Turn left and reach a junction, right, with the **Pine Knob Trail**, which can be used for returning to Campground C on SR 666 or back to the picnic area for a loop. Continue on the **Lakeside Trail** to the picnic area for a total of 3.2 miles around the lake.

USGS MAP: Gold Hill

ADDRESS AND INFORMATION: Bear Creek Lake State Park, 929 Oak Hill Rd., Cumberland, VA 23040; phone: 804-492-4410; fax: 804-429-9523. Available is a leaflet with map.

## FAIRY STONE STATE PARK
*Patrick and Henry Counties*

Fairy Stone State Park, established in 1936, is a 4,570-acre natural preserve in the foothills of the Blue Ridge Mountains. It has a 168-acre lake fed by Goblintown Creek, which flows into the adjoining Philpott Reservoir. The park is named for the famous lucky hexagonal crystals found in the southern tip of the park boundary. The crystals, called staurolite, are composed of iron aluminum silicate in small tan-brown and gray-blue forms of the Roman, Maltese, and St. Andrew's crosses. They have been formed by intense heat and pressure during the folding and crumpling of the Appalachian mountain chain.

A wide range of facilities include those for swimming, boating, fishing, hiking, bicycling, nature study, and tent and trailer camping. Also, housekeeping cabins are rented on a weekly basis Memorial Day through Labor Day and year round with a two-night minimum stay requirement. Newly renovated and opened in 2000, Fairy Stone Lodge (sleeps 16) and Fayerdale Hall Conference Center are popular for family and group gatherings. Reservations are available by calling 800-933-7275. The park has a number of short, easy to moderate hiking trails,

925–26 three of which connect. A separate one is the **Dam Spillway Trail**, a 1-mile, easy, round-trip path on the edge of the lake through a mixed forest. It is accessed from the nature center. For the physically impaired there is 0.1-mile **Handicapped Trail** 0.9 miles north on SR 623. It is a cement-paved trail to a picnic and fishing area in a cove by the lake.

ACCESS: From Bassett go 9 miles west on VA 57 and turn right on VA 346. After 1 mile is the park entrance and information center. (VA 57 continues west to VA 8, leading south to Stuart, and north to Woolwine.)

927 **Oak Hickory Trail**
LENGTH AND DIFFICULTY: 1.1 miles (2.1 km) round-trip; easy to moderate
TRAILHEAD: picnic area near the park entrance
DESCRIPTION: Where the road crosses the stream, look for a red-blazed trail sign and go right or left on the loop. Large trees include beech, oak, poplar, white pine, and maple. Parts of this serene path are mossy, with a rhododendron canopy. Deer are often seen in this area.

928–30 **Iron Mine Trail** (1.1 mi.), **Stuart's Knob Trail** (1.8 mi.), **Whiskey Run Trail** (2 mi.)
LENGTH AND DIFFICULTY: 4.9 miles (7.8 km) combined, round-trip; easy to moderate
FEATURES: iron mines, wildflowers, geological formations, scenic views
TRAILHEAD: Access on SR 623, 0.7 mile from park entrance, left.
DESCRIPTION: Ascend on a well-graded trail through periwinkle beds, fire pink, redbud, and a young mixed forest. At 0.2 mile is a junction with blue-blazed **Whiskey Run Trail**. Continue left through remains of iron mines and pass

junction with orange-blazed **Stuart's Knob Trail** at 0.5 mile. At 0.7 mile is a superb view of the park beach and lake. At 0.9 mile reach a gated open-shaft mine near a return to parking area. On **Stuart's Knob Trail** ascend steeply to a rocky knob. Heavy vegetation prevents scenic views. Return to the **Iron Mine Trail**. The **Whiskey Run Trail** branches off the **Iron Mine Trail**. It circles the base of Stuart's Knob for 1.5 miles before rejoining the **Iron Mine Trail** at a park overlook. Descend on the **Iron Mine Trail** to the parking lot.

USGS MAPS: Charity, Philpott Reservoir

ADDRESS AND INFORMATION: Fairy Stone State Park, 967 Fairystone Lake Dr., Stuart, VA 24171; phone: 276-930-2424; fax: 276-930-1136. Available are brochures and flyers on the history of the fairy stone legend and park outline map with trails.

## HOLLIDAY LAKE STATE PARK
*Buckingham and Appomattox Counties*

Established in 1972, the peaceful, 250-acre Holliday Lake State Park lies within the Buckingham-Appomattox State Forest. The park's major attraction is a 150-acre lake, offering boating and fishing as well as swimming at a spacious beach area. Canoes, rowboats, and paddle boats can be rented. Other facilities are a campground with water and electric hookups, store and concessions, picnic areas, visitor center, bathhouse, and several trails for hiking. In addition, the 12-mile multi-use **Carter Taylor Trail** in the Appomatox-Buckingham State Forest can be   931 accessed here.

ACCESS: On VA 24 east of the town of Appomattox and US 460, go 8 miles to SR 626, right. Follow SR 626 for 3 5 miles, turn left on SR 640 for 0.3 mile, and then right on SR 692 for 2.9 miles.

**Lakeshore Trail** (5.2 mi.), **Saunders Creek Trail** (0.2 mi.), **North Ridge Trail**   932–36
(0.4 mi.), **Laurel Trail** (1.3 mi.), **Dogwood Trail** (1 mi.)

LENGTH AND DIFFICULTY: 8.1 miles (12.9 km); easy to moderate

FEATURES: scenic views, lake, wildlife, fishing

TRAILHEAD: parking area near boat dock

DESCRIPTION: From the boat dock and bathhouse area begin the **Lakeshore Trail** either left or right for a loop. If hiking left, follow the dark-blue marker around the lake. Vegetation includes Virginia pine, shortleaf pine, oak, hickory, poplar, mountain laurel, red cedar, alder, white pine, green ash, dogwood, and numerous wildflowers. Reach lake overview at 0.4 mile on exceptionally well-graded trail. At 0.6 mile pass an access trail to campground. At 0.8 miles is a wooden observation deck overlooking the lake. At 1.3 miles you cross a wooden bridge over Holliday Creek. (A left after the bridge connects with the **Carter Taylor Trail** in the state forest.)

After crossing the bridge, continue right to a clearing and views of lake on right at 1.5 miles, and at forest road junction at 2.2 miles go straight ahead. Cross Forbes Creek, and reach rocky bluff with huckleberries at 2.7 miles. Descend a wooden stairway to a scenic cement bridge over the dam at 3.2 miles. Cross small stream in a cove, and follow upstream for 0.2 mile. Turn away from stream bank and reach paved gated road at 4.4 miles (right is entrance to 4-H Educational Center). Climb steps across road, descend to stream bank, follow through mature forest with beds of running cedar. Pass 1.3-mile **Laurel Trail**, left, and reach a bridge at the lake at 4.9 miles. Here is the **Saunder's Creek Trail**, an orange-blazed path left to the campground and right to the lake. Turn right and follow along lakeshore for another 0.3 mile to parking area. **North Ridge Trail**, a linear trail, and yellow-blazed **Dogwood Trail** are accessed from and near the picnic area.

USGS MAP: Holliday Lake

ADDRESS AND INFORMATION: Holliday Lake State Park, Rt. 2, Box 622, Appomattox, VA 24522; phone: 434-248-6308; fax: 434-248-6614.


## JAMES RIVER STATE PARK
*Buckingham County*

This parkland was constructed in the 1990s from the state's General Obligations Bond. It has 1,500 scenic acres on the east side of a bend of the James River with a 3-mile river frontage. There are two boat and canoe landings and five selected locations for fishing. Most of the park is forested with mixed hardwoods and scattered sections of Virginia pine. Meadows and hillside pastures are used for bird-watching trails, picnic areas, an amphitheater, three fishing ponds, and campgrounds. One of the fishing ponds and camping areas is more isolated in the northeast corner of the park. Other facilities are a visitor center, picnic and picnic shelter areas, and rest rooms. The park has a trail network of 15.9 miles, mainly old roads from former farms and pastureland, that includes spurs and connectors.

937–39    In addition to the trails described ahead, there is a 0.3-mile **Birdwalk Trail**, a 0.2-mile **Taylor Pond Trail**, and a 0.2-mile **Green Pond Trail**.

ACCESS: From Buckingham go west 17 miles on US 60 to Bent Creek and turn right (north) on SR 605; after 7 miles turn left on SR 606. From Amherst go 15 miles east on US 60 to Bent Creek and turn left on SR 605.

940–44    **Running Creek Trail** (3.1 mi.), **Branch Trail** (3.5 mi.), **Cabell Trail** (3.7 mi.), **Dixon Trail** (0.8 mi.), **River Trail** (2.4 mi.)

LENGTH AND DIFFICULTY: 14.3 miles (22 km); easy to moderate

CONNECTING/SPUR TRAILS: 2.1 miles

FEATURES: scenic river, historic sites, bird sanctuary

TRAILHEADS: The most central trailhead for hiking is a parking lot on the north side of the main road 0.1 mile east of the park office. For equestrians it is near the river on the first road to the left after entry into the park.

DESCRIPTION: The park's major trails are color coded with blazes and signage. Unless otherwise specified, all trails may be used by equestrians, hikers, and bicyclists. If hiking from the parking lot (115 yd. east of the park office) you may start north in the forest to connect with the **Cabell Trail** or **Branch Trail**. Or across the main road you can connect with the **Running Creek Trail**, which connects with both the **Cabell Trail** and **Branch Trail**. For this description the first routing is on the side of the park office to connect with the yellow-blazed **Running Creek Trail**. Stay right at the connection, and descend into grasslands that connect with the **Birdwalk Trail**, left. At 0.2 mile pass an option to take the **Running Creek Trail** ahead or to the left. If going ahead, come to an ascent and curve right among a patch of blackberry bushes. Curve left and descend to connect with orange-blazed **Cabell Trail** at 0.6 mile, but continue ahead 127 yards to the south end of blue-blazed **River Trail**. Turn left on the **Running Creek Trail**, pass a spur access left to picnic shelters #2 and #1, and after 0.2 mile cross the road that leads right to a campground in the meadow and near the river. Curve left and for the next 0.5 mile ascend, and cross three bridges and a ridge to connect left and right with another section of **Running Creek Trail**. Here a loop of 2 miles can be made by turning left and returning to the parking lot near the park office. To complete a longer loop, turn right on the **Running Creek Trail** and after 0.4 mile arrive at the main entrance road, but turn left. (Across the road begins the green-blazed **Branch Trail**.) Cross the campground road after another 0.3 mile and return to the parking lot near the park office at 3.2 miles.

If choosing to cross the entrance road to the **Branch Trail** descend to cross a small stream, ascend to a ridge, pass through a timber cut, and at 0.9 mile curve west and descend. At 1.3 miles there is a choice of staying left to cross a bridge, or turning right on a narrow path around Branch Pond. Cross the dam at 1.5 miles. Here the trail provides another option. Stay left and close to the lake edge for a foot trail or ascend a forest road of horseback riding. The pond has largemouth bass, sunfish, and catfish. At the upper end of the pond is a picnic shelter, primitive camping area, and short access to east side of pond on a bridge. (To the right on a gravel and gated road is an ascent and descent for 0.5 mi. to the dam. Also, this road connects with the **Cabell Trail** at the top of the ascent.) Continuing south on the gravel road, immediately leave the road into the woods for an ascent to parallel the road. (At 3.1 mi. is an orange-green-blazed connector trail, right. It goes 0.4 mi. to another connector trail where left is a 0.3-mi. return to the parking lot near the park office, or right on an orange-green blaze 0.4 mi. to the **Cabell Trail**.) If continuing on the **Branch**

**Trail** cross the Branch Pond Road and complete the loop at the entrance road at 3.5 miles.

For hiking the **Cabell Trail** from the parking lot near the park office, follow the orange-green blazes north. (At 0.3 mi. pass the orange-green connector trail to the **Branch Trail** described above.) Arrive at an intersection of the **Cabell Trail** and **Dixon Trail** at 0.7 mile. (The scenic **Cabell Trail** is named in honor of the Cabell families who were the first European settlers in the park area during the 1700s.) (The red-blazed **Dixon Trail** goes west and makes a horseshoe curve; it descends for 0.4 mi. to cross the park's main road. From there it ascends, then descends to cross a bridge and ends at an equestrian parking area on a side road from the main road.) The **Cabell Trail** goes right and left at the intersection. If going right, north, arrive at a gravel road, right, at 0.5 mile and turn left. (To the right is an access to Branch Pond and primitive campsite.) At 0.7 mile turn left where a former homesite is right. After a few yards there is a 0.2-mile spur trail right to the most scenic high spot of the park. It is a view of the confluence of the James and Tye Rivers. Continuing on the **Cabell Trail** descend to a gate at 1.2 miles. (To the right is a 0.3-mi. spur trail that descends to a picnic shelter and the main road. In 2003 there was not an overlook here.) From the gate pass a cemetery on the right, cross the main park road to a road, but veer right on a grassy area. At 1.5 miles pass a rest room and the "Appomattox" batteau that is on the left. Arrive at Green Hill Pond parking area where an asphalt loop trail with boardwalk bridges is around the pond. (To the right is an access road to the **River Trail**.) Ascend a grassy hill and pass by the amphitheater at 1.7 miles. At 1.8 miles turn left and ascend to cross a loop road and then cross the park main road at 2.4 miles. Continue ascent to reach the intersection with **Dixon Trail** for a loop at 3.1 miles. A return to the parking lot near the park office is 0.7 mile on the orange-green connector trail.

The 2.4-mile blue-blazed **River Trail** is linear, but it does make contact with the **Cabell Trail** and **Running Creek Trail** for partial loops. This trail has red-winged blackbirds and bob whites. If starting at Dixon Landing at the end of the main park road, hike right (downstream) for 0.2 mile to the north end of the trail. Backtrack and continue south near the river. Cross a bridge at 0.5 mile. After briefly following a road, turn right at 0.8 mile to cross a creek below Green Hill Pond, and pass another pond. At 1.5 miles bear left to hike around a stream in the meadow. Here is contact with the orange-blazed **Cabell Trail**. Return to the riverside and make contact with the **Running Creek Trail** at 2.4 miles, left and ahead. Follow the **Running Creek Trail** 0.2 mile to access the Canoe Landing and the campgrounds.

USGS MAPS: Gladstone, Shipman

ADDRESS AND INFORMATION: James River State Park, Rt. 1, Box 787, Gladstone, VA 24553; phone: 434-933-4355; fax: 434-933-8061. A park guide brochure is available.

## LAKE ANNA STATE PARK
*Spotsylvania County*

The 2,058-acre park is on a north side peninsula of Lake Anna, a large lake on the North Anna River in Louisa and Spotsylvania Counties southwest of Fredericksburg. The park opened to the public in 1983. Its land, and the land under the water, has been home to European settlers and their descendants since the early eighteenth century. They cut the trees from the sloping hills, farmed, and mined for iron, lead, and gold. Before them were the Maannahoack Sioux, fierce natives who held the colonists at bay for a century. The area is in the gold pyrite belt where in 1829 gold was found along Pigeon Run. A foundation site of the 1880s Goodwin Gold Mine still exists. Iron ore had been discovered early, and mining began in the 1720s. There are many historic sites to visit here, and at the park's visitor center are exhibits and displays of the area's natural and human history. Near the visitor center is a 0.3-mile interpretive loop trail around a preserved pond built by a former landowner. Access to the pond is easy for those who are physically handicapped, and a sheltered deck provides a place to observe waterfowl. Wooden platforms around the pond are for children and handicapped fishermen. Attractions are boating and fishing, swimming at a beach with bathhouse, a picnic area, boat rentals, and summer nature programs on the network of trails. A singular trail, the **Fisherman's Trail**, makes a 1-mile loop into the woods and 945 fields near the lake and passes through Picnic Area B. Access is from the boat launch and picnic parking area.

ACCESS: From I-95, exit 118, take SR 606 west at Thornburg to VA 208. After about 15.8 miles turn right on SR 601 and go 3.3 miles to park entrance, left. From US 522 it is about 8 miles east on VA 208 to a left turn on SR 601.

**Sawtooth Trail** (1.4 mi.), **Old Pond Trail** (0.3 mi.), **Railroad Ford Trail** (1.6 946–55 mi.), **Glenora Trail** (1.5 mi.), **Big Woods Trail** (1.1 mi.), **Cedar Run Trail** (0.8 mi.), **Turkey Run Trail** (1 mi.), **Mill Pond Trail** (0.9 mi.), **Pigeon Run Trail** (1.4 mi.), **Gold Hill Trail** (3.4 mi.)

LENGTH AND DIFFICULTY: 13.4 miles (21.4 km) combined, minus backtracks; easy

FEATURES: scenic views, historic sites, wildlife, wildflowers

TRAILHEADS: After entering the park, drive 1.8 miles to the park office or ahead to the visitor center.

DESCRIPTION: All these trails are described as a unit from the park office. The trails are color coded with exceptionally helpful signage at trailheads and connections. From here all trails can be hiked beginning north or south on the tan-blazed **Sawtooth Trail**. If starting south, cross an entrance road to Picnic Area C. (The road leads to parking space for equestrians and both the **Turkey Run Trail** and **Mill Pond Trail** at 0.4 mi.) Enter the forest on an old road among mixed hardwoods and scattered mountain laurel. After 0.8 mile from the park office, turn right on a hikers-only trail. Slightly descend over water bars and arrive at **Old Pond Trail** at 1 mile. Turn right to make a loop of 0.3 mile among cedars and across bridges to a pavilion and dam. (Here is access to the visitor center, rest rooms, beach, and picnic area.)

Continue the circuit by taking the red-blazed **Railroad Ford Trail** for hikers only along the lake's edge. There are cedar, beech, oak, honeysuckle, and sundrops. Fishermen have side trails to the lake. At 1.2 miles there is a turn away from the serpentine and scenic trail to a straight routing on an old railroad bed. (During World War I this old rail grade was used for mining lead and zinc to be used in armaments.) Complete the trail at 1.6 miles and rejoin **Sawtooth Trail**, left, and **Glenora Trail**, right. Follow the green-blazed multi-use **Glenora Trail** on an easy old road to a fork at 1.4 miles. To the right is a hiker's trail of only 0.1 mile to the site of an early 1800s plantation home called "Glenora." There are display signs about its history and the remains of an old smokehouse. Backtrack to **Big Woods Trail**, right. Follow it and cross a bridge at 0.8 mile and pass through a rocky area. At 1.1 miles intersect with yellow-blazed **Turkey Run Trail**, left and right. To the right is a hikers-only trail to a former homesite with chimney remains at 0.2 mile. Backtrack to the white-blazed **Cedar Run Trail**, right, and hike it for 0.8 mile, or continue ahead to stay on **Turkey Run Trail** for 1 mile. Near the end cross the park road to picnic area C. The road is 0.4 mile left to the park office.

To continue on the trail network, cross the road from the **Turkey Run Trail** to the blue-blazed **Mill Pond Trail**. Follow it to cross a stream and at 0.7 mile arrive at a power line and connection with the purple-blazed **Pigeon Run Trail**, left. Ahead, a hikers-only section of the **Mill Pond Trail** descends 0.2 mile to the nineteenth-century site of Hailey's Grist Mill. Backtrack. Follow the woods edge of the power line, descending and ascending for 0.2 mile; to the right is a lake cove. Coreopsis and other wildflowers are prominent. Turn left into the woods; on a descent are skunk cabbage, left. Cross a stream at 0.6 mile and ascend to contact **Gold Hill Trail**, right, at 1 mile. If making the circuit of the 3.4-mile black-blazed **Gold Hill Trail** return to the power line and reach a fork for making a circle at 0.6 mile. Either route from the sign provides an isolated passage. Backtrack from the fork. To continue on the **Pigeon Run Trail**, stay straight and connect with the **Sawtooth Trail** at 1.4 miles, left. From here the north section of the **Sawtooth Trail** parallels the entrance road south to the parking area at the park office at 0.7 mile.

USGS MAPS: Lake Anna West, Belmont

ADDRESS AND INFORMATION: Lake Anna State Park, 6800 Lawyers Rd., Spotsylvania, VA 22553; phone: 540-854-5503; fax: 540-854-5421. A trail brochure is available.

## OCCONEECHEE STATE PARK
*Mecklenburg County*

Leased from the U.S. Army Corp of Engineers in 1968, the 2,690-acre Occonee-chee State Park adjoins the John H. Kerr Reservoir near Clarksville. The park is named after the powerful Occoneechee Indians, who lived in the area from 1250 to 1676. They, like the Saponi and Tutelo Indians, traded furs from now-inundated islands until colonial rebels led by Nathaniel Bacon in 1676 massacred many of them, thereby breaking their stronghold. The survivors scattered into what is now North Carolina. Facilities include eighty-eight campsites (some with water and electric hookups), and popular activities are picnicking, boating, hiking, and summer interpretive programs. Bass fishing is a popular sport in the reservoir. Park camping facilities for tents and trailers are open from March 1 to December 1. Bathhouse, water, and electric hookups are available. (The **Panhandle Multi-Use Trail** is a 15-mi. linear route. Call the park office for information on its services to equestrians, bicyclists, and hikers.) 956

ACCESS: From the junction of US 58/15 and VA 49, across the bridge from Clarksville, go east on US 58 for 0.6 mile and turn right at park sign. Follow VA 364 for 0.5 mile to the park headquarters.

### Old Plantation Interpretive Trail 957
LENGTH AND DIFFICULTY: 1.2 miles (1.9 km) round-trip; easy
CONNECTING TRAILS: **Mossy Creek Trail** (0.7 mi.), **Warrior's Path Trail** (0.2 mi.), 958–61
   **Big Oak Trail** (0.6 mi.), **Connector Trail** (0.2 mi.)
FEATURES: historic site, nature study
TRAILHEAD: Terrace Garden parking area 0.1 mile south of park office
DESCRIPTION: Follow the red-blazed **Old Plantation Interpretive Trail** by the site of the Occoneechee plantation home of Dempsey Crudup into a forest of black and honey locust, black walnut, maple, oak, and cedar. At 0.2 mile pass the **Mossy Creek Trail**. (It extends right for 0.7 mi. to a large white oak stand, and to the park office.) On the **Old Plantation Interpretive Trail** follow a stream near beech and pine to a junction with the **Warrior's Path Trail**. (It leads 0.2 mi. right to parking area at the lakeshore.) After another 0.1 mile pass a junction with yellow-blazed **Big Oak Trail**, right. (It crosses the road near Campground B, and after a few yards it leaves the road at a huge white oak. It ascends to end near the entrance to Campground C in a group of large red and white oaks.) A yellow-blazed **Connector Trail** goes from Campground B to the **Old Plantation Interpretive Trail**.
USGS MAPS: Clarksville North and South, Tungsten
ADDRESS AND INFORMATION: Occoneechee State Park, 1192 Occoneechee Park Rd., Clarksville, VA 23927; phone: 434-374-2210; fax: 434-374-2210. Available is a brochure on park and fishing regulations.

## POCAHONTAS STATE PARK
*Chesterfield County*

Pocahontas State Park is southwest of Richmond and was established in 1946. It has 7,604 acres with 27 miles of roads for hiking. A 156-acre lake fed by Swift Creek is used for boating and fishing. Also provided are a large swimming pool, a bathhouse, areas for camping and picnicking, bicycle trails, hiking trails, wildlife exhibits, a visitor center, and a playground. Camping facilities are seasonal, but full services are between Memorial Day and Labor Day.

ACCESS: From the junction of VA 10 and SR 655 at Chesterfield Courthouse follow the park signs and go west on SR 655 for 3.8 miles, then turn right into park entrance on SR 780. Park office and parking area are another 1.5 miles away. (Access via I-95 is from exit 61; go west 7 mi. on VA 10 to Chesterfield Courthouse and SR 655.)

962 **Beaver Lake Nature Trail**
LENGTH AND DIFFICULTY: 2.6 miles (4.2 km) round-trip; easy
963–65 CONNECTING TRAILS: **Ground Pine Nature Trail** (1.2 mi.), **Third Branch Trail** (0.2 mi.), **Awareness Trail** (0.3 mi.)
FEATURES: historic site, lake, wildlife, wildflowers
TRAILHEAD: park visitor center
DESCRIPTION: Follow the blue-blazed trail down to Beaver Lake, which is bordered with tag alder; at 0.1 mile turn right and hike through a forest of large poplar, loblolly pine, oak, beech, and holly, with a ground cover of periwinkle. Pass old spring at 0.2 mile; a junction with yellow-blazed **Ground Pine Nature Trail**, extending right, is at 0.3 mile.

Continue through beds of ground pine and running cedar to lake overlooks at 0.5 mile and 0.7 mile. Cross boardwalk near large walnut, poplar, and sycamore stand at 0.8 mile. At 1.3 miles reach the **Third Branch Trail** and Old Mill Site. Turn left, cross stream, and continue circuit of the lake through a mixed forest. Arriving at the picturesque dam and spillway at 2.3 miles, descend, and cross footbridge below the dam. From there, a return to the visitor center can be made on the 0.3-mile **Awareness Trail**, which is marked in red, paved, and graded for wheelchair use (but may not have a sign). Return can also be made on the 0.1-mile spillway route to the junction with the **Beaver Lake Nature Trail**.

Another route, for a circuit of 3.8 miles to include half of the **Beaver Lake Nature Trail**, follows the trail signs for **Beaver Lake Nature Trail** from the visitor center to the junction with the **Ground Pine Nature Trail** at 0.3 mile. Turn right on the **Ground Pine Nature Trail** and go 0.2 mile to Crosstic Road, a bicycle trail. Turn left and follow the green-blazed bicycle trail across a cut left to Horner Road. Turn left again on Bottoms Road and, 2.2 miles from the visitor center, turn left off the bicycle trail onto the **Third Branch Trail**. Go 0.2 mile and make connections with the **Beaver Lake Nature Trail**. At that point turn right or left for the return to the visitor center.

USGS MAPS: Chesterfield, Beach

ADDRESS AND INFORMATION: Pocahontas State Park, 10301 State Park Rd., Chesterfield, VA 23832; phone: 804-796-4255; fax: 804-796-4004. Available are brochures and maps of the park and road network.


## SMITH MOUNTAIN LAKE STATE PARK
*Bedford County*

Smith Mountain Lake (20,500 acres) is the state's second largest lake. Constructed in the early 1960s the lake backs up the Roanoke and Blackwater Rivers for 40 miles in length and about 550 miles of shoreline in Franklin, Pittsylvania, and Bedford Counties. On the northern side of the lake is 1,506-acre Smith Mountain Lake State Park, which has four major peninsulas. Old tobacco barns and young forests attest to the farm life of the past. Water enthusiasts find the lake ideal for boating, skiing, and fishing. Each March the Smith Mountain Ruritans Bass Fishing Tournament is held here. The park offers a campground (electric hookups but no hot showers), a picnic area, a boat launch and rentals, and nature programs.

At the visitor center and parking area are two short trails. The 1-mile, yellow-blazed **Lake View Trail** makes a loop at the end of the peninsula near the shoreline. The 0.6-mile, blue-blazed **Tobacco Run Trail** passes a tobacco barn near the road before crossing to end at the lake. In the campground, near the park office, is the 0.5-mile, gold-blazed **Beech Wood Trail** loop. 966–68

ACCESS: From Bedford on US 460 drive south 13 miles on VA 122 to Moneta and take SR 608 for 6 miles. Turn right on SR 626 into the park. From US 29 in Altavista drive west on VA 342 for 15 miles to Woodford Corner and turn left on SR 626. Follow it directly 14 miles to the park.

### Chestnut Ridge Trail (1.7 mi.), Turtle Island Trail (1.3 mi.) 969–70

LENGTH AND DIFFICULTY: 3 miles (3.8 km) combined, round-trip; easy

FEATURES: wildlife, lake, scenic views, historic site

TRAILHEAD: parking area between park office and visitor center

DESCRIPTION: Begin across the road on the red-blazed **Chestnut Ridge Trail**. It makes a double loop, the first after 0.3 mile and again at 0.8 mile to the lakeside. In a forest of locust and sourwood among mountain laurel there are reminders of early farms, particularly tobacco. Begin the green-blazed **Turtle Island Trail** loop at the parking area. This interpretive trail is marked with posts and keyed to a trail guide. (There is a side trail to a wildlife-viewing blind for wheelchair users.) Hikers will see a forest succession study area, a soil nutrient cycle, a changing shoreline, a senescent forest, plant life, and animal habitats.

Among the Virginia pine and redbud are St.-John's-wort. At 0.6 mile is a footbridge to Turtle Island.

USGS MAP: Smith Mountain Dam

ADDRESS AND INFORMATION: Smith Mountain Lake State Park, 1235 State Park Rd., Huddleston, VA 24104; phone: 540-297-6066; fax: 540-297-1578. Available are brochure of park facilities and map.

## STAUNTON RIVER BATTLEFIELD STATE PARK
*Halifax and Charlotte Counties*

In 1995 this new 300-acre state park opened with a visitor center and museum of Civil War history. The displays are about the 492 Confederate old men and boys from Southside Virginia who assisted a stationed force of 296 soldiers under the command of Capt. B. L. Farinholt on the west side of the Staunton River, June 25, 1864. Their objective was to defend an important 0.1-mile railroad bridge over the Staunton River against a Union cavalry force with more than 5,000 men. The

971 Union army had to retreat. Today the **Fort Hill Trail** crosses the Staunton River on an old railroad bridge and on a high railroad bed for 1.2 miles to the post office of the community of Randolph. Backtrack to visitor center. The scenic trail route has views of wide pasturelands and two other bridge crossings. On the southwest corner of the Staunton River is a side trail to the Confederate earthworks. Also,

972 there is a 0.7-mile **Edgewood Nature Trail** that is self-guiding behind the visitor center. The trail makes a circle through the forest to two waterfowl observation platforms high above the Staunton River.

USGS MAP: Saxe

ACCESS: From South Boston drive 18 miles northeast to left on VA 92, and after 2 miles turn left on Black Walnut Road (SR 600). After 5.8 miles turn right on Fort Hill Trail (SR 855) to the park entrance, left. (On the way you passed a large electric generating station belonging to Virginia Power.)

ADDRESS AND INFORMATION: Staunton River Battlefield State Park, 1035 Fort Hill Trail, Randolph, VA 23962; phone: 434-454-4312; fax: 434-454-4313. Brochures are available.

## STAUNTON RIVER STATE PARK
*Halifax County*

Containing 1,287 acres of forest, meadows, and shorelines, the Staunton River State Park forms a peninsula into the 48,000-acre John H. Kerr Reservoir (also called Buggs Island Lake). By boat, it is about 15 miles upstream from the Occoneechee State Park. The park's history is associated with the Occoneechee Indians, who once controlled the area but were almost all annihilated or driven

*Fort Hill Trail, Staunton River Battlefield State Park*

into North Carolina by Nathaniel Bacon in 1676. Bacon's marauders were taking revenge on Indians in general because some Indians had murdered colonists on his estate near Richmond. Also in the park area, on June 25, 1864, a Union attack on the Richmond-Danville Railroad at the Staunton River Bridge was defeated by a Confederate group of old men and boys. In the late 1880s the Christian Social Colony settled on the peninsula, but it failed to find the expected utopia. Rich in history, the park was established in 1936, one of the six original state parks formed during the Great Depression. The park and river are named in honor of Capt. Henry Staunton, who commanded a company of soldiers to protect the early settlers from Indian attacks before the Revolutionary War.

In addition to deer, raccoon, wild turkey, and squirrel, the park also has several varieties of snakes; the copperhead is the only poisonous one. Snapping turtles and eastern box turtles also are seen in the park. During the early spring evenings a hiker can hear an orchestra of frogs—pickerel, bullfrogs, gray tree frogs, and spring peepers. Several species of waterfowl and wading birds, including geese, puddle ducks, diving ducks, osprey, and occasionally a great blue heron, can be seen. Multiple facilities include campsites, vacation cabins, an Olympic-size swimming pool, bathrooms, boat rentals and ramps, playgrounds, a visitor center, and nearly 10 miles of hiking trails. Activities include picnicking, fishing, tennis, interpretive tours, and nature study.

ACCESS: From US 58 and US 360 junction in eastern South Boston, go north on VA 360 for 5.3 miles to SR 613. Turn right on SR 613 and go 2.8 miles to Scottsburg. Turn right on VA 344 and go 8 miles to the park entrance.

973    **River Bank Trail**
LENGTH AND DIFFICULTY: 7.5 miles (12 km) round-trip; easy to moderate

974–79    CONNECTING TRAILS: **Tutelo Trail** (0.1 mi.), **Crow's Nest Trail** (0.5 mi.), **Robin's Roost Trail** (0.5 mi.), **Loblolly Trail** (0.7 mi.), **Campground Trail** (0.1 mi.), **Capt. Staunton's Loop Trail** (0.6 mi.)
FEATURES: waterfowl, scenic views, lake, wildflowers
TRAILHEAD: Parking area near the end of the peninsula
DESCRIPTION: From the entrance of the park, drive 1.7 miles to parking area in picnic area near the end of the peninsula. Begin hike on the blue-blazed **River Bank Trail** toward the tip of the peninsula at 0.3 mile. Views of the lake and shoreline are outstanding in all seasons. Follow the blazes right on a wide trail along the Dan River side of the lake through walnut, pine, locust, sourwood, hickory, cedar, and sweet gum. Spring and summer wildflowers flourish.

At 1.3 miles pass the white-blazed **Tutelo Trail** on right (which leads 0.1 mi. to a parking area and information center). At 1.4 miles and 1.8 miles pass through picnic areas. At 2.3 miles pass the orange-blazed **Crow's Nest Trail** on right (which leads 0.4 mi. to VA 344 in the center of the park). At 2.8 miles pass the yellow-blazed **Robin's Roost Trail** on right (which leads 0.5 mi. through a stand of pines to VA 344 in the park). The trail curves away from the lake at 3.3 miles, crosses VA 344 at 4.8 miles, and reaches a junction with the blue-blazed **Loblolly Trail** at 5.5 miles. (The **Loblolly Trail** goes right for 0.7 mi. to VA 344.) Continue ahead east along the Staunton River side of the lake at 6.2 miles, and pass a junction with the **Campground Trail** on the right (which leads 0.1 mi. to Campground A). At 6.4 miles pass the red-blazed **Capt. Staunton's Loop Trail**, with white markers (which goes right for 0.6 mi. to loop's trailhead at VA 344). Continue along scenic riverbank to park water plant and boat dock at 7.1 miles. Cross road, and return to parking area where hike began at 7.5 miles. The **Red Bank Trail** is now a multi-use trail for equestrians, hikers, and bicyclists. There is a major parking area for horse trailers immediately left after entering the park gate.

USGS MAP: Buffalo Springs
ADDRESS AND INFORMATION: Staunton River State Park, 1170 Staunton Trail, Scottsburg, VA 24589; phone: 434-572-4623; fax: 434-572-4650. Available are campground and park maps, brochures of park.

## TWIN LAKES STATE PARK
*Prince Edward County*

Located in the state's central piedmont, the double-lake, 349-acre Twin Lakes State Park adjoins the Gallion–Prince Edward State Forest. Goodwin Lake with 15 acres and Prince Edward Lake with 36 acres provide a tranquil area where the hiker can circle either body of water or, with a connector trail, hike around both. Wildlife is chiefly deer, quail, raccoon, beaver, squirrel, and wild turkey. Oak, hickory, and maple predominate in a mixed forest. The park has a campground, swimming beach, bathhouse, and group-use facilities. There are areas for boating, fishing, picnicking, nature study, and hiking. One of the trails, the **Dogwood** 980–82 **Hollow Trail**, is a self-guided interpretive trail with seven stops. From the park office the blue-blazed trail crosses the road and descends among mixed woods, ferns, and wildflowers. Recross a small stream and complete the loop after 1 mile. Another 1-mile loop trail is the **Goodwin Lake Nature Trail**. Access is at the parking area of the concession stand. It follows blue markers to the head of the lake, where there is likely to be evidence of beavers. Cross two bridges at 0.5 mile and 0.6 mile, cross the dam, and return to the picnic area and trail origin. (A **Connector Trail**, 0.3 mi., goes to **Otter's Path Trail**.)

ACCESS: From the junction of US 460/360 at Burkeville, go 4 miles southwest on US 360 to SR 613 and turn right. Go 1.5 miles on SR 613 to a junction of SR 629, where a large park sign gives directions to the park. Proceed right for 0.5 mile to the entrance of the day-use area.

### Otter's Path Trail                                                                 983
LENGTH AND DIFFICULTY: 4 miles (6.4 km) round-trip; moderate

FEATURES: cascades, wildlife, wildflowers

TRAILHEAD: Prince Edward Lake boat launch

DESCRIPTION: In either direction follow the orange markers around the lake. The trail winds around coves, up and down steep banks, and over mossy patches. If hiking right from the ramp, cross a cascading stream at 1.1 miles. At 2.1 miles cross a bridge near an active beaver dam and stroll through a white pine stand. Make a right at a barricade into a mature hardwood stand of maple, hickory, and beech along a small stream. At 2.8 miles return to the lake's edge, follow the trail through a mixed forest, and cross the dam and wooden walkway back to the parking area. (A **Connector Trail**, 0.3 mi., goes to the **Goodwin Lake Nature Trail**.)

ADDRESS AND INFORMATION: Twin Lakes State Park, 788 Twin Lakes Rd., Green Bay, VA 23942; phone: 434-392-3435; fax: 434-392-9406. Available for free are brochure and flyers; there is a fee for brochure on **Dogwood Hollow Trail**.

## Coastal Division

### BELLE ISLE STATE PARK
*Lancaster County*

This 733-acre tract was the first to be purchased with funds from the state's 1992 Parks and Recreation bond referendum. On the lower Northern Neck peninsula, it is on the northern side of the Rappahannock River. It is almost an island, with Mulberry Creek on the northwest and Deep Creek on the southeast. The park has eight types of wetlands. It was inhabited by Powhatan Indians before English settlers came to farm the area in the seventeenth century. The park has picnicking, bicycling, hiking, canoeing, and birding. There are bridle trails and a motor boat launch. Bel Air Mansion or the Bel Air Guest House can be rented for a
984–87  minimum of two nights. There are four trails on old farm roads. The **Watch House Trail** (0.5 mi.), one-way, signed red, is near the site of an old house used for guards to prevent poachers from stealing oysters. The **Neck Fields Trail** (1.2 mi.), one-way, signed green, is another river access trail through former farmlands. Crossing **Watch House Trail** is 0.3-mile yellow-signed **Mud Creek Trail** northwest to a boat launch, and 0.2-mile blue-signed **Porpoise Creek Trail** ends southeast to a playground area.

ACCESS: From the junction of VA 354 and SR 683, near Litwalton (3 mi. south of junction of VA 354 and VA 3), turn onto SR 683 to parking area.

ADDRESS AND INFORMATION: Belle Isle State Park, 1632 Belle Isle Rd., Lancaster, VA 22503; phone: 804-462-5030; fax: 804-462-0164.

### CALEDON NATURAL AREA
*King George County*

Bordered on the northern side by the Potomac River, this 2,579-acre preserve was donated to the commonwealth by Ann Hopewell Smoot in 1974. Designated a national natural landmark, the park and nearby area are a summer home to a large concentration of the noble-looking bald eagle. At the Smoot home, part of which is now a visitor center, are exhibits on the eagle and the park's history. Preservation of the eagle's habitat is the park's primary focus. Tours to view bald eagles are offered Saturdays and Sundays, by reservation only, from mid-June through August. The visitor center and nature store are closed Mondays and Tuesdays during the summer, but the natural area is open every day from 8 A.M. to sunset for hiking and picnicking.

988  (The 3.5-mi. **Boyd's Hole Trail**, a gravel road, leads to the Potomac River for eagle/bird-watching. It is open only from October 1 through March 31.)

ACCESS: From US 301, near Owens, drive west on VA 218 for 3.6 miles and turn right to park entrance.

**Fern Trail** (0.9 mi.), **Poplar Grove Trail** (0.8 mi.), **Laurel Glen Trail** (0.7 mi.), 989–93
**Benchmark Trail** (1.1 mi.), **Cedar Ridge Trail** (1.1 mi.)

LENGTH AND DIFFICULTY: 4.6 miles (7.4 km) combined, round-trip; easy to moderate

FEATURES: old-growth forest, birding, serenity

TRAILHEAD: from the visitor center parking area

DESCRIPTION: These five, color-coded, signed trails are connecting loops in the order listed. They surprisingly ascend and descend on forested hills close to marshlands and slow-moving creeks. The delightful trails weave through a forest of oak, beech, hickory, and tulip poplar among fern beds and mosses. Hawks, warblers, woodpeckers, chickadees, and goldfinches are among the bird species on the trails. Osprey and herons are in the eagle habitat.

USGS MAP: King George

ADDRESS AND INFORMATION: Caledon Natural Area, 11617 Caledon Rd., King George, VA 22485; phone: 540-663-3861; fax: 540-663-0818. Available are park map and nature adventure brochure.


## CHIPPOKES PLANTATION STATE PARK
*Surry County*

Chippokes Plantation State Park was established in 1967, but its 1,683 acres across the James River from Jamestown have an agricultural history of more than 380 years. When Capt. William Powell first patented the land, in 1619, he named the area in honor of an Indian chief, Choupouke, who had befriended the Jamestown settlers. Through the centuries the plantation area has retained its original boundaries and plantation atmosphere. The Chippokes Farm and Forestry Museum, located within the park, features artifacts that describe the history of Virginia's farm environment. The park fronts the James River and has more than 500 acres of cultivated and grazing lands. The large antebellum mansion on the property was constructed in 1854. Facilities include a visitor center, historic buildings, formal gardens, a campground with water and electric hookups, three rental cabins, a swimming pool, picnic area, hiking, biking, horse trails, and a fishing area. The paved **College Run Trail** is accessible for hiking and biking, and 994–96 extends 1.4 miles from the park's visitor center to the mansion. From the mansion parking area are two multi-use trails—the **James River Trail** and the **Lower Chippokes Creek Trail**, each 1 mile long. Horse trails follow the perimeters of farmlands.

USGS MAPS: Surry, Hog Island

ADDRESS AND INFORMATION: Chippokes Plantation State Park, 695 Chippokes Park Rd., Surry, VA 23883; phone: 757-294-3625/3728; fax: 757-294-3299. Available are a brochure with map of the park and a Farm and Forestry Museum brochure.

## FALSE CAPE STATE PARK

*City of Virginia Beach*

The 4,321-acre False Cape State Park is one of the few remaining undeveloped and undisturbed areas on the Atlantic Coast. A haven for waterfowl, the park is part of the Atlantic flyway, which aids a huge migratory bird population in winter. Located at the southeastern tip of the state between Back Bay NWR and the North Carolina state line, the park is a mile-wide barrier spit between the Atlantic Ocean and shallow Back Bay. There are 6 miles of pristine beach with dunes, maritime forests, and marshes. Although isolated, it is not totally undisturbed. There is a gravel road running through the park, providing access to Wash Woods Environmental Education Center. The center can accommodate up to twenty-two people overnight for the purpose of ecological studies. The park offers guided hikes, canoe/kayak tours, and bus tours. Other programs are offered under the joint effort of Virginia Marine Science Museum and the Virginia Institute of Marine Science. To manage the deer and feral hog population the park is closed one week (beginning the first Saturday) in October for the exclusive use of hunters. Recreational activities include fishing (crappie, perch, and bass in Back Bay), primitive camping, hiking, biking, and beachcombing.

ACCESS: From the southern end of US 60 (Pacific Ave.) at the beach in Virginia Beach, cross the bridge, and at 0.8 mile pass the Virginia Marine Science Museum on General Booth Boulevard. At 4.7 miles turn left on SR 615 (Princess Anne Rd.), go 0.8 mile, and turn left on Sandbridge Road. After 5.4 miles turn right on Sandpiper Road and continue 3.7 miles to Little Island Park. It is another 0.2 mile to the entrance of the Back Bay NWR and another 1.3 miles to the refuge visitor center and parking area. From here it is 3.8 miles to the state park entrance by hiking or biking. (From I-64 in west Virginia Beach take VA 407, exit 286 [Indian River Rd.] southeast to cross Princess Anne Rd. at Pungo at 12 mi. Cross the road, and after 1.1 mi. turn left on New Bridge Rd., and follow it 1.2 mi. to Sandbridge Rd. Follow it 3.1 mi. to Sandpiper Rd. and turn right. Follow it as described above.) If traveling by boat, drive south from Pungo on Princess Anne Road for 11.8 miles to Public Landing Road, left, and put in at the boat dock. It is about 6 miles across Back Bay to park dock landings at Barbour Hill, False Cape, and Wash Woods.

997–1006   **False Cape Main Trail** (4.2 mi.), **Barbour Hill Interpretive Trail** (2.4 mi.), **Barbour Hill Beach Trail** (0.7 mi.), **South Inlet Trail** (0.4 mi.), **False Cape Landing Trail** (0.4 mi.), **Ocean Bay Trail** (1 mi.), **Wash Woods Beach Trail** (0.6 mi.), **Wash Woods Interpretive Trail** (0.7 mi.), **Wash Woods Cemetery Trail** (0.5 mi.), **Dudley Island Trail** (3 mi.)

LENGTH AND DIFFICULTY: 13.9 miles (22.3 km) combined, one-way; combined backtracking 27.8 miles (44.5 km); easy

1007   CONNECTING TRAIL: **Back Bay Dike Trail** (3.8 mi.)

FEATURES: bay, Atlantic beach, wildlife, fishing, isolation

TRAILHEADS: three boat docks (see Access, above), and **Back Bay Dike Trail** (see Back Bay NWR in Chapter 8)

INTRODUCTION: Request a brochure about overnight camping, preparations, and regulations before leaving home (see Addresses and Information, below). Call about campsite availability. Free permits are required and can be obtained by calling 800-933-7275. If not accessing the park by boat across Back Bay, hikers may park their vehicles (for a fee) at Little Island Park, 3750 Sandpiper Road, at Sandbridge Beach. Backpack 5.3 miles from Little Island Park to the entrance of the state park through the refuge. Assigned campsites may be another 1.5 miles to 3 miles. Because the campsites are primitive, all water must be carried in and all trash carried out. Open fires are not permitted. Insect repellent, sunscreen, and a shade tarp are essential in hot weather. (Park officials recommend campers ride a bicycle instead of backpacking the 5.3 mi.) Permits are not required for day use. (If day hiking only, you may wish to ride a beach transporter, "The Terra Gator," through False Cape State Park and Back Bay National Wildlife Refuge. There is a fee, and it departs Little Island City Park at 9 A.M. and returns at 1 P.M. It operates weekends only from November 1 to March 31 [phone: 800-933-7275].)

DESCRIPTION: If planning to hike all the trails in the park and the **Back Bay Dike Trail** through the refuge and back, add 10.6 miles for a total of 27.8 miles. Beginning at the refuge visitor center and entering the park, follow the **Barbour Hill Interpretive Trail** for 0.7 mile to the park's contact station. At the park entrance is an observation deck for viewing wildfowl. At the contact station is a primitive rest room and information about the park. A ranger is usually stationed here, and the **Barbour Hill Interpretive Trail** continues right (west). At 0.7 mile a spur trail, east, goes left to Barbour Hill campsite and boat dock, and the interpretive trail bends right to make a loop back to the **Back Bay Dike Trail** (0.3 mi. from the park's entrance).

From the contact station the **False Cape Main Trail** (road) goes left 280 yards and turns right. Ahead is the **Barbour Hill Beach Trail** and beach campsite. Follow the main trail through the park, which is primarily forested with live oak, pine, wax myrtle, and yaupon. In a curve to the right is 0.4-mile **South Inlet Trail**. At 1 mile is an open area with a bog on the left and pleasant views of the bay on the right. After another 1 mile is an intersection where to the right is False Cape Landing campsite in a grassy field, and a boat dock by the bay. To the left, east, it is 0.4 miles on the **False Cape Landing Trail** to another campsite near the beach. Partially paralleling south of the **False Cape Landing Trail** is 1-mile **Ocean Bay Trail**. (False Cape received its name from mariners who falsely identified the slight curve in the beach for Cape Henry at Chesapeake Bay.) These are the last campsites on the journey south.

Continue on the main trail for 1.2 miles to another intersection. Here is a 0.3-

*False Cape Main Trail,
False Cape State Park*

mile road to the right to the ranger's quarters, and the 0.6-mile **Wash Woods Beach Trail** to the ocean on the left. Ahead on the main trail it is 0.1 mile to the **Wash Woods Interpretive Trail** left. It goes 0.2 mile over a high sand dune to an observation deck from which the bay and ocean can be seen with the woods and dunes in between. To the right is a junction with the **Wash Woods Cemetery Trail**, and ahead the interpretive trail goes 0.5 mile over dunes to the ocean. On the main trail it is 80 yards to a fork in the road. To the right it is 0.2 mile to the Wash Woods Environmental Educational Center (8.2 mi. from the refuge visitor center). Except for summer students involved in research at the center's dorms and classrooms, this area is usually quiet, almost ghostly. In this area a human settlement once developed, known mainly for its fishing and hunting. (Wash Woods received its name from the practice of using wood from shipwrecks to construct buildings.)

The most remote part of the park is ahead. From the left fork of the main trail begins the **Dudley Island Trail**; it is 0.4 mile in sand to the **Wash Woods Cemetery Trail**, which crosses the **Dudley Island Trail**. To the right it is 100 yards to the ruins of a Methodist church and a cemetery heavily shaded with live oaks and pine. To the left the **Wash Woods Cemetery Trail** passes over dunes to join the **Wash Woods Interpretive Trail**. The **Dudley Island Trail** continues ahead 2.6 miles to the Atlantic Ocean at the Virginia/North Carolina state line. Motor vehicles are not allowed on the trail; bicycles are. (Bicyclists may have to walk their bikes in some sandy areas.) On a route of sand, shrub, and solitude the trail passes Sheep House Hill and Stormonts Pond. A return loop can be made by hiking the beach to access the **Wash Woods Beach Trail** for a distance of 6.7 miles.

USGS MAP: Knotts Island

ADDRESSES AND INFORMATION: False Cape State Park, 4001 Sandpiper Rd., Virginia Beach, VA 23456 (this is a mailing address, not a park office); phone: 757-412-2300; fax: 757-412-2315. Camping permits can be obtained by calling 800-933-7275. Back Bay National Wildlife Refuge, 4005 Sandpiper Rd. (P.O. Box 6286), Virginia Beach, VA 23456; phone: 757-721-2412. Available are park and refuge map brochures, camping information.

## FIRST LANDING STATE PARK AND NATURAL AREA
*City of Virginia Beach*

Established in 1936 as one of the six original parks in the state system, the former Seashore State Park and Natural Area is now First Landing State Park and Natural Area. Remarkably preserved, it is a natural area and a national natural landmark and has national recreation trails. (The **Bald Cypress Trail** and **Cape Henry Trail** were designated as millennium trails by the White House.) Set in a metropolitan environment, it offers respite for those who wish a campsite in the dunes by the Chesapeake Bay or a cabin in the pines and oaks with tree frogs and songbirds. Rich in ecological succession, the 2,889-acre park has more than 600 species of plants. Many of its animal species are found in the mid-Atlantic states as well as the Carolinas. The area around the park has an impressive history. Near the park's campground are Cape Henry Memorial Landing Place, where the English landed in 1607 before settling in Jamestown, and the Old Cape Henry Lighthouse, the first built by the federal government in 1791. Both are in the Fort Story Military Reservation. On the beach area near the park is the city's Life-Saving Museum of Virginia and Virginia Marine Science Museum. The park includes facilities for boating, fishing, hiking, picnicking, bicycling, and nature study. There is a visitor information center and trail center, a large area of 222 campsites for tents and trailers, housekeeping cabins, and a grocery store. The visitor center is open from 9 A.M. to 6 P.M. in the summer. (Contact the center for hours during other seasons.) The new Chesapeake Bay Center has cooperative programming between university, local citizens, and the city of Virginia Beach. There are historical drama programs at the park's amphitheater about the First Landing. The park has a labyrinth of hiking trails, one of which, the **Cape Henry Trail**, is central to all the others. It extends the entire length of the park to a contact station on 64th Street, 0.2 mile from US 60.

ACCESS: From the junction of US 60 and US 13 near the Chesapeake Bay Bridge-

Tunnel go east on US 60 (Shore Dr.) for 4.5 miles. At a traffic signal turn right on VA 343, the park entrance, or turn left if entering the campground. If coming from the beach area of the city, go north on US 60 on Atlantic Avenue to Shore Drive.

1008–16 **Cape Henry Trail** (6 mi.), **Bald Cypress Trail** (1.5 mi.), **Osmanthus Trail** (3.1 mi.), **Fox Run Trail** (0.3 mi.), **Long Creek Trail** (4 mi.), **High Dune Trail** (0.2 mi.), **Kingfisher Trail** (0.6 mi.), **White Hill Lake Trail** (1.4 mi.), **Osprey Trail** (1.2 mi.)

LENGTH AND DIFFICULTY: 18.3 miles (30 km) combined, round-trip; easy

FEATURES: scenic views, marsh, swamp, wildlife, wildflowers

TRAILHEADS: parking lot at the trail center, or contact station on 64th Street of Atlantic Avenue at the beach

DESCRIPTION: All trails can be accessed from the trail center, but the immediate ones are the **Cape Henry Trail** and the **Bald Cypress Trail**. Connecting trails can be used to form loops of various distances. Camping is not allowed on any trail, and only the **Cape Henry Trail** is open for bicycling. One section of the dark-green-blazed **Cape Henry Trail** goes north and northwest from the trail center to Broad Bay for 1.1 miles. Backtrack. The second section goes southeast from the trail center, passing intersections with the **High Dune Trail**, right at 0.2 mile; the **Bald Cypress Trail** (for the second time), right and left at 0.4 mile; the **Kingfisher Trail**, right at 1.2 miles; and the **White Hill Lake Trail**, right at 2.4 miles. It reaches the contact station on 64th Street at 3.5 miles. Here is drinking water and a rest room. The last section crosses the road, turns right, meanders, but parallels with 64th Street to a parking area at Narrows boat ramp to complete the trail at 6 miles. Backtrack, or have a second vehicle waiting. On this wide, busy trail the treadway is usually dry. It is forested by oak, loblolly pine, sweet gum, ash, and holly.

The self-guiding, red-blazed **Bald Cypress Trail** begins at the trail center at a large trail display sign. It is handicapped accessible. Markers along the trail explain the uniqueness of the swamp forest, lagoons, plants, fish, birds, reptiles, and dunes. Visitors will hear spring peepers on spring nights, bullfrogs and the shrill of kingfishers in the summer, and chattering squirrels almost any season. At 0.3 mile the trail makes a junction with the blue-blazed **Osmanthus Trail** (which makes a loop and returns to the **Bald Cypress Trail** 0.2 mi. to the right). The **Osmanthus Trail** is wide, and sections are heavily draped with Spanish moss, an epiphyte. The trail goes deeply into the park and undulates on the dunes and swales. Some of the flora is the same as that on the **Bald Cypress Trail** and the **Cape Henry Trail**. Upon returning to the **Bald Cypress Trail** there will be more swamp and stately cypress. The trail is completed after crossing the wide **Cape Henry Trail**, passing the white-blazed **High Dune Trail**, and connecting with the yellow-blazed, leg-stretching **Fox Run Trail** to make a right turn for returning to the trail center.

The orange-blazed **Long Creek Trail** does not loop; it is a linear route, as is the **Cape Henry Trail**, to 64th Street. The trail begins on the entrance road, makes a junction with the **Fox Run Trail** at 0.4 mile, and at 1.4 miles makes a junction with the **Kingfisher Trail**, left. (The 0.6-mi. **Kingfisher Trail** serves as an excellent option for making a loop back to the trail center via the **Cape Henry Trail** for 3.6 mi.) At 1.6 miles the trail joins pink-blazed **White Hill Lake Trail**. (It goes 1.4 mi. ahead to a junction with the **Cape Henry Trail** for another loop option of 5.7 mi. to the trail center.) The **Long Creek Trail** turns right and crosses a cement bridge to pass between White Lake on the left and Broad Bay on the right. In this scenic area are sweet pepperbush, sensitive ferns, and wax myrtle. At 2.3 miles is a junction with green-blazed **Osprey Trail**, right. (The **Osprey Trail** descends steeply to a boardwalk and low level by the bay. From here are views of the US 60 bridge, northwest. To the left is a swamp and another boardwalk crossing with views of the bay. The trail meets the **Long Creek Trail** after 1.2 mi.) Continue on the **Long Creek Trail** on a wide old road and pass a damp area at 3.4 miles. Reach a junction with the **Osprey Trail** at 3.5 miles. On this trail and the **Osprey Trail** are multiple cuts through the forest made by bicyclists. Pass a gate and reach 64th Street at 4 miles. It is 0.6 mile left to the contact station, where a loop of 8.3 miles can be made by returning to the trail center on the **Cape Henry Trail**.

USGS MAP: Cape Henry

ADDRESS AND INFORMATION: First Landing State Park and Natural Area, 2500 Shore Dr., Virginia Beach, VA 23451; phone: 757-412-2300. Available for free are flyer with map and campground information, trail pamphlet. Books are on sale at visitor center.


## KIPTOPEKE STATE PARK
*Northampton County*

One of Virginia's newest and evolving state parks, Kiptopeke (meaning "Big Water" in the language of the Accawmack Indians) has 535 acres, purchased in 1992. At the site of the former Virginia Beach to Eastern Shore Ferry, there is nearly 1.5 miles of Chesapeake Bay beach frontage. The park has a campground with hookups, a yurt (part cabin, part tent), a picnic area with shelters, a store, an 1,800-foot-long fishing pier, a swimming area and bathhouse, and a scenic 1-mile **Baywood Trail**. The trail is across the road from the campground southeast to the 1017 beach, in primary and secondary dunes and forest to a hawk observation deck. Nearby is the Virginia Society of Ornithology migratory bird banding station and fields of songbirds and butterflies.

ACCESS: On US 13, 4 miles north of the northern end of the Chesapeake Bay Bridge-Tunnel, turn west on SR 704 (0.2 mi. on SR 645), opposite Cedar Grove.

ADDRESS AND INFORMATION: Kiptopeke State Park, 3540 Kiptopeke Dr., Cape

Charles, VA 23310; phone: 757-331-2267; fax: 757-331-4649. Available are leaflet and park map.

## LEESYLVANIA STATE PARK
*Prince William County*

Leesylvania, meaning "Lee's Woods," is the ancestral homesite of Henry Lee II and his wife, Lucy Grymes Lee. Here they farmed on a plantation, served as gracious colonial hosts, reared eight children, and were buried on one of the farm's mossy knolls. They were the grandparents of Robert E. Lee, whose father, Henry Lee III, was born here in 1756. He is best known as "Light Horse Harry" Lee. He was a member of the Continental Congress, governor of Virginia, and a member of the U.S. Congress. He is also known for his penned eulogy of his friend George Washington, "first in war, first in peace, and first in the hearts of his countrymen."

Today visitors will see only the ruins of the buildings at this noble estate, but its soil is secure, thanks to preservationists Don Curtis and Eleanor Lee Templeman. In 1978 the estate owner, philanthropist Daniel K. Ludwig, donated a large share of the property to the commonwealth for a state park, which opened in 1992. The park is located on a peninsula facing the Potomac River. On the northern side is Occoquan Bay, and on the southern side is Powells Creek. Across the Potomac is Cornwallis Neck in Maryland. The park has picnic grounds, a boat launch for
1018–19  boating and fishing, and trails. A short 0.4-mile loop, the **Bushey Point Trail**, is a stroll among ferns and spicebush to a sandy overlook at the Potomac River. It is near a parking area between the railroad and the boat launch and is handicapped accessible. Another forest trail is 1.4-mile **Powells Creek Trail**. At the trail entrance is a 150-million-year-old petrified stump. On the interpretive loop the trail descends to a scenic overlook of Powells Creek at 0.7 mile. The forest understory has papaw, mountain laurel, black cohosh, and cut-leaved toothwort. Access is at a parking lot, right, after the park entrance. A longer trail is described below.

ACCESS: From I-95, exit 156, south of Woodbridge, and the junction of SR 638 east, drive 1.6 miles to US 1. Turn right, go 0.2 mile, turn left on SR 610 (Neabsco Rd.) for 1.4 miles, and turn right to park entrance. The end of the road is 2.4 miles farther.

1020  **Lee's Woods Trail**
LENGTH AND DIFFICULTY: 2 miles (3.2 km); easy
FEATURES: scenic views, historic site
TRAILHEAD: parking area at the end of the road near picnic area
DESCRIPTION: Pass a monument in honor of Henry Lee III, father of Robert E. Lee, and approach the wide trail on a hillside. (If there is a pamphlet about the trail at a display box, take one for assistance in understanding the marker numbers.) At 0.2 mile is Freestone Point, a high bluff by the Potomac River. Here was an

artillery battery used by the Confederates in the Civil War. Algonquian Indians first used the river bluff to view hostile or friendly traffic. The trail passes views of Occoquan Bay on a side trail. Then, straight, it goes to marker #5, the homesite of John Fairfax. The home burned in 1910. (Fairfax served as an aid to Confederate general James Longstreet during the Civil War. He was with the general from Antietam to Appomattox.) At 1 mile is the homesite of Henry and Lucy Lee's plantation home, which burned in the 1790s. Beyond here and the Lees' gravesite is a descent to the 200-year-old Escaped Gardens. At 1.4 miles is a side trail to view hills cut by a railroad line in 1872. From here complete the loop on a wide trail.

USGS MAPS: Quantico, Indian Head

ADDRESS AND INFORMATION: Leesylvania State Park, 2001 Daniel Ludwig Dr., Woodbridge, VA 22191; phone: 703-670-0372; fax: 703-730-6552. Available are flyer of park information and map.


## MASON NECK STATE PARK
*Fairfax County*

Once the hunting and fishing grounds of Dogue Indians, this historic area's recorded history began in 1755, when George Mason, father of the Bill of Rights of the U.S. Constitution, constructed Gunston Hall, a colonial home. In the 1960s Friends of Mason Neck organized to preserve the peninsula from commercial and residential development. The result was a purchase of 5,000 acres by the Nature Conservancy, from which the park's 1,804 acres were purchased by the state in 1969. Adjoining the park on the northeast is Mason Neck NWR (see Chapter 8). Other adjoining properties are Pohick Bay Regional Park and Gunston Hall Historical Facility. On the southwestern side are Occoquan Bay and Belmont Bay. In addition to the habitat for bald eagle, the park accommodates at least 200 species of songbirds. Other wildlife includes deer, bobcat, and fox. The park has a visitor center, a picnic area, a canoe launch, and trails. The visitor center provides interpretive programs, children's programs, and canoe trips.

ACCESS: From US 1, junction with VA 242 (east to Gunston Hall), drive 4.3 miles to High Point Road, right. Pass the Mason Neck NWR parking lot after 0.7 mile and continue to the visitor center after another 2.9 miles.

**Beach Trail** (0.3 mi.), **Bay View Trail** (1 mi.), **Wilson Spring Trail** (0.7 mi.),     1021–24
**Kane's Creek Trail** (1 mi.)

LENGTH AND DIFFICULTY: 3 miles (4.8 km) combined, round-trip; easy

FEATURES: scenic views, birding, canoeing

TRAILHEAD: parking area at visitor center

DESCRIPTION: At the visitor center stroll 0.2 mile on the paved **Beach Trail** (wheelchair accessible) for a view of Belmont Bay. Then head to the south for hiking red-blazed **Bay View Trail**, an interpretive loop. At the fork choose the right and cross elevated boardwalks in the marsh, an excellent place for birding. At 0.5 mile make a small loop at a scenic bluff before curving north. Some of the vascular plants are papaw, mountain laurel, and blueberries. On the return, right, is yellow-blazed **Wilson Spring Trail**. Follow it through a hardwood forest of oak, ash, beech, and pine. Some of the trees are dead because of the gypsy moth. Cross the entrance road and reach a junction with the blue-blazed **Kane's Creek Trail**. It also makes a loop but has a side trail that requires about 0.2 mile of backtracking from a scenic view of Kane's Creek. Deer may be seen on this trail. Complete the loop through holly, ash, maple, and oak on a parallel with the entrance road to the visitor center.

USGS MAPS: Fort Belvoir, Indian Head

ADDRESS AND INFORMATION: Mason Neck State Park, 7301 High Point Rd., Lorton, VA 22079; phone: 703-550-0960; fax: 703-550-0654. Available are flyer of park facilities and map.


## WESTMORELAND STATE PARK
*Westmoreland County*

The 1,295-acre Westmoreland State Park is located on the northern edge of the Northern Neck, a peninsula between the Rappahannock and Potomac Rivers in the coastal plain. The area is rich in geological history, beginning about 127 million years ago, with remains of ancient marine life fossils found in the beach sediments. The area is also rich in political history. Adjoining the park on the east is Stratford, home of some of the Lee family and the birthplace of Robert E. Lee (see Leesylvania State Park in this chapter). Eight miles west in Wakefield is the birthplace of George Washington. Early owners of the park property were Nathaniel Pope, about 1650, and Thomas Lee, in 1716. The park was established in 1936, one of the original six in the state's park system.

Facilities include a visitor center, a nature center, campgrounds with hookups, primitive cabins in a campground, vacation cabins, an amphitheater, a bathhouse and swimming pool, a picnic area, playgrounds, rowboat and paddle boat rentals, a boat ramp, a camp store, a restaurant (with superb views of the Potomac), group camps, bridle and hiking trails, some facilities for the physically impaired, and the Potomac River Retreat, an upscale overnight facility accommodating up to sixteen. Some of the trails connect, and others serve as connectors between one facility and another. For example, the 0.5-mile, yellow-blazed beach trail goes from near the camp store to the beach and swimming pool area. The 0.4-mile, white-blazed **River Trail** connects west cabins with the west picnic area. The **Laurel Pond Trail**, a 1.4-mile, orange-blazed trail, goes from the parking area on the entrance road (across from Campground C) to the boat ramp. After 0.5 mile at

1025–26

Rock Spring Pond, the 0.5-mile, green-blazed **Rock Spring Trail** connects from 1027 the entrance road (across from the **Turkey Neck Trail**).

ACCESS: From junction of US 301 and VA 3, drive 17.5 miles east on VA 3 to VA 347, and turn left on park road.

**Big Meadow Trail** (0.6 mi.), **Turkey Neck Trail** (3.1 mi.), **Beaver Trail** (0.4 mi.) 1028–30
LENGTH AND DIFFICULTY: 4 miles (6.4 km) combined, round-trip; easy
FEATURES: scenic views, fossils, marsh, wildlife, geological formations
TRAILHEADS: Parking area near nature center, and on entrance road near campground B
DESCRIPTION: The red-blazed **Big Meadow Trail** has changed names and distance
  over the years, but it gets its most recent name from a large low area, partly
  marsh from beaver dams, on the eastern side of the park. Currently the trail is
  an interpretive route with markers keyed to a park brochure. It begins east of
  the visitor center at a median in the road to the east cabins. It descends on an
  old logging road, once an area whose floor was in a Miocene sea. In recent years
  the forest has become broadleaf with cherry, oak, beech, and tulip poplar. Its
  understory is dogwood, holly, sassafras, and papaw. At the last marker the trail
  turns left in a descent to the Potomac River and a sandy beach at 0.6 mile. Here
  are views of the jagged profile of Horsehead Cliffs. Backtrack to the main trail
  and continue ahead over a bridge to an observation deck in the meadow, also
  called Yellow Swamp, a name used because of its yellow hue in the summer.
  Here are shorebirds, and flowering plants such as white mallow, arum, and
  water rose. The blue-blazed **Turkey Neck Trail** begins here right and left. It
  makes a 2.3-mile loop but also has a spur west to pass a campground and exit at
  the entrance road. The loop is bisected by the 0.4-mile **Beaver Trail**. If taking
  the left, follow the edge of the meadow and beaver dams and cross occasional
  boardwalks. Turkeys or hawks may be seen or heard in the area. If not making
  the complete loop, turn left at the first left and pass a spur to Campground C at
  1.7 miles. Continue ahead to the entrance road, turn right, and walk back to the
  point of origin for a total of 4 miles.
USGS MAP: Stratford Hall
ADDRESS AND INFORMATION: Westmoreland State Park, 1650 State Park Rd., Montross, VA 22520; phone: 804-493-8821; fax: 804-493-8329. Available are brochure with park map and **Big Meadow Trail** brochure.


## YORK RIVER STATE PARK
*James City County*

York River State Park encompasses 2,505 acres of a valuable and sensitive estuarine environment where bluffs rise from a mixture of salt and fresh water. The

area has valuable Native American history of interest to archaeologists. For centuries it has been upper farmland bordered with hardwood forests and low brackish creeks. The park's northern border is the York River; through the center of the park is Taskinas Creek. Activities are boating and fishing (with access to the river on SR 605 [Croaker Landing Rd.] off SR 607 [Croaker Rd.] on the northwestern corner of the park). There are picnic areas near the visitor center, a freshwater pond nearby, and a trail network for hiking, biking, mountain biking, and horseback riding. There is a primitive group campground open from April 1 through November 30. Reservations are made through the park office. There are three equestrian trails, the longest of which is 2.6-mile **Meh-Te-Kos Trail**, and four trails are multiple-use for hiking and biking, the longest of which is 6-mile **Marl Ravine Trail**, an advanced mountain bike trail. All the trails connect, and some are short and clustered, which provides distance options for visitors. There is a 0.5-mile paved trail, self-interpreted, for wheelchair users around the day use area. The park is spacious, serene, and not crowded.

1031–32

ACCESS: From I-64, exit 231 (11 mi. north of Williamsburg), take Croaker exit north on SR 607 for 0.7 mile. Turn right on SR 606, go 1.6 miles, and turn left on SR 696 (York River State Park Rd.) for 1.9 miles to visitor center.

1033–40 **Woodstock Pond Trail** (1.3 mi.), **Beaver Trail** (0.6 mi.), **Mattaponi Trail** (1.4 mi.), **Backbone Trail** (1.3 mi.), **Laurel Glen Trail** (1 mi.), **Pamunkey Trail** (0.8 mi.), **Powhatan Forks Trail** (1.4 mi.), **Majestic Oak Trail** (1 mi.)

LENGTH AND DIFFICULTY: 10.3 miles (17 km) combined, round-trip; moderate

FEATURES: scenic views, marsh, fossils, wildlife, historic site

TRAILHEAD: parking area near visitor center

DESCRIPTION: From the visitor center, walk north to views of the river, then turn right, downhill to the pond on the **Woodstock Pond Trail**, a physical fitness trail. It crosses the dam for a circle of the pond, but it also connects to the backcountry trails. The pond is a popular freshwater impoundment for blue gill and largemouth bass. A short trail, closer to the lake, is the **Beaver Trail**. At the eastern end of the dam begins the **Mattaponi Trail**. It affords excellent views of the river and provides access to an area of beach where the Yorktown formation regularly exposes 5-million-year-old marine fossils. The trail curves south in woodlands and crosses a bridge in a pocket marsh. At 1.7 miles the trail ends, but it picks up a short piece of the **Woodstock Pond Trail** before connecting with the **Backbone Trail** on an old woods service road. At 2 miles is a junction with **Laurel Glen Trail**, left, which makes a 1-mile loop in a community of ferns and mountain laurel. Continue on the **Backbone Trail** (which is used by both hikers and bikers) through woods and fields to the **Pamunkey Trail**, left, at 3.7 miles. Follow it 0.8 mile on top of a ridge and a descent to the edge of the York River. An observation tower provides scenic views of marsh and river. Backtrack to a spur trail left at 5.2 miles. Follow the spur 0.2 mile to an intersection for the

**Majestic Oak Trail**, left and right, and the **Powhatan Forks Trail** straight
ahead. Take the left, which, like the **Pamunkey Trail**, is on a ridgeline. It ends
near a large white oak at the river and connects with the northern fork of the
**Powhatan Forks Trail** over a 200-foot-long boardwalk in a tidal marsh. Follow
the **Powhatan Forks Trail** south to its eastern fork, left, for another view of the
river. Backtrack on the fork to the main **Powhatan Forks Trail** and turn left. It
connects with the **Majestic Oak Trail** at 8 miles. Turn left for a quick access to
the **Backbone Trail**, right and left. Take the right, follow it to the **Woodstock
Pond Trail**, take a left to parallel the entrance road, and return to the visitor
center at 9.7 miles.

USGS MAP: Gressitt

### Taskinas Creek Trail                                                             1041
LENGTH AND DIFFICULTY: 1.7 miles (2.7 km) round-trip; moderate
FEATURES: marsh, wildlife, wildflowers, birding
TRAILHEAD: parking area at visitor center
DESCRIPTION: Quiet hikers may see deer, songbirds, herons, and hawks. After 0.2
   mile on an old road, parallel to the main entrance road and through a field, turn
   right into the forest. At 0.4 mile are two huge twin oaks, and at 0.6 mile is a
   kiosk with information about the wildlife and brackish water of Taskinas Creek.
   Cross a 280-foot-long boardwalk through marsh cordgrass. Here, as at all tidal
   marshes, part of the area changes from aquatic to terrestrial twice daily because
   of the tides. Ascend and reach a scenic overlook of the marsh at 0.8 mile. Begin
   a climb and curve south to return through mountain laurel, galax, and open
   hardwood forest.

USGS MAP: Gressitt
ADDRESS AND INFORMATION: York River State Park, 5526 Riverview Rd., Williamsburg, VA 23188; phone: 757-566-3036; fax: 757-566-4013. Available are brochure
   on facilities with trail map and the "Life on Edge" brochure for trail guide.


# Natural Area Preserves

The Virginia Natural Area Preserves Act was systemized by the Natural Heritage
Program in 1989. It made the Department of Conservation and Recreation (DCR)
responsible for the establishment and management of a Natural Area Preserves
program. Such a direction meant long-term protection of the state's biodiversity.
In 1990 the DCR began management of areas in the state that had rare or declining
plants, animals, and unique terrain and minerals. Assisting these efforts was the
passage of the 1992 Virginia Park and Natural Areas Bond. Now the state owns
eighteen preserves, and sixteen others are owned by local government agencies,
universities, or organizations such as the Audubon Society and The Nature Con-

servancy. Those not owned by the state have a contract with the state to protect the property's future activities. In 2002 the thirty-four sites encompassed 23,200 acres of public and private properties and more than 150 protected rare species. Thirteen of the Natural Area Preserves are currently open to the public, and some have stewards or managers. Some of the areas are closed for protection of sensitive species or habitat or for more scientific study of the site. Those that are open may have some restrictions. Signs may include all or some of the following: No camping, fires, horses, bicycles, ATVs, firearms, unleashed pets, hunting, fishing, trapping, alcohol, removal of plants, animals, minerals, or historic artifacts. Public access is from sunrise to sunset and usually year round. If a site is private property, the visitor would need to contact the owner. Only preserves with trails and owned by the state have been selected for inclusion in this chapter.

ADDRESS AND INFORMATION: Virginia Department of Conservation and Recreation, 217 Governor St., Third Floor, Richmond, VA 23219; phone: 804-786-7951. A preserve guide and fact sheet are available. You will need the Adobe Acrobat reader to review or print from the following: <www.der.state.va.us/dnh/preserv.htm>.

**Buffalo Mountain Natural Area Preserve** has 1,000 acres in Floyd County and is
1042 owned by DCR. From the gated parking area ascend on a gravel road (**Buffalo Mountain Trail**) 0.7 mile to the summit (elev. 3,971 ft.). The spectacular views from the wind-swept dome include the Blue Ridge Mountain range to the east and mountains southwest in North Carolina. The summit has six communities of rare plants in Virginia. One is mountain rattlesnake root (*Prenanthes roanesis*). On the side of the summit lives the giant mealybug (*Puto kosztarabi*), found nowhere else in the world. The preserve system staff request that visitors stay on the rocky areas and not trample the mosses, grasses, and plants. Backtrack.

STEWARD INFORMATION: phone: 276-676-5673

ACCESS: On the Blue Ridge Parkway drive north from US 58 2.5 miles to mp 174, and turn left on SR 799 (Conner Grove Rd.). (If driving south from VA 8 at Tuggle Gap it is 11.3 mi.) Follow SR 799 1.4 miles to Halls Store Road, left. After another 1.4 miles turn left on SR 727 (Moles Rd.). After 1.3 miles (of which may be a gravel road) arrive in a narrow gap; turn sharply right, ascend, and arrive at a parking space after 1.1 miles.

**Bush Mill Stream Natural Area Preserve** has 103 acres in Northumberland
1043 County and is owned by DCR. Here is 1-mile **Deep Landing Trail** near a tidal area where the stream empties into Great Wicomico River. The area has both fresh and tidal waters. One rare species, a tiny shrimp-like animal, is known here as *Stygobromus indentatus*. In a variety of wetlands there are many species of birds, and one of Virginia's largest great blue heron rookeries is here. Some years as many as 200 pairs of herons raise their young here.

STEWARD INFORMATION: phone: 804-445-9117

ACCESS: From Warsaw take US 360 east 18 miles to Heathsville. Turn right (south) onto VA 201 and go 3.3 miles to SR 642; turn left near a church. After about 0.3 mile the preserve entrance is left, and the parking area is 0.1 mile on a gravel road.

**Hughlett Point Natural Area Preserve** with 204 acres is also in Northumberland County and owned by DCR. From the parking lot follow **Winter Water Trail** briefly 1044–45 to **Bay Shore Trail**, right, and at 0.6 mile arrive at Chesapeake Bay beach. Along the way are wildlife-viewing platforms and interpretive signs. This is a habitat for bald eagle, osprey, and northern harrier. The threatened northeastern beach tiger beetle (*Cicindela dorsalis dorsalis*) is here; to exist the beetles must remain undisturbed.

STEWARD INFORMATION: phone: 804-684-7577

ACCESS: From Kilmarnock, drive north 4 miles on VA 200 SR 606 and turn right (east). After 2 miles to SR 605 turn right (south) and go about 2 miles to the preserve parking area, left.

**North Landing River Natural Area Preserve** consists of 3,441 acres in three sections in Virginia Beach and is owned by DCR. (Nearby there are more than 10,000 acres protected by a coalition of public and private conservation organizations.) There are white cedar and pond pine forests. Bird-watching is popular. There is a 0.5-mile boardwalk pedestrian trail, and a canoe trail into a pocosin and freshwater tidal marsh.

STEWARD INFORMATION: phone: 757-925-2318

ACCESS: From I-64 in Chesapeake, drive south on VA 168 (Battlefield Blvd.) for 9 miles. After passing Hickory High School on the left, turn left on Hickory Road. Drive 0.8 mile until it ends at Centerville Turnpike. Turn right and almost immediately turn left on Head of River Road. Drive 6.5 miles until the road forks and bears left. Go 0.2 mile until the road ends at Blackwater Road. Turn left and go 0.6 mile to the preserve entrance, right. Then drive 0.7 mile to the end of a gravel access road, parking area, and trailhead.

**Pinnacle Natural Area Preserve** has 435 acres in Russell County and is owned by DCR. The Pinnacle is a towering 400-foot rock outcrop that has an assortment of geological features, including bedrock derived of corals, algae, and other marine organisms originating about a half million years ago. In the area are at least nine rare plants. One is Canby's mountain-lover (*Paxistima canbyii*). Park at the first parking lot and walk across the footbridge if the creek is flooded. After 0.8 mile on the **Big Cedar Creek Trail** pass the second parking lot. Follow the trail 0.3 mile to 1046–49 Big Falls, then 0.2 mile to a three-way trail split. Scenic **Pinnacle Overlook Trail** is right 0.1 mile. **Clinch River Trail** is 0.2 mile and **Cooper Ridge Trail** is 0.5 mile left. Backtrack.

STEWARD INFORMATION: phone: 276-676-5673

ACCESS: On US 19 Bus in Lebanon, drive west on VA 82. After 1.1 miles turn right on SR 640 (Glade Hollow Rd.). After 4.2 miles turn left on gravel road SR 721. Drive 0.8 mile to the parking lot, left.

**Poor Mountain Natural Area Preserve** encompasses 925 acres in Roanoke County. It is owned by DCR. Unique to this mountain (3,000 ft. elevation) is the world's largest population of the brilliant yellow piratebush (*Buckleya disticho-phylla*), a rare shrub. (In smaller units the shrub is found in Tennessee and North Carolina.) The mountain is named for its impoverished soils, developed from metamorphosed sandstone bedrock. There is a short hiking trail, but a longer distance is planned. (Although open to the public the preserve may periodically be closed for resource protection.)

STEWARD INFORMATION: phone: 540-265-5234 (or 804-692-0479)

ACCESS: From US 460 at Glenvar (near I-81, exit 132) take Poor Mountain Road (SR 612) across a bridge of the Roanoke River and drive 7 miles, some of which are on sharp switchbacks in ascent to a gate and parking area at the top of the mountain.

## State Forests

Virginia has eleven state forests with a total of 50,636 acres. They are managed for the purpose of multiple usage to include timber production, hunting, fishing, wildlife control, watershed protection, and forestry research. Within four of the forests are state parks for other recreational activities such as camping, hiking, picnicking, and swimming. The parks are Holliday Lake in Appomattox-Buckingham State Forest (19,535 acres); Twin Lakes in Prince Edward-Gallion State Forest (6,970 acres); Pocahontas in Pocahontas State Forest (5,783 acres); and Bear Creek Lake in Cumberland State Forest (16,233 acres). Although the forests have many gated roads for unnamed day hikes, only the Cumberland and Appomattox-Buckingham have designated specific and long routes with names.

1050    The Appomattox-Buckingham route is 12-mile **Carter Taylor Multi-Use Trail**. A parking access is in Holliday Lake State Park (described earlier in this chapter). The road-trail is mainly on public or forest roads with a short section in Holliday Lake State Park. Users (equestrians, bicyclists, hikers) will pass through replanted and protected areas of mixed hardwoods and pines. Wildlife includes deer, turkey, and small game. For detailed information and map, contact Appomattox-Buckingham State Forest, Rt. 3, Box 133, Dillwyn, VA 23936; phone: 434-983-2175. Another forest, 278-acre Zoar State Forest in King William County, has a 1-mile interpretive trail among old-growth trees by the Mattaponi River. To reach it from us 360 at Aylett, go north 1.6 miles on SR 600 to a parking area on the right. The **Willis River Trail** with 15.2 miles is described below.

## CUMBERLAND STATE FOREST
*Cumberland County*

### Willis River Trail

1051

LENGTH AND DIFFICULTY: 15.2 miles (24.3 km); moderate

FEATURES: wildlife, streams, historic site, wildflowers, scenery

TRAILHEADS: For the northern trailhead, leave the town of Cumberland (at us 60) and go north on SR 622 for 1.8 miles. Take the right fork on SR 623 and go 2.6 miles; bear right on SR 624 for 1.2 miles to SR 608. After 2.2 miles look for a narrow dirt road on the right, and go 0.4 mile to the parking area. For the southern trailhead go west 3.1 miles on us 60 from the town of Cumberland and turn right on SR 629. Follow it 3 miles to a parking and picnic area on the right at Winston Lake.

INTRODUCTION: A joint project by the Virginia Department of Forestry and the Old Dominion Appalachian Trail Club, the trail is marked by white blazes and usually receives annual maintenance. It is entirely on state property, but camping is not permitted. However, the trail has a short connector to Bear Creek Lake State Park, which does have a campground. State roads bisect the trail at six places, thus making short hikes an option. In a forest of hardwoods and pine, hikers are likely to see wildlife.

DESCRIPTION: Across the river from the parking area at the northern end is a swinging footbridge, but this is not in the trail's direction. Instead, go right from the parking area through patches of clubmoss and by large groves of mallow near the river marsh. At 0.7 mile reach SR 615. Turn left, cross Reynolds Creek bridge, and turn right off the road. Ascend and descend on low ridges and coves among squirrel cups, Christmas fern, and tall beech trees. At 1.7 miles rock-hop the creek in a scenic area, and slightly ascend. Pass near the stream again at 2.1 miles and 2.4 miles, then follow an old logging road to gravel SR 224 at 2.9 miles. Turn right and follow the road for 0.6 mile to turn left at a forest road gate. Enter a flat damp area with ferns and honeysuckle, cross Bonbrook Creek, and arrive at paved SR 224 at 4.8 miles. (Parking space is nearby.)

Descend on a gentle path to Willis River at 5.3 miles. Go upstream on an alluvial floodplain among oak, river birch, spicebush, sycamore, and papaw (which has ripe edible fruit in early September). Follow the boundary line of 27-acre Rock Quarry Natural Area. At 6.3 miles reach a grassy road turnaround. Turn left to Rock Quarry Road. (Here is an exit, left, for 0.4 mi. to SR 623.) Turn right on the grassy road and follow the trail 0.2 mile to another cul-de-sac. Enter the forest and descend through oaks and beech to a bluff and Willis River at 6.8 miles. Bear left, leaving the river edge, and go 0.4 mile before returning to the riverbank. Again bear left from the river; pass an enormous oak, and go through a floodplain with sparse understory for 0.1 mile to the riverbank. Follow upstream, turn left on grassy road, go 180 yards, turn right off road at 7.7 miles, and reach Horn Quarter Creek. Follow along the edge of the scenic rocky stream to a crossing. Ascend to a cul-de-sac of seeded road. Turn left and follow road past a large oak and grazing field on the right and a deep pit on the left. Turkey, deer, pheasant, dove, and quail are often seen here. Turn right off road with pines at 8.3 miles, onto an overgrown road. Reach SR 622 at 9 miles. Turn left for 65 yards to a junction of SR 622 and SR 623.

Follow SR 622 (or under a power line if not overgrown) for 0.5 mile to a junction with SR 629 (Oak Hill Rd.) at 9.5 miles. (Here SR 629 leads 0.8 mi. right to Bear Creek Lake State Park and 2.1 mi. farther south on SR 629 to the southern trailhead at Winston Lake.) Follow the trail into a stand of pine and cross a forest road at 10.2 miles. (To the right on the forest road it is 0.3 mi. to Bear Creek Lake State Park campground at paved road. From here it is 0.3 mi. left, downhill, on the road to the beach and concession stand. To the right is the campground, with showers, and 0.3 mi. to the park's entrance off SR 629 at the lake's dam.)

Continuing on the **Willis River Trail**, reach a junction with a spur trail, right, at 10.7 miles. (The spur trail is 0.4 mi. from the park's beach, parking area, and concession stand, accessed by either the park's **Lakeside Trail** or part of the **Pine Knob Trail**. On the way it passes the park's **Circumferential Trail**.) The **Willis River Trail** crosses a small stream and at 10.8 miles begins a parallel with Little Bear Creek, to cross it at 11.4 miles. The area has a number of patches of pinesap, ladies tresses, and papaw. Large river birch and sycamore are prominent. Raccoon, deer, squirrel, and songbirds are in the area. Follow around a steep bluff, return to edge of Little Bear Creek, turn right, and pass an open spring under large beeches at 12.1 miles. At 12.2 miles cross Bear Creek Forest Road. (On this road it is 1.8 mi. right to SR 629.)

Cross Bear Creek at 12.4 miles, where large bunches of liverwort are on the rock ledges. Follow open gated forest road to Booker Forest Road, turn left, and follow it to cross paved SR 628 at 13.3 miles. (It is 2 mi. left on SR 628 to US 60, and 1.2 mi. right to SR 629 and entrance to Cumberland State Forest office.) Descend gradually to a damp area with patches of yellow root and cardinal flowers near a brook at 13.6 miles. At 14.6 miles cross a stream in a rocky area near an old field of young saplings and gentian. Proceed left (south) of the 10-acre Winston Lake on a slope through acres of clubmoss in a mixed forest. At a junction with old CCC walkway turn right (there is a parking area across the road, left); descend on steps, and cross a footbridge to a parking and picnic area at 15.2 miles at exit to SR 629. (It is 3 mi. left [south] to US 60, and 1.1 mi. right [north] to SR 628. Another 1 mi. north on SR 629 is park entrance.)

ADDRESSES AND INFORMATION: Cumberland State Forest, Rt. 1, Box 139, Cumberland, VA 23040; phone: 804-492-4121; access is at the intersection of SR 628 and SR 629. Zoar State Forest, P.O. Box 246, Aylett, VA 23009; phone: 804-769-2655/2962; access is on SR 608, 0.2 mile northwest of intersection of US 360 and SR 600. Appomattox-Buckingham State Forest trailhead is in Holliday Lake State Park, described earlier in this chapter; phone: 434-248-6308. Virginia Division of Forestry, Box 3758, Charlottesville, VA 22903; phone: 434-977-6555.

# PART IV. County and Municipality Trails

*Two roads diverged in a wood, and I—*
*I took the one less traveled by,*
*and that has made all the difference.*
ROBERT FROST (1874–1963)

# 12. County Parks and Recreation Areas

Of Virginia's ninety-five counties, seventy-seven have parks and recreation departments. Locally operated, they are usually administered by a county board of commissioners, supervisors, or other government agencies. In planning their parks and recreation areas they may request assistance from the state's Division of Planning and Recreation Resources. The division can provide help with water conservation, environmental regulations, greenways, grants, and programs. Depending on funding and demographics, the counties may have a single park with basic facilities or multiple parks with multiple facilities and services, such as the 300 parks in Fairfax County. A few counties and towns combine their resources, such as Floyd County. Another combination, though governed separately, consists of the multiple parks of Richmond and Henrico County or Roanoke City and County in a metropolitan environment. About 25 percent of the county parks have trail systems—trails other than physical fitness or connector trails between facilities. They are described in this chapter. For a directory of the state's county and city recreation departments, call the Department of Conservation and Recreation in Richmond, 804-786-2556

## Albemarle County

Scenic Albemarle County is in central Virginia where gentle rolling pasture and farmlands support dairy and beef herds, estates, fields of race horses, apple and peach orchards, vineyards, and its upland boundary with the Shenandoah National Park/Skyland Drive. Included in the county are historic Monticello, home of President Thomas Jefferson; Ash Lawn-Highland, home of President James Monroe; and John Mitchi Tavern, one of Virginia's oldest homesteads. Charlottesville is the county seat and the location of the University of Virginia, founded by Thomas Jefferson. The county has six parks: Beaver Creek, Chris Greene, Darden Tower, Totier Creek, Mint Springs Valley, and Walnut Creek. Ivy Creek Natural Area is described under Charlottesville in Chapter 13.

## MINT SPRINGS VALLEY PARK

The valley, with a series of three small, terraced lakes, is surrounded by mountains on three sides. The water supply for the town of Crozet flowed from this valley until 1971, when Beaver Creek Reservoir was constructed. Since then the park has become an excellent area for hiking the serene old mountain roads through orchards and by ruins of old cabins. Activities at the park include swimming, fishing, boating, and nature study.

ACCESS: From I-64, exit 107, at US 250, go 1.7 miles to VA 240. Turn left and go 1.4 miles to Crozet. Pass under railroad bridge, turn left, and go 1.8 miles on SR 788, which becomes SR 684 to reach the park, left.

1052–55   **Lake Trail** (0.5 mi.), **Fire Trail** (1.8 mi.), **Big Survey Trail** (0.8 mi.), **Hollow Trail** (0.5 mi.)

LENGTH AND DIFFICULTY: 3.6 miles (5.8 km) combined, round-trip; moderate
FEATURES: scenic views, wildlife, historic site, tranquility, wildflowers
TRAILHEAD: behind the beach area
DESCRIPTION: The loop **Lake Trail** from the picnic shelter passes to the south of all three lakes. For the **Fire Trail**, begin northwest of the beach area and ascend on a wide trail past cottonwood trees and an old stone chimney. At 0.5 mile is a junction with the **Big Survey Trail**, right. (It loops up a rocky slope of Bucks Elbow Mountain and rejoins the **Fire Trail**.) Continue ahead on two saddles and a knoll to another junction of the **Big Survey Trail** and begin a descent. Reach a junction with the **Hollow Trail** at 1.1 miles. (The **Hollow Trail** connects from the picnic area along a stream between Bucks Elbow Mountain and Little Yellow Mountain.) Continue to 1.4 miles, where a sharp descent begins for a return to the picnic area. Vascular plants in the area are wildflowers, locust, walnut, cherry, maple, and tree of heaven.
USGS MAP: Crozet
ADDRESS AND INFORMATION: Albemarle County Parks and Recreation, 401 McIntire Rd., Charlottesville, VA 22901; phone: 434-296-5844. Available is a trail leaflet with map.

## WALNUT CREEK PARK

This park is a special and popular place for mountain bicycling. Although the park is promoted as a park with 15 miles of multi-use trails, bicycling dominates the trail usage. There are not any pedestrian or equestrian signs or trail user symbols other than bicycling. However, hikers and joggers are welcome and the park brochure requests the International Mountain Bicycling Association's rules be

1056   followed. This allows naturalists strolling on **Luke's Loop Trail** to view the scenic lake at leisure. The trails are well designed and are made possible by hundreds of hours of volunteer work. The network of trails pass by historic sites and cross bridges among rolling hills and through a mixed hardwood forest. In addition to bicycling, there are facilities for fishing and picnicking, and in the summer there is a beach for swimming near the beach house.

The trails are color coded and difficulty is rated as easy, intermediate, and most difficult. Users have greater options from the first parking lot. If using this lot, begin near the upper lake waters on **Entrance Trail/Jungle Trail** (1 mi.). It forks to cross a stream and connect with **Luke's Loop Trail** (1 mi.), or stays right to make an immediate connection with **Extreme Sports Trail** (1.5 mi.), south, or **Blazing Saddles Trail** (1 mi.), north. It also continues upstream a few yards to cross and connect with the park's longest trail, **Wilkins Way Trail** (4 mi., the only trail with most difficult routing). Within this western network are **Bike Factory Trail** (1 mi. and north near the park's gatehouse), short **Wahoo Way Trail** (0.25 mi.), **Fifth Pillar Trail** (1.3 mi.), **Chimney Trail** (0.7 mi. and named for its passage near an old homestead), and **Colleen's Corners Trail** (0.5 mi.). At the second parking lot there is access for the frequently chosen **Blue Wheel Trail** (2.2 mi. with a crossing of the dam and two loops to the south). At the second parking lot is also the south end of **Extreme Sports Trail** and access to the **Entrance Trail/ Jungle Trail**. It connects with the first parking lot and along the way there is the **Kid's Trail** (0.25 mi.).

USGS MAP: Alberene

ACCESS: From I-64, exit 118, at south Charlottesville, drive south 6 miles on US 29 to Red Hill Rd. (SR 708), left. After 2.7 miles turn right on SR 631 at Olivet United Methodist Church. After 0.5 mile turn left to arrive at the first parking lot.

1057–67

# Arlington County

Arlington County, the state's smallest (26 sq. mi.), formed in 1920, is land that was ceded to the federal government as part of the District of Columbia in 1789, then retroceded to Virginia in 1846. It is notable for its history and national landmarks: Arlington House, Arlington National Cemetery, Fort Myer, Washington National Airport, the Pentagon, and George Washington Memorial Parkway. It also has outstanding recreational areas. There are two northern Virginia regional parks and more than ninety-four county parks, forty of which have designated hike/ bike trail systems with a 7.5-mile bicycle trail along Four Mile Run (see Chapter 9). Additionally, a portion of the **Washington and Old Dominion (W&OD) Rail-road Trail** follows Four Mile Run from Alexandria through the county to the city of Falls Church and beyond. There is also a 5.5-mile bicycle trail along I-66 that joins the **W&OD Railroad Trail**. (It is recommended that hikers unfamiliar with the parks and trail network in Arlington first go to the Lubber Run Community

Center office at 300 N. Park Dr. for orientation with the public open-space map. The office also has current information on area campgrounds.) The first three trails described below end at the Potomac River.

USGS MAPS: Falls Church, Washington West, Annandale, Alexandria

### GLEBE ROAD PARK

1068  Gulf Branch Nature Center is here, an excellent educational facility. The **Gulf Branch Nature Trail** extends 1.3 miles in a 37-acre, dense forest with tall poplar and oak along Gulf Branch to the Potomac River (0.5 mi. southeast of the Chain Bridge). This is a serene area amid the continual sounds of jetliners, where chipmunks, squirrels, raccoons, owls, and songbirds ignore the noise pollution. Wildflowers are prominent.

ACCESS: From the junction of US 29 (Lee Hwy.) and Military Road, follow Military Road north to 3608 Military Road; phone: 703-558-2340.

### ZACHARY TAYLOR PARK

1069  The 1.1-mile **Donaldson Run Trail** leads under tall hardwoods, along a stream valley, to the Potomac River. The 44-acre park has a 1.5-mile hiking/biking trail that extends from Military Road west to Yorktown Boulevard. The forest has an understory of haw, maple, and spicebush. (Adjoining the park near the river is Potomac Overlook Regional Park. See Chapter 14.)

ACCESS: From junction of US 29 (Lee Hwy.) and Military Road, follow Military Road to 30th Street. Turn right on 30th Street to the parking area.

### WINDY RUN PARK

1070  In a park of 13 acres the 1.4-mile **Windy Run Trail** descends to the Potomac River, only 1.5 miles upriver from Key Bridge. A remarkable trail, it begins from the parking area in a cul-de-sac of Kenmore Street. It crosses a stream three times under large oak, poplar, and beech. Wild hydrangea, spicebush, and goat's-beard adorn the trail border. A surprise awaits the hiker at the river, where a glistening stream of water falls 45 feet in a flume. A descent can be made on the right of the stream by a railing to an enchanting part of the forest below.

ACCESS: From the George Washington Memorial Parkway take Spout Run Parkway to Lorcom Lane and go three blocks to Kenmore Street, right.

### GLENCARLYN PARK

1071–72  Long Branch Nature Center is here. Within 98 acres, the **Long Branch Nature Trail** and the **Glencarlyn Park Trail** connect and provide 1.5 miles of trail to the

8-mile **Arlington County Bicycle Trail**. (The bicycle trail can also be hiked along 1073 Four Mile Run to facilities such as picnic areas, lighted tennis courts, and comfort stations in other parks—Barcroft, Bluemont, Bon Air, and East Falls Church.)

ACCESS: From Arlington Boulevard (US 50) turn south to 625 South Carlin Springs Road, between Northern Virginia Doctors' Hospital and Glencarlyn Elementary School; phone: 703-558-2742.

ADDRESS AND INFORMATION: Arlington County Parks and Recreation, #1 Courthouse Plaza, Suite 414, 2100 Clarendon Blvd., Arlington, VA 22201; phone: 703-358-4747.

# Campbell County

### LONG ISLAND PARK

Away from the noise of interstate highways and the smog of the cities is Long Island Park on the banks of the Staunton River. Only the occasional zephyr-like sound of a Norfolk & Western train competes with the gurgling rapids below a basin of still water. Families come here to fish, picnic at shelters (which can be reserved), and play games in a grassy meadow. From a parking area near the highway the 1.2-mile **Long Island Trail** follows the riverside to Hill Creek. A 1074 return can loop past a railroad trestle and garlands of honeysuckle on red cedar and redbud to the picnic area and riverside for a total of 2.4 miles. This bucolic park is a joint project of the Virginia Department of Game and Inland Fisheries, Virginia Commission on Outdoor Recreation, and Campbell County Recreation Department.

USGS MAP. Long Island

ACCESS: From Gladys on US 501 follow SR 761 south for 6.6 miles; from Brookneal on US 501 follow SR 633 west for 7.6 miles; from Cody on VA 40 follow SR 640 north for 5 miles to a turn left on SR 639 for 0.8 mile, and right on SR 761 for 1.8 miles.

ADDRESS AND INFORMATION: Campbell County Recreation Department, P.O. Box 369, Rustburg, VA 24588; phone: 434-332-9570.

# Chesterfield County

### HENRICUS HISTORICAL PARK

In 1986 the resurrection of the Citie of Henricus on the James River began with the establishment of Henricus Historical Park. It was financed by Chesterfield County, Henrico County, Henrico Doctors' Hospital, the city of Richmond, Tarmac-LoneStar Inc., and others. With a wealth of history, the 1.3-mile **Henricus** 1075 **Trail** is a wide, scenic route from Dutch Gap boat launch to the high bluff of

Henricus. Sir Thomas Dale and his crew built an outpost here in 1611. The next year he established Mount Malady, a forty-bed hospital (retreat) for the colonists. He also planned a university, but all his dreams were lost in the Indian massacre of 1622. The trail, with occasional elevated walkways, is shaded by river birch and sycamore to observation decks, interpretive signs, monuments, and superior views of the river. Backtrack for a total of 2.6 miles.

USGS MAPS: Dutch Gap, Drewrys Bluff

ACCESS: From I-95, exit 61, at VA 10 (toward Hopewell) go 0.2 mile on VA 10 (first traffic light) and turn left on SR 732 (Old Stage Rd.) and go 2 miles to parking area by the river.


## POINT OF ROCKS PARK

Opened in 1980, the park has 182 acres of diverse natural areas and historical significance. The area has been the site of Native American villages, a colonial plantation, a customs wharf, major Civil War encampments, and red ocher mining. It now provides multiple recreational facilities for fall fields and courts, picnicking, and heritage and nature study of the Ashton Creek Marsh.

ACCESS: From I-95, exit 61, at VA 10 (toward Hopewell) take VA 10 east for 5 miles to SR 746. Turn right and go 2 miles to the park.

1076–78 **Ashton Creek Trail** (0.5 mi.), **Woodthrush Trail** (0.7 mi.), **Cobbs Wharf Trail** (1.3 mi.)

LENGTH AND DIFFICULTY: 2.5 miles (4 km) combined, round-trip; easy

FEATURES: historic site, marsh, wildlife, wildflowers

TRAILHEAD: At visitor cabin from nearest picnic parking area

DESCRIPTION: Begin at the homestead display and enter the forest at the trail signs. The **Ashton Creek Trail** is a self-guiding nature study trail and crosses Cobblestone Creek where there are quartzite stones. It connects with a loop of the **Woodthrush Trail**, after which it connects with the **Cobbs Wharf Trail**, right and left. (To the right the trail ends at Ruffin Mill Rd.) Follow the trail left to Ashton Creek Marsh. A spur trail is on boardwalks to an observation deck in the marsh of arum, cattails, and cordgrass. Return to the main trail, reach another observation deck at 0.8 mile with views of the marsh, and again at 1.3 miles. To the right is a Civil War battery site, and ahead are views of the Appomattox River. Return by a meadow on the left.

USGS MAPS: Chester, Hopewell


## ROCKWOOD PARK

The 162-acre Rockwood Park, Chesterfield County's first park, opened in 1975. Its facilities are expansive with multiple picnic areas, ball courts and fields, and a unique area for community vegetable garden plots. In the undeveloped natural area of the park there is wildlife in a mixed hardwood forest and a swamp area along Falling Creek. The park staff provide extensive programs for nature study. The **Rockwood Nature Trail** is actually a network of easy, color-coded paths. 1078-A Entrance is at the trails parking area. Follow the YCC sign on white blazes. At 0.1 mile is a blue-marked trail to the left and a green-marked trail on the right. The white-blazed trail ends at 0.3 mile, and an orange-blazed trail goes left and right through mature hardwoods. There are clubmosses, ferns, and wildflowers. If taking the right, follow the edge of the lake and reach a paved road near a physical fitness area at 0.7 mile. Follow the road, right, back to the lake and pick up the orange-marked trail at 1.2 miles. Pass a marsh, explore three side trails to the left, and reach a gravel road at 1.9 miles. Return to the parking area at 2.1 miles. Mileage for all connecting trails is a total of 3.4 miles.

USGS MAP: Chesterfield

ACCESS: From US 360 and SR 653 junction, southwest of Richmond, take SR 653 north for 0.1 mile and turn right to park entrance. Continue for 0.4 mile to parking area for trail entrance.

ADDRESS AND INFORMATION: Chesterfield County Parks and Recreation, P.O. Box 40, Chesterfield, VA 23832; phone: 804-748-1623. Available are brochures and maps on all parks.


# Clarke County

### CLARKE COUNTY PARK

The park's mission statement is to "provide quality and wholesome recreational opportunities for all citizens of Clarke County." A visit to this outstanding park soon illustrates it succeeds in its mission. Among its twenty facilities are sports fields (with emphasis on Little League), tennis courts, playground, swimming pool, and picnic shelters. Programs range from arts and crafts to aerobics, general interest workshops, gardening, social dinners and dances, and trips and tours.

Circling the park complex is beautiful and paved 1.8-mile **Park Trail**. An easy 1079 access is from the parking area near the swimming pool; hike clockwise. Pass the tennis court and at 0.3 mile the recreational center. After Little League fields enter a forest of mixed hardwoods and conifers. At 0.7 mile is an open meadow, and at 0.8 mile are rows of pine followed by an electrical voltage station. There is a scenic pastoral area near agricultural fields at 1.5 miles. Pass hedges, cross the entrance road, and return to the parking area at 1.8 miles.

ACCESS: The park is located on the south side of West Main Street (VA 7 Bus) 0.3 mile east of VA 7 divide in Berryville.

ADDRESS AND INFORMATION: Clarke County Parks and Recreation, 225 Al Smith

Circle, Berryville, VA 22611; phone: 540-955-5140; fax: 540-955-5049. "The Core," a publication of programs and activities, is available.

## Fairfax County

The Fairfax County Park Authority maintains more than 386 parks and recreational facilities (including 5 nature/visitor centers and 8 indoor recreation centers) for one of the finest county park systems in Virginia and in the nation.

In 1950, when the Virginia General Assembly passed the Park Authorities Act, the Fairfax County Board of Supervisors began immediately to adopt a resolution for creating a park authority. Since then more than 19,326 acres have been acquired to provide the best in services to the citizens of the metropolitan area. In addition to the usual sports facilities and bicycle routes, there is a park with a working farm of the 1930s, an indoor ice rink, restored landmarks, and historic sites. Other facilities include a horticultural center and eight golf courses. In addition to an incomparable record of wise and effective management, the county has developed a master plan for facilities to serve future generations. Hikers may wish to examine the master plan and the *Annual Register of Parks and Facilities* at the park authority's headquarters. Each quarter of the year the county publishes *Parktakes*, a magazine of more than 100 pages about park classes, programs, and events as varied as aquatics, garden and farm workshops, fencing, roller hockey tournaments, boat races, and concerts.

Descriptions of the county's numerous parks would fill a volume. For this guidebook some short and long trails suggested by the park authority are described to reflect trail, facility, and camping variety. Covered in the regional parks section of this guidebook, Chapter 14, under the Northern Virginia Regional Park Authority (of which Fairfax County is a member), are the **W&OD Railroad Trail** (also called the **W&OD Trail**), Bull Run–Occoquan Regional Park trails, Fountainhead Park trails, and Pohick Bay trails. The Great Falls Park trails and the **Mount Vernon Trail** are listed with national park trails in Chapter 9. (Not covered, by request, are twenty-four trails under the aegis of ninety-three private clubs and organizations in the county with recreational facilities.) The county's five nature/visitor centers are at Annandale Park (see entry, below); Riverbend Park (see entry, below); Hidden Pond Park (8511 Greeley Blvd., Springfield, VA 22150, phone: 703- 451-9588); Ellanor C. Lawrence Park (see entry, below); and Huntley Meadows Park (see entry, below).

ACCESS TO PARK AUTHORITY HEADQUARTERS: From I-495, take exit 49 (I-66 west) to US 50 west and west on Ox Road South. Turn left onto Monument Drive, follow Monument approximately 0.5 mile to Government Center Parkway. Take the first right and follow it to the Hervity Building at 12055 Government Center Parkway, Fairfax, VA 22035; phone: 703-324-8700.

## ANNANDALE PARK

In addition to recreational facilities, this park has the Hidden Oaks Nature Center and the 0.3-mile loop, interpretive **Old Oak Nature Trail**. The trailhead is on the 1080 approach to the right of the nature center, through large white oaks and by a small steam with scattered gum, pine, mountain laurel, and wildflowers.

ACCESS: From I-495, exit 52B, at Little River Turnpike (VA 236), east to the left at the first traffic light at Hummer Road. Take Hummer Road for three blocks to Royce Street, turn left, and go to the nature center parking on the left at the corner of Linda Lane.

ADDRESS AND INFORMATION: Annandale Park, 4030 Hummer Rd., Annandale, VA 22003; phone: 703-941-1065.

## BURKE LAKE PARK/SOUTH RUN STREAM VALLEY PARK

In the 894-acre Burke Lake Park there are trails, facilities for tent or trailer camping, fishing (for musky, bass, walleye, and sunfish), and boating in the 218-acre lake. Also, there is picnicking, golfing, and bicycling. The park is open all year, but camping is seasonal (check with the park for spring opening and autumn closing).

ACCESS: From I-495, exit 54A, go west on Braddock Road to left on Burke Lake Road. Turn left on Ox Road and go to park entrance on the left, or from Fairfax County Parkway (SR 7100) take Burke Lake Road south to Ox Road (VA 123), left to park entrance on the left. Another access is from I-95 and Occoquan junction; take VA 123, Ox Road, north for 8 miles.

**Burke Lake Trail** (4.7 mi.), **Beaver Cove Nature Trail** (0.7 mi.), **South Run** 1081–83
**Stream Valley Trail** (3.8 mi.)
LENGTH AND DIFFICULTY: 9.9 miles (15.8 km) combined, round-trip; easy
FEATURES: scenic views, wildlife, wildflowers, fishing
TRAILHEADS: family campground or the marina
DESCRIPTION: From the park entrance and information center, follow the road left for 1.2 miles to the end of the road, and park at camp store visitor parking. Take the **Beaver Cove Nature Trail**, hiking 0.7 mile to a junction with the lake trail. If turning right, proceed along the lake border through poplar, oak, beech, aspen, and beds of ferns among partridge berry. Pass the family campground and begin a gravel physical fitness trail, which ends, or begins, east of the par-three golf course. Cross a stream near Burke Lake Road at 1.8 miles and continue around the lake, reaching the marina at 2.9 miles. Follow the trail to the dam at 3.8 miles. After crossing the dam continue to follow along the lake edge in and out of coves and through hardwoods with scattered pine. Complete the **Burke Lake Trail** at 5.4 miles and return to the trailhead on the **Beaver Cove Nature Trail** for a total of 6.1 miles.

South Run Stream Valley Park includes 340 acres and is situated between

Burke Lake Park and the Pohick Stream Valley. It has a 3.8-mile paved treadway named **South Run Stream Valley Trail**, and it goes through a wooded stream valley where a few sections are moderately steep. The trail may be accessed from the dam end of the **Burke Lake Trail** or from South Run District Park (turn at Reservation Dr. into the park from the Fairfax County Parkway).

USGS MAP: Fairfax

ADDRESS AND INFORMATION: Burke Lake Park, 7315 Ox Rd., Fairfax Station, VA 22039; phone: 703-323-6600. Available is a brochure with park facilities, map, and campground sites.

## SCOTTS RUN NATURE PRESERVE

Halfway between the Arlington County line and Great Falls Park on the Potomac River is Scotts Run Nature Preserve, with 337 acres. Mainly a conservation area, its major activities are fishing, hiking, and nature study. It has easy, round-trip, 2.9-mile **Scotts Run Trail**. Access to it is at the parking area. Follow it on a frequently used path downstream near river birch, sumac, dogwood, and locust with spots of tag alder and redbud. Rock-hop the stream, but notice that the trail can be hiked on either side. Approach a defile with rocky terrain and a steep ascent to the ridge on the left for an excellent view of the Potomac River. Descend to a rocky gorge with pools and cascades. Under a heavy cover of hemlock, mountain laurel, and witch hazel, the mosses and lichens give the ambience of a Blue Ridge Mountains glen. Wildflowers bloom between the base of the cascades and the narrow Potomac River beach. Backtrack to parking area.

USGS MAP: Falls Church

ACCESS: From I-495, VA 193 (Georgetown Pike), go west on Georgetown Pike for 0.7 mile to parking entrance on the right. (Exit from the parking area into traffic is dangerous.)

ADDRESSES AND INFORMATION: Scotts Run Nature Preserve, 7400 Georgetown Pike, McLean, VA 22102; phone: 703-759-3211. (For information, contact Riverbend Nature Center, 8814 Jeffery Rd., Great Falls, VA 22066; phone: 703- 759-3211.)

## ELLANOR C. LAWRENCE PARK/
## ROCKY RUN STREAM VALLEY PARK

Formerly the Walney Farm, this exceptionally beautiful 640-acre park was donated to the county in 1971 by Ellanor C. Lawrence and her husband David Lawrence, the founder and publisher of *U.S. News and World Report*. In accordance with Mrs. Lawrence's wishes, the park offers a visitor center, ballfields, fitness trail, historic buildings, archaeological sites, and educational programs. A short interpretive **Nature Trail** is near the amphitheater.

The 235-acre Rocky Run Stream Valley Park has the easy multi-use 3-mile trail,    1086
**Rocky Run Stream Valley Trail**. It runs from Fairfax County Parkway to Ellanor C. Lawrence Park. Its main natural feature is forested wetlands. Access is at
the Cabell's Mill parking area.

ACCESS: From I-495, exit 49, go west on I-66 for 11 miles to exit 53 on VA 28. Turn
right (north) on Sully Road to first right, Walney Road. Cabell's Mill is 0.5 mile on
the right and the visitor center is 1 mile on the left.

ADDRESS AND INFORMATION: Lawrence Park, 5040 Walney Rd., Chantilly, VA
22021; phone: 703-631-0013.

## HUNTLEY MEADOWS PARK

Nestled in Fairfax County's Hybla Valley, this park is a natural island in the vast
suburban sea of northern Virginia. Its 1,261 acres harbor majestic mature forests,
wildflower-speckled meadows, and acres of wetlands bursting with life. It is ideal
wildlife habitat for beavers, otters, herons, ducks, deer, and many songbird and
butterfly varieties as well as a host of other animals. Facilities include a visitor center with exhibits and an auditorium, a 0.6-mile boardwalk wetland trail
known as the **Heron Trail**, and 2-mile **Hike-Bike Trail**. The **Heron Trail** is an    1087–89
interpretive trail that meanders through the park with signs about the natural
habitats of plants and animals and has a side trail, the 0.4-mile **Pond Trail**. There
is also a wildlife observation tower for viewing waterfowl.

ACCESS: From I-495, exit 177A, go south 3.5 miles on US 1 (Richmond Hwy.) to
Lockheed Boulevard and turn right. Go 0.5 mile to park entrance on the left at
Harrison Lane.

ADDRESS AND INFORMATION: Huntley Meadows Park, 3701 Lockheed Blvd.,
Alexandria, VA 22306; phone: 703-768-2525.

## LAKE FAIRFAX PARK

Another of the county's excellent parks for camping is Lake Fairfax Park, with 476
acres, including an 18-acre lake. Although the park is open year round, the campground is seasonal, usually from March to November (check with the office for
dates). There are 135 campsites, 76 of which have hookups. Other facilities include
the Water Mine, an outdoor swimming pool enveloped by a lazy river, pedal boat
rental, fishing, a carousel, picnicking, and sports on athletic fields. Entrance to the
0.8-mile **Lake Fairfax Nature Trail** begins at campsite C21. Additionally, part of    1090–91
the 5-mile **Rails to River Trail** passes through the park. (This equestrian trail
connects south to the W&OD Regional Park trail at Michael Faraday Court, and
north from Lake Fairfax Park across Hunter Mill Rd. at Colvin Run Creek to
Leesburg Pike [VA 7] near Colvin Run Mill, then along Difficult Run Stream Valley

to Great Falls National Park and the Potomac River. For more information, contact Colvin Run Mill Park, 10017 Colvin Run Rd., Great Falls, VA 22066; phone: 703-759-2771.)

ACCESS: From I-495, exit 47A, take Leesburg Pike (VA 7) west for 6.5 miles to left on Baron Cameron Avenue (SR 606). Go 0.5 mile and turn left on Lake Fairfax Drive to park entrance.

ADDRESS AND INFORMATION: Lake Fairfax Park, 1400 Lake Fairfax Dr., Reston, VA 22090; phone: 703-471-5414.

## MASON DISTRICT PARK

This 121-acre park is centrally located in Fairfax County and is unique because of its historic landmarks. It has ballfields and courts, a picnic area, and forests and meadows with a history of 400 years of land use. The park's trails have been designed to preserve the land features. The 1.3-mile **Mason District Trail** is mostly through the forest but connects with the **Nature Trail** and a 0.6-mile jogging/exercise trail.

ACCESS: From I-495, exit 52B, take VA 236 (Little River Tpk.) east for 2 miles to turn left on John Marr Drive, and right on VA 244 (Columbia Pike) to park entrance on the right.

ADDRESS AND INFORMATION: Mason District Park, 6621 Columbia Pike, Annandale, VA 22003; phone: 703-941-1730.

1092–93

## RIVERBEND PARK

The 409-acre Riverbend Park is an outstanding preserve for maintaining the natural beauty of the Potomac River shoreline. It has a visitor center overlooking the river and a nature center tucked back in the forest. All trails can begin or make connections at the nature center.

ACCESS: From I-495, exit 44 (or at the visitor center), take VA 193 (Georgetown Pike) west for 5 miles and turn right on Riverbend Road. Go 2 miles on Riverbend Road to Jeffery Road, turn right, and proceed 1.5 miles to the park entrance.

1094–98    Paw Paw Passage Trail (1.2 mi.), Potomac Heritage Trail (1.7 mi.), Upland Trail (1 mi.), Center Trail (0.3 mi.), Duff and Stuff Trail (0.2 mi.)
LENGTH AND DIFFICULTY: 5.5 miles (8.8 km) combined, round-trip; easy
FEATURES: scenic views, wildlife, wildflowers, fishing
TRAILHEADS: from the nature center
DESCRIPTION: The **Paw Paw Passage Trail** is a loop from the nature center connecting with the **Potomac Heritage Trail**. Go left at the sign, descending to a spur trail on the right for an exhibit area and overlook. Pass the pond, turn sharply right, and follow the **Potomac Heritage Trail** down the river for 1.7

miles. Along the floodplain grow huge beech, poplar, elm, basswood, birch, and sycamore. In the understory are large patches of papaw (also spelled *pawpaw*), holly, ironwood, and spicebush. Wildflowers and ferns are commonplace. The springtime display of trilliums and bluebells is exceptional.

Pass the visitor center and picnic area on the way to a junction with the **Upland Trail**, right. It can be followed back to the nature center on rolling terrain among tall trees and by a number of spur trails right and left. Or continue another 1 mile on the **Potomac Heritage Trail** to a junction with the **Center Trail** and its 0.3 mile to the nature center. (The **Potomac Heritage Trail** connects with the **River Trail** at the boundary of Great Falls Park. It does not connect with a trail by the same name downriver in the George Washington National Memorial Parkway.) Back at the nature center is the **Duff and Stuff Trail**, which is paved, self-guiding, and useful for the physically disabled. Other natural surface trails in the forest can be used for horseback riding.

USGS MAPS: Seneca, Rockville

ADDRESS AND INFORMATION: Riverbend Park Nature Center, 8814 Jeffery Rd., Great Falls, VA 22066; phone: 703-759-3211. The visitor center is located at 8700 Potomac Hill St. Available are brochures and trail maps.

## WAKEFIELD AND LAKE ACCOTINK PARKS

These two parks are connected only by the **Accotink Stream Valley Trail**, which passes by Accotink Creek under the Braddock Road bridge west near I-495. Wakefield Park's 290 acres provide an exceptionally broad list of outdoor and indoor activities, including athletic fields, tennis courts, bicycle and hiking trails, picnic areas, and facilities for the physically disabled. At Lake Accotink, which has 482 acres and is south of Wakefield, facilities emphasize outdoor water sports, picnicking, and hiking. The bike/hike trails provide a linear route in Wakefield Park and a loop around the lake in Lake Accotink Park.

ACCESS: To Wakefield Park, leave I-495, exit 54A, on SR 620 (Braddock Rd.) west for 0.2 mile to park entrance on the right. For Lake Accotink Park, leave I-495, exit 54B, on SR 620 (Braddock Rd.) east for 0.5 mile and turn right on Heming Avenue to park's rear entrance. Or, from I-95, exit 169 (south of its intersection with I-495), turn west on SR 644 (Old Keene Mill Rd.), and at end of access ramps turn right on Backlick Road. Follow it to Highland Street and make a left to the marina entrance on the right.

### Accotink Stream Valley Trail 1099

LENGTH AND DIFFICULTY: 6 miles (6.4 km), round-trip; easy

FEATURES: scenic area, waterfowl, wildflowers, fishing, historic site

TRAILHEADS: parking lot at Wakefield Recreation Center, or parking lot at Lake Accotink Park marina

DESCRIPTION: If entering from Wakefield Park, follow the trail by the recreation building to the parking area and into the forest on a wide trail. Go downstream and under the Braddock Road bridge to parallel the Accotink Creek south. The forest is chiefly river birch, sycamore, oak, ash, basswood, and wildflowers. Pass a marsh and follow the trail near the edge of the lake. Join a physical fitness trail for the last 0.7 mile to the marina area at Lake Accotink park.

Another access is from Eakin Community Park. To reach the park take I-495, exit 52B to VA 236 (Little River Tpk.) east for 1.5 miles. Turn left on Prosperity Avenue to Eakin Community Park entrance and parking on the right. Users on the easy trail are bikers, in-line skaters, joggers, and walkers. The trail is in Accotink Stream Valley Park, which encompasses more than 700 acres. The stream valley includes community parks Eakin Mantua, Eakin Community, Howery Field, Brookfield, Byron Avenue, Pohick Estates, as well as Wakefield and Lake Accotink (described ahead with another trail by the same name). Trailheads are at Eakin Community Park, US 50 service drive near Nutley Road, and King Arthur Road. The two missing links (with a total of 7.5 mi.) in this trail will eventually connect it through Wakefield Park to Lake Accotink Park. Plans are for completion in 2003/4, and it will comprise the middle section of a planned **Cross County Trail**. Eventually the **Cross County Trail** would run from the Occoquan in the south to Great Falls and the Potomac in the north for 44 miles.

USGS MAP: Annandale

ADDRESSES AND INFORMATION: Wakefield Park, 8100 Braddock Rd., Annandale, VA 22003; phone: 703-321-7080. Lake Accotink Park, 7500 Accotink Park Rd., Springfield, VA 22152; phone: 703-569-3464. Available are brochures and maps of bicycle and canoe trails and park facilities.


## WOLFTRAP STREAM VALLEY PARK

This park is a forest corridor with Wolftrap Creek running through it. On the northern end of the park are Wolf Trails Park and Springlake Park, both small areas, but together the parks provide a beautiful and peaceful area for 4-foot-wide, asphalt **Wolftrap Stream Valley Trail** (formerly **Waverly/Wolftrap Trail**). It begins at the Creek Crossing Road west of Westwood Golf Course in Vienna. The trail meanders north for 1 mile to SR 677 (Old Courthouse Rd.). (The park is near to and south of Wolftrap Farm Park, and southeast of Meadowlark Gardens Regional Park.)

ACCESS: From I-495, exit 11, go west on VA 123 into Vienna and turn right on SR 675 (Beulah Rd.). Go two blocks and turn right on Creek Crossing Road to park entrance. Or, continue north on Beulah Road to Abbotsford Drive and turn right.

ADDRESS AND INFORMATION: Wolftrap Stream Valley Park, 1801 Abbotsford Dr., Vienna, VA 22180; phone: 703-255-1800.

# Fauquier County

The county is in the upper piedmont of the state, between the Blue Ridge Mountains in the west and Manassas in the east. It is known for its large pasturelands and thoroughbred horse farms. In the center of the county is Warrenton, the historic county seat. With the assistance of the county, town, and local organization leaders, the paved 1.5-mile **Warrenton Branch Greenway** is a landmark. Its northwest trailhead is downtown Warrenton at Depot Restaurant. Here is a restored caboose that was donated by the Norfolk and Western Railroad and restored by the Piedmont Railroaders. Access here is on Fourth Street. The southeastern trailhead is at a parking area cul-de-sac at the end of the Old Meetze Road, which is off Meetze Road, less than 1 mile east of the intersection with Lee Street and Expressway US 15/17/29. 1102

## JOHN MARSHALL BIRTHPLACE PARK

This 5-acre historic area has a footpath round-trip of 1.1 miles to a memorial site honoring John Marshall, the fourth chief justice of the United States. The **John Marshall Birthplace Trail** follows a shady passageway among locust, cedar, and honeysuckle. At the parking lot entrance are a number of markers providing information about the birthplace and other historical information. 1103

ACCESS: From the intersection of US 17 and VA 28 go northeast 3 miles to Germantown Road (SR 649) and turn right. Drive 0.3 mile (including crossing a railroad) to a small parking lot and sign, left.

## C. M. CROCKETT PARK

Expansive grassland and a lake make this park an outstanding example of public land in service to citizens. There is a boat launch and rentals, and fishing at Germantown Lake, picnic shelters, play area, disc golf, challenge course, and amphitheater. It has three named trails: **Four Seasons Nature Trail** consists of three loops totaling 1.2 miles. It meanders through a mature forest area near the lake, and in the wintertime can be used for cross-country skiing. The **Picnic Loop Trail** is 0.6 mile on a gravel path that loops around the shelters and playgrounds. And the longest trail, **Bluebird Cross Country Trail**, follows the lake shoreline and crosses the dam and meadows for 1.9 miles. If hiking counterclockwise, follow the sign to the lake. Pass under tall oaks and exit to cross a low side of the dam. You will see blue bird boxes and bluebirds in season. Arrive at the other end of the dam at 0.8 mile and return on the top of the dam. The scenery is superb and the grassy trail is a sweeping 24 feet wide. At 1.2 miles begin a loop around the wide spillway among grasses and clover for a return to the parking area. This trail also serves as a cross-country ski trail. 1104–6

ACCESS: If leaving the Marshall Park, at VA 28, turn right, north, and after 1.4 miles turn left on Meetze Road (SR 643). After 1 mile turn left on SR 602 and after another 0.6 mile right is the Crockett Park entrance.

### RADY PARK

1107   Every town or city should have a park like this where the songbirds are singing and the trail is easy for strolling. It has a grassy meadow for soccer, a clearwater stream, tall tree forest, rest rooms, picnic area, and paved **Rady Park Trail** (0.7 mi. including a spur to Bear Wallow Rd.). Additionally, there is a bridge over the stream away from the paved trail to an earthen walk among a landscaped floral garden. Native bunches of yellow flag iris grow near the stream bank.

ACCESS: From the intersection of US 17 and US 17 Bus, north of the city, drive southeast on US 17 Bus (Broadway Ave.) and after 0.3 mile turn right on Foxcroft Road. Take the next right, Evans Avenue, to the park entrance, right.

ADDRESS AND INFORMATION: Fauquier County Parks and Recreation, Administrative Office, 62 Culpeper St., Warrenton, VA 20186; phone: 540-347-6896; fax: 540-347-6898.

## Fluvanna County

Fluvanna County's Department of Parks and Recreation and volunteer nonprofit organizations have been successful in creating a large trail system for public service. One of the citizens' groups is Heritage Trail Foundation, whose mission is to use the **Fluvanna Heritage Trail** to connect with scenic and historic sites in and near the village of Palmyra, the county seat. In the process the trail system would support the Fluvanna County Historical Society, and the environmental emphasis of the Rivanna Conservation Society. The **Fluvanna Heritage Trail** system is ongoing with plans to connect with the Palmyra Elementary School, and to eventually have a nature center and outdoor classroom.

1108–10   The **Fluvanna Heritage Trail** is a combination of trails, the longest of which is 3-mile **River Bluff Trail**, and used by equestrians and pedestrians. The trail is between a west and east entrance off the north side of VA 53, northwest from Palmyra. To access the east entrance from the junction of US 15 and VA 53 in Palmyra drive west 0.4 mile on VA 53 and turn right. Here is an open grassy hill with a parking area, rest room, picnic area, and kiosk at a grove of walnut and wild cherry trees. From here begins both the **River Bluff Trail**, left, and the 0.5-mile **Sandy Beach Trail** (honoring Julie King), right. The latter has a pea gravel surface designed for usage of pedestrians only and the physically disabled. After 0.3 mile among a field of wildflowers the trail enters a river forest of tall hardwoods to a meadow and scenic Rivanna River. Backtrack, or return by a connection in the forest to ascend 0.5 mile on the **River Bluff Trail**.

If following the mile-posted **River Bluff Trail** upstream, west, cross a bridge at 0.4 mile, followed by an ascent on an old road. The trail undulates on the hillside, then descends to hug the river, and passes spurs and connections with loops. Mainly a hardwood forest, there are also cedar, pine, papaw, and spicebush. There are connections with unnamed and additional horse trails. At 2 miles is an access to a bluff for River Overlook. Ascend to the Pole Barns near the empty Haden House at Pleasant Grove. Here is the west entrance to the **Fluvanna Heritage Trail** system. Facilities here are picnic shelter, soccer fields, rest room, and a side road west of the Haden House to a parking area for the **Heritage Birding Trail**. This 1-mile trail has three interconnecting loops in an open field. Vehicular access to this west entrance is 1.4 miles west on VA 53 from the east entrance. (From here it is 15.1 mi. northwest on VA 53 to VA 20 near Charlottesville.)

USGS MAPS: Palmyra, Boyd Tavern

ADDRESSES AND INFORMATION: Fluvanna County Department of Parks and Recreation, P.O. Box 128, Fork Union, VA 23055; phone: 434-842-3150; fax: 434-842-1015. Fluvanna Heritage Trail Foundation, P.O. Box 501, Palmyra, VA 22963; Rivanna Conservation Society, P.O. Box 141, Palmyra, VA 22963; phone: 434-589-7576. Free brochures available.

## Gloucester County

### TINDALL'S POINT PARK

From the parking area at Gloucester Point follow the trail signs to display stations on easy, 0.5-mile **Tindall's Point Trail**. Here is information on the Revolutionary War and Civil War fortifications at a scenic overlook of the York River. A picnic area adjoins the trail.

USGS MAP: Claybank

ACCESS: From Yorktown cross the Coleman Memorial Bridge on US 17 north and enter Gloucester County. Park on the left at the end of the bridge.

### BEAVERDAM PARK

Beaverdam Park is part of Beaverdam Reservoir, which includes a 635-acre lake for fishing and boating. Among the eighteen fish species present, some are largemouth bass, six kinds of sunfish, white perch, channel catfish, redfin pickerel, and white perch. The park's other major attraction is a 10-mile network of eight multiuse (hiking, bicycling, and equestrian) loop trails and a nature trail. The trail system is frequently on old roads in a forest mainly of yellow poplar, sycamore, sweet gum, American holly, beech, oaks, pines, dogwood, buckeye, and iron-wood. If hiking from the northwest entrance, off Fary's Mill Road parking area, pass the sign board for **Beaverdam Trail** and descend 130 feet to a fork for Loop #1. Choose the left fork in wet seasons. After the first loop of 1 mile enter Loop #2, where points of interest are ferns, wild grape, views of lake, ridges, and lagoon with wood ducks. In Loop #3 are other ridges, and at a marsh with bridges are cattail, jewelweed, and arrow arum. At 2.7 miles enter a small loop of Loop #4, which has a horseshoe curve to the lake. The longest (317 ft.) boardwalk crossing, Swan Bridge, is at 3.4 miles in a marsh with cattail and cardinal flower. In Loop #5 is a resting bench at 3.7 miles and another at 4.3 miles where short Loop #6 begins. The loop ends at double bridges over an inlet at 4.7 miles. For the next 2.5 miles the trail weaves in and out of coves where blue lobelia and mistflower bloom, crosses small bridges, passes near scenic views of the lake, and arrives at an intersection of paths and old roads at 7.3 miles. To the right is a group camping area (reservations required), privies, and beautiful views of the lake. From here the **East Fork Loop Horse Trail** and a separate **Beaverdam Nature Trail** parallel each other to the 80-foot Morgan Bridge over an inlet at 8.4 miles. Cross another bridge, pass scenic views and side trails to the lake. (At 9.4 mi. a multi-use trail ascends left to a parking area outside the main gate.) Arrive at the parking area and ranger station at lakeside at 10 miles.

USGS MAP: Claybank

ACCESS: To main entrance from US 17 Bus/VA 14 in Gloucester, drive north 2.3 miles on SR 616 (Roaring Springs Rd.). For the Fary's Mill Road entrance drive west 3.2 miles from Roaring Springs Road on VA 14 to US 17 Bus for 3.2 miles and turn right on Fary's Mill Road. After 2.5 miles turn right to a parking area.

ADDRESSES AND INFORMATION: Gloucester County Parks and Recreation, P.O. Box 157, Gloucester, VA 23061; phone: 804-693-2355. Beaverdam Park, 8687 Roaring Springs Rd., Gloucester, VA 23061; phone 804-693-2107. Free trail map available.

## Hanover County

Formed in 1720, this historic county is the birthplace of Patrick Henry and Henry Clay. Although the county is a few miles north of metropolitan Richmond, the state's capital, it is about 23 percent agricultural and 66 percent forest. Ashland (founded 1858) is the county's largest town and home of Randolph Macon College (1830). Only 7 miles east of there is the town of Hanover, the county seat. Between the towns is north-south running I-95. The county's progressive parks and recreation system contains seven parks. Those with trails are described ahead.

The round-trip 0.9-mile **Ashland Trolley Line Trail** follows a historic section of the old Ashland-Richmond Trolley Line. The level walking and bicycling trail is paralleled on the east by a power line and a low forest with undergrowth of sumac and bracken. On the west side is a pristine hardwood forest. To access from I-95 exit 92, drive west on VA 54 for 0.7 mile and turn left on US 1. After 0.9 mile turn right on Ashcake Road, and after 0.8 mile cross a railroad to immediately turn left on Center Street Road. After 1 mile turn left on Gwathmey Church Road to cross a railroad. At 0.2 mile park left at a power line post.

There are two parks with walking-jogging trails. To access the trail at Courthouse Park, drive east from Ashland at I-95 on VA 54 for 6 miles to US 301. Turn right (south), pass the Hanover Courthouse, and after 1 mile turn left into the park. The 0.5-mile gravel **Courthouse Park Trail** is in an open area. Among other 1117–18 facilities are soccer and athletic fields and a roller hockey rink. The gravel 0.3-mile **Pole Green Park Trail** begins at the parking lot, enters the forest, and descends into a beautiful hardwood forest to make a loop. It has a side trail that forks north to exit near the community center. A backtrack can be 1 mile round-trip. Access from I-295 exit 38 east is on Pole Green Road. After 4.1 miles turn left at Pole Green Park and Elementary School. Turn right after 0.2 mile. Other facilities at the park are picnic shelters, horse ring with stable area, skateboard park, and ballfields.

## COLD HARBOR BATTLEFIELD PARK

This 50-acre park features the main **Cold Harbor Battlefield Trail**, side trails to 1119 rifle trenches and artillery pits, and the Garthright House for a total of 1.2 miles round-trip. On the trail there are interpretive signs concerning the Civil War battle of June 1, 1864. About 13,000 Federal and 5,000 Confederate troops were killed, wounded, or captured. Federal forces withdrew with plans to reorganize at Petersburg and Richmond. From the parking lot follow a wide gravel treadway into the hardwood forest, and at 100 yards pass a side trail, right, to the Garthright House, which was a Union hospital during the fighting and later was used by the Confederates. Arrive at a fork at 0.2 mile to make a circle for the return.

ACCESS: From I-295, exit 34 east, take Craighton Road; drive 1 mile and turn right on VA 156 (Cold Harbor Rd., also called Battlefield Park Rd.). After 1.7 miles pass Gaines Mill National Battlefield Park access on Watt House Road, right, and continue another 0.3 mile to Richmond National Battlefield (also called Cold Harbor Battlefield Park), left. Ahead it is 0.6 mile right to Cold Harbor Battlefield Park (a Hanover County park).

## NORTH ANNA BATTLEFIELD PARK

On this 75-acre historic and sacred park is **North Anna Battlefield Trail**. The park 1120 was made possible by General Crushed Stone Company and donated to the county in 1996. Including the side trails and backtracking, the trail is 2.7 miles. There are ten interpretive signs on the Ox Road portion trail discussing the Civil War battle of May 23–26, 1864. This educational walk can be accepted seriously because of the vivid educational descriptions. Historians claim that the earthworks you see are among the best preserved of the war. Although the Union Army of the Potomac was repulsed, it regrouped to move closer to Richmond. Its logistics were superior to those of General Lee's Army of Northern Virginia. During this battle General Lee was sick, and this may have prompted a statement on one of the trail's signs: "Lee failed to follow the movement of his opponent, and forever lost the opportunity offered by the North Anna River to destroy the Union Army."

From the parking lot follow the professionally designed trail through a deciduous forest with scattered holly. Descend on steps to follow an easy walk on pea gravel. At 0.2 mile is a credit sign for the interpretive work. If you first follow the main trail to its end at 0.8 mile, there is an observation platform where you may hear and see part of the North Anna River. There is another deck at sign #7. Here and elsewhere, the trenches were unforested in 1864. At the trail entrance is a monument honoring all the men who lost their lives here, and a specific memorial to a Wisconsin corporal. Part of a poem from his relatives reads, "Love and tears for the blue, tears and love for the gray."

ACCESS: From I-95, exit 98, drive west 0.7 mile on VA 30 to US 1. Turn right and after 1.5 miles on US 1, turn left on SR 684 (Verdon Rd.). After 2.5 miles turn right at park sign and drive 0.6 mile through a forest to the parking lot and trail entrance.

## POOR FARM PARK

The 205-acre Poor Farm Park is located in the South Anna District near Stagg Creek, behind Patrick Henry High School and Liberty Middle School. The park is open for day use only. The picnic area with shelters is on a grassy hill, where large trees provide a forest cover. Other facilities are soccer fields, volleyball courts, an archery range, horseshoe pits, an amphitheater, a **Nature Trail**, and a trail for mountain bikes. The **Patrick Henry Cross-County Trail** and other unnamed trails connect for a total of 2.8 miles, plus at least 2 miles of old logging roads near Stagg Creek. The forest is mixed hardwoods and pines with an understory of shrubs and wildflowers.

1121–22

ACCESS: From junction of I-95, exit 92, and VA 54 go west on VA 54 for 4.8 miles to SR 810 and turn left. Entrance is at the end of SR 810.

ADDRESSES AND INFORMATION: Hanover County Parks and Recreation, 13017 Taylor Complex Lane, Ashland, VA 23005; phone: 804-365-4695. Seasonal details of park activities published for public use. For area and Civil War information, contact Ashland/Hanover Visitor Center, 112 North Ave., Ashland, VA 23005; phone: 804-752-6766.

# Henrico County

There are thirty parks spread over this county, which almost circles the city of Richmond except the south side. Since 1934 the county has successfully provided public recreational facilities and programs of outstanding merit. More than 2.5 million visitors are served annually, and the park system goes beyond athletic fields, swimming pools, picnic shelters, and trails. There are cultural arts programs, museums, nature centers, community centers, and special educational activities for children and senior citizens. Many of its current facilities have been made possible by a citizens' vote in a 1989 bond referendum. A record of its services indicates the county lives up to its mission "to enhance the quality of life and to foster a sense of well being and community for the citizens of Henrico County." Some of the parks have trails that are mainly multi-use or specified as an exercise trail. Others that focus more on nature are identified here. (See Chapter 13 for trails inside Richmond's city limits.)

## CRUMP MEMORIAL PARK

Half of this 150-acre day-use park is Meadow Farm Museum, a living history site. There is a nineteenth-century farmhouse, an 1850 doctor's office, a smokehouse, an orchard, a barn, farm animals, a blacksmith shop, and a family cemetery. (The park is open year round, but the museum is closed on Mondays, and December through February. For information on Old Fourth of July Festival and Harvest Festival, call 804-672-5106/1367.) At the parking area east, downstream, is 0.3-mile **River Birch Trail**, a loop among knobby white oaks and around North Run 1123–24 Creek. To access the 0.5-mile loop, self-guiding **North Run Creek Trail**, walk up the hill to the farm barn and go left. The forest is mixed hardwood and pine. At marker #9 is a side trail to a field of wild roses.

ACCESS: From I-295, exit 45, turn south on Woodman Road to first street on the right, Mountain Road, and follow it 1.7 miles to park entrance on the right.

## DEEP RUN PARK

A day-use 167-acre facility with two lakes, picnic shelters, play areas, ballfields and courts, nature pavilion and boardwalk, and a beautiful 2.4-mile **Deep Run Trail**. 1125 It is multi-use for bicyclists, walkers, roller skaters, skateboarders, and runners. One section of the trail is on a historic coal pit railroad. Among future plans are additional trails and paths.

ACCESS: From I-64, exit 180, turn south on Gaskins Road. After 1.2 miles turn west (right) on Ridgefield Parkway for 0.4 mile right.

## DOREY PARK

This 400-acre park is the county's largest. Out in the countryside, it has a recreation center housed in a modified 1920s dairy barn. The park's facilities include four lighted baseball fields, tennis courts, picnic shelters, horse ring and horse trails, playground, fishing lake, disc golf course, exercise trail, and **Dorey Park Nature Trail**. To access the trail use the lake parking lot and hike west of the lake for 0.1 mile to the forest, and stay right. Follow the signs for hiking a 1.2-mile loop through a mixture of tall hardwoods and pines. There are signs with common and botanical names of plants. Resting benches have been made available by Eagle Scouts. After crossing a pipeline easement and disc golf course leave the woods and pass the east side of the lake for a return.

ACCESS: From I-295, exit 22B, follow VA 5 (New Market Rd.) west 0.6 mile and turn right on Doran Road. After 2 miles turn left on Darbytown Road. After 0.6 mile turn left at park entrance.

## DUNNCROFT/CASTLE POINT PARK

The park has picnic shelters, rest rooms, playing field, disc golf course, and a **Nature Trail**. From the parking lot, the **Nature Trail** enters the forest left of the rest room. In a combination of old and new growth forest the wide pea gravel trail winds 0.4 mile to a neighborhood street. Backtrack. (Paralleling the trail part of the way are some of the disc golf course tees.)

ACCESS: From I-295, exit 49, take US 33 (Staples Mill Rd.) east and after 0.3 mile turn right on Springfield Road. After another 0.3 mile turn left on Francestown Road and go 0.7 mile for a left entrance into the park.

## ECHO LAKE PARK

With an 8-acre stocked lake and pier for fishing, this 24-acre day-use park has picnic areas, a playground, and 0.7-mile **Echo Lake Trail** around the lake. The trail has a nature observation blind and footbridges; lake and grassy shore have mallards and Canada geese.

ACCESS: From I-295, exit 49, turn south on US 33 (Staples Mill Rd.) for 0.4 mile, and turn west (right) on Springfield Road for 0.5 mile left.

## HIDDEN CREEK PARK

A unique feature of this park is its memorial to the shuttle "Challenger" crew. It has a picnic area and shelter, play equipment, an open play area, tennis courts, and a special 0.4-mile **Hidden Creek Nature Trail**. The gentle earthen trail meanders through a forest of mixed hardwoods and requires backtracking. It is accessible from the parking area near the park office.

ACCESS: On I-64 take exit 192 on US 360 (Mechanicsville Tpk.) northeast and immediately turn right on Bloom Lane. Drive 0.1 mile to turn left on Appolo Road. After a block turn right on Cleary Street, drive 0.6 mile, and turn left on Broadway Lane. The park entrance is ahead.

## THREE LAKES PARK

The 18 acres of lakes are next to each other and separated by earthen dams. **Three** 1130 **Lakes Trail** makes loops around the lakes for 1.5 miles. There is an observation deck for lake views. Nearby is a play equipment area and picnic shelters. Unique to this 90-acre day-use park is a nature center with one of the largest outdoor aquariums in Virginia. The park is open daily, but the nature center is closed Mondays and December through February (call 804-262-4822 for more information).

ACCESS: From I-95, exit 82, turn northeast on US 301 (Chamberlayne Rd.); go 0.8 mile, turn right on Wilkinson Road, and go 0.9 mile south to Sausiluta Drive, right.

## VAWTER STREET PARK

In this 352-acre, day-use park is Glen Lea Recreation Area, which has a picnic area and ballfields. The park's special feature is the 0.8-mile **Chickahominy River** 1131 **Trail**. It begins at the southeastern corner of the parking lot, then drops suddenly into a forest of tall trees and fern beds with a deep ravine on the right. After 0.2 mile it reaches a field and crosses under a power line to follow the margin of the forest for about 0.2 mile. It turns left into wetland woods, follows a small dike ridge, crosses a boardwalk, and forks. Either fork goes about 250 yards to the marshy edge of the Chickahominy River and the raucous squawk of surprised waterfowl. Backtrack.

USGS MAP: Richmond

ACCESS: From US 360 intersection, go west on E. Laburnum Avenue and turn right on Vawter Avenue, or from VA 627 (Richmond-Henrico Tpk.) go east 0.8 mile and turn left. It is 0.7 mile to the parking area, right.

ADDRESS AND INFORMATION: Henrico County Recreation and Parks, 8600 Dixon Power Dr. (P.O. Box 27032), Richmond, VA 23273; phone: 804-672-5100. Available are parks brochure, flyers with park maps.

# Isle of Wight County

## CARROLLTON NIKE PARK

Facilities at this park are ballfields, picnic areas, a ramp for boating and fishing, and ramps for skateboarding. There are also two scenic trails. One is the 0.6-mile
**1132** **Nike Park Nature Trail**. It is a wide and scenic trail to an observation deck at the marsh of Jones Creek. In a pleasant passage it crosses five bridges and curves through tall pines and oaks with an understory of wax myrtle. There are songbirds and waterfowl. The trail loops back to the parking area. The other trail is 2.6-mile
**1133** **Nike Park Bike Trail**, used both by hikers and bikers. From the parking area slightly descend toward the forest and begin at a trail sign. Weave through a beautiful forest of mixed hardwoods and pines. Some of the understory has wildflowers, ferns, and devil's walking sticks. Fragrant yellow jessamine decorates some of the trees and shrubs. Marsh grasses are nearby as the path goes from curve to curve. At 0.3 mile is a picnic table near a small peninsula, where herons and egrets may be seen. The trail changes direction at 1 mile with a left curve past agricultural fields, then a sharp curve left at 1.7 miles. At 2 miles the forest trail ends at a Naval Signal Station. Backtrack, or walk out to the highway at 2.1 miles and complete the loop to the parking area at 2.6 miles.

ACCESS: From junction of US 258 and VA 10/32 at Benns Church (south of Smithfield), go northeast on US 258 to park sign. Turn left on SR 665 to Carrollton and go 3.2 miles; turn left on SR 669 and go 1 mile to park entrance on the left.

## FORT BOYKIN HISTORIC PARK

This tranquil and scenic historic site sits on a high cliff by the James River and is named in honor of Maj. Francis Boykin of the American Revolution. The fort was a strategic military post from 1623, when Capt. John Smith constructed a star-shaped salient, to 1862, when the fort was shelled and burned by Union gunboats. For the next forty-six years the fort lay in ruins, entangled with vines and briars. From 1908 to 1978 it changed private ownership at least five times. Each owner, including the late sisters Ella, Elizabeth, and Susan Jordan, landscaped or cared for the historic shrine. The sisters willed the property to the commonwealth, which in turn leased it to the county for fifty years.

**1134**      From the parking area, follow the signs on the 0.5-mile **Fort Boykin Trail**. Go over the salient and turn right to the second largest black walnut tree in the state. Meander to the other interpretive markers, to magazine sites, a chimney plinth, Greer Gardens, and magnificent views of the James River. The park is open from 9 A.M. to dusk Wednesdays through Sundays.

ACCESS: From the Pagan River bridge in downtown Smithfield, drive north on VA 10 (Church St.) for 1.5 miles to a fork and take SR 674 (Blount's Corner Rd.) for

1.1 miles to SR 673 (Morgart's Beach Rd.), and turn right. Go 1 mile to parking area on the left.

ADDRESS AND INFORMATION: Isle of Wight County Public Recreational Facilities Authority, 13036 Nike Park Rd., Carrollton, VA 23314; phone: 757-357-2291. Available is a brochure with map.

## James City County

This historic and scenic county is the home of Jamestown Island, an island where English settlement began in America, May 13, 1607. The island is now a component of Colonial National Historical Park. The county is surrounded by rivers, creeks, marsh areas, historic sites, and cities. The county's west border is with the Chickahominy River and Charles City County, and it shares its north boundary with New Kent County and Ware Creek. The eastern border is with York River, Gloucester County, York County, and Williamsburg City. South is Surry County, the James River, and the Newport News city limits.

Within the past ten years the county has experienced dramatic growth in parks and recreational facilities. As in some other counties in the state, efforts have been made by James City Parks and Recreation to provide multi-use trail systems in its new recreational areas. They will be mentioned ahead, but only the pedestrian trails will be described. Mid-County Park has 19 acres with the usual ballfields and courts, picnic shelters, and a children's playground known as Kidsburg. Its 0.7-mile **Mid-County Park Trail** is paved. Access is west on VA 5 from VA 199 for a right 1135 turn on Ironbound Road. After 1 mile the park entrance is on the left. The park is open year round.

Community Center Park, also in the heart of the county, has indoor facilities that include a swimming pool. Its outside facilities have ballfields and a 1-mile paved multi-use walk that connects with neighborhood sidewalks. Access from the intersection of VA 5 and VA 199 is north on VA 199 to Longhill Road, right. After 0.5 mile turn left.

District Park Sports Complex has 492 acres with ballfields and courts, picnic areas, and indoor facilities. A network of multi-use trails is planned to connect with a 1-mile paved trail now in use, and a nature trail is also planned. Access is off VA 199 on Longhill Road, west. After 2 miles turn right on **Warhill Trail** (road) to 1136 its end. District Park has 676 acres with a plan for an extensive network of multi-use trails to include equestrian usage. A nature trail (pedestrian only) is planned for completion by 2004. Access is west from VA 199 on Longhill Road for 4 miles to Centerville Road. The entrance is straight ahead.

The county will be part of a new trail system known as the **Williamsburg** 1137 **Historic Necklace Trail**. It was selected as a White House Millennium Trail in 2002, and the trails originate in Yorktown to terminate at the James City County

District Park. It will be a 31-mile corridor that links thirteen nationally significant historical sites with the historic triangle of Jamestown, Yorktown, and Colonial Williamsburg. Although presently accessible by vehicular traffic, bicycles, and pedestrians, plans include a multi-use trail along the Colonial Parkway, west on Greensprings Road (VA 5), and north on Centerville Road to District Park. Plans are for it to connect with the TransAmerica Bike Route US 76 and the 55-mile Capital-to-Capital Bikeway by 2007. Two of the county's parks with hiking/walking trails are Greensprings Greenway and Little Creek Reservoir Park, described below.

## GREENSPRINGS GREENWAY

The Greensprings Greenway represents environmental protection for both historical preservation and recreation enhancements within 400 acres near Jamestown and between the James River and Powhatan Creek. The area is part of the Powhatan Creek Watershed and is recognized as perhaps the most environmentally significant natural area in the James/York peninsula. The farmland surrounding the area is Mainland Farm, considered by some to be the oldest continuously cultivated farm in America. In this area is 2-mile **Greensprings Trail**, which has superior design and construction. Open to pedestrians only, the trail was awarded the Best New Recreation Facility in Virginia by the Virginia Recreation and Parks Society in 1999. Exceptionally well blazed and signed for spur usage, the trail has fifty signs with information on environmentally or historically significant interpretive sites. With an easy and natural treadway, the design avoids wet areas with the use of many boardwalks and two long bridges. Trees include tulip tree, sweet gum, maple, and scattered loblolly pine. More than 175 species of birds and waterfowl have been identified and catalogued along the trail. The Greenway is open year round from sunrise to sunset.

1138

If beginning at the trailhead signpost, and following clockwise, pass through a hardwood forest with drainage toward a marsh. At 0.6 mile is a spur trail to St. George Boulevard. At 0.7 mile is another spur (proposed to access the Powhatan Creek Area). At 1.4 miles pass a spur (Loop 4, which accesses a residential area), and curve right to cross a bridge. Another spur (Loop 3, which accesses Fieldcrest Run residential area) is left at 1.5 miles. A highlight of the trail begins at a 546-foot bridge over a marsh. Here are osprey nests, heron, egret, bittern, and many species of songbirds. Osprey season is usually from March to October. White-blooming lizard's tail is among the marsh grasses. At 1.7 miles is a spur (Loop 2, which accesses a pond with cattails, a route to another spur, left, and to the James River High School grounds, right). Continue right on the main trail, complete the loop, turn left, and return to parking area near the school tennis courts at 2 miles.

USGS MAPS: Surry, Norge

ACCESS: From I-64, exit 242 west on VA 199, drive 5.5 miles to junction west on

*Greensprings Trail, James City County*

VA 5 (John Tyler Hwy.); turn left, west, on VA 5 and after 3.1 miles turn left at James River High School (across the road from Green Springs Plantation residential entrance). Drive past the school entrance and park near the tennis courts from the corner of Eagle Way and Reade's Way. Trailhead has a sign at the forest edge.

## LITTLE CREEK RESERVOIR PARK

The 38-acre scenic park is at the shores of a 996-acre reservoir. Facilities include fishing piers, boat ramp and boat rentals, picnic shelters, rest rooms, and concession building. The park is a popular location for fishing. Among the fourteen fish categories are blue catfish, bluegill, chain pickerel, largemouth bass, yellow perch, and channel catfish. Although not completed at this writing, a 1-mile **Little Creek Reservoir Nature Trail** is planned. It is located on a peninsula 1139 with superb vistas from a gazebo overlook. (May be open only on weekends from December to February.)

ACCESS: If driving south on I-64, exit 227, follow VA 30 for 2 miles, connect with US 60 to follow it south. After 2 miles to Toano, turn right on Forge Road. After another 2 miles turn left on Lakeview Drive. The park entrance and office is on the right.

ADDRESS AND INFORMATION: James City County Parks and Recreation, 5249-C Olde Towne Rd., Williamsburg, VA 23188; phone: 757-259-3200/3209; fax: 757-259-3203 (phone for Little Creek Reservoir Park is 757-566-1702).

## King George County

### BARNESFIELD PARK

This park is in Mathias Point Neck with its eastern boundary at the Potomac River. It has a 3.4-mile round-trip, backcountry road-trail and 0.2-mile **Wayside Trail** from the parking area at the eastern end of the ballfields. Osprey have built nests in the park, and usually a family is at the top of a ballfield lighting pole. The **Wayside Trail** meanders through a dense growth of saplings and honeysuckle, crosses a service road, enters a pine grove, and descends on banks of shells to the shore of the Potomac River. From this point are views of the river and the Nice Memorial Bridge spanning the river to Maryland. A hike on the dead-end road-trail to a lake offers a quiet area for birding and observing wildlife. The park also has other unnamed paths, one of which follows an old former highway west from the entrance road.

USGS MAP: Dahlgren

ACCESS: On US 301, north side, at approach to the Potomac River Bridge (Nice Memorial), 3.1 miles east of VA 206 crossroads.

ADDRESS AND INFORMATION: King George County, P.O. Box 71, King George, VA 22485; phone: 540-775-4FUN.

## Lancaster County

### HICKORY HOLLOW TRAIL

Lancaster County is a coastal farming area bordered by the Rappahannock River on the south and known for its scenic bays, branches, and breezy beach points. It has only one public trail, the easy, 4-mile **Hickory Hollow Trail**. It is an exceptionally good example of a trail prepared for educational purposes. There are forty-five different signs describing, with an unusual degree of detail, the species

1140

1141

of trees, shrubs, and wildflowers near Western Branch. Some of the trees are oak, hickory, elm, black gum, green ash, and red maple. At 0.2 mile the trail forks left to make the long loop.

USGS MAP: Lancaster

ACCESS: From the town of Lancaster, drive 0.6 mile east; on VA 3, pass the school and turn left on SR 604 for 0.3 mile left to parking area.

ADDRESS AND INFORMATION: Public Works Department, P.O. Box 167, Lancaster, VA 22503; phone: 804-462-5129.


# Loudoun County

This county has twelve county parks and two regional parks. Its eastern border is Fairfax County and its western border is Clarke County in Virginia and Jefferson County in West Virginia. Two mountain ridges (Catoctin Mountain and Short Hill Mountain) are parallel to the most western ridges of the Blue Ridge. On the latter is the **Appalachian Trail**. Enhancing the scenic Blue Ridge is the scenic Potomac River on the county's north boundary with Montgomery and Frederick Counties in Maryland. The county was formed in 1757 and was the location of a major artery of traffic for commerce and passage west to the Shenandoah Valley. Of the 40 miles of the **Washington and Old Dominion (W&OD) Railroad Trail**, a multiple-use trail, 22.4 miles are from Herndon west through Loudoun County to Purcellville. Also in the county is Red Rock Wilderness Overlook Regional Park with its **Loblolly Trail**. Both this trail and the **W&OD Railroad Trail** are de- 1142 scribed under Northern Virginia Regional Park Authority in Chapter 14. Among the county's parks with trails are Claude Moore Park, Franklin Park, and Banshee Reeks Nature Preserve.

ADDRESS AND INFORMATION: Loudoun County Department of Parks, Recreation and Community Services, 1 Harrison St., SE, 4th Floor, Leesburg, VA 20177; phone: 703-771-5663; fax: 703-771-5354. Maps and brochures are available.

The major facilities of the 203-acre Franklin Park are nine sports fields, an outdoor swimming pool, picnic shelters, children's playground, and (to be constructed) a 300-seat theater. New forests are being created by planting thousands of seedlings, and there are two floral gardens. The park plans include a dual trail system, one about 3 miles long that circles the park's boundary for hikers and cross-country track, and a second more internal trail for equestrians and mountain bikers. Access is off VA 7 Bus on Franklin Park Drive, south, about halfway between Roundhill and Purcellville. Address is 17501 Franklin Park Dr., Purcellville, VA 20132; phone: 540-338-7603.

Banshee Reeks Nature Preserve has 695 acres of farm fields, forests, ponds, and streams. A historic manor house serves as park office, and there are other buildings. Educational programs are provided on nature trails, and a nature trail is planned for those with physical disabilities. Among the current nature trails are **Beaver Creek Trail** (1-mi. loop) that passes old silos toward a pond. Connecting with the trail is **Cathedral Trail** (1-mi. loop), a passage through a forest of large tulip and beech trees. Other trails are **Cedar Valley Trail** (1-mi. loop), and **Eastern Water Cress Trail** and **Western Water Cress Trail** (each 0.5 mi.). **Bank Barn Trail** is 1 mile one way, and **Snipe Trail** is 0.5 mile. Other walks are **Big Meadow Trail** and **Twin Springs Trail** for a 0.5-mile loop. **Springhouse Run Trail** is a 0.2-mile self-guided nature trail with ten labeled stops. (You may wish to call in advance for open hours and services.) For access from Leesburg south on US 15 Bus take SR 621 (Evergreen Mills Rd.) for 5 miles to turn right on SR 771 (The Woods Rd.). After 1 mile turn left to entrance. Address is 21085 The Woods Rd., Leesburg, VA 20175; phone: 703-669-0316; web: <www.bansheereeks.org>.

1143–52

## CLAUDE MOORE PARK

The 357-acre Claude Moore Park is named in honor of Claude Moore, M.D. (1892–1991), who purchased the historic Lanesville property in 1941. After his retirement from George Washington University Medical School, he served on the National Wildlife Federation's board of directors. He transferred the land to the Federation in 1975, and the Federation protected it until 1986 when Loudoun County began the process of purchase (completed by 1990). The park is in two major sections. The north section has an entrance east from Cascades Parkway on Vestal's Gap Road, and the immediate second entrance is on Lanesville Road east from Cascades Parkway. The Vestal's Gap section has parking areas, visitor center, and Lanesville Heritage Area. Here is 0.6 mile of the original route of the Vestal's Gap Road (1722), Frogshackle Log Cabin, Lanesville House (late 1700s), barns, boarding school house, tenant home, and other outbuildings. At the second entrance are parking areas, Sportsplex, and Loudoun Heritage Farm Museum. The museum has 30 acres of interpretive farming and a 10,000-square-foot exhibit hall. Among the exhibits are a general store, and items to document ten generations of agricultural life since 1719. There is also a working blacksmith shop and, during the summer, a petting zoo. On the west side of the museum are three lakes for catch-and-release fishing (largemouth bass, channel catfish, and bluegill). The park offers educational programs for all age groups, and special events for special days such as National Trails Day and Fourth of July. Bicycling is allowed only on paved areas. There are seven lighted softball/baseball fields. Surrounding and connecting all these fantastic facilities are eight trails and at least ten interconnecting short trails to make about 11 miles for hiking.

ACCESS: In Sterling on VA 7 go south 1 mile on Cascades Parkway to Vestal's Gap Road and Claude Moore Park entrance, left.

LENGTH AND DIFFICULTY: 3.5 miles (5.6 km); easy

CONNECTING TRAILS: **Little Stoney Mountain Trail** (3 mi.), **Hickory Nut Trail** 1154–59 (0.5 mi.), **Old Oak Trail** (0.8 mi.), **Southern Woods Trail** (0.8 mi.), **Beaver Slide Trail** (0.2 mi.), **Black Willow Spring Trail** (0.2 mi.)

FEATURES: old-growth forest, historic sites, marsh, streams, wildflowers, birds

TRAILHEADS: Begin at the Vestal's Gap Road park entrance, north and before you arrive at the parking area. Other connecting trails leave from behind the visitor center, on Vestal's Road east, and from parking areas on Loudoun Park Lane.

INTRODUCTION: The hiking trail system has numerous crossings and connections. To avoid confusion request a trail map at the visitor center. It will show the names of the trails and their blaze colors. It will also indicate the many short connector trails blazed in yellow. This will allow you to cut from trail to trail depending on your time and interest.

DESCRIPTION: If beginning clockwise on the blue-blazed **Scout Trail** loop, start at the most immediate trail, left after entering Vestal's Gap Road to the parking area. Pass yellow-blazed short connecting trails right to red-blazed **Hickory Nut Trail** (0.5 mi.) and orange-blazed **Old Oak Trail** (0.8 mi.) loop. Stay on the **Scout Trail** and cross white-blazed **Little Stoney Mountain Trail** (3 mi.) twice before curving south to cross Vestal's Gap Road at 1.1 miles. Along the way you pass through cedar, honeysuckle, walnut, Virginia pine, oak, and hickory, and by resting seats at 0.4 mile and 0.5 mile. Turn right on a gravel road with a power line, then leave it, left, at a parking area (for Loudoun Heritage Farm Museum). Pass left of the soccer field and cross a footbridge at 1.3 miles. Pass a marsh and cross another footbridge. (Park View High School is across the park boundary, left.) At 1.8 miles turn right at a juncture with **Southern Woods Trail**, left and right. (To the left it is 0.1 mi. to West Church St.) Turn right on **Southern Woods Trail**, and after 375 feet turn left. (The **Southern Woods Trail** goes ahead 30 yd. to cross **Little Stoney Mountain Trail**, left and right.) In an open hardwood forest pass resting benches and join **Little Stoney Mountain Trail** at 2.3 miles. Stay joined to cross **Southern Woods Trail** and Loudoun Park Lane into a cedar grove. Cross two footbridges near each other at 2.7 miles. At 2.8 miles **Little Stoney Mountain Trail** goes left and **Scout Trail** continues right. After 95 yards meet pink-blazed **Beaver Slide Trail** (0.2 mi.). (It goes to the south beaver pond dam, where it can also make a connection with **Little Stoney Mountain Trail**, right, and green-blazed **Black Willow Spring Trail** [0.2 mi.] left.) Continue on **Scout Trail** and at a resting bench notice there is a green blaze for the **Black Willow Spring Trail**, right, at 3.1 miles. Connect and follow briefly with **Little Stoney Mountain Trail** before leaving it left to arrive at Vestal's Gap Road at 3.5 miles.

ADDRESS AND INFORMATION: Claude Moore Park, 21544 Cascades Parkway, Ster-

*Black Willow Spring Trail,*
*Claude Moore Park,*
*Loudoun County*

ling, VA 20164; phone: 703-444-1275. (Loudoun Heritage Farm Museum is same address, but phone number is 703-421-5322.) Maps and brochures are available.

## New Kent County

Historic and rural New Kent County is geographically bordered by rivers and creeks. On the north side is Pamunkey River and on the south side is Chickahominy River. The northwest area has Black Creek and in the southeast is Ware Creek drainage from Diascund Creek Reservoir to York River. Running through the county is I-64 between Richmond and Williamsburg. The county was formed in the mid-1600s, and its agricultural lands and historic sites remain part of its appeal to local citizens and visitors. It is the only county in the nation with the birthplace and marriage place of two national presidential wives—Martha Danridge Custis, wife of President George Washington, and Letitia Christian Tyler, wife of President John Tyler.

The county recently acquired about 140 acres of a 565-acre tract of the Chesa-

peake Forest Products Company. On this property has been the popular **Warren-** 1160
**eye Nature Trail**. It had three blazed loops and forty-nine educational markers
that described trees, wildlife, and wildflowers. The longest loop was 2.9 miles and
if followed counterclockwise it passed under a power line at 1.4 miles before a
descent to a stream and then an ascent to the site of Warreneye Church, built in
1703. After an overlook at 2.1 miles the trail descended to a stream for a return
or circuit on the **Marl Loop Trail** at 2.4 miles. The county had not made a final 1161
decision on trail maintenance or relocation at the time of this book's publication. Visitors may consult the New Kent Parks and Recreation office for updated
information.

USGS MAP: West Point

ACCESS: From I-64, exit 220 (east of Richmond), take VA 33 northeast for 3.8
miles to the Warreneye Nature Trail parking area on the right.

ADDRESSES AND INFORMATION: New Kent Parks and Recreation, 12007 Courthouse Circle (P.O. Box 50), New Kent, VA 23224; phone: 804-966-8502; web:
<www.co.new-kent.va.us>. New Kent Historical Society, P.O. Box 24, New Kent,
VA 23124.


# Northampton County

## INDIANTOWN PARK

The 52-acre Indiantown Park, on Virginia's Eastern Shore, is a converted U.S.
government camera site. The historic area is adjacent to an old Native American
village and the Pocahontas Farm. Financial assistance from public and private
sources and volunteer work made it possible for the county's first park to open.
Among its facilities are a recreational center, a swimming pool, ballfields, picnic
areas, and 1.5-mile **Indiantown Nature Trail**. It begins between the parking lot 1162
and the softball field. Forming a loop, the trail passes an Indian burial ground
among hardwoods and pines.

USGS MAP: Cheriton

ACCESS: From US 13 at Eastville, go east on SR 631 for 2 miles to park entrance.

ADDRESS AND INFORMATION: Northampton County Parks and Recreation, P.O.
Box 847, Eastville, VA 23347; phone: 757-678-5179.


# Patrick County

Fairy Stone State Park is east of Stuart in this county (see Chapter 11, Piedmont
Division), and west of Stuart is the birthplace of Gen. J. E. B. Stuart, General Lee's
top cavalry commander. General Stuart died in Richmond on May 12, 1864, from

war injuries. The county's seat of government, Taylorsville, was renamed Stuart in his honor. (See Laurel Hill, General Stuart's birthplace, in Chapter 16.) The county's south border is North Carolina and northwest boundary is the Blue Ridge Parkway. The county also has the historic Reynolds Homestead near the county's eastern border. West of Stuart on US 58 near the top of the mountains is De Hart Botanical Gardens (see Chapter 16), and farther west 1.8 miles is Fred Clifton Park with a picnic area and Lovers Leap, a scenic overlook of Smith River Valley. Among the county's parks are four with trails. The shortest and most unique trail is **1163** **Nature Walk**, centered between a tennis area and picnic area at I. C. De Hart Memorial Park. Access from the juncture of VA 8 and VA 40 in Woolwine is 2.6 miles east on VA 40 to park entrance, left. At Patrick Springs Park, there is a ball-**1164** field, playground, picnic area, community building, and 0.3-mile **Patrick Springs Trail**. It makes a loop by a stream partly in woods with tall trees, chinquapins, and wildflowers. Access is off US 58 on Patrick Springs Road (SR 680) immediately right and shortly to Ball Park Road, left.

## DE HART PARK

This park has ball courts and fields, picnic shelters, playground, swimming pool, **1165** and 0.5-mile lighted and paved **De Hart Park Trail**. The trail makes a loop around a large meadow through which is a stream. The park was made possible by the late Alice De Hart of the Woolwine vicinity.

ACCESS: In Stuart from the junction of US 58 Bus and VA 8, drive north 0.4 mile to Johnson Street and Industrial Park, right. After a short descent, the park entrance is right. Access from the new US 58, bypassing the town's east side, descends west on Johnson Street to park entrance, left.

## MOUNTAIN TOP PARK

**1166** Near Vesta on the Blue Ridge Mountains, this park includes the 0.5-mile **Mountain Top Trail**. A nature trail, it makes a circle around a large ballfield. In the process it descends partly around the field and grassy areas into the woods. About halfway it passes through a dense forest of rhododendron and crosses a small stream where there are ferns and wildflowers. The park also has other athletic fields and tennis courts.

ACCESS: After 1.5 miles west on US 58 from the post office in Vesta, turn left at entrance. (Ahead 0.1 mi. on US 58 is a store and SR 264.) From the Blue Ridge Parkway and Meadows of Dan east on US 58, the park entrance is right after 2.5 miles.

ADDRESS AND INFORMATION: Patrick County Recreation Department, P.O. Box 506, Stuart, VA 24171; phone: 276-694-3917

# Prince William County

The Prince William County Park Authority, created in 1977 from the previous parks and recreation agency, has fifty-one recreational parks with approximately 3,000 acres. Additional recreational areas are associated with the public school system and with the cities of Manassas and Manassas Park. Two parks have trails that focus on nature study.

## VETERANS MEMORIAL PARK

The easy, 0.8-mile **Veterans Memorial Nature Trail** has two decks for observing     1167
migratory and local waterfowl, forest succession, wetland plants, flowers, and wildlife. White marsh mallow and water lilies are prevalent in the summer.

USGS MAP: Occoquan

ACCESS: In Woodbridge at junction of US 1 and SR 636 (Veterans Dr.) (at Featherstone Shopping Center), go east 1.9 miles on Featherstone Road to Veterans' Drive and parking area, left.

ADDRESSES AND INFORMATION: Veterans Memorial Park, 14300 Veterans Dr., Woodbridge, VA 22191; phone: 703-491-2183. County office: Prince William County Park Authority, 14420 Bristow Rd., Manassas, VA 20112; phone: 703-792-7060.

## LOCUST SHADE REGIONAL PARK

This 778-acre day-use park has a lake, a golf course, a marina with boat rentals, ballfields and tennis courts, picnic areas, playgrounds, and two loop trails. Access to **Locust Shade Trail** is at the fourth parking lot, left, after the park entrance.     1168
Ascend on a hill as part of a nature trail near a fence of I-95, descend, pass side trail right to ballfield, and go under a power line. Cross a footbridge at 0.5 mile, and 200 feet farther is a bridge, right, which is part of the loop. Continue ahead, upstream in a peaceful forest away from the sound of I-95 traffic. At 1.2 miles curve right within the sound of SR 619 traffic. Begin descent from hill at 1.6 miles and cross the wooden footbridge at 2.2 miles to complete the loop. Return to fourth parking lot at 2.8 miles.

Another easy trail is the forested **South Trail**, a 1.4-mile loop whose trailhead is     1169
at the far end of the second parking area (closer to the park's entrance). After 0.1 mile it divides. If going right, cross a footbridge, ascend to a ridge, and follow its crest. Descend, cross a stream in a beech grove, and at 0.7 mile turn left on an old road for a return to the parking area. (At the trailhead there is a 0.2-mi. connecting trail to the fourth parking lot.)

USGS MAP: Quantico

ACCESS: From I-95, exit 151, go east on SR 619 (Joplin Rd.) for 0.4 mile, turn right on US 1, and after 1.3 miles turn right into park.

ADDRESSES AND INFORMATION: Locust Shade Regional Park, 4701 Locust Shade Dr., Triangle, VA 22172; phone: 703-221-8579. County office: Prince William County Park Authority, 14420 Bristow Rd., Manassas, VA 20112; phone: 703-792-7060.

## Roanoke County

Roanoke County has forty-eight parks, and properties for camps, activity centers, and public school recreation areas, spread widely throughout the county on a total of 840 acres. The Department of Parks and Recreation has a combined park system with the Roanoke County School Board and the Roanoke County Board of Supervisors. The county also operates parks in the town of Vinton, and on properties that connect with Salem. Some parks emphasize preservation and natural areas. Those with trails are described below.

### GARST MILL PARK/MUD LICK CREEK GREENWAY

This beautiful green valley has a paved 0.6-mile greenway through a former farm meadow with Mud Lick Creek winding through the center. The artful trail design goes south from Halevan Road to Cresthill Drive. Near the parking lot is a children's playground and rest room facilities. The park is managed by Roanoke County Parks.

ACCESS: From VA 419 at Cave Spring, drive north 0.5 mile on Bramleton Avenue (US 221) and turn left at the Shell station onto Garst Mill Road. After 1 mile turn left at the silo onto Halevan Road. Park entrance is left.

### GLEN COVE PARK

1170 The 0.5-mile self-guiding **Nature Trail** loops through a 16-acre forest and by a stream. Emphasis here is on herbaceous plants and small mammals.

ACCESS: In northwestern Roanoke, follow either Cove Road or Peter's Creek Road east off VA 419 between US 460 and I-81.

### HANGING ROCK BATTLEFIELD TRAIL

This 1.9-mile abandoned railroad trail received its name from a Civil War battle. After a defeat in Lynchburg of Union forces led by Gen. David Hunter, his wagon column of supplies and artillery retreated toward New Castle. The retreat was delayed by a narrow passage and rocky bluffs through this gap at Mason Creek. Confederate general Robert Ransom's cavalry was in pursuit, and on June 21, 1864, General Ransom sent General John McCausland to strike the retreating Union forces. Damage was done to the Union's supply of weapons and ammunitions, and troops were captured. Soon additional Union infantry and cavalry arrived and General McCausland had to abandon the gap.

If beginning at the north trailhead, follow the trail under VA 419 highway bridge to Mason Creek. Rock-hop across, or if the water is too high return to cross on the bridge. Pass the Orange Market, a convenience store, and cross Kessler Mill Road to the old railroad. For the next 0.2 mile are history markers and maps about the Hanging Rock military encounter. The signage was made possible by the Hanging Rock Battlefield and Railway Preservation Foundation, the former Catawba Branch of the Norfolk and Western Railway, and the United Daughters of Confederacy Monuments. On a scenic and pleasant passage, go under I-81 bridge at 0.6 mile and by other markers at 0.7 mile, 1.2 miles, and 1.3 miles. Cross Kessler Mill Road at 1.5 miles where passage is close to private homes. The trail ends at 1.9 miles at a parking area on the west side of Kessler Mill Road, opposite from Resco Steel Products. Some of the plant life seen along the trail are bloodroot, fire pink, wild flax, silktree, basket willow, redbud, and ferns.

USGS MAP: Salem

ACCESS: From I-81 take Salem exit 141 and turn northwest onto Electric Road (VA 419). After 0.4 mile turn right on Dutch Oven Road to the parking area, left, for the northern trailhead. The southern trailhead is off East Main Street (US 460) in Salem onto Kessler Mill Road north for 0.4 mile.


## HAPPY HOLLOW GARDENS

These gardens were presented to Roanoke County by the H. B. Wharton and Foster Burgess families in 1998. In the gardens are a connecting combination of foot trails that create 1 mile of streamside sections and ascending and descending routes. From the parking lot the access begins on the **Azalea Trail** across a board-  1171–75
walk, also accessible for wheelchairs. After 0.1 mile is a picnic table to the left, and the **Chestnut Trail** turns right. Other trails that follow are **Spice Bush Trail**, **White Pine Trail**, and **Big Oak Trail**. The park's botanical emphasis is on both native plant species and ornamental plantings. The park has an amphitheater and a picnic area.

USGS MAP: Bent Mountain

ACCESS: Take Mount Chestnut Road (SR 692) off Bent Mountain Road (US 211) and go 2.3 miles up the mountain. Turn left at the park entrance. Mount Chestnut Road is 0.3 mile south of Poages Mill Church of the Brethren on US 211, or 4.3 miles south on US 211 from VA 419 junction in Roanoke.


## WOLF CREEK GREENWAY

This 1.6-mile greenway connects two parks, a shopping center, a medical facility, three schools, and a number of subdivisions in a combined area of Roanoke

County and the town of Vinton that adjoins the city of Roanoke on the west side. A suggested beginning for either walking or bicycling, particularly if you do not have a shuttle vehicle, is to start at Goode Park. Its entrance is on SR 961 on the north side of Washington Avenue (VA 24) 1.1 miles west of the Blue Ridge Parkway intersection, and across the highway from County Crossing Store.

From the parking area start north at the ball park and directional sign to Stonebridge Park. At 0.5 mile cross Tulip Lane to soon juncture with an interpretive trail that identifies box elder, black gum, basswood, hickory, and other trees. Pass Terrier Baseball Field and enter a grove of maples to exit at William Byrd Schools and nearby Stonebridge Park at 0.7 mile. Backtrack.

To continue south on the greenway, follow the trail out of Goode Park to an underpass of Washington Avenue at 0.3 mile. Cross Wolf Creek on a bridge. At 0.5 mile is a Roanoke Valley Greenway sign and a 100-yard access route, right, to a parking area at Lynn Haven Baptist Church. At 0.9 mile arrive at Hardy Road (SR 634). Backtrack, unless you have a shuttle car parked to the right, a parking courtesy of private landowners. On Hardy Road west it is 0.5 mile to VA 24 (Bypass Rd.).

USGS MAPS: Roanoke, Stewartsville

ACCESS: See descriptions above.

ADDRESSES AND INFORMATION: Roanoke County Department of Parks, Recreation, and Tourism, 1206 Kessler Mill Rd., Salem, VA 24153; phone: 540-387-6078; fax: 540-387-6146. Roanoke City Parks and Recreation, 210 Reserve Ave., Roanoke, VA 24016; phone: 540-853-2236. (A brochure of the major trails in the metropolitan area is available.) Salem Parks and Recreation, 216 South Broad St., Salem, VA 24153; phone: 540-375-3057. Roanoke Valley Greenways, P.O. Box 29800, Roanoke, VA 24018; phone: 540-776-7159 (commissioned by local governments). Pathfinders for Greenways, P.O. Box 8553, Roanoke, VA 24014; phone: 540-766-7159; fax: 540-772-2108 (a nonprofit organization that assists in coordinating volunteer services and fund-raising for the trails).

## Rockbridge County

### LAKE ROBERTSON PARK

Named in honor of Senator A. Willis Robertson, a devoted conservationist, this park has 581 acres of hills and meadows and a 31-acre lake stocked with bass and sunfish on the eastern slopes of North Mountain. The park has a swimming pool and bathhouse, tennis courts, ballfields, picnic areas with shelter, boat concessions, children's playground, trail network, a campground (with hookups), and a boat ramp. Hunting is allowed during fall and spring game seasons outside the developed areas. (One of the sponsoring agencies for the county is the Virginia Commission of Game and Inland Fisheries.)

ACCESS: From US 11 junction with VA 251 in Lexington, drive west on VA 251 for 10.6 miles. Turn left on SR 770 in Collierstown, and after 1.3 miles turn right on SR 652 to the park.

**Nature Trail** (0.5 mi.), **Grouse Haven Trail** (1.4 mi.), **Fox Path Trail** (0.25 mi.),     1176–84
**Squirrel Run Trail** (0.5 mi.), **Hawk Creek Trail** (1.1 mi.), **Deer Lick Trail** (1 mi.), **Turkey Roost Trail** (1.7 mi.), **Opossum Pass Trail** (0.5 mi.), **Lake Trail** (1.6 mi.)

LENGTH AND DIFFICULTY: 7.5 miles (12 km) combined, round-trip; easy to difficult

FEATURES: scenic views, wildlife, shrubs/wildflowers, lake

TRAILHEADS: from campground, picnic shelter, or boat house

DESCRIPTION: For a short loop or backtracking consider the **Nature Trail** from the picnic area across the entrance road from the office. Ascend the ridge to an access trail to the **Lake Trail**, left, but follow the **Nature Trail** right among hemlocks and other tree identification signs down the hill to an open field. To your right is the swimming pool and children's playground. Reenter the woods to ascend past white ash and pitch pine. At 0.5 mile exit at the park's entrance road. Backtrack or walk up the entrance road 0.1 mile to the park office. If hiking the **Lake Trail** from the picnic area and its juncture with the **Nature Trail**, descend toward the lake where you can turn right or left. If descending right it is 0.3 mile to the dam where you can cross and make a loop. If descending left you have scenic views of the lake and beach on a descent to cross a footbridge and arrive at the boat launch parking area after 0.3 mile. From there go upstream and clockwise complete the 1.6-mile **Lake Trail**.

If making a loop from the campground pass through campsites #25 and #26, where trail signs give direction. It is suggested you use a park map in your choice of loops through the hardwood forest. There are numerous ridges and hollows. Ascend on the **Grouse Haven Trail** to a shelter (not to be used for camping or fires) at 1.4 miles. (Here is 0.2-mi. **Fox Path Trail**, which makes a shortcut to **Hawk Creek Trail**.) Ahead is **Squirrel Run Trail**, which makes a connection with **Hawk Creek Trail**, right. (A descent on this trail back to the campground makes a 2.6-mi. loop.) If continuing on **Squirrel Run Trail**, make a connection with **Deer Lick Trail**, right, and another shelter (not to be used for camping or fires). (A descent on this trail back to the campground makes a 3.1-mi. loop.) From the **Deer Lick Trail** the **Squirrel Run Trail** goes 0.1 mile farther north and becomes **Turkey Roost Trail**. (A descent on this trail toward the lake and up to the campground makes a 4-mi. loop.)

Hikers not staying at the campground may wish to use a route from the parking area at the lake boat launch. If this is chosen go up the hollow from the lake to cross the road and enter the forest on an old road for the **Deer Lick Trail**. (At 0.1 mile is an access road left that leads 0.2 mile up the ridge to a small amphitheater and park office area.) Continue up the hollow, then steeply on a ridge at 0.4 mile. Shagbark hickory is here. At 0.7 mile pass **Opossum Pass Trail**. (It is a 0.5-mi. connector between **Deer Lick Trail** and **Turkey Roost Trail**.) Ascend to 1.1 miles to meet **Squirrel Run Trail**, right and left. (Here is also the shelter mentioned above.) Turn right and after 0.1 mile the trail becomes **Turkey Roost Trail**. Descend on switchbacks, cross a footbridge at 1.9 miles. Ascend; arrive at a divide of **Turkey Roost Trail** and north side of **Lake Trail** at 2.2 miles. Follow **Turkey Roost Trail** and descend on a limestone formation at 2.5 miles. Return to the lake parking area for a 2.9-mile loop.

USGS MAP: Collierstown

ADDRESS AND INFORMATION: Lake Robertson Park and Rockbridge County Parks and Recreation, 106 Lake Robertson Dr., Lexington, VA 24450; phone: 540-463-4164. A free brochure is available.

# Shenandoah County

This scenic county is in the Shenandoah Valley with the North Fork of the Shenandoah River flowing northeast through the county's center. On the west is the Shenandoah Mountain range and border of West Virginia, and east is the Massanutten Mountain range in the Lee Ranger District of George Washington National Forest (see Chapter 1). In the county is Shenandoah Caverns, New Market Battlefield, and a ribbon of recreational parks (some with paved walking and fitness trails) at public schools and towns along US 11 (Old Valley Pike Rd.). Plans are for a new and expansive park (151 acres) to be constructed southeast of Strasburg.

### SHENANDOAH COUNTY PARK

With 67.5 acres the park has tennis courts, ballfields, picnic area, playground, and two trails. One is **Toms Brook Trail**, a 0.2-mile round-trip grassy trail to a Civil War monument. The other trail, **Shenandoah County Park Trail**, makes a loop around the sport fields for 0.8 mile. It serves as both a fitness trail with marked stations and a walking trail. It passes through open fields among cedars, through a hardwood forest, and connects with the **Tuscarora Trail**. (East on the **Tuscarora Trail** it is 35.8 mi. to the **Appalachian Trail**, and west 20.4 mi. for its entry into West Virginia [see Chapter 1].)

ACCESS: On US 11 (between Woodstock and Strasburg) in Maurertown at Mountain Brethren Church, drive 0.7 mile north from the church to park entrance, right.

ADDRESS AND INFORMATION: Department of Parks and Recreation, 508 Piccadilly St., Edinburg, VA 22824; phone: 540-984-3030; fax: 540-984-8032; e-mail: <parks@co.shenandoah.va.us>. Brochures and county maps available.

1185–86

# Stafford County

### CURTIS MEMORIAL PARK

The 565-acre Curtis Memorial Park, dedicated to property donors Jesse and Emma Curtis, is Stafford County's answer to recreational needs for its citizens. The park is exceptionally well landscaped and meticulously maintained. Its facilities include an Olympic-size swimming pool, picnic areas, tennis courts, ballfields, and a 91-acre lake stocked for fishing. The county has seventeen other parks, some affiliated with the public school system. Behind the park office parking area is the easy, 0.4-mile **Cedar Path Nature Trail**. It has an outstanding display of vascular 1187 plants: hardwoods, pine and cedar, wild orchids and azaleas, huckleberry, ferns, lichens, and clubmoss.

ACCESS: From I-95 in Fredericksburg drive west on US 17 for 5.2 miles to SR 612. Turn right for 2 miles to the park entrance.

ADDRESS AND INFORMATION: Stafford County Parks and Recreation, 58 Curtis Lane, Hartwood, VA 22406; phone: 540-752-5632.

# Wythe County

This county is situated between part of Mount Rogers National Recreation Area, to the south, and Walker Mountain range, to its north, both part of Jefferson National Forest. In its center is a long valley where Wytheville, the county seat of government, is located. The scenic county is considered a "vacation land" with popular attractions such as New River Trail State Park, Shot Tower Historical State Park, Raven Cliff Furnace, Little Dry Run Wilderness, and Big Walker Mountain Scenic Byway with a lookout. The settlers who named a community here "Rural Retreat" knew what they were doing. Certainly the park described below is a retreat. The village of Rural Retreat is the home of the founder of the soft drink Dr. Pepper.

### RURAL RETREAT LAKE AND CAMPGROUND

This serene and well-designed county park is outstanding by any standards. It is open year round, and nature assists with average spring and summer temperatures of 74°. There are primitive and full service camping sites with water and electricity, deluxe swimming pool (open daily from Memorial Day through Labor Day), picnic areas and pavilions, boat ramp and row boat rentals, fishing (muskie, northern pike, and bass), and two hiking trails. To hike the **Lake Trail** drive to the 1188 parking area by the lake at picnic shelter #1. Enter the forest and follow the trail along the lakeshore through hardwoods, white pine, lavender knapweed and wild azaleas. (Campground accesses are to the right.) Cross the dam at 0.7 mile. After ascending hills and passing lake coves, follow an old road to a gate at 1.8 miles. Either backtrack for a 3.6-mile hike, or follow the paved roads with all left turns to pass the park office/snack bar at 2.7 miles, and return to picnic shelter #1 at 3.3 miles. A double loop can be made on the **Pond Trail**. If hiking from the picnic parking area on a grassy hill, ascend into the woods to the corner of shelter #4. For hiking clockwise, continue up the ridge to curve right for a descent. At 0.3 mile pass a short connector trail in the loop. Continue to descend into a hollow of hardwoods and black cohosh. Ascend steeply, take a sharp right, and descend to a trail fork at 0.6 mile. Left is to a bridge and lake where you enter a meadow. By the lake are willow and hazelnut. Arrive at the park entrance road at 0.8 mile. Backtrack. At the fork, stay left and return to picnic shelter #4 and parking area at 1.2 miles.

ACCESS: From I-81, exit 60, drive south 3.2 miles on VA 90 to pass through the village of Rural Retreat where VA 90 becomes SR 749. Turn right on SR 677 and after 1.5 miles turn left on SR 678 for 0.3 mile to office, left.

ADDRESSES AND INFORMATION: Rural Retreat Lake and Campground, 250 Lake Rd., Rural Retreat, VA 24358; phone: 276-686-4331; fax: 276-686-8323. Wythe County Department of Parks and Recreation, 225 South Fourth St., Wytheville, VA 24352; phone: 276-223-6022; fax: 276-223-6091. Free brochures are available.

*He hath no leisure who useth it not.*
GEORGE HERBERT (1593–1633)

# 13. Municipal Parks and Recreation Areas

There are nearly 1,000 communities, towns, and cities in the Old Dominion. About 190 are incorporated, and 45 are independent municipalities. Virginia Beach is the largest. Names reflect the history of honoring places of inhabitants' origins and people, and natural environments such as Forest, Blue Grass, Clover, Ivy, Catalpa, Hickory, Oak Grove, Laurel, Linden, Piney River, Poplar Hill, Walnut Point, Oyster, Fishersville, Deerfield, Raven, Birdsnest, and many more like them. Although the names of Eden and Xanadu are not found, there are plenty of other place names that reflect idyllic beauty. Some are Buena Vista, Roseland, Ocean View, and Grand View.

Parks and recreation departments are in seventy-two towns and cities. Under city government they usually have a supervisor, manager, or director with a budget approved by a city council or other government body. Towns may not be as independent because of county government jurisdiction or combination policies or programs. Planning assistance for the parks is available from the state's Division of Planning and Recreation Resources. The assistance includes water conservation, environmental regulations, grants, greenways, and recreational programs. Parks that have trail systems, other than physical fitness or service trails between facilities, are described in this chapter. For a directory of the state's town, city, and county parks and recreation departments, call 804-786-2556 at the state Department of Conservation and Recreation in Richmond.

## Alexandria

The area was settled in 1670, but its historic townhouses and Potomac River waterfront shops did not develop until surveyors John West Jr. and George Washington laid out streets and equal-size blocks in 1749. In 1789 the town was ceded to the District of Columbia, as was adjoining Arlington County. In 1846 Alexandria was returned to Virginia at the citizens' request. Walks in the historic district can begin at the visitor bureau at the William Ramsay House, the city's oldest (1724). It is at 221 King and Fairfax Streets. The city has more than forty-five parks and a network of bicycle trails. Some are walking trails that connect for a 7.5-mile

389

continuous hike from Ramsay Nature Center at the western edge of the city east to the Potomac River.

## DORA KELLEY NATURE PARK

1190    The Ramsay Nature Center, at the western end of the William Ramsay School on Sanger Avenue, is the western trailhead for the easy 1.5-mile **Dora Kelley Trail**. The center has information about the twenty-eight numbered interpretive posts on the trail. Begin at the western end of Sanger Avenue and descend to rocky Holmes Run to turn left. Continue along the stream on a paved bike/hike trail. The guideposts identify trees, shrubs, flowers, and animals among tall oaks and hickories. Cross the creek near a scenic rocky area and then cross Beauregard Street into the Holmes Scenic Easement.

ACCESS: From Shirley Memorial Highway, I-395, exit 4, go northwest on Seminary Road to Beauregard Street. Turn left and go 0.8 mile to Sanger Avenue, right, for entrance to the parking area at the Ramsay Nature Center and end of Sanger Avenue.

## BROOKVALLEY PARK AND HOLMES RUN

1191    The **Dora Kelley Trail** connects here with the 1.8-mile **Holmes Run Trail** under I-395. The trail continues southeast, crosses under Duke Street, and continues along Holmes Run to Eisenhower Avenue. Most of this easy trail meanders through a predominantly residential neighborhood featuring a variety of views and vistas, play equipment for children, and picnic areas. The trail also includes Alexandria's Bicentennial Tree, a 200-year-old willow oak.

ACCESS: From Ramsay School follow Sanger Avenue southeast to cross Beauregard Street and I-395 to Van Dorn Street. Turn right and after one block turn left on Taney Street, then right on Ripley Street to Holmes Run Parkway and the western trailhead. For the eastern trailhead continue south on Van Dorn Street 1.6 miles (from Taney St.) to Eisenhower Street. Turn left and follow it 1.7 miles into Hensley Park and across the stream to Cameron Run Regional Park and trail intersection.

## CAMERON RUN REGIONAL PARK

1192    From here the 3.8-mile **Cameron Run Trail** passes through a forested area, crosses a bridge at Lake Cook, crosses Eisenhower Avenue, and parallels the road. After 1.4 miles pass the cloverleaf of Telegraph Road, which intersects with the noise pollution of I-95/495. Pass the Eisenhower Avenue metro station and at 2.4 miles enter a gated trail to a vacant area before arriving at Payne Street and another gate. Turn north to Wilkes Street and make a right to descend to the waterfront area at

Pomander Park. Here is a juncture, right and left, with the **Mount Vernon Trail** (see Chapter 9). The **Jones Point Trail** is 0.5 mile on the right. 1193

ACCESS: From Cameron Run Regional Park drive east on Eisenhower Avenue to Holland Lane. Turn left to a right turn on Duke Street. Follow it to Union Street and turn right to the Marina and Pomander Parks.

ADDRESSES AND INFORMATION: Department of Recreation, Parks and Cultural Activities, 1108 Jefferson St., Alexandria, VA 22314; phone: 703-838-4343. Available are trail and bike maps. Ramsay Nature Center, 5700 Sanger Ave., Alexandria, VA 22311; phone: 703-838-4829.

# Bedford

As with many other places in Virginia, Bedford continues to have its charm, and makes efforts to respect its history and honor its quality of life. It was established in 1782 with the name of Liberty, and since then has shown its community pride. There is an advertising slogan of "the world's best little town." Its geographic location is in the town's favor. Only a dozen miles northwest are the Peaks of Otter and the Blue Ridge Parkway, and the Jefferson National Forest. Smith Mountain Lake State Park is 28 miles south of town. In addition to its parks with trails, it has a town center walking tour that can include twenty-one historic sites within a ten-block area, or advance to a 3-mile tour to include other residential and cultural sites. Bedford's town center was listed on the National Register of Historic Places in 1984. If you walk "centertown" you will see architectural beauty in arches, decorative cornices, and cartouches.

The town's Department of Parks, Recreation, and Cemeteries is another example of the community's pride. Not only does it maintain eight parks for recreational and cultural experiences, it maintains a complete city cemetery system as a public service. This means care for as many as 30,000 monuments and markers, including those for the deceased from the Revolutionary War to the present. Bedford lost more soldiers on D-Day in World War II than any other American town or city in percentage of population. A magnificent National D-Day Memorial is located on the north side of US 460 Bypass.

One of the town's parks is Poplar Park, where a yellow poplar, also called tulip tree (*Liriodendron tulipifera*), is treasured for its age and circumference of 31 feet, the nation's largest. Access from VA 43 (south of US 460 Bypass) is left on Smith Street, then left on Grand Arbre Drive. Immediately left is the parking area with picnic tables.

In 5.5-acre Reynolds Memorial Park there is a 0.4-mile paved **Reynolds Nature Trail**. It makes a loop in the gardenlike cove of tall sycamore, poplar, and other trees to include a locust grove. There are picnic shelters, gazebos, and bronze sculptures. One sculpture is of Michael David Reynolds, who died at age seven and 1194 for whom the park is named. Access from the junction of VA 122 and US 460 Bus is west 1.5 miles on US 460 Bus to parking, left.

## LIBERTY LAKE PARK

This 60-acre park with diverse services has ballfields and courts, a lake and pier for fishing, skateboard pod, roller-skating loop, community building, picnic shelters, play areas, nature trails, exercise trail, and a multi-handicapped accessible trail. After entering the park, the park office is left. Descend to the lake and take a one-way right to a parking area, left. Across the road and at the hardwood forest edge is a signboard with the multicolor trails network. Here is the beginning of green-blazed 0.4-mile **Pioneer Trail**. It is an easy, paved, exercise trail with twenty stations, and usable by the physically impaired. Beginning counterclockwise proceed 0.1 mile to a junction with the red-blazed 0.9-mile **Challenge Trail** and yellow-blazed 0.7-mile **Liberty Trail**, right. If following right ascend on a ridge slope where the **Liberty Trail** goes left to make a shortcut back to **Pioneer Trail**. Continue to ascend, then curve left into a cove among an understory of spicebush, ferns, wildflowers, and running cedar. Descend and at 0.3 mile rejoin the **Pioneer Trail** and **Liberty Trail**. Take a right and after 57 yards leave the **Pioneer Trail** and continue on the **Liberty Trail** and **Challenge Trail**. After 88 feet the **Liberty Trail** forks left. Ascend on the **Challenge Trail** to the top of a ridge and turn left, east, and then north. Descend to a junction. (Ahead is a 0.1-mi. spur of the **Challenge Trail** to Hilltop picnic shelter, northeast of ballpark #3. Backtrack.) To the left at the junction, descend on **Challenge Trail** to rejoin the **Pioneer Trail** at 0.8 mile. Here either turn left to complete some of the loop sections, or continue ahead at the forest edge to complete a loop of 0.9 mile (1.1 mi. if you include the Hilltop spur) to the network signboard and where you began.

ACCESS: From US 460 Bypass south of town, turn onto VA 122 south (Burks Hill Rd. and South Mountain Lake exit) and drive 0.5 mile to park entrance, left.

ADDRESS AND INFORMATION: Bedford Parks, Recreation, and Cemeteries, 939 Burks Hills Rd. (P.O. Drawer 807), Bedford, VA 24523; phone: 540-586-7161; fax: 540-586-7164. Brochures and information packet available.

# Blacksburg

Blacksburg is a university town with more than 26,000 students enrolled in Virginia Polytechnic Institute and State University (VPI & SU, founded 1872). It houses the Museum of Geological Sciences. Off US 460 near the university entrance is Smithfield Plantation (1773), the home of three state governors: James P. Preston, John Buchanan, and John Floyd. Framed in the Great Valley with sweeping pastoral surroundings, the city has a complementary backdrop with Brush Mountain in the JNF. The town has eighteen parks with facilities to provide a wide range of recreational activities, including 21.3 miles of asphalt trails. In the planning stages are another 20.7 miles by 2010. With such a network users can have a greenway connection from downtown shopping centers to urban malls and to golf courses, schools, residential areas, VPI & SU, historic sites, and to interconnect with the 5.7-mile **Huckleberry Line Trail**, described below.

Other trails are **Wyatt Farm Trail** (1.4 mi.) and **Woodbine Trail** (0.7 mi.) near    1198–99
Primrose Lane Park in the north part of the town off US 460 Bus (North Main St.) onto Vinyard Avenue. Near it, but between US 406 Bus and US 460 Bypass, is **Shenandoah Bike Trail** and Park with 2.5 miles. Access is east from US 406 Bypass    1200
on Tom's Creek Road to Patrick Henry Drive and left on Progress Street. If coming from US 406 Bus, turn west on Patrick Henry Drive to Progress Street, right. For **Deerfield/Brookfield Trail** (1.1 mi.) go west on Tom's Creek Drive 1 mile from US    1201–2
406 Bypass and turn right on Deerfield Drive. For **Hethwood Trail** (4 mi. combination of bicycle trails) turn off US 460 Bypass onto Prices Ford Road (toward Winfrey Fields and Kipps Elementary School/Blacksburg Middle School). Turn left on Heather Drive and park on the side of the road near the lake.

Another trail is the **Ellett Valley Nature Trail**, an easy, 2-mile double loop in    1203–6
Ellett Valley Park. From its parking area on Jennell Road the trail enters a gate and soon forks for a 1-mile loop or a 2-mile loop. It is self-guiding with interpretive markers and has three side loops named the **Earth Awareness Trail**, the **Micro Trail**, and the **Cycle of Life Trail**. The forest has oak, tulip poplar, black locust, hickory, and maple in climax groves. The trail passes an old farm site and a spring. (For group hikers, a tour guide is available from the park office.)

USGS MAP: Blacksburg

ACCESS: To reach the **Ellett Valley Nature Trail** take SR 642 (Jennell Rd.) off US 460 and follow it 2.3 miles to a narrow entrance on the right. Also, from US 460B (South Main St.) take SR 603 (Ellett Rd.) to Jennell Road and turn right. Go 0.2 mile to trail entrance, left.

## Huckleberry Line Trail    1207

LENGTH AND DIFFICULTY: 5.7 miles (10.7 km); easy

CONNECTING TRAILS: **Bicentennial Trail** (0.5 mi.), and greenway trails to Lane    1208
    Stadium, Southgate Drive, and VPI & SU campus, golf course, and airport

FEATURES: scenic railroad grade and meadows, forests and flowers, historic sites

TRAILHEADS: Northeast access is off South Main Street on Clay Street and parking
    area behind the Montgomery-Floyd Regional Library between Clay and Miller
    Streets. Southwest access is northwest corner of the parking area at New River
    Valley Mall off intersection of US 460 onto VA 114 (Peppers Ferry Boulevard).

DESCRIPTION: If beginning at the northeast trailhead in downtown Blacksburg,
    examine the kiosk at the entrance on Miller Street. (From this point you can

*Huckleberry Line Trail, Blacksburg*

walk the **Bicentennial Trail** on the sidewalks northeast on Miller St. to turn left on Draper St. Follow it to cross Clay, Washington, Wall, and Roanoke Streets to end at College St.) On the straight and shaded **Huckleberry Line Trail** arrive 0.7 mile at a kiosk for bicycle routes between VPI & SU campus and the airport. Leave the old railroad bed and make a sharp curve right beside fences. Cross Tech Center Drive at 1.4 miles. Pass through a hardwood forest with large white oaks at 1.5 miles, then slightly descend to enter an underpass tunnel of US 460 at 1.7 miles. Turn left and for 0.4 mile parallel the highway boundary by a hedge fence. At 2.3 miles pass through another section of forest. Cross an intersection with Mabry Lane and Hearth Drive at 2.8 miles. Parallel a fork of Slate Creek at milepost 3. After passing a connection with SR 1218 and SR 808 enter a young forest and onto the original Huckleberry Line track at 3.4 miles. At 3.9 miles is Hightop Road and other roads to approach Coal Miners' Heritage Park at the east base of Price Mountain. There is a viaduct and open mine pit at 4.5 miles. In a scenic area and on a high steel bridge cross Norfolk & Western Railroad at 4.9 miles. Cross an access railroad spur to Corning Glass Company at 5.5 miles, and to a scenic ending at 5.7 miles at New River Valley Mall.

USGS MAP: Blacksburg

ADDRESSES AND INFORMATION: Department of Parks and Recreation, 615 Patrick Henry Dr., Blacksburg, VA 24060; phone: 540-961-1135. Available are a brochure and trail map. Planning and Engineering Department, 300 South Main St., Blacksburg, VA 24062; phone: 540-961-1126; web: <www.blacksburg.va.us>. Museum of Geological Sciences, phone: 540-231-6029.

## Buena Vista

At the edge of the Shenandoah Valley, east of Lexington, the town's eastern boundary adjoins the GW&JNF, and only 5 miles east is the BRP. In the forest the **Indian** 1209–11 **Gap Trail** and the **Reservoir Hollow Trail** have termini in the town. These trails lead to the **Elephant Mountain Trail** for an outstanding view of Buena Vista (meaning "good view"). (See Chapter 1, Glenwood/Pedlar Ranger District.) In addition, the town has its own trail in the 315-acre Glen Maury Park. The 2.2-mile, easy **Glen Maury Nature Trail** follows an interconnecting system of sloping wood-  1212 land and grassy bald trails. The trail begins from the parking area at the multipurpose building and extends to the Maury River. Other activities at the park are swimming in an Olympic-size pool, picnicking, fishing, camping (with full service), and horseback riding. There are also ballfields, playgrounds, and a mountaintop pavilion with a grand view of the town.

USGS MAP: Buena Vista

ACCESS: In downtown Buena Vista take 10th Street west from Magnolia Avenue (US 501) for 0.3 mile to park entrance across the Maury River bridge.

ADDRESS AND INFORMATION: Glen Maury Park (and Buena Vista Department of Parks and Recreation), 2039 Sycamore Ave., Buena Vista, VA 24416; phone: 540-261-7321.

## Charlottesville

Almost in the center of the state, this area is the birthplace of Thomas Jefferson, whose accomplishments include the design and founding of the University of Virginia (1819). Having examined the classical architecture of Europe, Jefferson combined the styles to create an academic quadrangle with lawns, white colonnaded buildings, serpentine walls, gardens, and the inimitable rotunda. His home, Monticello, 3 miles east of the university, illustrates one of America's most classic architectural designs. Jefferson's interest in the natural environment is illustrated by his initiation and planning of the epic Lewis and Clark Expedition in 1804–6. (George Rogers Clark was born 2 mi. north of the city. A memorial is on W. Main St. east of the university.) One of the city's major parks is Pen Municipal Park.

## PEN MUNICIPAL PARK

1213 The 285-acre tract borders a bend in the Rivanna River. It has an eighteen-hole golf course, tennis courts, ballfields, picnic shelters, a children's playground, and special trails. One unique 0.5-mile trail is the **Physical Fitness Course/Nature Trail**. The course includes exercise stations for wheelchair individuals, or blind participants, or needs for cardiovascular conditioning. The picturesque and paved trail with twenty stations can also be used for jogging, baby carriage strolling, and nature interpretation. A brochure provides eighteen descriptions of such plants as autumn olive, chicory, spicebush, wild pear, black willow, and box elder. Near a

1214 small bridge begins the **Rivanna River Trail**. It is a wide treadway on a base of wood chips that first ascends a hillside near a row of large cedars, then descends to a level area on the banks of the Rivanna River. At 0.6 mile is an overlook of the river. From there the grassy trail remains shaded by tall sycamore, ash, yellow poplar, and hackberry. Among the trees are cardinals, catbirds, goldfinches, and many more. A thick understory has red mulberry, multiflora rose, and wild privet. Rabbits, groundhogs, foxes, and deer may be seen. Another river overlook is at 1.3 miles. Backtrack.

ACCESS: From US 250 in north Charlottesville, drive 2 miles north on Park Street, which becomes Rio Road, and turn right at Pen Park sign (SR 768). Arrive at the picnic shelter parking area after 0.6 mile.

## IVY CREEK NATURAL AREA

Charlottesville's Department of Parks and Recreation and the Albemarle County Department of Parks and Recreation jointly hold in perpetuity the 215 acres of Ivy Creek Natural Area for free use by the public. In addition, the private, nonprofit Ivy Creek Foundation assists the city and county in planning and protecting the preserve. There are more than 400 species of plants and 80 species of birds here. Garden and civic clubs provide community support for landscaping, an information kiosk, a reference library, and birdhouses.

ACCESS: From US 29 north in Charlottesville, take SR 743 (Hydraulic Rd.) west for 2.3 miles to the entrance, left.

1215 **Ivy Creek Nature Trail**
LENGTH AND DIFFICULTY: 5.7 miles (9.1 km) combined, round-trip; easy
FEATURES: historic site, streams, lake, wildlife, wildflowers
TRAILHEAD: parking area
DESCRIPTION: The trail system is graded, well designed, and carefully mowed in the open fields. It has thirteen interconnecting short trails that make loops within loops. Among the tree species present are maple, oak, walnut, beech, cherry, and poplar. Conifers include cedar, pine, and hemlock. Bird-watching is popular here. For the quiet enjoyment of all visitors, pets are not allowed. From

the parking area begin the hike by following the signs at a kiosk (and Virginia's first public solar composting rest rooms) to a restored farm barn. (To the right is 0.1-mi. **Wheelchair Trail**.) Hike straight ahead on the **Blue Trail** (0.5 mi.), partly in a field and in hardwoods. Pass a spring and connect with the **White Trail** (0.4 mi.), which goes left to the barn and right to cross cascading Martin's Branch at 0.8 miles. After hiking the **Yellow Trail** (0.4 mi.) loop, which is partly beside South Rivanna Reservoir, return to the **White Trail**, turn right, and connect with the **Orange Trail** (0.9 mi.) at 1.4 miles. (To the left is the **Red Trail**.) Turn right and follow the trail at the edge of the field until meeting the **Alternate Trail** (0.2 mi.). (It connects with the **Yellow Trail**, curves through the forest to a cove at the lake and reconnects with the **Orange Trail**.) Here the hiker has an option. To the right is the **Peninsula Trail** (0.7 mi.), which makes a loop through a mature forest to the lake. To the left the **Orange Trail** continues to meander in a circle until it rejoins the **White Trail** and the **Red Trail** (0.9 mi.) at 3.2 miles. (Along the way on the **Orange Trail** is the picturesque **Green Trail** [0.2 mi.], a circle and a shortcut to the **Red Trail**.)

Continue on the **Red Trail**, cross a stream, and at a pipeline clearing fork left to stay on the **Red Trail**, or go right to follow the **Woods Trail** (0.7 mi.). (It goes through a forest to cross the headwaters of Martin's Creek before returning to the **Red Trail**.) After crossing Martin's Creek and a tributary reach the **Field Trail** (0.4 mi.). (It ascends to near SR 743, passes a forest succession plot, and returns to the parking lot. Along the way the **School Trail** [0.3 mi.] is on the left. It goes to the **Watchable Wildlife Trail** [0.1 mi.] for a return to the parking lot.) Continue on the **Red Trail** to its junction at 5.6 miles with the **White Trail**. Turn right and complete the trail at the barn.

USGS MAPS: Charlottesville West and East

ADDRESSES AND INFORMATION: Charlottesville Parks, P.O. Box 911, Charlottesville, VA 22902; phone: 434-970-3101; fax: 434-970-3589. Available are a brochure and map of parks. Ivy Creek Foundation, P.O. Box 956, Charlottesville, VA 22902; phone: 434-973-7772. Available are brochure and information on Ivy Creek Natural Area and free guided tours.

## Chesapeake

In 1963 the city of South Norfolk and Norfolk County became the new city of Chesapeake. With 353 square miles it became the second largest city in the state. It adjoins Portsmouth and Norfolk on the northern boundary, Virginia Beach on the east, North Carolina on the south, and the city of Suffolk on the west. More than half of the Great Dismal Swamp NWR and most all of Lake Drummond are within the city's boundaries, and the intracoastal waterway passes through the eastern edge of the refuge and the northeastern corner of the city. Waterways crisscross the entire city, whose elevation is an average of 12 feet. From the western swamps and marshes originates the Northwest River; it leaves the southeastern corner of the city and flows into Currituck Sound of North Carolina.

Chesapeake Parks and Recreation has fifteen parks with three others in the planning stage. There are seven community centers and seven specialty facilities (such as senior centers or art centers). Outdoor recreational facilities have a total of 1,194 acres, the largest of which is 763 acres at Northwest River Park. The parks are concentrated in the north-central part of the city, an area with greater population density. Some of the parks have unnamed footpaths, or exercise trails, and mountain bike trails. They include Deep Creek Lock Park, Great Bridge Lock Park, Indian River Park, Oak Grove Lake Park, and Southwestern Park. Two parks with named trails are described below.

## INDIAN RIVER PARK

Near the northeast boundary of Chesapeake with the city of Virginia Beach is 91-acre forested Indian River Park. Towering oaks, yellow poplar, and pine are over sections of dense undergrowth, ferns, and vines. Songbirds are prominent.

1229     Through the elongated park is an unblazed but interconnecting **Indian River Trail**. It is used mainly by mountain bikers, walkers, and joggers. The trail system can include a loop and some spurs northwest for 0.7 mile, and further southeast with a crossing under a power line for another 1 mile. The latter route accesses Paramount Avenue.

ACCESS: From I-64 (Hampton Roads Beltway), exit 289, turn northwest on Greenbrier Parkway. Drive 0.8 mile to US 13 (Military Hwy.) and turn right. Drive 1.1 miles and turn right on narrow Rokeby Avenue. After 0.2 mile park on the right in a grassy field at the park sign.

## NORTHWEST RIVER PARK

Where Indian Creek flows into the Northwest River is the location of the city's 763-acre Northwest River Park. Carefully planned to protect the natural environment and to provide a variety of outdoor recreation experiences for the entire family, it is set apart from urban demographics. A quiet place (except for noise from naval aircraft flights), it is an extraordinary laboratory for nature study. There are 160 species of birds, 150 species of herbaceous plants (including 7 species of wild orchids), and 136 species of ferns, clubmosses, shrubs, trees, and vines. Wild mammals are chiefly deer, squirrel, mink, nutria, raccoon, and otter. There are 18 species of snakes (including 3 species of poisonous reptiles) and 16 species of fish. Activities include fishing, hiking, nature study, and boating (a ramp is provided). There are equestrian trails, picnic shelters, a children's playground, canoe rentals, facilities for camping (tents and recreational vehicles), and a visitor center. On the eastern side of the visitor center is 210-yard **Fragrance Trail**. It is a loop 1230 that has Braille signs for the visually impaired. Among the more than forty plants are dwarf wild azalea, sweet bay, silky camellia, fragrant sumac, and bigleaf snowbell.

ACCESS: If following VA 168 (Bus) from I-64, exit 190, drive south on VA 168 (Bus) (Battlefield Blvd.) 11.8 miles to Indian Creek Road on the left (at food mart). Turn left and go 4.1 miles to the park entrance, right. If following Great Bridge Bypass (also VA 168) from I-64, exit 191, drive south 6.2 miles to Hillcrest Parkway and exit to go left (east) to join VA 168 (Bus) (Battlefield Blvd.). Turn right and after 3.7 miles arrive at Indian Creek Road, left.

**Indian Creek Trail** (1.9 mi.), **Shuttle Trail** (1.3 mi.), **Deer Island Trail** (0.8 mi.), 1231–37 **Otter Point Trail** (0.8 mi.), **Wood Duck Slough Trail** (0.3 mi.), **Molly Mitchell Trail** (1.3 mi.), **Rein Memorial Trail** (0.2 mi.)

LENGTH AND DIFFICULTY: 6.6 miles (9.6 km) combined, round-trip; easy
FEATURES: waterfowl, wetlands and marsh, wildlife, wildflowers
TRAILHEAD: visitor center
DESCRIPTION: These trails connect for short or long loops. The longest loop is described here. From the visitor center, facing the lake, follow the left side of the lake to a grassy knoll and trail sign for the **Indian Creek Trail**. (To the left of the trail entrance is the flower garden and the **Shuttle Trail**. The **Shuttle Trail** is a dead-end road used for hiking or vehicular traffic to Southern Terminal, the southern end of the **Indian Creek Trail**.) After entering the woods, cross a bridge over the lake and reach a junction with the **Deer Island Trail**, left and right, at 0.2 mile. (The **Deer Island Trail** follows an old road left for 0.7 mi. to the **Shuttle Trail**. It passes a walk-in backcountry camping area and canoeing access and crosses a scenic footbridge. To the right it goes 0.1 mi. to the park's recreational vehicle campground.)

Continuing on the **Indian Creek Trail** (25 yd. right on the **Deer Island Trail** and off to the left), pass through a forest of sweet gum, maple, poplar, oaks, and beech. There are large patches of Christmas fern and wild ginger. Cross a bridle trail at 0.7 mile, a boardwalk at 1 mile, and another at 1.6 miles in Moonshine Meadow. At 1.8 miles is a view of a long boardwalk, but bear left to cross a small stream and exit at the **Shuttle Trail** near a pond and picnic shelter at 1.9 miles, the end of the trail. To the right it is 0.1 mile to a beautiful grassy area and a view of Northwest River. Here is a picnic area and a building for canoe rentals. To the right is 0.2-mile **Rein Memorial Trail**, a long boardwalk into the marsh of Indian Creek.

To complete the long loop, continue on 0.8-mile **Otter Point Trail** (30 yd. north of the southern terminus of the **Indian Creek Trail** on the **Shuttle Trail**) to Smith Creek, but turn away from the creek to reconnect with the **Shuttle Trail** at 2.7 miles. Turn right, and after a few yards turn right on 0.3-mile

**Wood Duck Slough Trail** to a bridge in a damp area with cypress, trout lily, and pennywort. Cross Blue Heron Bridge and reach a junction with the **Molly Mitchell Trail** at 3 miles. Pass through a forest of large beech and sweet gum with an understory of switchcane. After crossing three more bridges arrive at picnic area #4 at 4.1 miles. Reach the northern trailhead at the parking area at 4.2 miles and the visitor center at 4.3 miles.

USGS MAP: Moyock

ADDRESS AND INFORMATION: Northwest River Park, 1733 Indian Creek Rd., Chesapeake, VA 23322; phone: 757-421-7151/3145.

## OAKGROVE LAKE PARK

In great contrast to the design and usage of Indian River Park forest trails, this 130-acre park, of which 70 acres is a lake, has a 1.5-mile sunny loop. Manicured with a 1238 wide trail of wood chips, the scenic **Oak Grove Lake Trail** circles the lake and is marked every one-tenth of a mile. It passes through grassy meadows with hardwoods and pines on the outside perimeter. Waterfowl and songbirds are plentiful. The beautiful lake, established from a borrow pit, is stocked with bluegill and largemouth bass.

ACCESS: From I-64 (Hampton Roads Beltway) turn off at exit 290 south on VA 168 (Battlefield Blvd.). After 0.7 mile turn right at the second traffic light, Volvo Parkway. After 0.5 mile turn right onto Byron Street. Turn left into the park entrance after 0.2 mile.

## WESTERN BRANCH PARK

Western Branch Park, with 35 acres, has spacious ballfields and courts (including lighted tennis courts). There are also picnic shelters and a children's play area. 1239 The 1-mile **Western Branch Trail** makes intermittent curves in and out of the forest on the east side of the park entrance road, beginning with the children's playground and ending at the last ballfield fence corner at the road's end. (At the end and across the road's cul-de-sac, west, is another 0.2-mile trail in an open forest of hardwoods and pine.) On the **Western Branch Trail** there are sections with a base of wood chips. The forest canopy is mainly oak, pine, sycamore, and poplar, and an understory of bayleaf, laurel, and dogwood. Among the wildflowers are lobelia and ageratum. Songbirds are prominent.

ACCESS: From I-664, exit 11B, drive 0.6 mile east on Portsmouth Boulevard (SR 337) and turn right at the first traffic light. To the left is Western Branch Community Center. Stay right and ahead to enter Western Branch Park.

ADDRESSES AND INFORMATION: Western Branch Community Center, 4437 Portsmouth Blvd., Chesapeake, VA 23321; phone: 757-465-0211. Chesapeake Parks and Recreation, 112 Mann Dr. (P.O. Box 15225), Chesapeake, VA 23328; phone: 757-

382-6411; fax: 757-382-8418. Available are brochures and seasonal guide information for all parks.

# Danville

Founded in 1792, this city by the Dan River is one of industry, commerce, culture, and recreation. It is internationally known for the largest single-unit textile mill in the world. The City's Museum of Fine Arts and History is located in the former Mansion of Major W. T. Sutherlin, the site of the last capitol of the Southern Confederacy. During the 1990s the city's government referred to itself as a "world class organization." Among its activities was the advancement of new recreational projects. As with the cities of Lynchburg and Roanoke, Danville developed rail trails. At Ballou Park between West Main Street and Park Avenue North is the **Ballou Park Nature Trail**. For 0.7 mile it circles through a magnificent preserve   1240 with a mature forest. The city's largest park is the Dan Daniel Memorial Park.

## DAN DANIEL MEMORIAL PARK

This 170-acre park has three soccer fields, an American Legion baseball field, little league fields, amphitheater, nature center, picnic shelters, volleyball courts, nature trails, a 1.5-mile mountain bike trail, and part of the **Riverwalk Trail** described ahead. The 0.4-mile **Hidden Valley Trail** was constructed by Eagle Scouts.   1241 The trail begins from the American Legion baseball field parking area and ascends north to a ridge. On the approach to the amphitheater, it turns left and descends into a hollow with large trees, wildflowers, and stream. It ends at the baseball field overflow-parking lot, west. (At the amphitheater there is a connection trail from the **Hidden Valley Trail** to **Doe Run Trail**.)

The **Turkey Trot Trail** begins north from the soccer fields parking area. Also   1242–43 constructed by Eagle Scouts, it ascends in a hardwood forest and crosses the park's entrance road at 0.4 mile to connect with the 0.3-mile circuitous **Doe Run Trail**. The trail has a bridge over a small stream among large beech trees. Backtrack, or take the connector trail to the **Hidden Valley Trail**.

USGS MAP: Danville

ACCESS: From Main Street intersection drive east of Danville on US 58/360 for 1.6 miles and take US 29 exit south. After 1.3 miles turn right to the park's entrance. If arriving from the south on US 29, take exit right to River Park Drive and turn left to enter the park.

### Crossing-of-the-Dan Riverwalk   1244

LENGTH AND DIFFICULTY: 3.2 miles (5.1 km); easy
FEATURES: scenic river views, historic

TRAILHEADS: To access the west end of the trail, downtown, from US 58, cross the Main Street bridge over the Dan River and turn left on Craghead Street. After 0.8 mile turn left to the Danville Community Market and large parking area. To access the east end of the trail follow the directions to the Dan Daniel Memorial Park, above, but turn opposite across US 29 expressway to enter River Park Drive. After 0.8 mile turn right on Stinson Drive to the parking area at Anglers Park.

DESCRIPTION: If selecting the west end follow the trail sign to a steel bridge and scenic crossing of the Dan River. On the north side of the river descend to a landscaped area of flowers and shrubs and asphalt trail. The trail is popular for hikers, bicyclists, joggers, anglers, and strollers. Curve left under the bridge, then pass under a railroad bridge at 0.4 mile. Cross another steel bridge over Fall Creek. Ahead is a rest room on the left. The riverwalk passes through a meadow to the left and a major boundary of tall trees at the riverside on the right. There are resting benches and spur trails to the riverside for scenery and fishing. Enter a forest and arrive at a parking lot, left, and near the little league fields in Dan Daniel Memorial Park at 1.4 miles.

Continue downstream through another meadow and shady trees by the river known as the Blackberry Run Section. Pass under the US 29 expressway at 1.7 miles. Picnic tables and resting benches are along the way. Skillful engineering provides a winding greenway across streams, in combinations of forests and sunny meadows, and accesses for river viewing to a parking area in Anglers Park at 3.2 miles. Here is a boat ramp. Backtrack or use the US 29 expressway described above.

USGS MAP: Danville

1245 Richmond/Danville Rail-Trail

LENGTH AND DIFFICULTY: 5.5 miles (8.8 km); easy

FEATURES: isolated, bucolic, wildlife, history

TRAILHEADS: At the intersection of US 58/360 and VA 62, east of Danville, drive north on Ringgold Depot Road (SR 726) for 2.6 miles and turn left on Ringgold Depot Lane to Ringgold Station and parking lot. This is the western trailhead. For the eastern trailhead stay on US 58/360 east and after 3.8 miles turn left on Hackberry Road (SR 656) toward the community of Sutherlin. The road becomes Carter Trail Road briefly before Kerns Church Road to a parking lot, left, at 3.2 miles.

DESCRIPTION: This section of the Richmond/Danville Railroad was completed in 1855. In 1865 Jefferson Davis rode this rail line to the Sutherlin Mansion in Danville, and a number of U.S. presidents, including Grover Cleveland, used this route for political campaigning. Because of the lack of business a hundred years later, the line closed in 1958. Today, this route has become useful again with a pea gravel surface for recreational services only, such as hiking,

*Crossing-of-the-Dan Riverwalk, Danville*

bicycling, or running. The straight line appears endless and peaceful. Wildlife is commonplace and it is a birder's paradise. Brown thrush make certain that you know they are there. If choosing to begin at the east trailhead, pass a former lake on the right, but pass at 0.8 mile a lake and swamp with cattails and willows, part of Barker Creek. Sections of forest provide shade, but on sunny banks from railway cuts are flowers such as Virginia silene, wild quinine, and coral honeysuckle. Pass under Rock Springs Road bridge at 2.1 miles. The forest opens to pastureland at 3.2 miles, and Sandy Creek is crossed at 3.5 miles. Cross a road near a cemetery at 4 miles, and pass under Ringgold Depot Road at 5.2 miles. Arrive at the railroad station, which has a Norfolk and Western caboose, and parking area, at 5.5 miles.

USGS MAPS: Ringgold, Milton

ADDRESS AND INFORMATION: Danville Parks and Recreation, P.O. Box 3300, Danville, VA 24543-3300; phone: 434-799-5215; fax: 434-797-8996. A Dan Daniel Memorial Park brochure is available.

## Falls Church

The **W&OD Railroad Trail** goes 1.3 miles through Falls Church on its route from Arlington to Purcellville. (See Northern Virginia Regional Park Authority, Chapter 14.) The city also has a short trail in Berman Park.

ADDRESS AND INFORMATION: Department of Recreation and Parks, 223 Little Falls St., Falls Church, VA 22046; phone: 703-241-5077.

## Fredericksburg

The city of Fredericksburg, halfway between Richmond and Washington, D.C., is on the southern side of the Rappahannock River. It was authorized to be developed by the general assembly in 1727 and to be named in honor of Frederick, Prince of Wales, the eldest son of King George II. (Frederick's eldest son, George III, was king during the American Revolution.) During the Civil War the town was caught in the center of battles, but many of the buildings were not destroyed. Today, the historic district is maintained, and a 1-mile walking tour is worthwhile. In the space of about eight by five blocks there are at least twenty historic sites. Among them are the Mary Washington house and grave and the James Monroe Museum (see Chapter 6 for national military parks). Begin the walk at the city visitor center at 706 Caroline Street.

The city shares administrative jurisdiction with Stafford County for four parks, three of which are across the river in Falmouth. They are Falmouth Waterfront Park, St. Claire Brooks Memorial Park, and John Lee Pratt Memorial Park. These day-use parks have facilities for picnicking and fishing, tennis courts, ballfields, and unnamed trails between facilities. In Falmouth Waterfront Park is the 1.2-mile
1246 **St. Brooks Trail**, which begins at the northern corner of the parking area for picnic area B. It goes to the corner of the woods under a power line and crosses a wide bridge. It descends into a deep ravine near a stream where a heavy canopy is formed by tall beech, tulip poplar, and a variety of oaks. Part of a light understory contains skunk cabbage, papaw, and mountain laurel. The trail exits at River Road near a parking area. Backtrack, or make a loop by walking upriver on a 0.5-mile trail in a forest of ash, elm, and sycamore to a parking area and softball field. Cross the road, ascend to picnic area A, turn right, and walk right away from the baseball field to picnic area C parking area. Turn left in the parking lot to the point of origin. Access to the park is off US 1 in Falmouth east on Prince Street, which becomes Butler Road; park entrance is on the right.

The city has its own parks, such as Motts Run Reservoir Park, Canal Park, Snowden Park, Riverside Drive Park, and Alum Spring Park. The 35-acre Alum Spring Park, with picnic shelter, tables, and grills, and located within the city of
1247 Fredericksburg, is filled with natural and historic attractions. The 1-mile **Alum**

**Spring Trail** winds through the hardwoods along scenic Hazel Run, past the former sites of an icehouse and gristmill, and along a unique sandstone cliff. Water dripping from under the cliff carries alum, a mineral that is deposited in the white layers of rock. The mineral was used in colonial times to preserve meat. After the cliffs, continue counterclockwise to an old railroad bed of the Virginia Central Railroad, closed in 1984. Pass through the picnic area and return to cross a first-class bridge at the park entrance. Access from US 1 on VA 3 is 0.1 mile east to Greenbrier Drive, right, for 0.4 mile. Other city parks with trails are described below.

## CANAL PARK, OLD MILL PARK, AND RIVERSIDE DRIVE PARK

Although these parks are near each other and focus on different facilities and services, they are all water oriented and provide an exciting loop trail through a historic section of the city. The first 1.3 miles of the wide, paved trail follow a canal and are designed for bikers, hikers, birders, joggers, and strollers. The remainder of the route is on sidewalks or grassy paths of the other parks.

ACCESS: From US 1 take Fall Hill Avenue west 0.7 mile to the parking lot, left, at VEPCO Canal bridge.

**Canal Park Trail**                                                                 1248
LENGTH AND DIFFICULTY: 3.2 miles (5.1 km); easy
FEATURES: canal, waterfowl, scenic views, historic sites, wildflowers
TRAILHEAD: parking lot at VEPCO Canal bridge
DESCRIPTION: Begin at the trail bridge over the canal and follow beside the canal
   through overhanging willow, elm, and ash. White mallow and cattails are on
   the right side in marshes. At 0.3 mile is a connector bridge and access right and
   left to residential and office areas. Pass under US 1 at 0.7 mile and by an access
   ramp. Pass another access footbridge at 0.9 mile. There is a lake to the right
   with waterfowl and songbirds. Cross Washington Street at 1.2 miles. (To the
   right on Washington St. in the second block is the Mary Washington Monument
   and Grave.) Cross Canal Street and a footbridge at 1.3 miles. Reach Princess
   Anne Street (US 1/17B) at 1.6 miles.

   The canal goes underground here, and the trail turns right to immediately
turn left on Ford Street to Caroline Street for a left turn. Follow Caroline Street
past markers and at 2 miles pass the entrance to Old Mill Park, right. (The park
offers day-use facilities for picnicking and fishing and children's playgrounds.)
At 2.3 miles pass under US 1/17 (which accesses Caroline St.). Enter Riverside
Park and pass historic markers of old mills, one of which is the Francis Thorton
Mill at 2.6 miles. Here is also the legendary Indian punch bowl and scenic views
of and foot access to the Rappahannock River. Continue upriver and cross Hill
Avenue to the sidewalk at 3.1 miles for a return to the parking lot. (Across the

road is the Rappahannock Outdoor Educational Center, which provides rentals, sales, and classes in canoeing, tubing, rafting, and kayaking.)
USGS MAP: Fredericksburg

## MOTTS RUN RESERVOIR AND PARK

This 860-acre park is located in Spotsylvania County but owned and operated by the city of Fredericksburg. The 160-acre lake is the drinking supply for the city and county and is a popular spot for fishing, boating, picnicking, and hiking. Five miles of manicured hiking trails, maintained by Eagle Scouts, are on the north side of the lake. The park is open April 1 through October 31; however, hikers may park at the gate and walk the trails year round. There are some restrictions: no wading or swimming in the lake; no firearms or fireworks; no motorized vehicles, bicycles, or horses on the trails; no alcohol; and no camping.

ACCESS: From I-95, exit 130, go 1 mile west on VA 3; turn right on Bragg Rd. After 0.8 mile turn left on River Rd. for 2.4 miles.

1249–55 **Hidden Creek Trail** (1.1 mi.), **Osprey Point Trail** (0.4 mi.), **Turkey Ridge Trail** (0.6 mi.), **Possum Path Trail** (0.1 mi.), **Mine Run Trail** (2.1 mi.), **Lakeview Trail** (0.4 mi.), **Laurel Trail** (0.4 mi.)

LENGTH AND DIFFICULTY: 5.1 miles (8.2 km), combined, some round-trips; easy to
  moderate
FEATURES: wildlife, streams, scenic lake, wildflowers
TRAILHEAD: lake parking area (except parking at the gate when it is closed)
DESCRIPTION: From the boat launch parking area go east and enter the trailhead
  of the blue-blazed **Hidden Creek Trail** in a hardwood forest. Arrive at the loop
  divide at 0.1 mile and bear right. At 0.2 mile pass **Osprey Point Trail**, right,
  which descends 0.2 mile to the lake. After 75 yards there is a shortcut trail, left,
  that reduces the loop length by 0.3 mile. After a long curve, pass the shortcut
  trail and descend. Through patches of mountain laurel continue descent to
  cross two bridges and return to the parking lot at 1.1 miles.
      To hike the yellow-blazed **Turkey Ridge Trail**, follow the gravel trail from the
  boat launch parking lot, pass the fishing decks, and at a picnic area notice the
  trailhead, right. Ascend east, then curve north on the hilltop. Arrive at the
  orange-blazed **Mine Run Trail** at 0.3 miles. (To complete the **Turkey Ridge
  Trail** bear left and down the hill to pass 0.1-mi. **Possum Path Trail** [a side loop
  carpeted with running cedar], and return to the trailhead at 0.6 mi.)
      Continuing on the hilly route of **Mine Run Trail** follow a well-maintained
  trail through an open oak forest. Cross a transcontinental line and make a
  juncture with green-blazed **Lakeview Trail**, left at 0.2 mile. After another 0.2
  mile make a juncture with purple-blazed **Laurel Trail**, left. Pass a wood pile to
  your right. At 0.7 mile cross a small bridge, followed by another among moun-

tain laurel and pink azalea at 0.8 mile. At 1 mile descend on a curve, then after 100 yards reach rocky Mine Run. Here is a peaceful passage to rest among the ferns, mountain laurel, and birch. Backtrack.

On the return to **Laurel Trail**, a descent on an old road could be made. If chosen pass a natural spring, left, at 0.1 mile and reach the lakeside at 0.2 mile. (To your left is **Bank Fishing Trail**; it follows a narrow path along the shore and in the process crosses a footbridge among an alder grove. After 0.2 mi. it connects with **Lakeview Trail**, left. Here you could ascend **Lakeview Trail** on switchbacks to rejoin **Mine Run Trail** after 0.2 mi., or follow the **Lakeview Trail** ahead to its trailhead at the picnic area by the lake at 0.4 mi.) 1256

USGS MAP: Salem Church

ADDRESSES AND INFORMATION: Fredericksburg-Stafford County Park Authority, Saint Clair Brooks Park, P.O. Box 433, Fredericksburg, VA 22404; phone: 540-373-7909. Available is a brochure with map of the parks. Fredericksburg Recreation Department, 408 Canal St., Fredericksburg, VA 22401; phone: 540-372-1158. Rappahannock Outdoor Educational Center, 3219 Fall Hill Ave., Fredericksburg, VA 22401; phone: 540-371-5085. Fredericksburg Visitor Center, 706 Caroline St., Fredericksburg, VA 22401; phone: 540-373-1776.

## Front Royal

Front Royal is an ideal town for hikers. Not only does the town have excellent parks, recreation facilities, and hiker amenities, it is surrounded by trails and natural areas. It is the northern gateway to lofty Skyline Drive and the **Dickey Ridge Trail** in the Shenandoah National Park. On its western edge is white water on the South Fork of the Shenandoah River; on the northeastern corner of the GWNF is the long **Massanutten Mountain Trail**, and to the east for 3.2 miles on US 522 is the **AT**. For an underground trail, on the southern edge of town there is Skyline Caverns, with its rare, flowerlike calcite crystal formations. On the northern edge of town is I-66 on its route from Washington, D.C., to nearby I-81 at Strasburg. 1257

A historic town with shrines, museums, and cemeteries related to the Civil War, it has also honored its citizens after its founding in 1788. Its park services include recreational, social, and cultural activities for all ages. Its largest of ten parks is Municipal Park, which has the Bing Crosby Stadium on 8th Street. Across Happy Creek from the stadium is the imaginative Happy Creek Fantasyland for children. Trails by the creekside lead to a castlelike, multilevel wooden structure with interconnecting tunnels, slides, bridges, and ladders. Upstream, on Commerce Avenue for 1 mile, is the **Happy Creek Trail**, a 0.7-mile scenic paved bike and hike trail among flowering shrubs, arched bridges, and an arboretum. Entrance is at Prospect Street or Front Street from E. Main Street. 1258

ADDRESS AND INFORMATION: Parks and Recreation Department, 200 E. 8th St., Front Royal, VA 22630; phone: 540-635-7750. Available is a brochure on seasonal activities. For Skyline Caverns, call 540-635-4545.

## Hampton

The historic city of Hampton was settled in 1610 in Kecoughtan Indian territory. Its survival and continuous functioning makes the city the oldest location in America where English is spoken. Strategically located at the mouth of the James River on the Chesapeake Bay, it was vulnerable to the wars of 1776, 1812, and 1861, but it survived them all. Historic sites are at Casement Museum and Fort Monroe at the end of US 258. Among the city parks and preserves are Grandview Preserve 1259 and Sandy Bottom Nature Park described ahead. Additionally, there is **Matteson Trail**, a special 3-mile multi-use paved trail that circles in a natural area one of Hampton's finest golf courses. Usage is by walkers, joggers, in-line skaters, and bicyclists. Access is from I-64, exit 261A if eastbound onto Hampton Roads Center Parkway east to Magruder Boulevard left. (If westbound, an exit can be at I-64, exit 262 northbound on Magruder Blvd.) Follow Magruder Boulevard 0.5 mile to Butler Farm Road, left. The trail access is via Sentara Health and Fitness Center.

### GRANDVIEW PRESERVE

1260 At Grandview Preserve is a 4.5-mile round-trip walk on the **Grandview Preserve Trail**. This easy and scenic route from the Chesapeake Bay to the Back River offers views of waterfowl and wetlands filled with sumac, wax myrtle, cattail, and switchcane. It passes Hawkins Pond, right, on a wide access trail to the beach at 0.4 mile. Turn left and walk on the beach toward the Back River and the end of the beach and sand dunes. Backtrack.

ACCESS: From I-64, exit 268, drive northeast on Mallory Street 0.5 mile to Mercury Boulevard and turn left. Go 0.3 mile and turn right on Old Buckroe Road. Follow it to Silver Isles Boulevard, turn right, and after 0.1 mile turn left on Beach Road. Go 2.6 miles and turn left on State Park Drive. (Observe parking signs.)

ADDRESSES AND INFORMATION: Department of Parks and Recreation, 22 Lincoln St., Hampton, VA 23669; phone: 757-727-8347; fax: 757-727-8313. For Fort Monroe: Department of the Army, HHC Fort Monroe Bldg., Fort Monroe, VA 23551; phone: 757-727-2092.

### SANDY BOTTOM NATURE PARK

This 456-acre park is an outstanding example of what a city can successfully accomplish in developing a recreational, educational, and wildlife management facility from borrow pits and garbage dumps. Part of the park was unspoiled upland pristine forests with loblolly pine and cedar, and hardwoods such as sweet gum, beech, maple, and oak. Near the entrance to the park is Sandy Bottom Lake with game fish such as bluegill, catfish, and largemouth bass. Park visitors may fish from the pier or rent a boat. Also near the entrance is a 10,000-square-foot nature center. Among the live animal displays are snakes and turtles. Of the nine connecting trails all may be used by hikers and bicyclists except **Osprey Point Trail** and a separate trail, **Wood Duck Trail**, for pedestrians only. Other facilities include picnic shelters, tent cabins, individual and group campsites, children's playground, and canoeing. In 2003 a 55-acre northwest section of the park was under construction to restore the area to its original condition from a borrow pit. The result will include partial swampland with a canoe route and boardwalks.

**Old Crystal Trail** (2.1 mi.), **Osprey Point Trail** (0.2 mi.), **New Market Trail** (1.5  1261–70 mi.), **Shelton Trail** (0.7 mi.), **Red Fox Trail** (0.4 mi.), **Fallen Oak Trail** (1.1 mi.), **Black Cherry Trail** (0.2 mi.), **Buck Rub Trail** (0.1 mi.), **Lake Trail** (0.7 mi.), **Wood Duck Trail** (0.7 mi.)

LENGTH AND DIFFICULTY: 7.7 miles (12.3 km) combined, round-trip; easy
FEATURES: scenic lake areas, observation decks, birding
TRAILHEAD: parking lot at visitor center
DESCRIPTION: If hiking counterclockwise from the visitor center go north on gravel
**Old Crystal Trail** (yellow blazed). After 0.1 mile turn left around the lake. (To the right you can see another lake where the **Lake Trail** can be easily accessed from the visitor center parking area.) At 0.2 mile is a fork where you may have to turn right until construction is completed on the left by the lake. (To the right is a constant sound distraction from the traffic on I-64.) At 1 mile you may continue on the **Old Crystal Trail**, left, or begin **New Market Trail** (blue blazed), which continues to parallel I-64. Along the trail are sycamore, beech, and devil's walking stick. At 1.5 miles turn left under a power line. Turn left again at 1.6 miles; a deep drainage ditch is right. Curve left at 2.2 miles onto **Shelton Trail** (orange blazed). The open forest floor is a gentle pathway. Return to **New Market Trail** at 2.9 miles for either a backtrack or continuing on the **Old Crystal Trail** for a return loop of 5 miles. Along the way are color-blazed connecting options with **Red Fox Trail**, **Fallen Oak Trail**, **Black Cherry Trail**, **Buck Rub Trail**, and the scenic two-story Great Blue Heron Observation Platform. At **Fallen Oak Trail** are easy accesses to singular or group campgrounds. After passing a canoe dock, **Osprey Point Trail**, and tent cabins--all to the left—arrive at a rest room and parking area. Nearby is the children's playground and picnic shelters, right. Returning to the visitor center you may have hiked from 7 to 8.5 miles, depending on your double circuit or backtracking on short trails. To the south of the visitor center parking area are two accesses on the entrance road to 0.7-mile **Wood Duck Trail** loop in the forest.

ACCESS: From I-64, exit 261A to Hampton Roads Center Parkway west. Cross Big Bethel Road (SR 600) and make a right into the park entrance.

ADDRESS AND INFORMATION: Sandy Bottom Nature Park, 1255 Big Bethel Rd., Hampton, VA 23666; phone: 757-825-4657; fax: 757-825-4658; e-mail: <sbottom2 @hampton.gov>. Brochure with map is available.

## Herndon

1271 The **W&OD Railroad Trail** has a 2.4-mile stretch through Herndon on its way from Arlington to Purcellville. (See Northern Virginia Regional Park Authority, Chapter 14.) The 0.7-mile **Sugarland Run Trail** connects SR 606, Elden Street, to the **W&OD Railroad Trail**.

ADDRESS AND INFORMATION: Herndon Parks and Recreation, 814 Ferndale Ave. (P.O. Box 427), Herndon, VA 22070; phone: 703-435-6868.

## Lexington

Founded in 1777, Lexington is the county seat of Rockingham County in the Shenandoah Valley. In its historic residential and downtown districts is a sixteen-block section of homes, churches, museums, burial shrines, shops and stores, and universities. It is the home of Washington and Lee University (founded in 1749), the nation's sixth oldest, where Robert E. Lee served as president from 1865 until his death in 1870. It is also the home of Virginia Military Institute (founded in 1839), the nation's oldest state-supported military college. Here Thomas J. "Stonewall" Jackson taught military tactics and math for ten years before the Civil War. Both of these Confederate heroes are buried in Lexington. The city has three diverse trails: one is a sidewalk trail in the historic districts, another is semi-urban by a stream, and the longest is in the countryside with its origin in the city. It is the **Chessie Nature Trail**, described in Chapter 16. The other trails are described here.

1272 **Lee-Jackson and VMI-Marshall Tour Trail**

LENGTH AND DIFFICULTY: 2 miles (3.3 km) combined, round-trip; easy

FEATURES: historic site, museums, churches, gardens

TRAILHEAD: visitor parking lot on Washington Street

DESCRIPTION: From Main Street go 1 ½ blocks east on Washington Street to the visitor information center and parking lot. After receiving guide maps, follow 8 blocks of historic Lexington on the Lee-Jackson route to Lee's and Jackson's homes, universities, churches, and burial shrines. Pass the front campus of Washington and Lee University, regarded as one of the most beautiful campuses in the nation. Continue on the hike to VMI's George C. Marshall Museum and the parade ground to form a loop back to Washington Street. In addition, a 16-block hike tracing 215 years of American history can continue (see guide map) in the residential and business area. (Approximate time for combined urban hike is four hours.)

USGS MAP: Lexington

ADDRESS AND INFORMATION: Lexington Visitor Center, 102 E. Washington St., Lexington, VA 24450; phone: 540-463-3777. Available are brochures and maps.


## WOODS CREEK PARK

A day-use park, it is partly city public property and partly the grounds of Washington and Lee University and Virginia Military Institute. It is a tranquil greenway with a diversity of woodlands, meadows, songbirds, squirrels, spring peepers, bluets and meadow violets, and sections of an old railroad grade. It is favored by hikers, joggers, strollers, and picnickers.

ACCESS: For the northeastern trailhead, turn off US 11/11B at its fork at the southern end of Maury River Bridge on short Moses Mill Road (which becomes short Jordan's Point Rd. to the parking area, right). For the southwestern trailhead, take Jordan Street northwest from US 11B (downtown Main St.) to Pendleton Place, left, at the parking lot of Waddell School.

### Woods Creek Trail                                                    1273
LENGTH AND DIFFICULTY: 2.1 miles (3.4 km); easy
FEATURES: historic sites, scenery, geological formations, wildlife, wildflowers
TRAILHEADS: see Access, above.
DESCRIPTION: If hiking from Jordan's Point Road (also known as VMI Island), hike back 90 yards from the parking area to a service road, right. The road divides here, and if there is not a trail sign, take the left fork, which is also part of a physical fitness section. To the left is Woods Creek. At 0.4 mile pass right of VMI tennis courts, and at 0.6 mile cross a paved road to follow an old railroad grade. Turn left from a parking area and descend to the creekside. Here are tall maples, sycamores, and tulip poplars with scattered papaw in the understory. At 1.2 miles go under an old railroad culvert, close to the stream. Pass through part of Washington and Lee campus and under US 60 bridge, cross a low footbridge, and slightly ascend into white pines at 1.5 miles. At 1.6 miles cross Lime Kiln Road and bridge over Woods Creek. To the left are play fields, picnic areas, and open fields. The trail now becomes asphalt with pine bark and gravel on side trails. Cross Jordan Street, pass a small dam to the right, and cross a stream at 1.9 miles. Reach the end of the trail on crafted stone steps at the corner of Stonewall Street and Ross Road at 2.1 miles. It is 0.1 mile left to Waddell Elementary School and parking area.

Backtrack, or follow an alternate street route to northeastern trailhead: Walk east on Jordan Street one block and turn left on Jackson Street. Follow it to Preston Street, turn right, then left on Lee Avenue to Washington Street. Turn left and go around the Lee Episcopal Church onto the front lawns of Washington and Lee campus. Pass the Lee Chapel, come onto Letcher Avenue, and enter the campus of VMI. Follow straight on VMI Parade Street to Richardson Hall, pass other halls, and curve right to a junction with Institute Hill Street, left. Follow it past the VMI Hospital, turn left on the next street, and descend to join Moses Hill Road for a left.

USGS MAP: Lexington

ADDRESSES AND INFORMATION: Lexington Public Works, 890 Shop Rd., Lexington, VA 24450; phone: 540-463-3154; fax: 540-464-4198; or Lexington Visitor Center (see above). Available are brochures of city and Woods Creek Park.


## Luray

The town of Luray is in the center of Page County and in a long beautiful valley with its eastern boundary at the north end of Shenandoah National Park and Skyline Drive, and its western boundary with Massanutten Mountain and Shenandoah County. The town was founded in 1812 and is internationally known for the large Luray Caverns. Unique to the caverns is a formation that can produce symphonic music. There are four parks (total of 200 acres) with recreational facilities in Luray, of which Lake Arrowhead is the largest and has hiking trails. One of the other parks, Luray Recreation Park, features lighted ballfields and a designed wooden playground accessible to the disabled. There is also a fitness trail with fibar service approved by ADA guidelines.

Lake Arrowhead Park has 134 acres, 34 of which are the lake. There is a white sand beach for swimming. Fishing and boating are also allowed. There are five picnic shelters, a site for beach volleyball, playground, and accessible rest rooms

1274 for the disabled. If hiking **Lake Arrowhead Trail** clockwise, park near the maintenance shop or the entrance to the ballfield and walk the road to the dam. On the dam are outstanding views of the lake and forests, a colorful scene in autumn or at sunset. Reach the east end of the dam at 0.5 mile and turn right to follow a narrow trail on the lakeside. You may see signs of beavers along the way. Cross board-

1275–77 walks in the forest, and at 0.8 mile the Boy Scout **Beaver Nature Trail** doubles with the lake trail. Cross more boardwalks. Also in this area, pass **Bob White Trail** and at 1.1 miles pass **Tomahawk Trail**, both short connecting paths to the left that access a Boy Scout Camping Area. Arrive at a parking area near picnic shelter #1 and follow either the access road or the grassy area near the beach west to picnic shelter #4 at 1.3 miles for completion of the trail loop. The picnic shelters are provided by Luray community organizations.

ACCESS: In Luray on US 211 Bus take Reservoir Road (SR 669) (which becomes Fairview Rd.) 2.5 miles to SR 611 and stop sign. Turn right, then immediately left to continue on SR 669. After another 1.3 miles (watch for Lake Arrowhead signs) turn left to enter the park.

ADDRESS AND INFORMATION: Luray Parks and Recreation Department, 45 E. Main St., Luray, VA 22835; phone: 540-743-5511. Lake Arrowhead phone: 540-743-6475. Brochures and map available.

# Lynchburg

Lynchburg was settled in 1759 and was named for John Lynch, who built the first commercial buildings, a ferryhouse and a tobacco warehouse, by the James River above Horseford Crossing. It was the beginning of what is today the state's second largest city west of Richmond and a center for business, industry, and commerce in central Virginia. The city is 15 miles southeast of the BRP, the George Washington and Jefferson National Forests, and the AT. The route to these great attractions from Lynchburg is VA 130, a scenic state byway. To the southwest of the city is magnificent Smith Mountain Lake, and to the east is Buckingham-Appomattox State Forest. A historic city of museums, mansions, colleges, and Civil War shrines, it is also near the restored Thomas Jefferson personal retreat, Poplar Forest, begun in 1806. (Access is southwest of the city off US 221 on SR 661.) While the city treasures its human history, it also preserves its natural history. With a citywide system of diverse parks, it has set aside more than 900 acres. One of the oldest city parks is Riverside Park on Rivermont Avenue. Here is 1-mile **Alpine Trail** to the Miller-Clayton House (1791) and the keel of the packet boat 1278 *Marshall*. The city's largest park is Blackwater Creek Natural Area with 300 acres and 7 miles of unpaved treadway. The Blackwater Creek Natural Area also contains a portion of the James River Heritage Trail system, a multi-use asphalt route. Future plans are to extend the **James River Heritage Trail** east to Appomattox Courthouse and west to the D-Day Memorial in the city of Bedford. Also included are a **Heritage Park Bike/Hike Trail** and the **Ivy Creek Bike/ Hike Trail**.

## BLACKWATER CREEK NATURAL AREA

This carefully planned and constructed area for preserving the natural environment is located in the heart of the city. A basically undisturbed area, it is a day-use facility for hiking, bicycling, and picnicking. Within the area is the 115-acre Ruskin Freer Nature Preserve. It provides a good example of forestry succession. Along the creekside and on the high bluffs of the gorge are hardwoods such as oak, tulip poplar, hickory, beech, sycamore, and ironwood. The understory has dogwood, redbud, mountain laurel, Scotch broom, ferns, and wildflowers. Deer and wild turkey may be seen, and there are many species of songbirds.

1279 **Blackwater Creek Trail**

LENGTH AND DIFFICULTY: 5.2 miles (8.3 km); easy to moderate

1280–84 CONNECTING TRAILS: **Hollin's Mill Bikeway** (1.7 mi.), **Blackwater Creek Bikeway** also called **James River Heritage Trail** (3.4 mi.), **Ruskin Freer Lower Trail** (0.4 mi.), **Ruskin Freer Upper Trail** (0.7 mi.), **Beaver Trail** (1.6 mi.)

FEATURES: creek, gorge, historic sites, wildflowers, scenery

TRAILHEADS: This natural area has multiple accesses, but two main trailheads are emphasized. To reach the Hollin's Mill Road access parking area from US 29, downtown, take exit 1 on Main Street northwest, which becomes Rivermont Drive. Cross Blackwater Creek Bridge and turn left on Bedford Avenue at the top of the hill. After 0.7 mile turn left on Hollin's Mill Road and go 0.7 mile (pass a scenic waterfall on the right) to Blackwater Creek Natural Area parking lot, right, at Hollin's Mill dam. The most southwest trailhead access is at Blackwater Creek Athletic Area. From US 29 turn off at exit 3A and B and go northwest on Kemper Street (US 501 Bus). Proceed 1.3 miles and turn left on Murrell Road, which becomes Lakeside Drive, and go 0.8 mile to the second traffic light (a five-way intersection) and turn right on Monticello Avenue. Go 0.3 mile to Blackwater Creek Athletic Area parking lot on the right. (Accesses between the trailheads are described ahead.)

DESCRIPTION: (If beginning from Hollin's Mill Rd. parking lot, you will notice the **Hollin's Mill Bikeway** descends beneath Hollins Mill Road via a low-water crossing to follow Blackwater Creek downstream. It terminates at the lower end of Cabell St., near Point of Honor at 1.3 mi. A planned bridge will connect it with **Blackwater Creek Bikeway** and **Riverwalk** near the John Lynch Bridge.) Begin the **Blackwater Creek Trail** and **Hollin's Mill Bikeway** together upstream from the parking lot on a wide asphalt trail. At 0.3 mile the **Hollin's Mill Bikeway** goes left and the **Blackwater Creek Trail** goes right into a meadow. (The **Hollin's Mill Bikeway** goes another 0.1 mile to end at a connection, right and left, with **Blackwater Creek Bikeway**.) (See **Blackwater Creek Bikeway** description ahead.)

On the **Blackwater Creek Trail** pass under a railroad trestle at 0.5 mile and a higher trestle at 0.6 mile. Large sycamores line the trail and the creek banks. In this area the graveled trail is wide and is used by park service personnel. At 1 mile on the left is an access trail to Jefferson Park, where there is a parking area. (Access to Jefferson Park from US 29 as described above to Blackwater Creek Athletic Area is the same except after 1.3 mi., just beyond Murrell Rd. traffic light, turn right on Hillcrest St., which soon becomes Caroline St. for a turn left on York St. to the park entrance, right.) At 1.6 miles, left, is a short access trail to Hillsdale Road, which becomes Tate Springs Road to connect with Langhorne

*Blackwater Creek Trail, Lynchburg*

Road (us 501 Bus). At 2 miles, right, is a swinging bridge over the creek. At the far end of the bridge there are two trails: To the left is the 0.4-mile **Ruskin Freer Lower Trail**, which leads to the 0.7-mile **Ruskin Freer Upper Trail**. They both make interloops and are easily accessible to Thomson Drive at 2.3 miles. (Thomson Dr. exits to Tate Springs Rd. to connect with Langhorne Rd. [us 501 Bus].) To the right at the bridge is **Beaver Trail**.

(The **Beaver Trail** is a single-track, dirt trail that climbs steadily to a high ridge overlooking the Blackwater Creek gorge. It then descends, gradually winding, through a ravine to pass beneath overhead power lines. The trail is linked to the **Blackwater Creek Bikeway** at intervals by short uphill connector trails marked by mileposts, and it is frequently in sight of the **Blackwater Creek Trail**, which is on the opposite side of the creek bank. At the Norfolk Southern Railroad high trestle the trail turns left and winds up switchbacks to end on the **Blackwater Creek Bikeway**. [On the **Bikeway**, left, it is 1.8 mi. southwest to the **Bikeway**'s Ed Page parking area at Old Langhorne Rd., and right it is 0.7 mi. northeast to a connection with **Hollin's Mill Bikeway**'s southern trailhead].)

Continuing on the **Blackwater Creek Trail**, cross the creek at 2.5 miles on a swinging bridge for a left turn to leave the loop trails. Ascend on a narrow footpath among wildflowers such as hepatica and saxifrage at 3 miles. Three connecting trails to the right give access to the **Blackwater Creek Bikeway**. Cross a swinging footbridge over Ivy Creek at 3.3 miles, near the confluence with Blackwater Creek. Turn left and follow a narrow path up Blackwater Creek; at 3.4 miles an access trail to the right ascends to Peninsular Street. At 3.7 miles arrive at a meadow. Pass autumn olives and cedars and go left to cross a footbridge over the creek for a turn right. Christmas fern is prominent in the rich soil between the rocks. On the approach to Langhorne Road, cross a foot-bridge on a pipeline to go under the street bridge, at 4.2 miles. At 4.5 miles the trail descends steep steps, left, to cross a low-water cement bridge for a right turn under Hill Street. The remainder of the trail follows a wide gravel road for 0.7 mile in a scenic combination of the hardwood forest and creekside vistas before opening into a large meadow. Here are playing fields and a picnic area. To the left is the parking area for Blackwater Creek Athletic Area.

1281 **Blackwater Creek Bikeway**

LENGTH AND DIFFICULTY: 3.1 miles (4.9 km); easy to moderate

1282–84,  CONNECTING TRAILS: **Ruskin Freer Upper Trail** (0.7 mi.), **Ruskin Freer Lower**
1279–80,  **Trail** (0.4 mi.), **Beaver Trail** (1.6 mi.), **Blackwater Creek Trail** also called
1285, 1287  **James River Heritage Trail** (5.2 mi.), **Hollin's Mill Bikeway** (3.4 mi.), **Kemper Street Station Trail** (1.1 mi.), **Riverwalk**, also called **James River Heritage Trail** (3.5 mi.)

FEATURES: historic sites, landscaping, gorge, railroad tunnel, creek, forest, wild-flowers

TRAILHEADS: There are multiple accesses, but only the two main trailheads are emphasized. The southwest trailhead is at Ed Page Parking Area on Old Lang-horne Road. A convenient access from US 29, exit 3A or B, is west on Kemper Street (US 501 Bus). Proceed for 2.9 miles (Kemper St. becomes Langhorne Rd.), pass Greek Orthodox Church, right, and immediately turn right on Old Lang-horne Road. Behind the church is the parking area, left. The northwest trailhead is technically at the west end of Jefferson Street, but there is not a parking area there. Instead, there is Percival's Island Parking Area near the east end of Jefferson Street. Access is off US 29, exit 1, near the south end of the James River Bridge. Turn west on Main Street and after 0.2 mile turn right for a descent on Washington Street. Pass the east end of Jefferson Street, cross a gated railroad crossing, and bear right to an immediate left for the parking area at 0.4 mile.

DESCRIPTION: This bicycle route is also an excellent asphalt passage for hikers, runners, bird-watchers, and strollers. Its professional landscaping, preservation of both natural and historic areas, and multiple accesses deserve outstanding credits to city government. This trail, as with the other park trails, is open only from sunrise to sunset. There are resting benches along the way and signposts to prevent users from becoming disoriented. There are no rest rooms. Two natural appeals to the trail are the spring fragrance of wild white roses, honeysuckle, and spicebush and the abundant mixture of music from the songbirds. An engineering appeal is the passage of the trail at one point through a lighted railroad tunnel.

If beginning at the Ed Page Parking Area, notice to the right the old railroad bed for future development of the trail to the west. Continue ahead on the abandoned, but paved railroad route. At 0.7 mile is a connecting trail that leads to the Ruskin Freer Nature Preserve. At 1 mile is the East Randolph Place parking lot, accessing the Rivermont area. The high fills in this area provide good views of the Blackwater Creek gorge. At 1.5 miles an old farm road descends on an easy treadway to the **Beaver Trail**, right, and at 1.8 miles is the downstream access to the **Beaver Trail**, right. This is just before passing beneath the high trestle of the Norfolk Southern Railroad and crossing the gorge on an old railway bridge. At 2 miles is the paved intersection where **Hollin's Mill Bikeway** is left, and the **Blackwater Creek Trail** is right and left. Farther to the right is the planned 1.1-mile **Kemper Street Station Trail**, but to the immediate left the paved **Blackwater Creek Bikeway** continues for another 1.1 miles. (This section is also called the **Tunnel Trail**.)    1286

Continue downstream and at 2.2 miles pass through the lighted 500-foot abandoned railroad tunnel. Ahead and to the left are high and scenic views of Blackwater Creek and the **Hollin's Mill Bikeway** below. The area has large tulip poplars, sycamores, and maples. Between the supports of three bridges are beds of joe-pye weed, clovers, and fleabanes. Arrive at a ramp of steps and a new brick walk at Jefferson Street at 3.1 miles.


## PERCIVAL'S ISLAND NATURAL AREA

**James River Heritage Trail (Riverwalk)**    1287
LENGTH AND DIFFICULTY: 3.5 miles (5.6 km); easy
CONNECTING TRAIL: **Blackwater Creek Bikeway**    1281

FEATURES: scenic river and island sections, historic railroad sites, wildlife

TRAILHEADS: The western trailhead of the **James River Heritage Trail** is the same as that for the **Blackwater Creek Bikeway**, but this description is only from the west end of Jefferson Street, which is also the eastern trailhead for **Blackwater Creek Bikeway**. Vehicular access from US 29, exit 1, is west on Main Street to Ninth Street where a right turn descends one block to Jefferson Street. The trail is right and left, but left does not have an official parking area. Parking for this trail is recommended at Percival's Island Natural Area parking, as described above for the eastern trailhead of **Blackwater Creek Bikeway**. Although there are two accesses on back roads at and near the east end of the trail, it is recommended you backtrack. Such an experience will provide a different scenic perspective.

DESCRIPTION: The **James River Heritage Trail** proceeds along Jefferson Street past historic warehouses of the Lower Basin of the city to the intersection with Washington Street. From here the trail turns left and crosses a gated railroad to Percival's Island parking lot at 0.6 mile. At the northwest corner of the lot is a **Riverwalk** sign and kiosk. At the eastern edge of the parking area is an agency for renting bicycles, wheelchairs, and stroller carriages. The trail is open from sunrise to sunset. There are resting benches along the way but no rest rooms. The island is known for its birding opportunities. In addition to many species of songbirds, hawks, owls, and the American eagle have been seen. The trail briefly goes upstream, then turns right to cross a 558-foot plate beam railroad bridge to Percival's Island Natural Area at 0.9 mile. Informational signs are along the 8-foot-wide paved trail. At 1 mile pass under the US 29 bridge, and at 1.1 miles is a blue-blazed 0.3-mile spur trail, right, to weave through dense and lush island trees and undergrowth. At a few points along the riverbanks are fishing holes. On the main flat and straight trail the passage is the historic site of a railroad service yard. At 1.4 miles is an example of a railroad mile marker ("4.5 mi."). Near 2 miles is a 300-foot-long steel truss bridge and crossing into Amherst County. For the remainder of the trail there are a number of "private" signs at access routes to scenic meadows. In 2003 the eastern trailhead was 0.1 mile beyond the 6.5 railroad mile marker (at 3.5 miles). To the left is an access road to Fertilizer Road. (It is accessible off US 29 in Madison Heights on VA 210. Drive 1 mi. and turn right at traffic light on Colony Rd. [SR 334]. Follow it about 0.9 mi., and after passing a large water tower pass through an intersection and proceed on SR 1013. After 0.4 mi. take a left on Fertilizer Rd. At its end is a very small turnaround.) (Plans are for extending the **Riverwalk** to Six-Mile Bridge and beyond.)

ADDRESS AND INFORMATION: Lynchburg Parks and Recreation Department, 301 Grove St., Lynchburg, VA 24501; phone: 434-847-1640; e-mail: <reedeah@ci. lynchburg.va.us>.

# New Market

The New Market Community Park provides an admirable service to its local citizens. The park was made possible by local leadership and the Virginia Outdoor Fund. It has a swimming pool, picnic table, lighted tennis courts, children's play area, ballfields, and a twenty-station paved 0.9-mile **New Market Trail** through a   1288 peaceful and manicured meadow with a locust grove. The town was settled in 1761 and is known for its early American and antique shops. The south town boundary is the south boundary of Shenandoah County, and near here on the east side of US 11 is Shenvalee Golf Resort. Four miles north of town on US 11 east is Shenandoah Caverns. (See Chapter 6 for information on nearby New Market Battlefield Historical Park; this chapter for the town of Woodstock; and Chapter 12 for Shenandoah County Park.)

ACCESS: From I-81, exit 264, drive east on Old Cross Road to US 11. Turn right and drive 0.4 mile to Stonewall Street and turn right. After 0.1 mile turn left at park sign.

ADDRESS AND INFORMATION: Department of Parks and Recreation, Shenandoah County, 508 Piccadilly St., Edinburg, VA 22824; phone 540-984-3030; fax: 540-984-8032.

# Newport News

The city is the base for the Newport News Shipbuilding Company (1886), the largest in the world. With Norfolk and Portsmouth, two cities across the James River from Newport News, the three cities constitute the port of Hampton Roads, one of the world's finest deep and natural harbors. The first settlers on this part of the peninsula were David Gookin and about sixty other Irishmen in either 1619 or 1621. The site's name, "Newportes Newes," had preceded them. One historical claim is that Capt. Christopher Newport's arrival with supplies, news from England, and additional colonists to the James River was good news. In the city are the Virginia War Museum (documents and artifacts from 1775 to the present); the Virginia Living Museum (zoology); the Mariners' Museum (maritime history, photography, and the 5-mi. **Noland Trail**); and the Newport News Park (the   1289 largest municipal park east of the Mississippi, and the third largest in the nation).

## NEWPORT NEWS PARK

The 8,065-acre park has more than 180 campsites; laundry facilities; twenty-four picnic shelters; two golf courses; playgrounds; boat ramps; boat and bike rentals (no swimming); bike, equestrian, and hiking trails; 25 miles of fire roads (which can be used for hiking); an arboretum; horse shows; concerts and other cultural activities; camper store; eighteen-hole disc golf course; fishing; children's programs; and the Discovery Center. In addition to the trails described below there is an 0.8-mile **Lakeside Nature Trail** that can be accessed from the parking lot for the fishing area concessions at the second entrance on the left after entering the park. The park is popular for nature study and birding. There are more than 190 species of birds, 30 species of mammals, and more than 30 species of amphibians and reptiles. The park is open year round. (It adjoins the Colonial National Historical Park.)

ACCESS: From SR 105 (Fort Eustis Blvd.), crossing of parallel routes I-64 (exit 250 from I-64) and SR 143, turn north on SR 143 (Jefferson Ave.), to the park entrance on the right.

1290

1291–93 **White Oak Trail** (2.8 mi.), **Wynn's Mill Historical Trail** (1.1 mi.), **Twin Forts Trail** (0.7 mi.)

LENGTH AND DIFFICULTY: 4.6 miles (7.4 km) combined, round-trip; easy
FEATURES: waterfowl, swamp, wildflowers, historic site, lake, overlooks
TRAILHEAD: from the Discovery Center
DESCRIPTION: From the parking area secure a trail guide pamphlet, which lists twenty-three stations, from the Discovery Center. Cross the entrance road and follow the signs for 0.1 mile to dam #1 bridge over the 380-acre Lee Hill Reservoir. At the northern end of the bridge is a junction with the 0.7-mile **Twin Forts Trail** on the left. (It makes a loop to examples of well-preserved Confederate earthworks, many with descriptive signage.) Continue right and pass through a hardwood forest of oak, elm, red mulberry, persimmon, hornbeam, and hazel alder. Among the ferns and clubmosses are closed gentian, orange-fringed orchid, and pink lady's-slipper. Deer, red foxes, salamanders, and squirrels frequent the area. At 1.3 miles is an old homesite and fire road. The **Wynn's Mill Historical Trail** goes straight across the fire road and returns near the swamp bridge. (The loop trail is 1.1 mi. and has some of the largest Confederate earthworks in the park. A water-powered gristmill once operated here. Some of the vascular plants on this trail are Indian pipe and devil's walking stick. It is also adjacent to a heron rookery.)

Continue on the **White Oak Trail** and at 1.7 miles cross the swamp bridge. Nearly 600 feet long, it weaves through a marsh with white ash, sycamore, and wild rose. Woodpeckers, kingfishers, herons, and hawks may be seen here. At 2.1 miles cross a bridge over Deer Creek and return to the parking lot at 2.8 miles on the **White Oak Trail** (or 4.6 mi. for all trails).

USGS MAP: Yorktown

## RIVERVIEW FARM PARK

This 300-acre park is in the process of developing additional recreational services such as another 1-mile paved loop of the **Riverview Farm Trail**, picnic shelters, 1294 and a spacious elevated boardwalk for superb views of the James River. At present, 1 mile of the 2-mile figure eight is open for walkers, runners, joggers, strollers, and bicyclists. The loop trail surface is level and open, and in a former farm field. With it are soccer fields, multiple units of children's playgrounds, and concessions. At the back of the park office is 0.1 mile **Wildflower Garden Trail**. It follows 1295 a paved pathway into a forest of large holly, white oak, and pine to a scenic serpentine boardwalk and observation platform into the river.

ACCESS: From US 60 (Warwick Blvd.), turn west on Boxley Boulevard. After 0.8 mile turn left on Menchville Road. After 0.4 mile pass Menchville High School, right, and after another 0.3 mile curve right to the parking area for the **Riverview Farm Trail**. For the **Wildflower Garden Trail**, continue ahead on Menchville Road (which becomes City Farm Rd.) for 0.5 mile to turn right, with the office left near a gate.

ADDRESS AND INFORMATION: City of Newport News Department of Parks and Recreation, 2400 Washington Ave., Newport News, VA 23607; phone: 757-886-7911 or 926-8451; fax: 757-926-8728. Available are brochures and maps of the park facilities and trails.

# Norfolk

Norfolk's location at the world's largest natural harbor made it an ideal place for English settlers in the 1630s. In 1682 the Virginia general assembly purchased 50 acres on the Elizabeth River, a tidal estuary, from Nicholas Wise, a carpenter and early settler. The purpose was to start a new town for manufactured products and commerce. By 1736 it was Virginia's largest town, and by the end of the nineteenth century it was a prosperous industrial city. Norfolk and its sister city, Portsmouth, became the headquarters of the Atlantic fleet. Fulfilling its early purpose, Norfolk has since become the oldest naval port in the United States and, with the U.S. naval base, houses the largest naval installation in the world. Norfolk, Newport News, and Portsmouth are known worldwide as Hampton Roads. But Norfolk is more than a major commercial and industrial seaport; it is also the cultural hub of Hampton Roads. Easily accessible by land, sea, and air, it provides museums (such as the Chrysler Museum, with art treasures of the past 5,000 years), historic houses, monuments, performing arts centers, recreational areas, the Virginia Zoological Park, and the Norfolk Botanical Gardens.

## NORFOLK BOTANICAL GARDENS

Unsurpassed in beauty, scope, and design, the 175-acre Norfolk Botanical Gardens has been home for the annual International Azalea Festival since 1954. The festival is held on a weekend in April. There are more than thirty special gardens here, with 12 miles of colorful intertwining paved trails for walking or riding a tram. The trails wind along the shorelines of Whitehurst and Mirrow Lakes. Moderate year-round temperatures encourage horticulturists to grow a wide range of plants found in both northern and southern climates. As a result there are a quarter-million azaleas of every known variety, 900 varieties of camellias, and 150 varieties of rhododendron. The gardens were established in 1931 and were expanded in 1958. A Japanese garden was created in 1962; a rose garden with more than 250 varieties and 4,000 plants was dedicated in 1976; and in 1992 a pavilion of tropical plants was added.

In addition, the gardens are a mecca for horticultural activities, including a botanical library and educational programs. Regional and local garden and nature clubs contribute to projects and sponsor floral shows. At least 145 species of birds have been sighted, either as residents or as migratory fowl. In addition to the trails there are boat tours. Hours of daily operation are weekdays 9 A.M. to 5 P.M., and 9 A.M. to 7 P.M. from April 15 to September 15. A small fee is charged.

ACCESS: Turn off I-64, exit 279, at Northview Avenue (east) and go 1 mile to Azalea Gardens Road, VA 192, on the left. After 0.6 mile turn right into the Botanical Gardens. Access is also possible from US 60; turn off on VA 170, Little Creek Road, and go 1.1 miles. Turn left on Azalea Gardens Road, VA 192.

ADDRESS AND INFORMATION: Department of Parks and Recreation, 501 Boush St., Norfolk, VA 23510; phone: 757-441-2400; fax: 757-441-5423. For Botanical Gardens general information, phone: 757-441-5830; for administrative office, phone: 757-441-5830. Available are brochures and list of seasonal blooming periods.

# Poquoson

The city of Poquoson is on the Virginia Peninsula. It is bordered by Plum Tree Island NWR on the east at Chesapeake Bay; the Langley Air Force Base, the NASA Research Center, the Back River, and the city of Hampton on the south; and the Poquoson River with coves, bays, and islands on the north. Poquoson City Park has an excellent swimming pool facility, plus areas for picnicking, ball games, and
1296 nature study on the 0.5-mile **Poquoson Nature Trail**. It is a serpentine pea-gravel loop through a forest of oak, pine, sweet gum, and holly.

ACCESS: From I-64, exit 256, take VA 171 for 3 miles to an intersection with Wythe Creek Road. Proceed ahead and VA 171 becomes Little Florida Road. Follow it 1 mile, turn left on Cedar Road, go 0.3 mile, and turn left to parking area. Municipal Park headquarters adjoins the ballfield.

ADDRESS AND INFORMATION: Poquoson Parks and Recreation, 830 Poquoson Ave., Poquoson, VA 23662; phone: 757-868-3580.

# Radford

In the heart of Radford is Wildwood Park, a 66-acre natural area. Connelly's Run flows through a riparian valley where the prominent trees are oak, tulip poplar, yellow buckeye, locust, white ash, mulberry, and red maple. Among the ferns and wildflowers are bee balm, wild phlox, and coltsfoot. On the western slopes is the 0.5-mile **Wildwood Nature Trail**, where there are additional species of wild-  1297
flowers. The park staff and a citizens group, Pathways for Radford, are planning a 10-mile network of bikeway/walkway trails to areas along the New River, Bissett Park, Wildwood Park, and into residential areas.

ACCESS: From I-81 and VA 177 junction, exit 109, go north 4.2 miles on VA 177 to US 11 in downtown Radford. Turn left and go a few blocks to the park on the left, behind Charter Federal Bank.

ADDRESS AND INFORMATION: Radford Recreation, Parks, Playground Commission, 29 First St., Radford, VA 24141; phone: 540-731-3633; fax: 540-633-2368; about 0.2 mile west of Wildwood Park.

# Richmond

The capital of Virginia, Richmond, is preeminently historic. In 1607, soon after the Jamestown landing, Capts. Christopher Newport and John Smith, with a party of nineteen other men, sailed up the James River to the falls, the present site of Richmond. Thomas Stegg established a trading post here in 1637, and by 1644 Fort Charles was built to protect the English settlers from Indian attacks. The fort's name was changed to Richmond in 1733. By 1737 William Byrd II had a town laid out on what is now Church Hill (east of the present capital). It was incorporated in 1742. It was at St. John's Church on Church Hill in 1775 that Patrick Henry made his famous challenge, "Give me liberty or give me death." When Virginia seceded from the Union in 1861, the seat of the Confederate government was moved from Montgomery, Alabama, to Richmond. As a result, the city became a major military objective of the Union forces for the next four years.

A modern city of skyscrapers, Richmond continues its historic leadership in commerce, marketing, industry, banking, medicine, and transportation. An educational center, it has distinguished universities, two of which are Virginia Commonwealth University and Medical College of Virginia, and the University of Richmond. Its cultural heritage and emphasis is exemplified in museums, churches, historic districts, monuments, shrines, libraries, art centers, and government buildings (the design for the capitol building was selected by Thomas Jefferson). Attention is also given to parks and recreation. There are more than sixty areas set aside for preservation, sports activities, and enjoyment of natural beauty. Some parks have trails, and outside the parks are some historic sidewalk trails. Both types of trails are described below. (See Henrico County, Chapter 12, for parks adjoining the city.) Also of interest are gardens in or near the city. Two examples are Ginter Botanical Gardens (off I-95, exit 80, on Lakeside Ave. north [SR 161]), and Bryan Park (at the same exit, on Hermitage Rd., south to Bellevue Ave., then right to the park).

## JAMES RIVER PARK

The James River Park property is in five sections. The Main Section is between the Robert E. Lee Bridge (US 1/301) and Powhite Parkway Bridge on the south side; Belle Isle Section is partly under the Lee Bridge; Texas Avenue Section is partly under the Boulevard Bridge on the north side; Pony Pasture Section is upriver on Riverside Drive on the south side near the Huguenot Bridge; and farther northwest is Huguenot Woods Section, partly under Huguenot Bridge on the south side. (The Texas Avenue Section, east of Maymont Park, has a parking area at the end of the street. Undesignated trails, such as fishermen's paths, go across the railroad to the river.) Trails on the other four sections are described below. The James River Park has a diversity of wildlife and botanical species. Fishing is excellent, hiking is easy, and the quality of white-water sports in a metropolitan area is unparalleled in the nation. Picnic facilities are provided, but camping and fires are not permitted. A visitor center, accessible by foot, is halfway between 22nd Street and 42nd Street on Riverside Drive.

ACCESS: From junction of Lee Bridge, US 1/301 south, and Riverside Drive, go west on Riverside Drive 0.3 mile to parking area on the right at 22nd Street.

1298–1301 **Geology Interpretive Trail** (0.8 mi.), **Riverside Trail** (0.8 mi.), **Meadow Trail** (0.6 mi.), **Buttermilk Trail** (1.4 mi.)
LENGTH AND DIFFICULTY: 3.6 miles (5.8 km) combined, round-trip; easy
FEATURES: scenic views, riverside, historic site, waterfowl
TRAILHEAD: See Access, above.
DESCRIPTION: Begin on the eastern end of the parking area; ascend steps to pedestrian bridge over the Southern Railway, and descend steps at 0.1 mile. To the left is the **Riverside Trail** and to the right is the **Geology Interpretive Trail**. (On the geology trail are cement walkways in places. At 0.4 mi. the trail ends at the former railroad bridge to Belle Isle. Backtrack.) To continue on the **River-**

**side Trail** cross a canal bridge at 0.3 mile, and at 0.8 mile turn right on a gravel park service road to the visitor center. The well-maintained **Meadow Trail** loops the visitor center.

Continue ahead and enter a forest at 1 mile, pass a picnic area at 1.3 miles, and climb the cement steps to the pedestrian bridge at 1.4 miles on the left. (The trail to the right continues to a picnic area at 0.3 mi. and to the Boulevard Park Drive Bridge [Nickle Bridge] at 0.5 mi.)

After crossing the pedestrian bridge, turn right and enter the **Buttermilk Trail**. (A climb up the rock steps leads to the 42nd St. parking area.) Follow the **Buttermilk Trail** by the old Netherwood Granite Quarry at 1.7 miles and cross the park service road at 2 miles. Continue through a mature hardwood forest, cross Reedy Creek, pass Buttermilk Spring on the right, and complete the loop of 2.8 miles at the 22nd Street parking area. Some of the vascular plants hikers will see on these trails are red elm, green ash, papaw, oak, hackberry, periwinkle, clubmosses, and tree of heaven.

USGS MAP: Richmond

## Belle Isle Trail 1302

This is an easy, 1-mile loop trail on an old road around the edges of Belle Isle. Another 0.2 mile is necessary to arrive on the island by the elevated footbridge under the Robert E. Lee Bridge. After descending from the footbridge, pass the remains of the Old Dominion Iron and Steel Factory and the area of the notorious Civil War prison for Federal enlisted men. Keep right on the old road, pass whitewater rapids, some class 4 and 5, and pass an old quarry pit lake. An old picnic area is here, and a spur trail left, up the hill, leads to a good view of the area. Curve around the end of the island and pass the remains of an old VEPCO hydropower plant. Oak, gum, papaw, soapwort, and sensitive ferns are along the trail. At 0.8 mile are the remains of an 1815 snuff factory. Come out of the woods, bear left for a completion of the loop, and begin the return on the footbridge at the sign and kiosk. Access to the island is closed at night.

USGS MAP: Richmond

ACCESS: If on the Downtown Expressway going east, take Byrd Street exit to 7th Street. Turn right and go to Tredegar Street and turn right to parking area. If going west on the expressway, take Canal Street and turn left on 10th Street to Tredegar Street. Otherwise take 5th Street south to Byrd Street, turn left, go two blocks and turn right on 7th Street to Tredegar Street.

## Pleasant Creek Trail 1303

The **Pleasant Creek Trail** with side trails is in the Pony Pasture Section of the James River Park. It is a popular area for sunbathing, fishing, hiking, nature study, birding, and tubing (at gentle rapids upriver from the parking lot). This area is considered the best birding location in metropolitan Richmond. Additionally, this is a good place for wildflower field trips into biotic zones, and aquatic biology study. Rest rooms and drinking water are at the ranger station. The easy, 1.3-mile

1304–6 loop is from the parking lot on a wide trail. Pass a side trail, left, the **Quiet Woods Trail**, at 0.4 mile. Continue ahead in a mature forest of sycamore, tulip poplar, and river birch to the James River at 0.7 mile. Turn left on a side trail, the **Forest Trail**, at 0.9 mile for a return on a wide trail in the Pony Pasture to the **River Access Trail** (a spur to the river), and to the parking lot.

USGS MAP: Bon Air

ACCESS: From the junction of Huguenot Road at the Huguenot Bridge and Riverside Drive, take Riverside Drive east, downriver for 1.8 miles to the parking lot on the left.

1307 ### Huguenot Woods Trail

The 1-mile round-trip **Huguenot Woods Trail** is in the Huguenot Woods Section of the James River Park, the farthest section upriver. This section has a boat ramp and an access to riverside fishing. From the parking lot walk out to an observation point, then follow the river's edge downriver through a mature floodplain forest for 0.5 mile to Rattlesnake Creek. Backtrack. There is also a 0.2-mile side trail halfway along the trail.

USGS MAP: Bon Air

ACCESS: From the Huguenot Bridge descend the ramp to Riverside Drive (southern end of bridge) and go upriver to Southampton Street parking area. Parking is also possible downriver opposite Oxford Parkway.

## FOREST HILL PARK

Forest Hill Park adjoins James River Park's Main Section on the north, and Forest Hill Avenue and US 60 on the south. Forest Hill is one of Richmond's famous seven hills. The park has a lake, a picnic area with pavilions, a tennis court, and a nature study area. Some unmarked trails extend along Reedy Creek, which flows

1308 through the park. The 1-mile round-trip **Reedy Creek Trail** follows an old road below the dam to Riverside Drive, where a connection can be made with the **Buttermilk Trail**. The park has large tulip poplar and beech trees, with banks of wildflowers and shrubs. Vehicles are not allowed in the park.

USGS MAP: Richmond

## MAYMONT PARK

Formerly Crenshaw's Dairy Farm, the 105 acres on the edge of Richmond purchased by Maj. James H. Dooley in 1886 became his estate, which he renamed in honor of his wife, the former Sallie O. May. At the death of the Dooleys in 1925 this magnificent English country estate was willed to the city of Richmond for "the pleasure of its citizens." It is operated by the private, nonprofit Maymont Founda-

*Garden Walk, Maymont Park, Richmond*

tion and is free to the public. There are four distinctive trails in the park, totaling approximately 4 miles. The **Historic Walk** has seven major points of interest, 1309–12 beginning at the carriage entrance and including the Dooley Mansion. On the **Garden Walk** are fifteen major areas, which include the Italian garden, the Japanese garden, and the wildflower garden. More than fifty trees are labeled on the **Tree Walk**, and the **Animal Walk** includes an aviary, a small and large mammal habitat, and other zoo features. A detailed map and walking-tour guide is available at the nature center information desk at the entrance from Hampton Street.

ACCESS: On The Boulevard (VA 161) going north, cross the James River bridge to Maymont Park on the right. Turn right on Shirley Lane to Spottswood entrance and parking area, right. Or from the parking area continue east to Shields Lake Drive in Byrd Park to park at the Nature and Visitor Center entrance, right. (Continuing east to Hampton St. is another parking area, right.)

ADDRESS AND INFORMATION: Maymont Park, Maymont Foundation, 1700 Hampton St., Richmond, VA 23220; phone: 804-358-7166. Available are brochures and map of the park.

Richmond has two downtown sidewalk trails with a common focus on Capitol Square. The **Old Dominion Trail**, the oldest, is a linear trail of 7.5 miles designed by the Robert E. Lee Council of the Boy Scouts. The **Richmond Walking Trail** has been designed by the Chamber of Commerce to loop around the Capitol Square at ten historic sites.

ACCESS: From any of the expressways, such as I-95, I-64, I-195, or I-295, turn off at the proper interchange that has signs for downtown. Follow signs to Broad Street and Capitol Square.

### 1313 Old Dominion Trail

LENGTH AND DIFFICULTY: 7.5 miles (12 km); easy to moderate

FEATURES: historic site, architecture, art, gardens

TRAILHEAD: corner of 24th Street and Broad Street

DESCRIPTION: Begin at the St. John's Church (est. 1741) at 24th Street and Broad. (In this church, in 1775 when George Washington, Thomas Jefferson, and other patriots were assembled at the Virginia Convention to discuss independence, Patrick Henry made his famous "liberty or death" speech.) After visiting inside the church, hike west on Broad Street to 12th Street at 0.9 mile, and turn right to Marshall Street, where a right turn leads half a block to the Egyptian Building (the only architecture of its type in America). Backtrack to the junction of 12th Street, proceed on Marshall Street to 11th Street, and take a left to Capitol Square. Reach the governor's mansion at 1.2 miles. After leaving the mansion enter the capitol building at 1.3 miles. Visit the Old Bell Tower at 1.6 miles, and leave the capitol grounds by the side gate, which exits on 9th Street.

Leaving the capitol grounds, turn left and proceed down 9th Street to Main Street. Turn right and hike on Main Street to Monroe Park at 2.4 miles. From Monroe Park pass the mosque and turn left on S. Cherry Street. Follow S. Cherry Street to the entrance of Hollywood Cemetery at 3 miles. Visit the burial sites of James Monroe, John Tyler, and Jefferson Davis. Backtrack to Main Street and turn left at 5 miles. Follow Main Street to the boulevard, and turn left on the boulevard at 6.3 miles. Stay on the boulevard (VA 161) past the carillon, through Byrd Park, and to Shirley Street. Turn left on Shirley Street at 7.4 miles and turn right for entry into Maymont Park parking area at 7.5 miles. Backtrack or have second vehicle.

### 1314 Richmond Walking Trail

This loop walk through midtown can take two hours, visiting the ten historic sites and walking from the origin, at the state capitol, to the John Marshall House. Circle east on Governor Street and to the James River and return by way of St. Paul's Episcopal Church on E. Grace, for approximately 1.5 miles. The detailed information and map from the state's visitor bureau is a must for this urban hike.

ADDRESSES AND INFORMATION: Contact Richmond Convention and Visitor Bureau, 550 E. Marshall St., Richmond, VA 23219; phone: 804-782-2777 or 800-370-9004. Richmond City Parks, Recreation, and Community Facilities, 900 E. Broad St., Richmond, VA 23219; phone: 804-780-5717, or 804-646-5733, or 804-646-0037; fax: 804-646-6931. Available are brochures of the city parks.

# Roanoke

The city of Roanoke is Virginia's largest city (nearly 100,000 population) west of Richmond. It is in the southwestern area of the Shenandoah Valley with an elevation of about 1,000 feet. At the metropolitan boundary to the south is Mill Mountain, and east is the Blue Ridge Parkway. North of the city are Fort Lewis Mountain and Brushy Mountain, where beyond is the Jefferson National Forest and the **Appalachian Trail**. On the west boundary of the city is the city of Salem, and on the east border is the town of Vinton. The city of Roanoke was settled in 1740 and incorporated in 1882. It is considered to be the medical, industrial, cultural, and convention city of western Virginia. The large and scenic metropolitan area has more than fifty-five parks and recreation sites. Local government leaders can be honored for creating such an expansive recreational system to serve the public. The major recreation parks with trails and greenway areas are alphabetically described below. (At the time of this writing in 2003, a trail under construction is in the Lick Run Corridor, a long greenway from Valley View Mall southeast to the historic downtown Roanoke Hotel. Part of the **Lick Run Greenway** has been completed 1315 from Valley View Mall southeast to Court St. for 1.2 mi. From the overpass of I-581 the 10-foot-wide paved route switchbacks to parallel Lick Run among meadows, shade trees, and wildflowers such as fragrant wild white roses. Contact Roanoke City Parks and Recreation for an update on it and other greenway developments.)

## MILL MOUNTAIN PARK

This large park is situated on a mountain that towers 800 feet above the city and bears the lighted Roanoke Star seen throughout the metropolitan area and for 50 miles in the Roanoke Valley. Here are the Mill Mountain Zoological Park, Wildflower Garden, picnic areas, and scenic overlooks of the city. From the star site the **Mill Mountain Star Trail** descends to Riverland Road near the Roanoke River. If 1316 beginning the hike at the top of the mountain, descend on an earthen path with switchbacks in a young hardwood forest of oaks. At 0.7 mile there is an overlook among Virginia pines. Cross Fishburn Parkway at 1.1 miles and continue the descent to a flat area in a forest with cherry, ash, and tulip poplar. At 1.4 miles exit the forest at a gravel road and turn left. A city water tower is right. Descend to a parking lot at Riverland Road at 1.6 miles.

ACCESS: From downtown Roanoke take exit 6 off I-581 at Elm Avenue (VA 24) west. Go two blocks and turn left onto Jefferson Street. Go 0.5 mile and turn left onto Walnut Avenue at the traffic light. Cross over the Walnut Avenue bridge and take the first left onto Piedmont Street, then an immediate right on Riverland Road. After 1.1 miles turn right onto a gravel driveway for the parking lot, left. This is the low-elevation trailhead. To drive to the high-elevation trailhead at the star site, stay east on Walnut Avenue, which becomes Fishburn Parkway to Mill Mountain Park. If access is from the Blue Ridge Parkway, turn off on the Mill Mountain Parkway Spur at milepost 120.5.

## MURRAY RUN GREENWAY/FISHBURN PARK

1317    As with the **Mill Mountain Star Trail**, the **Murray Run Trail** is an earthen or wood-chip pathway. But in contrast it is less defined because of unnamed spur routes to private homes. Running through the center of the trail is Brambleton Avenue, where Fishburn Park is on the east side with easy parking facilities. Hiking options are east to James Madison Junior High School and Western Community College, or northwest across Brambleton Avenue to Raleigh Court School and Patrick Henry High School. If choosing the east route, descend from the parking lot's tennis court and kiosk to the meadow below, where there are rest rooms, a children's play area, and a disk golf course. Go upstream, cross a footbridge over Murray Run at 0.2 mile, and turn left. Follow downstream through a beautiful forest of large sycamores, oaks, and white pines. Avoid uphill unofficial spurs and stay near the creek to a fork at 0.6 mile. The left fork leads to a bridge crossing of Murray Run and the disk golf course. The right fork crosses a footbridge and ascends on switchbacks to a back entrance road at James Madison Junior High School at 0.9 mile. To the right is the entrance of TV Channel 15 and McNeil Drive out to Colonial Avenue.

If choosing the northwest route, cross Brambleton Avenue and ascend west of Shenandoah Life Insurance property on the sidewalk of Montgomery Street. Watch for a turnoff, right, into the woods. Follow the footpath through a forest of tall trees and wildflowers. Near the top of a ridge is a 0.2-mile circle of a spur trail. Exit the forest to a meadow with a six-lane track course at 0.7 mile. Cross east of the ballfield to a parking area at Patrick Henry High School. Access here is from Grandin Road, two blocks southwest from the intersection of Brandon Avenue.

USGS MAPS: Roanoke, Garden City

ACCESS: If arriving from the south on Brambleton Avenue (US 221) watch for Fishburn Park on the right, and a view toward the Shenandoah Life Insurance location on the left. If arriving from the north take Brambleton Avenue south off Brandon Avenue.

*Roanoke River Greenway, Roanoke*

## ROANOKE RIVER GREENWAY/SMITH PARK

This scenic and unique greenway is more than a place for walking, bicycling, running, and pushing baby carriages. Instead it is the former and frequently flooded Wiley Drive, divided in the center with the west lane being a one-way greenway for low-speed (15 mph) vehicular traffic. The former center yellow line is now a narrow cement container with shrubs and flowers. The upstream access is at large Wasena Park, where there are picnic areas, ballfields, and elaborate skateboard facilities under Main Street Bridge. As a community service project the recreational center is a joint credit to the Roanoke City Sheriff's Office, and the Roanoke City and County Parks and Recreation Departments. From the parking area cross a low-water bridge over the Roanoke River where railing and swimming are forbidden, but fishing for stocked trout from the riverbank is allowed. All foot traffic is on the east half of the roadway. Through a grassy floodplain there are large sycamores beside the river and new trees and shrubs have been planted with new landscaping. Halfway on the greenway pass through Smith Park, where

1318

there are picnic tables, rest rooms, and a children's playground. Cross the Roanoke River on another low-water bridge and end at 1 mile near Franklin Road.

USGS MAP: Roanoke

ACCESS: From I-581, exit 6, go west on Elm Avenue, which becomes Elm/Main Street (US 221) through downtown and the old southwest area. Bear left to cross Wasena Bridge over the Roanoke River, and immediately turn left on Winona Avenue to the Wasena Park parking lot.

## TINKER CREEK GREENWAY

1319 Between Tinker Creek and an active railroad grade the paved 1-mile greenway is from Fallon Park east and underneath the railroad to the confluence of Tinker Creek and the Roanoke River where it passes under the railroad again. Parking is available at Fallon Park and on both sides of Dale Avenue. Shade trees and wildflowers are prominent.

USGS MAP: Roanoke

ACCESS: From I-581, exit 6, go east on Elm Avenue (VA 24), which becomes Dale Avenue, 1.5 miles to Fallon Park, left, or continue ahead to Greenway parking lot just beyond the railroad trestle.

ADDRESSES AND INFORMATION: Roanoke City Parks and Recreation, 210 Reserve Ave., Roanoke, VA 24016; phone: 540-853-2236. (A brochure of the major trails in the metropolitan area is available.) Roanoke Valley Greenways, P.O. Box 29800, Roanoke, VA 24018; phone: 540-776-7159. (Commissioned by local governments.) Pathfinders for Greenways, P.O. Box 8553, Roanoke, VA 24014; phone: 540-766-7159; fax: 540-772-2108. (A nonprofit organization that assists in coordinating volunteer services and fund-raising for the trails.)

## Salem

### ROANOKE RIVER GREENWAY/MOYER SPORTS COMPLEX

Salem, founded in 1802, is Roanoke County's seat of government and home to Roanoke College. Although sharing in the industrial and cultural history of the city of Roanoke, it has its own department of parks and recreation. The southern

1320–21 trailhead of the **Hanging Rock Battlefield Trail** is near East Main Street, and there are plans for cooperating with the city of Roanoke in greenway planning. An example of what has been started is the short 0.5-mile asphalt **Roanoke River Greenway/Moyer** for fast walkers, bikers, and runners, but the nearness to the scenic Roanoke River makes the route desirable for sauntering. There is an option to go fishing, or watch action at the adjoining sports complex, or to examine the wildflowers, boxelder, hackberry, and princess trees along the riverside. When you reach a dead end at the bank of a small stream, you can dream of the day when a bridge is built and the trail is extended downriver to connect with other greenways. Meanwhile, backtrack, leisurely.

ACCESS: From VA 419 turn west on Apperson Drive (US 11) toward Salem. Immediately after the first traffic light and before the Colorado Street bridge over the Roanoke River, turn left onto Riverside Drive. Follow it upstream and turn right on Eddy Avenue to cross the bridge and take first right to parking lot for the trail.

ADDRESS AND INFORMATION: Salem Parks and Recreation, 216 S. Broad St., Salem, VA 24153; phone: 540-375-3057.

# Suffolk

In 1974 Nansemond County and the city of Suffolk merged as Suffolk City, making its 430 square miles the largest city acreage in the state, but twelfth in population. The city boundary on the east includes part of the Great Dismal Swamp NWR. There are other swamps without drainage in the southern part of Suffolk's boundaries. Examples are Cypress, Moss, Quake, and Dragon swamps. North of the original city are Lake Meade, Western Branch Reservoir, and the Nansemond River, whose mouth is at the James River. These bring waterways to the old city limits and through half of the old county boundaries. In the northern area the city has two major parks.

## BENNETT'S CREEK PARK

This day-use park is a former U.S. Army Nike missile installation. It now features picnic areas with shelters, boat ramp access to the Nansemond and James Rivers, fishing, crabbing, a children's playground, and a scenic nature trail. Although the park is open year round, it is closed on Mondays and Tuesdays. The 0.9-mile **Florida Maple Trail** is an easy hike from the parking area and pier along Bennett's 1322 Creek. It crosses footbridges to a grove of beautiful Florida maples. Other trees are sycamore, locust, and ash. There are two lookouts to the marsh for viewing waterfowl. At 0.4 mile backtrack or turn left to exit in a field of clover for a return to the parking area.

USGS MAP: Chuckatuck

ACCESS: From US 17, 2 miles west of Belleville, take SR 626 (Shoulder Hill Rd.) south for 0.9 mile and turn right on SR 757 to the park.

## LONE STAR LAKES PARK

The eight man-made Lone Star Lakes are the focus of a water resource and recreation project acquired by the city in 1975 from Lone Star Industries. The day-use park has 490 acres of lakes and 682 acres of land surface. Developed from marl mining pits, the lakes have freshwater fish such as largemouth bass, bluegill, and crappie. In addition to fishing, other activities are boating (no swimming), picnicking, bicycling, horseback riding, birding, and hiking. There are four short trails and 10 miles of unpaved back roads for hiking and viewing wildlife. The park is open year round but is closed on Mondays and Tuesdays.

1323–26    To hike the 0.1-mile **Nature Trail**, turn left after entering the gate at the park office, then turn right to a parking area up from an embankment. Follow the sign through the woods and descend to Butler Lake. Backtrack or follow the paved road for a return. For the 0.1-mile **Cedar Creek Trail**, turn right on the road after the park entrance and look for a trail sign on the left. Constructed by a troop of Eagle Scouts, the trail loops through an embankment of hardwoods and vines. Drive ahead and take a fork left for 0.5 mile to a picnic area beside the lake and the 0.3-mile **Southern Lakes Trail**. It crosses a footbridge and winds through a damp lakeside before crossing a low ridge among hardwoods such as willow oak. It ends at a parking area on the alternate road from the fork. Backtrack. After another 0.5 mile on the road, park at a picnic area with 0.6-mile, double-loop **Lone Star Lake Trail**. The first loop is at the base of large marl banks, but the second loop undulates over the banks near Cedar Creek. Tall beech, ash, and locust are over sections of wax myrtle.

USGS MAP: Chuckatuck

ACCESS: From Suffolk follow VA 10/32 north from the junction of US 58/460 for 6.7 miles to Chuckatuck. Turn right to Bob House Parkway and to the park entrance after 0.5 mile.

ADDRESSES AND INFORMATION: Department of Parks and Recreation, 301 N. Main St. (P.O. Box 1858), Suffolk, VA 23439; phone: 757-925-6325; fax: 757-539-5179. Ranger station for Bennett's Creek Park: 757-484-3984; ranger station at Lone Star Lakes: 757-255-4308.


## Vienna

The **W&OD Railroad Trail** goes 2 miles through Vienna in Fairfax County. (See Northern Virginia Regional Park Authority, Chapter 14.) **Wildwood Park Trail** is a 0.5-mile paved connector between Niblick Drive (off Chain Bridge Rd. [VA 123]) to **W&OD Railroad Trail**, southeast. Another paved 0.3-mile connector trail is **Wolftrap Stream Valley Trail** from Ayr Hill Avenue (off Maple Ave. [VA 123], north-

1327    west two blocks on Beulah Rd. [SR 675]) to Fairfax County **Foxstone Park Trail** at Creek Crossing Road, northeast.

ADDRESS AND INFORMATION: Department of Parks and Recreation, Vienna Community Center, 120 Cherry St., SE, Vienna, VA 22180; phone: 703-255-6356; fax: 703-255-6399.

# Virginia Beach

Virginia's largest city in population, Virginia Beach is one of the most popular beach areas on the nation's East Coast. Its history is traced to the first landing of the Jamestown colonists at Cape Henry. In 1963 it merged with Princess Anne County, creating 255 square miles of land and 57 square miles of water with 290 miles of shoreline. It is known for its 28 miles of public beaches (particularly on the Atlantic Coast), boardwalks, water sports, and fishing on piers, bays, and lakes as well as Atlantic deep-sea fishing. Lynnhaven Bay and Rudee Inlet are popular for catching blue crabs, oysters, speckled trout, and flounder; Back Bay is known for freshwater fishing. The state sponsors the Virginia Saltwater Fishing Tournament from April to November. On General Booth Boulevard is the Virginia Marine Science Museum, with major exhibits of the state's marine environment. At the northeastern corner of the city is First Landing State Park, and at the southeastern corner is False Cape State Park (see Chapter 11). The city has over 175 public parks, most of which are community oriented with regular sports activities. Red Wing Park is an example of a community park, and it has gardens and a nature trail.

### RED WING PARK

One of the city's oldest parks, it is also among the most beautiful. Red Wing Gardens has special sections for roses, azaleas, natural areas, and a Japanese Garden. In the center of the park are multiple ballfields, and at the eastern end of the loop road are sheltered picnic areas. From the parking area is the triple-loop, 0.8-mile **Red Wing Nature Trail**. Color coded, it weaves through the pine, ash, 1328 elm, and maple forest to a swamp with lizard tails and royal and sensitive ferns.

USGS MAP: Virginia Beach

ACCESS: At the junction of Oceana Boulevard and General Booth Boulevard (3 mi. south from US 60 at the beach on General Booth Blvd.), go east into the park.

ADDRESSES AND INFORMATION: Department of Parks and Recreation, Municipal Center Bldg. #21, 2408 Courthouse Dr., Virginia Beach, VA 23456; phone: 757-563-1100. Virginia Marine Science Museum, 717 General Booth Blvd., Virginia Beach, VA 23451; phone: 757-437-4949.

# Williamsburg

Settled in 1633 and known as Middle Plantation, its name was changed to Williamsburg in 1699 when it became the state's capital. It remained the seat of government until 1780, when the capital was moved to Richmond. During that colonial period of eighty-one years it was the center of the state's political power, social charm, and cultural advancement. It had the nation's second oldest college, the College of William and Mary (1693), Virginia's first printing press and newspaper, and the philosophical and intellectual seeds of independence with George Mason's Declaration of Rights. For nearly 150 years after the capital was changed, Williamsburg remained a quiet college town with many of its historic buildings in decay or decline. In 1926 Williamsburg's lifestyle and future dramatically changed under the influence of W. A. R. Goodwin, rector of Bruton Parish Church, and the financial backing of John D. Rockefeller Jr. to restore the capital area. Today the restored section, known as the Historic Area, 1 mile long by a half-mile wide, is a popular national attraction. The city is between the James and the York Rivers, and between Jamestown and Yorktown on the Colonial Parkway. Highway 5 from here to Richmond is one of Virginia's scenic byways. Visitors will find more than restoration; there are museums, gardens, and parks. The major park is Waller Mill Park.

## WALLER MILL PARK

With nearly 3,000 acres, of which 343 acres are dual lakes, this day-use park is a haven for wildlife. Located at the northern edge of the city, it provides boating (no gasoline powered), fishing (for largemouth bass, crappie, and bluegill), canoeing and pedal boats (rentals available), picnicking, bicycling, nature study, and hiking all year. One unique feature is a Seniors Walking Course with fourteen stretching-exercise stations near the upper parking lot. There is also the 4.5-mile **Dogwood Mountain Bike Trail** at the upper portion of the reservoir.

1329

The park has 1.5-mile **Bayberry Nature Trail**, which is self-guiding with seventy-five interpretive markers about plants, wildlife, mosses, vines, and other points of interest. It begins from the parking lot on a floating bridge and continues to a fork for making a loop. Another loop is the 2.6-mile **Lookout Tower Trail**. It begins from the lower end of the parking lot and follows trail signs. It crosses an old railroad grade to the edge of the lake. After 0.3 mile there is an observation deck. At the trail's fork either direction may be taken for the loop completion. Deer and turkey may be sighted on the trail, and vascular plants include ironwood, black and sweet gum, oaks, hazelnut, red maple, and loblolly pine.

1330–31

USGS MAP: Williamsburg

ACCESS: At junction of I-64, exit 243, and SR 143, turn west and immediately turn right on Rochambeau Drive. Go 1.2 miles, turn left on SR 645 (Airport Rd.), and go 0.4 mile to entrance on left. (SR 645 connects with US 60.)

ADDRESSES AND INFORMATION: Department of Parks and Recreation, 202 Quarterpath Rd., Williamsburg, VA 23185; phone: 757-259-3760; Waller Mill Park, phone: 757-259-3778. Available are a leaflet about facilities and a pamphlet trail guide. Visitor Center at Colonial Parkway and VA 132, phone: 800-HISTORY, or 757-229-1733.

# Woodstock

This historic and well-groomed town was founded in 1761. It is located in the center of Shenandoah County, and is the county seat of government. Among its historic sites are Massanutten Military Academy, and the oldest courthouse in use west of the Blue Ridge Mountains. There are two recreational areas inside the town limits. One is at Central High School with its baseball and football (lighted) fields, basketball courts, track, picnic shelter, and 0.5-mile **Central High School** 1332 **Nature Trail**. The trail descends north and down a gravel road from a south side parking area of the main building. It circles in a pine forest with resting benches. Access to the school from South Main Street is west on Reservoir Road (VA 42) and across the railroad to a turn left.

The W. O. Riley Park has a swimming pool, tennis courts, picnic shelter, soccer field, basketball children's maze, and paved 0.3-mile **Riley Park Trail**. Near it is an 1333 alluring arboretum on a hillside. Access from South Main Street is on West Spring Street five blocks to Washington Street, left.

Outside the edge of town is appropriately named Riverview Park. Its 17 acres are on hills above the North Fork of the Shenandoah River. Enhancing the grand views is 0.7-mile **Effinger Trail**. It undulates in a mixed hardwood forest with 1334 scattered cedars and pines, crosses bridges in the hollow, and forms a blazed two-loop route. Built by Boy Scout Troop #54 of Edinburg, the trail honors John Ignatious Von Effinger. (He lived in Woodstock and was the chief commander of bodyguards for Gen. George Washington in the Revolutionary War.) Access from downtown off Main Street is 0.2 mile on East Court Street. Turn left on Water Street a few yards and turn right on Cemetery Road. After 0.8 mile arrive at French Woods Road. Turn right and then you will be in sight of the park, left.

ACCESS: Both I-81 and US II are north-south highways through Woodstock; take exit 283 on I-81.

ADDRESSES AND INFORMATION: Town Office, 135 North Main St., Woodstock, VA 22664; phone: 540-459-3621. Department of Parks and Recreation, Shenandoah County, 508 Piccadilly St., Edinburg, VA 22824; phone: 540-984-3030; fax: 540-984-8032. Maps and brochures are available.

# PART V. Regional, Military, and Private Trails

# 14. Regional Parks

## Northern Virginia Regional Park Authority

*Arlington, Fairfax, and Loudoun Counties, and Cities
of Alexandria, Fairfax, and Falls Church*

The Northern Virginia Regional Park Authority (NVRPA) is the result of combined efforts in the 1950s of a group of conservationists, the Northern Virginia Planning District Commission, and local governments of Fairfax and Arlington counties and the city of Falls Church. They united to protect some of the natural heritage from suburban encroachment, and their remarkable wisdom and foresight led to organizing the regional park system in 1959 under the Virginia Park Authorities Act. Since then Loudoun County and the cities of Fairfax and Alexandria have been added. Functioning under a twelve-member board, the park authority plans, acquires, develops, and operates regional parks and other sites in nineteen locations. With good management it uses revenue-producing sources for 72 percent of its annual budget. Management employs a professional staff of 90 and more than 200 part-time employees.

The park authority provides an extraordinary variety of public recreational, educational, and cultural activities. In more than 10,000 acres, there are historic homes; gardens; swimming pools; campgrounds; picnic areas; golf courses; club and conference centers; ballfields; playgrounds; lakes and streams for boating, canoeing, fishing, and kayaking; bridle paths; concert halls; nature trails; the 45-mile **W&OD Railroad Trail**; and many other facilities and activities. The parks that have named trails are described below.

ACCESS TO NVRPA HEADQUARTERS: From I-66 junction with VA 123 in the city of Fairfax, go 4.3 miles on VA 123 (Ox Rd.), south, to junction with SR 654 (Popes Head Rd.). A sign is at the corner, right. From I-95, exit 160, go north on VA 123 (at first Gordon Blvd., but becomes Ox Rd. for 11.5 mi. before crossing the Occoquan River bridge).

ADDRESS AND INFORMATION: NVRPA, 5400 Ox Rd., Fairfax Station, VA 22039; phone: 703-352-5900; fax: 703-273-0905; web: <www.nvrpa.org>. Available are magazines, brochures, flyers for all parks, and summer calendar of events.

441

This 5,000-acre park and recreational complex of Bull Run–Occoquan is northern Virginia's largest park system. It includes six separate (but sometimes with adjoining property lines) areas: Bull Run Regional Park, Hemlock Overlook Regional Park Center for Outdoor Education, Bull Run Marina, Fountainhead Regional Park, Sandy Run Regional Park, and Occoquan Regional Park stretching more than 25 miles. Among the facilities are those for hiking and nature study, plus about 30 miles of shoreline for fishing, boating, lake cruises, and rowboat rentals. There are picnic grounds, visitor centers, playgrounds, a swimming pool, indoor archery range, historic sites, bike and bridle trails, and many cultural and educational programs. Camping with electrical and water hookups and an outdoor concert center are at Bull Run Regional Park. These connecting parks along the creeks and rivers offer more than the above recreational opportunities; they have forests and marshes for the preservation of wildlife and a water supply for many of the residents in this area.

## Bull Run Regional Park

This large park is best known for its wide range of activities. Its spacious fields can accommodate thousands of people for activities such as music festivals, contests, or soccer tournaments. It has a family campground with 150 sites, plus all amenities. There are campgrounds for Scouts and children's playgrounds. It has Virginia's only public sporting clay skeet and trap shooting center and indoor archery range. Its trails pass through hundreds of acres of Virginia bluebells. Its season is from the first of March through November, but the swimming pool is open from Memorial Day through Labor Day weekend.

1335 The 1.5-mile, yellow-blazed **Bull Run Nature Trail** may be the most beautiful wildflower trail in Virginia, particularly in mid-April, when the Virginia bluebells (*Mertensia virginica*) carpet the forest floor. Many other wildflowers are in profusion in the open forest of birch and ash. The trail begins at the visitor center and forms a loop by Cub Run and Bull Run. It touches another loop trail, the 1.8-mile, white-blazed trail that circles the campground pool and azalea garden. Also, it connects with the blue-blazed **Bull Run–Occoquan Trail** described below.

1336 **Bull Run–Occoquan Trail**
LENGTH AND DIFFICULTY: 17.7 miles (38.3 km); moderate
FEATURES: wildlife, wildflowers, streams, historic site
TRAILHEADS: parking area near group camps B and C in Bull Run Regional Park for northwestern trailhead; parking area at Fountainhead Regional Park for the southeastern end
INTRODUCTION: In addition to the two trailheads, there are three access points in between. This long trail has an intriguing name, which is part English for non-tide waters ("runs" or "rundles"), and part Taux or Doag Indian for "end of the

water." The trail is also called the **BROT** and the **Blue Trail** (not to be confused with the former **Big Blue Trail**). The trail passes through a sanctuary for deer, doves, bullfrogs, and bald eagles; a forest of tall beech and birch; and beds of bluebells and bluets. Its treadway is in hemlock groves and on floodplains, muddy ravines, hillsides, rock formations, and patches of ferns and mosses. There are reminders of the Civil War and remnants of pioneer homesites. Camping and campfires are not allowed, except at Bull Run Regional Park, which is open from mid-March through November. Although horseback riding is permitted, hunting, bicycling, and use of motorized vehicles are prohibited. Hikers are requested to carry plenty of potable water and a map (available from the visitor center) and to hike with a companion.

DESCRIPTION: Begin the hike downstream. Soon after the start, there is a unique joining of two large sycamores on the stream bank. Other trees in the area are locust, ash, and elm. Cross Cub Run on a footbridge, follow close to Bull Run, and go under Ordway Road bridge. At 1.7 miles reach a year-round parking access at VA 28 (Centreville Rd.). (Access from I-66, exit 53, in Centreville is south on VA 28 to the last road on the right before the Bull Run bridge. If driving north on VA 28, the route is from Manassas.) At Little Rocky Run, Johnny Moore Creek, and Popes Head Creek, cross large stepping-stones if bridges are absent. Pass through a rocky section and reach Hemlock Overlook Regional Park at 6.6 miles. Here is a year-round access point from SR 615 (Yates Ford Rd.). (Yates Ford Rd. is from SR 641 [Kincheloe Rd.] south of the town of Clifton.) George Mason University operates an environmental education center here.

At 11.3 miles is Bull Run Marina, where SR 641 (Kincheloe Rd.) joins SR 612 (Old Yates Ford Rd.). The boat ramp is on the northern side of the road. Clifton is north and Manassas is southwest on SR 612. Accessibility here is by a seasonal permit (contact Fountainhead Regional Park, 703-250-9124, for permit information). Continue ahead and cross Wolf Run and Stilwell Run. Complete the trail in Fountainhead Regional Park at 17.7 miles. Access here is on SR 727, which is off SR 647 (Hampton Rd.). Accessible season is from mid-March to mid-November, with boat launching facilities, canoe and boat rentals, picnic area, rest rooms, and telephone. (Plans are for continuing the trail to Sandy Run Regional Park downstream at the end of Van Thompson Rd., off SR 647 [Hampton Rd.]).

USGS MAPS: Manassas, Independence Hill, Occoquan

ACCESS: From junction of VA 28 and US 29 in Centreville, go west 3 miles on US 29 to Bull Run Park sign on Bull Run Post Office Road, left, and go 2 miles to park entrance.

ADDRESS AND INFORMATION: Bull Run Regional Park, 7700 Bull Run Dr., Centreville, VA 22020; phone: 703-631-0550 or 703-352-5900. Available are a park brochure and trail map.

### Hemlock Overlook Regional Park

This park has limited facilities for the public unless reserved for group programs through the George Mason University Environmental Education Center. All trails, however, are open without prior arrangement. There are five short trails here for a total of 3 miles. One extends from the parking lot past the pond. Others, on steep terrain, are spurs from the blue-blazed **Bull Run–Occoquan Trail** at the riverside, and another trail connects from Yates Ford Road to the old power plant and dam site.

ACCESS: From the town of Clifton go south on SR 645 (Clifton Rd.) for 0.7 mile and turn right on SR 615 (Yates Ford Rd.) to the park.

ADDRESS AND INFORMATION: Hemlock Overlook Regional Park, 13220 Yates Ford Rd., Clifton, VA 22024; phone: 703-993-4354.

### Bull Run Marina

The park has three unnamed but blazed trails. One is a joint 1.3-mile route with the blue-blazed **Bull Run–Occoquan Trail**; another is a 1.3-mile, orange-blazed trail from the Kincheloe Road junction with Old Yates Ford Road parking area; and the other is a 1.2-mile, yellow-blazed trail forming a loop from the visitor center. Both orange- and yellow-marked trails connect with the **Bull Run–Occoquan Trail**. Here, as at other places near Bull Run, is evidence of deer, beaver, turkey, raccoon, and wildfowl. The park is a practice site for several area school crew teams. Anglers and boaters may purchase seasonal passes.

ACCESS: From the junction in the city of Fairfax with VA 236 (Main St.) and VA 123 (Chain Bridge Rd., which becomes Ox Rd., S) drive south on VA 123. Go 8 miles to SR 643 (Henderson Rd.) and turn right. Go 5 miles to Old Yates Road, turn left on SR 612, and go 1 mile to the park.

ADDRESS AND INFORMATION: Bull Run Marina, 12619 Old Yates Ford Rd., Clifton, VA 22024; phone: 703-993-4354.

### Fountainhead Regional Park

A seasonal park, it is open from mid-March to mid-November. There is a tackle and bait store, a place for boat launching and boat and canoe rentals, a place for picnicking, rest rooms, and a telephone. The park is the southeastern terminus of the **Bull Run–Occoquan Trail**. Other trails here are a 1-mile, yellow-blazed trail; a 2-mile, white-blazed trail; and a 5.5-mile mountain bike trail. The first goes left from the parking lot, and the second goes right; both are circular paths and are self-guiding. Hikers can take the yellow-blazed trail entry to the **Bull Run–Occoquan Trail** for 3 miles over hillsides, sometimes through rocky areas with hemlock, rhododendron, ferns, mountain laurel, and clubmosses.

ACCESS: See directions above for Bull Run Marina, except after 1.9 miles on SR 643 (Henderson Rd.) turn left on SR 647 (Hampton Rd.), and turn right after 1.7 miles to reach the park.

ADDRESS AND INFORMATION: Fountainhead Regional Park, 10875 Hampton Rd., Fairfax Station, VA 22039; phone: 703-250-9124 or 703-352-5900.

## Occoquan Regional Park

One of six parks along Bull Run, Occoquan Reservoir, and the Occoquan River, this 400-acre historic park is diagonally across the river from the town of Occoquan. The park's entrance lane is lined with sycamores, and the entrance to the ballfields is lined with golden raintrees. Near soccer fields #3 and #4 is an old brick kiln that was operated by inmates of a prison that used to be in the park area. The paved, 2-mile **Occoquan River Trail** parallels the entrance road and   1337 passes picnic areas en route to the riverside. It then ascends to the ballfields and circles a batting cage. The park has an excellent dock with a boat ramp and year-round boat storage. There is a snack bar and visitor center, open from mid-March through November.

USGS MAP: Fort Belvoir

ACCESS: From I-95, exit 160 (south of the Occoquan River bridge), take VA 123 north for 1.6 miles to park entrance on the right. (From Fairfax, drive south on VA 123 to the park entrance on the left.)

ADDRESS AND INFORMATION: Occoquan Regional Park, 9520 Ox Rd., Lorton, VA 22079; phone: 703-690-2121 or 703-352-5900. Available is a park brochure and map.

## MEADOWLARK BOTANICAL GARDENS REGIONAL PARK

Paved and mulched trails lead the visitor through 95 acres of natural and landscaped gardens in this magnificent park. Quiet and classic in design, the main **Meadowlark Botanical Gardens Trail** has a number of side trails along its 1.2-   1338 mile circuit, which starts from and returns to the visitor center. Along the way are the native tree collection, the hosta garden, the daylily collection (with hybrids of tan-pink, salmon, brilliant red, and deep burgundy), the azalea woods, the herb garden, the cherry collection, Siberian iris, conifer collection, and the lilac gardens. There are three gazebos (one in each lake) and grassy hillsides of open space where one can sit on benches and watch birds. The park is open daily. Near the visitor center to the left is 0.3-mile **Nature Trail**, which enters the forest of   1339 Virginia pine, maple, oak, and dogwood on a wide gravel path to a large gazebo. The indoor garden atmosphere of The Atrium allows year-round enjoyment of the gardens.

USGS MAP: Vienna

ACCESS: From I-495, exit 10, take the Leesburg Pike, VA 7, northwest 4.5 miles to SR 702 (Beulah Rd.), and turn left. After crossing a bridge over the Washington Dulles Expressway (no access here) the highway becomes SR 675. After 1.6 miles from VA 7 the park is on the right.

ADDRESS AND INFORMATION: Meadowlark Botanical Gardens Regional Park, 9750 Meadowlark Gardens Ct., Vienna, VA 22182; phone: 703-255-3631. Available for free are newsletter and brochures; books are on sale at visitor center.

## POHICK BAY REGIONAL PARK

This park is open all year, and the large swimming pool is open from Memorial Day weekend to Labor Day weekend. On the Pohick Bay (Pohick is the Algonquin Indian word for "water place") of the Mason Neck peninsula, this beautiful area has an excellent family campground with full service. There are facilities for boating, sailing, birding, golfing, picnicking, horseback riding (4 mi. trail), and nature study (see Chapter 8 for nearby Mason Neck NWR, and Chapter 11 for Mason Neck State Park). There are two trails here, plus connectors. The **Yellow Trail** is 1.4 miles long and begins near the park gatehouse. It makes a junction with the **Blue Trail**, which goes 1.6 miles to boat ramp and visitor center. The **Orange Trail** is 0.6 mile from the junction of the **Yellow Trail** and the **Blue Trail** to campsites #118/119 and to the entrance road parking area.

1340–42

USGS MAP: Fort Belvoir

ACCESS: From US 1 junction with VA 242, near Lorton, go 3.2 miles east on VA 242 to Pohick Bay Drive park entrance, left.

ADDRESS AND INFORMATION: Pohick Bay Regional Park, 6501 Pohick Bay Dr., Lorton, VA 22079; phone: 703-339-6104.

## POTOMAC OVERLOOK REGIONAL PARK

Open all year for day use only, the 100-acre park has a nature center with archaeological and wildlife displays. The park is between the George Washington Memorial Parkway (no access) on the east, Donaldson Run on the northwest, and Zachary Taylor Park on the southwest (see Chapter 12). Near the picnic area and comfort station is the 0.6-mile, green-blazed **Nature Trail** entrance. It makes a loop to the Potomac palisades for views of Georgetown and downriver to the Washington Monument 5 miles away. The 1.1-mile **Blue Trail** connects with the **Nature Trail**, makes a loop around the visitor center, and connects with the 0.3-mile **Donaldson Trail**. It connects with the **Donaldson Run Trail** left to Zachary Taylor Park, and right to the **Potomac Heritage Trail**. These trails have large oak, maple, and tulip poplar trees with an understory of haw and dogwood.

1343–46

USGS MAP: Washington West

ACCESS: From the George Washington Memorial Parkway (northwest at Key Bridge), exit at Spout Run Parkway, turn right on Lorcom Lane, and go five blocks to turn right on Military Road. After three blocks on Military Road turn right on Marcey Road and into the park.

ADDRESS AND INFORMATION: phone: 703-528-5406 (see NVRPA address, above)

## RED ROCK WILDERNESS OVERLOOK REGIONAL PARK

This 67-acre sanctuary is on the bank of the Potomac River near Leesburg in Loudoun County, near Harrison Island. Open all year, it is a tranquil preserve of forest and flowers and away from the noise of traffic. From the parking area the **Loblolly Trail** has five connecting trails: the **Hemlock Trail**, the **Holly Trail**, the  1347–52 **Spruce Trail**, the **White Pine Trail**, and the **Sweetbay Trail** for a total of 3 miles. They follow ridges and converge at Cattail Branch, which flows into Goose Creek. At the northeastern point of the **Loblolly Trail** are three overlooks from the sheer cliffs of the Potomac to the river and into the hills of Maryland.

USGS MAP: Leesburg

ACCESS: From US 15 in Leesburg go 1.5 miles east on SR 773 (Edwards Ferry Rd.) to parking area on left.

ADDRESS AND INFORMATION: phone: 703-352-5900 (see NVRPA address, above)


## UPTON HILL REGIONAL PARK

Entry to the 1-mile **Upton Hill Trail** can be either east of the reflecting pool or east  1353 of the swimming pool complex, in this 26-acre park. Situated in a densely populated area, the tall poplars and oaks of the park provide a forest oasis. The reflection pool is surrounded by beautiful gardens and a gazebo sits over the water. The park is open all year, but the swimming pools are open from Memorial Day weekend to Labor Day weekend.

ACCESS: From I-95, exit 8, drive east 3.6 miles on US 50 (Arlington Blvd.) to Seven Corners (southeastern edge of Falls Church), and turn left on Wilson Boulevard. Drive 0.6 mile and turn right on Patrick Henry Drive at 6060 Wilson Boulevard.

ADDRESS AND INFORMATION: phone: 703-534-3437 (see NVRPA address, above)


## WASHINGTON & OLD DOMINION RAILROAD REGIONAL PARK

Dramatically different from any other park in the regional system, this is a 100-foot-wide and 45-mile-long corridor from Shirlington to Purcellville. Its remarkable feature is the **W&OD Railroad Trail**, constructed on the railroad bed of the  1354 former Washington and Old Dominion Railroad, which operated from 1859 to 1968. It was severely damaged during the Civil War but was rebuilt. Passengers gave the railroad the sobriquet of "The Virginia Creeper" (not to be confused with another "Virginia Creeper" in the JNF). The reality of this trail did not come easily. It took money and years of negotiating to retain the right-of-way. Actually, the corridor has two trails. The 8-foot- or 10-foot-wide asphalt route in a shadeless passage is for strollers, joggers, hikers, and bikers. Parallel to it on natural surface, which receives some shade in the summer, is a 30.5-mile route for equestrians and hikers. This trail is shorter because it begins in Vienna on its northwestern route. The paved trail begins at the city limits of Alexandria and passes through Arlington County, Falls Church, Fairfax County, Vienna, Reston, Loudoun County, Herndon, and Leesburg to Purcellville.

The regional park system is continuing its safety programs. An example is a bridge over major traffic arteries such as VA 28 near Dulles Airport and VA 7 in Falls Church. Other changes have been the construction of a trail that links the **W&OD Railroad Trail** with a wayside park for trail users in the city of Fairfax. (There is a dream to link the **W&OD Railroad Trail** to the **AT** with a 9-mile foot trail.) Trail scenery is diverse: high-rise condominiums, shopping centers, suburban homes and lawns, gardens, ponds, streams, bridges, meadows, cattle crossings, farms, forests, and the interminable power line. There are more than 450 species of wildflowers and about 100 species of birds seen on the trail. A rare and treasured trail, it is a gift the citizens have given to themselves. Their creeper and cinders have become the hikers' and bikers' Champs Élysées.

Hikers unfamiliar with the trail and its metro environment should at least have the "Playing it Safe on the W&OD" map, distributed free from the **W&OD Railroad Trail** office or the park authority office. If planning an all-day trip or a through-hike, purchase the 54-page detailed guidebook with maps (see Address and Information, below). The guide has information on how to prepare for the trip, safety and security, street accesses, mileposts, courtesy for multiple-use trail traffic, fast food restaurants, rest rooms, telephones, and emergency aid. For bikers there is a list of repair shops, and for equestrians, water sources and accesses. Request a list of places to stay overnight (no camping on the trail). There are motels, hotels, and bed and breakfast inns, but campgrounds are rare. At 16.5 miles is one option: At the intersection of Sunset Hills Road and Wiehle Avenue in Reston, go north on Wiehle Avenue for about 1.3 miles to turn right on North Shore Drive. Follow it right around Ring Road to Hunt Club Road, and follow it to a right turn on Lake Fairfax Drive into Lake Fairfax Park and campground for a total of about 3 miles (see Address and Information, below).

ACCESS: The southeastern trailhead is at the intersection of Shirlington Road and Four Mile Run Drive. Take exit 6 off I-395 and go north two short blocks (each with a traffic light) on Shirlington Road. The trail parallels Four Mile Run Drive northwest. (Here at the trailhead the **W&OD Railroad Trail** connects southeast with the **Anderson Bikeway** [also called **Four Mile Run Bike Trail**] at the pedestrian overpass of I-395 for another downstream connection with the NPS **Mount Vernon Trail** [see Chapter 9]). The northwestern trailhead for the **W&OD Railroad Trail** in Purcellville is one block off Main Street (VA 7) on 21st Street (SR 690) to O Street.

ADDRESS AND INFORMATION: Available are free brochures and summer calendars of events, brochures on individual parks with maps, and *Discover Your Regional Parks* magazine. There is a nominal charge for the *W&OD Trail Guide*.

1355

W&OD Trail Office, 21293 Smiths Switch Rd., Ashburn, VA 20147; phone: 703-729-0596; fax: 703-724-0898; web: <www.wodfriends.org>.

## Upper Valley Regional Park Authority
*Augusta County*

The Upper Valley Regional Park Authority was formed in 1966 between the city of Harrisonburg and the counties of Augusta and Rockingham. The city of Staunton was included the following year. The first acquisition was Natural Chimneys in 1970, followed by the Grand Caverns in 1974. The parks operate independently because of different facilities and activities. User fees make them almost self-supporting.

### GRAND CAVERNS REGIONAL PARK

These limestone caverns were formerly known as Cave Hill and later as Weyer's Cave. There are three major entrances on the hillside at the southwestern edge of the town of Grottoes, but only one entrance is open to the public now. It is not known who discovered the first cave in the 1780s, but it was on the property of John Madison, a friend of Thomas Jefferson, who explored it and drew a map of the interior. In 1804 Bernard Weyer, a seventeen-year-old trapper, discovered the Grand Caverns, the entrance open today, and in 1835 the Fountain Cave was discovered by Edmund Weast. The subterranean 0.7-mile trail in Grand Caverns passes gigantic stalactites and stalagmites into chambers as large as the 5,000-square-foot Grand Ballroom. The caverns are one of only fourteen caves in the nation designated natural landmarks by the Department of the Interior. Guided tours begin every thirty minutes daily from 9 A.M. to 5 P.M. from April 1 through October, weekends in March, and by group reservations from November through February.

At a small stone wall, near the inclined walkway to the caverns, is white-blazed **Grand Caverns Nature Trail**. It ascends through basswood, redbud, locust, and 1356 wildflowers such as goat's-beard and Virginia bluebells. There are overlooks at 0.3 mile and 0.4 mile of the South Fork of the Shenandoah River and the Blue Ridge Mountains beyond. Backtrack for a total distance of 0.9 mile. The park also has a swimming pool, a ballfield, and a picnic area. From picnic shelter #4 is a hike-bike trail around the perimeter of the park.

USGS MAP: Grottoes

ACCESS: From I-81, exit 235, and US 11, go east 6 miles on VA 256 to the town of Grottoes, and right on SR 825. The park is on the right; cross the bridge to the parking area. Access also from US 340 in Grottoes; go west on VA 256 and turn left on SR 825.

## NATURAL CHIMNEYS REGIONAL PARK

The 134-acre park is at Mt. Solon, southwest of the town of Bridgewater and northwest of Grand Caverns. Its spectacular natural beauty is a group of seven limestone chimneys ranging from 65 to 120 feet high. More than 500 million years old, the chimneys contain iron, magnesium, and chert on the top. Because the chimneys appear castlelike, they inspired a jousting tournament on the meadow at the base of the chimneys in 1821. It has become the Natural Chimneys Jousting Tournament, America's oldest continuously held sports event, and is staged each year on the third Saturday in August. Held the third Saturday in June is the annual National Jousting Hall of Fame Tournament. Excellent for bird-watching, the park has 125 species of birds. The park is open year round.

1357     There is a 3-mile, easy **Natural Chimneys Nature Trail** in the park. It begins from the visitor center parking area, follows a sign to the right, and ascends a graded treadway. It passes a shelter and an access road and reaches a chimneys overlook at 1.5 miles. It descends to a picnic shelter and parking area. From here it turns right to follow through and around the chimneys, where six exhibit signs explain the unique rock formations. The return is on the road from the parking area to the visitor center. The park has full camping services from March through November and limited services the other months. There are hookups for electricity and water. There are also biking trails, picnic shelters, a camp store, a laundry, a swimming pool, and playgrounds.

USGS MAP: Parnassus

ACCESS: From I-81, exit 240, go 3.5 miles west on VA 257 to Bridgewater. Turn left on VA 42 for 3.8 miles to SR 747. Turn right, go 3.5 miles to Mt. Solon, and then right on SR 731 for 0.6 mile to park entrance.

ADDRESS AND INFORMATION: Natural Chimneys Regional Park, Mt. Solon, VA 22843; phone: 540-350-2510. For information, call 540-249-5729. Available is a brochure with map.

# 15. U.S. Army Corps of Engineers and Military Areas

## U.S. Army Corps of Engineers

### JOHN W. FLANNAGAN RESERVOIR
*Dickenson County*

Completed in 1964, the reservoir retains rainfall from a 221-square-mile watershed and stores the waters of the Cranesnest and Pound Rivers. The dam is 250 feet high and 916 feet long, creating a 1,145-acre lake, 40 miles of shoreline, and 7,130 acres surrounding the lake. Its northwestern border adjoins the Clinch Ranger District of the JNF and is within sight of Pine Mountain, the divide between Virginia and Kentucky. It is named for a congressman who served the Ninth Virginia District from 1931 to 1949 and who was influential in flood control for the Appalachian highlands. There are fourteen recreation areas, all near the water. These include two campgrounds, five boat launch areas, and five picnic areas. There are two trails, both on the northern side of the lake, but a new trail system is under study on the southern side near the Cranesnest Campground.

#### Lower Twin Area

The Lower Twin Campground is a peaceful hollow with a dock, a boat ramp at the lake, hot showers (no hookups), a waste disposal unit, and a picnic area. Two trails begin here. The easy, 0.8-mile loop **Trail of Trees** begins at a sign near campsite #15. It crosses a footbridge, follows upstream, ascends, and returns from a the side of a ridge. Along the way are oak, beech, hemlock, rhododendron, and a closed coal mine. The other trail, 1.7-mile **Twin Eagle Trail**, is a moderate, linear trail between the Lower Twin Branch and the Upper Twin Branch. It begins on the side of the hill on the approach to the dock from the campground. It traverses a hillside among redbud, basswood, locust, and oak. At 1.5 miles it descends steeply to cross a branch over a footbridge. It enters a field, the site of an old campground. After 115 yards it reaches an old paved road, where it turns right. Follow it to a gate and parking space on SR 611. Backtrack or use a second car.

1358–59

USGS MAPS: Haysi, Clintwood

ACCESS: To access the dam from the town of Haysi and VA 80, go west 3.4 miles on VA 63 and turn right on SR 614. After 0.5 miles turn right on SR 739 and follow it 3.3 miles to a junction with SR 611. (Along the way are the dam crossing and the reservoir office on the left.) (On SR 611 right it is 0.9 mi. to a mountain grocery store and another 10 mi. to Breaks Interstate Park.) On SR 611, turn left and after 0.7 mile southwest turn left on SR 683. Go 0.4 mile to the Lower Twin Campground gate. It is another 0.3 mile to the dock. To reach the western end of the **Twin Eagle Trail**, return to SR 611, turn left, and after 1.2 miles park at the gate on the left.

ADDRESS AND INFORMATION: Flannagan Reservoir, Rt. 1, Box 268, Haysi, VA 24256; phone: 276-835-9544. Available is a brochure with map and facilities list.

## JOHN H. KERR RESERVOIR

*Mecklenburg, Charlotte, and Halifax Counties*

This large, 50,000-acre reservoir has 37,500 acres in Virginia and 12,500 acres in North Carolina and is managed by the U.S. Army Corps of Engineers. It was completed in 1952. Its watershed is 9,580 square miles of the entire Roanoke River (Staunton) basin, and it has 800 miles of shoreline. Its dam is 2,786 feet wide and 189 feet high. It is a popular lake for boating, fishing, and waterskiing. North Bend Park has a fishing pier for the physically disabled. The Corps manages nine picnic areas and five campgrounds (some with hookups) with hot showers. (There are campgrounds and other facilities on the North Carolina side, south of the dam, also. In addition, there are two state parks upriver—Occoneechee State Park and Staunton River State Park. See Chapter 11.) Below the dam is 169-acre Bugg's Island, named for Samuel Bugg and family, who were early settlers. Before English settlement the river basin was dominated by the Occoneechee Indians from 1250 to 1676, when they were killed or scattered by Nathaniel Bacon and his followers. Although called Bugg's Island Lake by many Virginians, the reservoir was named in honor of a North Carolina congressman who was influential in federal funding of the reservoir project.

1360    The reservoir area has two trails. An easy, round-trip trail, the **Liberty Hill Trail**, is 1.5 miles. It is accessible at the parking area of Liberty Hill Cemetery on the southern end of the dam. It meanders down to the riverbank through a forest of hickory, pine, gum, and oak. Scenic views of Bugg's Island and the river channel below the dam to Lake Gaston are part of the appeal of the trail. The other trail is described below.

1361    **Robert Munford Trail**
LENGTH AND DIFFICULTY: 7.4 miles (11.8 km); easy
FEATURES: lake views, historic site, wildlife
TRAILHEADS: Access to eastern trailhead: from US 58 at the western edge of Boydton, go 0.2 mile on Jefferson Street (SR 756) and turn right. Stay on SR 705 for 7

miles to parking area on right at BSA Camp Eagle Point. (It is 0.4 mi. ahead to Eagle Point boat ramp and scenic shore area.) Access to western trailhead: same as above, except after 4.4 miles on SR 705 from SR 756 turn right on SR 823 and drive 2 miles to parking area on left.

DESCRIPTION: Originally the **Eagle Point Trail**, the white-blazed trail follows the northern edge of Kerr Lake, in and out of coves, and skirts the slopes of peninsulas. The forest is mature hardwoods with scattered Virginia pine and cedar. Wildlife is mainly deer, raccoon, squirrel, fox, snakes, and some wild pigs. The hardwoods offer fine fall colors. If beginning at the eastern trailhead, descend, pass a large oak, and go under power lines at 0.5 mile, 1.1 miles, and 1.3 miles. At 1.8 miles is an open view of the lake and a picnic area. Cross a number of small streams between rolling hills and cross the last stream at 3.6 miles. (Trail distance may vary 0.2 mi. here because of choice of stream crossing, depending on water levels.) Ascend among patches of running cedar. Cross an old road at 4 miles and pass a white oak with a 14-foot circumference. Cross another old road at 4.2 miles. Enter the edge of a field, cross an old road at 5.5 miles, and arrive at a historic cemetery at 6 miles. Pass through the edge of a field, turn left, and follow an old road past two huge post oaks for a turn left. Follow the road to the gate and the western trailhead at 7.4 miles. Backtrack, or have a second vehicle.

USGS MAPS: Kerr Dam, Tungsten

ADDRESS AND INFORMATION: John H. Kerr Reservoir, 1930 Mays Chapel Rd., Boydton, VA 23917; phone: 434-738-6143 or 738-6143; fax: 434-738-6541.

## PHILPOTT LAKE
*Franklin, Henry, and Patrick Counties*

The 10,000 acres of Philpott Lake and surrounding lands were authorized by Congress in 1944 to be developed for flood control, hydroelectric power, and recreation. Construction by the U.S. Army Corps of Engineers began in 1948, and the project was completed for full operation in 1953. The clear, blue-green lake encompasses 3,000 acres and has a shoreline of 100 miles. A total of 5,000 acres are leased to the Virginia Commission of Game and Inland Fisheries for wildlife management purposes. Fairy Stone State Park adjoins the boundary on the west, and nearby, downriver and southeast, are the community of Philpott and the town of Bassett. Public facilities include boat launching ramps, nature trails, and areas for fishing, water skiing, picnicking, camping, hunting, and nature study. Camping is allowed in six of the twelve recreational areas. The campgrounds are open from April 1 through October 31, unless otherwise stated below.

### Philpott Park and Overlook
This area offers the most spectacular views of the gorge, dam, and lake. One of the islands seen upriver is Turkey Island, west of the larger Deer Island. There is one

1362  trail here. To follow the **Smith River Trail**, follow the sign at the scenic overlook parking area. Descend on switchbacks for 0.1 mile to the top of the dam. Continue descending the switchbacks, reaching the base of the dam at 0.3 mile. Follow the twenty-one interpretive trail signs down the Smith River with a guide booklet provided by the Visitor Assistance Center. Reach the trail's end at 0.7 mile at a large, nine-pronged sycamore. Other vegetation on the trail includes hemlock, beech, poplar, and rhododendron. Backtrack for a moderate to strenuous ascent.

USGS MAP: Philpott Reservoir

ACCESS: From downtown Bassett go west on VA 57 for 2 miles to junction with SR 904. Turn right on SR 904 and go 1.2 miles to the Visitor Assistance Center and visitor exhibit, and parking area at the overlook.

## Goose Point Park

1363  This area has public boat ramps, a campground, picnicking, swimming, hot showers, and a nature trail. The **Goose Point Trail** is an easy 0.5-mile hike from the campground along the lake to an amphitheater. The forest is mixed with hardwoods and pines, and there is a scenic view from the peninsula. Except for the campground, the park is open year round. (Camping reservations are not required here.)

USGS MAP: Philpott Reservoir

ACCESS: From downtown Bassett go west on VA 57 for 7.5 miles to SR 822 and turn right. Follow it for 5.3 miles to Goose Point Park.

## Jamison Mill Park

1364  The 0.7-mile **Jamison Mill Trail** is an easy round-trip that begins in the picnic area near the entrance. In addition to a picnic area there is a fishing area and a campground with hot showers. Begin the hike across the road on the right side of the river against a rocky bluff. Cross a small bridge in an area of trout lilies, spring beauty, mayapples, and ground cedar. Ascend through a hemlock forest and at 0.2 mile join an old road. Turn left for an excellent view of the campground below. At 0.4 mile reach a paved area; return to the bridge over the river and to the picnic area parking at 0.7 miles.

USGS MAP: Philpott Reservoir

ACCESS: From the town of Ferrum take SR 623 southwest for 3.8 miles to junction with SR 605 and turn left. Drive 1.2 miles to junction with SR 780 and turn right. Follow it 1.9 miles to Jamison Mill.

## Salthouse Branch Recreation Area

This beautiful area is on the eastern side of the lake near a peninsula and Deer Island. Secluded, it has a good family campground with hot showers. It also has a picnic area, a boat launch, and a place to swim. Vascular plants are oak, maple,

tulip poplar, beech, pine, and rhododendron. **Salthouse Branch Nature Trail** is a    1365
0.5-mile interpretive trail with twenty stops on an easy loop. Access to it is from
the campground at the trail signs. It crosses three streams. (Camping reservations are not required here. Portions of the park are open all year, but not the
campground.)

USGS MAP: Philpott Reservoir

ACCESS: From the town of Henry drive west on SR 605 for 1.7 miles to junction
with SR 798. Take SR 798 on the left for 1.4 miles to junction with SR 773 and follow
it 0.4 mile to enter the recreation area.

ADDRESS AND INFORMATION: Visitor Assistance Center, 1058 Philpott Dam Rd.,
Bassett, VA 24055; phone: 276-629-2703. Available is a brochure with map and
recreation facilities.

# Military Installations

Virginia has 372,692 acres of military lands, of which 174,198 are seasonally available for public hunting, fishing, and hiking. Another 1,141 acres are designated for
other recreational activities. Fort A. P. Hill, one of the largest of nine U.S. Army
installations in the state, has outstanding space for Boy Scout camping. Similar
arrangements can be made at Quantico Marine Base. (Trails for hiking or field
trips for nature study are no longer provided at Fort Pickett Military Reservation.)
For information on camping, trails, travel, and recreational activities on Virginia's
military bases, request the *Armed Forces Recreation Areas Travel Guide*, DOD PA-15,
from any of the addresses below.

### FORT A. P. HILL MILITARY RESERVATION
*Caroline County*

The A. P. Hill Military Reservation, named in honor of Civil War general Ambrose
Powell Hill, includes a 212-acre tract of land set aside for the Boy Scouts of America. Other visitor hiking is also allowed. In this area, hiking is permitted once
requests to use the facility are approved. Group participation in hiking exercises is
allowed in designated areas during specific times of the year, if such activities do
not interfere with training of military personnel. Written requests are mandatory.
The request should state the desired dates and purpose, and hikers must be self-
sufficient. If desired, long hikes can be arranged outside the BSA area. Among the
miles to walk is 1-mile **Beaverdam Pond Trail**. It is a right turn across the drain of    1366–67
the lake; 0.7-mile **Scout Trail** (an interpretive trail) off Travis Lake Road at the
corner of Spring Road; and a new 3- to 4-mile trail under construction. Visitors
must have a permanent ID card and driver's license to be admitted.

ACCESS: From junction of VA 2 and US 301 in Bowling Green go northeast 2.2 miles on US 301 to main entrance, left.

ADDRESS AND INFORMATION: Commander: Attn: DPTMS, Hq. Fort A. P. Hill, Bowling Green, VA 22427; phone: 804-633-8624 or 804-633-8338 (main office, 804-633-8710); fax: 804-633-8406.

## QUANTICO MARINE BASE

*Stafford, Prince William, and Fauquier Counties*

The Quantico Marine Base has 61,000 acres of woodlands and 420 acres of lakes. Designated areas around the lakes and open fields can accommodate from 200 to 1,800 campers in groups. The campers must be self-sufficient; it is not a camp for public recreational vehicles. There are 15 miles of streams open to the public for fishing with proper licenses. Trails are unnamed, except the fitness trail, and are within the designated areas. It is advisable to call in advance about services and restrictions.

ACCESS: Off I-95, exit 147, turn east across US 1 on SR 619 (near Triangle) into base and sentry gate.

ADDRESS AND INFORMATION: Commanding General, REC BR (B37), ATTN: Lunga Park, Marine Corps Base, 3250 Catlin Ave., Quantico, VA 22134; phone: 703-640-6395 (office); 703-784-5270 (store); fax: 703-695-6395.

*Not what we give, but what we share—*
*For the gift without the giver is bare.*
JAMES RUSSELL LOWELL (1819–1891)

# 16. Private and Special Holdings

There are hundreds of trails on private property in Virginia, most of which are short walks in natural or formal gardens. Some are open to the public during annual April Historic Garden Week (usually the last week of April). Others are longer treks in forests or on farms for hunting, fishing, horseback riding, or viewing scenic points of interest. A few are at large industrial research corporations or forest products companies. In addition, there are well-maintained trails at private resorts, where guests of the resort can enjoy hiking or bicycling the trails. An example is The Homestead, where 100 miles of scenic trails blend into the 15,000-acre estate (P.O. Box 2000, Hot Springs, VA 24445; phone: 540-839-5500; fax: 540-839-7850). There are two other resorts where trails not only are used by guests but are open to the public, with the expectation that users will inform the main office of their plans and provide whatever information may be needed. These are Wintergreen Resort, with 13,000 acres and 30 miles of trails near Reeds Gap (P.O. Box 468, Nellysford, VA 22958; phone: 434-325-2200 [reservations 800-325-2200]), and the 11,000-acre Mountain Lake Resort (115 Hotel Circle, Pembroke, VA 24136; phone: 540-951-1819; fax: 540-626-7172). (Some of the trails at Wintergreen Resort are 0.7-mile **Brimstone Trail**, 0.7 mile **Cedar Cliffs** 1368–75 **Main Trail**, 1-mile **Cedar Cliffs North Trail**, 1.1-mile **Fortunes Ridge Trail**, 1.8-mile **Loggers Alley Trail**, 3-mile **Old Appalachian Trail**, 1.5-mile **Pedlars Edge Trail**, and 0.5-mile **Upper Shamokin Gorge Trail**.)

There are a few colleges and universities in the state that have nature trails, botanical pathways, or historic walkways. Virginia Military Institute (VMI) has the longest trail, the 7.3-mile **Chessie Trail**, described in this chapter. Virginia Polytechnic Institute and State University (VPI&SU) provides part of the 5.7-mile **Huckleberry Line Trail**, described in Chapter 13. For information on some short trails at other collegiate institutions call the following: College of William and Mary in Williamsburg at 757-253-4000 about trails near the Wildflower Refuge and Lake Matoaka; Rappahannock Community College in Warsaw at 804-333-6700 and in Glenn at 804-758-6705 about the pathways of the **Virginia Birding and Wildlife Trail**. The same trail also recognizes the nature paths in the woodlands at Richard Bland College in Petersburg, phone: 804-862-6247. The **University of** 1376 **Virginia Academic Walk** in Charlottesville covers a 0.6-mile tour of academic and architectural points in the Thomas Jefferson "Academic Village." Call the Rotunda for a guide map, 434-924-0311, or pick up the material at the office between 9 A.M. and 4:45 P.M. daily.

The following listed properties have trails open to the public, with restrictions as described.

## De Hart Botanical Gardens

This natural 200-acre garden has an outstanding display of wildflowers such as trillium, firepink, crested dwarf iris, and orchids. In a forest of hardwoods and scattered evergreens, the understory has groves of purple rhododendron, mountain laurel, and redbud over ground covers of galax and running cedar. Scenic rock formations, deep coves, and clear mountain streamlets are part of the 3-mile

1377 **De Hart Mountain Trail** loop. The private gardens are open to the public without charge, in all seasons, during daylight hours only. No camping. Elevation change is easy to difficult.

From the gated entrance follow signs and ascend on an old road, turn left at a ridge, and follow the scenic ridgeline west. At 0.7 mile turn right and descend gradually on switchbacks. Reach a cove among a large spread of mayapples at 1.3 miles, turn left and parallel a spring-fed stream. At 1.6 miles cross the stream and

1378 immediately turn left on the **Waterfall Trail**, a short side trail to another switchback for a view of a 20-foot waterfall. Backtrack, ascend and descend to pass a stone chimney at a pioneer homesite at 1.7 miles. In the springtime there is a wide display of daffodils. After crossing the small streams ascend to a ridge at 2 miles. Curve right and after switchbacks arrive at the top of a rocky peak (2,610 ft.) at 2.6 miles. Here is a spectacular view of Smith River Valley, and beyond to Rocky Knob at the Blue Ridge Parkway. Descend 105 yards to complete the loop, left, for a backtrack to US 58.

USGS MAP: Stuart

ACCESS: From the east at intersection of US 58 and VA 8 (3 mi. north of Stuart) follow US 58 west 3.6 miles to garden signs in a long curve right. There is space here for about four cars. From the west Vesta post office, drive east on US 58 for 4.2 miles to signs in long curve left.

ADDRESS AND INFORMATION: De Hart Botanical Gardens, Inc., 3585 US 401 South, Louisburg, NC 27549; phone: 919-496-4771 or 276-930-2285.

## Lake Laura

Between the north-south ranges of Supin Lick Mountain and the Great North Mountain is a slender valley where places have names like Happy Valley Road,

Orkney Springs, and Bird Haven. Here is also the large Bryce Resort, the community of Bayse, and near it all is Lake Laura. It was made possible with the cooperation of Bryce Resort and the Virginia Department of Game and Inland Fisheries. A multi-use trail for hiking fishing, bicycling, and horseback riding circles the beautiful lake. The lake area also has parklike fee facilities open from May 25 to September 2: a swimming pool, tennis courts, and picnic area. Canoeing and fishing are allowed in the lake at specific hours. Not allowed are camping, gasoline-powered boats, seining, and firearms. Hikers and bicyclists may use the trail at anytime during daylight hours. Equestrians need a schedule and should call 540-856-8100. There is more than one access to the lake, but the one described below corresponds to the main access from I-81.

From the parking area at the base of the dam, ascend the **Lake Laura Trail** on a $\quad$ 1379 system of thirty-seven steps. Hike clockwise to pass the spillway, left. At 0.1 mile enter the forest of locust, pine, and oak, and begin the lakeside trip that passes through five coves. The trail is between the lakefront and private homes on the slopes. Follow an old road at 0.6 mile and cross Stoney Creek at the dam's headwaters at 1 mile. To the left is private property with a meadow and farm barn. Continuing the circle, stay close to the lake's edge and enter a cove with ferns and wildflowers. After ascending an open and partly forested slope the lake scenery becomes magnificent. Descend, and at a fork in the trail stay right to cross the dam. Return to the parking area at 2.5 miles.

ACCESS: From I-81, exit 273, drive west on VA 263 for 10.8 miles. Watch closely for a narrow entrance (Arnold Road) to the parking area, left. Ahead it is 0.2 mile to the bottom of the hill where the road (SR 836) to Bryce Resort office goes right. To the left VA 263 continues and there is a gas station and grocery store. It is here that you may need to ask for directions if you missed the lake entrance. In that case you would return on VA 263 to cross the bridge at 0.1 mile (where there is a small sign for "nature trail" that is separate from, but near to, the Lake Laura Trail parking area below the dam), then another 0.1 mile to turn right. The entrance road is 0.2 mile to the parking area.

ADDRESS AND INFORMATION: Bryce Resort, P.O. Box 3, Basye, VA 22810; phone: 540-856-2121; fax: 540-856-8567.

## Laurel Hill

The birthplace and boyhood home of Major General James Ewell Brown (Jeb) Stuart, C.S.A. (1833–1864) is Laurel Hill. Although the former plantation farm consisted of 1,500 acres, a 75-acre section that includes the birthplace has been acquired. The historic site has been made possible by the J. E. B. Stuart Birthplace Preservation Trust, founded by historian Thomas D. Perry and others in 1991. The trust is managed by a nonprofit Board of Directors.

1380    **Laurel Hill Walking Trail** passes by twelve historic sites and begins at the office parking area. Site #1 has a historic marker, placed at the park's entrance in 1930 by the State of Virginia. Site #3 lists the property as on the Virginia Historic Register and the Register of Historic Places since 1998. Other sites are graveyards, former building sites, and an overlook of the Ararat River. The trail can range from 0.5-mile round-trip to 2 miles round-trip. Access to site #12 (the grave of Stuart's great grandfather, William Letcher) can be by vehicle on SR 749. The gravesite has a claim to being Patrick County's oldest marked grave. A brochure is available for the location.

ACCESS: From the town of Stuart, drive 4 miles south on VA 8 to VA 103; turn right (west). After another 9 miles turn right on SR 773 (Ararat Hwy.), and drive 10.9 miles to Laurel Hill entrance, right. From downtown in Mount Airy, North Carolina, drive northeast 0.2 mile on NC 103 (Pine St.) and turn left, north, on NC 104 (Riverside Dr.). After 4.8 miles enter Virginia where the road becomes SR 773, and 0.7 mile farther to entrance, left.

ADDRESS AND INFORMATION: J. E. B. Stuart Birthplace, Inc., P.O. Box 240 (1091 Ararat Hwy.), Ararat, VA 24053; phone: 276-251-1833; e-mail: laurelhill@jebstuart .org. (Inquire about symposiums and spring and fall encampments.)

## Mariners' Museum Park

The Mariners' Museum Park in Newport News is the state's foremost museum of nautical history. There are displays and exhibits in galleries that chronicle the development of ship building, navigation, and oceanography. Among the exhibits are artifacts representing 3,000 years of maritime science. The museum is a non-profit educational facility developed in the 1930s and made possible by philanthropists Archer and Anna Hyatt Huntington (for whom the 2,500-acre Huntington Beach State Park in South Carolina is named). Within the park's 550 acres is 167-acre Lake Maury, named for Matthew F. Maury, U.S. naval officer and hydrographer from Spotsylvania County. Around the lake is the **Noland Trail**, the state's finest private trail open to the public. It passes through a mature forest of jack pine, sweet gum, oak, maple, and magnolia and is home to more than 435 species of vascular plants. There are more than 110 species of birds. The museum is open daily except Christmas Day.

1381    **Noland Trail**
LENGTH AND DIFFICULTY: 5 miles (8 km); easy
FEATURES: scenic views, lake, wildflowers, historic site
TRAILHEAD: parking lot at the museum
DESCRIPTION: The **Noland Trail** was completed in 1991 and was made possible by

the financial generosity of Lloyd Noland Jr., a local businessman. The trail is well designed and has fourteen bridges crossing quiet coves. There is a granite mileage marker every 0.5 mile, and parts of the trail are usable by the physically impaired. Begin the trail from the entrance road at the northern side of the museum's parking area. At 0.2 mile is an overlook of the lake and the museum buildings before crossing a curved bridge at 0.4 mile. There is another overlook of the lake at 0.6 mile near tall pines and an understory of dogwood, mountain laurel, and blueberry. Pass a wildlife meadow and then cross a service road at 1.3 miles. There is a large white oak near a side trail, the **Indian File Trail**, at 1.8    1382 miles. The side trail rejoins the main trail at an overlook at 2 miles. Another side trail goes to an overlook on a peninsula a few yards ahead. At 3.1 miles the trail leaves a grassy area and crosses the lake's dam at Museum Drive. On the western side is a parking lot and a large spreading water oak. This area offers scenic views of both the lake and the James River. Ascend on a grassy knoll to historic monuments and reenter the forest. There is another fine view of the lake at 3.5 miles. For the next 1.5 miles the trail crosses three more bridges in lowlands with bayberry and buttonwood. There are also beds of jewelweed, mandrake, galax, and wild petunia. Complete the trail at the southern edge of the museum and parking area.

USGS MAP: Mulberry Island

ACCESS: From I-64, exit 258-A, drive 3 miles west on US 17 (Clyde Morris Dr.), cross VA 143 to SR 312, and at US 60 (Warwick Blvd.), cross to Museum Drive.

ADDRESS AND INFORMATION: Mariners' Museum Park, Museum Dr., Newport News, VA 23601; phone: 757-595-0368. Available for free is a trail brochure and map; books are on sale in the gift shop.


# MeadWestvaco

When it comes to wildflower pilgrimages, no one does it better than MeadWestvaco (West Virginia Pulp and Paper Company). An example is the company's group tour in April on the 0.8-mile **Buffalo Creek Interpretive Trail**. Otherwise,    1383–86 visitors hike on their own to see about seventy-five species of wildflowers on this and three other trails: 0.8-mile **Pine Field Trail** loop, 0.3-mile **Oak Ridge Trail**, and 1-mile **Hemlock Loop Trail**. The flowers peak from mid-April to mid-May. Among them are green and gold (*Chrysogonum virginianum*) and yellow lady's-slipper (*Cypripedium calceolus*). There are both lowland and upland hardwoods and conifers such as hemlock and white pine. Wildlife includes turkey, woodcock, deer, and songbirds. The trail begins at a parking area near Buffalo Creek bridge. It turns left of the field and passes to the right of a hemlock forest. Before the first footbridge, **Oak Ridge Trail** goes left into coves and returns to the main trail after the second footbridge. The **Hemlock Loop Trail** also leaves the main trail on the left. Near its completion the **Pine Field Trail** goes left for a loop. After a footbridge the **Hemlock Loop Trail** returns to the main trail where to the left the **Buffalo Creek Interpretive Trail** ends at Buffalo Creek. Backtrack. The Buffalo Creek Nature Area of 125 acres is registered with the Virginia Native Plant Registry. (In addition to the forests here in Campbell and Bedford Counties, Westvaco has forests in twenty-three other counties for a total of nearly 245,000 acres.

USGS MAP: Lynch Station

ACCESS: From US 29, south of Lynchburg, go west 6.2 miles to Evington on VA 24. From Evington continue west for 2.5 miles to the county line and a parking area on the left near Buffalo Creek bridge. (It is 19.3 mi. west to US 460 in Bedford.)

ADDRESS AND INFORMATION: MeadWestvaco, Route 4, Box 134, Appomattox, VA 24522; phone: 434-352-7132. Available is a brochure with map.

## The Nature Conservancy

Formed in 1950, The Nature Conservancy is a private conservation organization with more than 1 million members dedicated to the preservation of natural environments. Through its action and cooperation with public and private agencies, it has been responsible for protecting more than 11 million acres of natural diversity in more than 2,000 natural sanctuaries in all fifty states, the Virgin Islands, Canada, and elsewhere. The conservancy acquires funding from individual contributors, foundation grants, corporate gifts, and investments. It publishes the *Nature Conservancy News*.

The Virginia chapter was established in 1960, and since then its members have been active in acquiring and protecting 250,000 acres of forests, islands, wetlands, and significant wildlife sanctuaries, of which 65,000 acres are owned by the Conservancy. In 2003 there were thirty-two preserves, some of which offer a variety of hiking and naturalist activities for day use only. Two examples of preserves owned by The Nature Conservancy—Bottom Creek Gorge Preserve and Brownsville Farm—with officially named trails are described below. Many of the preserves have seasonal openings or are open only on weekends or during specific hours; others are open with permission only. Visitors are advised to contact the Charlottesville office for a permission statement with guidelines and brochures about the preserves. Within the guidelines the following are permitted: hiking, nature study, bird-watching, and photography. Not permitted are biking, horseback riding, hunting, fishing, trapping, camping, swimming, rock climbing, caving, use of ATVs, pets, picking of flowers (also berries, nuts, or mushrooms), and removing any part of the natural landscape.

INFORMATION: Virginia State Chapter Office, The Nature Conservancy, 490

Westfield Rd., Charlottesville, VA 22901; phone: 434-295-6106; fax: 434-979-0370; web: <www.nature.org/wherewework/northamerica/states/virginia/preserves>. The website has information on all places the Conservancy protects and a schedule of field trips and events.

## BOTTOM CREEK GORGE PRESERVE

This preserve encompasses 657 acres with magnificent scenery of Bottom Creek and Bent Mountain waterfalls. In the gorge are slopes of granite and shale that near the top becomes loose scree. The forests has virgin hemlocks and many species of wildflowers and birds. The preserve is open Saturday and Sunday from dawn to dusk. There are three named trails (plus a waterfall overlook path): **Duval Trail** (1.4 mi.); **Johnston Trail** (0.8 mi.); and **Knight Trail** (1.5 mi.). A trail 1387–89 map should be at the kiosk where the trail network begins.

ACCESS: From Cave Spring, in southwest Roanoke, at intersection of US 221 and VS 419, drive south 13.8 miles on US 221 to SR 644, right. (This is past the community of Bent Mountain.) Descend 1.1 miles to fork and stay right on SR 669. Continue straight for 2.5 miles (do not use SR 607 [Bottom Creek Rd.]) and turn right at a T. After 1.3 miles cross a bridge. Turn left at a sign to ascend on a gravel road to a gate and parking area. Walk 0.8 mile on entrance road to interpretive kiosk. If approaching from the town of Floyd, drive 19.7 miles northeast on US 221 and turn left on SR 644.

## VIRGINIA COAST RESERVE/BROWNSVILLE SEASIDE FARM

This preserve consists of 1,000 acres of scenic woodlands, a freshwater pond, and salt marshes. It is near The Hammocks at Hog Island Bay. The farm is headquarters for The Nature Conservancy's Virginia Coast Reserve. From the parking area there is **Brownsville Birding Trail**, a 3-mile round-trip route starting under a 1390 canopy of willow oak, sweet gum, and maple. After 0.7 mile there is a grassy field and freshwater pond. After passing a greenhouse, there is an observation deck at 1.1 miles. The trail ends in the hummocks after crossing a causeway. The Delmarva fox squirrel is protected in the hummocks. In addition to the marshes of needle rush and sedges, the main feature is birdlife, such as cedar waxwing, heron, egret, osprey, marsh wren, fish crow, and red-tail hawk.

INFORMATION: Virginia Coast Reserve, P.O. Box 158, Nassawadox, VA 23413; phone: 757-442-3049. Call for reservations to visit the trail.

ACCESS: In Nassawadox, from US 13 at traffic light, drive 0.2 mile east on Rogers Drive to SR 600 (Seaside Rd.) and turn left. After 0.2 mile turn right on SR 608 (Brownsville Rd.). After 1 mile turn right to The Nature Conservancy office and park at the trail user sign.

# Pinnacles of Dan Hydro Development

The 3,640-acre Pinnacles of Dan Hydro Development, near the BRP, is owned by the city of Danville and is under city, state, and federal regulation. Two dams— Talbott and Townes—on the Dan River are 75 miles west of the city in Patrick County. At the Townes Dam a pipeline channels water over trestles and through a sealed tunnel on the western side of the gorge to the power plant downriver. Between the pipeline's tunnel and the river are three pinnacles with breathtaking, panoramic views of the gorge. As recently as the early 1950s the route of the AT was through the gorge and over these sharp peaks. The route, and the Devil's Stairsteps on the eastern side of the gorge, had been chosen by Myron Avery and other Appalachian Trail Conference officials. When Earl Shaffer, the first through-hiker, hiked from Georgia to Maine in the summer of 1948, he wrote, "This couple of miles was probably the most rugged and most spectacular segment of the Trail."

Although the property is publicly owned, its description is placed in a special property category in this book because of its uniqueness. The public should be aware that the city of Danville allows fishing, hiking, backpacking, camping, and nature study as a voluntary public service and not by public mandate. To preserve this rugged wilderness-type area and to provide safety for all visitors, there are some necessary restrictions. First, a free written permit is required and must be carried by the visitor at all times. Permits may be acquired in Danville or at the site of the hydro development. In Danville, permits can be obtained at the Electric Department, Utilities Service Building, 1040 Monument Street (phone: 434-799-5270), Monday through Friday from 8 A.M. to 5 P.M. (Hours may change; call in advance.) At the site, the preferred location to obtain a request is the power plant on SR 648 (Kibler Valley Rd.) for 24-hour-a-day service. Permits are also available from a ranger at the top of the canyon rim parking area gate to the Townes Dam each day at about 7:15 A.M. and 2:45 P.M. (If the ranger is not at the gate because of other unexpected work, visitors should drive down the mountain on SR 614 to the power plant [see Access, below].) Prohibited are campfires, hunting, firearms, fireworks, alcohol and illegal drugs, damage to plants and animals, swimming, littering, bicycles, motorcycles, ATVs, and pets. Fishing boats must be small and are limited to 5 hp. Visitors are reminded that they enter the gorge at their own risk.

1391–92    **Aqueduct Trail** (3 mi.), **Pinnacle Trail** (1.4 mi.)
LENGTH AND DIFFICULTY: 7.4 miles (10.8 km) combined, round-trip; strenuous
FEATURES: outstanding views, wildflowers, wildlife, rugged terrain
TRAILHEADS: Parking area at the end of SR 602 for northern trailhead; parking area at end of SR 648 for southern trailhead. (See Access, below.)
DESCRIPTION: From the parking area at the northern trailhead descend on the

*Pinnacle Trail, Pinnacles of Dan Hydro Development*

steep and narrow paved road for 0.7 mile to Townes Dam. Descend the steps below the dam to the **Aqueduct Trail**. Follow the aqueduct to a long and high trestle over Barnard Creek at 1.7 miles. After crossing, continue on a descent before climbing over a rocky area for ascension to a ridge and a junction left with the **Pinnacle Trail** at 2.1 miles. (From here the **Aqueduct Trail** descends on switchbacks to Kibler Valley and the power plant at 3 mi. Backtrack, or have a two-car arrangement.) Follow the **Pinnacle Trail** on the ridge to a low saddle and begin to climb steeply over precipitous rocks. There may be faint white blazes, a reminder of the **AT**'s original route over the peaks. Reach the highest pinnacle

(2,662 ft.) at 0.3 mile. Growing in the crevices of the rocks are scrub pine, mountain laurel, bleeding heart, galax, serviceberry, ferns, mosses, and lichens. Vultures soar on the updrafts, and unless the sound of the river rises from the gorge, there is silence. Ice and snow make this trail exceptionally dangerous. Backtrack.

If hiking farther east, descend, staying on the ridge spine and climbing over large boulders to the Dan River at 0.7 mile. Elevation loss from the highest peak is 1,100 feet. Backtrack. (The old **AT** crossed the river here and ascended on a steep, rocky spine called the Devil's Stairsteps to the top of the mountain, which is private property.)

USGS MAP: Meadows of Dan

ACCESS: For the northern trailhead, drive south from US 58 in Meadows of Dan (near the BRP) on SR 614 for 3.8 miles to a junction with SR 602. Turn left on SR 602 and go 1 mile to a parking area at the gate to Townes Dam. For the southern trailhead, drive north from VA 103 at Claudville on SR 773 for 1.5 miles to SR 648 (Kibler Valley Rd.) and follow it 5.8 miles to its end at the power plant. (For a road connection between the trailheads, continue south on SR 614 for 3.6 mi. to the community of Bell Spur. Descend 5.5 mi. to junction with SR 773 in the community of Carters Mill. Turn left, east, 3.3 mi. to junction with SR 648 and turn left. Drive 5.8 mi. to the power plant.)

ADDRESS AND INFORMATION: Pinnacles of Dan Hydroelectric Station, 6211 Kibler Valley Rd., Ararat, VA 24053; phone: 276-251-5141.


## Scheier Natural Area

The 100-acre Scheier Natural Area is owned and managed by the Rivanna Conservation Society. It is open daily and free to the public. In an effort to safeguard the ecological, scenic, and historic resources of the Rivanna and its watershed, the society has established rules and regulations for this preserve. The basic request is that the preserve be used only for walking on the three miles of trails, and observing the wildlife and plant life. From the parking area and kiosk follow the signage and the color-coded loop trails. All trails are designed for easy walking. If going counterclockwise, first follow the 0.8-mile **White Pine Trail** (yellow). Along the way you may see orchids, fox gloves, and wild azaleas among scattered beech groves and sunny sections of the hardwood forest. The trail connects with the 1.2-mile **Fern Trail** (red), and it crosses a small stream among tall hardwoods in the northwest section of the preserve. It connects with the 1-mile **Laurel Trail** (blue). It twice crosses a small stream where spicebush, mountain laurel, and ferns form a fragrant and gentle natural garden. On the trail crossing to a flat ridge there are light pink and white rabbit pea plants. From the **Laurel Trail** there is a short 0.4-mile **Ridge Trail** (white). Its major feature is a view from the bluffs of a fork of Cunningham Creek. The **Laurel Trail** completes the circles and makes a return to

*Virginia Living Museum Trail, Newport News*

the parking area. Across the road is the 0.6-mile round-trip **Pond Trail** (green) to 1397
a group of eight ponds. This is a haven for aquatic life.

USGS MAP: Fluvanna

ACCESS: From US 15 at the south edge of Palmyra, drive west 3.5 miles on SR 640
and turn right on SR 639. After about one-half mile is the preserve and parking
area, right. If coming from Charlottesville, follow VA 20 south, and turn left on VA
53 east. At Cunningham turn right onto SR 660/619, right, then left at a fork onto
SR 660. Continue to its end and turn right on SR 640 west. Then take an immediate
right on SR 639 as described above.

ADDRESS AND INFORMATION: Rivanna Conservation Society, P.O. Box 141, Palmyra, VA 22963: phone 434-589-7576. A brochure with map is available.


## Virginia Living Museum

The Virginia Living Museum is a unique combination of native wildlife park,
science museum, aquarium, botanical preserve, and planetarium. The facility

continues to expand. There is a new boardwalk that loops around Deer Park Lake

1398 with 10 acres of outdoor exhibits. On the 0.5-mile **Living Museum Nature Trail**, which begins at the back of the museum, there is a waterfowl nesting observation deck. Along the boardwalk is a coastal plain aviary and special sites for viewing bald eagle, fox, deer, turkey, and bobcat. Near the museum is a butterfly and wildflower garden. A new 62,000-square-foot museum is under construction. There is an admission charge, and the museum is open daily except Christmas Eve and Day, Thanksgiving, and New Year's Day.

ACCESS: From I-64, exit 258A, take the J. Clyde Morris Boulevard (US 17) south 2 miles and turn left at the museum entrance. (Ahead and on the boulevard across US 60 is Mariners' Museum.)

ADDRESS AND INFORMATION: Virginia Living Museum, 524 J. Clyde Morris Blvd., Newport News, VA 23601; phone: 757-595-1900; web: <www.valivingmuseum .org>.

## Virginia Military Institute

Of all the college and university trails in Virginia, the 7.3-mile **Chessie Nature Trail** is the longest and most unique. It has been owned and maintained by the VMI Foundation, Inc., an independent endowment agency for VMI, since 1979. The Chessie was developed by the foundation with the assistance of the Virginia Environmental Endowment, the Chesapeake and Ohio Railroad, the Commission on Outdoor Recreation, VMI, the Rockbridge Area Conservation Council, and many individual citizens. A day-use trail, it is used for hiking, birding, jogging, fishing, cross-country skiing, and picnicking. Bicycles and vehicles are not permitted. The trail is closed on Christmas Day. Sections of the trail are arbored with ash, sycamore, and mulberry, and other sections pass through open grassy meadows. Deer, fox, and many species of birds are likely to be seen.

1399 **Chessie Nature Trail**
LENGTH AND DIFFICULTY: 7.3 miles (11.7 km); easy
FEATURES: scenic views, historic site, river, wildflowers, geological formation
TRAILHEADS: For the western trailhead in Lexington, turn off Main Street at junction with fork of US 11/11B at the southern end of Maury River bridge onto short Moses Mill Road (which becomes short Jordan's Point Rd.), and follow it to the parking area on VMI Island. (This is also the parking area for the northeastern trailhead of the **Woods Creek Trail**.) For the eastern trailhead, park by the river near the junction of US 60 bridge and SR 608 in Buena Vista.
DESCRIPTION: From the parking area in Lexington follow the signs, cross a pedestrian bridge over the Maury River, and pass under the US 11 bridge. (Note: The

pedestrian bridge was washed away in a flood a few years ago. A new bridge is under construction and should be finished in 2003.) Before crossing the Mill Creek bridge there is a wye site where the trains turned around. At 1 mile the high cliffs are pocketed with bloodroot, trillium, columbine, fire pink, and meadow rue in the spring. Pass under an I-81 bridge at 2.5 miles. Cross a small bridge at 2.7 miles, and then pass through gates three times between 2.8 miles and 4 miles in a pastoral valley. At 4.1 miles is South River Lock on the right, the site of an old canal. Cross South River on a skillfully constructed 235-foot footbridge with C&O trusses. After 5.4 miles enter a field of wildflowers such as Virginia bluebells, chicory, soapwort, and nodding onions. On the right at 5.9 miles are remnants of the Ben Salem Lock. Pass cliffs of limestone veined with calcite and quartz (formed about 500 million years ago). At 6.6 miles pass the Zimmerman's Lock site, and cross a road at 6.9 miles. At 7.3 miles reach a junction with US 60 and SR 608, the completion of the trail. Backtrack or use a second vehicle.

USGS MAPS: Lexington, Glasgow, Buena Vista

ADDRESS AND INFORMATION: VMI Foundation, P.O. Box 932, Lexington, VA 24450; phone: 540-464-7287. Available is a brochure with map. Information is also available from the Lexington Visitors Bureau; phone: 540-463-3777.

## Westmoreland Berry Farm

There are other outstanding berry farms in Virginia, but none on such a grand scale beside the Rappahannock River with a trail network as this one. A historic 1,600-acre site, it was originally patented in 1641. By 1803 it was known as Leesville Plantation, with sweeping views from a hill to the lowland fields and the river. The current management raises sixteen different crops, including black, red, and purple raspberries; strawberries; blackberries; blueberries; peaches; and apricots. Fresh or preserved fruit is sold, and there is also a pick-your-own policy.

Request permission to hike the trails at the open-air market. From here descend on the farm road to the peach orchard, turn left at a brown shed on a smaller road, and go to the end of the road at a dam at 0.7 mile. Begin the **Main Trail** over a 1400 small berm beside an oak tree and cross the dam and stream to a field. Keep right in grasses and pink meadow beauty on an old road. At 0.2 mile turn right on the **Troy Creek Trail**. It follows an old road under tall oaks and beech with holly, 1401 laurel, and ferns in the understory. Hushed, remote, and inspiring repose, the area has large earthen mounds and scenic bluffs by Troy Creek. At 0.9 mile pass a marsh with waterfowl and songbirds. Reach a fork at 1.4 miles. (To the left the hiker can return to the dam at the edge of the field for a distance of 2 mi.) Continue right in a deep forest, stay right at a fork with the **Main Trail**, and reach a cabled gate at 2 miles. Backtrack, but go straight from the fork on the left. Pass a timber cut and reach a junction with the **Troy Creek Trail** at 2.6 miles. Follow the edge of the field for a return to the dam at 3.1 miles.

USGS MAP: Rollins Fork

ACCESS: From VA 3 (0.3 mi. east of the King George and Westmoreland Counties boundary) turn right on SR 634 and drive 0.9 mile. Turn right on SR 637 and drive 1.5 miles to sign and road on the right for 0.2 mile to the farm.

ADDRESS AND INFORMATION: Westmoreland Berry Farm, 1235 Berry Farm Lane, Oak Grove, VA 22443; phone: 804-224-9171 or 800-997-2377; fax: 804-224-8967; web: <www.westmorelandberryfarm.com>. Although the farm is open year round, the market store is open from April 1 to a week before Christmas. The farm is also the access to the Voorhees Nature Preserve, a 729-acre forest and tidal marsh on the northeast bank of the Rappahannock River. It has 4 miles of hiking trails on the linear **Carriage Road Trail** and the loop **Hollow Tree Trail**. Visitors must register at the farm store or office. For more information than the telephone numbers above, call The Nature Conserancy in Charlottesville at 434-295-6106.

1402–3

# Maps

In the maps that follow, trail numbers correspond with those in the margins of the pages where the trails are described. The trail numbers are also found in the index with the trail names, page numbers, and map designations. Some trail numbers may appear more than once if the trail is long—for example, the Appalachian Trail or the New River State Park Trail. Such trails are also shown by dotted lines. Due to lack of space, a few trail numbers may not be on the maps. The purpose of the maps is to provide general orientation. As recommended in the Introduction, hikers should have an official Virginia highway map, an atlas (such as the *Virginia Atlas and Gazetteer* by DeLorme mapping company), and/or a street map by ADC. Other street/road maps may be available from counties and cities. The National Geographic maps provide detailed topographic trail maps of national forests and parks. Although the state highway map uses a small rectangle for secondary roads, the actual road signs are a black-and-white circle. For a legend to the maps, see below.

## Abbreviations Used on Maps

| | | | |
|---|---|---|---|
| HP | —Historic Park | NS | —National Seashore |
| NA | —National Area | NWR | —National Wildlife Refuge |
| NB | —National Battlefield | RA | —Recreation Area |
| NBP | —National Battlefield Park | RP | —Regional Park |
| NF | —National Forest | SF | —State Forest |
| NHP | —National Historic Park | SP | —State Park |
| NM | —National Monument | WMA | —Wildlife Management Area |

## Legend

| | | | |
|---|---|---|---|
| ⑰ | Federal highways | ▨ | National Parks, forests, lakes, and rivers |
| ⑭ | Interstate highways | • 682 | Trail numbers |
| ⑯ | State primary highways | — · — | County line |
| 622 | State secondary highways | — · · — | State line |

# THE COUNTIES
## AND REGIONS OF VIRGINIA

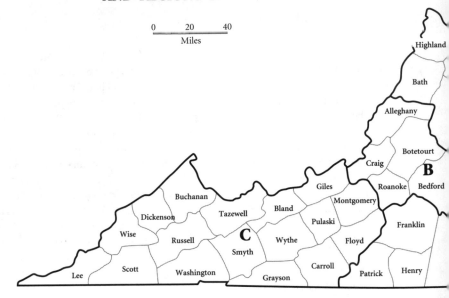

0     20     40

Miles

N

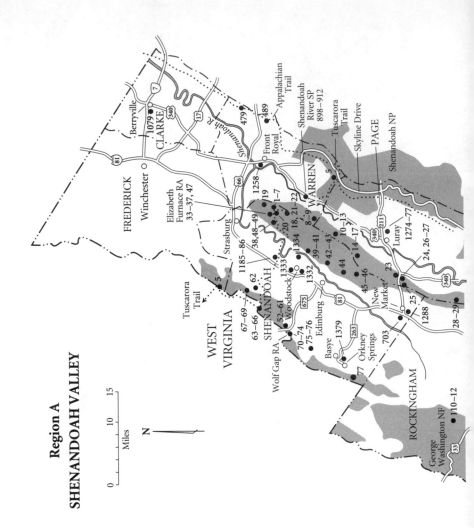

**Region A**
**SHENANDOAH VALLEY**

N

0   5   10   15
Miles

WEST VIRGINIA

Tuscarora Trail

FREDERICK

Winchester

CLARKE

Berryville

1079

7

340

81

17

66

Shenandoah R.

479

489

Front Royal

Appalachian Trail

Shenandoah River SP 898–912

Tuscarora Trail

Skyline Drive

Shenandoah NP

PAGE

WARREN

5

1258

19

1–7

38, 48–49

8–9

18, 21–22

20

1334

10–13

14–17

340

211

Luray

1274–77

24, 26–27

340

Elizabeth Furnace RA 33–37, 47

Strasburg

1185–86

62

5

1333

39–41

42–43

44

45–46

23

1332

25

1288

28–29

SHENANDOAH

Woodstock

52–61

675

Edinburg

1379

703

263

Orkney Springs

Basye

New Market

67–69

63–66

70–74

75–76

77

Wolf Gap RA

81

ROCKINGHAM

George Washington NF

33

110–12

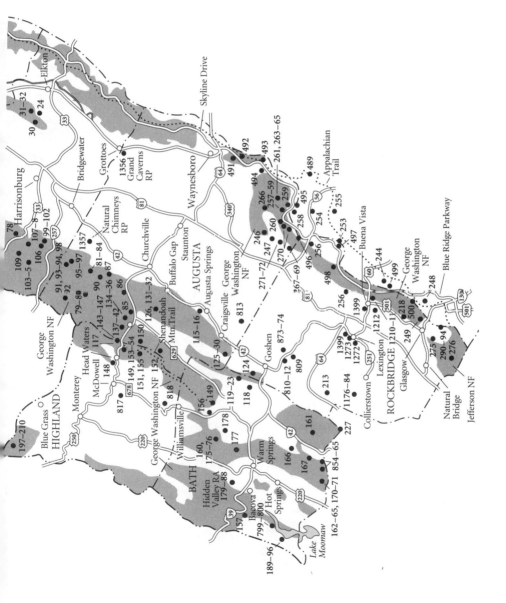

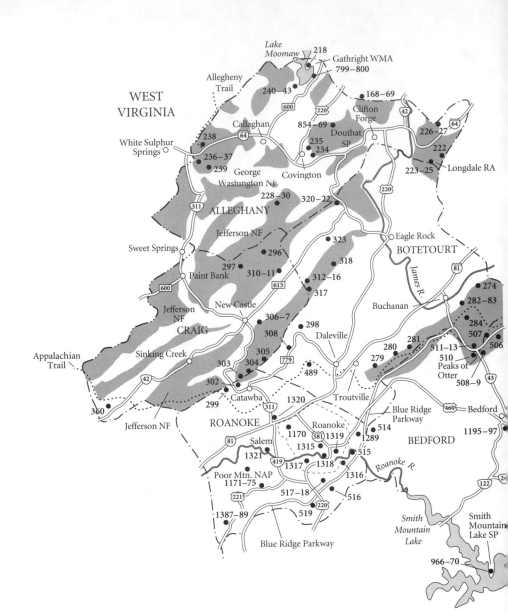

Lake
Moomaw
218
Gathright WMA
799–800

Allegheny
Trail

240–43

WEST
VIRGINIA

600

220

168–69

Clifton
Forge

42

64

226–27

Callaghan

854–69

Douthat
SP

222

White Sulphur
Springs

238

64

235
234

223–25

Longdale RA

236–37

239

George
Washington NF

Covington

220

228–30

320–22

311

ALLEGHANY

Jefferson NF

323

Eagle Rock

BOTETOURT

Sweet Springs

296

318

81

297

274

Paint Bank

310–11

312–16

James R.

282–83

600

615

317

Buchanan

284

Jefferson
NF

New Castle

306–7

298

307

281

507

511–13

506

CRAIG

308

Daleville

280

510

Sinking Creek

305

279

Peaks of
Otter

Appalachian
Trail

303

304

779

489

508–9

43

302

Catawba

Troutville

42

299

311

1320

Blue Ridge
Parkway

460

Bedford

360

ROANOKE

Roanoke

514

1195–97

81

1170

1319

1289

BEDFORD

Salem

581

1315

515

1321

419

1317

1318

1316

Roanoke R.

122

24

Poor Mtn. NAP
1171–75

517–18

516

221

Smith
Mountain
Lake

Smith
Mountain
Lake SP

1387–89

519

220

Blue Ridge Parkway

966–70

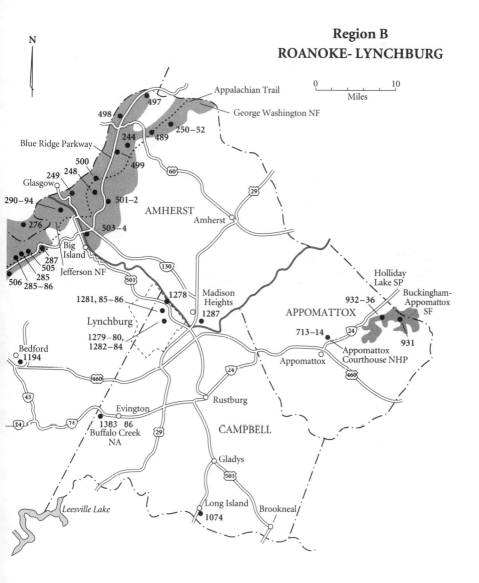

N

0        10
Miles

Appalachian Trail

497

498

George Washington NF

250–52

244        489

Blue Ridge Parkway

500

249    248

Glasgow

499

60

29

290–94

501–2

AMHERST

Amherst

276

503–4

Big
Island

130

287

505

Jefferson NF

501

506    285

285–86

1281, 85–86

1278

Madison
Heights

Lynchburg

1287

1279–80,
1282–84

Bedford

1194

460

43

24        74

Evington

1383  86

Buffalo Creek
NA

29

Rustburg

CAMPBELL

Leesville Lake

Gladys

501

Long Island

Brookneal

1074

Holliday
Lake SP

932–36

Buckingham-
Appomattox
SF

APPOMATTOX

713–14

24

931

Appomattox
Courthouse NHP

Appomattox

460

24

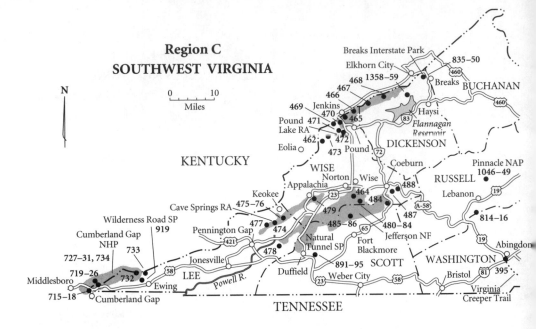

**Region C**
**SOUTHWEST VIRGINIA**

N

0        10
Miles

Breaks Interstate Park

835–50

Elkhorn City

468 1358–59

Breaks BUCHANAN

467

460

466

Haysi

469 Jenkins

470

83

Flannagan
Reservoir

Pound 471

465

Lake RA

462

472

DICKENSON

Eolia

473 Pound

72

KENTUCKY

Coeburn

Pinnacle NAP
1046–49

WISE

RUSSELL

Norton  Wise

488

Appalachia

Lebanon

19

Keokee

475–76

464

484

814–16

Cave Springs RA

479

487

A-58

477

485–86

480–84

Wilderness Road SP

474

65

Jefferson NF

919

480–84

Pennington Gap

19

Cumberland Gap
NHP

733

478

Natural
Tunnel SP

Fort
Blackmore

Abingdon

727–31, 734

421

SCOTT

WASHINGTON

719–26

732

Jonesville

Duffield

891–95

81

395

Middlesboro

58

LEE

Powell R.

Weber City

Bristol

715–18

Ewing

23

58

Virginia
Creeper Trail

Cumberland Gap

TENNESSEE

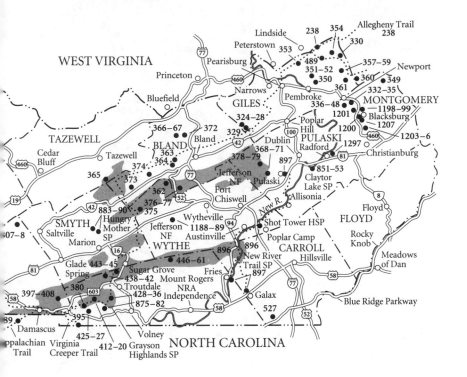

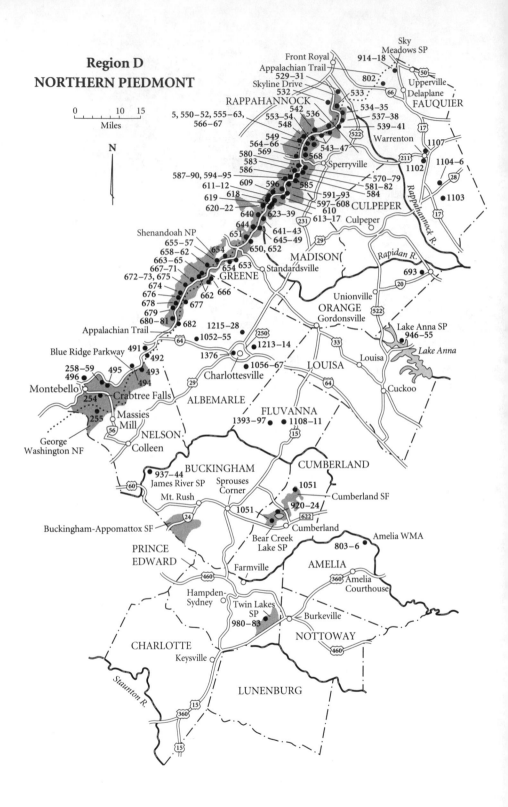

# Region D
# NORTHERN PIEDMONT

0    10   15
Miles

N

Sky
Meadows SP
914–18
Front Royal
Appalachian Trail          802
529–31
Skyline Drive                      Upperville
532          533          Delaplane
RAPPAHANNOCK                       FAUQUIER
5, 550–52, 555–63,          542   536   534–35
566–67          553–54          537–38
548          539–41
549          Warrenton   1107
564–66          543–47
580   569          1104–6
583          1102
586          Sperryville          1103
587–90, 594–95
611–12   609   596   585          570–79
619   618          581–82
620–22   640          591–93   584
623–39          597–608   CULPEPER
644          610
641–43          613–17   Culpeper
Shenandoah NP          651   645–49
655–57          650, 652          Rapidan R.
658–62   654          MADISON          693
663–65          653          20
667–71   654          Standardsville
672–73, 675   674          Unionville
676   662   666          ORANGE          522
678          677          Gordonsville
679   682   1215–28
680–81          1052–55   1213–14          Lake Anna SP
Appalachian Trail          250          946–55
Blue Ridge Parkway   491   1376   1056–67          Lake Anna
492          LOUISA
258–59   495   493          Charlottesville          Louisa
496          494          29          64
Montebello   254          ALBEMARLE          Cuckoo
255   Crabtree Falls          FLUVANNA
Massies          1393–97   1108–11
Mill   56          15
George   NELSON
Washington NF   Colleen
BUCKINGHAM          CUMBERLAND
937–44          1051
James River SP   Sprouses          Cumberland SF
Corner          920–24
Mt. Rush          1051   622
1051          Cumberland          Amelia WMA
Buckingham-Appomattox SF          Bear Creek          803–6
Lake SP          AMELIA
PRINCE          Farmville          360   Amelia
EDWARD          460          Courthouse
Hampden-
Sydney   Twin Lakes          Burkeville
SP          NOTTOWAY
980–83          460
CHARLOTTE          Keysville
Staunton R.
LUNENBURG
15
360
15

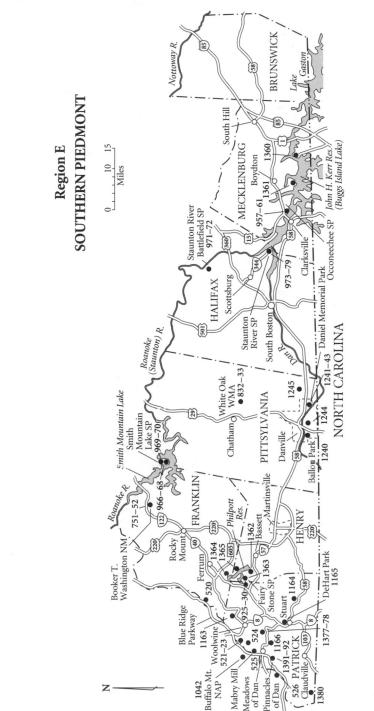

**Region E**
**SOUTHERN PIEDMONT**

0   5   10   15
Miles

N

Booker T.
Washington NM

Nottoway R.

85

58

BRUNSWICK

Lake
Gaston

South Hill

85

11

MECKLENBURG

Boydton

1360

1361

957–61

John H. Kerr Res.
(Buggs Island Lake)

15

360

Staunton River
Battlefield SP
971–72

HALIFAX

Scottsburg

344

Clarksville

973–79

Occoneechee SP

Daniel Memorial Park

58

NORTH CAROLINA

Roanoke
(Staunton) R.

501

Staunton
River SP

South Boston

1241–43

Dan R.

Smith Mountain Lake

Smith
Mountain
Lake SP
969–70

White Oak
WMA
832–33

29

Chatham

PITTSYLVANIA

1245

1244

Danville

1240

Ballou Park

58

Roanoke R.

966–68

751–52

122

FRANKLIN

Philpott
Res.

1362

Bassett

Martinsville

HENRY

220

57

220

1165

DeHart Park

Rocky
Mount

40

220

1364

1365

605

Ferrum

520

Fairy
Stone SP
1363

1164

Stuart

58

8

Blue Ridge
Parkway
1163

Woolwine
521–23

524

925–30

8

103

1166

1391–92

PATRICK

526
Claudville

1377–78

8

1042

Buffalo Mt.
NAP

Mabry Mill

Meadows
of Dan

525

Pinnacles
of Dan

1380

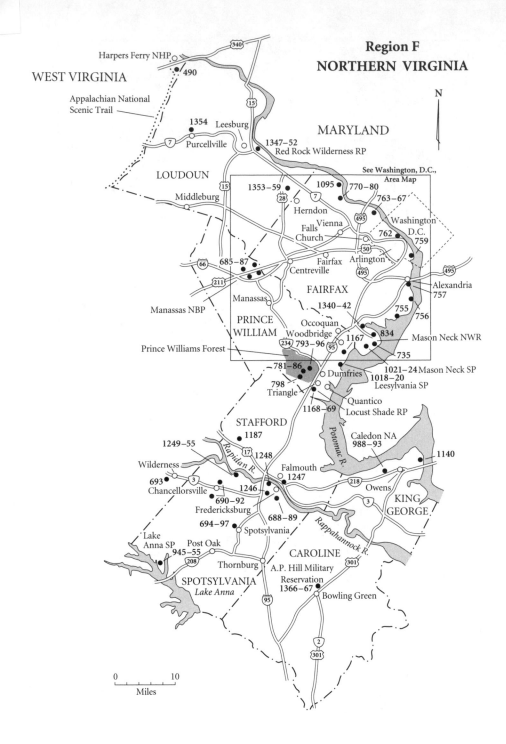

Region F
NORTHERN VIRGINIA

N

WEST VIRGINIA

Harpers Ferry NHP
490

Appalachian National
Scenic Trail

1354    Leesburg

Purcellville

1347–52
Red Rock Wilderness RP

MARYLAND

See Washington, D.C.,
Area Map

LOUDOUN

Middleburg

1353–59    1095    770–80

763–67

Herndon

Vienna

Falls
Church

Washington
D.C.

762
759

Fairfax    Arlington

Centreville

Alexandria
757

FAIRFAX

685–87

Manassas

Manassas NBP

PRINCE
WILLIAM

1340–42

Occoquan

Woodbridge

Prince Williams Forest

234    793–96    95

1167    834

755

756

Mason Neck NWR

735

781–86

Dumfries

798
Triangle

1021–24  Mason Neck SP
1018–20
Leesylvania SP

1168–69

Quantico
Locust Shade RP

STAFFORD    1187

Caledon NA
988–93

1140

1249–55    1248

Wilderness

693
Chancellorsville

690–92

Fredericksburg

694–97

Lake
Anna SP    Post Oak

945–55
208

Thornburg

SPOTSYLVANIA
Lake Anna

1246

Falmouth
1247

Owens

218

KING
GEORGE

688–89

Spotsylvania

CAROLINE

A.P. Hill Military
Reservation
1366–67

Bowling Green

0        10
Miles

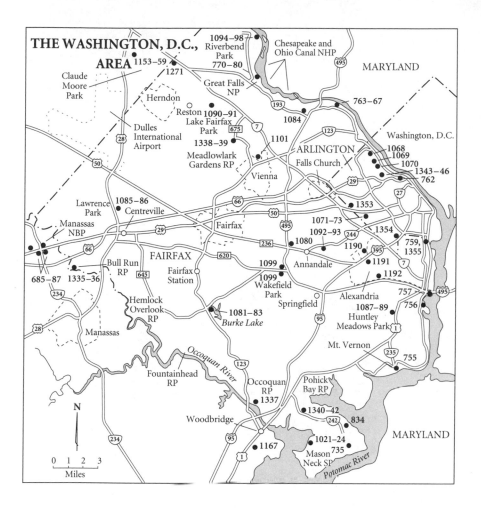

# THE WASHINGTON, D.C., AREA

Claude Moore Park

Herndon

Dulles International Airport

Reston

Lake Fairfax Park

Meadowlark Gardens RP

Vienna

Riverbend Park

Great Falls NP

Chesapeake and Ohio Canal NHP

MARYLAND

Washington, D.C.

ARLINGTON

Falls Church

Lawrence Park

Manassas NBP

Centreville

Fairfax

Annandale

Alexandria

FAIRFAX

Bull Run RP

Fairfax Station

Wakefield Park

Springfield

Huntley Meadows Park

Manassas

Hemlock Overlook RP

Burke Lake

Mt. Vernon

Fountainhead RP

Occoquan RP

Pohick Bay RP

Woodbridge

Mason Neck SP

MARYLAND

*Occoquan River*

*Potomac River*

N

0  1  2  3
Miles

1094–98
770–80
1153–59
1271
1090–91
1338–39
1101
1084
763–67
1068
1069
1070
1343–46
762
1085–86
1353
685–87
1335–36
1071–73
1092–93
1080
1190
1354
759, 1355
1099
1099
1191
1192
757
756
755
1081–83
1087–89
1337
1340–42
834
1167
1021–24
735

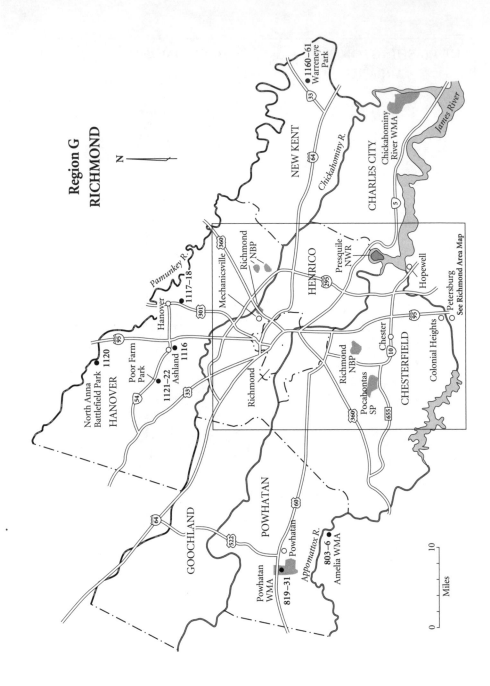

Region G
RICHMOND

N

1160–61
Warreneye
Park

33

NEW KENT

Chickahominy R.

64

CHARLES CITY

Chickahominy
River WMA

James River

5

Richmond
NBP

Mechanicsville

HENRICO

Presquile
NWR

295

Hopewell

Petersburg
See Richmond Area Map

Pamunkey R.

360

1117–18

Hanover

301

Hanover

95

Poor Farm
Park

54

1121–22
Ashland

1116

33

North Anna
Battlefield Park

1120

HANOVER

Richmond

95

Richmond
NBP

Chester

10

Pocahontas
SP

360

655

CHESTERFIELD

Colonial Heights

64

GOOCHLAND

522

POWHATAN

60

Powhatan

Appomattox R.

Powhatan
WMA

819–31

803–6
Amelia WMA

0

10

Miles

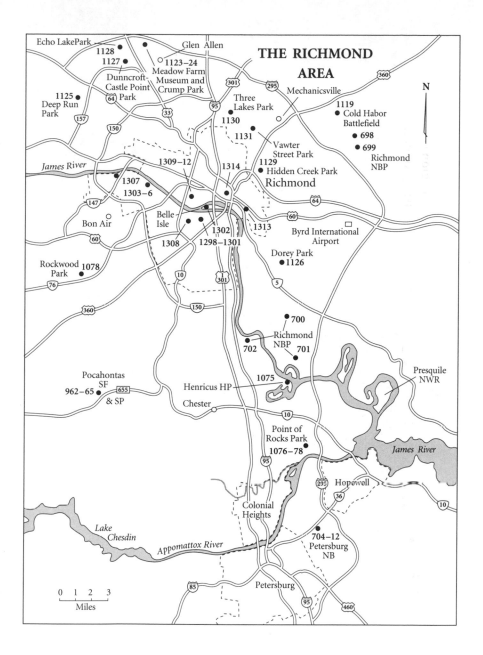

THE RICHMOND
AREA

N

Echo LakePark
1128
1127
Dunncroft-
Castle Point
Park
1125
Deep Run
Park

Glen Allen
1123–24
Meadow Farm
Museum and
Crump Park

Mechanicsville

1130
Three
Lakes Park
1131

1119
Cold Habor
Battlefield
698
699
Richmond
NBP

James River
1309–12
1307
1303–6

1314
Vawter
Street Park
1129
Hidden Creek Park
Richmond

Bon Air
Belle
Isle
1302
1308  1298–1301
1313
64
60

Byrd International
Airport
Dorey Park
1126

Rockwood
Park  1078

700

Richmond
NBP
702  701

Pocahontas
SF
962–65
& SP

Henricus HP
Chester

1075

Presquile
NWR

James River

Point of
Rocks Park
1076–78

Hopewell

Lake
Chesdin
Appomattox River

Colonial
Heights

704–12
Petersburg
NB

0  1  2  3
Miles

Petersburg

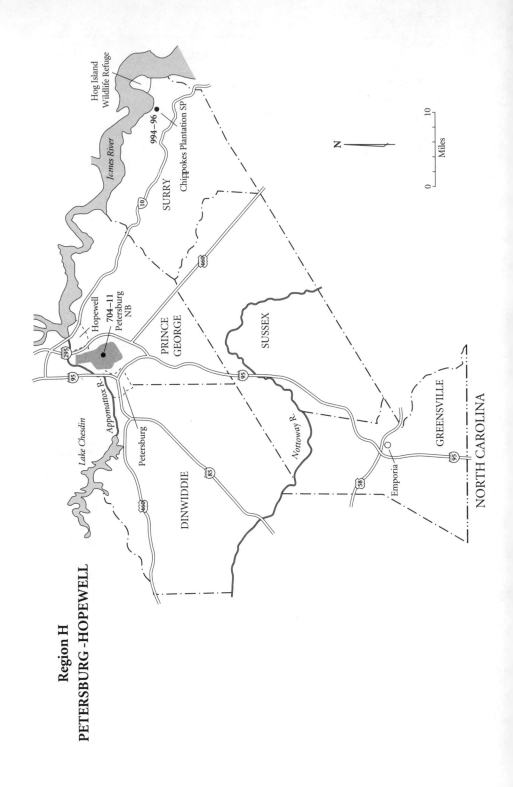

# Region H
# PETERSBURG-HOPEWELL

Hog Island
Wildlife Refuge

*James River*

994–96

Chippokes Plantation SP

SURRY

10

Hopewell

704–11
Petersburg NB

PRINCE
GEORGE

*Lake Chesdin*

*Appomattox R.*

295

95

Petersburg

460

DINWIDDIE

85

SUSSEX

95

*Nottoway R.*

GREENSVILLE

58

95

Emporia

NORTH CAROLINA

N

0    10

Miles

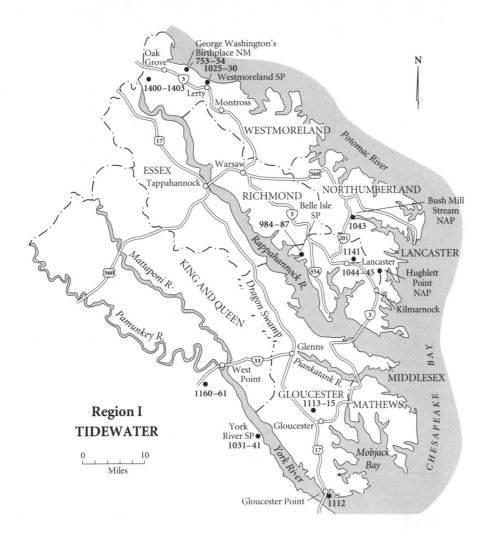

George Washington's
Birthplace NM
**753–54**
**1025–30**
Westmoreland SP

Oak
Grove

**1400–1403**
Lerty

Montross

WESTMORELAND

Potomac River

N

17

Warsaw

ESSEX
Tappahannock

RICHMOND

Belle Isle
SP

**984–87**

NORTHUMBERLAND

Bush Mill
Stream
NAP

3

360

**1043**

201

**1141**

LANCASTER

Lancaster

354

**1044–45**

Hughlett
Point
NAP

3

Kilmarnock

Mattaponi R.

KING AND QUEEN

Rappahannock R.

Dragon Swamp

360

Pamunkey R.

Glenns

33

West
Point

**1160–61**

Piankatank R.

GLOUCESTER

**1113–15**

MIDDLESEX

MATHEWS

BAY

Region I
TIDEWATER

York
River SP
**1031–41**

Gloucester

Mobjack
Bay

0        10
Miles

York River

Gloucester Point

**1112**

CHESAPEAKE

BAY

N

York River
SP

1031–41

1139

JAMES
CITY

1136

Williamsburg

1329–31

YORK

1135

1138

James River

684

Jamestown

994–96
Chippokes
Plantation SP

Fort
Boykin HP
Smithfield

1134

Carrollton Nike
Park

ISLE OF
WIGHT

460

Nottoway R.

Franklin

58

SOUTHAMPTON

SUFFOLK

13

NORTH CAROLINA

# Region J
# HAMPTON ROADS

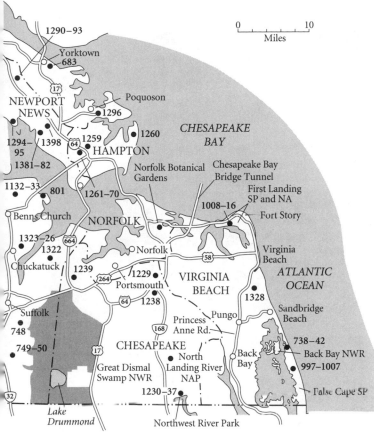

0 ___ 10
Miles

1290–93

Yorktown
683

17

Poquoson

NEWPORT NEWS
1296

CHESAPEAKE BAY

1260

1294–95 / 1398
1259
64
HAMPTON

1381–82

Norfolk Botanical Gardens

Chesapeake Bay Bridge Tunnel

1132–33   801
1261–70

First Landing SP and NA

1008–16

Fort Story

Benns Church

NORFOLK

1323–26
1322
664

Norfolk

Virginia Beach

Chuckatuck
1239

264
1229

ATLANTIC OCEAN

58

Portsmouth
VIRGINIA BEACH

Suffolk
64
1238

1328

748

Princess Anne Rd.

Pungo

Sandbridge Beach

168

749–50

17

CHESAPEAKE

North Landing River NAP

Back Bay

738–42

Back Bay NWR

997–1007

Great Dismal Swamp NWR

32

1230–37

False Cape SP

Lake Drummond

Northwest River Park

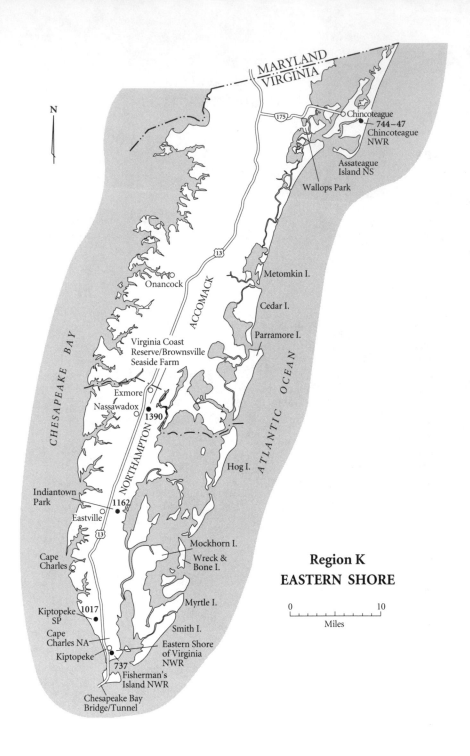

N

MARYLAND
VIRGINIA

175

Chincoteague
744–47
Chincoteague
NWR

Assateague
Island NS

Wallops Park

13

ACCOMACK

Metomkin I.

Onancock

Cedar I.

Parramore I.

Virginia Coast
Reserve/Brownsville
Seaside Farm

CHESAPEAKE BAY

Exmore
Nassawadox
1390

NORTHAMPTON

ATLANTIC OCEAN

Hog I.

Indiantown
Park
1162

Eastville

13

Mockhorn I.

Wreck &
Bone I.

Cape
Charles

Region K
EASTERN SHORE

Myrtle I.

0                    10

Miles

Kiptopeke
SP
1017

Smith I.

Cape
Charles NA

Eastern Shore
of Virginia
NWR

Kiptopeke

737

Fisherman's
Island NWR

Chesapeake Bay
Bridge/Tunnel

# APPENDIX A. Sources of Information

The addresses of national, state, and local forests, parks, recreation areas, historic sites, gardens, and other areas are provided in the text. The following agencies, organizations, and clubs are also valuable sources of information.

## U.S. Congress

Committee on Agriculture (House)
Longworth House Office Bldg., Rm. 1301
Washington, DC 20515
(Phone: 202-225-2171; fax: 202-225-0917; web: <www.agriculture.house.gov>)
(Topics include forest resources, wildlife)

Committee on Agriculture, Nutrition, and Forestry (Senate)
Russell Bldg., Rm. 328-A
Washington, DC 20510
(Phone: 202-224-2035; web: <www.senate.gov/-agriculture>)
(Topics include forestry, wilderness)

Committee on Energy and Natural Resources (Senate)
Dirksen Bldg., Rm. SD-364
Washington, DC 20510
(Phone: 202-224-4971; fax: 202-224-6163)
(Topics include minerals, national parks, recreation areas, scenic rivers, historical sites, military parks)

Committee on Environment and Public Works (Senate)
Dirksen Bldg., Rm. SD-458
Washington, DC 20510
(Phone: 202-224-6167; fax: 202-224-1273; web: <epw.senate.gov>)
(Topics include environmental policy and research, fisheries, wildlife)

## U.S. Government/Executive Branch

Army Corps of Engineers
441 G St.
Washington, DC 20314
(Phone: 202-761-0010)

> District Office (Flannagan)
> 502 Eighth St.
> Huntington, WV 25701
> (Phone: 304-529-5395; fax: 304-529-5591;
> web:
> <www.intra.lrh.usace.army.mil>)

> District Office (Philpott and Kerr)
> P.O. Box 1890
> Wilmington, NC 28402
> (Phone: 910-251-4501; fax: 910-251-4185;
> web: <www.usace.army.mil>)

Council on Environmental Quality
722 Jackson Place NW
Washington, DC 20503
(Phone: 202-456-6224; fax: 202-456-2710)

Department of Agriculture
1400 Independence Ave. SW
Washington, DC 20250
(Phone: 202-720-8732)

> Forest Service
> P.O. Box 96090
> Washington, DC 20090
> (Phone: 202-205-8333; fax:
> 202-205-1599; web: <www.fs.fed.us>)

> Forest Service Regional (#8) Office
> 1720 Peachtree Rd. NW, Suite 800
> Atlanta, GA 30309
> (Phone: 404-347-4178; fax: 404-347-4821)

>> George Washington and Jefferson
>> National Forests
>> 5162 Valleypointe Parkway
>> Roanoke, VA 24019
>> (Phone: 540-265-5100;
>> fax: 540-265-5145; web: <www.
>> southernregion.fs.fed.us/gwj>)

Department of Commerce
National Oceanic and Atmospheric
   Administration
Hoover Bldg., Rm. 5128
14th and Constitution Ave. NW
Washington, DC 20230
(Phone: 202-482-3436; fax: 202-408-9674;
   web: <www.noaa.gov>)

Department of the Interior
1849 C St. NW
Washington, DC 20240
(Phone: 202-208-6843; fax: 202-219-0910;
   web: <www.nps.gov>)

> Bureau of Land Management
> 1849 C St. NW
> Washington, DC 20240
> (Phone: 202-208-3801;
>    fax: 202-208-5242;
>    web: <www.blm.gov>)

> National Park Service
> US Custom House
> 200 Chestnut St., 5th Floor
> Philadelphia, PA 19106
> (Phone: 215-597-7013;
>    web: <www.nps.gov>)

>> Regional Director (Southeast)
>> 1875 Century Blvd.
>> Atlanta, GA 30345
>> (Phone: 404-679-4000;
>>    fax: 404-679-4006)

> U.S. Fish and Wildlife Service
> 1849 C St., Rm. 3012
> Washington, DC 20240
> (Phone: 202-208-5634; fax:
>    202-208-7407; <web: www.fws.gov>)

## U.S. Government/Independent Agencies

Advisory Council on Historic Preservation
1100 Pennsylvania Ave. NW, #809
Washington, DC 20004
(Phone: 202-606-8503; fax: 202-606-8672;
  web: <www.achp.gov>)

Environmental Protection Agency
1200 Pennsylvania Ave. NW
Washington, DC 20460
(Phone: 202-260-2090; fax: 202-564-4613;
  web: <www.epa.gov>)

## National Regional Commissions

Appalachian Regional Commission
1666 Connecticut Ave. NW, Suite 700
Washington, DC 20009
(Phone: 202-884-7700; fax: 202-844-7691;
  web: <www.arc.gov>)

Atlantic State Marine Fisheries Commission
1444 Eye St. NW, 6th Floor
Washington, DC 20005
(Phone: 202-289-6400; fax: 202-289-6051;
  web: <www.asmfc.org>)

Interstate Commission on the Potomac
  River Basin
6110 Executive Blvd., Suite 300
Rockville, MD 20852
(Phone: 301-984-1908; fax: 301-984-5841;
  web: <www.potomacriver.org>)

Marine Mammal Commission
4340 East-West Highway, Rm. 905
Bethesda, MD 20824
(Phone: 301-540-0087; fax: 301-504-0099)

Migratory Bird Conservation Commission
1849 C St., NW
Washington, DC 20240
(Phone: 703-358-1716; fax: 703-358-2223)

## National and Regional Organizations (Nongovernment and Nonprofit)

Alliance for the Chesapeake Bay
P.O. Box 1981
Richmond, VA 23218
(Phone: 804-775-0951; fax: 804-775-0954;
  web: <www.alliancechesbay.org>

American Bass Association, Inc.
P.O. Box 896
Gate City, VA 24251
(Phone: 540-253-5780; fax: 540-253-5782)

American Birding Association
P.O. Box 6599
Colorado Springs, CO 80934
(Phone: 719-578-9703; fax: 719-578-1480)

American Camping Association, Inc.
5000 State Rd., 67N
Martinsville, IN 46151
(Phone: 765-342-8456; fax: 765-342-2065;
  web: <www.acacamps.org>)

American Cave Conservation Association
199 East Main St.
Horse Cave, KY 42749
(Phone: 502-786-1466; web:
    <www.cavern.org/acca.htm>)

American Federation of Mineralogical
    Societies, Inc.
Central Office, P.O. Box 891
Oklahoma City, OK 73189
(Phone: 405-682-2936)

American Fisheries Society
5410 Grosvenor La., Suite 110
Bethesda, MD 20814
(Phone: 301-897-8616; fax: 301-897-8616
    or 8096)

American Forests
P.O. Box 2002
Washington, DC 20013
(Phone: 202-955-4500; fax: 202-955-4588;
    web: <www.Americanforests.org>)

American Geographical Society
120 Wall St.
New York, NY 10005
(Phone: 212-422-5456; fax: 212-422-5480)

American Hiking Society
1422 Fenwick Lane
Silver Spring, MD 20910
(Phone: 301-565-6704; fax: 301-565-6714;
    web: <www.americanhiking.org>)

American Rivers
1025 Vermont Ave. NW
Washington, DC 20005
(Phone: 202-347-7550;
fax: 202-347-9240; web:
    <www.americanrivers.org>)

Appalachian Mountain Club
5 Joy St.
Boston, MA 02108
(Phone: 617-523-0636; fax: 617-523-6617;
    web: <www.outdoors.org>)

Appalachian Trail Conference
P.O. Box 807
Harpers Ferry, WV 25425
(Phone: 304-535-6331; fax: 304- 535-2667;
    web: <www.appalachiantrail.org>)

Audubon Naturalists Society
    (Central Atlantic)
8940 Jones Mill Rd.
Chevy Chase, MD 20815
(Phone: 301-652-9188; fax: 301-951-7179;
    web: <www.audubonnaturalist.org>)

Boy Scouts of America (National)
P.O. Box 152079
Irving, TX 75015
(Phone: 972-580-2000; web:
    <www.bsa.scouting.org>)
(Call for information on state chapters.)

Camp Fire, Inc.
4601 Madison Ave.
Kansas City, MO 64112
(Phone: 816-756-1950; fax: 816-756-0258;
    web: <www.campfireusa.org>)

Chesapeake Bay Foundation, Inc.
6 Herndon Ave.
Annapolis, MD 21403
(Phone: 410-268-8833; fax: 410-280-3513;
    web: <www.cbf.org>)

Clean Water Action
4455 Connecticut Ave. NW
Washington, DC 20008
(Phone: 202-985-0420)

Cousteau Society
870 Greenbrier Cir.
Chesapeake, VA 23320
(Phone: 757-523-9335)

Defenders of Wildlife
1101 14th St. NW
Washington, DC 20005
(Phone: 202-682-9400; fax: 202-682-1311;
    web: <www.defenders.org>)

Ducks Unlimited, Inc.
One Waterfowl Way
Memphis, TN 38120
(Phone: 901-758-3825; fax: 901-758-3850)

Environmental Defense Fund, Inc.
1875 Connecticut Ave.
Washington, DC 20009
(Phone: 202-387-3500; fax: 202-234-6049;
    web: <www.environmentaldefense.
    org>)

Friends of the Earth
1025 Vermont Ave. NW
Washington, DC 20005
(Phone: 202-783-7400; fax: 202-783-0444;
    web: <www.foe.org>)

Friends of the Blue Ridge Parkway
2301 Hendersonville Rd.
Arden, NC 28704
(Phone: 800-228-7275)
and
3536 Brambleton Ave. SW
Roanoke, VA 24018
(Phone: 540-772-7900)

Girl Scouts of the U.S.A.
420 Fifth Ave.
New York, NY 10018
(Phone: 212-852-8000;
fax: 212-852-6509; web:
    <www.girlscouts.org>)
(Call for information on state chapters.)

National Arbor Day Foundation
211 North 12th St., Suite 501
Lincoln, NE 68508
(Phone: 402-474-5655; web:
    <www.arborday.org>)

National Audubon Society
700 Broadway
New York, NY 10003
(Phone: 212-979-3000;
fax: 212-979-3188; web:
    <www.audubon.org>)

National Geographic Society
1145 17th St. NW
Washington, DC 20036
(Phone: 800-647-5463; web:
    <www.nationalgeographic.com>)

National Parks and Conservation
    Association
1300 19th St. NW
Washington, DC 20036
(Phone: 800-628-7275; web:
    <www.npca.org>)

National Recreation and Park Association
22377 Belmont Ridge Rd.
Ashburn, VA 20148
(Phone: 703-858-0784; fax: 703-858-0794;
    web: <www.nrpa.org>)

National Speleological Society
2813 Cave Ave.
Huntsville, AL 35810
(Phone: 256-852-1300; fax: 256-851-9241;
    web: <www.caves.org>)

National Wildlife Federation
11100 Wildlife Center Dr.
Reston, VA 20190
(Phone: 703-438-6000; fax: 703-442-7332;
    web: <www.nwf.org>)

The Nature Conservancy
4245 North Fairfax Dr., Suite 100
Arlington, VA 22203
(Phone: 703-841-5300; fax: 703-841-1283;
    web: <www.nature.org>)

Rails-to-Trails Conservancy
1100 17th St. NW, 10th Floor
Washington, DC 20036
(Phone: 202-331-9696; web:
    <www.railstrails.org>)

Sierra Club
730 Polk St.
San Francisco, CA 94109
(Phone: 415-776-2211)

Smithsonian Institution
1000 Jefferson Dr. sw
Washington, DC 20560
(Phone: 202-357-2700; web:
  <www.si.edu>)

Trout Unlimited
1500 Wilson Blvd.
Arlington, VA 22209
(Phone: 703-522-0200; fax: 703-284-9400;
  web: <www.tu.org>)

Izaak Walton League of America, Inc.
1401 Wilson Blvd. (Level B)
Arlington, VA 22209
(Phone: 703-528-1818)

The Wilderness Society
1615 M St. NW
Washington, DC 20036
(Phone: 202-833-2300 and 800-THE WILD;
  web: <www.wilderness.org>)

## Virginia State Agencies

Department of Conservation and
  Recreation
203 Governor St., Suite 302
Richmond, VA 23219
(Phone: 804-786-6124; web:
  <www.dcr.state.va.us>)

  Division of Natural Heritage
  217 Governor St., 3rd Floor
  Richmond, VA 23219
  (Phone: 804-786-7951; fax: 804-371-2674;
    web: <www.dcr.state.va.us/dnh>)

  Division of Soil and Water Conservation
  203 Governor St., Suite 206
  Richmond, VA 23219
  (Phone: 804-786-2064; web:
    <www.dcr.state.va.us>)

  Division of State Parks
  203 Governor St., Suite 306
  Richmond, VA 23219
  (Phone: 804-692-0403; fax:
    804-786-9294; web:
    <www.dcr.state.va.us>)

Department of Game and Inland Fisheries
4010 W. Broad St. (Box 11104)
Richmond, VA 23230
(Phone: 804-367-1000; web:
  <www.dgif.state.va.us>)
(Publishes *Virginia Wildlife*)

Department of Highways and
  Transportation
1401 E. Broad St. (Central Office);
  also 1221 E. Broad St.
Richmond, VA 23219
(Phone: 804-786-2264 [Enhancements];
  804-371-6752 [Environmental Programs];
  web: <www.vdot.state.va.us>)
(Highway Helpline for road conditions,
  instate: 800-367-7623, out-of-state:
  804-786-3181)

Department of Mines, Minerals,
  and Energy
202 Ninth St. Office Bldg.
Richmond, VA 23219
(Phone: 540-523-8119; fax: 804-692-3237)

Piedmont Environmental Council
P.O. Box 460
Warrenton, VA 22186
(Phone: 703-347-2334 or 804-977-2033)

Virginia Division of Forestry
900 Natural Resources Dr., Suite 800
Charlottesville, VA 22903
(Phone: 804-977-6555; fax: 804-296-2369;
  web: <www.dof.state.va.us>)

Virginia Division of Tourism
1021 E. Cary St. (Tower II)
Richmond, VA 23219
(Phone: 804-786-2051)
(Publishes *Virginia Travel Guide*, free)
(Write or call the Virginia Division of
   Tourism for an address list of Virginia's
   local bicycle clubs.)

Virginia Museum of Natural History
1001 Douglas Ave.
Martinsville, VA 24112
(Phone: 276-666-8600; fax: 276-632-6487;
   web: <www.vmnh.org>)

Izaak Walton League of America
   (Virginia Division)
5235 Richardson Dr.
Fairfax, VA 22032
(Phone: 703-361-5729)

## Virginia Citizens' Organizations

Appalachian Trail Conference
   (Headquarters)
P.O. Box 807
Harpers Ferry, WV 25425
(Phone: 304-535-6331; fax: 304-535-2667;
   web: <www.appalachiantrail.org>)

   Mount Rogers A.T. Club
   24198 Green Spring Rd.
   Abingdon, VA 24211

   Natural Bridge A.T. Club
   P.O. Box 3010
   Lynchburg, VA 24503
   (Web: <www.nbatc.org>)

   Old Dominion A.T. Club
   P.O. Box 25283
   Richmond, VA 23260
   (Web: <www.ODATC.org>)

   Piedmont A.T. Hikers
   P.O. Box 4423
   Greensboro, NC 27404
   (Web: <www.path-at.org>)

   Potomac A.T. Club
   118 Park St. SE
   Vienna, VA 22180
   (Phone: 703-242-0693; web:
      <www.patc.net>)

   Roanoke A.T. Club
   P.O. Box 12282
   Roanoke, VA 24024
   (Web: <www.ratc.org>)

   Tidewater A.T. Club
   P.O. Box 8246
   Norfolk, VA 23503
   (Web: <www.tidewateratc.com>)

   Virginia Tech A.T. Club
   P.O. Box 538
   Blacksburg, VA 24060
   (Web: <www.fbox.vt.edu/org/
      outing/>)

BikeWalk Virginia
P.O. Box 203
Williamsburg, VA 23187
(Phone: 757-229-0507; fax: 757-259-2372;
   web: <www.bikewalkvirginia.org>)

Sierra Club (Virginia Chapter)
6 North 6th St.
Richmond, VA 23219
(Phone: 804-225-9112; fax: 804-225-9114;
   web: <www.sierraclubva.org>)

Virginia Conservation Network
1001 East Broad St., Suite LL35C
Richmond, VA 23219
(Phone: 804-644-0283; fax: 804-644-0286;
  web: <www.vcnva.org>)

Virginia Environmental Council
P.O. Box 460 (5 Horner St.)
Warrenton, VA 20188
(Phone: 540-347-2334; fax: 540-349-9003;
  web: <www.pecva.org>)

Virginia Forestry Association
8810B Patterson Ave.
Richmond, VA 23229
(Phone: 804-741-0836; fax: 804-741-0838;
  web: <www.vaforestry.org>)

Virginia Native Plant Society
400 Blanly Farm Land, Unit 2
Boyce, VA 22620
(Phone: 540-837-1600; fax: 540-837-1512;
  web: <www.vnps.org>)

Virginia Society of Ornithology
7451 Little River Turnpike, #202
Annandale, VA 22003
(Phone: 703-305-7381 or 256-8275)

Virginia Trails Association
P.O. Box 1132
Ashland, VA 23005
(Phone: 804-798-4160)

Wildlife Center of Virginia
P.O. Box 557
Waynesboro, VA 22980
(Phone: 540-942-9453; fax: 540-943-9453)

Wildlife Society (Virginia Chapter)
2503 Brunswick Rd.
Charlottesville, VA 22903
(Phone: 434-295-4681; fax: 434-975-1005)

# APPENDIX B. Federal and State Endangered and Threatened Species in Virginia

An endangered species is one that is in danger of extinction throughout all or a significant portion of its range. A threatened species is one that is likely to become an endangered species within the foreseeable future throughout all or a significant portion of its range. In this table, F = Federal, S = State, E = Endangered, and T = Threatened. Virginia also has seventy-nine animal species of "state special concern" (SSC), not a legal status.

| COMMON NAME | SCIENTIFIC NAME | STATUS |
|---|---|---|

## Fauna

### AMPHIBIANS

*Frogs*

| | | |
|---|---|---|
| Barking treefrog | *Hyla gratiosa* | ST |

*Salamanders*

| | | |
|---|---|---|
| Eastern tiger salamander | *Ambystoma tigrinum* | SE |
| Mabee's salamander | *Ambystoma mabeei* | ST |
| Shenandoah salamander | *Plethodon shenandoah* | FE, SE |

### BIRDS

| | | |
|---|---|---|
| Bachman's sparrow | *Aimophila aestivalis* | ST |
| Bachman's warbler | *Vermivora bachmanii* | FE, SE |
| Bald eagle | *Haliaeetus leucocephalus* | FT, ST |
| Bewick's wren | *Thryomanes bewickii* | SE |
| Gull-billed tern | *Sterna nilotica* | ST |
| Henslow's sparrow | *Ammodramus henslowii* | ST |
| Kirtland's warbler | *Dendroica kirtlandi* | FE, SE |
| Loggerhead shrike | *Lanius ludovicianus* | ST |
| Peregrine falcon | *Falco peregrinus* | ST |
| Piping plover | *Charadrius melodus* | FT, ST |
| Red-cockaded woodpecker | *Picoides borealis* | FE, SE |
| Roseate tern | *Sterna dougallii* | FE, SE |
| Upland sandpiper | *Bartramia longicauda* | ST |
| Wilson's plover | *Charadrius wilsonia* | SE |

## FRESHWATER CRUSTACEANS

| Common Name | Scientific Name | Status |
|---|---|---|
| Lee County Cave isopod | *Lirceus usdagulun* | FE, SE |
| Madison Cave amphipod | *Stygobromus stegerorum* | ST |
| Madison Cave isopod | *Antrolina lira* | FT, ST |

## FRESHWATER FISHES

| Common Name | Scientific Name | Status |
|---|---|---|
| Blackbanded sunfish | *Enneacanthus chaetodon* | SE |
| Carolina darter | *Etheostoma collis* | ST |
| Duskytail darter | *Etheostoma* sp. | FE, SE |
| Emerald shiner | *Notropis atherinoides* | ST |
| Greenfin darter | *Etheostoma chlorobranchium* | ST |
| Longhead darter | *Percina macrocephala* | ST |
| Orangefin madtom | *Noturus gilberti* | ST |
| Paddlefish | *Polyodon spathula* | ST |
| Roanoke logperch | *Percina rex* | FE, SE |
| Sharphead darter | *Etheostoma acuticeps* | SE |
| Shortnose sturgeon | *Acipenser brevirostrum* | FE, SE |
| Slender chub | *Erimystax cahni* | FT, ST |
| Spotfin chub | *Cyprinella monacha* | FT, ST |
| Steelcolor shiner | *Cyprinella whipplei* | ST |
| Tennessee dace | *Phoxinus tennesseensis* | SE |
| Tippecanoe darter | *Etheostoma tippecanoe* | ST |
| Variegate darter | *Etheostoma variatum* | SE |
| Western sand darter | *Ammocrypta clara* | ST |
| Whitemouth shiner | *Notropis alborus* | ST |
| Yellowfin madtom | *Noturus flavipinnis* | FT, ST |

## MAMMALS

| Common Name | Scientific Name | Status |
|---|---|---|
| Delmarva Peninsula fox squirrel | *Sciurus niger cinereus* | FE, SE |
| Dismal Swamp southeastern shrew | *Sorex longirostris fisheri* | ST |
| Eastern big-eared bat | *Plecotus rafinesquii macrotis* | SE |
| Eastern cougar | *Felis concolor couguar* | FE, SE |
| Gray bat | *Myotis grisescens* | FE, SE |
| Indiana bat | *Myotis sodalis* | FE, SE |
| Northern flying squirrel | *Glaucomys sabrinus* | FE, SE |
| Rock vole | *Microtus chrotorrhinus* | SE |
| Snowshoe hare | *Lepus americanus* | SE |
| Virginia big-eared bat | *Plecotus townsendii virginianus* | FE, SE |
| Water shrew | *Sorex palustris* | SE |

## MARINE MAMMALS

| Common Name | Scientific Name | Status |
|---|---|---|
| Blue whale | *Balaenoptera musculus* | FE, SE |
| Fin whale | *Balaenoptera physalus* | FE, SE |

| COMMON NAME | SCIENTIFIC NAME | STATUS |
|---|---|---|
| West Indian manatee | *Trichechus manatus* | FE, SE |
| Humpback whale | *Megaptera novaeangliae* | FE, SE |
| Northern right whale | *Eubalaena glacialis* | FE, SE |
| Sei whale | *Balaenoptera borealis* | FE, SE |
| Sperm whale | *Physeter catodon* | FE, SE |

### MILLIPEDES

| | | |
|---|---|---|
| Ellett Valley pseudotremia | *Pseudotremia cavernarum* | ST |
| Laurel Creek xystodesmid | *Sigmoria whiteheadi* | ST |

### MOLLUSKS

*Freshwater and Land Snails*

| | | |
|---|---|---|
| Brown supercoil | *Paravitrea septadens* | ST |
| Rubble coil | *Helicodiscus lirellus* | SE |
| Shaggy coil | *Helicodiscus diadema* | SE |
| Spiny riversnail | *Io fluvialis* | ST |
| Spirit supercoil | *Paravitrea hera* | SE |
| Unthanks Cave snail | *Holsingeria unthanksensis* | SE |
| Virginia coil | *Polygyriscus virginicus* | FE, SE |

*Freshwater Mussels*

| | | |
|---|---|---|
| Appalachian monkeyface mussel | *Quadrula sparsa* | FE, SE |
| Atlantic pigtoe mussel | *Fusconaia masoni* | ST |
| Birdwing pearlymussel | *Lemiox rimosus* | FE, SE |
| Black sandshell mussel | *Ligumia recta* | ST |
| Brook floater mussel | *Alasmidonta varicosa* | SE |
| Cracking pearlymussel | *Hemistena lata* | FE, SE |
| Cumberland bean mussel | *Villosa trabalis* | FE, SE |
| Cumberland combshell mussel | *Epioblasma brevidens* | FE, SE |
| Cumberland monkeyface mussel | *Quadrula intermedia* | FE, SE |
| Deertoe mussel | *Truncilla truncata* | SE |
| Dromedary pearlymussel | *Dromus dromas* | FE, SE |
| Dwarf wedge mussel | *Alasmidonta heterodon* | FE, SE |
| Elephant-ear mussel | *Elliptio crassidens* | SE |
| Fanshell mussel | *Cyprogenia stegaria (=irorata)* | FE, SE |
| Fine-rayed pigtoe mussel | *Fusconaia cuneolus* | FE, SE |
| Fragile papershell mussel | *Leptodea fragilis* | ST |
| Green blossom mussel | *Epioblasma torulosa gubernaculum* | FE, SE |
| James spiny mussel | *Pleurobema collina* | FE, SE |
| Little-wing pearlymussel | *Pegias fabula* | FE, SE |
| Ohio pigtoe mussel | *Pleurobema cordatum* | SE |
| Oyster mussel | *Epioblasma capsaeformis* | FE, SE |
| Pimpleback mussel | *Quadrula pustulosa pustulosa* | ST |
| Pink mucket mussel | *Lampsilis abrupta (=orbiculata)* | FE, SE |

| COMMON NAME | SCIENTIFIC NAME | STATUS |
|---|---|---|
| Pink pigtoe mussel | *Pleurobema rubrum* | SE |
| Purple bean mussel | *Villosa perpurpurea* | FE, SE |
| Purple lilliput mussel | *Toxolasma lividus* | SE |
| Rough pigtoe mussel | *Pleurobema plenum* | FE, SE |
| Rough rabbitsfoot mussel | *Quadrula cylindrica strigillata* | FE, SE |
| Sheepnose mussel | *Plethobasus cyphyus* | ST |
| Shiny pigtoe mussel | *Fusconaia cor* | FE, SE |
| Slabside pearlymussel | *Lexingtonia dolabelloides* | ST |
| Slippershell mussel | *Alasmidonta viridis* | SE |
| Snuffbox mussel | *Epioblasma triquetra* | SE |
| Spectaclecase mussel | *Cumberlandia monodonta* | SE |
| Tan riffleshell mussel | *Epioblasma florentina walkeri* | FE, SE |
| Tennessee heelsplitter mussel | *Lasmigona holstonia* | SE |

**REPTILES**

*Lizards*

| | | |
|---|---|---|
| Eastern glass lizard | *Ophisaurus ventralis* | ST |

*Snakes*

| | | |
|---|---|---|
| Canebrake rattlesnake | *Crotalus horridus atricaudatus* | SE |

*Turtles*

| | | |
|---|---|---|
| Atlantic green sea turtle | *Chelonia mydas* | FT, ST |
| Bog turtle | *Clemmys muhlenbergii* | FT, SE |
| Eastern chicken turtle | *Deirochelys reticularia* | SE |
| Hawksbill sea turtle | *Eretmochelys imbricata* | FE, SE |
| Kemp's Ridley sea turtle | *Lepidochelys kempi* | FE, SE |
| Leatherback sea turtle | *Dermochelys coriacea* | FE, SE |
| Loggerhead sea turtle | *Caretta caretta* | FT, ST |
| Wood turtle | *Clemmys insculpta* | ST |

## Flora

| | | |
|---|---|---|
| Chaffseed | *Schwalbea americana* | FE, SE |
| Eastern prairie fringed orchid | *Plantanthera leucophaea* | FT, ST |
| Eastern prairie fringed orchid | *Plantanthera leucophaea* | FT, ST |
| Ginseng | *Panax quinquefolius* | FT, ST |
| Harper's fimbristylis | *Fimbristylis prepusilla* | FE, SE |
| Long-stalked holly | *Ilex collina* | SE |
| Mat-forming water hyssop | *Bacopa stragula* | SE |
| Michaux's sumac | *Rhus michauxii* | FE, SE |
| Nestronia | *Nestronia umbellula* | SE |
| Northeastern bullrush | *Scirpus ancistrochaetus* | FE, SE |
| Peters mountain mallow | *Iliamna corei* | FE, SE |
| Piratebush | *Buckleya distichophylla* | SE |

| COMMON NAME | SCIENTIFIC NAME | STATUS |
|---|---|---|
| Seabeach pigweed | *Amaranthus pumilus* | FT, ST |
| Sensitive joint-vetch | *Aeschynomene virginica* | FT, ST |
| Shale barren rock-cress | *Arabis serotina* | FE, SE |
| Small anthered bittercress | *Cardamine micranthera* | FE, SE |
| Small-whorled pogonia | *Isotria medeoloides* | FT, SE |
| Smooth coneflower | *Echinacea laevigata* | FE, SE |
| Swamp pink | *Helonias bullata* | FT, SE |
| Variable sedge | *Carex polymorpha* | SE |
| Virginia round-leaf birch | *Betula uber* | FT, SE |
| Virginia sneezeweed | *Helenium virginicum* | FT, SE |
| Virginia spiraea | *Spiraea virginiana* | FT, SE |

# APPENDIX C. Trails for Special People

The following lists of trails are offered as examples of trails that are particularly suited for three categories of special people: adventurous backpackers (rugged, secluded, wilderness-type trails of moderate to strenuous difficulty); families with young children (short walks of 0.1 mi. to 1.5 mi. on easy terrain offering scenic views and emphasizing animals and plants); and people with disabilities (PWD) (easy, short, usually paved trails for enjoying scenery, plant life, and fishing). Hikers and backpackers will notice many more trails in these and other categories throughout the book.

## Adventurous Backpackers

Allegheny Trail (three sections, 36.5 mi., linear)

Appalachian National Scenic Trail (550. mi., linear)

Tuscarora Trail (55.3 mi., linear)

Chief Benge/Little Stony Creek/Pickem Mountain Trails (22.6 mi., linear)

Dike/False Cape Trails (32.6 mi., round-trip)

Fore Mountain/Middle Mountain Trails (22.1 mi., linear)

Iron Mountain Trail (57 mi., linear)

Little Wilson Creek Wilderness Trails (23.7 mi., circuit connections, and backtrack)

Massanutten Mountain Trails (East, South, West) (91.4 mi., linear)

New River State Park Trail (55.2 mi., linear)

North Mountain (North)/Crawford Mountain Trails (22.3 mi., linear)

North Mountain (South)/Lick Branch Trails (17.9 mi., linear)

Oliver Mountain/Brushy Lick Trails (15.7 mi., circuit and backtrack)

Pine Mountain Trail (26.2 mi., linear)

Ramsey Draft/Bald Ridge Trails (17.9 mi., circuit)

Rich Hole/White Rock Tower Trails (12 mi., linear)

Ridge/Ewing Trails (19 mi., linear)

Ridge/Saddle/Old Rag Fire Road/AT/ Nicholson Hollow Trails (19.5 mi., circuit)

Rock Castle Gorge Trail (10.6 mi., circuit)

Shenandoah Mountain Trail (North, South) (28.3 mi., linear)

Stone Mountain Trail (13.5 mi., linear)

Virginia Creeper Trail (34.1 mi., linear)

Whetstone Ridge Trail (11.4 mi., linear)

Wild Oak Trail (25.9 mi., circuit)

Willis River Trail (15.2 mi., linear)

## Families with Young Children

Alpine Trail (1.0 mi.)
Alum Spring Trail (1.0 mi.)
Ashton Creek Trail (0.5 mi.)
Augusta Springs Wetland Trail (0.6 mi.)
Bald Cypress Trail (1.5 mi.)
Barn Wharf Trail (0.4 mi.)
Bayberry Nature Trail (1.5 mi.)
Bay View Trail (1.0 mi.)
Baywood Trail (1.0 mi.)
Beartree Lake Trail (1.0 mi.)
Belle Isle Trail (1.2 mi.)
Birdwalk Trail (0.3 mi.)
Bluebell Loop Trail (1.3 mi.)
Braley Pond Trail (0.6 mi.)
Buffalo Creek Trail (0.8 mi.)
Buffalo Mountain Trail (1.4 mi.)
Bull Run Nature Trail (1.5 mi.)
Cave Mountain Lake Trail (0.8 mi.)
Charcoal Trail (0.6 mi.)
Children's Forest Trail (0.3 mi.)
Cock's Comb Trail (0.4 mi.)
Confederate Breastworks Trail (0.5 mi.)
Dismal Town Boardwalk Trail (0.9 mi.)
Dune Trail (0.2 mi.)
Dyke Trail (1.0 mi.)
Eastern Shore Nature Trail (0.5 mi.)
Echo Lake Trail (0.7 mi.)
Elk Run Trail (0.8 mi.)
Farms to Forest Trail (1.1 mi.)
Fenwick Nature Trail (1.0 mi.)
Fenwick Wetlands Trail (0.8 mi.)
Fisherman's Trail (1.0 mi.)
Fort Boykin Trail (0.5 mi.)
Geology Interpretive Trail (0.8 mi.)
Goodwin Lake Nature Trail (0.3 mi.)
Green Leaf Nature Trail (0.7 mi.)
Greenstone Trail (0.3 mi.)
Guest River Gorge Trail (1.0 mi. of 5.8 mi.)
Hanging Rock Trail (0.7 mi.)
Henry Hill Trail (1.2 mi.)
Heron Trail (0.6 mi.)
Hiawatha Nature Trail (0.9 mi.)
Hidden Valley Trail (West) (1.0 mi.)
Hog Pen Trail (1.8 mi., backtrack)
Hurricane Knob Nature Trail (1.0 mi.)

James River Trail (at Chippokes, 0.5 mi.)
Jones Point Trail (0.5 mi.)
Kennedy Peak Trail (0.3 mi.)
Lakeside Trail (at Sherando, 1.0 mi.)
Lakeside Trail (at Bear Creek, 0.8 mi.)
Lake Trail (at Mint Springs, 0.5 mi.)
Limberlost Nature Trail (1.3 mi.)
Living Museum Nature Trail (0.5 mi.)
Long Island Trail (1.2 mi.)
Lover's Leap Trail (0.5 mi.)
Mountain Farm Trail (0.4 mi.)
Mountain Industry Trail (0.4 mi.)
Meadowlark Botanical Gardens Trail
    (1.2 mi.)
Meadow Spring Trail (0.5 mi.)
Molly's Pioneer Trail (0.6 mi.)
New Market Battlefield Trail (1.0 mi.)
Nike Park Nature Trail (0.6 mi.)
North Mountain Overlook Trail (0.2 mi.)
Old Plantation Interpretive Trail (1.2 mi.)
Pandapas Pond Trail (0.7 mi.)
Phillips Creek Trail (1.0 mi.)
Pig Iron Trail (0.3 mi.)
Powells Creek Trail (1.4 mi.)
Ragged Island Trail (0.5 mi.)
Reynolds Nature Trail (0.4 mi.)
Richmond Walking Trail (1.5 mi.)
Ridge Trail (0.5 mi.)
River Loop Trail (1.0 mi.)
Roaring Run Falls Trail
Ruskin Freer Trails (1.1 mi.)
Salthouse Branch Nature Trail (0.5 mi.)
Sandy Beach Trail (1.0 mi.)
Snead Farm Loop Trail (0.8 mi.)
Stony Fork Nature Trail (1.0 mi.)
Three Lakes Trail (0.7 mi.)
Trail of Trees (0.5 mi.)
Todd Lake Trail (1.1 mi.)
Tunnel Trail (0.3 mi.)
Turtle Island Trail (1.3 mi.)
Unaka Nature Trail (1.0 mi.)
Virginia's Walk (1.3 mi.)
Whispering Water Trail (0.5 mi.)
Wildflower Trail (0.5 mi.)
Woodland Trail (1.6 mi.)

## People with Disabilities (PWD)

Awareness Trail (0.3 mi.)
Azalea Trail (0.3 mi.)
Bald Cypress Trail (first loop of 1.5 mi.)
Beartree Lake Trail (1.0 mi.) (fishing)
Cherokee Trail (0.2 mi.) (fishing)
Children's Forest Trail (0.3 mi.)
Discovery Way Trail (0.2 mi.)
Duff and Stuff Trail (0.2 mi.)
Fenwick Wetlands Trail (0.8 mi.) (fishing)
Fragrance Trail (Braille) (0.1 mi.)
Guest River Gorge Trail (first 1 mi. of 5.8 mi.)
Handicapped Trail (0.1 mi.)
Happy Creek Trail ((0.5 mi.)

Kelly Bridge Trail (0.2 mi.) (fishing)
Lake Anna State Park (0.3 mi. to pond)
Limberlost Nature Trail (1.3 mi.)
Lions Tale Trail (Braille) (0.3 mi.)
Massanutten Story Book Trail (0.6 mi., includes backtrack)
North Mountain Overlook Trail (0.2 mi.)
Pandapas Pond Loop Trail (0.7 mi.) (fishing)
Pine Grove Forest Trail (0.2 mi.)
Rhododendron Trail (0.1 mi.) (on North Mountain)
Wetland's Boardwalk Trail (0.2 mi.)
Wheelchair Trail (0.1 mi.)

# Bibliography

## Manuscripts

Abstracts and Transcripts from Original Colonial Papers, I–X. Virginia Public Library, Richmond.

Anderson, Robert, and William Nelson. Letterbooks. Alderman Library, University of Virginia, Charlottesville.

British Colonial Papers (1625). Library of Congress, Washington, D.C.

Colonial Papers, 1710–1720. Archives Division, Virginia State Library, Richmond.

Virginia Miscellaneous Papers, 1606–1863. Manuscripts Division, Library of Congress, Washington, D.C.

## Maps

Maps Division, Alderman Library, University of Virginia, Charlottesville. Includes the *John Smith Map of 1608*, *Nova Virginia Tabula Map of 1671*, and the *W. E. Myer Map of 1928*.

Municipal and County Maps (current). Various publishers, coverage, and scale. Examples are *Street Map of the Virginia Peninsula* (Hampton–Newport News–Yorktown–Poquoson–York County–James City County and Williamsburg), Dolph Map Co.; *Street Map of Richmond and Petersburg*, Rand McNally; *County of Fairfax Public Parks*, Fairfax County Park Authority; *ADC's Street Map of Richmond and Vicinity*, *Prince William County*, *Northern Virginia*, and others, Langenscheidt Publishing Group. Local chambers of commerce usually have street maps of towns, cities, and counties.

National Geographic Society. Trails Illustrated Maps for all George Washington and Jefferson National Forests districts. Map numbers: 786, 787, 788, 789, 791, 792, and 793. In addition, map number 228 is for Shenandoah National Park. Scales: 1 inch = 1.18 mile.

NPS. Maps of the Blue Ridge Parkway. Scale is based on mileposts.

———. Maps of Shenandoah National Park. Published by Potomac Appalachian Trail Club. Best maps are North, Central, South (nos. 9, 10, and 11), and a general map of the park published by the NPS. Scale: $\frac{5}{16}$ inch = 1 mile.

USFS. District maps of Virginia and West Virginia. District headquarters. Scales: 1 inch = 1 mile or 1 inch = 1.3 miles (current).

———. Maps of the Appalachian Trail (recreation guides). Maps cover the trail from Mount Rogers National Recreation Area to the northern end in Virginia and through Maryland.

———. Maps of Virginia and West Virginia. USFS Headquarters, Roanoke. Scale: 1:126,720 (current).

USGS. Maps of Virginia. (Also, modified USFS topographical maps, which show
boundaries.) There are 788 maps listed. 1:24,000 scale of 7 ½-minute series.
*Virginia Atlas and Gazetteer Map*. DeLorme Mapping Company of Yarmouth, Maine. Full
state map with topographical scale. (See details in this book's Introduction.)
Virginia Department of Transportation. Official highway map (current) and 95 county
maps (current). Richmond.


## Public Documents

Commonwealth of Virginia. Department of Conservation and Recreation, Division of
Planning and Recreation Resources. *Virginia Outdoor Plan*. Richmond, 2002.
——. Department of Game and Inland Fisheries. *Discover Our Wild Side (Virginia Birding
and Wildlife Trail)*. Richmond, 2002.
GWNF. *Comments and Responses of the EIS for the Revised Land and Resource Management
Plan*. Harrisonburg, Va., 1993.
——. *George Washington National Forest Final Revised Land and Resource Management Plan*.
Harrisonburg, Va., 1993.
——. *Record of Decision of the Final Environment Impact Statement*. Harrisonburg, Va., 1993.
——. *A Summary of the Final EIS*. Harrisonburg, Va., 1993.
JNF. *Final Environmental Impact Statement*. Roanoke, Va.
——. *Jefferson National Forest Land and Resource Management Plan*. Roanoke, Va., 2003.


## Books, Theses, and Articles

### ALLIED RECREATION
Bowen, John. *Adventuring in the Chesapeake Bay Area*. San Francisco: Sierra Club Books,
1999.
Gooch, Bob. *Virginia Fishing Guide*. Charlottesville: University Press of Virginia, 1992.
——. *Enjoying Virginia Outdoors*. Charlottesville: University Press, of Virginia, 2000.
Skinner, Charlie, and Elizabeth Skinner. *Bicycling the Blue Ridge*. Birmingham, Ala.:
Menasha Ridge Press/Globe Pequot (distributor), 1999.

### FLORA AND FAUNA
Alderman, J. Anthony. *Wildflowers of the Blue Ridge Parkway*. Chapel Hill: University of
North Carolina Press, 1997.
Angier, Bradford. *Feasting Free on Wild Edibles*. Harrisonburg, Pa.: Stackpole, 2002.
Bull, John, and John Farrand Jr. *The Audubon Society Field Guide to North American Birds:
Eastern Region*. New York: Alfred A. Knopf, 1977.
Cunningham, Paul. "The Gentle Melancholy of Trees." *American Artist*, June 1994.
Gupton, Oscar W., and Fred W. Swope. *Wildflowers of the Shenandoah Valley and Blue Ridge
Mountains*. Charlottesville: University Press of Virginia, 2002.
——. *Trees and Shrubs of Virginia*. Charlottesville: University Press of Virginia, 2002.
Linzey, Donald W., and Michael J. Clifford. *Snakes of Virginia*. Charlottesville: University
Press of Virginia, 1995.

——. *Mammals of Virginia*. Blacksburg, Va.: McDonald and Woodward
Publishing/University of Tennessee Press (distributor), 1998.

Martof, Bernard S., William M. Palmer, Joseph R. Bailey, and Julian R. Harrison.
*Amphibians and Reptiles of the Carolinas and Virginia*. Chapel Hill: University of North
Carolina Press, 1980.

Simpson, Marcus B., Jr. *Birds of the Blue Ridge Mountains*. Chapel Hill: University of North
Carolina Press, 1992.

Stokes, Donald W. *Field Guide to Birds*. New York: Little Brown and Company, 1996.

——. *Field Guide to Observing Insects*. New York: Little Brown and Company, 1998.

Strausbaugh, P. D., and Earl L. Core. *Flora of West Virginia*. Vols. 1–4. 2d ed. Morgantown:
West Virginia University Books, 1973.

Webster, William David, James F. Parnell, and Walter C. Biggs. *Mammals of the Carolinas,
Virginia, and Maryland*. Chapel Hill: University of North Carolina Press, 1985.

## HISTORY

Abernethy, Thomas Perkins. *The South in the New Nation*. Baton Rouge: Louisiana State
University Press, 1961.

——. *Three Virginia Frontiers*. Baton Rouge: Louisiana State University Press, 1962.

Alvord, Clarence W., and Lee Bidgood. *The First Explorations of the Trans-Allegheny Region
of the Virginians, 1650-1674*. Cleveland: Arthur Clark, 1996.

Bartram, William. *The Travels of William Bartram, 1791*. Naturalist's ed. Edited by Francis
Harper. Athens: University of Georgia Press, 1998.

Beverley, Robert. *The History and Present State of Virginia*. Edited by Louis B. Wright.
Charlottesville: University Press of Virginia, 1968.

Briceland, Alan. *Westward from Virginia: Exploration of Virginia-Carolina Frontier*.
Charlottesville: University Press of Virginia, 1987.

Brooks, Maurice. *The Appalachians*. Morgantown, W.Va.: Seneca Books, 1998.

Cooke, John Esten. *Virginia: A History of the People*. Edited by Horace Scudder. Boston:
Houghton Mifflin, 1887. Reprint, New York: AMS Press, 1973.

De Hart, Allen. "Colonial History of Prince George County, Virginia." M.A. thesis,
University of Virginia, Charlottesville, 1957.

Heatwole, Henry. *Shenandoah National Park and Guide to Skyline Drive*. Luray, Va.:
Shenandoah Natural History Association, 1990.

Jolley, Harley E. *The Blue Ridge Parkway*. Knoxville: University of Tennessee Press, 1969.

Lederer, John. *The Discoveries of John Lederer*. 1672. Reprint, edited by William P.
Cumming, Charlottesville: University Press of Virginia, 1958.

Lord, William G. *Blue Ridge Parkway Guide*. Birmingham, Ala.: Menasha Ridge
Press/Globe Pequot Press (distributor), 1992. Flora and fauna included in addition to
history.

Raeburn, Paul. "Can This Man Save Our Forests?" *Popular Science*, June 1994.

Rountree, Helen C. *Pocahontas's People: The Powhatan Indians of Virginia through Four
Centuries*. Norman: University of Oklahoma Press, 1996.

——. *Eastern Shore Indians of Virginia and Maryland*. Edited by Thomas E. Davidson.
Charlottesville: University Press of Virginia, 1998.

Williams, Ted. "Can the Forest Service Heal Itself?" *Wildlife Conservation*,
September/October 1994.

## TRAIL GEAR AND SUPPLIES

Angier, Bradford. *How to Stay Alive in the Woods*. New York: Blackdog and Leventhal, 2001.

Axcell, Claudia, Diana Cook, and Vikki Kinmont. *Simple Foods for the Pack*. San Francisco: Sierra Club Books, 1986.

Fletcher, Colin. *The Complete Walker IV*. New York: Alfred A. Knopf, 2002.

Gorman, Stephen. *Winter Camping*. Boston: Appalachian Mountain Club Books, 1999.

Greenspan, Rick, and Hal Kahn. *The Camper's Companion*. San Francisco: Foghorn Press, 2001.

McHugh, Gretchen. *The Hungry Hikers Book of Good Cooking*. New York: Alfred A. Knopf, 1993.

Randall, Glenn. *Outward Bound Backpacker Handbook*. New York: Lyons Press/Globe, 2000.

## TRAIL GUIDES

Adkins, Leonard M. *Walking the Blue Ridge: A Guide to the Trails of the Blue Ridge Parkway*. Chapel Hill: University of North Carolina Press, 1992.

*Appalachian Trail Guide: Maryland and Northern Virginia*. 16th ed. Edited by Melissa Lanning. Vienna, Va.: Potomac Appalachian Trail Club, 2000.

*Appalachian Trail Guide: Shenandoah National Park*. 12th ed. Edited by Lee Sheaffer (maps by Dave Pierce). Vienna, Va.: Potomac Appalachian Trail Club, 1999.

*Appalachian Trail Guide: Central Virginia*. 1st ed. Edited by Bob Ellinwood. Harpers Ferry, W.Va.: Appalachian Trail Conference, 2001.

*Appalachian Trail Guide: Southeast Virginia*. 2nd ed. Edited by Vaughn Thomas. Harpers Ferry, W.Va.: Appalachian Trail Conference, 2002.

De Hart, Allen. *Hiking the Mountain State: The Trails of West Virginia*. Boston: Appalachian Mountain Club, 1997. Includes trails of Jefferson and George Washington national forests in West Virginia.

De Hart, Allen, and Bruce Sundquist. *Monongahela National Forest Hiking Guide*. Charleston, W.Va.: West Virginia Highlands Conservancy, 1999. Includes topographical maps of trails connecting to Virginia trails.

Denton, James W. *Circuit Hikes in Shenandoah National Park*. Vienna, Va.: Potomac Appalachian Trail Club, 1996.

Finley, Lon, and Tom Horsch. *Mountain Biking the Appalachians*. Winston-Salem, N.C.: John F. Blair, Publisher, 1998.

Garvey, Edward B. *The New Appalachian Trail*. Birmingham, Ala.: Menasha Ridge Press, 1997.

Kohlbrenner, Wil. *Guide to Massanutten Mountain Hiking Trails*. Rev. ed. Vienna, Va.: Potomac Appalachian Trail Club, 2000. (The Potomac Appalachian Trail Club [PATC] has about eighty additional books and maps. Call for list at 703-242-0693.)

## WILDERNESS

Hart, John. *Walking Softly in the Wilderness*. San Francisco: Sierra Club Books, 1998.

Hampton, Bruce, and David Cole. *Soft Paths: How to Enjoy the Wilderness without Harming It*. Harrisonburg, Pa.: Stackpole, 1994.

Hodgson, Michael. *The Basic Essentials of Minimizing Impact on the Wilderness*. Merrillville, Ind.: ICS, 1991.

Horan, Jack. *Where Nature Reigns*. Asheboro, N.C.: Down Home Press, 1997.

Schimelpfenig, Tod, and Linda Lindsey. *Wilderness First Aid*. Lander, Wyo.: National Outdoor Leadership School, 2000.

# General Index

University of Virginia Biological Station, 148, 151
Upper Valley Regional Park Authority, 449
Upton Hill Regional Park, 447

Vawter Street Park, 369
Veterans Memorial Park, 381
Virginia Coast Reserve, 463
Virginia Commonwealth University, 423–24
Virginia Fish Cultural Station, 37, 39
Virginia Institute of Marine Science, 326
Virginia Living Museum, 419, 467–68
Virginia Marine Science Museum, 326, 329
Virginia Military Institute, 243, 348–49, 410–12, 457, 468–69
Virginia Polytechnic Institute and State University (Virginia Tech), 154, 194, 392, 457
Virginia Society of Ornithology, 331
Virginia War Museum, 419
Virginia Zoological Park, 421

Wakefield and Lake Accotink Parks, 359–60
Waller Mill Park, 436
Walnut Creek Park, 348–49
Walnut Flats Campground, 144–46
Waonaze Peak, 49
Warren County, 33, 37, 304
Warwick House, 92, 93
Washington and Lee University, 410–12
Washington & Old Dominion Railroad Regional Park, 447–49
Washington County, 162, 166, 275, 279
Wash Woods Environmental Education Center, 326, 328
Waterfalls. *See descriptions of individual trails*
Weather, 20–21
Western Branch Park, 400–401

Westmoreland Berry Farm, 469–70
Westmoreland County, 261, 334, 358
Westmoreland State Park, 287, 334–35
West Virginia Scenic Trails Association, 9, 107, 136, 150
Whetstone Ridge and South Mountain Area, 116
White Oak WMA, 284–85
White Pine Horse Camp, 144–46
White Rocks Campground, 146, 249
Whitetop Laurel Creek Area, 162–66
Wildcat Mountain Area, 125–26
Wilderness Battlefield, 240–41
Wilderness Road Campground, 247, 248, 249, 250, 288
Wilderness Road State Park, 308
Wildflowers. *See "Feature" sections under trail headings; descriptions of individual parks, preserves, and natural areas*
Wildlife. *See Chapters 1, 2, 3, 5, 8, 10, and 11 passim*
Wildlife Center of Virginia, 32
Wildwood Park, 423
Windy Run Park, 350
Wintergreen Resort, 457
Wise County, 121, 179, 181, 183, 186
Wolf Creek Picnic Area, 154
Wolf Gap Campground, 35
Wolf Gap Recreation Area, 51, 53, 54
Wolftrap Stream Valley Park, 360
Woods Creek Park, 411–12
Woodstock Lookout Tower, 47, 49
Worcester County, Md., 260
Wythe County, 155, 156, 298, 387

York County, 235
York River State Park, 287, 288, 335–37

Zachary Taylor Park, 350

# Trail Index

Most trails mentioned in the book are listed below, whether they are merely connectors, have limited usage, or receive a full descriptive treatment. The first numbers are page numbers. Boldface numbers refer to the trail numbers that appear in the outside margins of the text, next to the trail descriptions; these correspond with the same numbers on the maps. Trail names and page numbers not followed by boldface numbers are either older names (now superseded), historic trails not in current use, short trails mentioned in introductions, or connecting trails that may originate outside Virginia.

CCC Trail, 282–83; **825**; Map G

CCC Trail, 296; **887**; Map C

Cedar Cliffs Main Trail, 457; **1369**; Map D

Cedar Cliffs North Trail, 457; **1370**; Map D

Cedar Creek Trail, 51, 53; **62**; Map A

Cedar Creek Trail, 434; **1324**; Map J

Cedar Path Nature Trail, 387; **1187**; Map F

Cedar Ridge Trail, 325; **993**; Map F

Cedar Run Trail, 227; **593**; Map D

Cedar Run Trail, 215–16; **951**; Maps D and F

Cedar Valley Trail, 376; **1145**; Map F

Cellar Mountain Trail, 120; **271**; Map B

Center Creek Trail, 289; **841**; Map C

Center Trail, 298; **893**; Map C

Center Trail, 358; **1097**; Map F

Central High School Nature Trail, 437; **1332**; Map A

Chadwell Gap Trail, 248–50; **732**; Map C

Challenge Trail, 392; **1196**; Map B

Chancellorsville History Trail, 239–40; **691**; Map F

Channel Rock Trail, 154

Charcoal Trail, 36–38; **4**; Map A

Charlie Thomas Trail, 228; **625**; Map D

Cherokee Trail, 146; **331**; Map C

Chessie Nature Trail, 468–69; **1399**; Map A

Chestnut Flat Spring Trail, 73–74; **130**; Map A

Chestnut Ridge Trail, 166–67; **404**; Map C

Chestnut Ridge Trail, 58

Chestnut Ridge Trail, 211; **517**; Map B

Chestnut Ridge Trail, 319; **969**; Maps B and E

Chestnut Trail, 383; **1172**; Map B

Chickahominy River Trail, 369; **1131**; Map G

Chief Benge Scout Trail, 186–87; **480**; Map C

Children's Forest Horse Trail, 123; **230**; Map B

Children's Forest Long Loop Trail, 103; **229**; Map B

Children's Forest Trail, 103; **228**; Map B

Chimney Hollow Trail, 74–75; **131**; Map A

Chimney Trail, 349; **1064**; Map D

Chopawamsic Trail, 268; **790**; Map F

Christian Run Trail, 95; **202**; Map B

Circumferential Trail, 309; **923**; Map D

Citation Trail, 154; **370**; Map C

Clark Mountain Trail, 162; **386**; Map C

Clay Lick Trail, 69–70; **114**; Map A

Claytor Lake Trail, 290; **851**; Map C

Clean Sweep Trail, 304–6; **903**; Map A

Cliffside Trail, 169–71; **414**; Map C

Cliff Trail, 66–67; **106**; Map A

Cliff Trail, 188; **265**; Map B

Clinch Mountain Trail, 276; **807**; Map C

Clinch River Trail, 399; **1048**; Map C

Cobbler Mountain Trail, 91–92; **182**; Map A

Cobbs Wharf Trail, 352; **1078**; Map G

Cock's Comb Trail, 98; **213**; Map B

Cold Harbor Battlefield Trail, 365; **1119**; Map G

Cold Harbor Trail, 242; **698**; Map G

Cold Springs Run Trail, 95–96; **200**; Map A

Cold Spring Trail, 73–74; **129**; Map A

Cold Spring Trail, 120; **272**; Map B

Cold Spring Trail, 289; **848**; Map C

Coles Trail, 99; **218**; Map B

Colleen's Corners Trail, 349; **1065**; Map D

College Run Trail, 325; **994**; Map H

Colson Trail, 248; **726**; Map C

Comers Creek Fall Trail, 173–74; **441**; Map C

Comers Creek Trail, 173–74; **442**; Map C

Comers Rock Trail, 177; **459**; Map C

Compton Gap Fire Road, 220; **535**; Map D

Compton Peak Trail, 219; **534**; Map D

Confederate Breastworks Trail, 71; **117**; Map A

Connector Trail, 317; **961**; Map E

Connector Trail, 323; Map D

Conservancy Trail, 148–49; **351**; Map C

Conway River Fire Road, 229; **641**; Map D

Cookie Trail, 61; **96**; Map A

Cook's Trail, 304–6; **904**; Map A

Cooper Ridge Trail, 339; **1049**; Map C

Corbin Cabin Cutoff Trail, 225; **584**; Map D

Corbin Hollow Trail, 227; **604**; Map D

Corbin Mountain Trail, 226; **602**; Map D

Cornelius Creek Trail, 128–29; **286**; Map B

Cotoctin Trail, 206; **493**; Map D

Counts Cabin Trail, 179, 181; **468**; Map C

Courthouse Park Trail, 365; **1117**; Map G

Cove Branch Trail, 134; **297**; Map B

Cove Mountain Trail, 127–28; **283**; Map B

Cove Trail, 99; **216**; Map B

Crabtree Falls Trail, 114–16; **254**; Map B

Craig Creek Trail, 144; **323**; Map B

Poplar Grove Trail, 325; **990**; Map F

Poquoson Nature Trail, 423; **1296**; Map J

Porpoise Creek Trail, 324; **987**; Map I

Possum Path Trail, 406; **1252**; Map F

Potomac Heritage Trail, 262, 358–59; **758/1095**; Map F

Pound Lake Trail, 179; **463**; Map C

Poverty Creek Connector Trail, 147; **333**; Map C

Poverty Creek Trail, 147; **342**; Map C

Powell Mountain Trail, 49; **51**; Map A

Powell Mountain Trail, 229; **640**; Map D

Powell's Creek Trail, 232; **1019**; Map F

Powerline Trail, 147; **343**; Map C

Power Line Trail, 282; **831**; Map G

Powhatan Forks Trail, 336–37; **1039**; Map I

Price Broad Mountain Trail, 140–42; **317**; Map B

Prickley Pear Trail, 147; **344**; Map C

Priest (Overlook) Trail, The, 206; **495**; Map D

Prospectors Trail, 289; **845**; Map C

Purchase Ridge Trail, 298; **895**; Map C

Pine Field Trail, 461–62; **1384**; Map B


Quantico Falls Trail, 267; **783**; Map F

Queen Anne Lake Trail, 147; **345**; Map C

Quiet Woods Trail, 426; **1304**; Map G


Racer Camp Hollow Trail, 51, 53; **58**; Map

Raccoon Branch Nature Trail, 175; **445**; Map C

Rader Mountain Trail, 69; **113**; Map A

Rady Park Trail, 362; **1107**; Map D

Ragged Island Trail, 274; **801**; Maps D and G

Raider's Run Trail, 296; **883**; Map C

Railroad Ford Trail, 315–16; **948**; Maps D and F

Rails to River Trail, 357; **1091**; Map F

Ramsey's Draft Trail, 77–79; **137**; Map A

Rapidan Fire Road, 228; **623**; Map D

Raven Cliff Trail, 176; **454**; Map C

Raven Cliff Furnace Trail, 177; **458**; Map C

Red Branch Trail, 276; **808**; Map C

Red Bud Trail, 282; **828**; Map G

Red Fox Trail, 182; **470**; Map C

Red Fox Trail, 409; **1265**; Map J

Red Gate Fire Road, 228; **618**; Map D

Red Oak Trail, 282–83; **830**; Map G

Redtail Ridge Trail, 304–6; **908**; Map A

Red Trail, 397; **1221**; Map D

Red Wing Nature Trail, 435; **1328**; Map J

Reed Creek Trail, 129–30; **289**; Map B

Reedy Creek Trail, 426; **1308**; Map G

Rein Memorial Trail, 399; **1237**; Map J

Reservoir Hollow Trail, 395; **1210**; Map A

Reynolds Nature Trail, 391; **1194**; Map B

Rhododendron Gap Trail, 170; **422**; Map C

Rhododendron Trail, 98; **211**; Map B

Rhododendron Trail, 295; **879**; Map C

Ribble Trail, 146; **328**; Map C

Rich Hole Trail, 102; **226**; Map B

Richmond/Danville Rail-Trail, 402; **1245**; Map E

Richmond Walking Trail, 428; **1314**; Map G

Ridge Trail, 154; **371**; Map C

Ridge Trail, 218; **528**; Map D

Ridge Trail, 247–50; **727**; Map C

Ridge Trail, 265–66; **772**; Map F

Ridge Trail, 288; **835**; Map C

Ridge Trail, 296; **890**; Map C

Ridge Trail, 466; **1396**; Map D

Riley Park Trail, 437; **1333**; Map A

Riprap Trail, 234; **678**; Map D

Rivanna River Trail, 396; **1214**; Map D

River Access Trail, 426; **1306**; Map D

River Bank Trail, 332; **973**; Map E

Riverbend Equestrian Trail, 265–66; **777**; Map F

River Birch Trail, 367; **1123**; Map G

River Bluff Trail, 362–63; **1109**; Map D

River Loop Trail, 91–92; **181**; Map A

Riverside Trail, 424; **1299**; Map G

River Trail, 264; **763**; Map F

River Trail, 289; **846**; Map C

River Trail, 312–14; **944**; Map D

River Trail, 334; **1025**; Map I

River Walk, 416

Riverview Farm Trail, 421; **1294**; Map J

Road Hollow Trail, 77–80; **139/144**; Map A

Roanoke Mountain Summit Trail, 211; **516**; Map B

Roanoke River Greenway/Moyer, 423–33; **1321**; Map B

Roanoke River Greenway/Smith Park, 431; **1318**; Map B

Roanoke River Trail, 210–11; **515**; Map B

Roanoke Valley Horse Trail, 211; **518**; Map B
Roaring Fork Trail, 154; **365**; Map C
Roaring Run Falls and Loop Trail, 142–43; **320**; Map B
Roaring Run Trail, 43–45; **27**; Map A
Robert Munford Trail, 452; **1361**; Map E
Robertson Mountain Trail, 227; **605**; Map D
Robin's Roost Trail, 322; **976**; Map E
Rock Castle Gorge Trail, 212–13; **521**; Map E
Rock Creek Trail, 263; **760**; Map F
Rock House Ridge Trail, 294; **875**; Map C
Rock Shelter Trail, 93
Rock Spring Trail, 334–35; **1027**; Map I
Rockwood Nature Trail, 353; **1078-A**; Map G
Rocky Branch Trail, 223; **566**; Map D
Rocky Mountain Run Trail, 231; **660**; Map D
Rocky Mount Trail, 231; **655**; Map D
Rocky Run Stream Valley Trail, 357; **1086**; Map F
Rocky Run Trail, 57; **78**; Map A
Rockytop Trail, 231; **661**; Map D
Rose River Fire Road, 227; **613**; Map D
Rose River Loop Trail, 227–28; **615**; Map D
Ross Camp Hollow Trail, 292–93; **868**; Map B
Round Meadow Creek Trail, 214; **526**; Map E
Round Mountain Trail, 154; **372**; Map C
Running Cedar Trail, 309; **921**; Map D
Running Creek Trail, 312–14; **940**; Map D
Rush Trail, 166; **405**; Map C
Ruskin Freer Lower Trail, 414–15; **1282**; Map B
Ruskin Freer Upper Trail, 414–15; **1283**; Map B

Saddleback Mountain Trail, 230; **652**; Map B
Saddle Gap Trail, 111; **248**; Map B
Saddle Trail, 227; **607**; Map D
Saint Brooks Trail, 404; **1246**; Map F
Saint Mary's Gorge Trail, 19; **268**; Map B
Saint Mary's Trail, 119–20; **267**; Map B
Salamander Trail, 227; **612**; Map D
Salthouse Branch Nature Trail, 455; **1365**; Map E
Salt Pond Ridge Trail, 87–88; **164**; Map A

Salt Stump Trail, 87–88, 291; **173**; Maps A and B
Sam Ramsey Hunter Access Trail, 72; **122**; Map A
Sams Ridge Trail, 224; **576**; Map D
Sand Spring Mountain Trail, 61–62, 64; **93**; Map A
Sandy Beach Trail, 362–63; **1110**; Map D
Sandy Gap Trail, 87–88; **170**; Map A
Saponi Trail, 285; **833**; Map E
Saponi Trail, 8
Sartain Trail, 152; **361**; Map C
Sarver Trail, 147–48; **349**; Map C
Saunders Trail, 162; **390**; Map C
Saunders Creek Trail, 311–12; **933**; Map B
Sawmill Hollow Trail, 304–6; **909**; Map A
Sawtooth Trail, 315; **946**; Maps D and F
Scales Trail, 172–73; **430**; Map C
School Trail, 397; **1227**; Map D
Scothorn Gap Trail, 37, 42, 43; **16**; Map A
Scotts Run Trail, 356; **1084**; Map F
Scout Trail, 376–77; **1153**; Map F
Scout Trail, 455–56; **1367**; Map F
Seaside Trail, 253–55; **739**; Map J
Second Mountain Trail, 44, 46; **32**; Map A
Seven Bar None Trail, 46, 49; **43**; Map A
Sevenmile Mountain Trail, 135–36; **301**; Map B
Seven Sisters Trail, 155; **377**; Map C
Shady Ridge Trail, 290; **853**; Map C
Sharp Top Trail, 209–10; **510**; Map B
Shaw Gap Trail, 162; **392**; Map C
Shawl Gap Trail, 37–40; **2**; Map A
Shawl Gap/Tuscarora Trail, 38; **18**; Map A
Shaws Fork Trail, 81; **151**; Map A
Shaws Ridge Trail, 81; **148**; Map A
Shelton Trail, 409; **1264**; Map J
Shenandoah Bike Trail, 393; **1200**; Map C
Shenandoah County Park Trail, 386; **1186**; Map A
Shenandoah Mountain Trail (North), 77–79; **143**; Map A
Shenandoah Mountain Trail (South), 81–83; **149**; Map A
Sherman Gap Trail, 37–40; **6**; Map A
Shoe Creek Trail, 116; **255**; Map B
Short Loop Trail, 244; **709**; Map G
Short Ridge Trail, 72; **121**; Map A